Using PageMaker® 4 for Windows™

Sharyn Venit

que®

Using PageMaker® 4 for Windows™

Copyright© 1991 by Que® Corporation.

All rights reserved. Printed in the United States of America. No part of this book may be used or reproduced in any form or by any means, or stored in a database or retrieval system, without prior written permission of the publisher except in the case of brief quotations embodied in critical articles and reviews. Making copies of any part of this book for any purpose other than your own personal use is a violation of United States copyright laws. For information, address Que Corporation, 11711 N. College Ave., Carmel, IN 46032.

Library of Congress Catalog No.: 90-63263

ISBN 0-88022-645-5

This book is sold *as is*, without warranty of any kind, either express or implied, respecting the contents of this book, including but not limited to implied warranties for the book's quality, performance, merchantability, or fitness for any particular purpose. Neither Que Corporation nor its dealers or distributors shall be liable to the purchaser or any other person or entity with respect to any liability, loss, or damage caused or alleged to be caused directly or indirectly by this book.

94 93 92 91   4 3

Interpretation of the printing code: the rightmost double-digit number is the year of the book's printing; the rightmost single-digit number, the number of the book's printing. For example, a printing code of 91-1 shows that the first printing of the book occurred in 1991.

This book is based on Aldus PageMaker Version 4.0 and the earlier Version 3.0.

Publisher: Lloyd J. Short

Associate Publisher: Karen A. Bluestein

Acquisitions Manager: Terrie Lynn Solomon

Product Development Manager: Mary Bednarek

Managing Editor: Paul Boger

Book Designer: Scott Cook

Production Team: Hilary Adams, Sandy Grieshop, Denny Hager, Bill Hurley, Bob LaRoche, Howard Peirce, Tad Ringo, Louise Shinault, Bruce Steed, Johnna VanHoose, Lisa Wilson

Product Director
Shelley O'Hara

Production Editor
Gregory Robertson

Editors
Sharon Boller
Dennis G. Frazier
Beth Hoger
Heidi Weas Muller
Susan Shaw

Technical Editor
Ron Holmes

*Composed in Garamond and Macmillan
by Que Corporation*

About the Author

Sharyn Venit

Sharyn Venit began working in the publishing industry as a proofreader and layout artist when page proofs were delivered on galleys and pasted up manually. She learned letterpress techniques ("...as an art form") in 1979, and she has directed the publication departments of several software companies. Her rich background in all aspects of publishing is reflected in this book and her other writings—more than ten books and hundreds of articles about using computers for publishing. Her articles have appeared in national magazines, including *PC Computing*, *PC Magazine*, *PC Week*, and *Publish!* Her articles include reviews of laser printers and typesetters, page layout applications, drawing applications, and word processing software. She designed and produced the original *PageMaker Classroom* training materials for Aldus Corporation. Venit is one of the founders of TechArt, Inc., a graphic design and production shop in San Francisco, and a company where PageMaker has been a primary tool since it was first introduced in 1985.

TRADEMARK ACKNOWLEDGMENTS

Que Corporation has made every effort to supply trademark information about company names, products, and services mentioned in this book. Trademarks indicated below were derived from various sources. Que Corporation cannot attest to the accuracy of this information.

1-2-3 and Symphony are registered trademarks of Lotus Development Corporation.

Agfa is a registered trademark of Agfa-Gevaert A.G.

Aldus PageMaker is a registered trademark and Aldus Freehand and Aldus Freelance Plus are trademarks of Aldus Corporation.

AutoCAD is a registered trademark of Autodesk, Inc.

Bitstream is a registered trademark of Bitstream, Inc.

Canon is a registered trademark of Canon, Inc.

Compugraphic is a registered trademark and 9600G is a trademark of Agfa Corporation.

CorelDRAW! is a trademark of Corel Systems Corporation.

EPSON is a registered trademark of Seiko Epson Corporation.

HP and LaserJet are registered trademarks of Hewlett-Packard Company.

IBM is a registered trademark of International Business Machines.

Linotronic is a registered trademark of Linotype-Hell Company.

Macintosh, LaserWriter, and Apple are registered trademarks of Apple Computer, Inc.

Micrografx is a registered trademark and In*A*Vision and Micrografx Designer are trademarks of Micrografx, Inc.

Microsoft is a registered trademark of Microsoft Corporation.

Microtek Lab is a registered trademark of Microtek Lab, Inc.

PC Paintbrush, Publisher's Paintbrush, and Publisher's Type Foundry are registered trademarks of Z-Soft Corporation.

PostScript is a registered trademark and Adobe Illustrator is a trademark of Adobe Systems, Inc.

QMS and ColorScript are registered trademarks of QMS, Inc.

ACKNOWLEDGMENTS

My greatest appreciation goes to Diane Burns, my business partner and coauthor on the first two editions of this book, whose enthusiasm and patience helped carry us through all the trials and celebrate the many triumphs that we experienced as pioneers in desktop publishing. Many of the tips you will find throughout this book are fruits of the lessons Diane and I learned in trying to deliver camera-ready copy—on time—to diverse and demanding clients at TechArt.

This book would not have been possible without the help and cooperation of TechArt's clients and staff, including the following: Aldus Corporation; American Electronics Association; Ben Bowermeister, Aldus Corporation; Chris Chenard; Laurie Deutsch, McCutchen, Doyle, and Brown and Enerson; Leticia Gueverra, TechArt San Francisco; Ike Computer Company; Judy Jacobson, Aldus Corporation; Know How, Inc.; Denise Lever, TechArt San Francisco; Sam Louie, TechArt San Francisco; Grace Moore, TechArt San Francisco; Laura Murphy, TechArt San Francisco; National Association of Professional Women (NAPW); Barry Owen; Pacific Heights; Shana Penn, stylist; Emily Rosenberg, Venture Development Service; Mike Sherwood, Aldus Corporation; Robert Sheridan; David Smith, designer; TechArt San Francisco; Thompson and Company; and Zablocki Printing Company.

Special thanks to Reyna Cowan, Berkeley, California, for her extensive writing and editing of text and preparing of figures for the second and third editions of this book, and to Lisa Pletka for her help in developing the illustrations for the third edition.

CONVENTIONS USED IN THIS BOOK

The conventions used in this book have been established to help you learn to use the program quickly and easily. Menu names begin with uppercase letters (File menu). PageMaker commands, dialog box names and options, and menu options also are written with initial uppercase letters.

Names of files and directories are written in all uppercase letters (WINDOWS3, NEWS.TXT).

PageMaker tools and icons are written in all lowercase letters (text tool).

Any text the user should type is in *italic type* or on a line by itself.

Icons in the margins indicate information that is relevant to PageMaker 4.0.

Messages that appear on-screen are in a `special typeface`.

Tips have a shaded background.

Cautions and warnings are enclosed in a box with a shadow around it.

Contents at a Glance

Introduction 1

Part I The Production Process with PageMaker

Chapter 1	Introducing PageMaker and Desktop Publishing	9
Chapter 2	Getting Started	33
Chapter 3	Creating a New Publication	67
Chapter 4	Typing, Importing, and Editing Text	121
Chapter 5	Formatting Text	167
Chapter 6	Working with Graphics	209
Chapter 7	Managing Large Documents and Linked Files	247
Chapter 8	Printing	281
Chapter 9	Making Color Separations	323

Part II Designing and Producing Different Types of Publications

Chapter 10	Typography	349
Chapter 11	PageMaker as a Design Tool	383

Part III Examples of Publications Created Using PageMaker

Chapter 12	Creating Business Reports, Books, and Manuals	415
Chapter 13	Creating Newsletters and Similar Publications	457
Chapter 14	Creating Overhead Transparencies, Slides, and Handouts	489
Chapter 15	Creating Brochures, Price Lists, and Directories	517
Chapter 16	Creating Fliers and Display Ads	551

Glossary 569

Table of Contents

Introduction 1
Why a Book about PageMaker? 1
Who Should Use This Book? 2
What Is in This Book? 2
Part I—The Production Process with PageMaker 3
Part II—Designing and Producing Different Types of Publications .. 4
Part III—Examples of Publications Created Using PageMaker 5
Glossary 6

I The Production Process with PageMaker

1 Introducing PageMaker and Desktop Publishing 9
The Information Age 10
Development of Desktop Publishing 10
    Using Low-Cost Equipment 12
    Using High-Resolution Printers 12
    Using Different Typefaces 13
    Merging Text and Graphics 14
Desktop Publishing: The Melting Pot 15
    Typesetting Traditions 15
    Design Traditions 16
    Printing Traditions 16
    Computing Traditions 17
PageMaker 17
    PageMaker and Word Processors 19
    PageMaker and Graphics Programs 24
    The Final PageMaker Publication 24
PageMaker and the Publishing Cycle 25
    Division of Responsibilities 26
    Steps in the Production Process 27
    Quality, Economy, and Deadline 30
Chapter Summary 31

2 Getting Started 33
Reviewing Hardware Requirements 34
    Printers 35
    Scanners 35

Using PageMaker 4 for Windows

  Installing PageMaker 36
    Naming the PageMaker Directory 38
    Selecting Filters 39
  Managing Files 40
  Starting PageMaker 41
    Starting PageMaker from Windows 42
    Starting PageMaker from DOS 42
    Starting the Program and Opening a Document 44
  Using PageMaker 44
    Opening a Document 44
    Reviewing the Publication Window 47
    Controlling the Display 53
    Changing the Appearance of the Mouse Pointer 55
    Selecting with the Pointer and Text Tools 57
  Getting Help 60
  Reviewing the Basic Steps in Creating a Document 62
  Chapter Summary 65

3 Creating a New Publication 67
  Understanding PageMaker Terms 68
  Opening a Publication 69
    Opening a PageMaker 4.0 Publication 69
    Transferring a Publication from the Macintosh to the PC 71
  Entering Page Setup Specifications 72
    Specifying Page Size 73
    Setting Page Orientation 76
    Designating the Number of Pages 76
    Assigning a Starting Page Number 78
    Selecting a Format for Page Numbers 79
    Working with Double-Sided Publications 80
    Restarting Page Numbers 83
    Specifying Page Margins 84
    Specifying the Target Printer 87
    Building the Publication 88
  Setting Preferences 88
  Adding Master-Page Elements 91
    Creating a Master Grid 93
    Setting Column Guides 93
    Creating Nonprinting Guides 96

Table of Contents

    Typing Running Heads and Running Feet 102
    Numbering Pages Automatically 103
    Adding Graphic Elements to Master Pages 104
    Hiding Master-Page Items 105
    Copying Master Guides 106
Working with Pages 107
    Changing the Views of a Page 107
    Inserting and Removing Pages 109
    Turning Pages 113
Using the Edit Menu Commands 114
    Deleting and Copying Objects 114
    Pasting Objects 116
    Undoing Your Most Recent Action 116
    Reversing All Changes Made Since the Last Save 117
Developing Efficient Procedures 117
Chapter Summary 119

4 Typing, Importing, and Editing Text 121

Typing Text in Layout View 122
Importing Text with the Place Command 124
    Specifying Text Flow 127
    Using the Drag-Place Feature 130
    Placing Text on the Pasteboard 130
    Formatted Text versus Unformatted Text 131
Moving and Sizing Text Blocks 136
    Moving a Text Block 137
    Sizing a Text Block 138
    Breaking a Column of Text into Several Blocks 141
    Merging a Series of Text Blocks 143
    Rotating a Text Block 144
Editing Text in Layout View 144
    Inserting Text 145
    Selecting Text 146
    Selecting a Whole Text File 147
    Using the Clipboard 147
Typing and Editing Text in the Story Editor 149
    Displaying the Story Window 149
    Adding Text in the Story Window 152
    Finding and Changing Text in Story View 152

xiii

Using PageMaker 4 for Windows

    Using the Spelling Checker 156
    Using the Table Editor 158
        Creating a Table 158
        Importing Data into the Table Editor 163
        Exporting from the Table Editor 164
        Importing a Table into PageMaker 165
        Editing a Table in PageMaker 166
    Chapter Summary 166

5   Formatting Text 167

    Reviewing Default Settings 168
    Changing Type Specifications 169
        Specifying Font Name and Size 170
        Specifying Leading 171
        Specifying Position and Case 171
        Changing Character Width and Tracking 173
        Specifying Color 173
        Specifying Type Style 174
        Using Menu Commands 174
        Using Keyboard Shortcuts 174
    Defining Paragraph Formats 175
        Indenting Paragraphs 176
        Setting Paragraph Spacing 177
        Aligning Paragraphs 178
        Selecting a Dictionary for Hyphenation and Spelling 179
        Controlling Breaks 180
        Including a Paragraph in the Table of Contents 181
        Adding Rules 181
        Aligning Text to the Horizontal Grid 183
        Controlling Spacing 184
        Using the Indents/Tabs Command 187
        Controlling Hyphenation 191
    Using Style Sheets 195
        Viewing Styles 196
        Adding New Styles 197
        Editing Styles 202
        Formatting Text by Using Styles 203
    Copy Fitting 203
    Chapter Summary 207

xiv

Table of Contents

6   Working with Graphics 209
    Drawing with the Toolbox Tools 210
        Drawing Straight Lines 211
        Creating Boxes 211
        Creating Circles and Ovals 212
        Editing Toolbox Graphics 213
        Changing Lines Widths and Fill Patterns 216
    Importing Graphics Created in Other Programs 217
        Object-Oriented Graphics 221
        Encapsulated PostScript Format 224
        Bit-Mapped Graphics 224
        Scanned Images 225
    Editing Imported Graphics 227
        Trimming Imported Graphics 228
        Controlling Paint and TIFF Graphics Image 229
    Pasting Graphics from the Clipboard 232
    Layering Objects 234
        Placing Objects in the Background 234
        Bringing Objects to the Foreground 235
    Wrapping Text around Graphics 235
    Creating a Custom-Shaped Graphic Boundary 239
    Using Inline Graphics 242
        Creating an Inline Graphic 243
        Including Symbols in Text 244
        Handling Figure Captions 244
    Chapter Summary 245

7   Managing Large Documents and Linked Files 247
    Managing Linked Text and Graphics Documents 248
        Linking Graphic Files 248
        Setting Default Link Options 250
        Checking or Changing Link Settings 251
        Changing Link Options for Individual Files 254
        Updating Linked Files 256
    Using the Book Command 256
    Creating a Table of Contents 258
        Identifying Table of Contents Entries 258
        Generating a Table of Contents 258
        Editing a Generated Table of Contents 261

Creating an Index 262
　　Identifying Index Entries 262
　　Selecting Page Reference Options 264
　　Selecting Cross-Reference Options 266
　　Selecting Topics from a List 266
　　Editing the Index 268
　　Generating an Index 271
Organizing Your Disk Files 274
　　Decide on Naming Conventions 275
　　Copy All Project Files onto One Hard Disk 275
　　Set Up Project-Specific Directories 275
　　Back Up All Files Regularly 276
Reviewing Some Workgroup Scenarios 276
　　Networked Workgroup Scenario 276
　　Nonnetworked Workgroup Scenario 278
Chapter Summary 279

8 Printing 281

Knowing Your Printers 281
　　Printers Supported by PageMaker and Windows 3.0 282
　　Resolution 282
　　Paper Stock, Size, and Print Area 283
　　Types of Fonts 284
Installing the Printer 287
　　Adding Printers through the Windows Control Panel 287
　　Choosing the Target Printer through PageMaker 294
Downloading Soft Fonts 297
　　Installing Soft Fonts 297
　　Downloading Permanently or Temporarily 303
　　Using Soft Fonts 305
Using the Print Command 305
　　Specifying the Number of Copies 306
　　Printing a Range of Pages 307
　　Reducing and Enlarging Pages 307
　　Printing Double-Sided Copies 308
　　Printing Thumbnails 309
　　Printing Crop Marks 310
　　Using Fast Rules 311
　　Printing in Color 311

Table of Contents

    Printing Books 312
    Printing Blank Pages 312
    Printing Parts of Pages 312
    Selecting the Printer 314
    Changing Printer Specifications 314
    Using the Print Manager 316
    Stopping the Printing Process 318
Printing a Publication to a Disk 318
    Creating a Printable Disk File 319
    Printing the Disk File from DOS 319
    Changing Systems 320
    Using Service Bureaus 320
Chapter Summary 321

9   Making Color Separations 323

Assigning Spot Colors in PageMaker 324
    Editing Existing Colors 325
    Creating New Colors 328
    Removing Colors 329
    Copying Colors 329
Applying Colors 330
    Applying Color to Text 331
    Applying Color to PageMaker Graphics 331
    Applying Color to Imported Graphics 332
Proofing Colors On-Screen 333
Printing in Color with Color Printers 334
    Comps or Proofs 335
    Short-Run Color Publications 335
    Presentation Materials 336
Printing in Color with Offset Printing 337
    Understanding Spot-Color Offset Printing 338
    Deciding between Spot Color and Process Color 338
    Printing Spot-Color Overlays 339
    Marking Mechanicals for Solid Spot Color 343
    Specifying Colors for Offset Printing 343
    Preparing a PageMaker Publication for Process Color
        Printing 345
Chapter Summary 345

xvii

II Designing and Producing Different Types of Publications

10 Typography 349
Understanding Fonts 349
    Typeface 351
    Size 353
    Style 354
Working with PageMaker's Font List 356
    Changing the Default Font 356
    Installing Fonts 356
    Using a Type Manager 361
Planning Your Design Specifications 362
    Choosing the Fonts 362
    Mixing Typefaces 365
    Choosing Automatic or Forced Leading 366
    Kerning Headlines and Titles 370
    Handling Captions 372
    Inserting Symbols in Text 372
    Creating Fractions in PageMaker 373
Fitting Copy 376
    Copy Casting 376
    Adjusting the Column Width 379
    Adjusting the Leading 379
    Using Hyphenation and Justification 380
    Controlling Word and Letter Spacing 381
Chapter Summary 381

11 PageMaker as a Design Tool 383
Creating Design Alternatives 384
    Identifying the Essential Elements 385
    Looking at Unique Design Features 387
Building a Template 389
    Defining the Standards 391
    Defining the Page Setup 392
    Identifying the Target Printer 395
    Selecting a Unit of Measure 395
    Displaying Rulers 396

Setting Defaults on the Type Menu 396
Setting Defaults on Style Sheets 397
Creating a Grid System 397
Identifying Common Text and Graphic Elements 400
Adding Standard Elements to Numbered Pages 402
Determining the Number of Templates Required 403
Adding Instructions for Working with the Template 404
Creating Specifications for Other Programs 405
Designing Page Layouts before Entering Content 406
Going beyond PageMaker 408
Chapter Summary 412

III Examples of Publications Created Using PageMaker

12 Creating Business Reports, Books, and Manuals 415
Design Principles 417
Production Tips 425
Examples 427
Chapter Summary 456

13 Creating Newsletters and Similar Publications 457
Design Principles 459
Production Tips 462
Examples 467
Chapter Summary 487

14 Creating Overhead Transparencies, Slides, and Handouts 489
Design Principles 491
Production Tips 495
Examples 498
Chapter Summary 516

15 Creating Brochures, Price Lists, and Directories 517
Design Principles 519
Production Tips 521

xix

	Examples 524
	Chapter Summary 550
16	**Creating Fliers and Display Ads** **551**
	Design Principles 551
	Production Tips 554
	Examples 555
	Glossary **569**

Introduction

PageMaker, by Aldus Corporation, is one of the most sophisticated page-layout programs for microcomputers on the market today. First released for the Macintosh computer in July 1985, and later for IBM ATs, AT compatibles, and IBM PS/2 computers, PageMaker is credited with starting the desktop publishing revolution.

Desktop publishing uses personal computers to produce typeset-quality text and clean graphic images, merge the text and graphics on the same page, and then print full pages on a high-resolution laser printer or typesetter. With desktop publishing, you eliminate the need for rulers, ink pens, blue lines, boards, wax, tape, screens, and X-ACTO knives as you produce final camera-ready pages for offset printing or photocopier reproduction.

PageMaker is an especially easy-to-use desktop publishing program. With it, you perform all your production tasks on a screen that displays an exact image of your page as it will be printed. (Some font types require additional soft fonts or cartridges for you to print what you see on-screen.) Because of the program's power and sophistication, almost any user can produce professional publications with a minimum investment in equipment and software.

Why a Book about PageMaker?

Although PageMaker basics are easy to learn, developing efficient operating techniques can take months. Moreover, the fact that the *program* is capable of producing beautiful publications does not guarantee that every *user* is capable of producing beautiful documents without getting advice from professional designers or studying graphic design.

Using PageMaker 4 for Windows helps solve the problems of the less experienced user. This book offers tips to help you design and produce a wide variety of documents. The documents included range from short brochures and fliers to full-length books and reports.

This book is not intended as a substitute for the excellent Aldus documentation. Instead, *Using PageMaker 4 for Windows* is a practical guide that goes beyond the basics of the manual and provides practical examples and hints for using the program in a production environment. This edition incorporates the features in PageMaker 4.0, including the new Story Editor and the Book feature for linking several PageMaker publications.

Who Should Use This Book?

No matter what your background and experience, you will need to learn new methods and terms when you enter the world of desktop publishing. This book brings together the special vocabularies of the typesetter, designer, word processor, and computer operator to explain clearly the concepts from these disciplines, which are merged in desktop publishing applications.

This book is intended for professional designers, typesetters, publishers, people in corporate publishing departments, and independent publishers who already are using or considering using PageMaker. The numerous examples demonstrate the wide range of possibilities with PageMaker. By studying these examples and tips, users can improve the appearance of their documents, as well as reduce the overall production time.

Although this book is addressed specifically to PC and PS/2 users, those persons using PageMaker on the Macintosh also will find these examples and suggestions useful.

What Is in This Book?

PageMaker 4.0 offers many more features than previous versions. You now can use PageMaker's Story Editor to edit text quickly. The Story Editor also includes a spelling checker and a search-and-replace feature. Typographic controls have been expanded to enable finer adjustments of line spacing, letter spacing, and point sizes, as well as direct control over the size and position of subscripts and superscripts. You now can generate automatically a table of contents and an index. You also can associate a series of PageMaker publications as a "book" with automatic adjustment of page numbers between sections. These capabilities and other new or enhanced features of PageMaker 4.0 are described in *Using PageMaker 4 for Windows*.

Part I of the book (Chapters 1-9) addresses PageMaker's basic features and describes the steps involved in producing a publication. Part II (Chapters 10-11) offers specific advice about defining the type specifications and designing and producing different types of publications. Part III (Chapters 12-16) presents examples of publications produced by PageMaker and highlights specific design and production tips. If you already are using PageMaker on the PC (or Version 4.0 on the Macintosh), you may want to skim Part I, looking for tips; read Part II; and use Part III as a reference source when you have a specific production problem.

Part I—The Production Process with PageMaker

The information in Part I (Chapters 1-9) lays a foundation. Chapter 1, "Introducing PageMaker and Desktop Publishing," defines desktop publishing and describes PageMaker's basic functions. After comparing PageMaker with word processing and graphics programs, the chapter describes the final form of a page created in PageMaker and gives an overview of the production process.

Chapter 2, "Getting Started," discusses the equipment required to run PageMaker and provides a list of optional equipment and compatible software programs. Then comes a discussion of the steps for installing and starting the program for the first time, with descriptions of the opening screens and menu commands. This chapter also offers a quick summary of the steps necessary to produce a complete PageMaker publication.

Chapter 3, "Creating a New Publication," presents detailed instructions and tips for laying out a document page-by-page and step-by-step. This chapter illustrates how to use PageMaker's ruler line, master page grid, and automatic page numbering capability. The chapter also offers specific tips on creating layouts that call for mixed formats (such as different numbers of columns from page to page).

Chapter 4, "Typing, Importing, and Editing Text," discusses the methods of placing text on a page in PageMaker (i.e., typing directly on the page, typing in PageMaker 4.0's Story Editor, or importing text from other sources), and distinguishes between formatting in a word processing program and formatting in PageMaker.

Chapter 5, "Formatting Text," demonstrates the techniques you use to edit and format text after it is in PageMaker, including changing paragraph formats (alignment and spacing) and character formats (font, leading, and kerning).

Chapter 6, "Working with Graphics," describes PageMaker's built-in graphics tools and tells how to bring in graphics created in other programs. You learn how to scale and crop graphics and how to position graphics on a page, including wrapping text around graphics and anchoring graphics within the text. You also see the difference between object-oriented and bit-mapped graphics.

Chapter 7, "Managing Large Documents and Linked Files," describes how to manage large documents using PageMaker 4.0's new features, including expanded capabilities for linking imported files to a PageMaker publication, associating a series of PageMaker publications through the Book command, and generating a table of contents and index. This chapter also offers suggestions for organizing your disk files and managing files in workgroups.

Chapter 8, "Printing," takes you through the steps involved in printing with different printers, including Apple's LaserWriter, Hewlett-Packard's LaserJet, and Allied's Linotronic typesetters. You learn how to work with multiple printers and how to print thumbnails and tabloid-size newspapers.

Chapter 9, "Making Color Separations," introduces you to PageMaker's color capabilities. You learn how to produce a camera-ready color document using PageMaker's color overlay feature, and how to add new dimensions to your publication with spot color.

Part II—Designing and Producing Different Types of Publications

Part II (Chapters 10 and 11) focuses on design decisions.

Chapter 10, "Typography," begins with a discussion from the typographer's view of a document—specifically, how to select fonts for a document. The chapter also tells which fonts are available for each printer, how you install the fonts, and how you create new fonts. As a result, you learn what fonts, font sizes, and font styles are available for your printer before you start the design process. You also learn how to work with a limited font selection. The chapter contains definitions and illustrations of leading and kerning and gives special tips on copy fitting.

Chapter 11, "PageMaker as a Design Tool," explores the process of designing with PageMaker, including developing a series of design alternatives for a single document and using master pages and templates to standardize a series of documents. This chapter offers special tips for creating design specifications for files from different sources, including word processors and graphics programs. In this chapter, you also find tips about preparing pages for the offset printer, including photographs and color separations.

Part III—Examples of Publications Created Using PageMaker

Part III (Chapters 12-16) offers numerous examples of different types of documents. These examples illustrate specific design principles and production tips that are given in Part II. The examples also demonstrate the range of fonts available with different printers.

Chapter 12, "Creating Business Reports, Books, and Manuals," describes some specific design and production ideas that you can use in creating reports, manuals, and books.

Chapter 13, "Creating Newsletters and Similar Publications," covers design features and production problems for documents that use columns, have "interrupted" text (text that is continued several pages later), and share some other characteristics.

Chapter 14, "Creating Overhead Transparencies, Slides, and Handouts," uses examples to show how to work with these "presentation" materials. Graphics play a major role in this type of publication.

Chapter 15, "Creating Brochures, Price Lists, and Directories," provides examples of these common publications. They are promotional materials, but come in a wide variety of formats.

Chapter 16, "Creating Fliers and Display Ads," explains how to approach these short documents that often come in nonstandard sizes.

Glossary

The Glossary includes terms used on PageMaker's menus and dialog boxes as well as traditional terms used in typesetting, design, and printing.

Enjoy *Using PageMaker 4 for Windows*, and make use of the many helpful tips in this book. You can profit from them by cutting down on the amount of time you need to put together your documents and the number of mistakes you make. These tips can help you create attractive and professional publications that fulfill your objectives.

Part I

The Production Process with PageMaker

Includes

Introducing PageMaker and Desktop Publishing

Getting Started

Creating a New Publication

Typing, Importing, and Editing Text

Formatting Text

Working with Graphics

Managing Large Documents and Linked Files

Printing

Making Color Separations

Part I introduces PageMaker's outstanding features and the basic steps of the production process. You learn about the equipment needed to install PageMaker, the tools for creating text and graphics in PageMaker, and the methods of bringing text and graphics from other applications into PageMaker.

Part I also teaches you how to edit and format text and graphics in PageMaker itself. In short, Part I gets you started in using PageMaker.

Introducing PageMaker and Desktop Publishing

PageMaker is a page-layout program with which you can compose a complete publication—including text and graphics—and preview full pages on-screen before printing the publication on a high-resolution printer or typesetter. In combining text and graphics created in PageMaker or imported from other software programs, PageMaker's tools and commands can perform the functions of the layout artist's tools and materials: typeset galleys of text, photographic reproductions of line art, halftones of photographs, pens, pressure-sensitive tapes, knives, wax, blue lines, boards, and acetate overlays. PageMaker 4.0 also incorporates the functions of a word processor, including automatic indexing, automatic generation of tables of contents, search and replace operations, and spelling checks.

Created by Aldus Corporation for the Macintosh computer and LaserWriter printer in 1985, PageMaker helped launch the desktop publishing revolution. This book tells you how to use PageMaker for desktop publishing on your IBM AT and its compatibles. You also will find tips and suggestions that can be applied to using PageMaker on Macintosh computers.

This chapter is an introduction for readers who are not already familiar with PageMaker and desktop publishing. If you are familiar with other desktop publishing applications, skip to Chapter 3 for an overview of how Page-Maker works. If you are familiar with Version 3.0 of PageMaker, skip ahead in this chapter to the summary of new features available in Version 4.0. You then can skim Chapters 3 through 8 to look for the 4.0 icon in the margin next to paragraphs that describe new features.

In this chapter, you see how desktop publishing has evolved from technological breakthroughs in a number of different fields and how desktop publishing is changing the way printed pages are produced in many different communication areas. You learn about PageMaker's basic capabilities by examining a page that was produced using PageMaker and several other programs. You also get an overview of the production process itself.

The Information Age

The emergence of desktop publishing technology reflects the fact that we live in an information society. Measured in terms of the number of people involved in production, the United States produces more information than manufactured goods. Each person probably spends more time consuming information than consuming tangible items, such as food or clothes.

A tremendous amount of information is generated daily. With so much information floating around, how can people consume and digest facts important to them? When reading a publication, how can you absorb all the information you need to know as quickly as possible? How can an author or publisher catch the reader's attention? The answer, of course, is to design the information to invite the reader's attention, to include headings and subheadings that make skimming the material for key points easy, and to include illustrations that can convey complex ideas much more quickly than words.

Desktop publishing enables you to create the kinds of effective, eye-catching publications that you need in this information age.

Development of Desktop Publishing

The term *desktop publishing* did not exist before 1985. The phrase originally was coined by one of PageMaker's designers, Paul Brainerd, the president of Aldus Corporation. The term quickly caught on as a way to describe the combined results of technological changes in the computer and publishing industries.

Chapter 1: Introducing PageMaker and Desktop Publishing

First, the cost of microcomputer equipment for on-screen graphics processing dropped noticeably. New breakthroughs in laser technology also reduced drastically the price of high-resolution printers and typesetters. To take advantage of the new laser printers, type manufacturers began designing new typefaces or adapting traditional typeface designs for the desktop publisher. Software developers realized that these breakthroughs in hardware technology had opened the way for the creation of programs, such as PageMaker, that merge text and graphics directly on-screen. These developments formed the basis of complete publishing systems assembled for extremely low prices (see fig. 1.1).

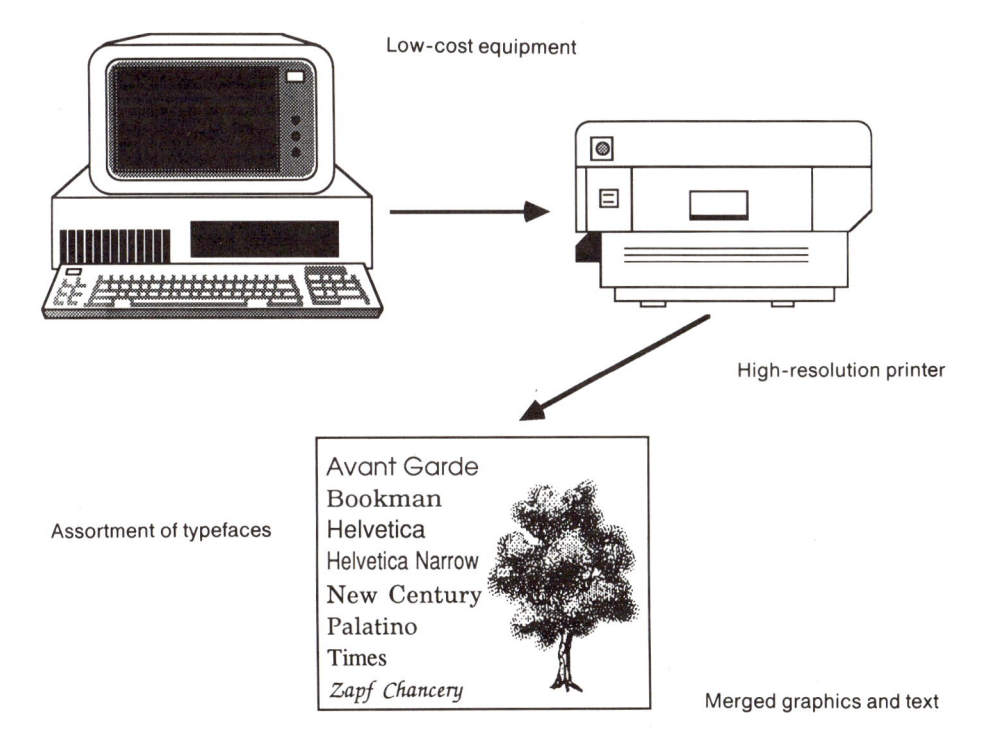

Fig. 1.1. Elements of desktop publishing.

This combination of capabilities, embodied in PageMaker, has had a tremendous impact on typesetters, designers, professional publishers, corporate publications departments, and small businesses (as well as those who dream of producing their own great novels). To understand the significance of these capabilities, you need to understand the factors discussed in the following sections—the roots of desktop publishing.

Using Low-Cost Equipment

The cost of personal computers has fallen significantly during the past ten years and continues to fall relative to the power and capabilities of the equipment. Owning a personal computer once meant a $5,000 investment in a simple computer with no software and little memory. Now, many PCs that are priced under $2,000 include the extra memory and graphics capabilities required for desktop publishing functions.

PageMaker 4.0 runs under Windows 3.0 and requires at least 2 megabytes (2M) of memory and a graphics card. Chapter 2 describes in more detail the equipment requirements for running PageMaker.

Using High-Resolution Printers

Since the introduction of laser technology into the desktop market, high-resolution printers and typesetters have replaced dot-matrix and fixed character-set printers in the office environment. Many offices, therefore, already are equipped for desktop publishing, even if they do not think of themselves as publishers.

Printer *resolution* is a measure of the sharpness of the edges of printed characters and graphics. Resolution commonly is measured by the number of dots, or spots, per inch (dpi). For example, dot-matrix printers print both text and graphics by pushing pins onto the ribbon that strikes the paper. The resolution of the image is limited by the number of thin metal rods the manufacturer puts in the print head. The common resolution for dot-matrix printers is 120 dots per inch. This resolution is considered coarse compared with the resolution of typesetting equipment, which uses a different technology to print images at 1,200 or 2,400 dots per inch (see fig. 1.2). Typesetting equipment, however, can cost from $20,000 to more than $100,000.

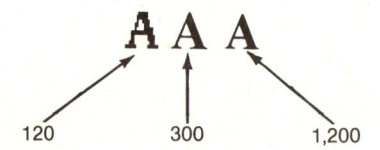

A A A
120   300   1,200

Fig. 1.2. Characters printed at 120, 300, and 1,200 dots per inch.

The revolution in printer technology began when Canon introduced the 300-dots-per-inch laser engine that is used in many printers now available for less than $5,000, such as Apple's LaserWriter series of printers (used to print the example shown in figure 1.2) and Hewlett-Packard's LaserJet series. Other manufacturers also have introduced laser printers that print 400 or 600 dots per inch. Linotype's Linotronic and other PostScript imagesetters use the same laser technology to phototypeset images at 1,200 or 2,400 dots per inch. PageMaker was designed to take full advantage of these printers' capabilities. Chapter 8 describes in greater detail the types of printers that are compatible with PageMaker.

To the untrained eye, publications printed at 300, 1,200, and 2,400 dpi appear the same. The text looks typeset at all three of these settings. As a result, desktop publishers can achieve—with PageMaker and a $3,000 printer—the same results that previously required an investment of more than $20,000.

Professional typesetters and others in the graphics industry, however, can see the difference between 300 and 1,200 dots per inch, and this difference can affect the appearance of the final publication when it is reproduced with offset printing. These professionals can get the best results from PageMaker with $30,000 worth of typesetting equipment, or they can use one of the many typesetting service bureaus that offer printing services for PageMaker publications.

Using Different Typefaces

The changes in printers naturally led to changes in typefaces for these printers. A *typeface* defines the appearance of a character. For example, Courier and Helvetica are two different typefaces. Desktop publishing introduces a broader range of typefaces than ever was possible in most office environments. Not so long ago, a typewriter had only one typeface—pica or elite. More recently, you could change the typeface in your typewriter or printer by changing the daisywheel or type element; but each publication usually showed only one typeface throughout—Courier, for example. You could mix boldface and normal characters on a page, but you couldn't mix normal characters and italic. Dot-matrix printers enabled you to mix normal, boldface, and italic characters and to print different sizes of letters, but the jaggedness of the output is considered inferior to the output of letter-quality printers (see fig. 1.3).

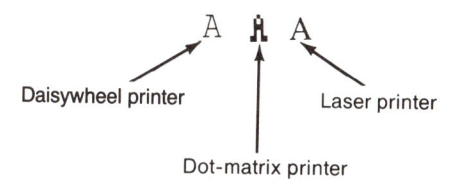

Fig. 1.3. Typefaces from a daisywheel printer, a dot-matrix printer, and a laser printer.

With desktop publishing's software and hardware components, you can print a variety of typefaces, styles, and sizes in a single publication. These features vary among printers, but any laser printer offers more than two options—the limit for most letter-quality printers. Desktop publishing offers as many typefaces as professional typesetting, and new typefaces are added to the list almost daily. Chapter 5 describes typefaces and how they are applied in PageMaker.

Merging Text and Graphics

As a result of these changes in technology, programs were developed to merge text and graphics. Merging text and graphics on-screen is not new; professional page-composition systems have been doing this for years. *Time* magazine, for example, started composing pages on a computer more than 15 years ago. Time, Inc., however, paid more than $250,000 for that system. Meanwhile, most publishers continued to use X-ACTO knives and wax to paste up printed text and line art on boards—usually slow and tedious work.

Before 1984, microcomputer users were able to produce text with word processing programs and graphics with their spreadsheet or drawing programs, but the output from the various programs rarely was merged on-screen or on paper. Instead, reports were assembled with all the graphics in an appendix, for example, or the graphics were printed on pages without text and merged with the text pages later. A few adventurous departments, using scissors and glue, left spaces in the text and inserted the graphics later.

PageMaker was one of the first page-composition packages that actually eliminated pasteup. Today PageMaker users can merge text with graphics and print fully composed pages. The basic tools of on-screen pasteup are the computer (with its various programs) and a high-resolution printer. With PageMaker, you can create text and graphics, and you can incorporate text and graphics from other programs. You then can copy and scale the graphics directly on-screen. After the layout of all the pages is finished, any change made on one page automatically shifts linked text on following pages. Chapters 3 through 6 describe the process of laying out pages in PageMaker.

With PageMaker, you can see on-screen how the page actually will look when printed. PageMaker is an approximate *WYSIWYG* system (pronounced *wizzy-wig*), meaning that "what you see is what you get." In other words, you can see graphics and text on-screen as they will appear on the printed page (with slight variations due to the different resolutions of the screen and printer). Only two such packages were available for the IBM PC before 1984, and both cost more than $5,000.

As you can see, desktop publishing is a result of technological breakthroughs in several fields. The fact that desktop publishing programs are personal computer applications means that many individuals and businesses already have desktop publishing facilities. Even though these users might not consider themselves publishers, they are beginning to realize that these new capabilities have the potential of making all printed communications more effective.

Desktop Publishing: The Melting Pot

Desktop publishing merges traditions from four disciplines: typesetting, graphic design, printing, and computing. Each discipline has its own set of technical terms and standards. Professionals from these fields find that they need to add a few terms to their vocabularies to "speak" desktop publishing. Users are discovering, for example, that terms such as *spot, dot,* and *pixel* can mean the same thing and that each area of expertise has something to teach the others.

Typesetting Traditions

Typesetters work with codes: one code sets the typeface, another sets the style, another the size, and so on. The disadvantage of the code-based systems is that they are difficult to learn. Furthermore, many typesetting machines lack the capability of previewing exactly how the text will look when printed; the typesetters have to print the text through the photochemical typesetting device to find any errors in the coding.

The advantage of traditional typesetting is precision. Most typesetting systems enable you to set the spacing between lines and letters in finer increments than are possible with PageMaker (which offers increments in type size and leading as small as one tenth of a point). Typesetters might need to adjust their demands and expectations slightly to match the capabilities of desktop publishing systems, but desktop publishing does not have to mean inferior typographic quality. Chapters 5 and 10 describe PageMaker's typographic controls in detail.

Although menu-driven systems such as PageMaker can be slower than typesetting machines, some typesetters welcome desktop publishing's low-cost WYSIWYG screens, short learning curve, and economical printing options. At the same time, desktop publishers can learn something from typesetters. For example, the typesetter can tell you how many words or characters of a certain typeface and size will fit in a given space. You learn several copy-fitting tricks in Chapter 10.

Design Traditions

Professional designers take pride in their ability to take a client's tastes and ideas and translate them into beautiful finished products. In the past, the process of transferring design ideas to paper has been painstaking and time-consuming, as reflected in the fees charged for design services.

With PageMaker, you can rough out design ideas quickly and deliver what looks like finished work rather than the traditional penciled sketches of the preliminary stages. In many cases, the efforts of producing a design idea with PageMaker are not lost, because the files can be fine-tuned for final production. Furthermore, files can be duplicated and modified for other publications in the same series or for similar publications in another series. In the long run, the efficiency of designing with desktop publishing techniques can be passed on to clients in the form of lower design fees.

Initially, some professional designers might balk at the idea of using a computer for such creative tasks (not to mention the lower billing amounts that result). These factors, however, can increase demand for design services at all levels.

The fact that even amateurs can produce attractive designs with PageMaker seems a bit frightening to professionals. Good design, however, always will require the knowledge and skills of the design trade. You learn some of these design principles in Chapters 11 through 16 in addition to production methods that help you match the designer's tradition of excellence with the business community's demand for expediency.

Printing Traditions

Not long ago, to make multiple copies of a publication, you had to take your masters to an offset printer to get the best results. More recently, some copy equipment has been improved to the point of producing good-quality reproductions. In either case, the result depended on the condition of the original page. You needed clean, clear, black images on white paper.

Now, laser printers print the entire image, including gray scales, directly on any color paper you choose. You can print hundreds of "originals" for immediate distribution. If you take the same image to an offset printer, however, you may find that the camera used in the printing process does not see the image the same way you do. In later chapters, you learn how to prepare your master for offset printing. You also learn the vocabulary you need to communicate with the printer, who is accustomed to dealing with graphics professionals. Chapter 9 specifically discusses the issues involved in preparing publications to be printed in color.

Computing Traditions

The final elements in the desktop publishing "melting pot" come directly from the computer industry. *Pixels* and *screen fonts*, *ports* and *baud rates*, *icons* and *menus* are terms that you will become familiar with as you move into desktop publishing from the other trades.

Throughout this book, you find production tips for getting the most out of your computer, for using PageMaker commands, for using Windows 3.0 commands, and for implementing other procedures unique to computer operation. You learn the importance of developing good "housekeeping" habits for your disk files, just as many designers practice good housekeeping with the papers and tools in their studios.

PageMaker

This chapter has discussed desktop publishing in general, using PageMaker as an example. What about PageMaker itself? How is PageMaker similar to and different from other programs you might be using on your computer? Table 1.1 itemizes the new features that have been added in PageMaker 4.0. The remainder of this section describes PageMaker's features as they compare to other packages you already might be using.

**Table 1.1
New Features Added in PageMaker 4.0**

Story Editor—a built-in word processor that offers

- Faster text editing than in Layout view
- Spelling checker
- Search and replace capability

Style sheet feature adds Next Style option to change styles automatically when you start a new line.

Enhanced typographic controls:

- Ruled lines that are part of paragraph format
- Inline graphics—graphics that can be embedded within paragraphs
- Text rotation capability (90 degrees)
- Capability to stretch and condense characters
- Size control of small caps, superscripts, and subscripts
- Automatic widow and orphan control
- Forced page breaks or column breaks as a text attribute
- Type set in any size from 4 points to 650 points and size adjustment and leading in one-tenth-point increments

New features for multiple-chapter publications:

- 999-page limit per publication
- Automatic table of contents and index generation
- Association of several publications as chapters that compose a book and automatic repagination as needed
- Compound page numbers, including page number prefixes and choice of Arabic or Roman numerals

Enhanced file management for linked text and graphics files:

- Option to link external graphic files or to incorporate them to be stored as part of the PageMaker publication, with individual link management for each imported file
- Option to update a publication graphic automatically when the external graphics file changes

Business publication support:

- Table Editor for creating rows and columns of data quickly and easily
- Option to import spreadsheets, graphs, charts, and data from spreadsheet and database programs
- 35 templates for creating business cards, memos, newsletters, and so on

Printing enhancements:

- Capability to print directly to color printers
- Open Prepress Interface (OPI) support for image scanning by high-end prepress color systems

Each of these features is described in detail in Chapters 3 through 8. Look for the PageMaker 4.0 icon in the margin next to paragraphs that introduce new features.

PageMaker is a page-composition program. PageMaker enables you to compose pages using elements created in other programs and in PageMaker. Figure 1.4 shows examples of several types of publications that you can produce using PageMaker.

You can type text directly into PageMaker, or you can type text using your word processor and then import that text into PageMaker. You can create simple graphics directly in PageMaker, and you can bring in graphics that were created using a graphics program such as Windows Draw or PC Paintbrush. After the graphics are in PageMaker, you easily can move the graphics around on the page, change their size and shape, add color, duplicate the graphics, or delete them.

PageMaker and Word Processors

You can type text in PageMaker much the way that you type text with your word processor. The text in the page-layout view on the PageMaker screen looks very nearly as it will when you print the page. Because PageMaker was designed as a graphics-oriented program, earlier versions were much slower for word processing than true word processing programs, which are designed for speed. For this reason, PageMaker 4.0 introduces the Story Editor—a built-in word processor that enables you to type and edit text as quickly as you can in most word processors. The Story Editor is described in greater detail in Chapter 4.

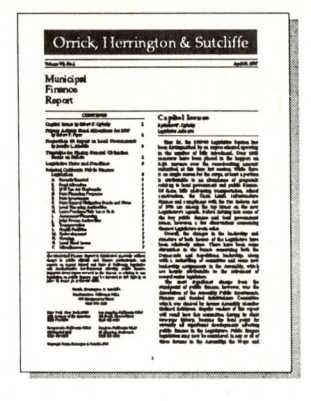

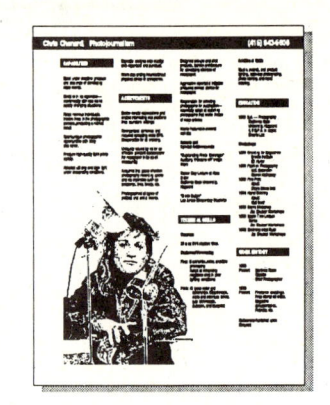

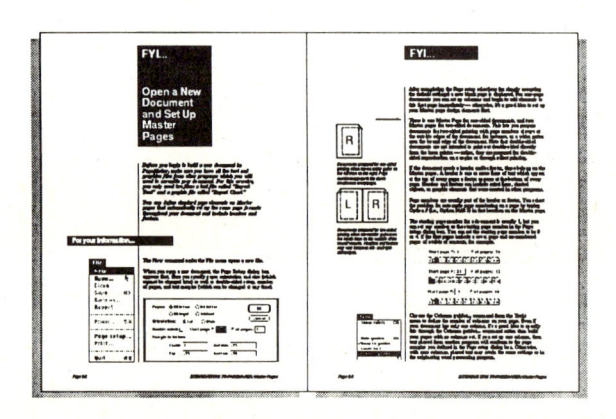

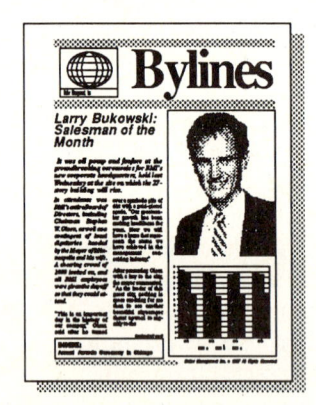

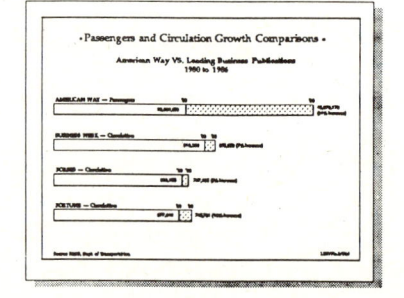

20 Part I: The Production Process with PageMaker

Fig. 1.4. Publications produced using PageMaker.

In addition, the Story Editor offers several special word processing functions, including a global search and replace feature and a spelling checker. In fact, you now can use PageMaker as a stand-alone word processing package. If you choose to use a word processor for your initial text entry, or if you will be assembling your publications using text collected from a variety of sources, PageMaker enables you to import text from most word processing applications, as described in Chapter 4.

On the other hand, if you do not already own a copy of PageMaker but use an advanced word processing package such as WordPerfect 5.1, you might question investing in a page-layout application such as PageMaker when your word processor can do the same thing.

Since the dawn of desktop publishing, word processing applications have been evolving to perform more like page-layout applications. Page-layout applications first offered the capability to use different typefaces in a publication, and now most word processors offer that capability. Desktop publishing introduced WYSIWYG, and now many word processors are WYSIWYG—especially when run under Microsoft Windows. Page-layout applications enabled you to create and import graphics, and now word processors enable you to create and import graphics. You can expect these two application areas to merge even further as time goes on.

So, why would you invest in a page-layout application that costs $795 (PageMaker) when you can get the same results from your word processor for $495 (WordPerfect and Microsoft Word for Windows)? The following sections detail nine differences that remain between word processing and page-layout applications—nine reasons that designers and typographers choose PageMaker over traditional word processing applications.

Typographic Controls

PageMaker enables you to adjust in fine increments the spacing between characters, words, and lines. You can use this feature to make type fit a given space or to give a page a custom look. The feature is used most often, however, to adjust large fonts in headlines, banners, and logos. In the early days, PageMaker met with heavy criticism for enabling you to adjust leading only in half-point increments; therefore, recent versions enable you to adjust leading and point size in one-tenth-point increments. A point is 1/72nd of an inch—0.0139 inches. Typographers are accustomed to working with these small numbers.

Word processors, on the other hand, often are designed to measure distance in inches. The old standard on typewriters was six lines per inch. Spacing between lines (i.e., "leading") could be set as single-line, line-and-a-half, or double spacing. Although some word processors enable you to adjust leading in finer increments, their adjustment capabilities do not equal those of PageMaker. Some word processors enable you to expand or condense type by adjusting the space between all selected characters—a process called *tracking*. PageMaker offers tracking as well as kerning, which is a more complete type of control over spacing between characters.

Irregular Text Wrap

PageMaker offers an automatic text wrap feature that includes an irregular text wrap capability—PageMaker can wrap text around the edges of nonrectangular graphics. With a word processor, you can force an irregular wrap by inserting carriage returns manually, but you also need layering capability (described later in this chapter) to force the text to cross the rectangular bounding box that holds the imported graphic. Text wrap is described in Chapter 6.

Graphics Tools

PageMaker incorporates the basic graphics tools that you find in drawing applications—lines, rectangles, and ovals. Word processing programs like WordPerfect and Microsoft Word also enable you to create lines or boxes as part of the text, but they do not have an oval tool. Word processing applications also do not include fill capability for solid shapes or a wide variety of line styles. In addition, PageMaker offers image manipulation tools for imported scans.

Layers

Another distinguishing feature is PageMaker's capability to work in layers. You can layer graphics and text on top of each other. The most common use of this feature is to place text on a shaded background, but you also can layer text on top of imported graphics to achieve special effects, as often seen in magazines and newspapers. You can layer graphics on top of one another as well.

Master Pages

Almost all word processors have the capability to create running headers or footers that appear on every page. In some word processing applications, you can include graphics in the headers or footers. PageMaker takes this capability one step further by enabling you to create master pages. A *master page* contains the basic grid and other elements appearing on every page of the publication. You can put text or graphic elements anywhere on a master page—not just in the header or footer—and these elements will appear on every page in the publication.

Bleeds between Pages

Sometimes you see an illustration or a simple graphic element (such as a line or a box) that runs off the edge of a page or crosses from one page to the facing page—a situation known as a *bleed*. Bleeds are possible with PageMaker but currently impossible with any word processing applications. Bleeds are described and shown in Chapters 12 and 15.

Color Separations

Some word processing applications (such as Microsoft Word) enable you to apply different colors within a document for printing on a color printer. These applications do not enable you (as PageMaker does) to print the color separations necessary for offset printing in color.

Efficiency

The final pages printed from a word processing application and PageMaker might look the same. If you plan to produce a large volume of complex page layouts, however, you should compare time spent producing a page using a word processing application versus using PageMaker. Page-layout applications compete heavily on efficiency; factors such as screen redraw speed and number of steps required to position a graphic affect the purchase decision for many publishers. Word processors, on the other hand, still compete primarily on their text-handling features; the capability to incorporate graphics and to create complex page layouts is just icing on the cake. The fact that text-handling features are available with word processing applications might affect the purchase decision, but the efficiency of the process is less important.

Printing Speeds

Word processors originally were designed to print words only. To keep a good share of the market from switching to page-layout applications, word processing programs more recently have added the capability to create and import graphics. Word processors, however, haven't yet provided the capability to print pages with graphics quickly—a PageMaker capability that appeals to professional publishers who produce hundreds of pages a day.

PageMaker and Graphics Programs

You can draw simple graphics, such as lines, boxes, and circles, directly in PageMaker; or you can bring in graphics from other programs (as described in Chapter 6). Graphic images that have been brought into PageMaker can be scaled and cropped to fit the allotted space on individual pages. Like most drawing programs, PageMaker has menus of available lines and fill patterns for graphic objects. PageMaker also enables you to add color to your graphic images, as described in Chapter 8.

If you are accustomed to using a graphics program as a stand-alone package to produce one-page documents such as fliers and advertisements, you should know that PageMaker offers additional benefits. Most drawing programs accommodate some form of text entry but do not handle text formatting, such as columnar layouts and tabular data, as readily as Pagemaker does. Furthermore, most graphics programs do not handle multiple pages. By working directly with a draw or paint program, however, you can use some of the more sophisticated features not offered directly in PageMaker, such as airbrush effects, blends, and pixel-by-pixel image manipulation. You also can use a paint program to clean up images that have been digitized with a scanner. These images then can be imported into PageMaker.

The Final PageMaker Publication

A completed PageMaker publication can be composed of text and graphics created entirely in PageMaker or created with elements brought in from other programs. Figure 1.5 shows a typical page created using PageMaker. The text was typed in a word processing program (Microsoft Word). The text then was moved into PageMaker with the PageMaker's Place command. The bar graph was created in 1-2-3. The graphic logo—a globe—was created in a drawing program (Windows Draw). A scanned image was modified using PC Paintbrush before the image was placed on the PageMaker page. Some of the short text elements, such as the banner text across the top of the page, were typed directly into PageMaker. Other text, such as the headline, was modified using PageMaker's Style Sheet option. Hairline rules and boxes were added with PageMaker's graphics tools. Running feet and automatic page numbering were set up on the publication's master page, the page that contains the basic grid and other elements appearing on every page of the publication.

Fig. 1.5. A page created using PageMaker.

Figure 1.5 shows you what is possible with PageMaker. The rest of the book shows you how to create such a publication.

PageMaker and the Publishing Cycle

PageMaker brings together functions that at one time were divided among many people at different locations. For example, before desktop publishing, a typist might have typed the text of a newsletter and sent the file, on paper or on disk, to the typesetter for formatting and typesetting. Meanwhile, the graphics department might have used a computer or pens and ink to create the graphic images for an outside service to photostat to the correct size. Eventually, the galleys of type and the reproductions of the figures would reach a drafting table, where the layout artist would use X-ACTO knives and wax to trim the paper and paste it down on boards into final pages.

With PageMaker, the same person can type the text, draw the graphics, and compose the pages on-screen. Just because one person is performing all the steps does not mean that the steps themselves are much different. The person responsible for the entire production, however, may be strong in some areas and weak in others. Many desktop publishing departments, therefore, still divide the desktop publishing tasks among different people. When the production team is small (as is common in desktop environments), weak spots still can develop in the production cycle—areas in which no one on the team has experience. This book provides tips in areas of expertise where you and your team may be lacking.

Division of Responsibilities

Even if one person produces the publication, responsibilities still can be divided conceptually among different publishing roles: production manager, author, editor, copy editor, designer, illustrator, and production crew.

The production manager oversees the entire project, makes sure that everyone else involved meets the schedule, or adjusts the schedule as needed. The production manager also should make sure that efficient file management procedures are followed throughout the project, as described in Chapters 12 through 16.

The author delivers complete, accurate text, probably on a disk. An author also can format the text if he or she knows the final design specifications.

An editor then reviews the text and graphics to be sure that the publication is clear and complete. The copy editor reads the text and graphics for grammatical, typographical, and formatting errors and makes sure that all references to figures or other sections or pages of the publication are accurate. The editors also may be responsible for tone and content.

The designer determines the overall appearance of the pages: paper size and orientation, margins, and basic grid structure. The designer specifies the typefaces, sizes, and styles to be used in the publication and also may specify fill patterns or treatments for all illustrations. The illustrator produces the graphics files that will be placed on the page. In some cases, the illustrator may be the author or the designer.

Finally, the production crew includes anyone who sits at the computer and uses PageMaker to assemble the pages. The production crew also may format the text if the author has not done the formatting.

As stated previously, these responsibilities may be performed by one person or divided among several people, depending on the situation. A knowledge of these functions will help you more easily produce high-quality work with PageMaker.

Steps in the Production Process

Whether you produce a publication on your own or with a team, you can set up an efficient production schedule if you recognize the steps involved in a typical production cycle. Some of these steps can take place at the same time, and some projects may drop some steps or call for a slightly different sequence. A typical production schedule showing relationships among the following steps is shown in a Gannt chart in figure 1.6. (A Gannt chart shows the length of time allowed for each project task and the period of time during which the task must be completed to meet the schedule—that is, the earliest start and latest finish dates.)

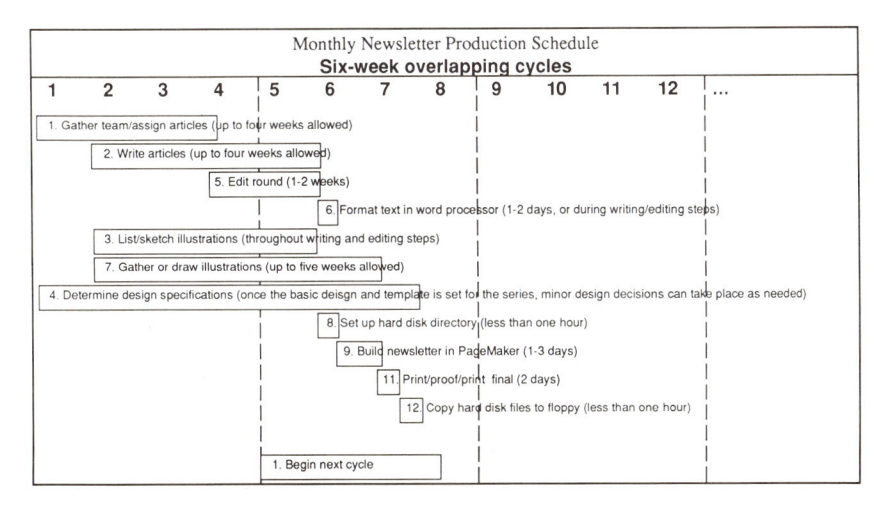

```
                Monthly Newsletter Production Schedule
                     Six-week overlapping cycles
  1    2    3    4    5    6    7    8    9    10   11   12   ...
  | 1. Gather team/assign articles (up to four weeks allowed) |
       | 2. Write articles (up to four weeks allowed) |
            | 5. Edit round (1-2 weeks) |
                 | 6. Format text in word processor (1-2 days, or during writing/editing steps) |
       | 3. List/sketch illustrations (throughout writing and editing steps) |
       | 7. Gather or draw illustrations (up to five weeks allowed) |
  | 4. Determine design specifications (once the basic deisgn and template is set for the series, minor design decisions can take place as needed) |
                 | 8. Set up hard disk directory (less than one hour) |
                 | 9. Build newsletter in PageMaker (1-3 days) |
                      | 11. Print/proof/print final (2 days) |
                      | 12. Copy hard disk files to floppy (less than one hour) |
                           | 1. Begin next cycle |
```

Fig. 1.6. A typical production schedule.

The typical steps in the production process are the following:

1. Gather the team, identify the division of responsibilities, and prepare the production schedule. The team can include the client ordering the work as well as the production group; or a "team" may be simply the talents of one individual who sketches a single timetable.

2. Write the text using PageMaker's Story Editor or a word processor. Even if the authors are not using the same type of computer that you will be using with PageMaker, almost any text can be converted or telecommunicated before the final PageMaker stage.

3. Sketch or list illustration ideas.

4. Determine the design specifications, including the following:

    - Typefaces, sizes, and styles for different elements within the text

    - Basic text format

      Will the paragraphs have a first line indentation? What spacewill be left between paragraphs? Will the text be justified? Will headings be flush left or centered?

    - Basic page layout or grid

      Includes page size, margins, orientation, number of columns, and positions of other nonprinting guides. Some of this information is required before you start a new PageMaker publication.

    - Final (maximum) size of illustrations, as well as typefaces, sizes, and styles to be used within the illustrations and in the captions

    - Final page count or the range of pages expected to be filled

      This count will help you to decide whether to divide a long publication into smaller publications or sections, to determine how to divide the publication, and to estimate the printing costs. The page count traditionally has been performed after the text is written because the design itself may be affected by the content and structure of the text. Often, the authors know the design specifications (including page count) before writing the text, enabling the authors to participate in the production by setting tabs and other format requirements.

5. Have one or more editors read the text for the following purposes:

    - One reading for accuracy and completeness of the content

    - One reading for grammar and consistency of usage

    - One reading to mark the text according to the design specifications

Most professionals find that one person cannot read on all these levels at one sitting. If you have only one reader, these readings should be done separately.

6. Edit and format the text with the word processor, or edit and format the text in PageMaker in step 10. If you are using PageMaker for editing, do as much editing as possible in the Story Editor.

7. Create the illustrations using the graphics program best suited for each, as follows:

    - Scanners can digitize photographs and line drawings that would be difficult to reproduce otherwise.

    - Paint programs are best for working with digitized images and for "fine art" illustrations—original artwork that is never modified or edited.

    - Drafting packages should be used for line art and technical illustrations.

    - Spreadsheets or graphing programs are most efficient for graphs that are derived from tables of numbers.

    - Some illustrations or graphic elements can be created directly in PageMaker.

8. Set up a single directory on the hard disk for this document or publication; move all text and graphics files into that directory. (Several small projects can be grouped into a single directory.)

9. Use PageMaker to create a master template for the entire publication (if the publication requires more than one publication file). The publication always includes the master page elements and can include a style sheet and elements on the numbered pages as well.

10. To build the publication, use the PageMaker tools to add elements and to insert the text and graphics files created in other programs.

11. Print the publication. (You will perform this step many times during the production cycle.)

12. When the project is finished, copy all files related to that publication onto one or more floppy disks or a removable hard disk for archiving. Save the disk files until the publication has been reproduced and distributed—or longer if the publication will be revised for later editions. (Don't forget to save files while you work on them; if your hard disk fails, you will need a backup copy of your work.)

Some of these steps are essential for any PageMaker production. Other steps, such as designing a publication from scratch, are considered advanced. If you are new to design, you probably should start with small projects that mimic other publication designs. After you have learned how to use PageMaker's basic features (described in Chapters 3 through 8) and tried building a few pages, you can tackle the advanced topics covered in Chapters 9 and 10. Table 1.2 indicates the level of each step and lists the chapters that provide information about each step.

**Table 1.2
Where To Find More Information**

Step	Level	Chapter
1	Basic	Chapter 1 (this section)
2	Basic	Chapter 4
3	Advanced	Chapter 10
4	Advanced	Chapters 10 and 11
5	Basic	(not covered in this book)
6	Basic	Chapter 4
	Advanced	Chapter 10
7	Basic	Chapter 6
8	Basic	Chapter 2
	Advanced	Chapter 7
9	Basic	Chapter 3
	Advanced	Chapter 11
10	Basic	Chapters 3, 4, 5, 6, 7, 9
11	Basic	Chapter 8
12	Basic	Chapter 7

Quality, Economy, and Deadline

More than almost any other business or activity, publishing is ruled by deadlines. For example, you cannot send out June's news in July. When the published document is part of a larger product package, the marketing or distribution group probably will want the publications finished as soon as the product is ready for shipment, even though you cannot write the text until the product is complete. For these reasons, the publication department usually is pushed to complete everything as quickly as possible. Professionals often must struggle to maintain the highest quality in their productions. In the end, you will find that no publication ever is perfect in the eyes of those who worked on it.

When you produced your business reports with a word processor and a letter-quality printer, you probably spent more time editing the content of the publication than you spent formatting the pages. With desktop publishing, you may find that the reverse is true; you will spend more time formatting than editing.

This reversal of formatting and editing will be especially true if your production group includes professional designers or typesetters who will not tolerate inconsistencies and misalignments. During the final stages, you will discover that what you see on a 72-dpi screen is not exactly what you get when you print with a 300-dpi laser printer. You then may have to make fine adjustments to the file to get exactly what you want.

You probably will need to print your publication more than once during the final production stages, so plan for several printings as part of the production schedule. Remember that printing time can be significant when you are producing a 400-page book with graphics.

Chapter Summary

The process of putting text and graphics on a page is changing drastically and quickly, thanks to the revolution called desktop publishing. PageMaker continues to hold an important position in this new field and has helped to transform the appearance of a wide range of printed communications. Some people believe that desktop publishing with personal computers will revolutionize our communications as significantly as Gutenberg's press did in the fifteenth century. In the end, of course, the real impact of this revolution will not be on the production methods alone, but also on the readers, who will benefit from the clearly formatted and illustrated publications.

Getting Started

PageMaker runs in the Microsoft Windows environment on a Personal Computer AT or compatible system. Although PageMaker can run on a 286 system, Aldus recommends using a 386 system for faster operation. PageMaker's 3 1/2-inch version runs on the IBM PS/2 and portable computers that can run under the Windows environment. Unlike previous versions of PageMaker, PageMaker 4.0 must run under Microsoft Windows 3.0, have a minimum of 2M of memory, a graphics card, and a hard disk of at least 20M for storage (Aldus recommends 40M).

This chapter presents basic steps concerning installing PageMaker and starting the program. You see how Windows works, and you learn how to use PageMaker efficiently.

The last section in the chapter contains a brief presentation of the steps involved in producing a document, from verifying the necessary disk files to printing the final copy. Later chapters provide more details and tips concerning the steps in this chapter. Beginners may need to refer to user's manuals concerning the Windows operating environment and DOS to find information not presented in this book.

If you have used PageMaker on the Macintosh, review the first part of this chapter to learn how Windows works on the IBM. If you are familiar with Windows 3.0, you can skip ahead to the section on installing PageMaker. If someone else has installed PageMaker on your system, find out whether you need to change to a particular directory, and then read the section called "Starting PageMaker." If you are new to both Windows and PageMaker, you should read this entire chapter before starting the installation process.

Reviewing Hardware Requirements

In addition to PageMaker, a full desktop publishing system includes a computer with a graphics board, a draft-quality dot-matrix printer, a high-resolution printer for final copies, and a scanning device. Before you install PageMaker on your system, be sure that your equipment meets PageMaker's minimum requirements. A system equipped to run Microsoft Windows usually can run PageMaker if it is equipped with enough memory.

PageMaker runs on IBM AT (80286 and 80386) and equivalent systems, IBM PS/2 computers, some WANG system models, Hewlett-Packard Vectra Systems PCs, VAXmate systems, and Apple's Macintosh computers. The term *IBM AT* indicates that the system includes a hard disk and some of the other elements shown in figure 2.1. Compatible PC systems that can run PageMaker must have a hard disk and include all the elements listed in figure 2.1.

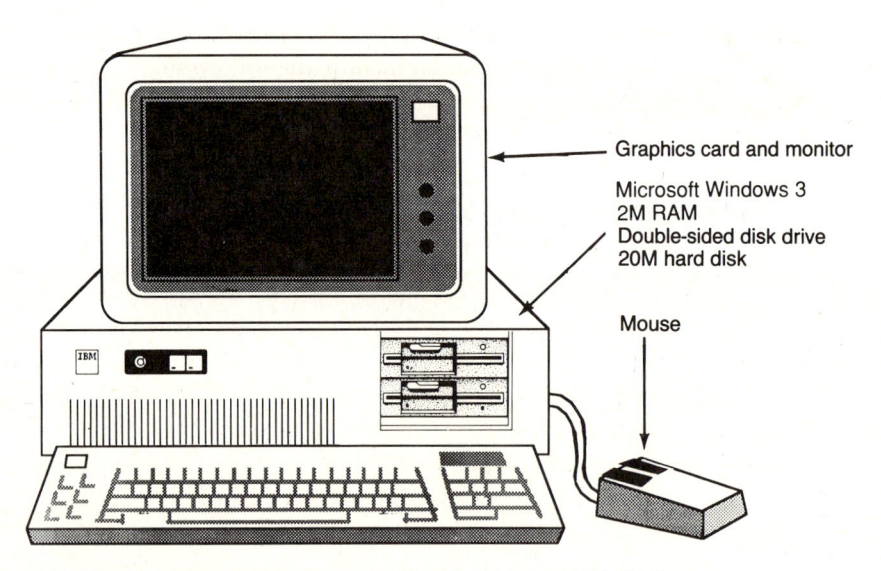

Fig. 2.1. Elements Required for running PageMaker on an IBM AT.

AT systems require a 20M hard disk and a double-sided disk drive that can read 1.2M 5 1/4-inch disks or 720K 3 1/2-inch disks. PageMaker needs at least an AT or compatible computer to run. An XT cannot run PageMaker. Be sure that your hard disk has 5M of free space before you install PageMaker. If you want to install all of the available drivers and all of the available templates, you need even more space on your hard disk.

PageMaker 4.0 requires 2M of RAM (random-access memory), but the program runs faster with more memory. With Windows 3.0 and a 386 AT machine, you can run programs simultaneously.

The PC also requires a graphics card, such as an Enhanced Graphics Adapter (EGA), Video Graphics Array (VGA), or Hercules Graphics Card, and a monochrome or color monitor that can display graphics. The better the screen resolution of your monitor, the more accurately your screen displays text and graphics. To work with Windows and PageMaker, you also need a pointing device, such as a mouse.

You should have DOS and Windows 3.0 on your system before you install PageMaker. PageMaker 4.0 will not work with any earlier version of Windows.

Printers

PageMaker documents can be printed on some dot-matrix printers, but the final printer usually is a laser printer or typesetter. At this writing, the printers supported by the program include the following:

- Hewlett-Packard (HP) LaserJet Series printers
- Apple LaserWriters
- Allied Linotronic 100 or 300
- Any PostScript printer
- Any PCL printer that is fully HP LaserJet compatible
- QMS ColorScript 100 and many compatible color printers

Your printer choice affects your options for selecting fonts on the menu. Chapter 8 explains printer drivers and fonts and how to choose different printers on a multiprinter network. For specific instructions on installing a particular printer, refer to the documentation provided with your equipment.

Scanners

If you expect to be using a lot of artwork that currently exists on paper but not on disk, consider investing in a scanner as part of your hardware configuration. Artwork on paper can be *digitized*, converted to a disk file PageMaker can use, with a scanning device. Digitized images are saved in one of the paint formats supported by PageMaker or in Microsoft's Tag

Image File Format (TIFF). Canon, Datacopy Corporation, DEST Corporation, Microtek Lab, Inc., Hewlett-Packard, Ricoh Systems, Inc., and others also make software to create scanned images that can be saved in one of these formats.

Installing PageMaker

Before you install PageMaker on your system, read this description of the installation process. The installation program leads you step-by-step through the installation process. Unlike earlier versions of PageMaker, PageMaker 4.0 does not ask you what kind of equipment you are using. The program relies on the choices you made during the installation of Microsoft Windows. If you make changes to your system after you install Windows, modify Windows to reflect those changes before you install PageMaker.

The installation process asks you for the directory names of the Aldus-related software and the PageMaker 4.0 directory. If you do not want to use the directory names suggested by Aldus, you should choose the names of these directories before you start the installation process. The installation program enables you to abort the process if you come to a question that you cannot answer.

The PageMaker package includes five 5 1/4-inch disks for installation on a 1.2M drive. These PageMaker disks are called Disk 1, Disk 2, Disk 3, Disk 4, and Printers Drivers for Windows 3.0.

Five 3 1/2-inch disks are needed for the 720K computers: Disk 1, Disk 2, Disk 3, Disk 4, and Disk 5.

If your system has only 360K disk drives, you can order the correct disks from Aldus.

Before you can install PageMaker, you must have Windows 3.0 on your hard disk. If you try to install the program without first starting Windows, you get the message `This program requires Microsoft Windows`, and the setup program does not start.

To begin installation of PageMaker, you must first enter Windows. You can start Windows in different ways, depending on how it was set up during installation. If you accept all of Windows' defaults during installation, you simply type *win* at the C prompt. If you did not have the installation program update your CONFIG.SYS and AUTOEXEC.BAT files, you might need to change to the Windows subdirectory before you type *win*. Some computers

Chapter 2: Getting Started

are configured so that you enter Windows automatically when you turn on the machine. Put Disk #1 into drive A of your computer. When you are in Windows, select the Run command from the File menu in Window's Program Manager (see fig. 2.2). In the dialog box, type

A:\ALDSETUP

and then click OK. Make sure that the Run Minimize box isn't checked off.

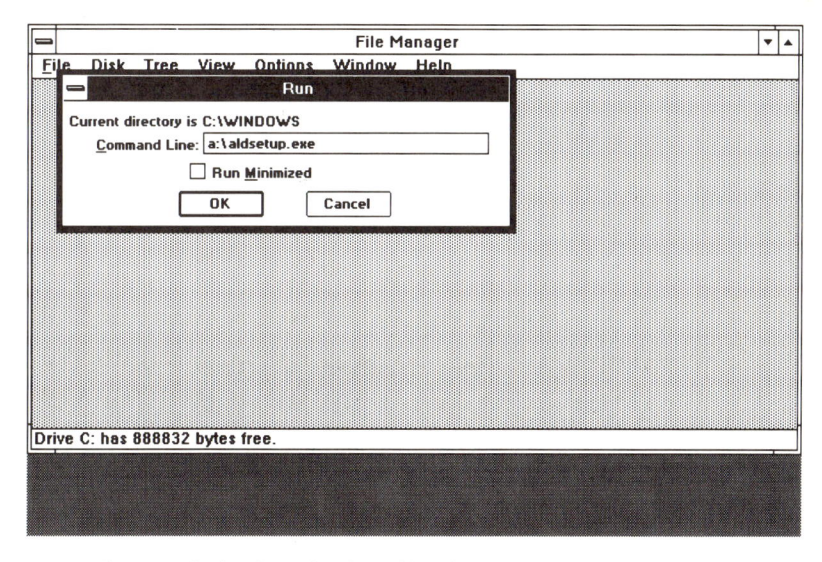

Fig. 2.2. The Run dialog box displayed by the Run command from the File menu in the Windows Program Manager.

Anytime during installation you can press Alt-X or highlight the Exit box to stop the process and cancel the installation. You usually press Enter or Alt-S to continue installation and view the next screen. The next screen shows you the main PageMaker Installation menu. You can install all the PageMaker options or a specific option, such as the template or tutorial files. The menu enables you to modify easily certain options without reinstalling all of PageMaker.

You first must decide where you want the Aldus files placed. The default choice places the files in drive C and in the Aldus directory, C:\ALDUS. If you want to modify the location of these files, start typing and C:\ALDUS is erased and replaced with whatever drive and directory you choose.

The second screen displayed during the installation process shows you the Aldus Setup Main Window (see fig. 2.3). Six categories of files for installation can be selected from the list in the dialog box: PageMaker, Tutorial, Filters, PostScript Templates, PCL Templates, and PostScript Font Metrics.

Part I: The Production Process with PageMaker

What this setup feature enables you to do is selectively install only parts of the full PageMaker package (if you want to save space on your hard disk and you do not need all of the templates, for example), reinstall parts of PageMaker (when you get an update of Version 4.0), or install additional filters (if you did not install all of them the first time).

PageMaker, Tutorial, and Filters are highlighted initially. You can select the three highlighted items or add the other options by clicking the mouse on the selections that you want. If you want to cancel a highlighted selection, click on the option, and it is deselected. After you have chosen the categories you want to install, click on the Setup box, or press Alt-S.

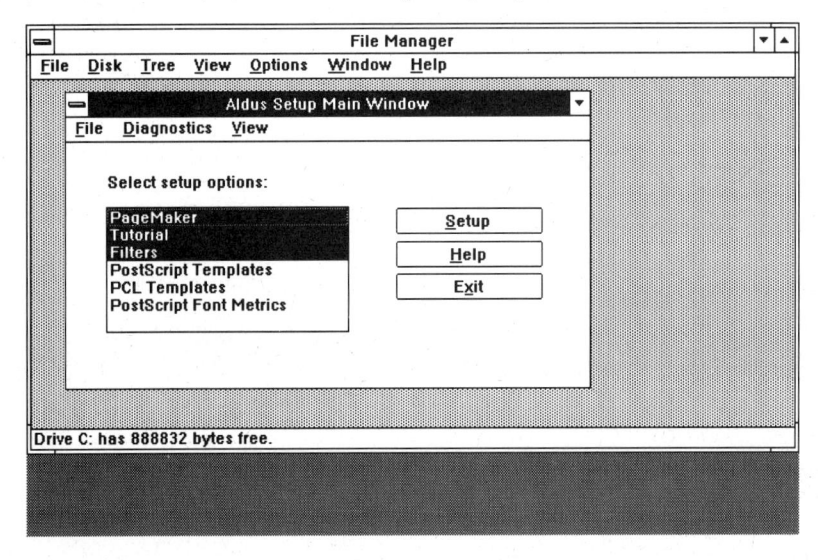

Fig. 2.3. The Aldus Setup Main Window.

Naming the PageMaker Directory

The next screen displayed during the installation process prompts you to select the directory that you want to use for the PageMaker program and related files. You can create a new directory or use one on your hard disk. If you use an established directory, specify the full path name of the directory. Type the name of the directory you want, or accept the suggested default path of C:\PM4. Press Enter.

After you select a directory for the PageMaker files, the installation program asks you for your name, company, and the serial number of your PageMaker program. Your serial number is printed on the master disks. Type the numbers and dashes exactly as they are listed. If you do not type the number correctly, the program will prompt you to try again, and the installation cannot continue without the correct serial number. If you cannot locate the serial number and you cancel the process, you must reinstall PageMaker from the beginning. The installation will not save the selections made up to this point.

In the following screen, the installation program asks you whether it should append your AUTOEXEC.BAT and CONFIG.SYS files so that your hard disk can find your PageMaker files. These files also tell your computer how many files to work with. If you click Enter, the installation program adds the following commands to your AUTOEXEC.BAT file:

PATH C:\PM4;C:\DOS

SET TEMP=C:\PM4

If you do not have a path created, PageMaker creates the path C:\PM4 and adds it to your batch file. The PATH command causes DOS to search all listed directories when you enter a command that is not found in the current directory. Enter the command *win pm4* from any directory to start PageMaker. The installation program also changes your CONFIG.SYS file to enhance the performance of PageMaker.

If you don't want PageMaker to make the changes, you can click No and modify the files yourself. You also can edit your AUTOEXEC.BAT and CONFIG.SYS files to make these changes.

Selecting Filters

PageMaker has the capability to use text and graphics from other programs. Because each program is different, PageMaker provides filters that can be used to import and export text and graphics. To import text from dBASE IV, for example, you must install the dBASE filter in PageMaker. PageMaker then can import the dBASE files, read them, and correctly place them into your document.

PageMaker now asks you which filters you want installed. You can select a few specific filters or all of the filters listed. On the bottom of the screen, the Select Filters dialog box shows you how much space is needed to install the selected filters and how much space you have left on your hard disk (see fig. 2.4). After you have selected the filters that you want, press Enter or Alt-S.

PageMaker then decompresses and copies all necessary files from the PageMaker disks. As the files are copied onto the hard disk, you see what percentage of files have been copied. This process takes 7-25 minutes, depending on the speed of your computer and the number of options you install. PageMaker signals you with a beep when it needs a different disk. To continue, you must insert the requested disk and press Enter.

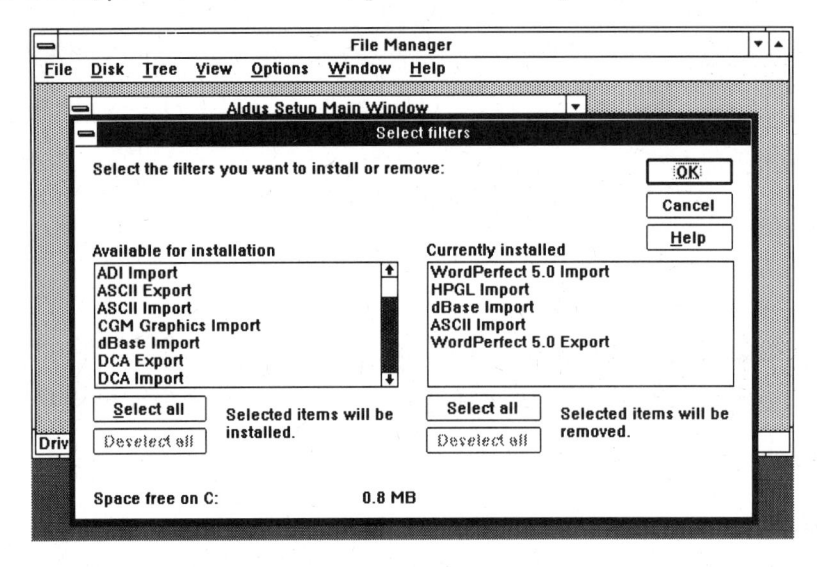

Fig. 2.4. The Select Filters dialog box.

After installing the program, PageMaker asks whether you want to exit PageMaker or reboot to take advantage of the changes made during installation. If you click the Enter key, the computer reboots, and PageMaker opens.

Managing Files

PageMaker requires a hard disk system to run on an IBM AT or a compatible system. You should use a hierarchical system of directories to organize all of your files. You also should organize your program files and your data files.

When you install PageMaker, the installation program sets up a directory structure for you. In the typical PageMaker setup, the directory named PM4 has five subdirectories. In figure 2.5, the subdirectories are named TUTORIAL, where tutorial files are stored; TEMPLATE, where style sheets are stored; SETUP, where all of the setup files are stored; PROXIMITY, where the dictionary and hyphenation files are stored; and FILTERS, where the filter files for programs that are imported or exported are stored.

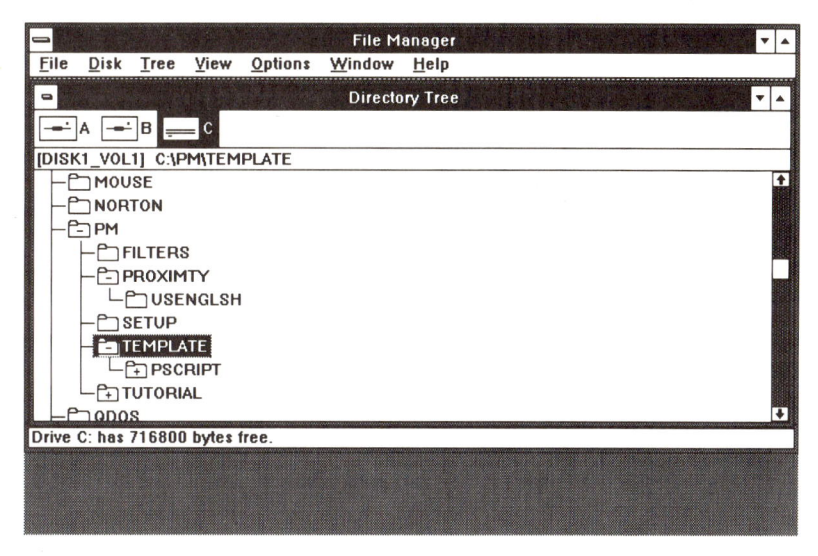

```
                          File Manager
  File   Disk   Tree   View   Options   Window   Help
                         Directory Tree
   A    B    C
 [DISK1_VOL1]  C:\PM\TEMPLATE
        ├─ MOUSE
        ├─ NORTON
        ├─ PM
        │    ├─ FILTERS
        │    ├─ PROXIMTY
        │    │    └─ USENGLSH
        │    ├─ SETUP
        │    ├─ TEMPLATE
        │    │    └─ PSCRIPT
        │    └─ TUTORIAL
        ├─ QDOS
 Drive C: has 716800 bytes free.
```

Fig. 2.5. *A typical hard disk directory for PageMaker.*

You usually have plenty of storage space when you work with a hard disk, but you easily can create so many files that you cannot view the complete list of files on-screen at once. More than one screen of file names can be an inconvenience. A more serious production problem is that you cannot track all the files used to create documents. You should create a separate directory or subdirectory outside the PM4 and WINDOWS directories for each project or long document. A directory map set up for a busy production network is shown in figure 2.6.

For more information on directory and file management, refer to your DOS or Windows manual, or see Que's *Using DOS* or *Using Microsoft Windows 3*, 2nd Edition.

Starting PageMaker

After PageMaker is installed, you can start the program from DOS or from Windows. This section explains how to start PageMaker from Windows or before Windows is started.

Part I: The Production Process with PageMaker

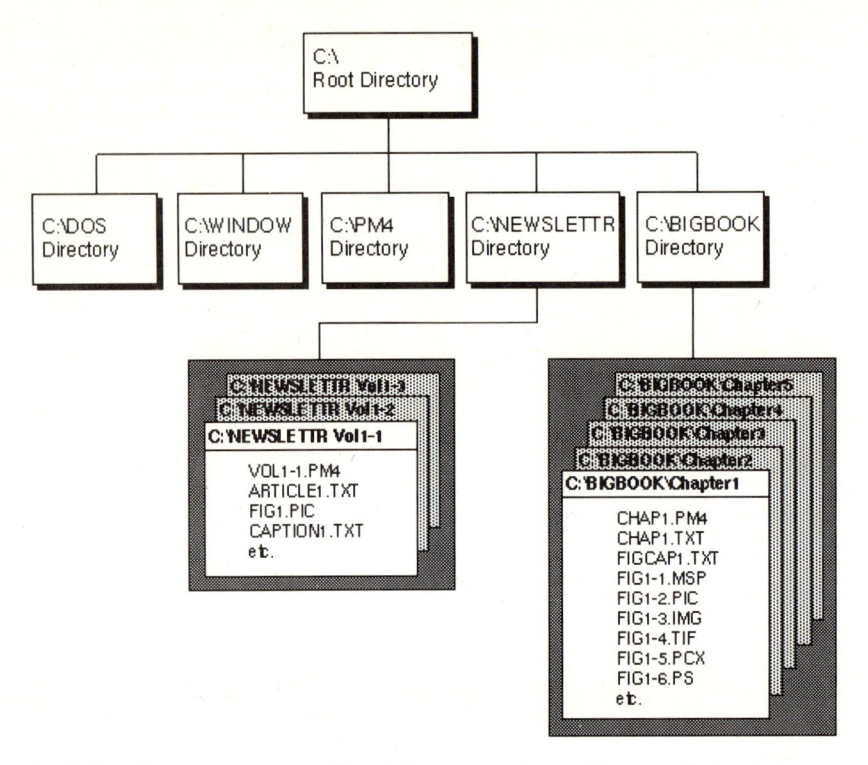

Fig. 2.6. A directory system with subdirectories devoted to specific projects.

Starting PageMaker from Windows

Before you can start PageMaker from Windows, you must start Windows. In the opening screen for Microsoft Windows, open the Aldus window by double-clicking the Aldus icon. Double-click the PageMaker icon to open PageMaker (see fig. 2.7).

Starting PageMaker from DOS

If your PATH line in the AUTOEXEC file shows `PATH C:\PM4;C:\DOS; C:\WINDOWS`, you can start PageMaker from any directory by typing *win pm4*.

Remember that during the installation process you were prompted to change your AUTOEXEC.BAT file. If you let the program change the file, this line was added to your PATH. If you did not okay the change, you must add the line now.

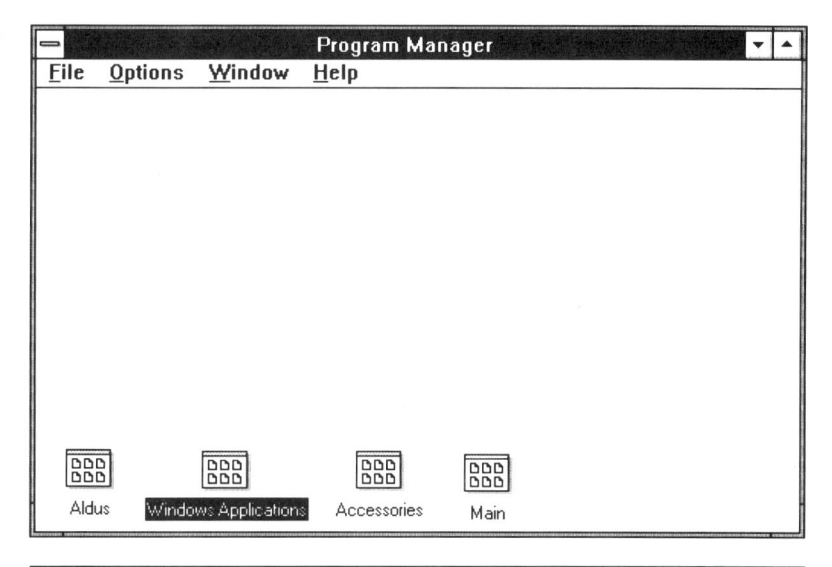

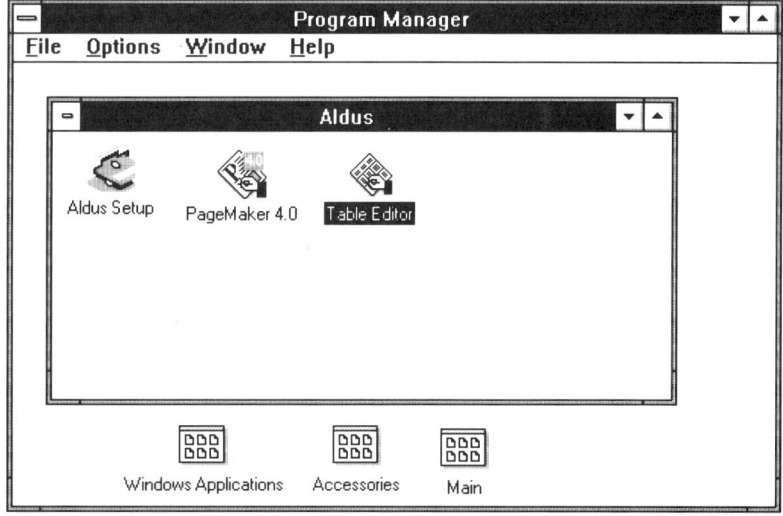

Fig. 2.7. The Microsoft Windows screen with the Aldus icon (top) and the Aldus window showing the PageMaker icon (bottom).

Starting the Program and Opening a Document

If you have created a PageMaker document and saved it in the current directory on disk, you can start PageMaker and open that document in one step from DOS by typing *win pm4 filename*, where *filename* is the name of the file you want to open.

If the file is not in the current directory, you can include the directory path in the command by typing *win pm4 C:\subdirectoryname\filename*.

In Windows, you can open a publication directly by choosing the Run command from the File menu and typing *pm4 filename* or *pm4 c:\subdirectoryname\filename*.

If you are running Windows, you can open a PageMaker document from the File Manager by double-clicking the document name. Otherwise, you can start PageMaker (using any of the aforementioned methods) and then use the Open command under the File menu as described in the next section.

Using PageMaker

When you start PageMaker, the opening screen displays the Aldus logo and information about your version of PageMaker. The opening fades to a new screen containing your name and PageMaker serial number and then becomes a new publication window. A row of menu titles is displayed along the top of the screen.

The following sections discuss basic program operations.

Opening a Document

You can use the New command or the Open command under the File menu to create a new publication or open an old one (see fig. 2.8). The following sections explain opening new and existing PageMaker documents.

Creating A New Document

You use the New command to start a publication from scratch. You first see the Page Setup dialog box. Use this box to specify characteristics of the

Chapter 2: Getting Started **45**

document. The <mark>Page Setup dialog box appears when you create a new document</mark> or use the File menu's Page setup command (see fig. 2.9). These options are explained in Chapter 3.

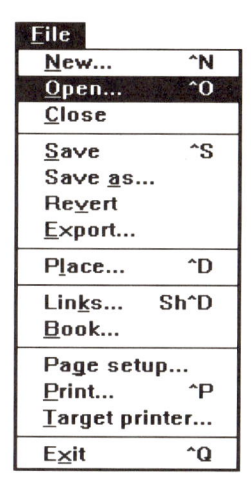

```
File
  New...          ^N
  Open...         ^O
  Close
  Save            ^S
  Save as...
  Revert
  Export...
  Place...        ^D
  Links...        Sh^D
  Book...
  Page setup...
  Print...        ^P
  Target printer...
  Exit            ^Q
```

Fig. 2.8. The PageMaker File Menu.

```
Page setup                                    OK
  Page: Letter                                Cancel
  Page dimensions: 8.5 × 11 inches
  Orientation: ● Tall  ○ Wide                 Numbers...
  Start page #: 1    Number of pages: 1
  Options: ☒ Double-sided  ☒ Facing pages
           ☐ Restart page numbering
  Margin in inches:
    Inside  1       Outside  0.75
    Top     0.75    Bottom   0.75
  Target printer:   PostScript Printer on LPT1:
```

Fig. 2.9. The Page Setup dialog box.

You can make changes to the page setup before the document is open, or you can keep PageMaker's defaults and simply click OK. After you close the Page Setup dialog box, PageMaker displays the blank page 1 of the untitled new document (see fig. 2.10).

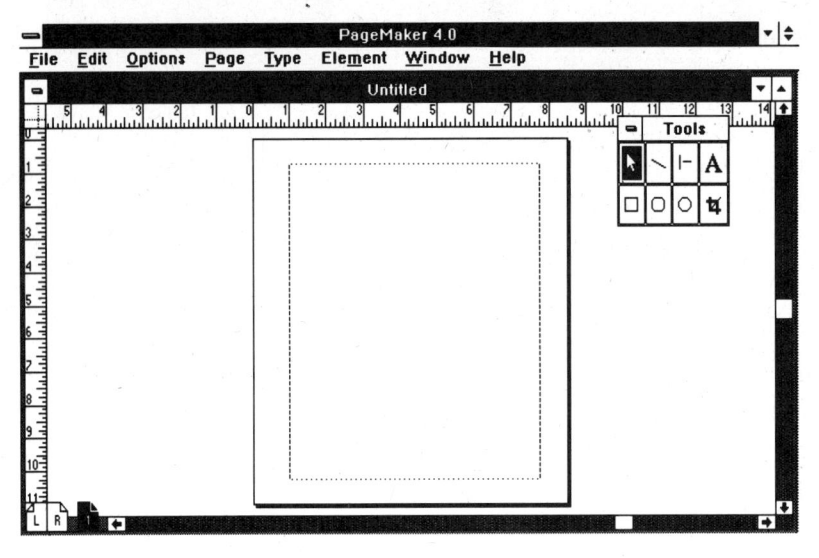

46 Part I: The Production Process with PageMaker

Fig. 2.10. Display of blank page 1 of new document.

Opening an Existing Publication

You use the Open command to open a template or publication that already exists. (PageMaker comes with a set of templates that you can use as starting points in creating your own publications.) When you use the Open command, PageMaker displays a dialog box that shows the list of PageMaker files on your disk. To choose the name of the file you want to open, first find the file name in the window (see fig. 2.11) by following these steps:

1. If the file name is not visible, drag the scroll bars to move down the list.

2. Click on [-A-], [-B-], or [-C-] to view the lists of files on other drives.

3. Click on [..] to view the list at the next higher directory level.

4. Click on a directory name, shown in brackets, to view the list at the next lower directory level (see fig. 2.11). Double-click on a directory name to view files within a subdirectory.

5. Click on the name of the file you want to open to highlight the file. Next, click Open on the File menu. You also can double-click the file name. PageMaker displays the page that was displayed when the file was last saved.

6. Click Copy in the Open dialog box to make a duplicate of the file as you are opening it. Click Cancel to stop the Open command.

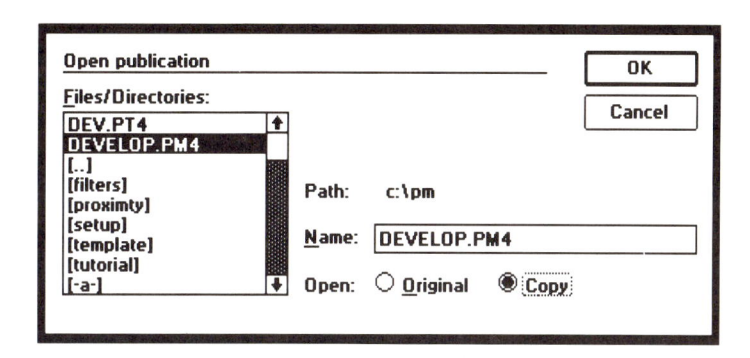

Fig. 2.11. Finding a file name in the Open Publication dialog box.

Reviewing the Publication Window

After a new or old publication is open, PageMaker displays pages in the publication window (see fig. 2.12). A quick look at the different elements of the publication window can give you an idea of the versatility of PageMaker.

The top title bar shows the name of the program (PageMaker 4.0) and includes the Control menu box on the left and the minimize and maximize arrows on the right—all standard features of any window in Microsoft Windows, described later in this chapter. Pull-down menu titles on the menu bar list PageMaker's command categories. The second title bar shows the publication name and includes the Control box menu and maximize and minimize arrows. In figure 2.12, the toolbox is displayed as a movable window with graphics tools and a text tool.

The page image shows the outline of the edges of the paper; the nonprinting guides on the page indicate margins, columns, or grid lines. The surrounding area serves as a pasteboard for storing text and graphics that have not been positioned on the page. The pointer shows the current position of the mouse and is used to select commands and objects on the page or pasteboard.

The scroll bars and rulers can be turned on or off. The page icons at the bottom of the screen show where you are in the document by highlighting the page number. Click on a page icon to turn to that page. The L and R pages are master pages. If you are working under the full Windows program, the icon for the Program Manager icon is displayed at the bottom left corner of the screen.

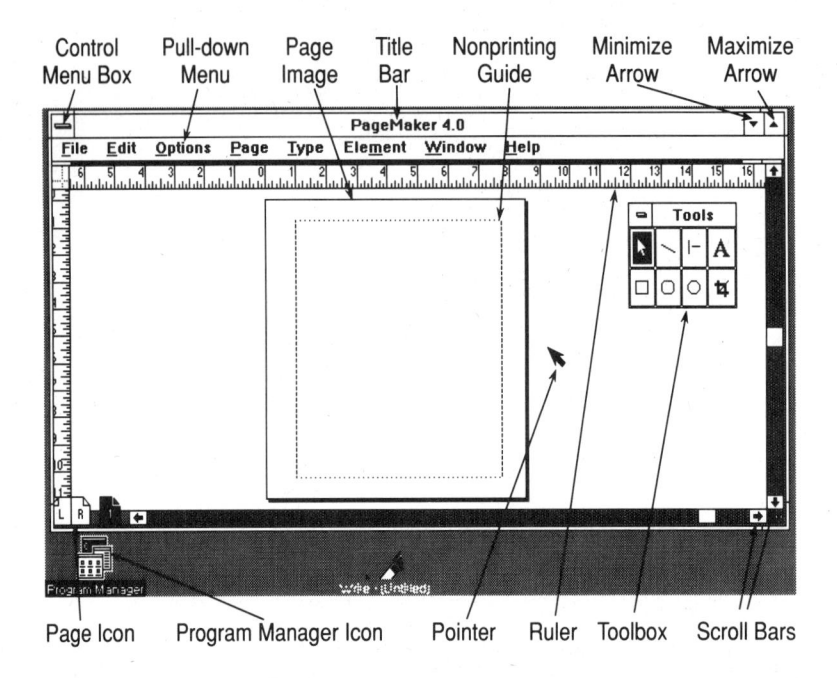

Fig. 2.12. The Publication window.

Using Pull-Down Menus

Menu titles appear along the menu bar at the top of the screen. When you position the pointer on a menu title and hold down the mouse button, the menu drops down the screen to show all the commands under that menu. You select a command by dragging the pointer down until the desired command is highlighted, and then you release the mouse button.

Some commands also have keyboard shortcuts, which are shown on the menu (see fig. 2.13). A caret (^) before a letter represents the Ctrl key. To execute the command, hold down the Ctrl key while you press the letter shown.

A check mark in front of a command indicates an on/off option. The feature is turned on if it is checked; you can turn off the feature by selecting the command. A right-facing triangle next to a command means that a submenu appears when you choose that command. The feature is turned off if it is not checked; you turn on the feature by selecting the command.

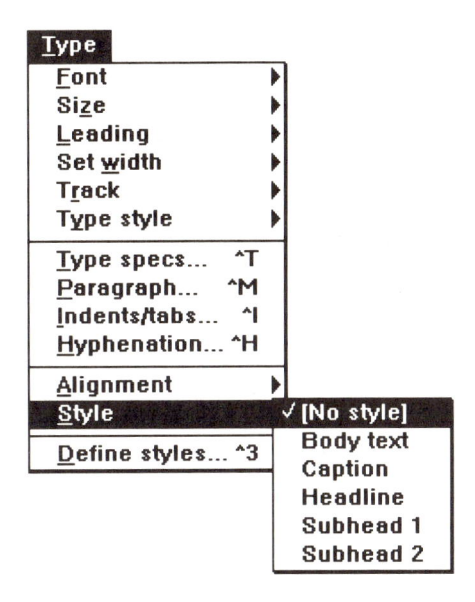

Fig. 2.13. The Type menu with the Style submenu showing.

An ellipsis (...) following a command indicates that a dialog box asking you for more information comes on-screen after you select the command. The dialog box also gives you a chance to cancel the command.

Using Dialog Boxes

When you select a menu option, a dialog box often appears (see again fig. 2.11). Table 2.1 explains how to use a dialog box.

**Table 2.1
Dialog Box Operations**

Click an option button to make a selection from a mutually exclusive list.

Click a check box to make a selection from a nonexclusive list.

Tab to or click a text entry box and type a value.

Click a name in a list to select the name.

Click a down-pointing arrow next to display a drop-down list and click an item to select it from the list.

Click OK to close the box with changes.

Click Cancel to close the box without recording any changes.

Reviewing the Toolbox Window

PageMaker's toolbox, shown in figure 2.14, is much like a conventional artist's collection of drawing tools. Pens, rulers, protractors, and knives are replaced by icons, which you select to perform the artist's work. The perpendicular-line tool draws lines at any angle divisible by 45 degrees, and the diagonal-line tool draws lines at any angle.

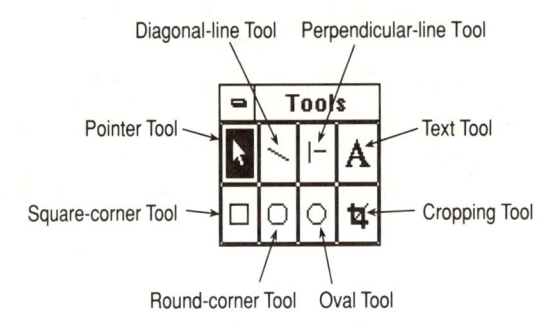

Fig. 2.14. The toolbox.

You can create boxes with squared or rounded corners. The square-corner tool draws rectangles with 90-degree corners. The rounded-corner tool draws rectangles with rounded corners. To draw circles or ovals, you choose the oval tool. The pointer tool selects objects, and the text tool edits and types text. You also can use the cropping tool to trim edges from graphics that you bring in from other programs.

To select any tool in the toolbox, click on the tool, or use the keyboard shortcuts shown in table 2.2.

Table 2.2
Keyboard Shortcuts for the Toolbox

Keys	Tool
Shift-F1	Pointer tool
Shift-F2	Diagonal-line tool
Shift-F3	Perpendicular-line tool
Shift-F4	Text tool
Shift-F5	Square-corner tool
Shift-F6	Rounded-corner tool
Shift-F7	Oval tool
Shift-F8	Cropping tool

The graphics created with tools from the toolbox are covered in Chapter 6.

The toolbox is a separate window on-screen. You can drag the window by its title bar to any position on-screen. You also can close the window by selecting the Toolbox command on the Windows menu. To redisplay the toolbox after you close the window, select the Toolbox command again.

Using the Control Menu

The top left corner of any window shows a small square with a thin bar: the Control menu icon. The Control menu lists the commands that are accessible from any program running under Windows (see fig. 2.15). These commands control the screen display by moving, sizing, closing, or switching between windows.

Fig. 2.15. The Control menu.

If two or more windows are open on-screen, you can adjust the size of each by using the Size command on the Control menu. When you select the Size command, the pointer changes to a four-headed arrow. By using the arrow keys on your keyboard, you can position and size the windows.

You also can use the mouse to resize a window. Place the pointer on the edge of the window and hold down the mouse button; the pointer changes to a two-headed arrow. Click on the window's border or corner that you want to resize, and then drag the pointer up or down. The highlighted borders mark the position of the window. When the window is in the correct location, release the mouse button (see fig. 2.16).

If two or more windows are open on-screen, you can enlarge one window to full-screen size by using the Maximize command on the Control menu or by clicking the up arrow in the upper right corner of the window. You can close a window without leaving the program by using the Minimize command under the Control menu or by clicking the down arrow in the upper right corner of the window. When you select the Minimize command, the selected window closes and is replaced by an icon at the bottom of the screen (see fig. 2.17). The window you most recently clicked on is the one selected and is displayed on top of other windows. To change any icon back to an open window, double-click the icon or drag the window.

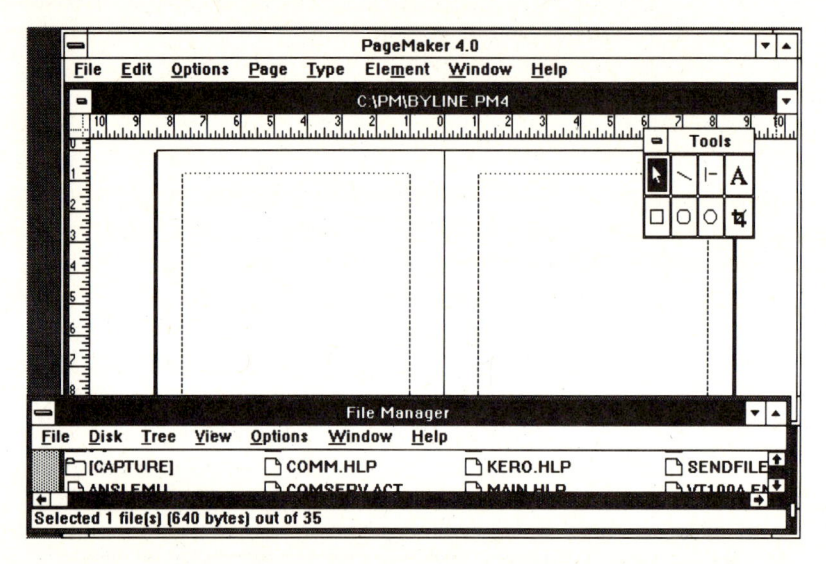

Fig. 2.16. Changing the size of a window with more than one window on-screen.

Fig. 2.17. An icon resulting from the Minimize command.

When two or more windows are displayed, you can rearrange them with the Move command. Select the Move command from the Control menu of the first window you want to move. Then click on the second window. The two windows change places.

You use the Close command on the Control menu to close a window and leave the program that is running in that window. When you use this command, most programs (including PageMaker) prompt you to save the file.

Controlling the Display

You often can see only a part of a page or a document on-screen. In PageMaker, you have three ways to move the page image around the screen. You can use the scroll bars to scroll vertically and horizontally. You can use the grabber hand to move the image in any direction. You can use the Page menu commands to jump to enlarged views of a particular area or reduce the page image to a smaller size. These techniques are described next.

Using the Scroll Bars

PageMaker's scroll bars operate the way other scroll bars work under Windows. To move the on-screen image in small increments, you click on an arrow. You click in the gray area of a scroll bar to jump up or down in the window in larger fixed increments. You drag the white portion of the scroll bar to move any distance. The position of the white box on the scroll bar indicates the position of the screen image relative to the whole page and the pasteboard (see fig. 2.18).

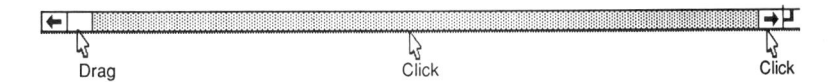

Fig. 2.18. A PageMaker scroll bar.

The distance that the image moves depends on the view you are using. The increments are smaller in enlarged views, such as 200%, than in reduced views, such as Fit in Window.

To turn off the scroll bars so that they are not displayed, select the Scroll Bars command from the Options menu. You then can see more of the page, and you can use any of the following techniques to move around on-screen. When the scroll bars are turned off, the page icons are also hidden, but you can use the Go to Page command on the Page menu to change pages.

To turn on the scroll bars, select the Scroll Bars command. This on/off switch shows a check mark next to the command when the scroll bars are turned on.

Using the Grabber Hand

In any view, you can use the grabber hand to drag the image in any direction. Hold down the Alt key while you press the main mouse button. When the pointer changes to a hand, you can drag the pointer in any direction to move the page image on-screen (see fig. 2.19). If you hold down both the Alt key and the Shift key, the grabber hand moves either horizontally or vertically, not diagonally.

Fig. 2.19. The grabber hand.

> **Moving around on the Page**
> The quickest way to move around on the screen is to use the grabber hand for diagonal or small movements.

Using the Page Menu

The Page menu offers seven commands for changing your view of the page; the Fit in Pasteboard command doesn't appear on the menu.

The following list gives the Ctrl-key equivalent of each command:

Command	Equivalent
Fit in Window	Ctrl-W
25% Size	Ctrl-0
50% Size	Ctrl-5
75% Size	Ctrl-7
Actual Size	Ctrl-1
200% Size	Ctrl-2
400% Size	Ctrl-4
Fit in Pasteboard	Ctrl-Shift-W

If your mouse has two or more buttons, you can use the secondary button to change views quickly. Pressing the secondary mouse button changes the view from any other view to Actual Size of the page. The Actual Size image is centered at the position of the pointer on the screen. If you are in the Actual Size view, pressing the secondary mouse button changes the view to Fit in Window.

Holding down the Shift key and pressing the secondary mouse button changes from any other view to a 200% Size view. The 200% Size image is centered at the position of the pointer on the screen. If you are in 200% Size, pressing the secondary mouse button changes you to the Actual Size view. See the Microsoft Windows installation guide for information about selecting the primary and secondary mouse buttons.

Changing Views of the Page

Use the secondary mouse button to toggle between Actual Size and Fit in Window.

Use the Shift key with the secondary mouse button to toggle between Actual Size and 200% Size.

Use the secondary mouse button to jump from Fit in Window view to close-up views of particular areas of the page by placing the pointer at the spot you want to see before you click. For example, toggling from Actual Size to Fit in Window and back to Actual Size of another part of the page can be faster than using the scroll bars or the grabber hand when moving diagonally for long distances.

Changing the Appearance of the Mouse Pointer

The appearance of the mouse pointer changes with what you are doing (see fig. 2.20). Any pointer can be used to select menu commands, toolbox options, page icons, or to use the scroll bars. The appearance of the pointer also indicates which other functions can be performed.

You use the arrow pointer, which appears whenever the pointer tool is selected in the toolbox, to select objects on the page. The I-beam appears when the text tool is selected in the toolbox. You use the I-beam to select portions of a block of text and to position the text insertion point. A crossbar appears when a graphics tool is selected in the toolbox. You use the crossbar to draw lines, boxes, and circles. When the cropping tool is selected in the toolbox, the pointer changes to the cropping icon. You use this icon to trim the edges of a graphic imported from another program.

The mouse pointer also takes a different appearance when you use the Place command to retrieve text or graphics from other programs. PageMaker has three text icons you can use to import text into PageMaker. Which icon is active depends on whether the autoflow option is on manual, semiautomatic, or automatic. The pencil icon indicates that you are importing a graphic from a draw program. You use the paintbrush icon to insert a graphic from a paint program. When you are placing a scanned image, the pointer becomes a box containing an X. The hourglass icon is displayed while the program is processing. You must wait until the hourglass changes into one of the other icons before you can continue working.

	Pointer:	Selects objects on the page
	I-beam:	Selects portions of a block of text, and positions the text insertion point
	Crossbar:	Draws lines, boxes, circles, and ovals
	Cropping tool:	Trims the edges from a graphic that is placed from another program
	Text icon:	Places text from another file
	Pencil icon:	Places a graphic from a draw-type program
	Paintbrush icon:	Places a graphic from a paint-type program
	X icon:	Places a scanned image
	PS icon:	Places an Encapsulated PostScript file
	Hourglass:	Indicates the program is processing—you wait until hourglass changes back to a different icon to continue
	Automatic text flow icon:	Flows text automatically from page to page
	Semiautomatic text flow icon:	Flows text semiautomatically from page to page, stopping text flow at the bottom of the text column

Fig. 2.20. Changes in the appearance of the pointer.

Selecting with the Pointer and Text Tools

Many PageMaker commands operate only on objects that have been selected on the page. An object is active as soon as it is drawn or placed on a page, or you can select objects with the pointer tool and the text tool. The three methods of selecting objects with the pointer tool are shown in figures 2.21, 2.22, and 2.23.

- Position the pointer over text or a graphic, and click once to select the text or graphic. If the handles are not displayed as expected, the object may be buried under other objects. You can hold down the Ctrl key and click again to select objects on the next layer down, or use the Send to Back and Bring to Front commands to dig out the object, as described in Chapter 6 (see fig. 2.21).

- Hold down the Shift key and click the pointer on several objects to select them all (see fig. 2.22).

- Position the pointer at one corner of the area that includes the objects to be selected, and drag the pointer diagonally to the opposite corner. Objects that are not completely encompassed are not selected (see fig. 2.23).

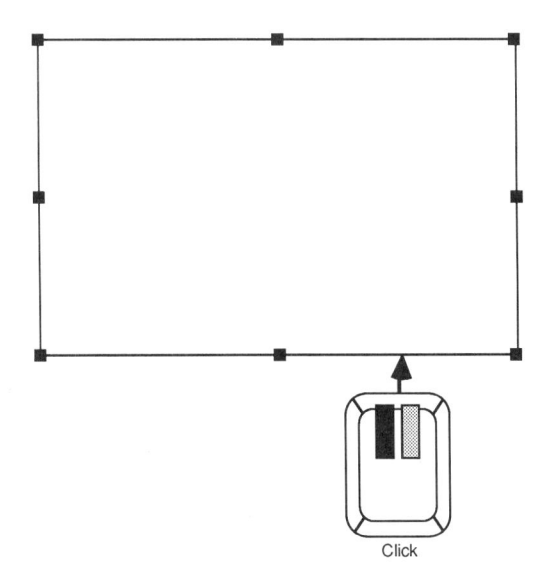

Fig. 2.21. *Clicking once to select text or a graphic.*

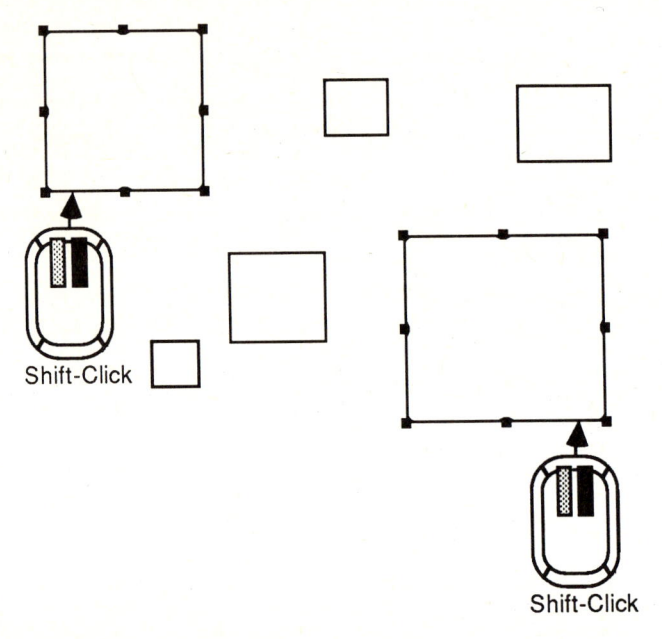

Fig. 2.22. *Using Shift-click to select several objects.*

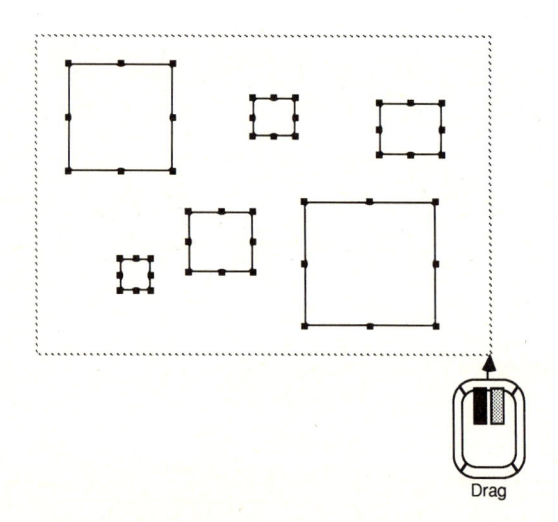

Fig. 2.23. *Dragging the pointer to select an area.*

The text tool is used to select portions of text within a block of text or to establish the text insertion point before typing new text. The methods of selecting text and insertion points with the text tool are shown in figures 2.24, 2.25, and 2.26.

Position the I-beam beside a character, and click the main mouse button to position the cursor with a line of text (see fig. 2.24). Use this method for inserting new text.

Double-click a word to select it (see fig. 2.25).

Drag the I-beam over the text to select it (see fig. 2.26).

Click the text tool once in a text block, and choose the Select All command from the Edit menu to select the entire article, such as the current text block plus all linked blocks.

Use the keyboard shortcuts shown in table 2.3.

This is a line of text

Click

Fig. 2.24. Positioning the I-beam to select a text insertion point.

This is a **line** of text

Double-click

Fig. 2.25. Selecting one word.

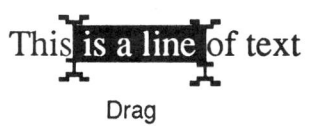

This **is a line** of text

Drag

Fig. 2.26. Dragging the I-beam to select text.

Table 2.3
Keystrokes Used To Move the Text Insertion Point

To move the text insertion point to:	Press:
Beginning of a line	Home
End of a line	End

continues

Table 2.3 *(continued)*

To move the text insertion point to:	Press:
Beginning of a sentence	Ctrl-Home
End of a sentence	Ctrl-End
Left one character	Left arrow
Right one character	Right arrow
Left one word	Ctrl-left arrow
Right one word	Ctrl-right arrow
Up one line	Up arrow
Down one line	Down arrow
Up one paragraph	Ctrl-up arrow
Down one paragraph	Ctrl-down arrow
Up one screen	PgUp
Down one screen	PgDn
Top of story	Ctrl-PgUp
Bottom of story	Ctrl-PgDn

Getting Help

When you have questions concerning commands and topics, you can receive help from the Help menu on the right of the menu bar. When you click on the Help menu, you can choose Index, Commands, Topics, Using PageMaker Help or About PageMaker (see fig. 2.27). The About PageMaker command tells you what version of the program you are using. Knowing the version of your program is important if you use the telephone hotline offered by Aldus to resolve any problems you have with the program. This service, available to registered owners, is well worth the subscription fee if you plan to do a great deal of production with PageMaker.

The Index command displays on-screen help (see fig. 2.28). By highlighting Index, you enter into a tiered help system. The first dialog box displays a list of the main help topics (see fig. 2.29). You can highlight the selected topic and then click on it, or you can double-click the topic. You then see a second list of the topics covered under your selected topic. When you double-click a topic in this list, you see detailed information on the topic (see fig. 2.29).

Chapter 2: Getting Started 61

Fig. 2.27. The Help Menu.

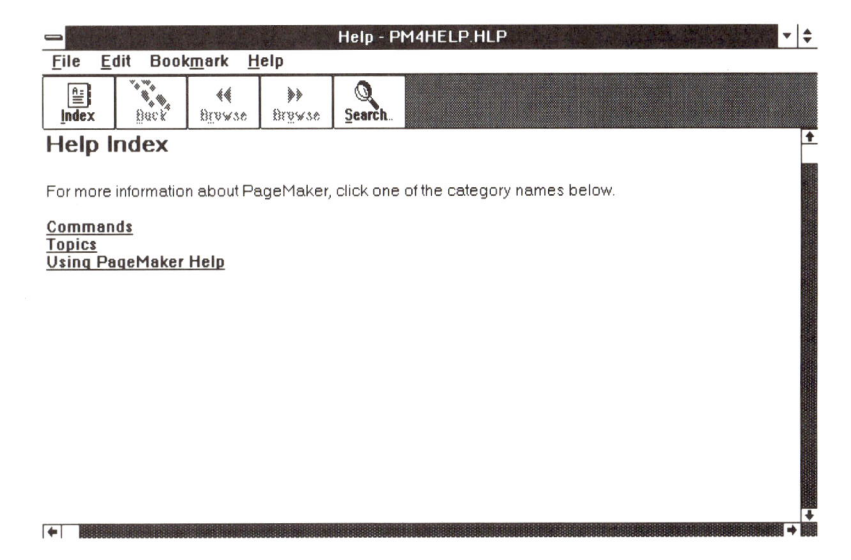

Fig. 2.28. The main help screen.

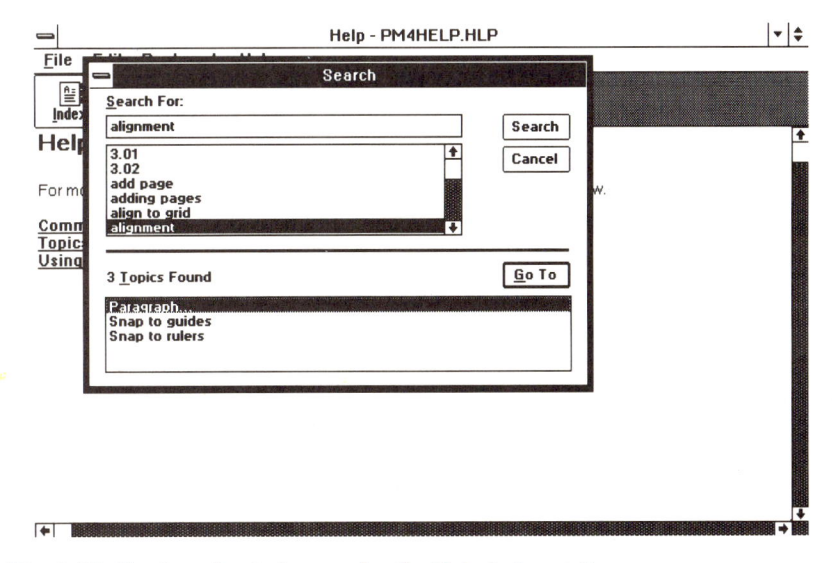

Fig. 2.29. The Search window under the Help Index option.

You also can use the Commands or the Topics commands from the Help menu to skip the index step. To help your searching, the top of the Help screen contains several button choices. By using the mouse you can click on Index, which lists the general topics; Back, which returns you to the previous screen; Browse, which enables you to look at any help screen; and Search, which enables you to highlight a word and find the relevant help screens (again see fig. 2.29).

Reviewing the Basic Steps in Creating a Document

Creating a document requires three steps: planning and designing your document, constructing the text and graphics with programs other than PageMaker, and producing the final version in PageMaker. Planning a document requires designing the appearance of the *page* (paper size and margins) and the appearance of the *type* (text formatting). You can decide such issues as page size, typeface, location of figures, and general appearance. Some decisions can be applied in the word processing and graphics programs that you use to create the document. The remaining specifications are made in PageMaker. After you understand the basic steps for creating a document, you understand how other detailed steps in this book relate to the process.

> *Note:* Save your files often by using the Save command from the File menu or typing Ctrl-S. While you are working on a document, it is stored in the computer's memory. Each time you save the document, the version in memory is copied to the disk. If the power fails or if you need to restart the computer, anything in the computer's memory is erased; but what you have saved on disk is preserved. For this reason, save your document often while you are working.

PageMaker also saves on disk interim versions of the document every time you insert, remove, turn a page, or touch the icon on the current page. These interim versions do not replace the latest version you saved on disk, but they are available when you reopen a document after a system failure.

PageMaker has a more sophisticated recovery program than other desktop publishing programs. When you use PageMaker's Revert command to cancel your current edits and revert to the last saved version, you return to the latest version you saved with the Save or Save As command. Interim versions saved by PageMaker are ignored by the Revert command.

> **When To Save a Document**
> - When you finish a page—before turning to another page
> - When you finish placing a long text file
> - When you finish placing, sizing, and cropping a graphic
> - As you are working, every 15 minutes or so
> - Before you print
> - Before you globally change type specs or format
> - After you make any changes to the master pages
> - At least once a week, back up your hard disk files to floppy disks in case of hard disk failure

The following overview of the steps involved in producing a document includes references to other chapters in which the steps are discussed in more detail:

1. Develop design specifications.

    Design specifications traditionally have been hand-written or typed and illustrated in rough pencil sketches. You can use PageMaker, however, as a design tool for developing specifications (see Chapter 11). This step includes deciding what type of printer you will use for the final production, because the choice of printer affects your type specifications (see Chapters 8 and 10).

2. Prepare text and graphics by using other programs.

    Although you can build documents from scratch by using PageMaker alone, most PageMaker documents are composed of text and graphics that have been created in other programs (see Chapters 4 and 6).

3. Start a new document.

    After the text and graphics have been prepared in other programs, you start PageMaker and begin building the document. In this step, you may begin with a new file, or you may begin with a *template file*, which is set with the design specifications (see Chapters 3 and 11).

4. Create the master pages.

    The master pages include the running heads, running feet, and other elements that appear on every page. These pages also may contain the underlying *grid*, a network of lines that appears on the screen but is not printed. This grid is used to align objects consistently on all pages of the document (see Chapters 3 and 10).

5. Change the grid as necessary on individual pages.

    The elements set on the master pages can be changed on individual pages of the document as you are working (see Chapters 3 and 10).

6. Place the text and graphics in the document.

    On each page of the document, you use the Place command to get text and graphics from other programs (see Chapters 3, 4, and 6). After text and graphics are in PageMaker, you can use PageMaker's tools and commands to edit the text (see Chapter 4), format the text (see Chapter 5), or manipulate the graphics (see Chapter 6). You can store imported graphics as part of the PageMaker publication or link external graphics files to the PageMaker publication (see Chapter 7).

7. Print the document.

    You should expect to print a document many times before you print the final version. Even if you have edited thoroughly the text and graphics before placing them on a page, you need to print drafts of the PageMaker publication to review for format and alignment. PageMaker is a WYSIWYG program: *What You See (on the screen) Is What You Get (on the printed page).* You always find some differences between the screen and the printed page, however, because of the differences in resolution. These discrepancies cannot be seen until you print the publication. You can find detailed information about printing in Chapter 8.

8. Close the publication.

    You can close one PageMaker file without leaving the PageMaker program altogether by using the Close command on the File menu. You also can close the current publication by using the New or Open commands on the File menu. If you have saved your document, PageMaker closes the publication and opens another publication when you use these commands. If you have not saved your document, PageMaker displays a dialog box asking whether you want to save the document before you close it and open another.

9. Close PageMaker.

   When you are working in a full Windows environment, you can run other programs without closing PageMaker. When you do want to leave PageMaker, however, you must use the Close command on the Control menu. PageMaker verifies that you have saved your current document. If you have not saved the current document, PageMaker displays a dialog box asking whether you want to save your changes as well as close PageMaker (see fig. 2.30).

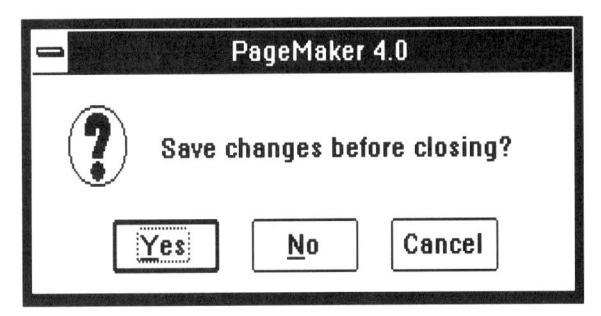

Fig. 2.30. Confirmation for saving a document.

   When you leave PageMaker under the full Windows program, you return to the Windows opening screen or to a full-screen view of the other windows that are open. When you leave PageMaker under the run-time version of Windows, you return to DOS.

10. Close Microsoft Windows.

    To leave the full Windows program, choose the Close command on the Control menu of the Windows Main window. The Windows program always asks you to confirm in a dialog box that you want to end the session.

Chapter Summary

The best way to learn PageMaker is to use it. If you have never used PageMaker, use the tutorial provided with the program to get a quick overview of the program's features. No matter what your level of experience, you can find many useful tips throughout this book for using PageMaker efficiently.

3

Creating a New Publication

This chapter takes you through the steps involved in creating a new publication. The discussion begins with the New command, which is used to create a PageMaker publication. The discussion then progresses through defining your preferences for the on-screen page display and setting up a master page with a page layout grid. You learn how to move through a multiple-page publication, and you receive tips on developing efficient procedures. You also are introduced to adding and editing text and graphics. (The procedures for adding and editing text and graphics are described in greater detail in Chapters 4 through 6.)

The chapter explains how to open a new PageMaker publication and then takes you through the following steps:

- Entering page-layout specifications in the Page Setup dialog box
- Defining your preferences for the on-screen page display
- Specifying standard layout elements on the master pages
- Using common editing commands from the Edit menu
- Using the Page menu commands to change views of the publication

Before starting to build a PageMaker publication, you can create text and complex graphics using other programs. Chapters 4, 5, and 6 explain how to use other programs to prepare text and graphics and how to bring the text and graphics into PageMaker. Chapters 4, 5, and 6 also describe how you can use PageMaker's tools to create text and graphics.

If you have never used PageMaker, you should read this chapter and the next three chapters carefully. Before launching your first major publication project, try creating a few short and simple publications. After you have become familiar with the basic operations described in Chapters 1 through 6, you will be ready to learn the more advanced features described in Chapter 7, such as how to associate a series of publications through the Book command, how to generate a table of contents and an index, how to link external text or graphics files to a publication, and how to manage changes in text and graphics files that are linked to the publication.

The steps in this chapter are described from the production perspective. The initial assumption is that the design specifications for the publication already are known and that the task is to build the publication according to those specifications. In Chapter 10, some of these same steps are reviewed from the designer's perspective, and basic design principles are discussed. Part III of this book (Chapters 12 through 16) provides examples of how these basic design principles have been applied in PageMaker publications.

Understanding PageMaker Terms

Many of the terms that describe elements in a PageMaker publication have been discussed in the preceding section. The following paragraphs provide a summary of the key terms used in this chapter. A file created using PageMaker is called a *publication*. A publication is composed of numbered pages and master pages. *Numbered pages* are the pages of the document that you print out. *Master pages* contain guides (margin guides, column guides, ruler guides) that help you position items consistently on document pages. Besides their nonprinting elements, master pages also can contain printing items (text and graphics) that appear repeatedly on multiple document pages.

Pages are displayed in *Layout view* as they will appear when printed, but you can view, type, and edit text more quickly in *Story view*. When the Layout view is displayed, you can use the area beyond the paper's edges as a *pasteboard* for storing elements that you have not yet positioned on a page.

The basic building block for text in PageMaker is the *text block*. Text blocks can be chained together to direct the flow of text from page to page or from block to block on the same page. The flow occurs automatically if you set *Autoflow* to on for imported text. PageMaker also enables you to chain a series of text blocks manually. The stream of text that flows through a chain of text boxes is called a *story*.

A series of PageMaker publications can be associated as a *book*. Imported graphics can be stored as part of the PageMaker publication or *linked* to the publication at the time of printing, as described in Chapter 7.

Opening a Publication

You can create a new document in PageMaker by starting the program, choosing New from the File menu, making entries in the Page Setup dialog box, and then positioning items on the first page. If the document you want to create is similar to other documents that you already have created, you might save time by opening the similar document, modifying the document, and saving the document under a different name. These two options (starting with a blank publication or cloning an existing publication) are described first. The rest of this chapter describes the steps in starting a document from scratch.

Opening a PageMaker 4.0 Publication

To open an existing publication that has been created using PageMaker, choose the Open command from the File menu. (You cannot have more than one PageMaker publication open at the same time. When you choose the Open command, PageMaker prompts you to save any currently open publication.)

When you choose the Open command from the File menu, PageMaker displays a dialog box that shows a list of PageMaker files on your disk. To choose the name of the file you want to open, first find the file name in the window (see fig. 3.1).

If the file name is not visible, drag the scroll bars to move down the list. Click [-A-] or [-B-] or [-C-] to view the list of files on other drives. Click [..] to view the list at the next higher directory level. Click a directory name (shown in brackets) to view the list at the next lower directory level. Double-click a directory name (in brackets) to view files within a subdirectory.

When you find the name of the publication you want to open, click on the file name to highlight it and then click Open Copy to make a duplicate of the file as you are opening it. (Note that if you simply double-click the file name, you open the original publication, unless it is a template, as described in this chapter and in Chapter 11). PageMaker displays the page that was displayed when the file was last saved.

Click Cancel to stop the Open command.

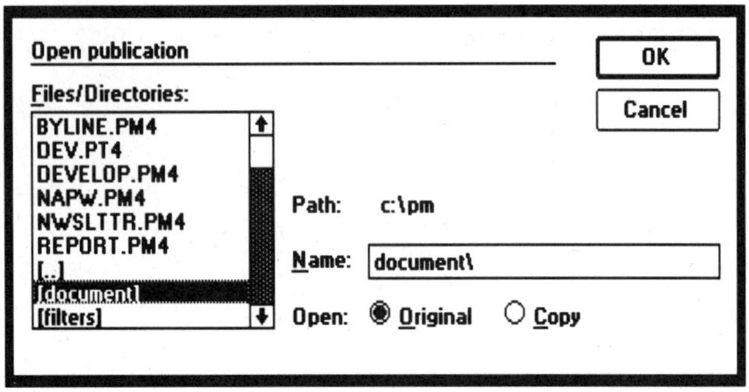

Fig. 3.1. Finding a file name in the Open Publication dialog box.

Starting a New Publication from a Template

PageMaker 4.0 comes with 35 templates for common business publications such as business cards, memos, and reports. Chapter 11 describes how you can create your own custom templates. You can save a lot of time by starting with a custom template that matches designs you use often, rather than creating every publication with the New command.

If the publication originally was created using PageMaker 4.0, the document will open with the same page view as when you last saved the publication. If the publication originally was created using PageMaker 3.0 or 3.01 for Windows or with PageMaker 3.0 for OS/2 Presentation Manager, PageMaker converts the publication to a Version 4.0 document and opens it as an untitled publication. As PageMaker converts the document to Version 4.0, the following effects can occur:

- The publication usually becomes smaller (that is, takes up less disk space).

- Line breaks within the text might change because PageMaker 4.0 is more precise in typographical controls.

- The length of text blocks might change because PageMaker 4.0 calculates leading more precisely than earlier versions.

- When you edit text in PageMaker 4.0, text might wrap around graphics that are part of the master page.

Transferring a Publication from the Macintosh to the PC

You can transfer PageMaker publications that were created on the Macintosh to a PC (and vice versa) through a network (such as AppleShare, Ethernet, or TOPS) or through telecommunications (using modems or a direct cable with appropriate software, such as MacLink Plus by DataViz, or LapLink Plus by Centram). Transfer the files in binary format (an option offered by the file transfer application) and transfer any linked graphic documents as well.

You also can transfer publications by using file disk drives that enable your PC to read Macintosh disks. MatchMaker by Micro Solutions Computer Products and the Copy II PC Deluxe Option Board by Central Point Software are examples of such file disk drives.

If the Macintosh publication originally was created using PageMaker 3.0, the document must first be converted to a 4.0 publication on the Macintosh. In transferring the publication to the PC, you also must give the publication a valid DOS name. Use the extension ".PM4" when you name the file.

In switching between the two platforms, PageMaker converts text, PageMaker formatting, PageMaker graphics, all bit-mapped graphics less than 64K, EPS graphics, low-resolution screen versions of large (more than 64K) scanned images, and graphics that have a complete copy stored in the publication. PageMaker does not transfer linked graphics or text files, graphics that do not have a complete copy stored in the publication, tables placed from the Table Editor, or special characters that the PC (ANSI character set) does not share with the Macintosh. You can transfer the linked files separately, however, and use the Link command to establish the new associations.

Type specifications are transferred if you use the same type of printer on both systems—such as a PostScript printer.

After you have opened a publication, you can add to or edit the document using any of the techniques described in the rest of this chapter and in Chapters 4 through 8. The next section describes the process of starting a new publication from scratch.

Entering Page Setup Specifications

When you begin creating a publication by using the New command on the File menu, PageMaker displays the Page Setup dialog box (see fig. 3.2). You use this box to specify the size of the sheets of paper you want to use, the orientation of the printed image, the text margins, the number of pages, the starting page number, and the page number format. You also indicate whether you will print and bind the publication as a two-sided publication.

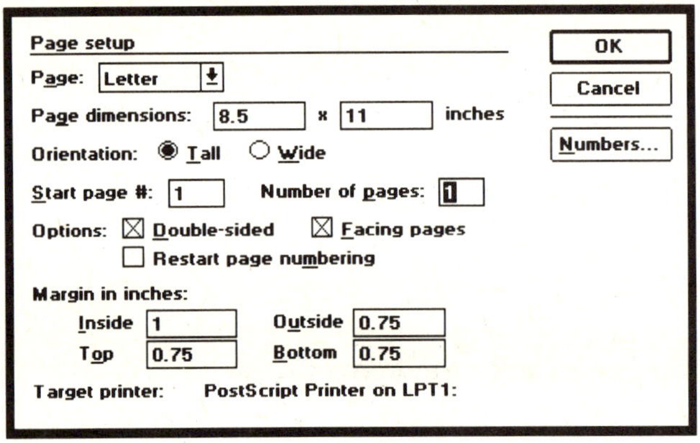

Fig. 3.2. The Page Setup dialog box with default settings.

Before making your selections in the Page Setup dialog box, you should plan the design of your publication. Why? Because the page's size, orientation, and margins are essential elements of the design specifications. Changing these settings after you have started building a publication might require moving text and graphics that already have been placed on pages.

Figure 3.3 shows how the settings in the Page Setup dialog box affect a page. Double-sided facing pages are displayed. The Page Size is defined in solid lines; the Orientation is Tall. The inside margin measure is applied to the right margin of left-hand pages and the left margin of right-hand pages. The dashed lines on the inside and outside margins indicate that a column guide is on the margin. The top and bottom margins are shown as dotted lines.

At any time during the production process, you can change the Page Setup options, which include double-sided printing, number of pages, and starting page number. To change the Page Setup options, use the Page Setup command on the File menu. The following sections explain what happens when you change these settings after you have started building the publication.

Chapter 3: Creating a New Publication 73

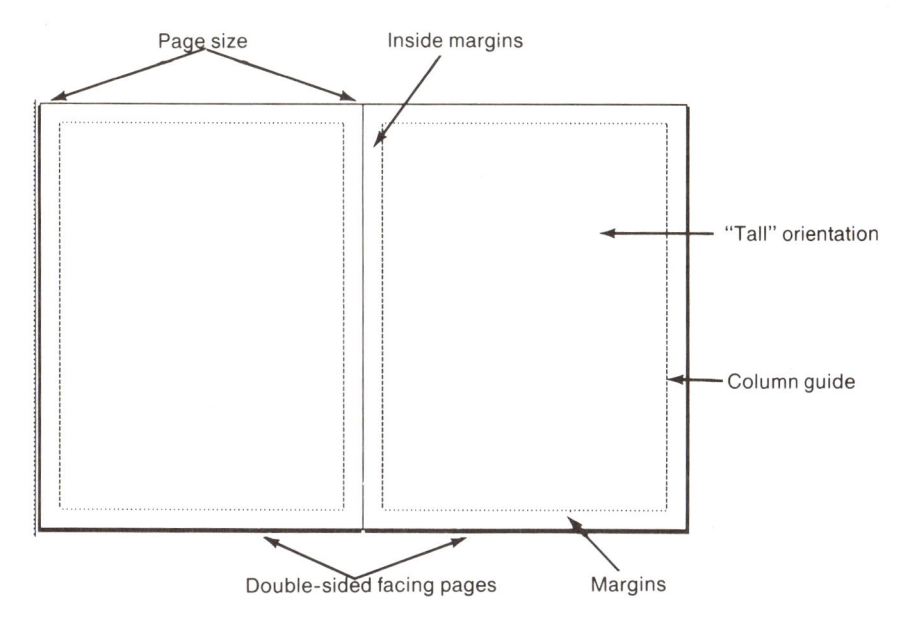

Fig. 3.3. How the Page Setup dialog box entries affect a page.

Changing the Defaults for Page Setup

If you choose the Page Setup command when no document is open, you can change the defaults that appear in the New dialog box when you use the New command. Use this method to change the paper size and orientation, single-sided/double-sided/facing-page settings, or margins to the values you use most frequently in your publications. Otherwise, if your publications have many different specifications, create a template that captures these values for each type of publication (as described in Chapter 11).

Specifying Page Size

In the File menu's Page Setup dialog box, PageMaker offers three predefined page sizes that match the standard American paper sizes (see table 3.1). You can, however, specify any size up to 17 by 22 inches. You specify page size by clicking on the arrow to the right of the current page size to display the drop-down list of Letter, Legal, Tabloid, and Custom size options.

If you choose one of the standard sizes, PageMaker fills in the dimensions automatically. Alternatively, you can enter any dimension (up to 17 by 22 inches) by tabbing into the dimension boxes and typing new values. If you follow this procedure, the Custom option is chosen automatically in the Page field.

Table 3.1
Standard Paper Sizes in PageMaker

Option	Size
Letter	8 1/2 by 11 inches
Legal	8 1/2 by 14 inches
Tabloid	11 by 17 inches
Custom	Any size up to 17 by 22 inches

Using the Keyboard To Make Dialog Box Entries

Throughout this book, instructions are given for making dialog box selections using the mouse. Most dialog boxes offer keyboard alternatives as well. To jump to any field, hold down the Alt key and press the letter that is underscored in the field title. For example, because the letter *a* is underscored in the word *Page*, you can jump to the Page Size field by holding the Alt key and pressing A (Alt-A). To view a drop-down list, keep holding down the Alt key and press the down-arrow key. To make a selection from a drop-down list, release the Alt key and press the up- or down-arrow key to select from the list. In some cases, the drop-down list closes when you press the arrow keys, but the selection shown in the field changes each time you press an arrow key. In other cases, the drop-down list might remain open as you press the arrow keys, and you can close it (after making your selection with the arrow keys) by pressing the Alt key.

Similarly, you can jump to a text box entry by holding down the Alt key and typing the letter underscored in the field name. You then can type the new text. You can select radio button fields or check mark fields by holding down the Alt key and typing the underscored letter in the field name. You can toggle (select or deselect) check mark fields by holding down the Alt key and typing the underscored letter in the field name.

The page size you specify in the Page Setup dialog box is not necessarily the same as the size of the sheets of paper that you will be feeding into a laser printer. Rather, ==the size you choose here dictates the measurements of the page border on the screen.== For example, you can specify Tabloid size and print the publication pages in sections on 8 1/2-by-11-inch sheets by using the Print command's Tile option, which is explained in Chapter 8. Figure 3.4 shows how 12-by-22-inch pages can be printed in four pieces on 8 1/2-by-11-inch paper, using the Print Command's Tile option.

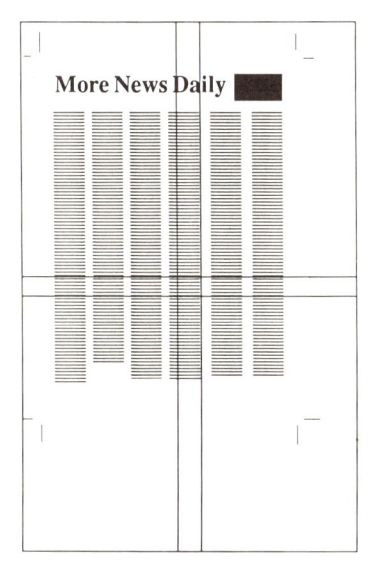

Fig. 3.4. Page printed by using the Tile option.

==If you choose a page size smaller than the sheets of paper on which you print, PageMaker prints the image in the center of the paper.== You can use the Crop Marks option in the Print Command dialog box to print crop marks that indicate the final trim size on the larger paper (see fig. 3.5).

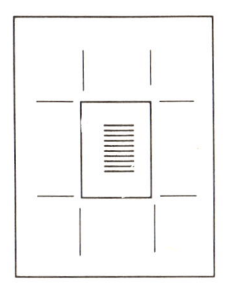

Fig. 3.5. Printing crop marks around page layouts smaller than the paper in the printer.

You can use the Page Setup command to change the page size after you have opened a publication, but PageMaker does not reposition the text and graphics (that already have been positioned) to match the new page size. On single-sided pages, PageMaker maintains the position of text and graphics relative to the top left margin corner. On facing pages, PageMaker centers the new page outline behind the text and graphics of the old page. If the new page is smaller than the old page, text and graphics spill over onto the pasteboard. In any case, you must reposition text and graphics individually on each page to meet the new page size and margins.

Setting Page Orientation

The width and length of each page also is affected by the Orientation option in the Page Setup dialog box. You can orient your pages to print Tall or Wide by clicking the appropriate button. The most common page size and orientation for business publications is Tall, 8 1/2 by 11 inches. Figure 3.6 shows a few variations:

  A. An 8 1/2-by-11-inch page with Tall orientation printed one sheet per page

  B. An 8 1/2-by-11-inch page with Wide orientation printed one sheet per page

  C. An 11-by-17-inch (tabloid) page with Tall orientation printed four sheets per page

  D. An 11-by-17-inch page with Wide orientation printed four sheets per page

You can use the Page Setup command to change the orientation after you have opened a publication, but PageMaker will not reposition the text and graphics (that already have been positioned) to match the new orientation. Text and graphics will spill over onto the pasteboard if they do not fit the new orientation, and you will have to reposition individually text and graphics on each page to adjust to the new orientation.

Designating the Number of Pages

PageMaker's default is set to create a one-page publication. You can, however, designate the number of pages before you start building the publication by typing a number in the # of Pages box in the Page Setup dialog box. If you do not know how many pages the publication will have, you can add or delete pages as you work by using the Insert Pages or Remove Pages commands on the Page menu. If you place text with the Autoflow option set to on, as described in Chapter 4, PageMaker inserts pages automatically as needed to accommodate the placed text. (After you open a new publication, you cannot change the number of pages by using the Page Setup dialog box.)

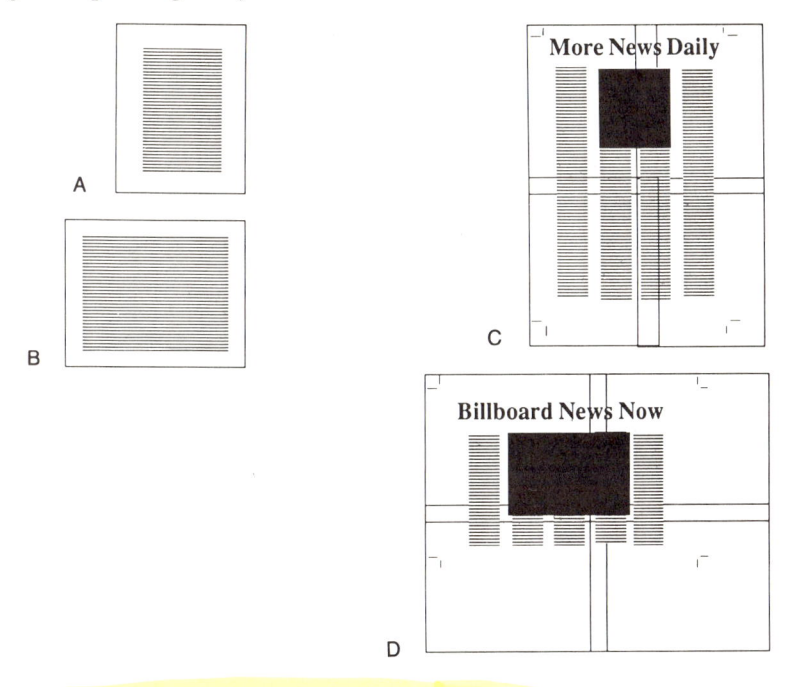

Fig. 3.6. Examples of page size and orientation settings.

A PageMaker 4.0 publication can be up to 999 pages long, but you will find working with smaller files more efficient. In long files, when you turn pages or make text edits that carry over to subsequent pages, response time is slow. Dividing a long publication into sections or chapters is good practice because you can work faster on smaller files. Another advantage is that you can set up a different running head and running foot for each chapter. (Running heads and feet usually are entered on the master pages, so they cannot be changed in the middle of a file.) The Book command, described in Chapter 7, enables you to associate a series of separate PageMaker documents as chapters in a book.

Another important consideration when you are deciding how many pages a single file will have is the size of the final publication in bytes. You want to be able to back up your publications on floppy disks for storage and transport purposes. Therefore, you need to keep the sizes of your files lower than the following limits:

- 360K for double-sided double-density 5 1/4-inch disks
- 1.2M for double-sided high-density 5 1/4-inch disks
- 720K for double-sided double-density 3 1/2-inch disks
- 1.44M for double-sided high-density 3 1/2-inch disks

> ### Checking the File Size as You Work
>
> When creating large publications, save your file frequently as you work. Periodically use the Save As command, and then open the Windows File Manager window to see how large your publication is. (You must use the Save As command to update the file size, date, and time last modified in the Windows File Manager window when simultaneously running PageMaker. If the file size does not appear next to the files listed in the Windows File Manager window, choose the Other command from the View menu and check off the details you want to view: size and time last modified.) Do not build a publication file that is too large for a floppy disk to hold; break large publications into sections or chapters.
>
> PageMaker also stores "ghost" memories of items or pages you have deleted when you use the Save command. You can use the Save As command to reclaim space in a publication that you reduced by editing, cutting, pasting, or deleting pages. You can reclaim as much as 30 percent of the publication's size. You can use the Preferences command, described later in this chapter, to make the Save command act like the Save As command, but each Save operation will be slower.

Assigning a Starting Page Number

You can start a publication with any page number up to 9999 by typing a number in the Number of Pages text box. For example, if you fill one file with 999 pages, the maximum number possible, you can continue building a second file that starts with page 1000. You also can specify the starting page number for publications that are divided into sections, with the first section starting on page 1 and the second section starting on page 20, for example.

You also can type a prefix as part of the page number on the master pages. You can opt to have the prefix appear in the automatically generated table of contents and index through the Page Numbering dialog box (described later in this chapter).

You can use the Page Setup command to change the starting page number of the publication at any time. PageMaker then renumbers all the pages in the publication. This process causes left-hand pages to become right-hand pages in double-sided publications, if you change a publication that starts on an odd-numbered page to start on an even-numbered page, or vice versa. You need to make adjustments for facing pages that formerly had elements that "bled" across the inside margins from one page to another and for pages that previously were inserted to force subsequent pages to be on the left or right.

> **Controlling Left-Hand and Right-Hand Page Positions**
>
> When preparing a publication for double-sided printing, be sure to account for and print every page, including blank left-hand pages that are needed to force new sections or chapters to start on right-hand pages. Having a numbered sheet for every page of the publication also helps whoever is printing or copying the publication before binding.

Note that you can use the Book command (described in Chapter 7) to assemble several PageMaker publications into one publication for the purpose of printing or generating a table of contents or an index. You still must use the Page Setup command, however, to set the starting page number for each section. The Book command does not change page numbers automatically.

Selecting a Format for Page Numbers

Click the Numbers button (new in Version 4.0) in the Page Setup dialog box if you want to use special page number formats. The Page Numbering dialog box (see fig. 3.7) offers five choices: Arabic Numeral (normal default), Upper or Lower (uppercase and lowercase, respectively) Roman numerals, and Upper or Lower Alphabetic characters.

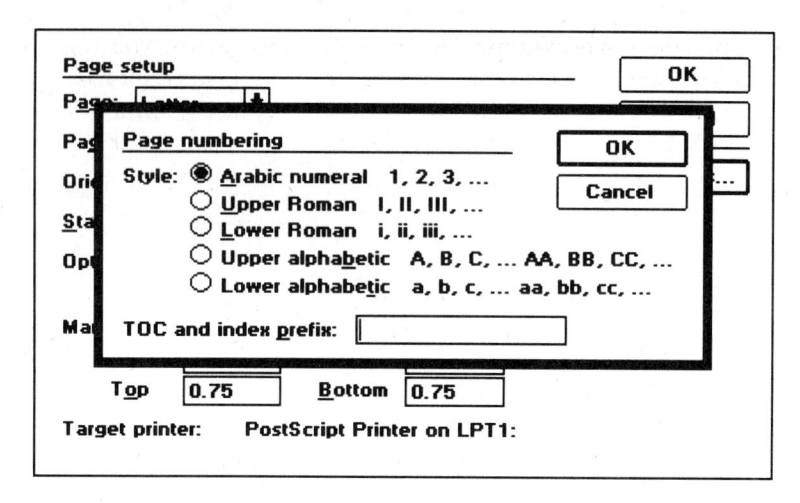

```
Page setup                                    OK
Pa┌──────────────────────────────────────┐
Pa│ Page numbering                    OK │
Or│  Style: ⦿ Arabic numeral  1, 2, 3, …  │
  │         ○ Upper Roman    I, II, III, … │ Cancel
Sta│         ○ Lower Roman    i, ii, iii, … │
Op│         ○ Upper alphabetic  A, B, C, … AA, BB, CC, … │
  │         ○ Lower alphabetic  a, b, c, … aa, bb, cc, … │
Ma│  TOC and index prefix: [        ]    │
  └──────────────────────────────────────┘
      Top  [0.75]     Bottom [0.75]
  Target printer:   PostScript Printer on LPT1:
```

Fig. 3.7. The Page Numbering dialog box.

You also can enter a prefix that appears in the automatically generated table of contents and index. This prefix does not automatically appear on each page, however, unless you type it as part of the page number on the master pages as described later in this chapter.

Working with Double-Sided Publications

You can make a double-sided publication by clicking the check box at the left of the Double-Sided field name. Alternatively, you can click anywhere on the field name to display an X in the box. The Double-Sided option is a toggle: if you click when the box is empty, you select the option and an X appears; if you click when an X is in the box, you deselect the option and the X disappears.

The Double-Sided option does not cause pages to be printed on both sides of the paper as the paper comes out of the laser printer. Rather, you use this option if you want to reproduce the final pages as a two-sided publication, using either xerographic or offset printing equipment. See figure 3.8 for examples.

When you choose the Double-Sided option, PageMaker applies the measure specified for the inside margin to the left margin of odd-numbered pages and to the right margin of even-numbered pages. The inside margin often is wider than the outside margin to accommodate binding. Double-sided publications have two master pages: one for even-numbered, or left-hand, pages and one for odd-numbered, or right-hand, pages. You can set up different running heads and running feet for left-hand and right-hand pages. Figure 3.9 shows the screen display for a single-sided publication. Figure 3.10 shows the screen display for a double-sided publication. Table 3.2 describes the differences between single- and double-sided publications.

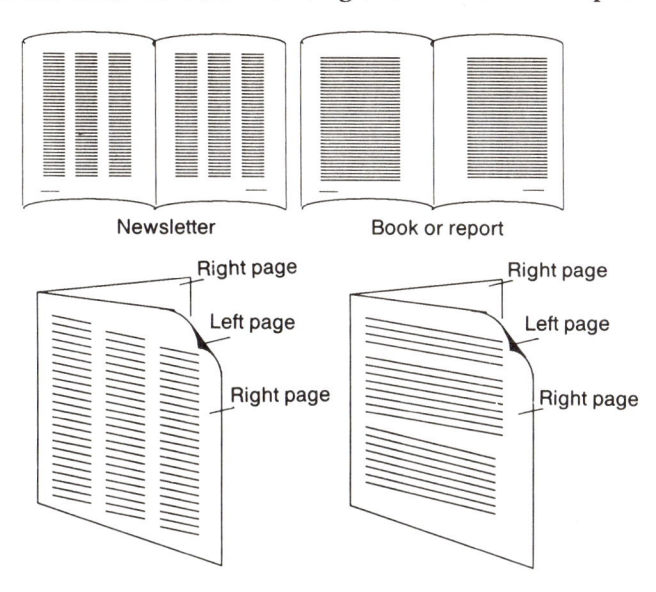

Fig. 3.8. Double-sided publications have facing-page spreads with odd-numbered pages on the right and even-numbered pages on the left.

Table 3.2
Single-Sided versus Double-Sided Publications

Single-Sided Publications	*Double-Sided Publications*
One page displayed at a time	Option of viewing one page at a time or two facing pages Option of "bleeding" an illustration across two pages
One master page or grid for all pages of the publication	Two master pages; one for left-hand (even-numbered) pages and one for right-hand, odd numbered pages
Same running head and different running foot on every page	Option of having heads and feet on left- and right-hand pages
Left margin wide enough to accommodate binding	Inside margins wide enough to accommodate binding

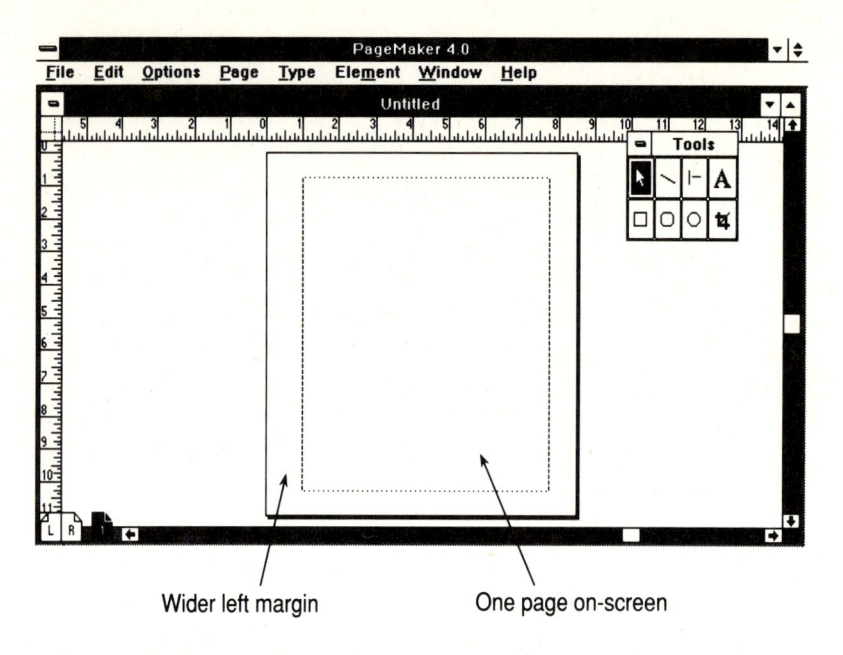

82 Part I: The Production Process with PageMaker

Fig. 3.9. Screen display for a single-sided publication.

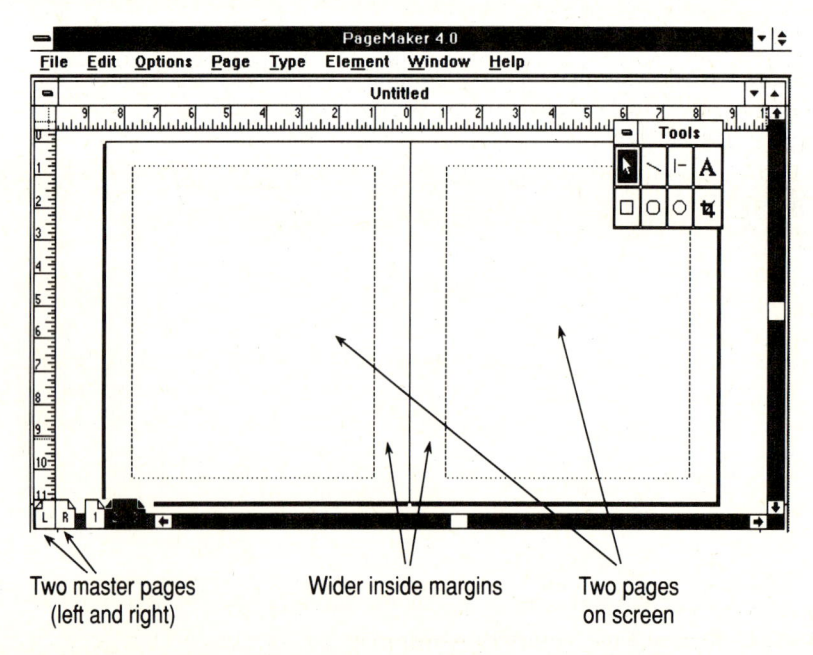

Fig. 3.10. Screen display for a double-sided publication.

If you select the Facing Pages option in addition to the Double-Sided option, you can view pages that face each other in double-sided publications. This feature can be useful when you are designing pages with graphics that bleed across the inside margin or when you want to be sure that the overall two-page layout is balanced (see Chapter 11).

You also can use the Facing Pages option as an efficiency tool. The process of laying out and changing pages is much quicker when you can see two pages at the same time.

You can use the Page Setup command to change the Double-Sided and Facing Pages options after you have opened a publication. If the publication is double-sided and you change to single-sided, the inside margin specification becomes the left margin on all pages, and the outside margin becomes the right margin. If the publication is single-sided and you change to double-sided, the left margin becomes the inside margin, and the right margin becomes the outside margin. If the publication has facing pages and you turn this option off, text and graphics that bleed across facing pages remain anchored to the left-facing page and spill onto the pasteboard, and you will have to reposition text and graphics individually on each page to meet the new page size and margins.

> ***Using the Double-Sided Option for Single-Sided Publications***
> **When building a long, single-sided publication, you can reduce the time you spend turning pages if you set up the document as a double-sided publication and view facing pages as you are working. If the right and left margins are equal, you can print the publication as a double-sided publication with identical left and right master pages. If the left and right margins are not equal, you must turn off the Double-Sided option before printing the final pages.**

You can set up a double-sided publication as a single-sided publication if the inside and outside margins are the same and the master pages are identical. In most cases, however, you should use the Double-Sided option for any publication that you plan to make double-sided, and you should turn off the Facing Pages option if you want to work on one page at a time.

Restarting Page Numbers

Click the Restart Page Numbering option in the Page Setup dialog box if you want the page numbering of the publication always to begin with the page number specified in the Start Page # box. Do not check the Restart Page Numbering box if you will be including this publication as part of a "book" assembled by PageMaker through the Book command, which is described in Chapter 7.

> ### Turning Off the Facing Pages Option for Heavy Pasteboard Use
>
> If your page layouts will not be affected by what is on the facing pages of a double-sided publication, and if you expect to use the pasteboard heavily as a work area during production, turn off the Facing Pages option and work on one page at a time. With the Facing Pages option turned off, you can see more of the pasteboard on each side of the page in reduced views (such as Fit in Window).
>
> In any case, work with the Facing Pages option turned on while you are setting up the master pages. This practice helps you align running heads and feet and horizontal guides on the two pages.

Specifying Page Margins

You enter measurements for the page margins in the Page Setup dialog box by clicking in or tabbing to the text boxes for the four margins and typing numeric values. The page margins entered in the Page Setup dialog box affect all pages of a publication, and this setting cannot be altered for individual pages. To change the text margins on individual pages, you must move the column guides, as described in the "Moving and Locking Guides" section of this chapter.

Margins are measured from the edges of the page; that is, margins are measured from the page size, which is not necessarily the paper size (as explained earlier in this chapter). The margins should reflect the limits to be used for text and column settings on numbered pages rather than the limits allowed for headers and footers and other master-page elements (see fig. 3.11). Margins also should be within the image area of your target printer—for example, the LaserJet will not print nearer than 0.5 inch to the edge of a page.

The margins are displayed in the unit of measure specified by the Preferences command in the Edit menu (see fig. 3.12). To specify margins in the Page Setup dialog box, you can enter any number, including decimals. If the unit of measure is specified as picas and points or ciceros (a European measure), you must include a *p* to separate the pica units from the points. For example, you enter a measurement of 4 picas and 6 points as *4p6*, as shown in table 3.3.

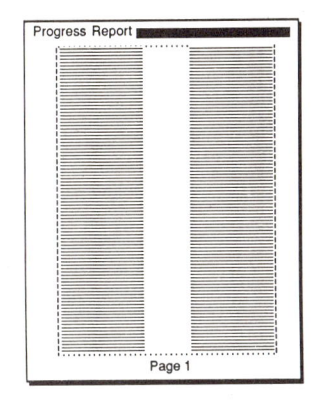

Fig. 3.11. Margins defining the text area limits and excluding the running head and foot.

Fig. 3.12. Determining the unit of measure for the margins in the Preferences dialog box.

Table 3.3
**Equivalent Measures:
Inches, Millimeters, Picas and Points, and Ciceros**

Size	Inches	Millimeters	Picas	Ciceros
	.04	1		
	.167		1p0	
	.177			1c0
	.25	6.36	1p6	1c4.9
	.5	12.7	3p0	2c9.9
	.75	19.06	4p6	4c2.8

continues

Table 3.3 *(continued)*

Size	Inches	Millimeters	Picas	Ciceros
	1	25.4	6p0	5c7.8
A5	5.827	148	34p11.6	32c10.7
B5	6.929	250	41p6.9	39c1.4
A4, A5	8.268	210	49p7.3	46c8
Letter, Legal	8.5	215.9	51p0	47c11.7
B5	9.842	176	59p.07	55c6.7
Letter, Tabloid	11	279.4	66p0	62c1.1
A4	11.693	297	70p1.9	66c
Legal	14	355.6	84p0	79c0.3
A3	16.535	420	99p2.6	93c4
Tabloid	17	431.8	102p0	95c11.5

Overriding the Unit of Measure

You can override the current unit of measure in the Page Setup dialog box (or any dialog box) by entering a one-character abbreviation for the unit of measure you want to specify (see fig. 3.13). Changing the unit of measure will not affect any text or graphics already on the page. To specify inches, enter *i* after the number (for example, *0.75i*). To specify millimeters, enter *m* after the number (as in *19.06m*). To specify picas and points, enter a *p* between the number of picas and the number of points (for instance, *4p6*). To specify picas only, enter a *p* after the number. To specify points only, type a *p* before the number. To specify ciceros, enter a *c* between the number of ciceros and the number of points (as in *4c2.8*).

The unit of measure shown on the publication ruler line always reflects the current unit of measure, as set with the Preferences command on the Edit menu, regardless of the unit of measure you enter in a dialog box (see "Setting Preferences" in this chapter).

You can use the Page Setup command to change the margins after you have opened a publication, but PageMaker will not reposition the text and graphics (that have already been positioned) to match the new margins. PageMaker maintains the position of text and graphics relative to the top left margin corner. You must manually reposition text and graphics to fit the new margins on each page, including text that was positioned using the old column guides.

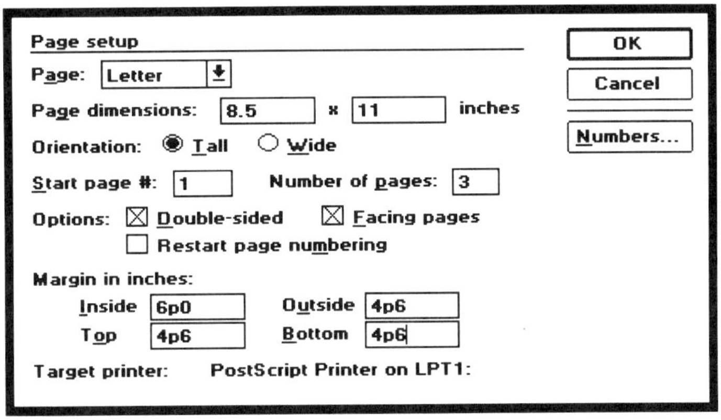

```
Page setup                                    OK
Page: [Letter ▼]                              Cancel
Page dimensions: [8.5] × [11] inches
Orientation:  ⦿ Tall   ○ Wide                 Numbers...
Start page #: [1]   Number of pages: [3]
Options:  ☒ Double-sided   ☒ Facing pages
          ☐ Restart page numbering
Margin in inches:
    Inside  [6p0]    Outside [4p6]
    Top     [4p6]    Bottom  [4p6]
Target printer:    PostScript Printer on LPT1:
```

Fig. 3.13. Overriding the current unit of measure (inches) by entering margins in picas in the Page Setup dialog box.

Specifying the Target Printer

The Page Setup dialog box shows which printer currently is the target printer. If the specified printer is not the printer you will be using for your final publication, you should change the target printer before you start building your publication, because the target printer selection can affect your choice of fonts. You change the target printer by selecting the Printer Setup command on the File menu. Alternatively, before you print, you select the target printer in the Print dialog box (see Chapter 7).

Before choosing the target printer, answer these questions: Does your installation have more than one type of printer? Are you using a font cartridge system, and do you have more than one cartridge? In both these cases, you should define the target printer that you will be using for the final printouts *before* you start a new publication, and you should stick with that setting throughout the production cycle. Otherwise, if you change printers in the middle of a publication, PageMaker asks you whether it should reformat the publication for the new printer, and the resulting publication may look different when printed.

For a discussion of the differences among printers, the methods available for installing and selecting printers, and the ways printers can affect your publication design and production, see Chapter 8.

Building the Publication

After you enter the initial specifications in the Page Setup dialog box, PageMaker displays a blank page with the default setting for column guides (see fig. 3.9). This page is page 1 of your publication. You can begin building a publication immediately by using the Place command to bring in text and graphics that you have prepared in other programs or by using PageMaker's built-in graphics and text tools. Usually, however, you will want to begin by setting your preferences for how PageMaker displays elements on the screen and by defining the master pages so that you can fit each page layout into an overall grid system. Those topics are presented next in that sequence. Remember, however, that you can change your Preferences settings at any time without affecting any of the work you have done in building pages. You also can set up or make changes to the master page at any time, but not all master-page changes are applied automatically to pages that you already have begun building.

Setting Preferences

You can customize the way PageMaker displays elements on-screen by using the Preferences command on the Edit menu. If you use the Preferences command when no publication is open, your selections apply to all new publications. If you use the Preferences command when a publication is open, your choices apply to that publication only. The Preferences dialog box (see fig. 3.14) shows the first set of options that you can customize.

In describing entries in the Preferences dialog box, steps using the mouse are described. Remember, however, that you also can use the keyboard to make dialog box entries, as described in a tip earlier in this chapter.

You can set the preferred measurement system to Inches, Inches Decimal, Millimeters, Picas (and points), or Ciceros by clicking on the arrow to the right of the current measurement system to display a drop-down list of systems. Next, drag the mouse to select a system. This setting determines the unit of measure displayed on the horizontal ruler and in most dialog boxes that show measurements (such as the Page Setup dialog box).

You can choose a different unit of measure for the vertical ruler by clicking on the arrow to the right of the current system for the vertical ruler to display a drop-down list of systems. Next, drag the mouse to select a system. If you choose Custom, you can set tick marks on the vertical ruler that match the leading of your text, entering (in the Points field to the right of the Vertical

Ruler field) the exact number of points between tick marks. If Snap To Rulers is turned on in the Options menu, PageMaker aligns the baselines of selected text to the vertical ruler's tick marks.

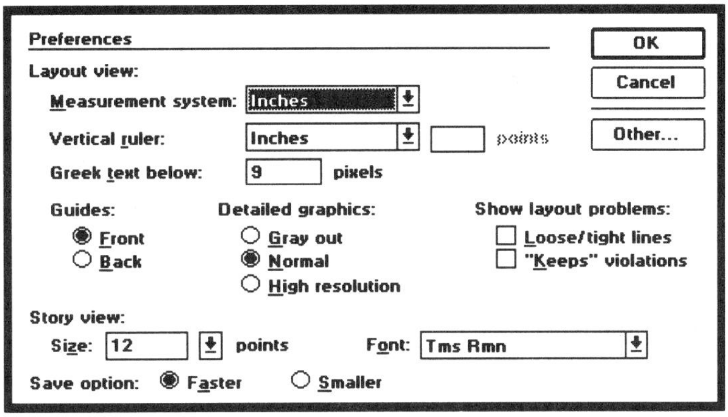

Fig. 3.14. The Preferences dialog box.

You can change the preferred unit of measure at any time without affecting the publication itself—only the ruler line and other displays that show measurements change. You may choose to work with one unit of measure throughout the production, or you may want to switch among the different units (for example, you might use picas for margins and columns, and inches for scaling figures).

The number of increments displayed along the ruler line varies, depending on the size in which you currently are viewing the page (see fig. 3.15). As you learned in Chapter 2, you can view pages in five different scales, from 200% Size to Fit in Window view. The ruler line shows finer increments of measure in enlarged views (such as 200% Size) than in reduced views.

PageMaker displays small-size type as gray bars in reduced views, such as Fit in Window view, to reduce the time required for screen refresh when you change views. The gray bars are called *greeked text*. The default setting is nine pixels, which means that if the text is nine pixels or smaller in the view chosen, the text will be greeked. By tabbing to the Greek Text Below box and typing a number, you can set the default smaller to reduce or eliminate greeking or higher to increase the amount of greeking. Greeking text affects the screen display only—not the way text prints out.

You can set nonprinting guides (margin guides, column guides, and ruler guides) to display in front of or in back of printing elements on the screen by clicking the radio button for Front or Back.

Part I: The Production Process with PageMaker

"Fit in window" (eighths of an inch)

"50% size" (sixteenths of an inch)

"75% size" (sixteenths of an inch)

Actual size (thirty-seconds of an inch)

"200% size" (thirty-seconds of an inch)

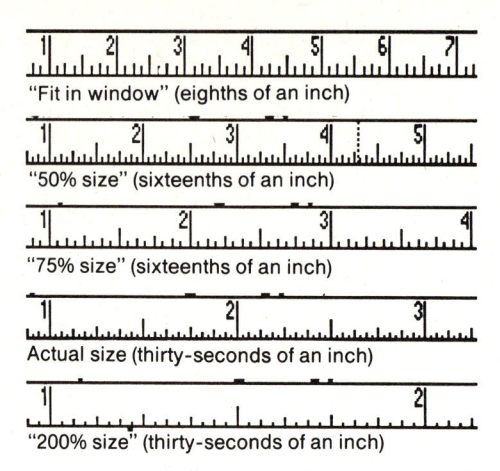

Fig. 3.15. Increments on the ruler line in different views of the page.

4.0 In Version 4.0, you can opt to view graphics normally, to gray them out, or to display them at high resolution by clicking on one of the three radio buttons below Detailed Graphics in the Preferences dialog box. Graying out graphics reduces redraw time, while displaying graphics at high resolution increases redraw time. At high-resolution, the graphics are displayed in sharper detail and can be displayed in color. These options affect the screen display only—not the way graphics print. To display the high-resolution version of linked graphics files, the graphic's link must be updated or the graphic must be stored as part of the publication (as described later in this chapter and in Chapter 6).

4.0 You can allow PageMaker to help you spot layout problems by clicking one or both of the check boxes below Show Layout Problems (in the Preferences dialog box). If you check Loose/Tight Lines, PageMaker highlights lines of text that have too much or too little spacing between words and letters as a result of the hyphenation and justification process. PageMaker bases its evaluation on the spacing limits you set in the Spacing Attributes dialog box (described in Chapter 5). If you check Keep Violations, PageMaker highlights lines that violate the Widow, Orphan, or Keep-With-Next controls that you set in the Paragraph Specifications dialog box (described in Chapter 5). (Violations can result when PageMaker cannot reconcile all the preferences you have set for Spacing, Keep-With-Next, and so on.)

4.0 You can select the font and size for text displayed in Story view. These font and size lists are drop-down lists that restrict the range of choices to fonts and sizes that facilitate fast screen display. You make selections by clicking on the arrows to the right of the values for Size and Font to display a drop-down list of choices. You then drag to highlight your choice.

You can opt to make the Save command run faster by clicking on the Faster radio button at the bottom of the dialog box. Choosing the Faster option might make files larger by including "ghost" memories of items or pages you have deleted. You also can make the Save command act like the Save As command, which results in smaller files. You can choose this option by clicking on the Smaller radio button at the bottom of the dialog box.

You can click the Other button in the Preferences dialog box to display the Screen Font Options dialog box (see fig. 3.16). In displaying screen fonts, PageMaker uses two methods in displaying large fonts or enlarged views of fonts of the screen (as when you are displaying a 36-point font in 200% view). Stretching is a faster method than using vector fonts, but vector fonts maintain better precision in the display. Your choice affects the screen display only, and not the way text prints out.

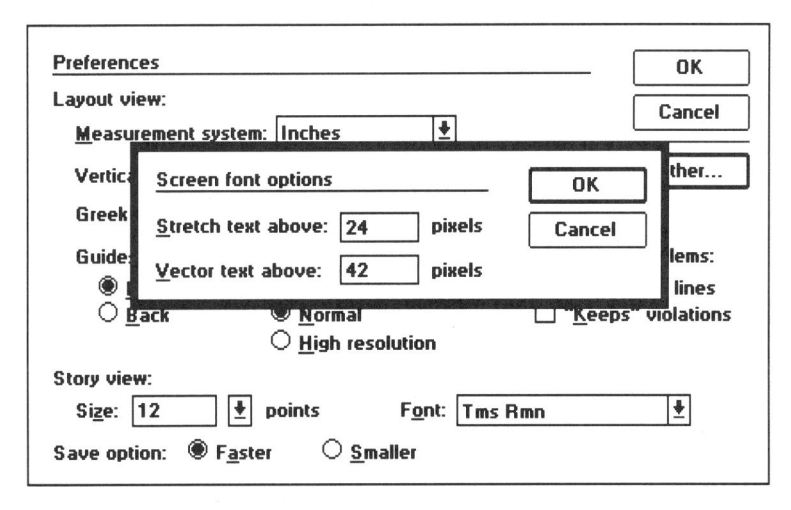

Fig. 3.16. The Screen Font Options dialog box.

Adding Master-Page Elements

PageMaker divides publications into two types of pages: master pages and numbered pages. Any text, graphics, or guides that you set on a master page appear on every page in the publication. Any text, graphics, or guides that you set on a numbered page are printed on that page only. If your publication is longer than two pages, you can save time by making basic settings on master pages.

Figure 3.17 shows elements that usually are on master pages. These elements include column guides, running heads and running feet, and nonprinting guides, which define the basic grid system underlying the publication's design. Settings made on the master pages can be changed on individual pages when necessary. You can move column guides, suppress running heads and running feet, hide all guides, or call the original master page settings back to the current page display.

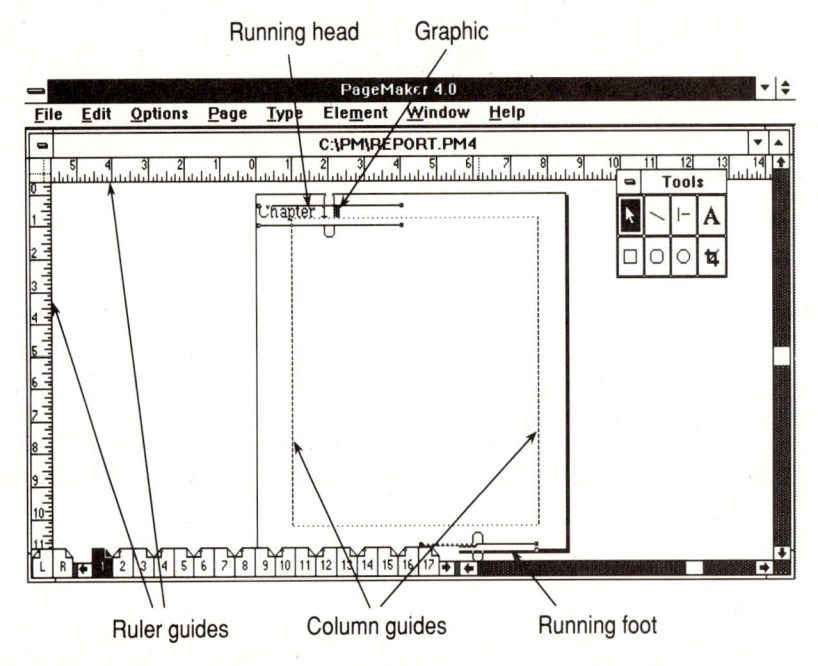

Fig. 3.17. A sample master page.

To turn to a master page, click on the page icon for the left or right master page. These icons are displayed at the bottom left of the screen. You also can use the Go To Page command on the Page menu and choose the left or right master page in the dialog box. When on the master page, you can use the techniques described in this chapter to set the column guides and other grid lines.

Left and right master pages have different effects on numbered pages. Elements set up on the right-hand master page appear on every page of a single-sided publication but only on odd-numbered pages of double-sided publications. Elements set up on the left-hand master page appear on all even-numbered pages of double-sided publications. If you select the Double-Sided and Facing Pages options in the Page Setup dialog box, you can work on both master pages at the same time because master pages appear on-screen simultaneously.

The following sequence of steps is typical for building a master page:

1. Set the column guides.

2. Display the rulers and position guides that are part of the grid, including horizontal guides for positioning the running heads and feet on the master pages.

3. Type the running head between the column guides and then drag the running head to the top of the page.

4. Add graphic elements.

5. Type the running foot between the column guides and then drag the running foot to the bottom of the page.

An example of a master page appears in figure 3.17.

Creating a Master Grid

You usually think of a grid as the page margins and column guides for a publication. Of course, margins and column guides are the basic elements of any grid system. Professional designers, however, often use much more elaborate grid systems, as described in Chapter 11. The grid can include ruler guides as well as graphic elements, such as hairline rules between columns. The principle in designing a grid for master pages is to identify all the basic elements that appear on every page throughout the publication.

Figure 3.18 shows some examples of grid systems used in a book, a manual, and a newsletter. For a more complete discussion of using the grid system in design, see Chapter 11. Chapters 12 through 16 provide examples of grids used in various publications, including those shown in figure 3.18.

The grid for left-hand pages may differ from that for right-hand pages. More likely, however, the grid itself will be the same on all pages; only the text of the running heads and running feet differs between pages. The following sections describe how to use the Column Guides command, how to set up other guides, and how to use other commands on the Options menu to set up your master grids (see fig. 3.19).

Setting Column Guides

PageMaker's default setting is for one column. With the Column Guides command on the Options menu, you can call up a dialog box to change this number (see fig. 3.20). If you have set the publication to be double-sided (in the Page Setup dialog box described earlier), you can set the same number of columns and space between columns on both master pages, or you can check the box beside Set Left and Right Pages Separately to make the dialog box display separate entries for left and right pages. Use the mouse or the Tab key to select the current entries in the boxes beside Number of Columns and Space Between Columns, and then type new values.

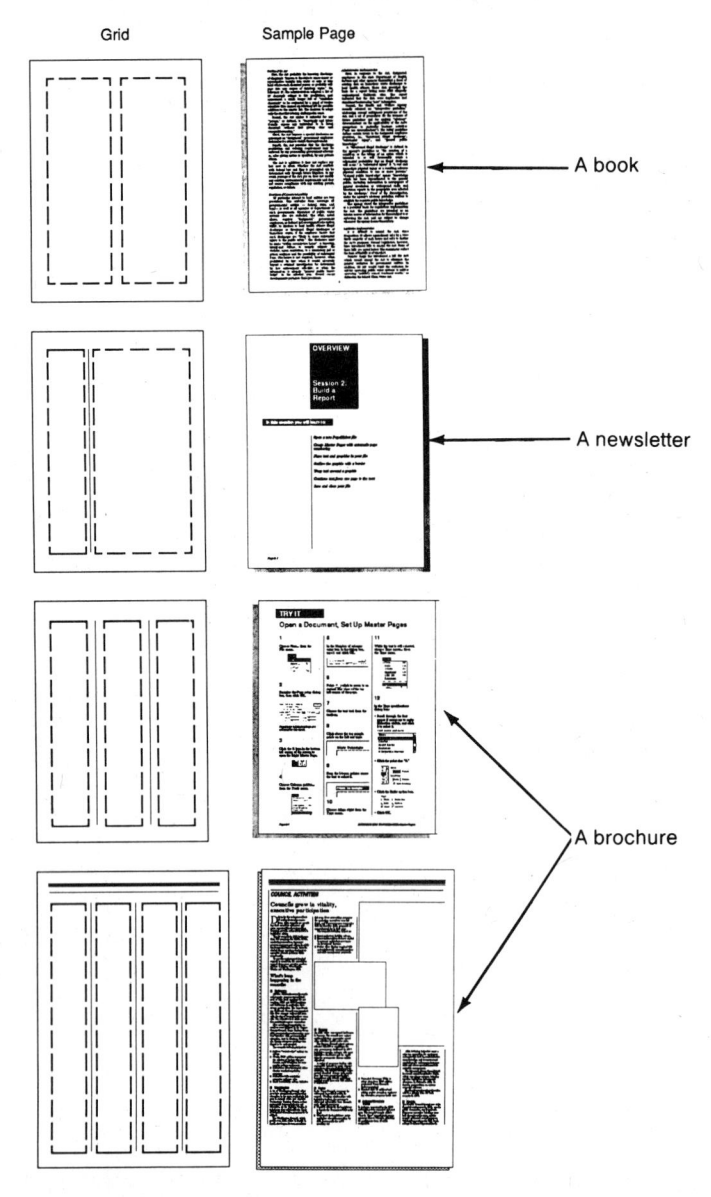

Fig. 3.18. Examples of grid systems and their uses.

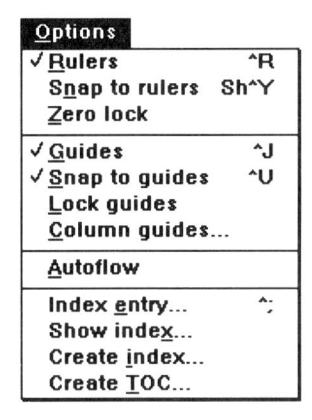

Fig. 3.19. The Options menu commands used to set up nonprinting guides.

Fig. 3.20. The Column Guides dialog box.

The column guides that you set up on the master pages apply to all numbered pages. You can change the column guides for individual pages, however, by turning to the numbered page and using the Column Guides command.

PageMaker imposes a maximum limit of 20 columns per page and a minimum column width of one-half inch. The maximum number of columns allowed on a page, therefore, is determined by the margins of the page and the space between the columns. In practice, you rarely reach this limit because most publications have no more than 5 columns on a page.

When you first select a number of columns and specify the amount of space you want between the columns, PageMaker takes these figures and divides the page into equal columns between the margins (see fig. 3.21). Column guides define the width of text that is placed or pasted in the column. Changes made through the Column Guides command do not affect text that already has been positioned on the page. After placing text in a column, you can change the column guides without affecting the text, and you can change the width of the text by dragging the text block handles, as explained in Chapter 4.

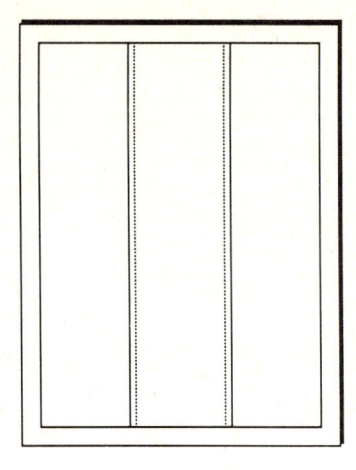

Fig. 3.21. A three-column page division.

To make columns unequal, you drag the column guides (see "Moving and Locking Guides"). Remember that changing column widths does not affect the width of blocks of text already on the page—only the width of new text placed or pasted into the column.

You cannot change the space between the columns except through the Column Guides dialog box. The space between columns is given or entered in the unit of measure currently selected through the Preferences command on the Edit menu. All columns on a page must have the same amount of space between them. Note that the space between columns is ignored in one-column layouts.

Creating Nonprinting Guides

Nonprinting guides include all the various dotted and dashed lines that are displayed in PageMaker but are not printed. These nonprinting guides include page margins, column guides, and ruler guides, as shown in figure 3.22. To specify page margins, you use the appropriate options in the Page Setup dialog box. To set up column guides, you use the Column Guides command, which is described in the preceding section.

In addition, you can drag up to 40 ruler guides from the ruler lines. To drag a guide from the ruler line, the horizontal and vertical rulers must be visible at the top and left of the Layout view. If the rulers are not displayed, choose Rulers (Ctrl-R) from the Options menu. Then place the pointer on the ruler line and hold down the mouse button until the pointer changes to a two-headed arrow. You then drag the pointer onto the page. You drag from the top ruler line to create horizontal guides; you drag from the left ruler line to create vertical guides. The dotted-line marker on the ruler line helps you position the guide. Ruler guides are useful for positioning objects on a page but do not directly affect the width of text (as column guides do) or the length of text (as the bottom page margin does).

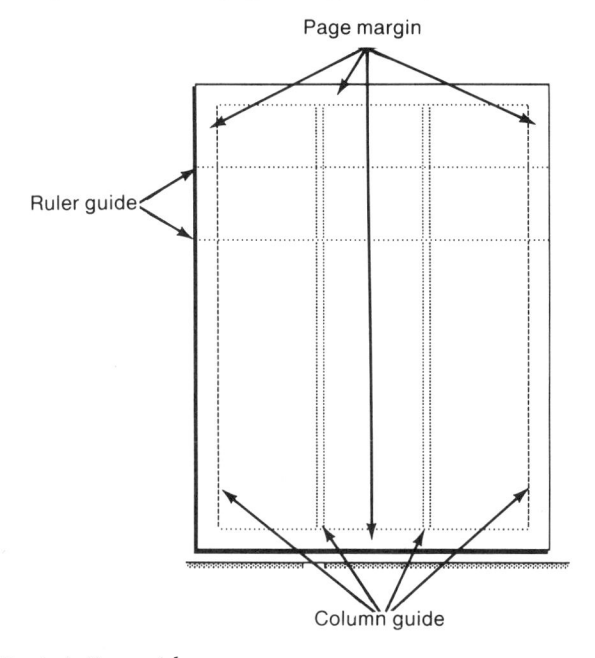

Fig. 3.22. Nonprinting guides.

Ruler guides that you position on master pages appear on all new or blank numbered pages, or you can use the Copy Master Guides command on the Page menu to show new ruler guides from a master page on a numbered page. Ruler guides that you position on a numbered page are displayed on that page only. You can reposition column guides and ruler guides by dragging them on the page. You can move these guides on numbered pages even if the guides originally were set up on the master page, and you can revert to the original master page guides at any time by choosing Copy Master Guides from the Page menu. Page margins cannot be moved except with the Page Setup command (described in "Specifying Page Margins" in this chapter).

Page margins, column guides, and ruler guides help align objects on a page. All three types of guides have a snap-to effect. Only column guides and ruler guides can be moved by dragging them on the page. Only margins and column guides cause text to wrap. Only the bottom page margin affects the length of the columns.

Using the Snap-To Effect

All nonprinting guides—page margins, column guides, and ruler guides—have a snap-to effect. The snap-to effect pulls the pointer, icons, and the edges of a graphic or block of text into position against the guide when you bring the object close to the guide (see fig. 3.23). This capability is extremely useful when you want to align objects quickly and precisely, especially when you are working in reduced views such as Fit in Window.

Sometimes, you may prefer to work with the snap-to effect turned off—for example, when you are forcing something into a position outside the basic grid structure. Suppose that you are drawing a hairline rule between two columns. You do not want the crossbar or the rule to snap to either column guide. To turn off the snap-to effect, use the Snap To Guides command on the Options menu (see fig. 3.19). Turning Snap To Guides on and off has no effect on text and graphics already on the page.

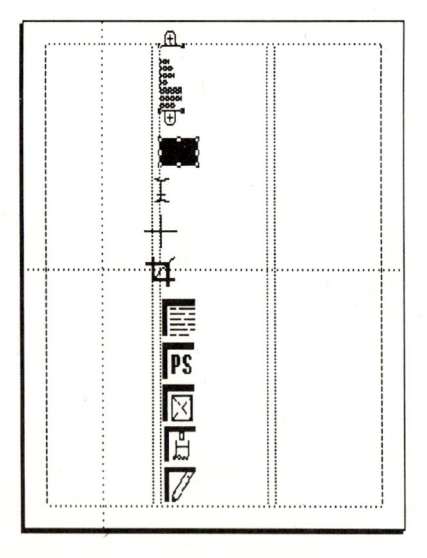

Fig. 3.23. The snap-to effect on icons, blocks of text, and graphics.

Moving and Locking Guides

To move a column guide or ruler guide, you put the pointer over the guide and hold down the mouse button. When the pointer changes to a two-headed arrow, you can drag the guide to a new location. Displaying the ruler lines (by choosing the Rulers command from the Options menu or pressing Ctrl-R) before moving column guides is good practice: you can use the rulers to help position the column guides precisely.

Figure 3.24 shows an example of a publication in which the column guides were moved to create custom layouts. The example is taken from Part III of this book. On the left side of the figure, the middle column guides of a two-column layout have been moved to the left to create a narrow left column and a wide right column. In the center example, columns have been arranged to create a wide right column and two narrow columns. In the example on the right, the column guides have been moved to create two columns: a wide left column and a narrow right column.

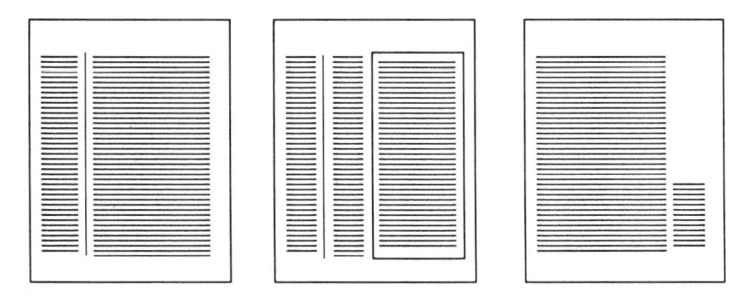

Fig. 3.24. Examples of publications with custom column settings.

To be sure that you do not move any guide inadvertently, you can use the Lock Guides command on the Options menu. The Lock Guides command works like a toggle switch. When the toggle is on, the command is checked on the menu; when the toggle is off, the command is not checked. The Lock Guides setting affects every page of the publication.

You can remove a ruler guide by dragging the guide off the page. To remove a column guide, however, you must use the Column Guides command and dialog box from the Options menu.

Using the Ruler Line

With the Rulers command on the Options menu, you can display or hide the horizontal and vertical rulers at the top and left of the screen. You use these

100 Part I: The Production Process with PageMaker

ruler lines to help place guides, text, and graphics on a page; to measure distances; and to draw or scale graphics to fit an area. To display the rulers, you select the Rulers command. The Rulers command is a toggle switch; you invoke the same command to turn the rulers on or off.

The on-screen position of the pointer or an object being moved is indicated by dotted markers on the rulers, as illustrated in figure 3.25. These markers can be helpful especially in aligning objects or drawing a graphic to exact size.

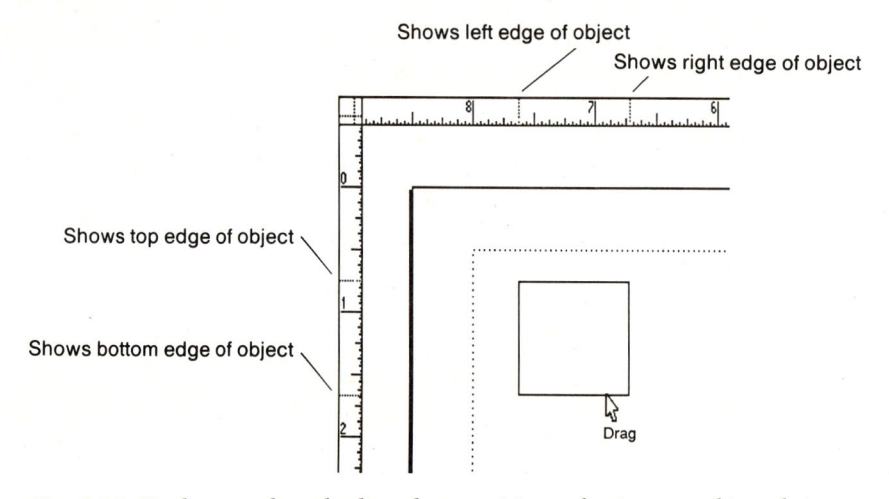

Fig. 3.25. Markers on the ruler line show positions of pointer or objects being moved, cropped, or scaled.

The screen must display the ruler lines before you can create nonprinting guides on the page, as described in the section "Creating Nonprinting Guides." You also must display the ruler lines before you can move their zero point, as described in the next section.

Changing the Zero Point

The *zero point* is where the top and left rulers intersect and begin measurement. Usually, the zero point falls at the top left corner of the page. In double-sided publications viewed with the Facing Pages option, the zero point falls at the inside edges of the facing pages.

Before you can change the zero point, the ruler line must be on the screen. To move the zero point, you put the pointer on the intersection point of the rulers and hold down the mouse button as you drag the marker to the new zero point location (see figs. 3.26 and 3.27). The measures on the ruler line then shift to the new point, as shown in fig. 3.28.

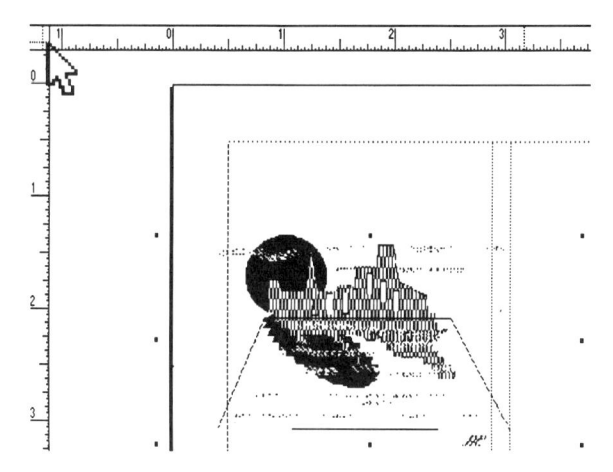

Fig. 3.26. Changing the zero point: the pointer at the intersection of the ruler lines.

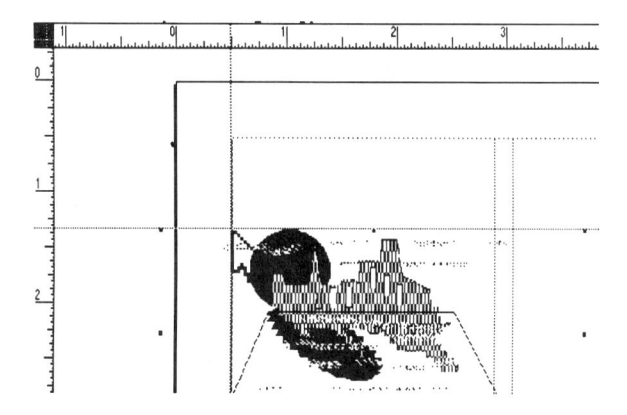

Fig. 3.27. Changing the zero point: dragging the marker to the new location.

When you move the zero point on one page, the new position appears on every page of the publication.

When To Move the Zero Point

You move the zero point when you want to measure the size of an object or scale a graphic or a column to match a specific size. When you want to position an object relative to other objects on the page, keep the zero point at the top left corner of the page.

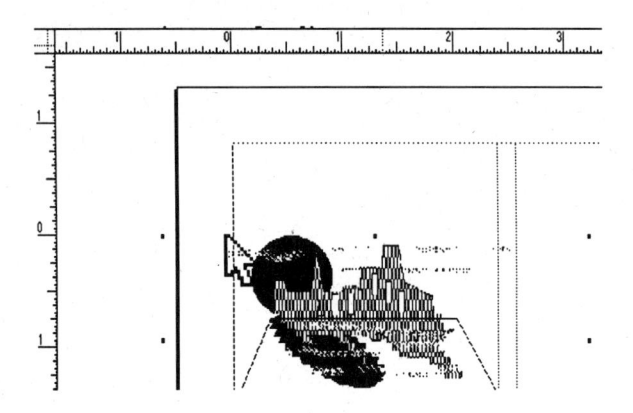

Fig. 3.28. Changing the zero point: the measures on the ruler line shift to the new point.

▸ 4.0 The Zero Lock command from the Options menu is a toggle command that enables you to lock the zero point so that it cannot be moved or to unlock the zero point if it is locked.

Typing Running Heads and Running Feet

Text entered on the master pages appears on every page of the publication unless the text is suppressed (see "Hiding Master-Page Items" in this chapter). This text can include page numbers as well as running heads and running feet that might identify the publication or the chapter.

You can type or place text on a master page the same way you type or place text on any other page (see Chapter 4). Usually, you type the text directly on the master pages because the text is short and does not have to be part of a continuous flow between the master page and other pages. To type text directly on a page in PageMaker, first select the text tool—the letter *A* in the top right corner of the toolbox. When you click the pointer on the text tool, the mouse pointer changes to an I-beam. Click the I-beam anywhere on the page to set an insertion point, and start typing. Chapter 4 describes additional methods of positioning text on a page, and Chapter 5 describes how to format the text (change the font, style, alignment, and so on).

> **Using Margins To Control Placed Text**
>
> Place the running heads and running feet outside the page margins, as shown in figure 3.29. Use the top and bottom margins to define the length of the columns when you place text on numbered pages.

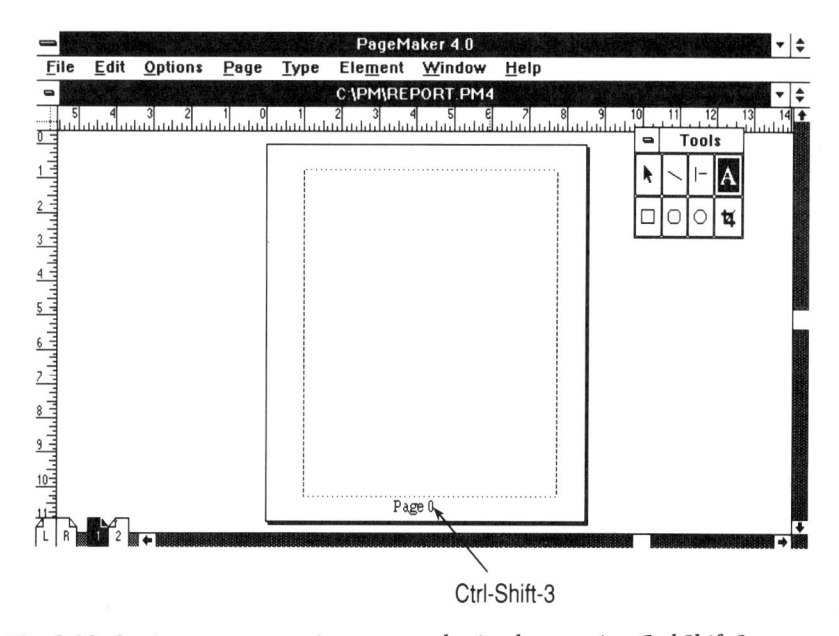

Fig. 3.29. Setting up automatic page numbering by pressing Ctrl-Shift-3.

If you already have placed ruler guides and customized column settings on several pages before you define the master page elements, those pages retain their original settings and do not pick up the master settings, unless you use the Copy Master Guides command, described in the section "Copying Master Guides."

Numbering Pages Automatically

You can set the starting page number in a publication through the New and Page Setup commands, as described earlier in this chapter. To have page numbers print out on publication pages, however, you must insert them as part of the text—usually on the master pages.

You create a page number by pressing Ctrl-Shift-3 (Ctrl-#) while typing with the text tool. When you press this keystroke combination on a single-sided master page or on a right-facing master page, RM appears at the text-insertion point on the master page. When you type Ctrl-Shift-3 on a left-facing master page, LM appears at the text-insertion point. You can format the page number as you would any other text: by selecting the page number with the text tool and setting type specifications.

Page numbers usually appear in a running head or foot on the master pages, but you can make PageMaker print page numbers anywhere on any page. If you enter the page numbers by pressing Ctrl-Shift-3 on the master pages, on subsequent pages the page numbers appear in the location set on the master pages. You also can set up page numbers by pressing Ctrl-Shift-3 on individual pages within a publication.

The most easily referenced parts of any book are the outer edges of the pages: the top or bottom left of even-numbered pages, and the top or bottom right of odd-numbered pages. Using these four positions makes page numbers and section names easy to find.

Adding Graphic Elements to Master Pages

In addition to containing text and guides, master pages can include graphics created in PageMaker or imported from other programs. For instance, the grid system may include hairline rules between columns. You can create or place graphics on a master page the same way you create or place text on any page in PageMaker. These techniques are described in Chapter 6.

Figure 3.30 shows sample master pages from Part III of this book; the example incorporates graphics on the master pages. The pages shown use PageMaker graphics to set off the grid and to incorporate a logo created in a graphics program.

Remember that you use master pages to make specific material appear on all or most pages of a publication. After you are on a numbered page of the publication, you can suppress all or parts of the master-page elements by using one of the techniques described in the following two sections.

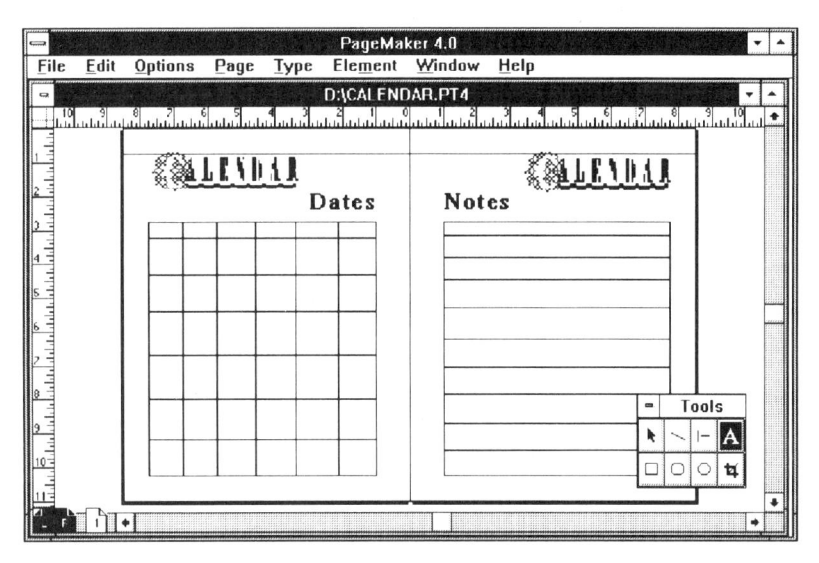

Fig. 3.30. Master pages including graphics from other programs.

Repeating Elements from One Master Page to Another

After setting up text and graphics on one master page, you can copy the text and graphics to the second master page in a facing-page publication. To copy the text and graphics to the second master page, follow this procedure: use the Edit menu's Select All command to select the entire group, and then use the Copy and Paste commands to copy and paste the group on the second master page.

When you have set up the master pages, you are ready to begin working on the first numbered page. Use the Place command on the File menu to bring in graphics and text from other programs, or use PageMaker's built-in text and graphics tools, as described in Chapters 4 through 6.

Hiding Master-Page Items

After building your master pages, you can eliminate all the master guides, text, and graphics from an individual numbered page by turning off the Display Master Items command on the Page menu.

You can use the Display Master Items command to eliminate all the master elements. You then can use PageMaker's text and graphics tools to add back only the elements you want to use on a selected page.

> ### Suppressing Parts of the Master-Page Elements
>
> If you want to suppress only some of the master-page elements, you can hide them by covering them with white boxes: rectangles created with PageMaker's square-corner tool and given a color of white (Paper in the Shades command's submenu) and a line style of None (in the Lines command's submenu). Figure 3.31 provides an example in which a white box at the top of the page hides the running head.
>
> This trick does not work with all printers; some printers cannot print reverse type or white boxes.

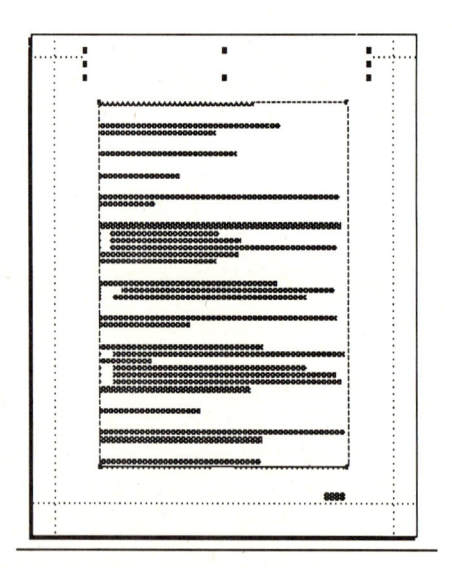

Fig. 3.31. Using a white box to hide the running head.

Copying Master Guides

Suppose that you have suppressed the display of all master elements by turning off the Display Master Items command when a numbered page is displayed on-screen. Or suppose that, on a numbered page, you have moved any of the column guides or ruler guides initially set up on the master pages. With the Copy Master Guides command on the Page menu, you can restore these guides. The Copy Master Guides command is useful in several situations:

- When you want to restore the master guides after changing them on a numbered page

- When you want to display the master guides on a page that you built before setting up the master page

    If you already have placed ruler guides and customized column settings on several pages before you define the master-page elements, those numbered pages retain their original settings and do not pick up the master settings unless you use the Copy Master Guides command.

- When you are using more than one grid system or column layout in a publication

    For example, if you want some pages to contain three equal columns and other pages to have a particular custom column setting, you set up the custom columns on the master pages and use the Column Guides command to switch to three columns (see Chapter 10).

Working with Pages

While building a publication, you can use the Page menu commands to move around on a page, to add or delete pages, or to turn from one page to another. Most of the Page menu commands have keyboard equivalents or mouse shortcuts. The Page menu commands are described in the following sections.

Changing the Views of a Page

The Page menu in PageMaker 4.0 lists seven different views that you can use on any page: Fit in Window (Ctrl-W), 25% Size (Ctrl-0), 50% Size (Ctrl-5), 75% Size (Ctrl-7), Actual Size (Ctrl-1), 200% Size (Ctrl-2), and 400% Size (Ctrl-4). The Page menu shows the keyboard shortcuts to the right of the commands. You can get a Fit in World view, which displays all of the pasteboard, by holding down the Shift key when you choose Fit in Window (Shift-Ctrl-W). In addition to using those shortcuts, you can click the secondary mouse button to switch to an Actual Size view of the pointer's position on the page or to toggle between Actual Size and Fit in Window. Hold down the Shift key and click the secondary mouse button to switch to a 200% Size view of the pointer's position.

You can turn to a Fit in Window view of any page, regardless of the view in which the page was left last, by holding down the Shift key as you click the mouse on a page icon. This method also works if you click on the icon for the current page.

To move around on the screen in any view, use one of the following methods:

- Use the scroll bars.
- To move the page on the screen, hold down the Alt key as you drag the grabber hand.
- To jump the text tool (the I-beam) from one place to another within a text block (and thereby jump to a new view of the page), use the keyboard shortcuts described in Chapter 4.

Starting a Page in the Fit in Window View

Start building each page by working in the Fit in Window view, letting the snap-to effect of the guides help you place text and graphics from other programs. To type or edit text or to draw graphics with PageMaker's tools, change to Actual Size, 75% Size, or 50% Size. Change to 200% Size to work with small type (eight points or fewer) and to align graphics and text precisely without using guides.

Saving Pages in Different Views

Some layout artists save the finished pages in their publications in Fit in Window view and the unfinished pages in a close-up view of where they left off with that page. This way, the layout artist can page through a publication quickly, making finishing touches after the first complete run-through. (Each page is saved in its last view.)

Inserting and Removing Pages

While you are working, you can insert and delete pages by using the Insert Pages and Remove Pages commands on the Page menu. With either command, you enter the number of pages to be inserted or deleted (see fig. 3.32).

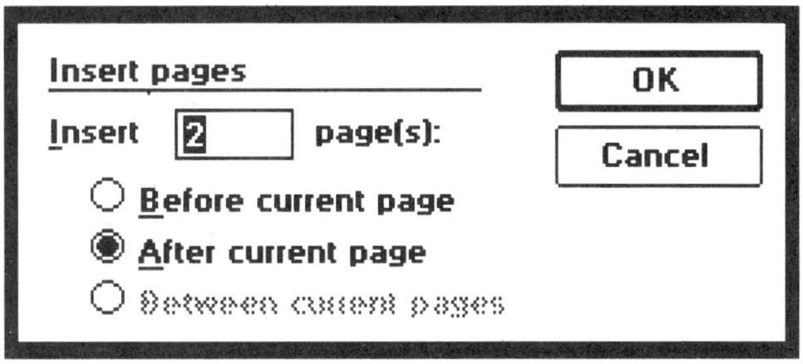

Fig. 3.32. Inserting new pages.

Page insertions and deletions in the publication are reflected in the page count displayed in the Page Setup dialog box. Chapter 4 describes how to continue text from one page to another when you are using the Insert Pages command.

When you delete pages, PageMaker warns you that you cannot restore their contents. If you delete a block of text from the middle of a multipage flow of text from the same source, PageMaker preserves the link between adjacent blocks, but the content of the deleted text block is lost. For example, before a block of text is deleted, the text in figure 3.33 flows through three columns. After the middle block of text is deleted, the text flows from the first column to the third column. To delete pages without losing their contents, you can use the pointer tool to select all of the page contents, drag the contents to the pasteboard area, and then delete the pages.

> ### *Enlarging Your View of the Pasteboard*
> When working with big graphics or large blocks of text on the pasteboard, you can obtain a wider view of the pasteboard by holding down the Shift key as you select the Fit in Window option (see fig. 3.34). This technique works if you select the option from the Page menu or if you press Ctrl-Shift-W, but not when you use the secondary mouse button to change to the Fit in Window view.

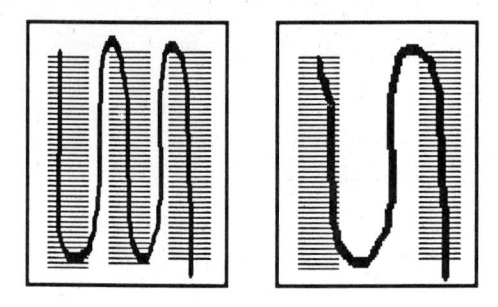

Fig. 3.33. The chain between adjacent text blocks is preserved after text deletion.

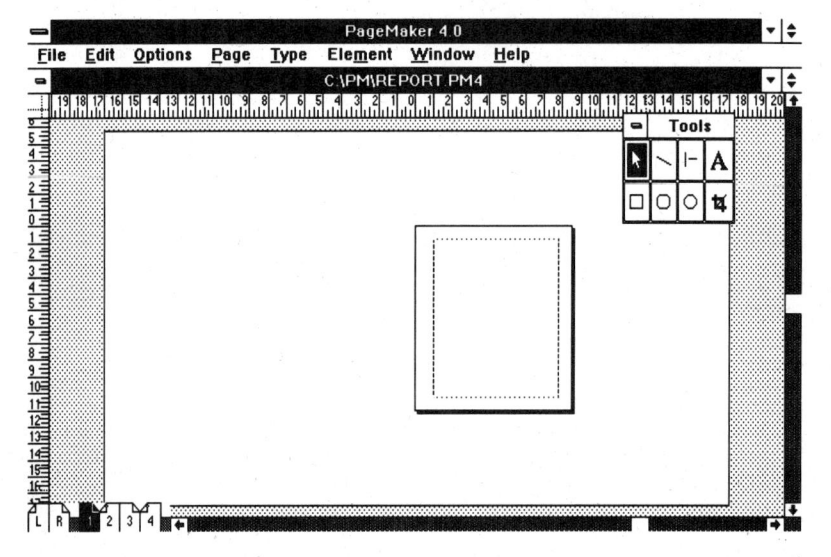

Fig. 3.34. Pressing Ctrl-Shift-W to get a wider view of the pasteboard area.

PageMaker has two methods for forcing a left-hand (even-numbered) page to become a right-hand (odd-numbered page). You can insert a blank page in front of the left-hand page. Alternatively, if you are working with a publication consisting of many sections, you can make each section a separate file, each of which starts with an odd-numbered page. Figure 3.35 illustrates these two methods.

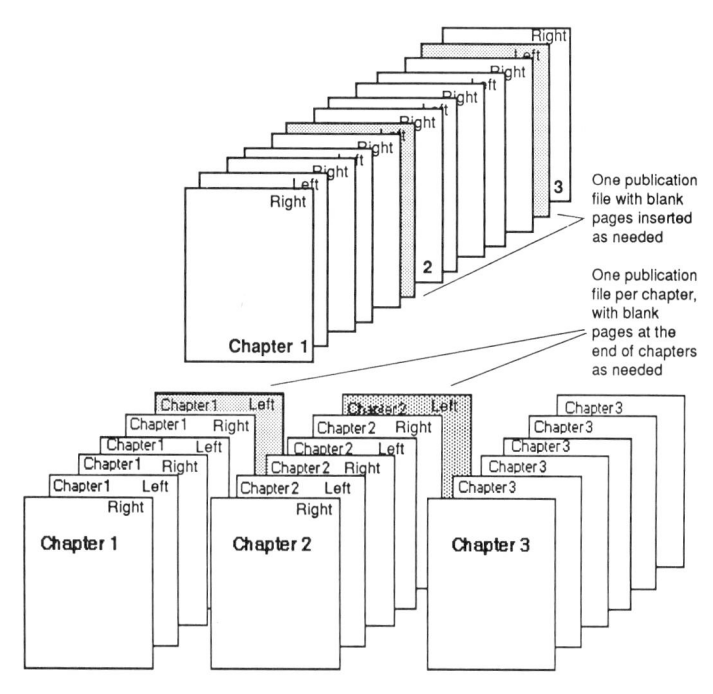

Fig. 3.35. Two ways of forcing new sections to start on right-hand pages.

If you insert pages between two facing pages, any items that extend across the boundaries between the two pages remain on the left-hand page. If you delete a left-hand page from a facing-page set and some elements overlap both pages, PageMaker deletes those elements. If you delete pages so that two new facing pages have more than 40 ruler guides (the maximum allowed for a pair of facing pages), PageMaker deletes some of the ruler guides on the right-hand page.

If you insert an odd number of pages into a double-sided facing-page layout, elements that were formerly set up to bleed from the left-hand to the right-hand page of a pair bleed onto the pasteboard. In figure 3.36, for example, elements bleed across pages 2 and 3. When a new page is inserted, the elements bleed from page 3 (the old page 2) onto the pasteboard, and the connection with page 4 (the old page 3) is lost (see fig. 3.37).

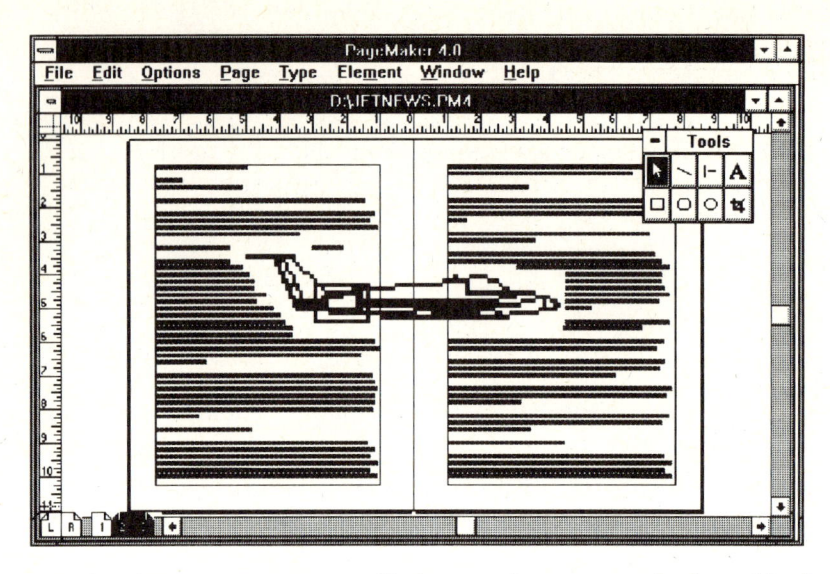

112 Part I: The Production Process with PageMaker

Fig. 3.36. Before one page is inserted before two facing pages, the figure bleeds across pages 2 and 3.

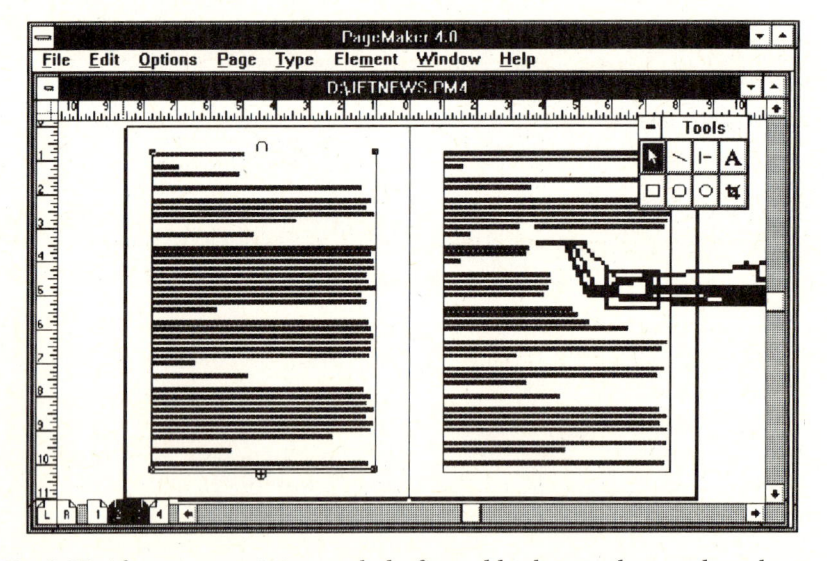

Fig. 3.37. After one page is inserted, the figure bleeds onto the pasteboard.

Turning Pages

You can move from page to page by clicking on the page icons at the bottom of the screen. If the publication is so large that not all the page icons fit on the bottom of the screen at one time, you can click on the arrows that appear at each end of the page icons (see fig. 3.38). Use one of the following methods:

- To scroll one page icon at a time in the direction of the arrow, position the mouse pointer on the arrow and click the main mouse button once.

- To keep the page icons scrolling, hold down the mouse button on an arrow.

- To jump half the number of page icons shown, place the mouse pointer over the scroll arrow and click with the secondary mouse button.

- To jump to the beginning or end of the page icon list, click on the third mouse button or hold down the Ctrl key and click once on an arrow.

Fig. 3.38. Scrolling through the page icons in large publications.

You also can jump to other parts of the publication by using the Go To Page command on the Page menu, or you can use keyboard shortcuts to jump one page forward or backward at a time. Use one of the following methods:

- To jump forward one page (or two pages in a double-sided publication with facing pages), hold down the Ctrl key and press the Tab key.

- To jump backward one page (or two pages in a double-sided publication with facing pages), hold down the Ctrl and Shift keys while you press the Tab key.

> ### *Changing Pages*
> You can change pages by using the keyboard shortcuts for jumping through an article with the text tool. In other words, you can jump to the end of an article in order to jump to the page on which the article ends. With the text tool selected and the I-beam placed within a block of text, you press Ctrl-PgUp to jump to the beginning of that text file. To jump to the end of a text file, you press Ctrl-PgDn.

> ### *Scrolling through Pages Automatically*
> You can have PageMaker page through a publication automatically—displaying pages sequentially like a continuous slide show—by holding the Shift key as you choose Go To Page from the Page menu. Click the mouse button to stop the slide show.

Using the Edit Menu Commands

After laying out all the pages with their essential elements, or while you are still building pages, you can use the Edit menu's commands to delete, copy, or move text or graphics. Most of these commands affect only the object (or objects) you select at the time you invoke the command. If you select nothing when you give the command, nothing happens. (This statement may seem obvious, but one of the most common mistakes beginners make is to execute a command without first selecting an object.) Basic methods of selecting text or objects are described in Chapter 2, and additional methods are described in Chapters 4 and 6.

Deleting and Copying Objects

The Cut, Copy, and Clear commands and the Backspace key affect all the blocks of text and graphics selected with the pointer tool or the phrases of text selected with the text tool.

First, select the object (or objects) by clicking or dragging the pointer tool (to select graphics or whole text blocks) or the text tool (to select parts of text within a block). To remove the selection from the page, from the Edit menu choose the Cut command (or press the keyboard shortcut, Shift-Del) or the Clear command (or use the keyboard shortcut, Del). Alternatively, press the Backspace key. To make a copy of the selected object, choose Copy (or press Ctrl-Ins), and then use the Paste command (described later in this chapter).

To move an object, select it with the pointer tool and drag the object to a new position nearby. Alternatively, you can select an object with the pointer tool or the text tool, choose the Cut (Shift-Del) command, and then choose the Paste command (described later in this chapter).

Both the Cut (Shift-Del) and Copy (Ctrl-Ins) commands put the selected object (or objects) in the Windows Clipboard. The Cut command removes the selected objects from the page, whereas the Copy command leaves the objects on the page and puts a copy of them in the Clipboard. The Clipboard is a temporary storage area that is active while you are working, but the Clipboard's contents are lost the next time you use the Cut or Copy command or when you leave Windows.

The Clipboard remains active throughout each Windows session. For example, suppose that you use Windows Draw to draw a graphic. You then copy the graphic to the Clipboard and open a PageMaker publication without leaving Windows. With the Paste command, you can pull the graphic from the Clipboard onto the page in PageMaker.

Similarly, you can use the Clipboard to paste selected objects from one PageMaker publication into another.

When you use the Clear command or the Del or Backspace key, PageMaker removes the selected object from the page; however, unlike the Cut command, PageMaker does not put the objects into the Clipboard. The only way to retrieve objects after using the Clear command or the Del or Backspace key is to invoke the Undo command immediately.

Preserving the Clipboard Contents

When you specifically do not want to replace the contents of the Clipboard, use the Clear command or the Del or Backspace key to delete text or graphics. Otherwise, use the Cut command and let the Clipboard serve as a temporary backup for later retrieval of the objects.

To remove objects from a page for indefinite storage and retrieval, move them onto the pasteboard instead of the Clipboard.

Pasting Objects

By using the Paste command (Shift-Ins) from the Edit menu, you can retrieve whatever was last put in the Clipboard with the Cut or Copy command and place that material on the page, usually in the center of the screen.

When objects first are pasted on the page, they already are selected; that is, you can see the handles of the pasted graphics and text. If you are pasting a group of objects, you can move the objects as a group by dragging the entire selection immediately after pasting the selection on the page. Otherwise, if you click the pointer off the selection, the object no longer is selected.

The Paste command is used most often to paste objects from one part of a PageMaker publication to another or from one PageMaker publication to another. For moving graphics or text from another program into PageMaker, you will find using the Place command more convenient (described in Chapters 4 and 6).

This statement has one exception. Suppose that you want to select only a small part of a word processing document or a drawing from another program. Rather than place the entire file and crop (cut off) the excess parts, a more convenient technique is to go into the word processing or graphics file under the Windows umbrella, select the desired parts, and copy them to the Clipboard. You then open the PageMaker publication and use the Paste command.

Undoing Your Most Recent Action

The Undo command on the Edit menu reverses the action taken immediately before the command is invoked; that is, immediately after making a mistake or changing your mind about an edit, you can use the Undo command to reverse that action. You should work cautiously when making major changes to a publication, such as changing the type specifications or formatting a whole block of text or story. Check the results of each action as you go along. The wording of the Undo command itself changes to describe the last action—for instance, Undo Move or Undo Stretch.

If PageMaker cannot reverse your last action, the Edit menu displays the words Cannot Undo in gray instead of the Undo command in black. Some actions you cannot reverse include the commands on the File menu (except Page Setup), the commands on the Lines and Shades submenus, view changes, scrolling, and selecting.

Reversing All Changes Made Since the Last Save

With the Revert command on the File menu, you can reverse all edits or changes you made since the last time you saved the publication. In other words, you can use the Revert command to restore a publication to the state the publication was in the last time you used the Save or Save As command. If you have not used either command since the last time you used the Open command, you restore the publication to the condition the publication was in before you opened it. PageMaker automatically saves a temporary copy of your file—called a *minisave*—on disk whenever you click a page icon, add or delete a page, or change the page setup. You can revert to the last minisave by holding down the Shift key as you select the Revert command.

> **Using the Save and Revert Commands**
>
> Save your publications often while you are working. Saving often enables you to use the Revert command to reverse your most recent changes.

Developing Efficient Procedures

After you build the master pages as described in the preceding sections, you begin the task of placing text and graphics on each page. A typical sequence of steps for each page is as follows:

1. Verify that the master-page elements are appropriate for the current numbered page. If column guides or ruler guides need to be changed for this page, adjust them as needed before placing text and graphics on the page. Commands that are used in this step include Column Guides, Rulers, and Display Master Items.

2. If your design specifications limit you to one or two variations in text and graphic formats, you can change the default settings to match the most common specifications or set up a style sheet so that each text variation has its own tag. (You can read more about

style sheets in Chapter 5.) Remember that you change the default settings for text and graphics by making menu selections while the pointer tool is selected.

3. Place text and graphics on the page. The following are general guidelines:

- Work in Fit in Window view at first to lay out the entire page. Change to Actual Size view to make fine adjustments.
- Use the Snap To Guides feature to help you position text and graphics against the guides on the page.
- Use the drag-place feature to scale a graphic as you are placing the graphic or to override the column width when placing text (see "Using the Drag-Place Feature" in Chapter 4).

4. Save your work often. Press Ctrl-S to execute the Save command or click the current page icon to cause a minisave. For more information on these two alternatives, see the preceding section, "Reversing All Changes Made since the Last Save."

Up to this point, you have learned that you should build master pages before creating individual pages, and that you easily can add or remove pages or hide master items on selected pages.

Chapters 4 through 6 explain how to place text and graphics on the pages by using the Place command or PageMaker's text and graphics tools. This sequence follows one common approach to building a publication: position and format all of the text first, then add the graphics.

When actually building a publication, however, you will find it helpful to study various methods or sequences of operations before deciding on the one that suits you best. The most efficient approach to building a publication varies according to the type of publication you are producing and your own preferences. In some cases, you assemble all the elements on one page at a time, refining every detail of that page layout before you go on to the next page. In other cases, you quickly position all or part of the elements on each page, working through the entire publication once before you go back to make fine adjustments. The question of whether to place text or graphics first also depends on the design of the publication and your personal preference.

In most cases, you should import all the text into the publication before you go back and do any text editing that was not done with the word processor. If you are placing unformatted text, be sure that the default paragraph format and type specifications match those specified for the bulk of the text so that you can fit the copy roughly on the pages as you go along. You can change the defaults for text by making selections on the Type menu with the pointer tool selected from the toolbox, as explained in Chapter 4, or by using style sheets, as explained in Chapter 5.

You should finish placing one whole text file before you start placing another. Placing an entire text file before going on to the next is not a requirement; you can work with as many "loose ends" of unplaced text as you like. In practice, however, you may find that working with more than two text files at a time is confusing.

Chapter Summary

This chapter explained the sequence of steps that you follow when building any publication with PageMaker:

1. Open a new publication.
2. Set up the master page elements and nonprinting grid lines.
3. Use the guides to arrange text and graphics on each page.

The next chapter explains the process of adding text to the publication, and Chapter 5 describes how to change the appearance of the text. Chapter 6 describes how to add graphics to the page and how to edit those graphics. Chapter 7 describes advanced features, such as how to associate a series of publications through the Book command, how to generate a table of contents and an index, how to link external text or graphics files to a publication, and how to manage changes in text and graphics files that are linked to the publication. Chapter 8 describes the printing process, and Chapter 9 describes how to apply color and print color publications.

Together, Chapters 3 through 9 present the commands and steps required for a complete production cycle (except for the design process). Part II offers basic guidelines to help you design your own publications, and Part III provides examples of publications that have been designed for efficient production, usefulness, and pleasing appearance.

Typing, Importing, and Editing Text

You can type text directly into PageMaker, and the Story Editor feature (introduced in Version 4.0) makes this option attractive. In previous versions of PageMaker, you had to work directly in page layout view when typing or editing text. Because the screen showed exactly what the text would look like when printed, typing and editing were relatively slow processes. You still can type and edit text in page layout view in Version 4.0, or you can type and edit text in the Story Editor, which displays text quickly in Story view, using a single font that does not reflect exactly the text's printed appearance. Story Editor also adds new features usually associated with word processors, such as global search and a spelling checker.

Alternatively, you can import text into PageMaker. The text can come from many sources, including word processing programs, tables created with the Table Editor, or databases and spreadsheets that have been saved in text format. PageMaker 4.0 also introduces the Table Editor, a separate utility you can use to create complex tables.

Although you can type text directly on a page in PageMaker, in most large projects you begin publications with text that has been prepared using a word processor. This situation occurs because most authors and editors use word processors, and the production team often uses PageMaker. In many cases, PageMaker can preserve the formatting done in the word processor—for example, type specifications, tabs, and paragraph alignment. In this chapter, you see how PageMaker handles text formatted in a word processing program. By understanding the capabilities of PageMaker and your word processor, you can decide whether to do most formatting during the word processing step or later when working in PageMaker.

This chapter shows you how to import text from word processing programs, how to type text into PageMaker, how to create tables using PageMaker 4.0, and how to select and edit text. You also learn how to control the position and size of text blocks. The steps that precede typing or placing text into PageMaker, such as setting up column guides, were presented in Chapter 3. In Chapter 5, you learn how to change the appearance of the text—with paragraph formatting and type specifications—after the text is placed on the page in PageMaker.

Typing Text in Layout View

Generally, you use PageMaker's text tool for editing and formatting text instead of for typing new text. With Version 4.0, most new text is typed in the Story Editor. On occasion, however, you still will want to use the text tool in Layout view (that is, the WYSIWYG view of the page, as opposed to Story view, which is displayed when you are using the Story Editor) to type short segments of text. In the next section, you see how the text tool operates as an input device. The text tool's common uses as a formatting device are described in Chapter 5. (See Chapter 1 for a discussion of the differences between PageMaker and word processing programs.) To type text directly on a page in PageMaker, you first select the text tool—the letter *A* in the top right corner of the toolbox. When you click the pointer on the text tool, the mouse pointer changes to an I-beam. Click the I-beam anywhere on the page to set an insertion point, and begin typing (see fig. 4.1).

The position of the typed text varies depending on where you click the I-beam to set the text insertion point. For instance, if you click the I-beam on an empty part of the page between two column guides, the text begins at the left column guide and wraps at the right column guide (see fig. 4.2).

If you click the I-beam on a page with no column guides, the new typed text wraps at the right margin. The typed text is in the default format, which usually is flush-left 12-point Times Roman type.

If you click the I-beam within an existing block of text, the typed text is inserted within that text block. This text has the same format as the text immediately to the left of the insertion point.

If you click the text insertion point on the pasteboard or a page with no column guides, the typed text begins wherever you click the insertion point. If you are working on a pasteboard, the text assumes the margin-to-margin width defined in the Page Setup dialog box.

You can create a text box using the drag-type feature by dragging the I-beam to form a boundary for the text (which is visible only when you drag the mouse). The typed text stays within the area specified by the boundary.

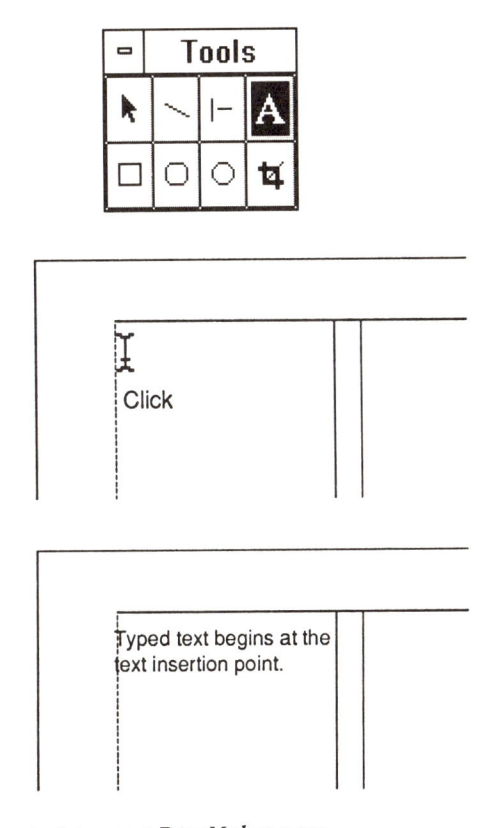

Fig. 4.1. Starting to type on a PageMaker page.

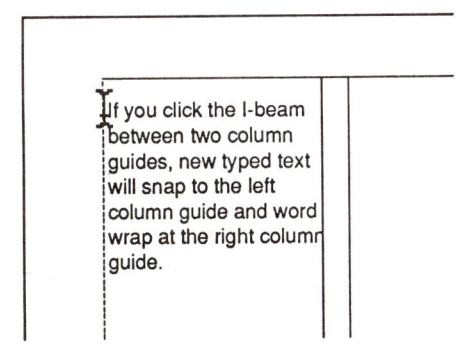

Fig. 4.2. Typed text.

If you want to type more text than will fit in the current text block, column, or page, you can use the techniques described later in this chapter to change the size or position of the text block or to create a series of chained text blocks.

Importing Text with the Place Command

You use the Place command to import text typed in a word processor or data saved as text-only (ASCII) from a spreadsheet, database, or noncompatible word processor. If the text has been formatted in a word processing program supported by PageMaker, PageMaker can preserve some of that formatting, saving you from duplicating the work (see "Importing Formatted Text" in this chapter, and see Chapter 5 for details). PageMaker 4.0 offers the additional option of dynamically linking imported text files to the publication so that changes made in the external file are reflected in the PageMaker publication, as described in Chapter 7.

To place text from an external text file into PageMaker, follow these steps:

1. Choose the Place command from the File menu (see fig. 4.3).

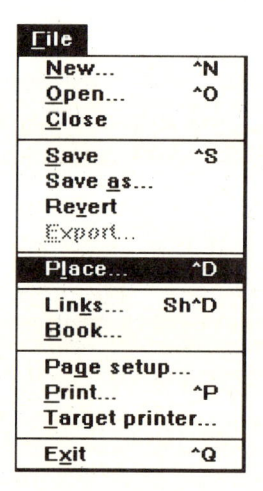

```
File
 New...           ^N
 Open...          ^O
 Close

 Save             ^S
 Save as...
 Revert
 Export...

 Place...         ^D

 Links...         Sh^D
 Book...

 Page setup...
 Print...         ^P
 Target printer...

 Exit             ^Q
```

Fig. 4.3. The File menu with Place selected.

PageMaker displays the Place File dialog box with a list of text and graphics files on your disk. If no file names appear in the list, you can use the techniques described in the next step to check all the directories and disk drives on your system. (If no file names are displayed after checking all directories and disk drives, your disk does not contain any text or graphic files that are recognized by PageMaker. You must install the correct filters for each file format you will be using by going through the installation procedures described in Chapter 2.)

2. In the Place File dialog box, find the name of the text file you want to place (see fig. 4.4).

   - If the file name is not visible, drag the scroll bars to move down the list.
   - Click [-A-], [-B-], or [-C-] to view the list of files on another drive.
   - Click [..] to view the list at the next higher directory level.
   - Click a directory name (shown in brackets) to view the list at the next lower directory level. Alternatively, double-click a directory name (shown in brackets) to view the files within a subdirectory.

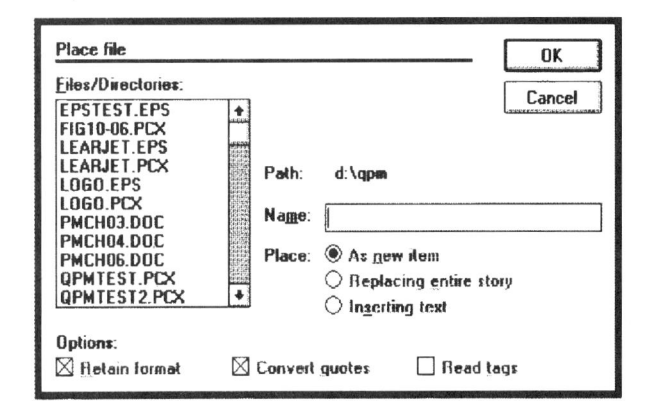

Fig. 4.4. The Place File dialog box.

Notice that you change directories and disks in the Place File dialog box by using the same techniques you learned in Chapter 2 for the Open Publication dialog box. The difference is that only PageMaker publications are listed in the dialog box with the Open command. The Place File dialog box lists only text and graphics files.

3. In the Place File dialog box, choose Retain Format to keep the formatting that was made in your word processing program (formatting is described later in this chapter). Choose Convert Quotes if you want to convert regular (straight) quotation marks to typesetting (opening and closing) quotation marks. And choose Read Tags if you want PageMaker to read the style tags that you set up in your word processing program. (See Chapter 5 for more information on style tags.)

You can select any or all of the options; an X appears in the box next to the option. To deselect an option, click on the box; the X disappears.

4. Select the file name by double-clicking it. Double-clicking is a shortcut for clicking once on the file name to select it and then clicking OK.

5. If your text file does not have an extension that represents a word processing program, such as WP for WordPerfect, a dialog box with the message `Do not know how to place text` appears. Specify the word processing program that the text came from by double-clicking the format. Table 4.1 (under "Importing Formatted Text" later in this chapter) lists the extensions for different word processing programs.

   The pointer changes to the manual or the automatic text flow icon (the next section discusses text flow options).

6. Position the text icon where you want the text to appear and then click.

   The text takes on the width of the column in which the text is placed or the width of the boundary created with the drag-place method, described in "Using the Drag-Place Feature." If Autoflow (described in the next section) is not active, the text stops flowing at the bottom of the column or when the text runs into another object on the page (see fig. 4.5).

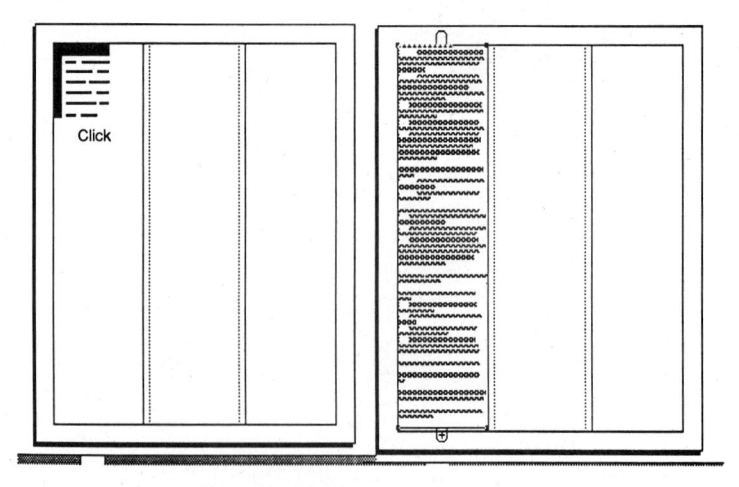

***Fig. 4.5.** The page before (left) and after (right) placing text with manual placing.*

Specifying Text Flow

PageMaker offers three ways of directing the flow of imported text: manual flow, automatic flow, or semiautomatic flow. You can select how you want the text to flow before importing the text, or you can switch between manual, semiautomatic, and automatic text flow after the text icon appears.

Manual text flow is active when the Autoflow command under the Options menu is not checked. Manual text flows to the bottom of the column or to the first object that blocks the text. The pointer tool automatically is selected when the text stops flowing, and the text appears in a *text block* framed in horizontal lines (called *windowshades*) at the top and bottom. In the middle of each windowshade is a *handle*. If the bottom handle is empty, then all of the story has been placed. If the bottom handle contains a down arrow, then there is more text to be placed. To continue placing the text manually, click on the handle at the bottom of the text block to reload the text placement icon, position the loaded text icon in a new column or page, and click to continue placing the text (see fig. 4.6).

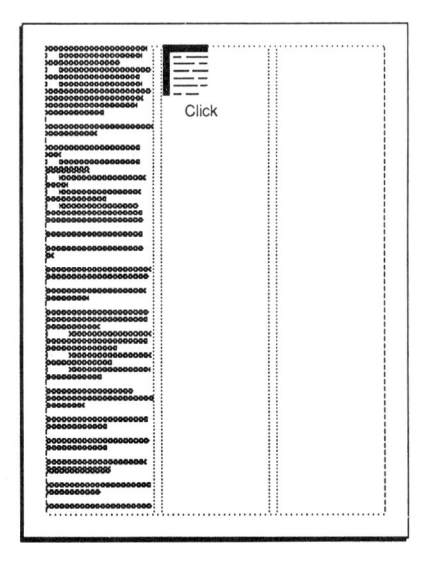

Fig. 4.6. Text icon positioned in next column.

When the page is filled but the last block still shows a down arrow in the bottom handle, you can continue the text to the next page by clicking the last handle on the page to get the text icon. You then have the following options:

- Click the icon of the page number to which you want to go.
- Select the Go to Page command from the Page menu.
- Select Insert Pages from the Page menu to create a new page.

Don't worry that the text icon changes to an arrow when you make a menu selection. The loaded text icon returns when you are back on a page.

When the next page is displayed, position the text icon on the page and click. The text file continues flowing on the page until reaching the bottom margin or another object.

A more efficient way to continue text from column to column or page to page is to use the Autoflow option. To activate automatic text flow, select Autoflow from the Options menu (if that option is not checked already). Autoflow places text continuously, wrapping text around previously placed graphics, filling all columns, and adding pages as needed until all the text is placed. Text stops when you click the main mouse button, when the text runs out, or when the publication reaches 999 pages.

If you stop the automatic text flow by clicking the main mouse button, you can extend or shorten the last text block by dragging the bottom windowshade with the pointer. You can resume the flow at any time by clicking the down-pointing arrow in the windowshade that marks the bottom of the flowed text when the text is selected with the pointer tool. This method yields a loaded text icon that you can click at the margin to continue the flow.

To activate semiautomatic text flow, hold down the Shift key when you are in manual or automatic mode. When you hold down the Shift key for semiautomatic flow, the text flows to the bottom of the column and stops, but the text placement icon remains loaded and ready for you to position. You then just click to continue the flow. The semiautomatic mode changes the text flow only temporarily. When you release the Shift key, the flow pattern reverts to manual or automatic at the end of the column, depending on which mode you were in prior to switching to semiautomatic mode.

Text placed from a single file remains connected as a story, regardless of how many columns or pages are spanned. Figure 4.7 shows that when text blocks are chained in a single file, any insertion or deletion of text selected with the text tool causes the text in chained blocks to move forward or backward to accommodate the change. If a block is selected with the pointer tool and deleted, the text in that block is deleted along with the text block itself, and chained blocks remain unchanged.

In the Autoflow mode, text can flow around graphics. With the Text Wrap command in the Options menu, you can specify how the text wraps around the graphic and where the text flows after the graphic. (See Chapter 5 for a discussion of the Text Wrap command.)

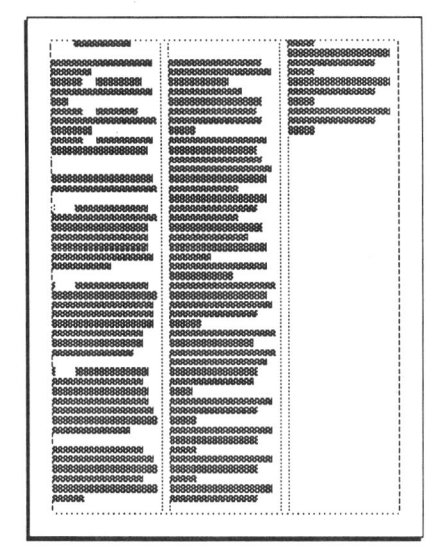

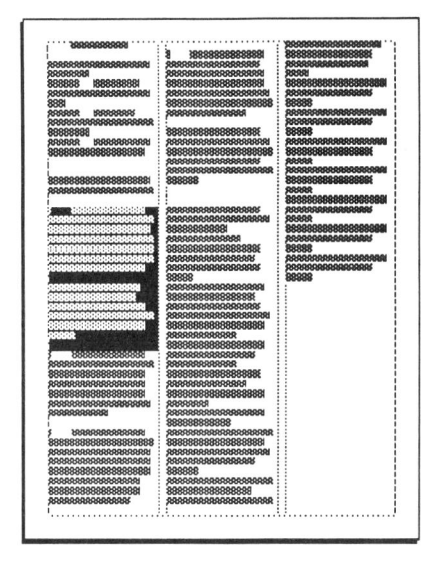

Fig. 4.7. Adding material within chained blocks of text causes other text to shift.

Switching between Manual Flow and Autoflow

You temporarily can switch the automatic flow to manual flow by pressing the Ctrl key and to semiautomatic flow by pressing the Shift key. Therefore, you can keep Autoflow on and switch easily to another option as needed. If, however, you frequently find your left index finger getting tired of holding the Ctrl key, switch Autoflow off.

If you usually do not want the text to flow automatically, make sure that Autoflow is not checked on the Options menu before you use the Place command. If you use the Place command and see that the automatic text flow icon is displayed, you can choose Autoflow from the Options menu to deselect that option before you position and click the loaded text icon. When you deselect Autoflow, the manual text icon appears. If you use the drag-place feature—holding the mouse and dragging the text icon to outline a text block—manual text placement is activated. Finally, if you start the text placement process with Autoflow selected, you can stop the flow by clicking the mouse button and then deselecting the Autoflow option before you continue to place the text.

> If you usually want the text to flow automatically, make sure that Autoflow is checked on the Options menu before you use the Place command. Otherwise, if you use the Place command and see that the manual text flow icon is displayed, you can choose Autoflow from the Options menu; the automatic text flow icon appears. Finally, if you start the text placement process with Autoflow unchecked, you can change to Autoflow whenever the manual flow stops.

> ### Using Different Views
>
> Work in the Fit in Window view when placing text from another program, but work in Actual Size view when typing or editing text. The text is greeked in the Fit in Window view so that you are unable to read the letters as you are typing. (To adjust the size of text that is greeked, change the size specified in the Preferences dialog box under the Edit menu.)
>
> Text may be greeked in the 75% Size and 50% Size views as well, depending on the resolution of your screen and the point size of the text.

Using the Drag-Place Feature

Usually, the line length of placed text depends on the width of the column in which you add the text. The drag-place feature is useful whenever you want to override the column guides for text or place a large graphic into a small area.

To use the drag-place feature, you define the width of the text by holding the mouse button and dragging the loaded text icon diagonally. An outline of a box appears on the page as you hold down the mouse button and drag. When you release the mouse button, the text you are placing takes on the dimensions of the box.

Placing Text on the Pasteboard

Usually, you place text from outside files directly into columns in Page-Maker. Under some conditions, however, you may want to place text directly on the pasteboard. For instance, you may want all the text to fit on one page; but when you fill the last column, you can see that more text remains in the source file. In figure 4.8, text was flowed onto the pasteboard to see how much overflow needed to be accommodated or edited out.

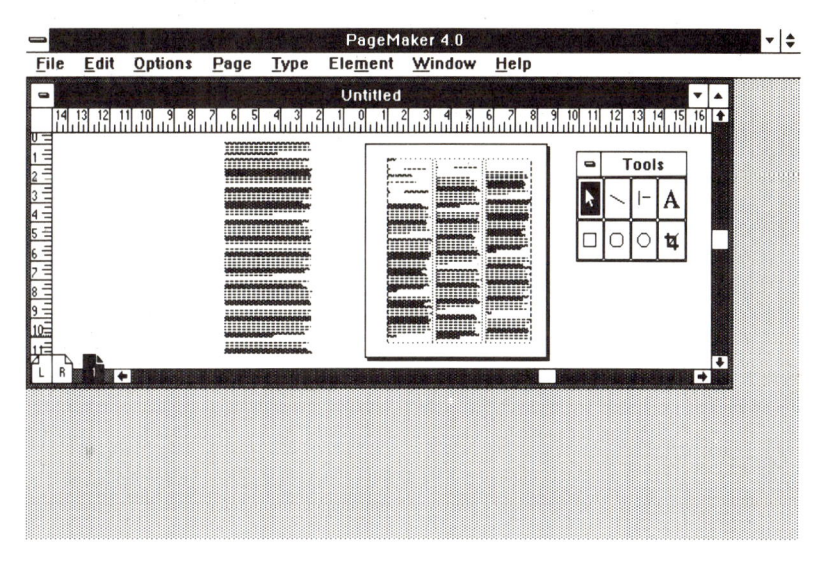

Fig. 4.8. Text flowed onto the pasteboard.

To place text on the pasteboard, use the Place command or click on the bottom of a text block that has not been placed completely to get the loaded text icon. Next, position the loaded text icon beyond the page boundaries that are displayed in Layout view and click. Text that you place on the pasteboard takes on the default width, which is determined by the page margins rather than the column guides.

Formatted Text versus Unformatted Text

When you import text that has been formatted in a word processing program, you have two options: you can retain the formats, or you can have the formats stripped out during the import process (as described in the following section). If the text to be placed is not already formatted in a word processing program, or if PageMaker does not support the word processor and cannot preserve its formatting, the text takes on PageMaker default formats and type specifications when imported. Figure 4.9 shows examples of formatted and unformatted text placed on a page in PageMaker. (See Chapter 5 for additional information about PageMaker's default formats and other methods of formatting text.)

This text was unformatted when placed in Page-Maker, and has taken on all default characteristics. All bold, underscore, and italic settings made in the word processing program are lost. Paragraph formatting is also lost.

This text was formatted in Windows Write *before* being placed in Page-Maker, and has retained **bold** and *italic* settings and justification (among other formatting specifications, which are not clearly evident).

Fig. 4.9. Unformatted (left) and formatted (right) text placed in PageMaker.

Importing Formatted Text

As long as you select the Retain Format option in the Place command dialog box, PageMaker preserves the formatting of text from word processing programs such as Windows Write, Microsoft Word, WordPerfect, WordStar, MultiMate, Lotus Manuscript, and XyWrite. In addition, PageMaker reads Document Content Architecture (DCA) files like those created by IBM DisplayWrite 3, SAMNA Word, Volkswriter 3, and WordStar 2000. These file names must have the appropriate extensions so that the files can be converted properly when placed in PageMaker with the Place command. Table 4.1 lists the programs and their extensions.

Table 4.1
Extensions for Different Word Processing Programs

Word Processor	Extension
DCA	DCA or RFT
Windows Write	WRI
Word	DOC
MultiMate	DOC
WordPerfect	WP
WordStar 3.3	WS
XyWrite III	XYW
Text-only ASCII files	TXT or ASC

Be sure to save your word processing files with these extensions if you want PageMaker to translate text-formatting commands when you use the Place command. PageMaker's text-importing capability is file-extension sensitive. If the extension (DOC, TXT, DCA, and so on) does not appear in the dialog box, another dialog box appears and prompts you for the extension.

Formatting characteristics preserved from most word processors include

- Left margin
- Left and right indents
- First-line indent
- Carriage returns
- Tabs

If your word processor offers different font selections, PageMaker may convert the type specifications. If the target printer does not support the type specifications set with that word processor, PageMaker substitutes a close match but remembers the initial specifications and uses them if you switch to a printer that supports them.

The right margin of your text is changed to match PageMaker's column width, with right margin indents preserved from some word processors. But PageMaker ignores specialized formatting commands such as running heads, running feet, footnotes, and the side-by-side command of Microsoft Word.

The example in figure 4.10 demonstrates how PageMaker preserves formats from compatible word processing programs. You can use PageMaker tools to implement any type specifications and formatting options not supported by the word processing program or not preserved in PageMaker (see Chapter 5).

If you want to test formatting commands not shown in figure 4.10, you should make your own test file and place the file in PageMaker.

Importing Unformatted Text

The three common sources of unformatted text are ASCII files from any word processor, data saved in ASCII format from a spreadsheet or database program, and text that has been telecommunicated through a central mailbox facility. You also can convert formatted text to unformatted text by deselecting the Retain Format option in the Place command dialog box.

Microsoft Word

This text was typed in Microsoft Word, in 10-point Times.

This paragraph has no indent. The ruler line was set with a normal (flush-left) tab at .5 inches and a decimal tab at 2 inches.
    Flush left   Decimal
    text   100.00
                          Centered Bold Text
                                          Flush-right Italic Text
                                              Bold Italic Text

    This paragraph has a normal indent at .25 inches in the word processor.

This paragraph has a reverse or "hanging" indent of .25 inches in the word processor.

        This line was set up with a left indent at 1 inch.

This line was set up with a right indent at 1 inch.

        This line was set up with left and right indents of 1 inch.

This paragraph is justified in the word processor. The default font and the menu list of fonts changes depending on what printer is selected. The menu in this case offered:

`Courier 12`
Helvetica 14
Times Roman 8 and 10

You can specify any size of text.

Fig. 4.10. Formatted Microsoft Word text placed in PageMaker.

Some sources of unformatted ASCII text force hard carriage returns at the end of every line. When you import ASCII text, PageMaker displays a dialog box that enables you to strip out extra carriage returns automatically (see fig. 4.11). You can choose to remove extra carriage returns at the end of every line or between paragraphs. You can specify that tables, lists, and indented lines are to retain carriage returns. You also can opt to replace three or more spaces with a tab character (for tables that were formatted using spaces) or to import the data in the monospace Courier font.

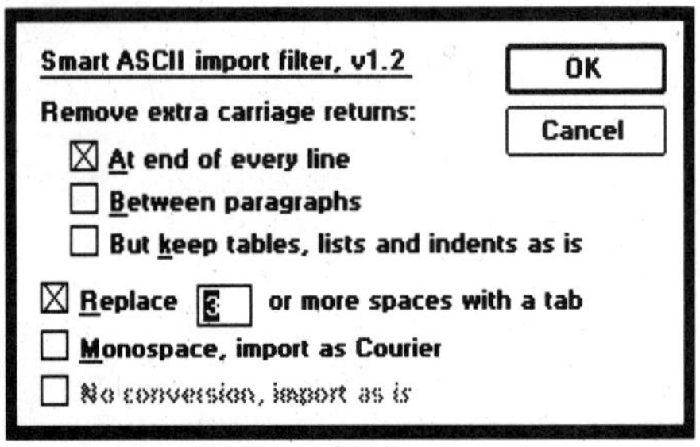

```
Smart ASCII import filter, v1.2          [ OK ]
Remove extra carriage returns:           [Cancel]
    [X] At end of every line
    [ ] Between paragraphs
    [ ] But keep tables, lists and indents as is
[X] Replace [3] or more spaces with a tab
[ ] Monospace, import as Courier
[ ] No conversion, import as is
```

Fig. 4.11. Smart ASCII Import Filter dialog box.

Initially, unformatted text takes on PageMaker's default type specifications and format. The default specifications also are applied to formatted text files if you place them by selecting the Text Only option in the Place command dialog box.

> ### *Choosing Not To Use the Retain Format Option*
>
> If your word processor is not capable of specifying the fonts you want in your publication, adjust the default settings in PageMaker to match the specifications for your publication's text. Place the files without highlighting the Retain Format option in the Place File dialog box.
>
> By changing the default settings first, you can see immediately how the text fills each page. This method is better than placing all the text in the wrong font and then using the Select All command to change the type specifications.

If your word processor is not supported directly by PageMaker, you still can place your text files in PageMaker if those files have been saved in the text-only option that most word processors offer. (If your word processor does not offer this option and is not otherwise supported by PageMaker, you may not be able to place your files in PageMaker.)

Most spreadsheet programs and database packages offer the option of saving data as text-only ASCII files. If your program uses the tab character as the delimiter, you can use PageMaker to set tabs on the ruler line, as described in Chapter 5. The data then should fall into columns.

If the other program uses commas or some other delimiter, you must convert these delimiters to tabs before the data can be arranged in columns. Sometimes the text-only files include quotation marks around fields that happened to use that delimiter as part of the data. In either case, you can further prepare the data by using the Change command in the Story Editor window (see "Finding and Changing Text in Story View" in this chapter).

Text can be telecommunicated from one computer to another directly or through a mailbox facility. If you are telecommunicating directly to another computer, you can preserve the formatting set up in many word processing programs. If you are sending your text through a mailbox facility, however, the text probably should be stored in ASCII format (text-only) so that you will receive text in this unformatted state.

Just like data saved from spreadsheets, you can format the telecommunicated text using your word processing program. Alternatively, you can place the text in PageMaker to be formatted directly within the program.

Moving and Sizing Text Blocks

When you select text by clicking on the text with the pointer tool in Layout view, your text appears as a text block framed at the top and bottom by horizontal lines (windowshades). In the middle of each windowshade is a handle, which looks like a square. A handle can be empty or contain a plus sign or down arrow. The handles disappear when the text block is no longer selected with the pointer tool or when the text tool is selected. A black *sizing square* is located at each end of a windowshade (see fig. 4.12).

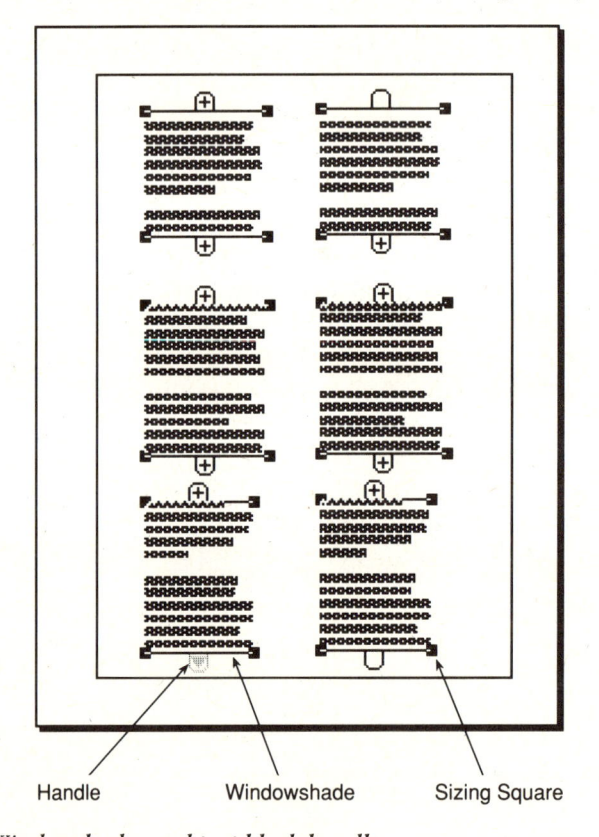

Fig. 4.12. Windowshades and text block handles.

Whether typed, placed, or pasted, text automatically becomes part of a text block on a page. A page can contain any number of text blocks. A full page of single-column text with no graphics might consist of one text block, but a two-column page of text must have at least two text blocks—one in each column. Text can flow from one block to another and from one page to another. Text that is connected in a flow of chained text boxes is called a *story*. A publication can be composed of many different stories, or chained text flows.

The symbols in the handles indicate whether the displayed text is chained to any other text in a publication. An empty top handle indicates that the block is the beginning of a story. A plus sign (+) in the top handle means that the text is continued from another block—that the text is not the beginning of the story. An empty bottom handle indicates that the block is the end of a story. A plus sign in the bottom handle means that another text block is chained to that block. A down arrow in the bottom handle indicates that the story contains more text and that you need to enlarge the text block or click on the bottom handle to get the text icon and continue placing the text on that page or on other pages.

You can move a block of text, change its size, or break up or combine text blocks by using the techniques described in the following sections.

Moving a Text Block

You use the pointer tool from the toolbox to move a block of text. Click anywhere on the block and hold down the mouse key as you drag the block in any direction (see figs. 4.13 and 4.14).

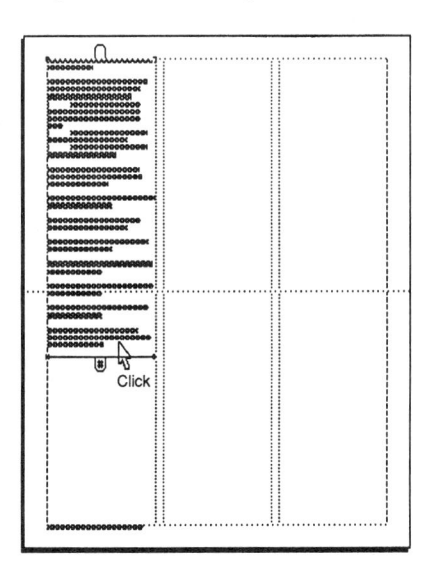

Fig. 4.13. Block of text ready to be moved.

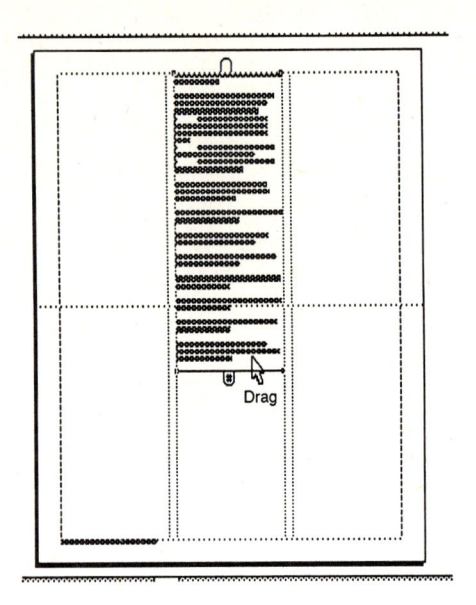

Fig. 4.14. Block of text after being moved.

Sizing a Text Block

After your text is on the page, you easily can change the length of the text block. Use the pointer tool to select the text block and display the handles; then drag the bottom handle up or down, as shown in figures 4.15 and 4.16. If this text block is connected to others, the extra text flows automatically into the next chained block when you shorten the first block. When you lengthen the block, additional text flows in from the next chained block.

You cannot lengthen a block of text beyond the text itself. If the end of the block is the end of the text—signified by an empty bottom handle—you cannot drag the bottom handle down any farther.

The width of a text block usually is determined by the column guides that you have set up using the Column Guides command under the Options menu, unless you use the drag-place or drag-type feature in placing or typing the text, as described in Chapter 3. Remember that you can create a text frame by dragging the mouse to form a box (which is visible only when you drag the mouse). The typed text then fills in the shape of the box and stops wherever the box stops. You also can drag the mouse to create a box to place text in the publication.

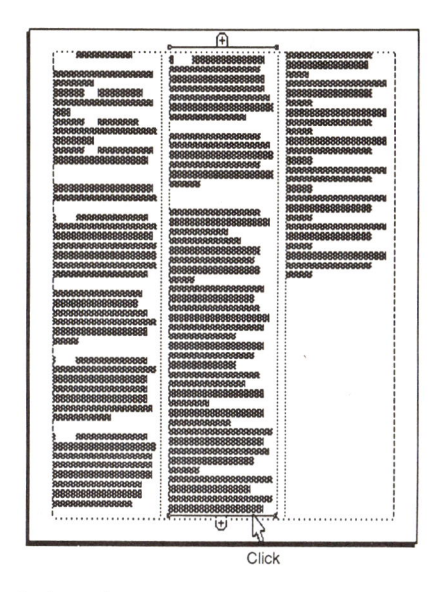

Fig. 4.15. Block of text before shortening.

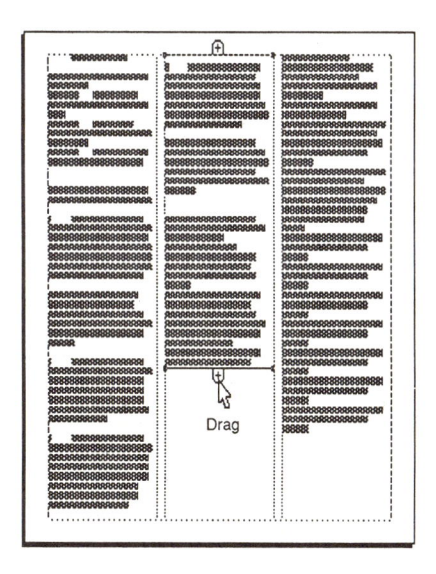

Fig. 4.16. Block of text after shortening.

After you have typed or placed text in a column, however, you can change the width of the text block. Use the pointer tool to select the text block, and then **drag** a corner of either windowshade to the left or right.

By dragging the corner of the windowshade, you change the width of the entire text block, and all the text in that block adjusts automatically. If you make a text block narrower, the overflow text flows into the next connected text block or becomes part of the text yet to be flowed. If you make a text block wider, additional text flows in from the next connected block or from the unflowed portion of the text file. To change the width and the length of a block in one motion, as shown in figure 4.17, follow these steps:

1. Position the pointer over the corner of a windowshade and hold down the mouse button to display a two-headed arrow.

2. Drag the mouse pointer in the direction you want to shape the text block.

3. Release the mouse button when the text block is the shape you want.

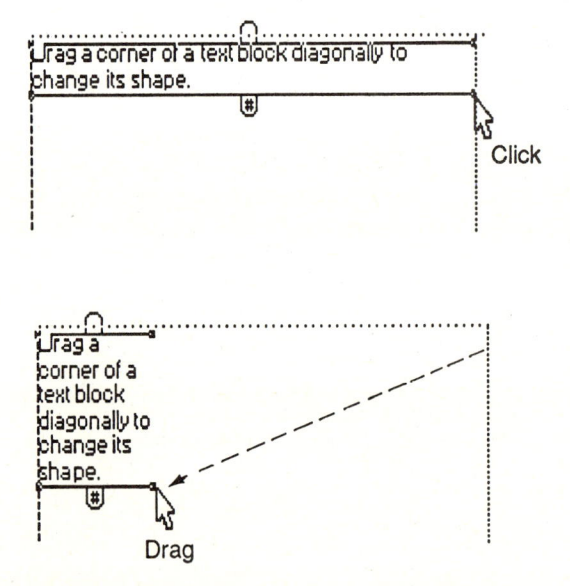

Fig. 4.17. Dragging the text handle diagonally to change text width and length.

Notice that you need not change the column guides to change the width of text after the text has been typed or placed in the column. The column guides are necessary only when you are first placing text, and the guides are a part of the publication's grid structure to which you can always return.

Breaking a Column of Text into Several Blocks

A column of text can include more than one text block. You can have several text blocks arising from several situations: when a column is composed of text placed from different files, when the text is typed as separate blocks, or when the text deliberately is broken up to accommodate special layout requirements (see fig. 4.18).

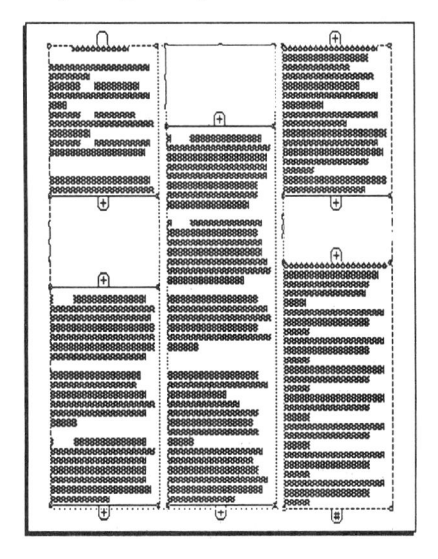

Fig. 4.18. Columns composed of several blocks of text.

Suppose that you want to break into two blocks the text shown in the middle column of figure 4.19. Follow these steps:

1. Select the block to be broken up to display its handles.

2. Drag the bottom handle up to shorten the block.

3. Click the plus sign in the bottom handle to get the text placement icon.

4. Click the text placement icon anywhere in the column below the top block (see fig. 4.20).

The text continues flowing as a second block of text, and a space is left between the two blocks (see fig. 4.21).

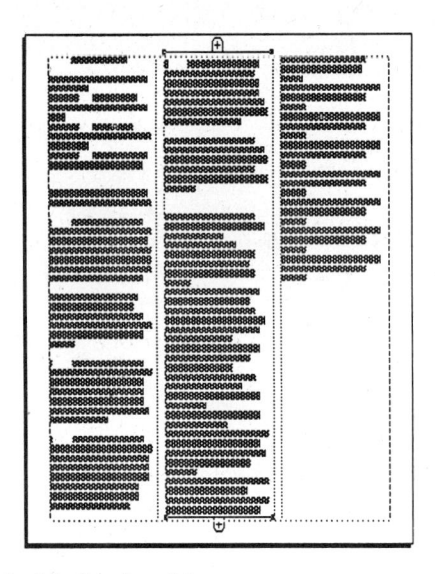

Fig. 4.19. Text block before breaking.

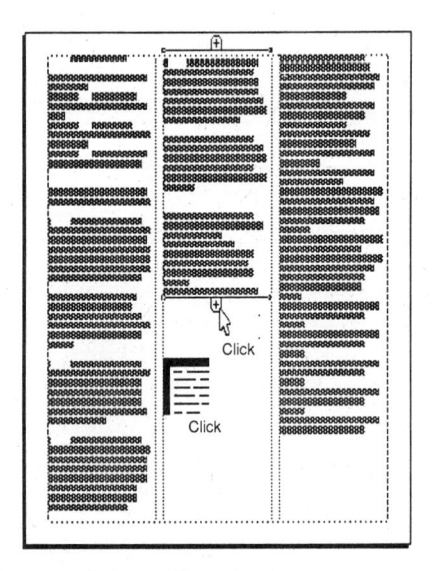

Fig. 4.20. Text icon ready to continue text.

With this method, you can break text into any number of blocks. Generally, you do not need to break text into blocks to make room for a graphic—you can use the automatic text wrap feature described in Chapter 6. If you want text to wrap around another text block, however, you do need to break the wrapping text into separate blocks.

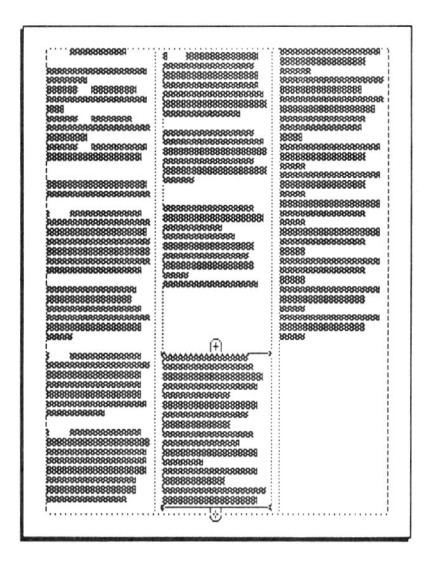

Fig. 4.21. Divided text block.

Merging a Series of Text Blocks

If two or more text blocks already are chained as a story, you can merge them into one text block by dragging the bottom handle of the first text block until it contains all of the text, as indicated by an empty bottom handle. If you want to delete a text block from the middle of a series of chained text blocks, first drag the bottom handle of the text block you want to delete upward to meet the top handle. This process squeezes all the text out of the block, enabling you to delete the block without losing any text. Next, drag downward the handle of the text block you want to keep, expanding the block until all of the text fits in that block.

If you want to merge or chain blocks of text that are not already chained as a single story, you must use the Cut and Paste commands from the Edit menu. If, for example, you have two separate text blocks that you want to chain, you first must merge them into one text block. To do so, use the text tool or the Select All command to select all the text in the second text block and choose the Cut command. Next, position the text insertion point at the end of the text in the first block and choose Paste. You then can expand the first text block to display all the text. Alternatively, you can break the block into a series of chained text blocks as described earlier in this chapter.

You also can cut and paste text between separate stories by working in multiple story windows under the Story Editor, as described later in this chapter.

Rotating a Text Block

‹4.0› PageMaker 4.0 introduces a Text Rotation feature with which you can rotate a text block in 90-degree increments. This feature is useful in creating special page designs in newsletters, magazines, fliers, or ads. You also can use this feature to rotate a whole page of text, thereby mixing Tall and Wide page orientations in a single publication. In Layout view, use the pointer tool to select a text block and choose Text Rotation from the Element menu. The Text Rotation dialog box enables you to rotate text in 90-degree increments by choosing one of the four rotation icons.

You can move or scale the rotated text block in Layout view, but you must switch to Story view to edit rotated text, as described later in this chapter.

If you have installed a type manager or are printing to a PostScript printer, the rotated text should print with the same precision as normal text. If you have not installed a type manager, some non-PostScript printers (including all PCL printers) will print rotated fonts in vector fonts composed of diagonal lines, giving the text a jagged edge.

Editing Text in Layout View

In preceding sections, you learned that to move or reshape a whole block of text, you use the pointer tool to select the text. To format or edit text in Layout view, you must select the text with the text tool.

You select the text tool by clicking the large *A* in the toolbox or by using the keyboard shortcut, Shift-F4. When you select the text tool, the pointer changes to an I-beam icon, as shown in figure 4.22. You use the I-beam to position the text-insertion point or to select text already on the page, as described in the following sections.

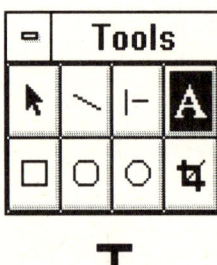

***Fig. 4.22.** The text tool I-beam icon.*

Inserting Text

If you want to insert new text in a text block, position the I-beam where you want the new text to begin. As you type, existing text shifts to make room for the inserted text.

You can move the text insertion point by using the mouse to move the I-beam pointer when the text tool is selected and clicking to position the text insertion point within a text block. You also can move the text insertion point by using the keyboard shortcuts listed in table 4.2.

Table 4.2
Shortcuts for Moving around On-Screen or in a Document

Key/Click Sequence	Result
Click once	Selects next point of insertion for new text from the keyboard
Left arrow, Right arrow	Moves the insertion point one character at a time to the left or right of the current point
Ctrl-left arrow, Ctrl-right arrow	Moves the insertion point one word at a time to the left or right
Home or up arrow, End or down arrow	Moves the insertion point one line at a time
Ctrl-Home, Ctrl-End	Moves the insertion point one sentence at a time
Ctrl-up arrow, Ctrl-down arrow	Moves the insertion point one paragraph at a time
PgUp, PgDn	Moves the insertion point a fixed distance determined by the view and the resolution of your screen
Ctrl-PgUp, Ctrl-PgDn	Moves the insertion point to the beginning or end of the article

You can replace text and insert new text by entering the text at the keyboard, as you do with a word processor. If you want to replace text, highlight the text to be replaced by dragging the I-beam over it (or by using any of the text selection methods described in the following section). Type new text from the keyboard. When you begin typing, the highlighted block of text is deleted; you do not have to delete the block before you begin typing.

Selecting Text

The most applicable method of selecting any amount of text within a block is to drag the I-beam over the text you want. Place the I-beam next to the first part of the text you want to select. Hold down the mouse button as you drag the I-beam to the end of the text to be selected. If necessary, the screen scrolls as you drag the I-beam down a column. When you release the mouse button, the selected text appears in reverse video (see fig. 4.23).

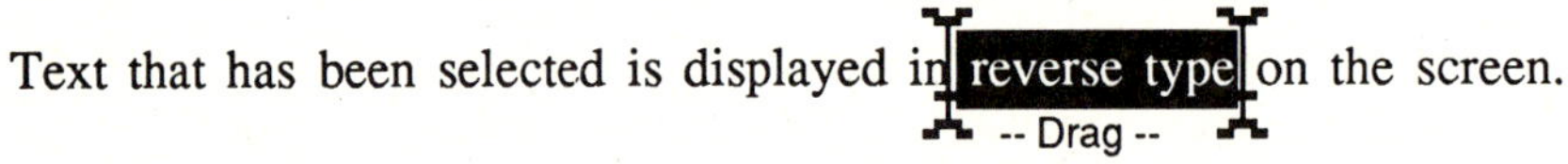

Text that has been selected is displayed in reverse type on the screen.
-- Drag --

Fig. 4.23. *Selecting text by dragging the I-beam.*

To place the text-insertion point within a text block, click the I-beam between two characters. To select a whole word (including the space that follows), double-click (click the mouse twice) with the I-beam on that word. To select a whole paragraph, triple-click with the I-beam in the paragraph. To select an entire text file (all the linked text blocks brought from the same text file, such as one story or article), click the I-beam anywhere in a text block and choose Select All from the Edit menu.

You can use many shortcut methods to select text groups, including segments crossing multiple blocks of linked text. These methods, described in table 4.3, involve clicking the mouse alone or with special keys. For example, to select the end of a text file, click the I-beam once to put the text-insertion point in front of the first word or character you want to select and press Shift-Ctrl-PgDn.

Table 4.3
Shortcuts for Moving the Text-Insertion Point and Selecting Text

Key/Click Sequence	Result
Click once	Selects next point of insertion for new text from keyboard
Click-drag	Selects a range of text character-by-character or line-by-line
Double-click	Selects whole word
Double-click-drag	Selects a range of text word-by-word
Click-Shift-click	Selects all the text between two insertion points

Each of the following selection methods sets the anchor point from which the following keyboard commands operate:

Shift-left arrow, Shift-right arrow	Extends or decreases the selection one character at a time to the left or right of the anchor point
Shift-Ctrl-left arrow, Shift-Ctrl-right arrow	Extends or decreases the selection one word at a time to the left or the right
Shift-Home or Shift-up arrow, Shift-End or Shift-down arrow	Extends or decreases the selection one line at a time
Shift-Ctrl-Home, Shift-Ctrl-End	Extends or decreases the selection one sentence at a time
Shift-Ctrl-up arrow, Shift-Ctrl-down arrow	Extends or decreases the selection one paragraph at a time
Shift-PgUp/Shift-PgDn	Extends or decreases the selection a fixed distance determined by the view and the resolution of your screen
Shift-Ctrl-PgUp, Shift-Ctrl-PgDn	Extends or decreases the selection to the beginning or the end of the article if the article ends or begins on the same page where the cursor is located

Selecting a Whole Text File

To select all the text in a story (a series of linked text blocks), use the Select All command. To issue this command, select the text tool and click anywhere in any block that is part of the continuous file. Specify Select All on the Edit menu or use the keyboard shortcut, Ctrl-A (see fig. 4.24).

Using the Clipboard

As described in Chapter 3, using the Paste command brings from the Clipboard text you have put there with the Cut or Copy commands. Because the Clipboard is a Windows feature, you can put text in the Clipboard while you are working in another program and then open the PageMaker publication to paste the text on the page. You also can use the Clipboard to paste text from one PageMaker publication to another or from one part of a publication to another.

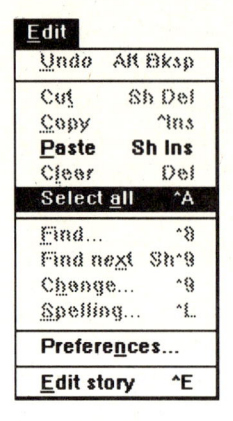

```
Edit
 Undo       Alt Bksp
 Cut        Sh Del
 Copy       ^Ins
 Paste      Sh Ins
 Clear      Del
 Select all ^A
 Find...    ^8
 Find next  Sh^8
 Change...  ^9
 Spelling... ^L
 Preferences...
 Edit story ^E
```

Fig. 4.24. The Select All command on the Edit menu.

Suppose that you start with the page shown in figure 4.25. To copy a block of text to the Clipboard and paste that text onto another page of your publication, follow these steps:

1. Select the text to be copied with the text tool (see fig. 4.25).

2. Choose the Copy command from the Edit menu. PageMaker copies the selected text to the Clipboard.

3. Select the placement for the new text by positioning the text insertion point within an existing text block or by clicking or drag-placing the text tool icon on a page or on the pasteboard.

    If you select the text tool when you paste, the pasted text appears at the text insertion point. If the pointer tool is selected when you paste, the pasted text appears in the center of the screen.

4. Choose the Paste command from the Edit menu.

    You can use one of the techniques described earlier in this chapter to position the pasted text block.

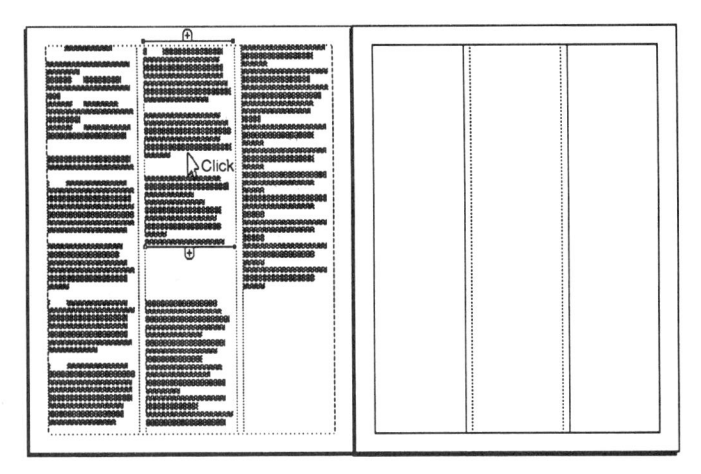

Fig. 4.25. Text block in column 2 selected to cut and paste.

Typing and Editing Text in the Story Editor

PageMaker 4.0 introduces the Story Editor feature, which offers several advantages over typing and editing text directly in the Layout view. The Story Editor enables you to enter and edit text much more quickly, because the text is displayed in a single screen font that you specify through the Preferences command, as described in Chapter 3. (The Story Editor window does not show the WYSIWYG view of the text.) You can use the Story Editor to edit rotated text, and you can open more than one story window at a time. In addition, the Story Editor offers a spelling checker and a search and replace feature. These features are described in the following sections.

Displaying the Story Window

Before you can use the Story Editor, a PageMaker publication must be open. When a publication is open, you can use the Story Editor to edit the text of an existing story or to create a new story in Story view—a window on the screen that displays text without showing the formatting that is evident in page layout view. (A story in PageMaker is a single text block, or all the text in a chained series of text blocks. Methods of chaining a series of text blocks are described earlier in this chapter.) A publication can include more than one story, and you can open multiple story windows under the Story Editor.

The four methods that you can use to open a story window are described in the following paragraphs.

1. The quickest way to switch to Story view is to triple-click on a text block with the pointer tool. You also can use the slower method of clicking once on the text block and then choosing Edit Story from the File menu (or use the keyboard shortcut Ctrl-E). In either case, the story window opens with the text insertion point at the beginning of the story.

2. With the text tool selected, position the text insertion point within a block of text in page layout view and choose Edit Story from the File menu (or use the keyboard shortcut Ctrl-E). The story window opens with the Story view at the text insertion point as selected in page layout view (see fig. 4.26).

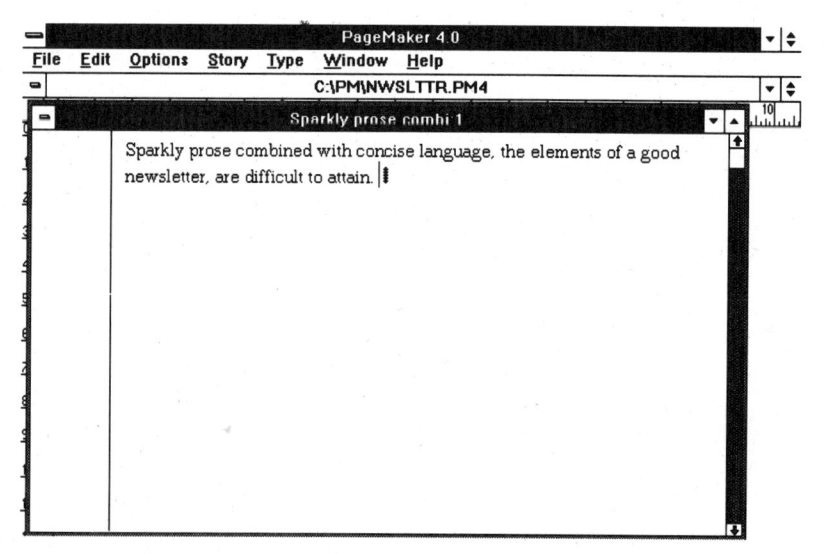

Fig. 4.26. The story window.

3. You can open a new, empty story window by choosing Edit Story from the File menu (or by using the keyboard shortcut Ctrl-E) when no text is selected and the text insertion point is not positioned in a text block in page layout view. (The next section describes how to enter text in a new story window.)

If a story window is already open but hidden behind another story window or the publication window, you can click on a visible part of the story window to bring it to the front. Alternatively, you can choose the window by name from the Window menu.

4. You can use the first three methods to open multiple story windows. You also can open a new, empty story window while a story window is displayed by choosing New Story from the Story menu.

The display in the story window has several characteristics that distinguish it from the publication window:

- The text in the story window is displayed in the single font selected through the Preferences dialog box, as described in Chapter 3. Actual page, column, and line breaks are not displayed in Story view. Inline graphics are displayed as markers only—actual graphics are not displayed.

- Each story window is named with the first few words of the story.

- The menu bar changes to display the Story menu. The Element and Page menus are not available.

- The toolbox is not available.

- You can format text by using the Colors and Styles palettes or by using commands under the Type menu, but format changes do not appear until you return to Layout view.

- The Display Style Names command from the Story menu enables you to view the assigned styles by name, as displayed in the left column beside the text.

- The Display command from the Options menu displays special characters such as carriage returns. When you change from Story view to Layout view, any changes made to the text in the story window will be reflected in the publication window. The display in the publication window, however, does not change as you work in the story window.

You can switch between the Story view and the Layout view by clicking on the windows or by choosing the windows by name from the Window menu. Using these methods, you return to the same view of the publication as before you opened the story window. By choosing Edit Layout from the Edit menu (or by using the keyboard shortcut Ctrl-E), you return to a Layout view with the text insertion point in the same position as it was in the story window.

You also can change from Story view to Layout view by closing the story window. The fastest way to close the story window is to double-click the Control menu icon in the upper left corner of the story window. You also can close the window by clicking the Control menu icon and choosing Minimize or Close, by choosing Place or Replace (Ctrl-D) from the File menu, or by choosing Close Story (Ctrl-W) from the Story menu (see fig. 4.27). When you close a new story window that contains new (unplaced) text, PageMaker displays a loaded text placement icon. You then can place the story in a publication, as described later in this chapter.

Fig. 4.27. The Story menu.

Adding Text in the Story Window

You can type text directly in the story window just as you would in any word processor. You can use the mouse to reposition the text insertion point and select text. The text selection methods described earlier in this chapter can be applied to select text in the Layout view or in the Story view.

You can use the Import command from the Story menu to import text or inline graphics (graphics that are anchored to the text as described in Chapter 6). The Import command dialog box is the same as the Place command dialog box, which is described later in this chapter. The only difference between the Place and Import commands is that the Place command results in a loaded text or graphics icon, whereas the Import command simply positions the imported text or graphics at the text insertion point as part of the story.

Imported graphics are represented by a graphics marker in the story window. You cannot view, resize, or crop the graphic until you return to the Layout view.

You can use the Export command from the File menu to export text from the Story Editor to an external text file. You also can export text from the Layout view, as described later in this chapter.

Finding and Changing Text in Story View

When a story window is active, the Find, Find Next, and Change commands are available on the Edit menu (see fig. 4.28). You can search for and change text (words or phrases and nonprinting characters) and text attributes (by

Chapter 4: Typing, Importing, and Editing Text   153

style names or fonts, styles, and sizes). You can search all stories in a publication at the same time, or you can search the current story or selected text.

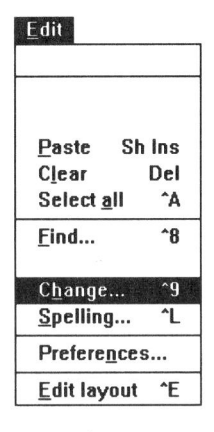

Fig. 4.28. Edit menu with Change active.

To search text for a phrase or specific text format that you want to replace with a new phrase or format, follow these steps:

1. Choose the Change command from the Edit menu. When you choose the Change command, the Change dialog box appears (see fig. 4.29).

Fig. 4.29. Special characters displayed in Story view.

2. In the Change dialog box, type the phrase you want to find in the Find What text box (see fig. 4.29).

    The phrase can include special characters such as nonbreaking spaces, tabs, and carriage returns. You must enter special characters in the Change dialog box using different keystrokes than you use when typing them in the text (see fig. 4.29).

Part I: The Production Process with PageMaker

3. Type the phrase with which you want to replace found text in the Change To text box (see fig. 4.30).

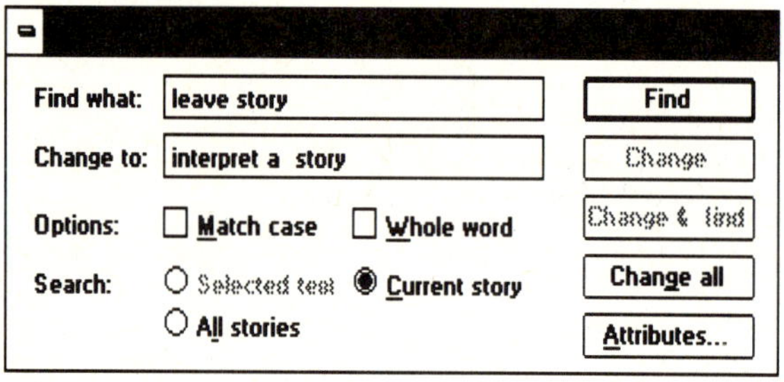

Fig. 4.30. Changing a phrase.

4. Click the Match Case check box if you want to find only those instances where the capitalization matches what you have typed in the Find What text box. Leave the Match Case box unchecked if you want PageMaker to search for all matches, regardless of case.

5. Click the Whole Word check box if you want to find only those instances where the Find What text is preceded by a space and followed by a space or a punctuation mark (such as a period). Leave the Whole Word check box unchecked if you want to find all the places where the combination of letters occurs. For example, leave the Whole Word check box unchecked if you want to find the words *ask*, *asking*, *asked*, *task*, and so on when you search for *ask*.

6. You can click Attributes to display a second dialog box (see fig. 4.31). You can use the Change Attributes dialog box to find and change the paragraph style (if a style sheet was used in formatting the text, as described in Chapter 5) or to find and change individual font/size/style combinations.

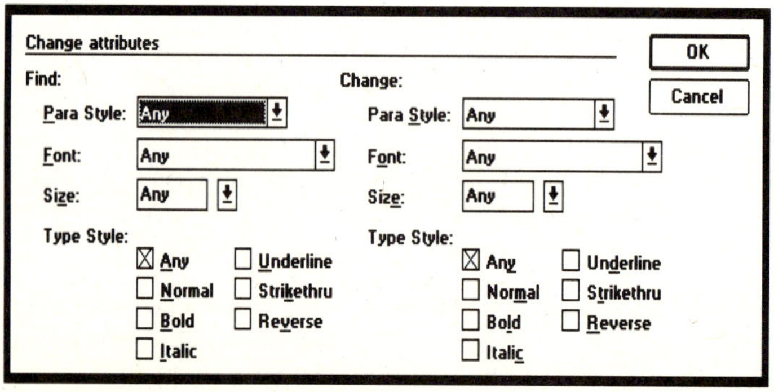

Fig. 4.31. The Change Attributes dialog box.

7. Click OK to exit the Change Attributes dialog box and return to the Change dialog box. Click Find to find the next occurrence only (and go on to step 8), or click Change All to substitute all occurrences of the found text with the text you entered in the Change To box.

   If no text was entered in the Change dialog box, all occurrences of the text attributes are changed as specified in the Change Attributes dialog box. If you entered text in the Change dialog box, only text that matches both the entered phrase and the text attributes is changed. If no text attributes are entered, any text that matches the entry in the Change dialog box is changed, and the text takes on the attributes of the found text.

8. If you clicked Find (rather than Change All), you selectively can keep or change each found occurrence: When PageMaker finds the next occurrence of the Find What text or attributes, that area is highlighted in the story window. You can click Find again if you do not want to change that text, or you can click Change or Change & Find to change the text as described in step 7.

When you use the Find command, the dialog boxes displayed are similar to those displayed when you use the Change command. With the Find dialog box, however, you enter search information only—not replace information (see figs. 4.32 and 4.33).

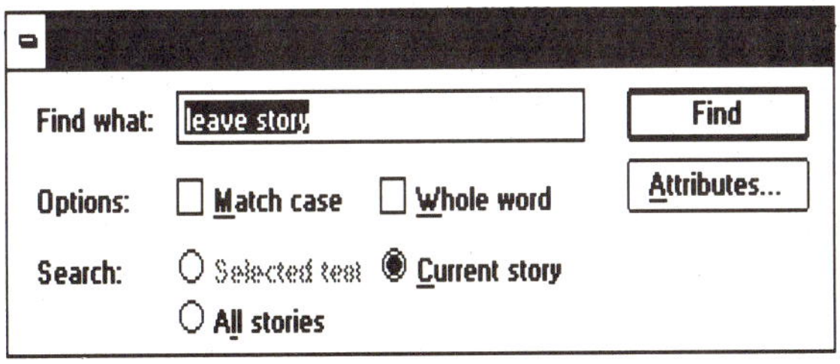

Fig. 4.32. The Find dialog box.

You can close the Find dialog box and jump quickly to the next occurrence of the text you last entered in the Find dialog box by choosing the Find Next command from the Edit menu (or by using the keyboard shortcut Shift-9).

Chapter 12 includes several examples of using global searches in formatting long publications such as books and manuals.

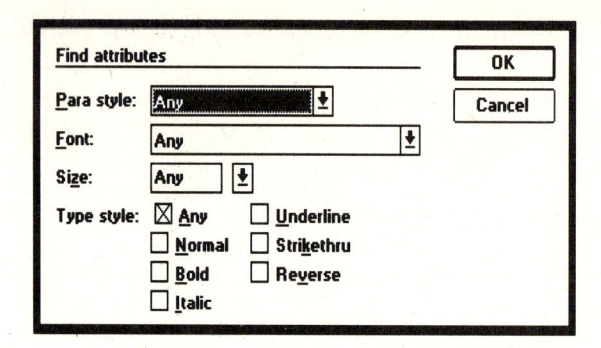

Fig. 4.33. The Attributes dialog box from the Find dialog box.

Using the Spelling Checker

PageMaker 4.0 introduces a spelling checker as part of the Story Editor. With a story window open and active, you can choose Spelling from the Edit menu. In the Spelling dialog box (see fig. 4.34), you can choose to check the spelling in all of a publication's stories at one time, in the current story only, or in selected text.

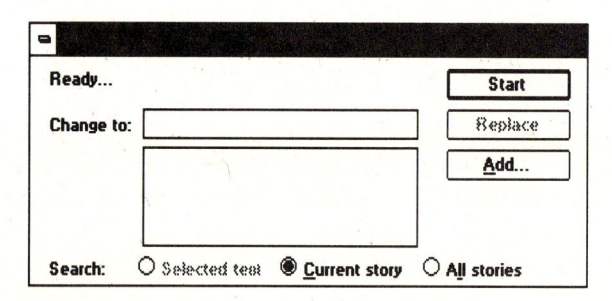

Fig. 4.34. The Spelling dialog box.

PageMaker searches the text and checks spelling against a 100,000-word U.S. English dictionary (or a dictionary that you create or select as described below). When PageMaker finds a word that is not in the dictionary, that word is displayed in the dialog box along with any close matches. PageMaker also locates duplicate words (two identical words in a row) and possible capitalization errors (lowercase words following a period and a space). You then can choose one of the following alternatives:

- Click Ignore to leave the word unchanged and go on with the search.

- Retype the word in the Change To text box, and then click Replace or press Enter to change the word and continue the search.

- Double-click on a word in the list of close matches to replace the found word and go on with the search.

    Alternatively, click once on a word in the list of close matches, and then click Replace.

- Click Add to add, edit, or remove a word in the dictionary (see fig. 4.35).

- Click on the Close box to close the Spelling dialog box and end the search.

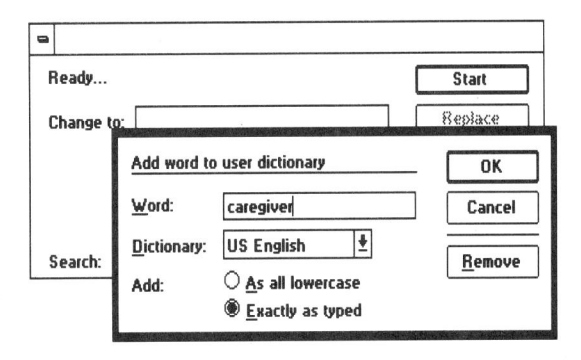

Fig. 4.35. Adding a word to the dictionary dialog box.

PageMaker comes with a 100,000-word dictionary in the U.S. English version or an 80,000-word dictionary in the International English version. You also can purchase other dictionaries from Aldus, including dictionaries in other languages and dictionaries for the medical and legal professions. You can use PageMaker's Dictionary Editor to create your own user dictionary (as an alternative to adding terms to the 100,000-word dictionary) or to combine two or more dictionaries.

If you have more than one dictionary in your PageMaker system, you can use the Paragraph command under the Type menu to choose the dictionary used in the spelling checker, as described in Chapter 5.

Using the Table Editor

4.0 Introduced with Version 4.0, the Table Editor is a stand-alone utility for creating and editing *tables*—text arranged in rows and columns. The Table Editor provides several benefits as an alternative to setting tabs with the Indents/Tabs command. The Table Editor offers you the flexibility of making the width and depth of each column or row easy to adjust, letting text wrap within each "cell," shading rows or columns, and creating rules between columns and rows. Chapters 12, 13, and 14 provide examples of tables created using the Table Editor.

Using the Table Editor is easy. You create a table using the Table Editor, export the table as a Windows Metafile graphic, and then place the table as a graphic in PageMaker. These steps are described in the following sections. The commands used in the Table Editor are similar to those used in other PageMaker modes. The following sections describe in detail only those commands that are unique to the Table Editor.

Creating a Table

To create a table, start the Table Editor by double-clicking the Table Editor icon in the Windows Applications window. The Table Setup dialog box (see fig. 4.36) prompts you to enter the basic characteristics of the table—each of which can be changed at any time through the Table Setup command. The table characteristics include number of columns, number of rows, table size, and the gutters between rows and columns.

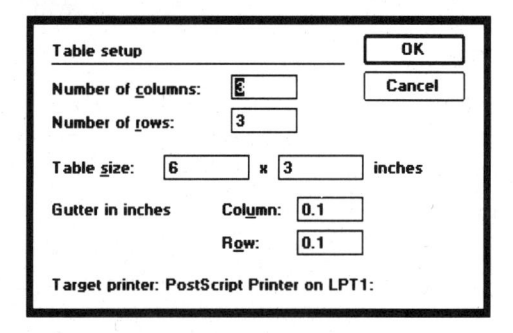

Fig. 4.36. The Table Setup dialog box.

When you click OK in the Table Setup dialog box, the screen displays a blank table (see fig. 4.37) that has numbers down the left side of the window to indicate rows and letters along the top of the window to indicate columns—following the conventions of most spreadsheet applications.

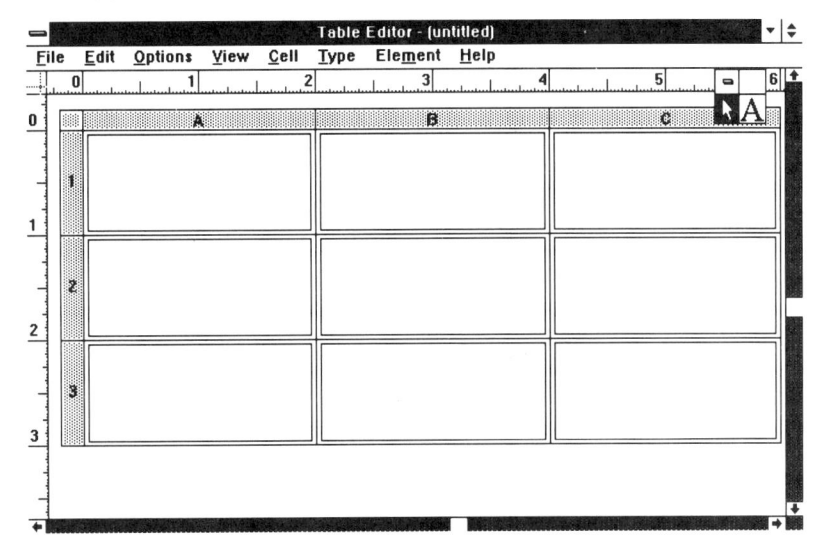

Fig. 4.37. A blank table.

You can hide or display the nonprinting grid labels and grid lines using the Grid Labels and Grid Lines commands on the Options menu.

Typing and Editing Text in Cells

To enter text in a cell (the intersection of a row and a column), select the text tool from the toolbox, click the cursor in a cell, and type. As you type, text wraps within the cell if the text line is wider than the column. You move to a new cell by moving the pointer to another cell and clicking, or by pressing Enter (to move down one cell) or Tab (to move right). If you want to force a new line within the current cell, press Shift-Enter.

You can select an entire row by clicking on the row label to the left of the window. Similarly, you can select an entire column by clicking on the column label at the top of the window. To select a group of rows or columns, drag along the labels at the left or top. You can select a group of cells—not necessarily entire rows or columns—by clicking in one cell and dragging to another. To select the entire table, click in the top left corner of the label bars.

You can select and edit text using the techniques described at the beginning of this chapter for selecting and editing text in PageMaker. You can format the text in a selected cell by using Type menu commands, which are the same as the corresponding commands on the Type menu in PageMaker (as described in Chapter 5). All text in a cell, however, must have the same format. You cannot format individual words or paragraphs.

If you select cell text with the text tool and choose the Cut or Copy command, only the text is cut or copied. If you select a cell with the pointer tool and choose the Cut or Copy command, the text, borders, and shade of the cell also are cut or copied (see "Changing the Cell Borders and Shades" in this chapter). When you paste the selection into another cell, the pasted text retains its format attributes if the new cell is empty. The pasted text takes on the new cell's attributes if that cell is not empty.

If a cell contains only numbers (plus the period, comma, or hyphen), you can use the Number Format command from the Cell menu to choose among nine number formats (see fig. 4.38).

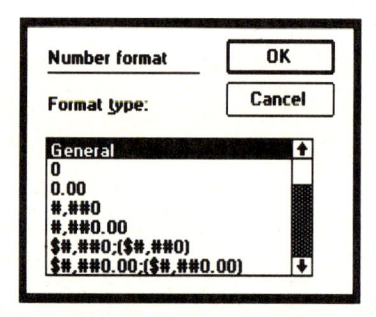

Fig. 4.38. The Number Format dialog box.

You also can calculate the sum of numbers contained in a row or column. To calculate a sum, drag the mouse pointer over a series of cells in one column or one row and choose Sum from the Cells menu. Next, click in the cell where you want the sum to appear. This action replaces the cell's previous contents. Numbers preceded by a minus sign are subtracted from positive numbers in calculating the sum.

Sizing the Table

You can resize a row or column by dragging a boundary in the band at the top or left of the table that shows row and column headings. Alternatively (or to size more than one row or column at a time), you can select a series of rows or columns and then choose the Row Height or Column Width commands from the Cell menu. In either case, when you change the size of a row or column, the adjacent row or column is adjusted automatically to preserve the width and height of the overall table. If you want to change the width or height of the table and preserve the width or height the adjacent columns or rows, hold down the Alt key as you drag the boundary.

The amount of text in the largest cell determines the minimum height of a row. You can decrease the height of a row only to the point that all text still fits in all cells. You can work around this limitation by decreasing the point size of the text, increasing the width of the column with the limiting cell, or decreasing the size of the gutters.

You can create a cell that crosses several rows or columns by selecting a range of cells and choosing Group from the Cell menu. The Table Editor considers the group of cells to be one cell, which the Table Editor identifies by the cell in the upper left corner. You can reverse this process at any time by selecting the cell and choosing Ungroup from the Cell menu. The text format, line style, and shade of the upper left corner cell of the range determines the format of the group.

You can add rows or columns by selecting a cell and choosing Insert from the Cell menu to display the Insert dialog box (see fig. 4.39). Type the number of rows or columns you want to insert, and then click Row or Column. When you click OK, new rows are added above or new columns are added to the left of the selected cell. The width of all columns or the height of all rows is adjusted to accommodate the new additions without changing the size of the table.

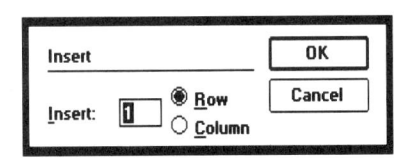

Fig. 4.39. The Insert dialog box.

You can add rows to the bottom or columns to the right side of a table with the File menu's Table Setup dialog box, as described earlier in this section.

You can delete a row or column by selecting the row or column (or a cell in the row or column) and choosing the Delete command from the Cell menu. In the Delete dialog box, you can specify whether you want to delete the row or the column of the current cell. The table shortens when you delete a row, but when you delete a column, the other columns adjust automatically to maintain the same table width. You cannot undo this delete operation.

Changing the Cell Borders and Shades

The Table Editor usually creates one-point rules between rows and columns. You can specify different borders by selecting any cell (or range of cells) and choosing Borders from the Cell menu. In the Borders dialog box (see fig. 4.40), you can specify that the next style you choose from the Line menu be applied to one or more of the four sides of the selection's perimeter (the horizontal and vertical borders of all cells in the selection) or to all of the interior cells in the selection.

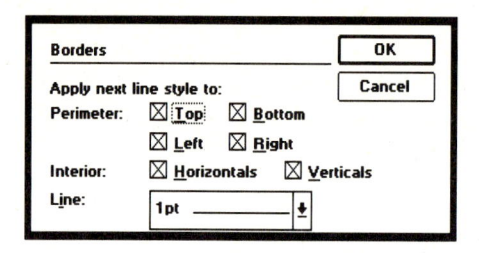

Fig. 4.40. The Borders dialog box.

After setting the borders, choose a style for the border lines from the Line menu (see fig. 4.41).

Setting the Same Lines Styles Repeatedly

The options you set in the Borders dialog box are saved until you change them. For example, if you want to make thick horizontal lines above two different, nonadjacent rows, you can select the first row, use the Borders command to specify the top perimeter, then choose a style from the Line menu. Next, select the second row above which you want a thick line and go directly to the Line menu. You need not use the Borders command again until you want to change the last selection.

You can define a shade for one or more cells by selecting the cells and choosing a shade from the Shades menu. If you select a range of rows, you can choose Alternate Rows from the Shades menu and then choose the shade you want—PageMaker applies the selected shade to every other row in the selection, beginning by shading the top row in the selection.

You can cut, copy, and paste line styles and shades from one cell to another. If you select a cell with the pointer tool and choose the Cut or Copy command from the Edit menu, the text, line styles, and shades are cut or copied from the selected cell. When you then use the Paste command, all cut or copied attributes are pasted into the new cell if the cell is empty. If the cell is not empty, the pasted text takes on the attributes of the new cell.

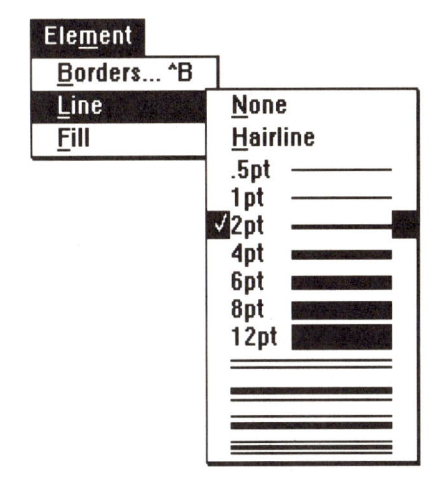

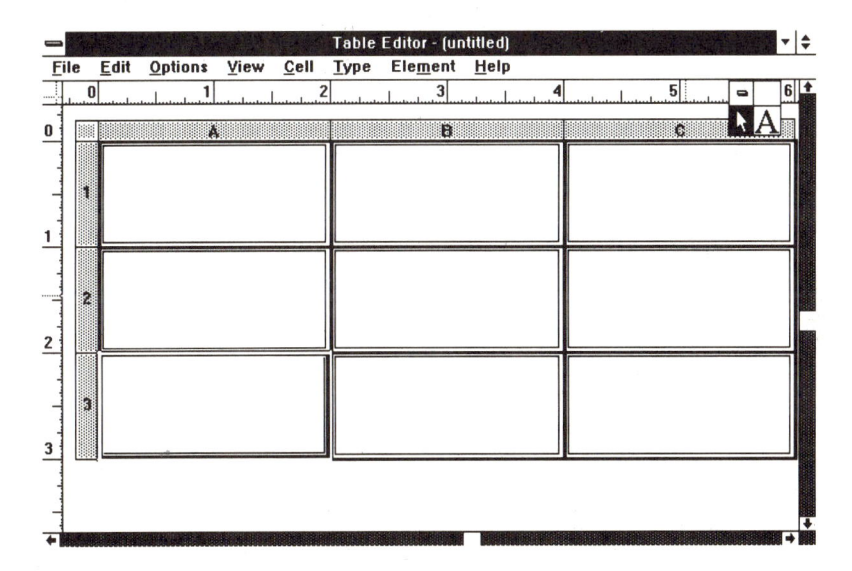

Chapter 4: Typing, Importing, and Editing Text **163**

Fig. 4.41. The Line menu selection and resulting cell borders.

Importing Data into the Table Editor

You can use the File menu's Import command to import tab-delimited or comma-delimited ASCII text into the Table Editor. The text formats can be imported from a word processor, a spreadsheet, or a database, as long as the file has been saved in ASCII text format. The delimiters (tabs or commas) determine the breaks between columns, while hard carriage returns determine the breaks between rows.

In the Import File dialog box, you can choose to replace the entire table with the imported data or to import the data into a preselected range of cells only. If the data to be imported represents more cells than are selected, the Table Editor displays an alert box. The alert box enables you to cancel the import or to import only the data that fits in the selected cells.

You can transpose rows and columns automatically as you import data. Before you select the Import command, choose the Define Flow option from the Edit menu. (The Define Flow option also determines how rows and columns behave when pasted with the Paste command.) In the Define Flow dialog box (see fig. 4.42), you can choose the usual Left to Right, Then Down flow, or the transposing Top to Bottom, Then Right flow.

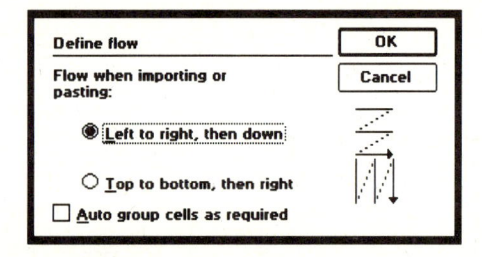

Fig. 4.42. The Define Flow dialog box.

To group cells automatically when you import or paste text that spans two or more cells in the original source, check Auto Group Cells as Required. For example, if you type a long title such as *Import/Export Figures between 1980 and 1990* in a spreadsheet cell, that text overflows across adjacent cells (if the cells are empty). In the Table Editor, however, the same title in a long cell text wraps to fit within the cell's width and makes the cell deeper to accommodate the text, unless you check Auto Group Cells as Required.

Exporting from the Table Editor

You should use the File menu's Save command often while building a table. This process saves the table in a format that can be edited by the Table Editor. To import a table from the Table Editor into PageMaker, you must use the Table Editor's Export command. The Export to File dialog box (see fig. 4.43) enables you to choose between two formats and to export the entire table or the selected range of cells only.

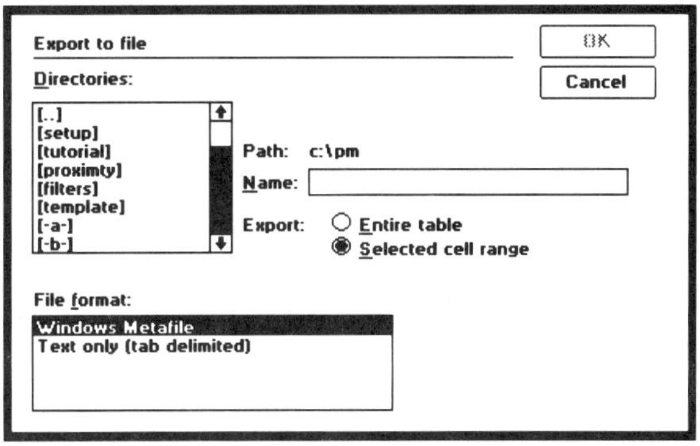

Chapter 4: Typing, Importing, and Editing Text **165**

Fig. 4.43. The Export to File dialog box.

If you export the table as text, the export file name receives the extension TXT, and the file retains none of its text formats, line styles, or shades. After you import the text into PageMaker, however, you can edit the text. If you export the table in Windows Metafile format (i.e., as a graphic), the export file receives the WMT extension, and the table is exported to PageMaker as a graphic. The table then can be scaled and cropped like any other graphic. If, however, you want to edit the table in PageMaker, you must use the techniques described later in this chapter.

Importing a Table into PageMaker

You can use the following three methods to import into PageMaker a table or selection of cells from the Table Editor:

- You can select cells in the Table Editor, choose the Copy command from the Edit menu, and then open the PageMaker publication and use the Paste command from the Edit menu.

- You can use the Place command while in Layout view in PageMaker to import the entire table.

- You can use the Import command while in Story view in PageMaker to import the entire table.

The Copy, Paste, Place, and Import commands are described in Chapter 3.

The imported table is linked to the PageMaker publication as described in Chapter 3. If you exported the table from the Table Editor in text format, the imported table is text and can be edited like any text in PageMaker. If you exported the table as a graphic, the imported table can be scaled or cropped, but you can edit the table only as described in the following section.

Editing a Table in PageMaker

To edit a table that has been created using the Table Editor and imported into PageMaker in Windows Metafile format (as a graphic), hold down the Ctrl key and triple-click anywhere inside the table. This process starts the Table Editor and opens the original table file with the TBL extension.

You can use the same methods to edit the table as you used to create the table. When you save the changes, the exported WMT file is updated automatically. The table in the PageMaker publication is updated automatically in the PageMaker publication if

- The link between the PageMaker publication and the WMT file is up to date, as shown in the Links dialog box (described in Chapter 7)
- The Update Automatically option is checked in the table's Link Options dialog box (described in Chapter 7)
- You opened the table directly through PageMaker and not through the Table Editor as a separate program running under Windows

If you update a table directly through the Table Editor, you must export the table in WMT format again to replace the older table in PageMaker. You must use the same name that was identified in the link with the PageMaker publication or use PageMaker's Place command to replace the older table.

Chapter Summary

Placing text in PageMaker is not difficult. You use the Place command to bring in long text files from other programs. You use the Paste command to bring in text that was cut or copied from another part of the publication. You can type text in the Story Editor or use the text tool from the toolbox to type text directly on a page.

To see how PageMaker handles text when you place it on a page, build a test file using you word processor. Try placing the test file twice—once with the Retain Format option selected and once with the Retain Format option deselected—to see how the situations differ.

When you are familiar with how PageMaker handles your files, you can decide intelligently how much preparation you want to do in your word processing program before placing text in PageMaker. After you have placed the text in PageMaker, you can use the commands and techniques explained in the next chapter to change the text's formatting.

5

Formatting Text

The capability to set type in different fonts and formats is an essential feature of any desktop publishing system. PageMaker's formatting features enable you to position, size, and align text on a page. In Chapter 4, you learned that PageMaker can incorporate some of the formatting attributes set up in your word processing program. After importing most documents into PageMaker, however, you usually will change the format of the text case-by-case or globally through a style sheet. This chapter explains how to change your publication's format and style by using PageMaker's text tools and Type menu to select and modify text.

The procedures and steps described in this chapter are part of the page layout process presented in Chapter 3. Chapter 4 described the range of formatting options available through PageMaker and to help you decide how much formatting and editing to do in advance by using your word processor, and how much to do directly in PageMaker. As Chapter 4 stresses, you should do as much editing—typing new text or changing the content of existing text—as possible by using the PageMaker 4.0 Story Editor or your word processor. The WYSIWYG screen in Layout view makes the program slower for text editing. On the other hand, you probably will want to do most of the text formatting—changing the appearance of the type—in the Layout view, where you can see the effects of changes as you make them, even though the same formatting can be done and will go faster in the Story view, where you cannot see the effects of the changes immediately.

Although PageMaker preserves the formatting from a word processor, at certain times you still need to do formatting in PageMaker. First, your word processor may not be capable of producing the type of formatting called for in your design specifications. Second, in the division of responsibilities on your team, the word processing user may only enter the text, while the designer using PageMaker does all the formatting.

PageMaker offers many different ways to format text. By using the text tool, you can change the type specifications for the whole publication or small segments of text. You can specify the alignment of text—left, right, centered, or justified—hyphenation, and fine increments for spacing between characters and lines. PageMaker 4.0 introduces the capability to set up rules that run above or below a paragraph as part of the text format, which is more efficient than using PageMaker's line tools to draw rules between paragraphs.

PageMaker also offers style sheets, which quickly apply character and paragraph formats in one step by associating a style name, or *tag*, with each paragraph. For example, a book's style sheet may include styles for the chapter title, three levels of headings, body text, and figure captions. A magazine or newsletter may have several styles for text, figure captions, article titles, and bylines.

Styles give publications a consistent appearance by ensuring that headlines, captions, and other similar blocks of text are the same throughout the publication. For each publication, you can create a new style sheet, modify an existing style sheet, or modify text without using a style sheet.

The commands described in this chapter change the appearance of the text: the shape and size of the characters, the distances between characters and lines, and the alignment of the text relative to the column guides or margins. Text commands can be applied in Layout view, where you see the effects of your changes immediately, or in Story view, where you cannot see the formatting.

Reviewing Default Settings

Text typed directly into PageMaker with the text tool uses the default characteristics unless you specify otherwise. Table 5.1 lists the default settings for all text in PageMaker.

If you apply the commands described in this chapter when no publication is open, you can change the defaults for all new publications. (Chapter 10 includes more tips about changing PageMaker's default settings.) If you apply these commands when a publication is open but no text is selected, you change the defaults for new text typed in the current publication. If you apply these commands when text is selected with the text tool, the changes apply to the selected text only.

Table 5.1
PageMaker's Text Defaults

Specification	Default
Font name	Times (or similar, if available on the target printer)
Size	12 point (or next size smaller)
Leading	Auto
Style	Normal
Position	Normal
Case	Normal
Hyphenation	Auto
Pair kerning	Above 12 points
Paragraph alignment	Left
Indents	None
Spacing between paragraphs	Zero
Tab stops	Every half inch

Changing Type Specifications

Type specifications determine the appearance of the text characters: the text font. All options for defining the type specifications of selected text can be entered in the Type Specifications dialog box (see fig. 5.1). Some options are repeated as commands on the Type menu and have keyboard shortcuts.

As Chapter 4 explains, you can change the default type specifications by using the Type menu commands when the pointer tool is selected. You can change the defaults when using the text tool only when no text is selected and the text insertion point is not positioned on the page, or you can change the defaults by using the Styles palette to redefine all the body text in the publication. The default specifications apply to new text typed in PageMaker and to unformatted text files brought into PageMaker.

You also can use the Type menu commands to change the specifications for text selected with the text tool. When you first display the Type menu or any of its associated dialog boxes, the screen displays the options that apply to the current selection.

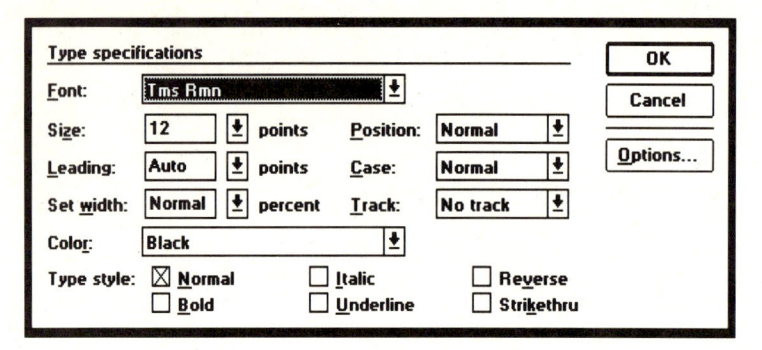

Fig. 5.1. The Type Specifications dialog box with settings for the current selection.

When you select the Type Specifications command (Ctrl-T) from the Type menu, the screen displays the Type Specifications dialog box. From this dialog box, you define the font name, size, leading, style, width, track, color, position, and case of the selected characters (see fig. 5.1). These specifications define a character's appearance. All options except case, color, and position also are available through other commands on the Type menu.

Specifying Font Name and Size

Traditionally, a *font* is a specific combination of typeface, size, and style. A *typeface* is the more general name. For example, 10-point Times italic is a different font from 12-point Times italic, but both are the same typeface (Times). Most desktop publishing applications reverse these traditional meanings and refer to typefaces as fonts, as done in the Type Specifications dialog box.

Typefaces and sizes are displayed in scrolling windows in the Type Specifications dialog box. To select a typeface, use the scroll bars to display the name you want and click that name to highlight it.

The typefaces appearing in the dialog box are determined by the printers and the typefaces you have installed through Windows. If you have installed more than one kind of printer, PageMaker displays only those typefaces that are designed for the *currently selected* printer. If you have installed more typefaces than the current printer or cartridge can handle, you should select only typefaces for which your printer is set up (see Chapter 8).

To select a size, scroll to any number in the size window and click that number. In the Size box, you can specify any size from 4 to 650 points in one-tenth point increments—not just the sizes listed on the scrolling menu.

PageMaker 4.0 introduces the new maximum of 650 points, up from 127 points in previous versions. Not all printers, however, handle all sizes of every typeface. You should enter a custom font size only if the current printer allows scalable fonts, such as a PostScript or a PLC-V series printer. Choosing a custom size on other types of printers may result in font substitution or in bit-mapped printing. (For a detailed discussion of printer fonts, see Chapter 10.)

Specifying Leading

Leading (rhymes with "heading") is a measure of the distance from the base of one line of text to the base of the next line (see fig. 5.2). If you specify Auto in the Leading box, PageMaker sets and adjusts the leading when you change the point size of the text. If you enter a specific value for the leading and you change the point size, you may need to change the leading too. Leading may be set to any value from 0 to 1300 points in one-tenth-point increments.

This is 10/11	This is 10/auto	This is 10/13	This is 10/20
Times: 10-point Times with 11-point leading.	Times: 10-point Times with automatic leading.	Times: 10-point Times with 13-point leading.	Times: 10-point Times with 20-point leading.

***Fig. 5.2.** Examples of different leading.*

With automatic leading selected, PageMaker sets leading at 120 percent of the point size to the nearest tenth of a point. For example, 10-point type gets 12-point leading. You can change the percentage value for automatic leading by choosing the Paragraph command from the Type menu and changing the Spacing option in the Paragraph Specifications dialog box.

To achieve a particular look, you may want to specify the leading precisely as part of the design specifications (see Chapters 10 and 11). Changing the leading also is a way to fit copy into a defined space. For example, you can adjust the leading to squeeze text on a tight page, to expand text to fill an area, or to force two columns to the same length (see Chapter 10).

Specifying Position and Case

The options for the Position of text are Normal, Superscript, and Subscript. Superscripts and subscripts may affect the leading where they occur. You can adjust your preferences for the size of superscripts and subscripts through the Type Options dialog box that is displayed when you click the Options button in the Type Specifications dialog box. Some printers cannot print superscripts and subscripts in all sizes.

You can convert any text to all caps or to small caps. Small caps usually are 70 percent of the height of full caps (see fig. 5.3), but you can adjust your preferences for the size of small caps through the Type Options dialog box that is displayed when you click the Options button in the Type Specifications dialog box.

> Normal capitalization
> ALL CAPS
> SMALL CAPS

Fig. 5.3. All caps and small caps.

‹4.0› You can click the Options button in the Type Specifications dialog box and set your own preferences for the size of small caps, superscripts, and subscripts and for the position of superscripts and subscripts. Values in the Type Options dialog box (see fig. 5.4) are entered as percentages of the font size. In specifying Superscript Position, a value of zero would position the superscript on the same baseline as the normal text, and a value of 100 would position the superscript at the top of the ascent of normal text. The default is 33.3 percent. A value of zero for the Subscript Position would put the subscript on the same baseline as normal text, and a value of 100 would position the subscript ascent at the baseline of normal text. The default is 33.3 percent.

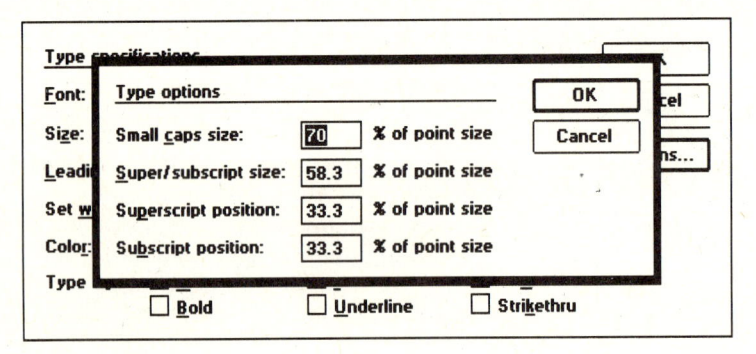

Type options		
Small caps size:	70	% of point size
Super/subscript size:	58.3	% of point size
Superscript position:	33.3	% of point size
Subscript position:	33.3	% of point size

OK / Cancel

☐ Bold ☐ Underline ☐ Strikethru

Fig. 5.4. The Type Options dialog box.

Changing Character Width and Tracking

The Set Width and Track options are new features added to the Type Specifications dialog box in Version 4.0. Set Width enables you to expand or compress the width of characters by specifying 1–250 percent in increments of one-tenth of a percent. Set Width works only if the selected printer supports scalable fonts, such as a PostScript or a PLC-V series printer. Choosing a custom width on other types of printers may result in font substitution or in bit-mapped printing.

A drop-down list appears when you click the arrow at the right of the Track field, itemizing PageMaker's tracking options, which range from Very Loose to Very Tight (see fig. 5.5). Tracking adds or subtracts a defined amount of space between letters in the selected range of text. The amount of change relates to the font and size of the text. If you change the font or size, therefore, the tracking amounts also adjust. (For more information on ways to kern the spaces between two letters manually, see Chapter 10.)

Very Loose Track	**CALENDAR**
No Track	**CALENDAR**
Very Tight Track	**CALENDAR**
70% Width	**CALENDAR**
Normal Width	**CALENDAR**
130% Width	**CALENDAR**

Fig. 5.5. Examples of different width and track settings.

Specifying Color

You can apply color to text through the Color palette or through the Color option in the Type Specifications dialog box. (Color is explained in detail in Chapter 9.)

Specifying Type Style

The six type styles listed in the Type Specifications dialog box also appear in a submenu from the Type Style command on the Type menu. The most common styles have keyboard equivalents:

F5 or Ctrl-Shift-space bar	Normal text
F6 or Ctrl-Shift-B	Boldface
F7 or Ctrl-Shift-I	Italic
F8 or Ctrl-Shift-U	Underscore

Using Menu Commands

You can change six settings from submenus of the Type menu, which is faster than opening the dialog box if you only want to change one variable. The command names that display submenus correspond to the field labels described in the previous sections: Font, Size, Leading, Set Width, Track, and Type Style.

Each command displays a submenu of choices. If you have a text selected, and the selected text shares the same characteristics, then the current setting shows a check on the submenu. If the selected text includes a mix of attributes, then nothing is checked on the submenu. If no text is selected, a check indicates the current default. The font list and size list reflect the fonts and sizes that are installed on your system and the selected printer.

For attributes that enable you to enter a wider range of values than can be displayed on the submenu—size, leading, and width—you can choose Other to display a dialog box that enables you to enter any value within the range supported by PageMaker.

Using Keyboard Shortcuts

Table 5.2 provides a list of keyboard shortcuts for changing type specifications. You turn off selected style settings by using the same function key that turns on the setting (a toggle). Notice that the keyboard shortcuts for some styles have changed or been expanded to include easy-to-remember Ctrl-Shift combinations with Version 4.0.

Table 5.2
Keyboard Shortcuts for Changing Type Specifications

Keys	Action
F5 or Ctrl-Shift-space bar	Returns text to normal style
F6 or Ctrl-Shift-B	Boldfaces text
F7 or Ctrl-Shift-I	Italicizes text
F8 or Ctrl-Shift-U	Underscores text
Ctrl-Shift-S	Strikes through text
F9 or Ctrl-Shift-V	Reverses text
Shift-F9	Decreases point size
Shift-F10	Increases point size
Ctrl-Shift-L	Aligns on left
Ctrl-Shift-C	Aligns in center
Ctrl-Shift-R	Aligns on right
Ctrl-Shift-J	Justifies
Ctrl-Shift-F	Force justifies
Ctrl-Shift-A	Sets automatic leading
Ctrl-Shift-X	Sets normal character width
Ctrl-Shift-Q	Turns off tracking

Defining Paragraph Formats

Type specifications define the appearance of individual characters, and paragraph specifications determine the relationships between characters, between lines, between paragraphs, and between the text and the column guides. Paragraph specifications apply to whole paragraphs, regardless of how much text is selected. In other words, when you select one of the commands that affect whole paragraphs—Paragraph, Indents/Tabs, or Hyphenation—the options you choose apply to all the text in any paragraph in which the text-insertion or selection point is positioned.

When you choose the Paragraph command from the Type menu, or use the keyboard shortcut Ctrl-M, the Paragraph Specifications dialog box appears (see fig. 5.6). You can select the options that affect paragraph indentation, alignment, breaks within and between paragraphs, rules (lines above or below paragraphs), and spacing between letters and words. You also can assign different dictionaries to different paragraphs to be used in hyphenating or checking spelling.

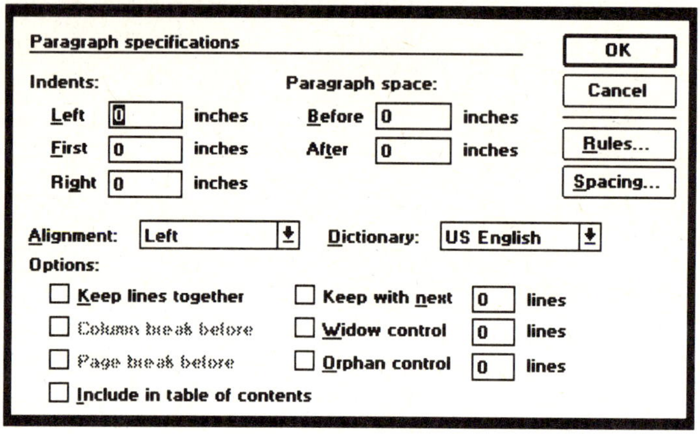

Fig. 5.6. The Paragraph Specifications dialog box.

Changes made in the Paragraph Specifications dialog box when text is selected are not reflected in the text on-screen until the dialog box is closed.

Indenting Paragraphs

The Paragraph Specifications dialog box enables you to set paragraph indentations. You also can set or change indentations by using the Indents/Tabs command from the Type menu, which is described later in this chapter. The difference between these two alternatives is that you can specify decimal increments for indentations with the Paragraph command, but you are limited to fixed increments on the ruler line if you use the Indents/Tabs command. Any changes made to the Indents/Tabs ruler line are reflected in the Page Specifications dialog box, and vice versa.

You may use three different indentation settings for any paragraph: Left indent, First line indent, and Right indent. The Right indent adjusts text from the right margin—the right side of the text block. Figure 5.7 shows how different Left and First line indentation settings affect the text and what those settings look like in the dialog box and on the Indents/Tabs ruler line. Notice that you can use these settings to create a hanging indentation. In the third example, the Left indent is set at 0.25 inches, and the First line indent is set at −0.25 inches. (For a description of how to change the indentation settings on the ruler line, see "Changing Indentation Settings on the Ruler Line" later in this chapter.)

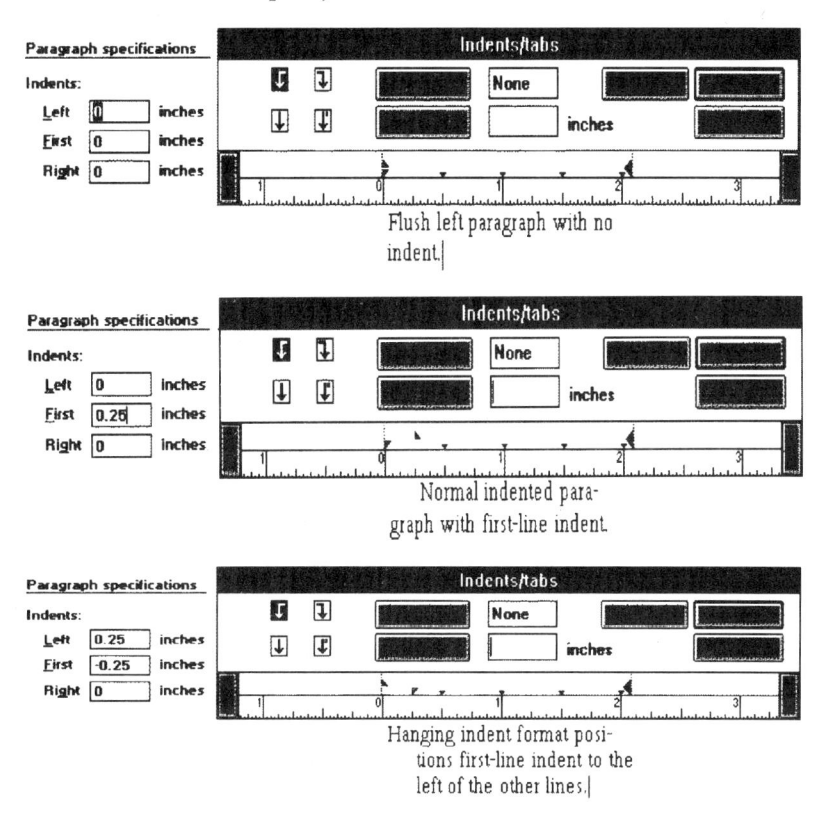

Fig. 5.7. Paragraph indentation settings.

The unit of measure shown in the dialog box reflects the current setting of the Preferences command on the Edit menu. You can use this command to work in inches, picas and points, centimeters, or ciceros (see Chapter 10), or you can enter values in any unit of measure by including the unit-of-measure abbreviation in the entry (see Chapter 3).

Setting Paragraph Spacing

You specify the spacing between paragraphs in the Paragraph Specifications dialog box (see fig. 5.8). When a new paragraph occurs, PageMaker increases the usual spacing between lines by the amounts entered in the Before and After boxes. The value you enter for spacing between paragraphs is added when a hard carriage return appears in the text.

Fig. 5.8. Specifying spacing between paragraphs.

This method of defining paragraph breaks yields more flexible results than using extra carriage returns (empty lines) to add space between paragraphs. The space before a paragraph is not added if the paragraph starts at the top of a column, for example, and you easily can adjust globally the space between paragraphs if you format by using style sheets (see "Using Style Sheets" later in this chapter).

> ### *Eliminating Double Carriage Returns*
> You can use the Change command in the Story Editor to replace globally all double carriage returns with one carriage return. If you are accustomed to double-spacing between paragraphs, however, you may want to experiment with the spacing setting on short publications before you decide to delete all double carriage returns in a long publication's text.

Aligning Paragraphs

PageMaker offers five alignment options for paragraphs: Align Left, Align Right, Align Center, Justify, or Force Justify. Forced justification, new in Version 4.0, justifies the last line of a paragraph, and this option also can force a single line of text to spread across a column or a text block, which sometimes is used in advertising or on stationery.

To specify alignment, use the Paragraph Specifications dialog box and select the alignment directly on the Type menu, choose an option from the Alignment submenu under the Type menu, or use the keyboard shortcuts for paragraph alignment (see fig. 5.9). Any changes made through the menu or keyboard also are reflected in the dialog box.

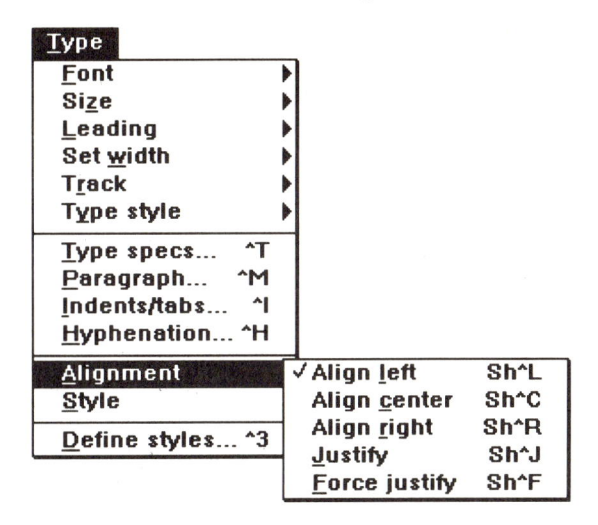

Fig. 5.9. The Alignment submenu with keyboard shortcuts for paragraph alignment.

Selecting a Dictionary for Hyphenation and Spelling

The Dictionary drop-down menu lists the installed language dictionaries that control hyphenation and check spelling. You can assign different dictionaries to different paragraphs within a publication, but using more than one dictionary slows down text composition and the spelling checker. To assign a special dictionary to a whole publication, no text should be selected when you choose the Paragraph command. To assign a special dictionary to all new publications, choose the Paragraph command when no publication is open. In either case, select a dictionary by clicking the arrow at the right of the Dictionary field to display the list of available dictionaries, drag the mouse to highlight the dictionary you want to select, and release the mouse button.

Controlling Breaks

Six of the options at the bottom of the Paragraph Specifications dialog box control the breaks within and between paragraphs, which are new features introduced in PageMaker 4.0. If you click Keep Lines Together, then the paragraph is not broken across columns or pages. If the entire paragraph cannot fit in the column, PageMaker starts it in the next column or on the next page. The Keep Lines Together option is useful for keeping together lines in a table.

You also can select Column Break Before or Page Break Before to force the corresponding break before a paragraph. These options sometimes are applied to heading levels that start new stories or new topics. If you click Keep with Next, then the paragraph is not separated from the paragraph that follows it, and you can specify how many lines of the next paragraph must appear with the current paragraph. The Keep with Next option is useful for setting any heading level.

> ### Setting Specifications for Subheads
> You should set any heading or subheading with the Keep Lines Together and the Keep with Next options. You also should keep the heading with at least two lines from the next paragraph or apply Widow Control to the next paragraph. If you create space below each heading by adding a carriage return, rather than using the preferred method of specifying space below, then you should keep the heading with at least the next three lines.

Using the Widow Control option enables you to specify the minimum number of lines that can fall at the end of a column or page before you start a new paragraph. If you set Widow Control to 1 line, for example, then PageMaker never lets one line of a paragraph end a column; the entire paragraph is pushed to the next column or page, unless at least two lines fit at the bottom of the column.

Using the Orphan Control option enables you to define the number of lines at the end of a paragraph that can be separated from the rest of the paragraph by a column break or a page break. If you set Orphan Control to 1 line, PageMaker never lets one line of a paragraph be pushed to the top of a new column or page; the entire paragraph is pushed to the next column or page, unless at least two lines fit at the top of the next column.

> **Conflicting Specifications**
>
> When PageMaker fits text in a column, it considers all rules for paragraph breaks. The specifications for adjacent paragraphs may conflict when trying to fit the space allowed in the column. If one paragraph, such as a heading, is set with the Keep with Next option, the next paragraph is part of a long table that is set with the Keep Lines Together option, and the column cannot fit both the heading and the table, PageMaker breaks one or more of the rules you have set.
>
> If you find that columns and pages are breaking in ways you did not expect or cannot control by adjusting the windowshade at the bottom of text blocks, check these settings for the paragraphs that are part of and adjacent to the breaks.

Including a Paragraph in the Table of Contents

Automatic generation of a table of contents is a feature new in PageMaker 4.0 (see Chapter 4). You can include any paragraph in the table of contents by checking the Include in Table of Contents option in this dialog box.

Adding Rules

PageMaker 4.0 enables you to specify rules (ruled lines) as part of the paragraph formatting. You can create lines above or below a selected paragraph through numerical specifications—instead of using one of PageMaker's drawing tools. Those lines automatically move with the text when the text is reflowed due to editing changes—without using the online graphics feature.

You can click the Rules button in the Paragraph Specifications dialog box to display the Paragraph Rules dialog box (see fig. 5.10) and set rules above or below a paragraph. Check the options Rule Above or Rule Below to add a ruled line above or below a paragraph.

A rule may be assigned a Line Style, Line Color, Line Width, and Indentation. This Line Style list is the same as the style list available from the Line submenu under the Element menu, except that you cannot reverse ruled lines that are part of the text. The Line Color list is the same as the color list available in the Color palette (see Chapter 8).

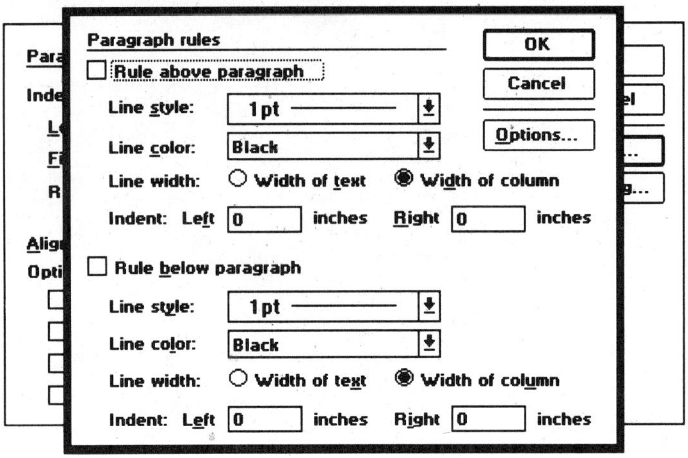

Fig. 5.10. The Paragraph Rules dialog box.

You can specify Line Width to be the width of the column or to match the line of text nearest the rule. You can adjust the length by specifying indentations from Left or Right by which the line will be shortened (by a positive value entry) or extended (by a negative value entry), relative to the text or column as specified in the Line Width setting.

Click the Options button to display the Paragraph Rule Options dialog box (see fig. 5.11) that enables you to control the distance of the lines from the text. With the controls set to Auto, the lines usually run along the top and bottom of the slug of the top line of the paragraph. The *slug* is the horizontal bar that contains a line of text and the leading. The slug normally is invisible, but you see it as a black bar behind white text when text is selected with the text tool.

To increase the distance between the text and the ruled lines, enter positive values in the Top or Bottom fields in the Paragraph Rules Options dialog box. You enter these values in the unit of measure listed in the dialog box, or use abbreviations for points and picas or other units of measure (see Chapter 3).

When the thickness of a rule is increased through the Style setting, the line is expanded *toward* the text from the edge of the slug. You can set wide rules above and below a one-line paragraph and reverse the type to display white type on a black background. (See Chapter 12 for more tips on using rules to set up reverse text on a black background.) Figure 5.12 shows examples of rules in text.

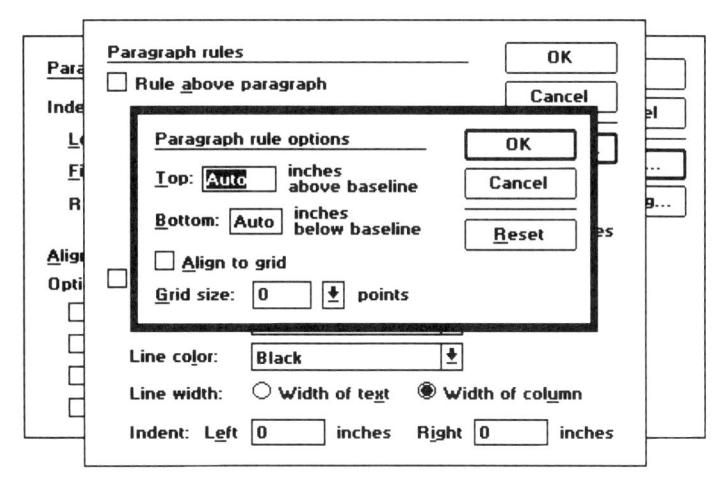

Fig. 5.11. Paragraph Rule Options dialog box.

Fig. 5.12. Examples of rules in text.

Aligning Text to the Horizontal Grid

Some publishers prefer to use the baselines of text to align horizontally across columns and pages. This preference primarily pertains to magazines and newspapers but can be desirable in any publication. Horizontally aligned baselines are easy to achieve when all of the text is the same size and has the same leading. This alignment is difficult to maintain, however, when paragraphs with rules, different sized headings, and figures are inserted.

To maintain alignment, select the Align to Grid option from the Paragraph Rule Options dialog box for any paragraph that adds space for rules, is a different size, or uses different leading than normal body copy (see fig. 5.13). Set the Grid Size in the Paragraph Rule Options dialog box to match the leading of the body copy.

Text set in 9-point Times. Text set in 9-point Times.	Text set in 9-point Times. Text set in 9-point Times. Text set in 9-point Times. Text set in 9-point Times. Text set in 9-point Times. Text set in 9-point Times. Text set in 9-point Times. Text set in 9-point Times. Text set in 9-point Times. Text set in 9-point Times. Text set in 9-point Times. Text set in 9-point Times.	Text set in 9-point Times. Text set in 9-point Times.
Paragraph set with 1-point ruled line above, and below, .1 inch from baseline.		Paragraph set with 1-point ruled line above, and below, .1 inch from baseline.
Text set in 9-point Times. Text set in 9-point Times.		Text set in 9-point Times. Text set in 9-point Times.

Fig. 5.13. Examples of text with Align to Grid (left) and without Align to Grid (right).

Controlling Spacing

In unjustified text, the amount of space between words and letters is determined by the font and kerning tables. In justified text, imperceptible amounts of space are added or deleted between letters and words to make the text fit between the left and right margins (see fig. 5.14). Generally, you should let PageMaker's default values control spacing, unless you have enough experience with typography that you feel comfortable changing these values, and you plan to proofread the copy carefully to check the effects of your spacing adjustments.

> In the process of justifying this paragraph, Page-Maker first adjusted the spacing between words (within the limits specified on the "Spacing..." dialog box). After this process, words that extended past the end of each line were broken at the hyphens (if any were inserted by PageMaker's automatic hyphenation process when the text was placed). Next, to make the line exactly flush at the right margin, spacing was adjusted between letters within the words (within the limits specified in the "Spacing..." dialog box). Finally, if the line was still not flush at the right margin, Page-Maker extended the space between words *beyond* the limits specified in the "Spacing..." dialog box.

Fig. 5.14. Justified text.

By clicking the Spacing button in the Paragraph Specifications dialog box, you display the Spacing Attributes dialog box, which controls the amount of space added or deleted between words and characters and adjusts the formula for automatic leading and the leading method.

You specify the spacing values as percentages. For example, 100 percent is equal to one normal space created by the space bar, as defined for that font (see fig. 5.15). You specify the following in the Spacing Attributes dialog box:

- The Minimum, Desired, and Maximum spaces allowed between *words*, in ranges from 0 percent to 500 percent. During the justification process, PageMaker starts with the desired space between each word on the line, and expands or condenses from that point within the limits specified as minimum and maximum. For unjustified text, the spacing specified in the Desired box is used throughout.

- The Minimum and Maximum allowed spacing for between *letters* when text is justified, in ranges from −200 percent to 200 percent. During the justification process, PageMaker adjusts the space between words first, as described in the previous paragraph, then adjusts the space between letters within words. These settings do not apply to unjustified text (0 percent is assumed).

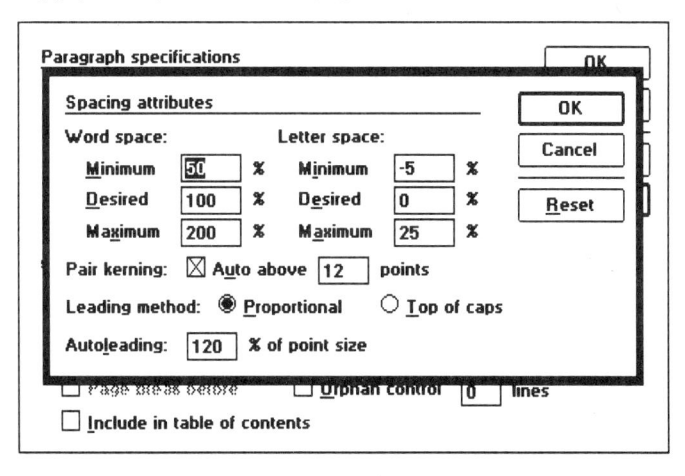

Fig. 5.15. The Spacing Attributes dialog box.

Activating Pair Kerning

Kerning refers to the fine adjustments made to the space between certain combinations of letters in order to achieve a balanced look. When kerning is not enabled, each character is assigned a specific width determined by the font selection and the character. Every 10-point Times italic A, for example, has the same width.

When kerning is enabled, the spacing between two letters is adjusted slightly in accordance with the values stored in PageMaker's table of kerning pairs. In figure 5.16, the space between the A and the V is smaller than the space between the V and the E because of the shapes of the letters. If the spacing between the different pairs is not adjusted or kerned, the A and V seem to be farther apart than the V and E. Kerned text generally looks better than unkerned text.

K N A V E   Monospaced

KNAVE   Proportionally spaced

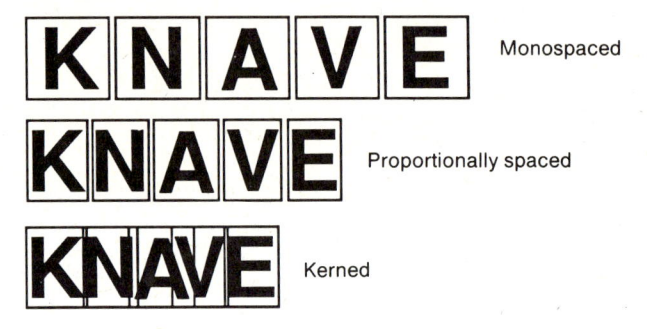

KNAVE   Kerned

Fig. 5.16. Monospaced, proportionally spaced, and kerned letters.

The Pair Kerning option in the Spacing Attributes dialog box activates automatic kerning for all text larger than 12 points in size. You change the point sizes at which kerning is turned off, or you may turn off all kerning for a publication or selected paragraphs.

> ### Using Automatic Kerning for Large Fonts Only
> Large fonts, such as those used for headlines, are more attractive when kerned. Pages are displayed and printed more quickly if kerning is turned off for small point sizes. If you do not want to turn off kerning entirely, you can set kerning to a number higher than any point size you are using.

All printers do not support kerning, but PageMaker offers kerning capability for the printers that can support it. (For more information on the pros and cons of kerning and ways to kern the spaces between letters manually, see Chapter 10.)

Changing the Leading Method or Formula

You can change the method of leading and the formula for automatic leading through the Spacing Attributes dialog box. With normal Proportional leading, the baseline of each line of text is placed two-thirds of the page down from the top of the slug. The Top of Caps leading option places the baseline a distance from the top of the slug equal to the height of the tallest font ascender in the line. Autoleading usually is 120 percent of the point size of the type style. You can change this percentage for selected paragraphs. Selecting individual paragraphs is a handy method for making copy fit a limited amount of available space (see "Copy Fitting" later in this chapter).

Using the Indents/Tabs Command

When you invoke the Indents/Tabs command, the screen displays a ruler line that you use to set or change tabs and indentation settings for selected paragraphs: left text margin, first-line indent, right text margin, flush-left tab, flush-right tab, center tab, and decimal tab (see fig. 5.17). Changes made to the indentation settings on the ruler line also are reflected in the Paragraph Specifications dialog box, as described earlier in this chapter under "Indenting Paragraphs." You define indentation by entering numeric values in the Paragraph Specifications dialog box, or you can achieve the same results by clicking and dragging icons on the ruler line.

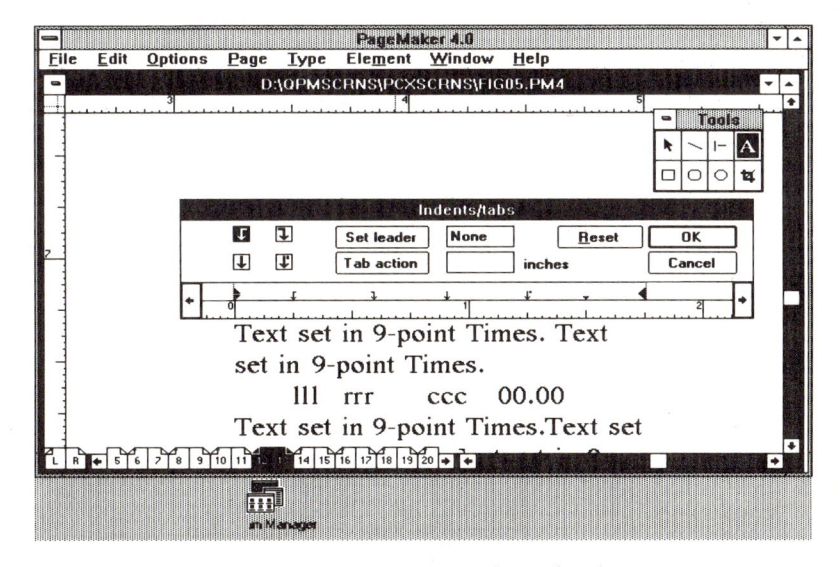

Fig. 5.17. Ruler line and icons representing tabs and indentation settings.

PageMaker sets default tabs every 0.5 inch on the ruler line. If you set tabs in the word processing program before placing the text, PageMaker's ruler lines change to reflect those settings.

To display the ruler line, choose the Indents/Tabs command on the Type menu. If the pointer tool is selected when you invoke this command, the ruler line displays the default settings for the publication, and the changes you make affect the next paragraph you type. If the text tool is selected, the settings you see on the ruler and the changes you make apply only to the selected paragraphs.

The ruler line window first appears in the center of the screen, but you can move the window and use the scroll bars to put it over the text you want to format (see fig. 5.18). This procedure is not necessary if you want to base all your settings on measured values rather than on the screen image.

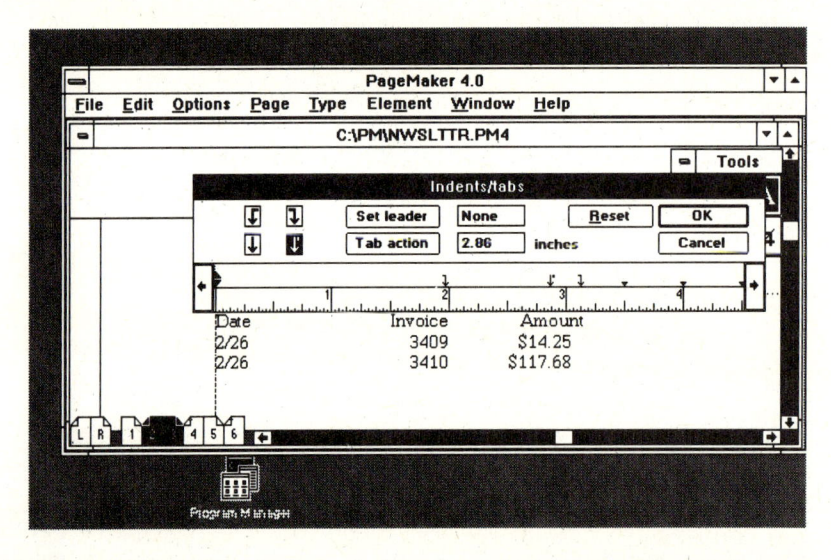

Fig. 5.18. Placing the ruler line window above the text to be formatted.

The Indents/Tabs ruler always is displayed in the scale that matches the screen view; the ruler shows a wider measure in the Fit in Window view than in Actual Size, for example. When you are working in close views, you may not be able to see the left and right margins at once in the Indents/Tabs dialog box. Use the scroll arrows at the ends of the ruler to see extensions of the measure.

Changes made on the ruler line are not reflected on-screen until you close the ruler line window. Changes made to the ruler line affect only the selected text. Changes made with the pointer or text tools without any text selected become the new default values. These changes also can be saved within a style.

> ### Positioning the Indents/Tabs Ruler above the Column
>
> The Indents/Tabs dialog box is a window that can be moved on-screen by dragging the title bar with the pointer. You also can use the scrolling arrows at each end of the ruler to move it inside the window. For convenience in setting tabs and indents, position the zero point of the Indents/Tabs ruler above the left column guide of the text.

> ### Using the Table Editor Instead of Tabs
>
> As an alternative to setting tabs directly in page layout view, you can use the Table Editor utility that comes with PageMaker to create complex tables in which each row/column entry is a *cell* with margins that can contain paragraphs. (The Table Editor is discussed in Chapter 4.)

Changing Indentation Settings on the Ruler Line

The three indentation variables—Left indentation, First line indentation, and Right indentation—were described in detail earlier in this chapter under "Indenting Paragraphs," where you learned how to adjust these settings through the Paragraph Specifications dialog box. These three settings are represented by three icons on the Indents/Tabs ruler line:

- The Left indentation icon is the bottom half of a triangle that appears at the zero point on the ruler line when all indentation is set at zero (the default).

- The First line indentation icon is the top half of a triangle that appears at the zero point when indentation is set at zero.

- The right indentation icon is the triangle that appears at the right margin on the ruler line when indentation is set at zero.

To move the Right indentation icon, click the icon with the mouse pointer and drag it to the left. (You cannot force the Right indentation to the right, beyond the width of the text block.)

To move the First line indentation icon independently, click and drag it. To move the Left indentation icon independently, hold the Shift key as you click and drag the icon.

Changes made to the ruler line are reflected in the text after you close the ruler window.

Adding and Deleting Tabs

Default tabs are displayed as small triangles on the ruler line. You can move these tabs by dragging them, or you can delete them by dragging them off the ruler. The first new tab you add then deletes all default tabs to the left of it.

To add a tab, define the type of tab by clicking one of the icons for a left, right, center, or decimal tab (see fig. 5.18). Select the Set Leader option. A tab *leader* is a character that fills in the space between two tab stops. You can select a line of periods, hyphens, or underscores; or you can define your own leader characters by clicking the fourth option and typing one character or two alternating characters in the box.

After defining the tab, set it by clicking just above the ruler line where you want to set the tab. The numeric value of the new tab position appears in the ruler line window. To move a tab, click on the tab marker and hold down the mouse button as you drag the tab horizontally along the ruler line. As you move a tab, the ruler line window displays the current ruler measure. You can add, delete, move, or repeat a tab by selecting a tab icon or an existing tab on the ruler line, typing a numeric position in the Position field, and then choosing an option from the Tab Action drop-down menu. The Repeat option sets a series of tabs at the increment of the distance between the highlighted tab and the zero point on the ruler line.

After you set a tab stop, you can move or delete it, but you cannot change the tab's alignment or leader settings. If you want to change these settings, you must delete the tab and create another one with new settings. To delete individual tabs, click on the tab marker and hold down the mouse button as you drag the tab down to the bottom of the ruler line, or select the tab and choose Delete from the Tab Action drop-down menu.

Settings are limited to the increments on the ruler line. The number of increments per unit of measure depends on the size in which you are working on-screen. For example, when working in 200% size, you can use smaller increments than when you work in a reduced view of the page. You cannot set more than 40 tab stops on the ruler line. If you try to add a tab and find that PageMaker does not accept it, the ruler line may already have 40 tabs set.

After tab stops are set on the ruler line, text with tab characters falls into place below each tab stop after you close the ruler window. You add tab characters to align text by positioning the I-beam for text insertion and pressing the Tab key.

Copying the Indents/Tabs

You can copy a ruler line from one paragraph to subsequent paragraphs. Select the text you want to change, beginning with the paragraph that has the ruler you want to copy and including the subsequent paragraphs that you want to match the first one. When the ruler line appears, it shows only the settings that apply to the first paragraph selected (see fig. 5.19). Make any change to the ruler, such as adding a tab, and then close the ruler line window. The new ruler line applies to all the selected text and can be saved within a style. You must make at least one change to the ruler line for any changes to be registered in the text.

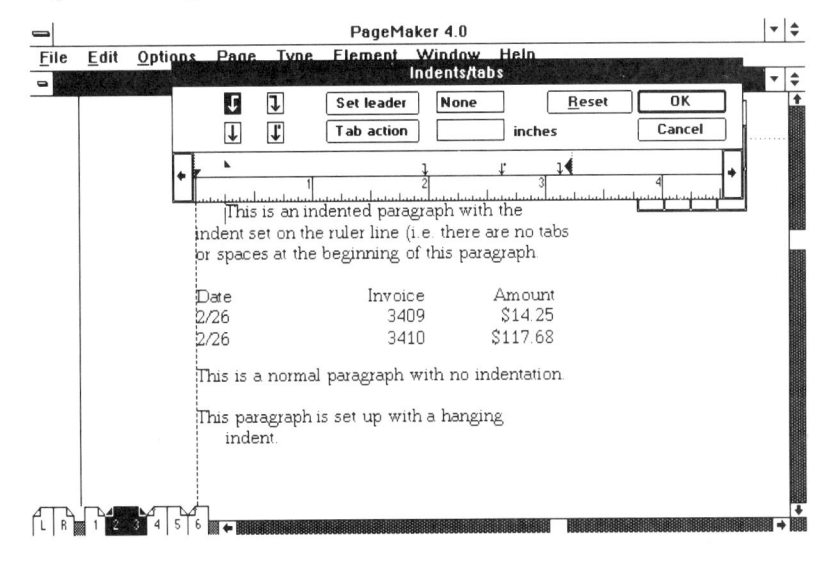

Fig. 5.19. Ruler line showing settings for first selected paragraph.

Controlling Hyphenation

PageMaker usually hyphenates text as you are typing or placing the text on the page. The program searches for each word in a Houghton-Mifflin dictionary containing more than 110,000 terms and a supplementary dictionary containing words added by you. The process is instantaneous. Through the Hyphenation dialog box, you can turn off hyphenation, add terms to the dictionary, and control hyphenation at any time on a case-by-case basis. The following are descriptions of these options:

- You can display the Hyphenation dialog box (see fig. 5.20) by choosing the Hyphenation command from the Type menu or by choosing the Hyphenation options when you are defining styles.

The basic option is to turn hyphenation on or off. If hyphenation is on, you can choose from three methods of hyphenation: Manual Only, Manual Plus Dictionary, or Manual Plus Algorithm. If hyphenation is turned off, PageMaker suppresses all hyphenation, even the discretionary hyphens.

```
Hyphenation                              OK
Hyphenation:  ● On    ○ Off
              ○ Manual only              Cancel
              ● Manual plus dictionary
              ○ Manual plus algorithm    Add...
Limit consecutive hyphens to:  [No limit]
Hyphenation zone:  [0.5]  inches
```

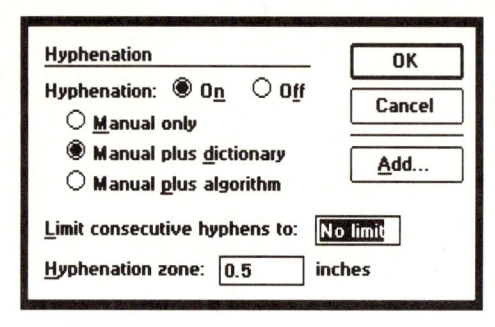

Fig. 5.20. The Hyphenation dialog box.

- If Manual Only is selected, PageMaker hyphenates words that contain discretionary hyphens. To insert discretionary hyphens manually within words, press Ctrl and the hyphen key simultaneously. You can insert these discretionary hyphens by using the word processor before the text is placed, or you can enter them in the Story Editor or the Layout view in PageMaker. Discretionary hyphens behave the same way as automatic hyphens: They appear on-screen and in print only when they fall at the end of a line.

Deciding When To Use Manual Only

You generally select Manual Only if you only want to minimize the amount of hyphenation in a very short publication. Don't insert any discretionary hyphens until you have finished all other editing and formatting in Layout view. Insert discretionary hyphens selectively to eliminate wide right margins at the end of unjustified lines or wide rivers of white within justified text.

Selecting Manual Plus Dictionary is a more efficient method of correcting many wide ragged-right margins or wide rivers. Select Manual Plus Dictionary, set a wide but acceptable Hyphenation Zone, and limit the number of hyphens in a row to one.

- With the Manual Plus Dictionary option selected, PageMaker hyphenates words containing discretionary hyphens and words it finds in the dictionary. If a conflict arises, the discretionary hyphens prevail.

> ### *Entering Discretionary Hyphens Only Once*
> You need enter the discretionary hyphens only once per word per publication, and PageMaker hyphenates that word the same way wherever appropriate. You delete discretionary hyphens as you do any other character: by selecting them and pressing the backspace key.

- With Manual Plus Algorithm selected, words may be hyphenated at discretionary hyphens, at dictionary hyphens, or by the dictionary algorithm. This method provides the greatest range of flexibility in hyphenating. Using Manual Plus Algorithm generally reduces the amount of white space in hyphenated text through increased hyphenation.

You can limit consecutive hyphens to a specified number by typing any number from 1 to 255 or by typing the words *no limit*.

The Hyphenation Zone determines the width of the space you want to allow at the end lines of unjustified text before hyphenating. If you allow a 0.5 inch hyphenation zone, for example, then a word that starts within 0.5 inch of the right margin or right indentation setting is forced to the next line. Words that start to the left of the 0.5-inch zone are hyphenated if possible.

A narrow hyphenation zone results in a great deal of hyphenation. The wider the hyphenation zone, the more ragged the right margin is. When hyphenation is turned off, the hyphenation zone is the length of the longest word in the text.

> ### *Getting Fewer Hyphens*
> Turn on hyphenation for justified text. During the justification process, PageMaker adjusts the spaces between words or letters, hyphenates words when necessary, and, if necessary, expands the space between words beyond the maximum allowed. If you want fewer hyphens, turn off justification and use flush-left text, or expand the allowance for word and letter spacing in the Spacing Attributes dialog box.

Changing Hyphenation on a Case-by-Case Basis

If hyphenation is turned on, you can suppress hyphenation for individual words by typing a discretionary hyphen in front of them. To override the dictionary hyphenation breaks for a word, you can insert a discretionary hyphen at the preferred break in the word on the page. If you want to change the way a word is hyphenated in all cases, you can add or remove words from the dictionary.

Adding Words to the Dictionary

4.0

Click the Add option in the Hyphenation dialog box if you want to add a word to the dictionary. The Add Word to User Dictionary dialog box is new in Version 4.0 (see fig. 5.21).

If you select a word in the text before choosing the Hyphenation command and choosing Add, the selected word is displayed in this dialog box with current hyphenation possibilities displayed as tildes (~). You can edit the displayed word, or you can type any word and enter tildes where you want to allow hyphenation.

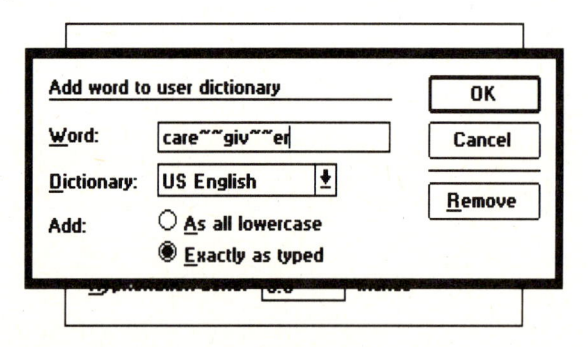

Fig. 5.21. Add Word to User Dictionary dialog box.

You can enter up to three tildes at each hyphenation point: one tilde indicates the most preferable break, two tildes indicates the next preferable, and three tildes indicates the least preferable but allowable break points. If you never want the word hyphenated, type a tilde at the beginning of the word in this dialog box.

If you have installed more than one dictionary, you can choose to add words to other dictionaries by selecting the desired option from the Dictionary drop-down menu that is displayed when you click the arrow to the right of the Dictionary field in the Add Word to User Dictionary dialog box. If you add a word that is already in the dictionary, the new hyphenation replaces the old. Choose Remove to remove the word from the dictionary. You can use the PageMaker 4.0 Dictionary Editor to combine dictionaries from earlier versions of PageMaker or from word processors with a PageMaker 4.0 dictionary.

Using Style Sheets

The electronic style sheet is one of the most powerful yet least used features of desktop publishing applications. A *style sheet* is a collection of shortcuts for applying type specifications—character attributes and paragraph formats—used throughout the publication. A style sheet system enables you to define the character attributes and paragraph format for each type of text element in a publication: major headings, subheadings, captions, and body text. After you design a style sheet for a publication, you can format the text by using short keystroke commands or menu selections rather than using several commands to format each paragraph.

Character-specific formats include all attributes that are applied by using the Font, Size, Leading, Set Width, Track, and Type Style commands from the Type menu. Many entries made with these commands also can be made through the single dialog box displayed by the Type Specifications command or by using keyboard shortcuts. The quickest method of applying complex formats, however, is with a style sheet.

Paragraph-specific formatting includes all settings that are applied using the Paragraph, Indents/Tabs, Hyphenation, and Alignment commands from the Type menu. Many of the entries made through these commands also can be made by using keyboard shortcuts. With a style sheet, however, you can apply the character attributes and the paragraph formats in one step.

In designing a style sheet, you define a number of styles by name or tag—one for each heading or paragraph format in your publication. The process of formatting characters and paragraphs with a style sheet can take place in PageMaker or in Microsoft Word. Style sheets created in Microsoft Word can be imported along with the text into PageMaker if the Microsoft Word import/export filter has been installed.

Styles set the format specifications for different types of paragraphs. A paragraph in PageMaker includes all the text between two hard carriage returns. If you want to modify part of a paragraph, use the text-modifying capabilities of PageMaker by highlighting those words with a mouse and changing their attributes, not the style sheet feature. If you want to modify entire paragraphs, use the style sheet function to change the attributes of the entire paragraph.

Each style has two major elements: the style name—for example, Head—and the attributes of the text the style describes—for example, 24-point Helvetica, centered, bold text. A series of styles becomes a style sheet. PageMaker comes with a default style sheet that includes five styles and additional sample style sheets you can use and modify for your publications. These style sheets are located in PageMaker's template subdirectory, if you opted to install the templates that come with PageMaker.

Viewing Styles

To view the styles that have been set for your publication, choose Style from the Type menu to see the list of styles in the submenu, or choose Style Palette (Ctrl-Y) from the Window menu to display the Styles palette. The Styles palette, like the toolbox and Color palette, is first displayed near the top right corner of the publication window (see fig. 5.22). You can drag the title bar to move it anywhere on the screen, and you can drag the border to resize the palette.

```
┌─────────────────────┐
│ ▬ │     Styles      │
├─────────────────────┤
│ [No style]          │
│ Body text           │
│ Caption             │
│ Headline            │
│ Subhead 1           │
│ Subhead 2           │
└─────────────────────┘
```

Fig. 5.22. *The Styles palette.*

The style of the selected text is highlighted in the Styles palette. A plus sign (+) follows the style name if the format of the selected text has been further modified by using commands under the Type menu.

An asterisk (*) following a style name indicates that the style already was defined in the text when it was imported from a word processor. PageMaker removes the asterisk if you modify the style by using the Define Styles command after it has been imported.

You also can view the styles that have been applied to each paragraph in Story view. First, select the text tool and position the insertion point anywhere in the story you want to edit. Choose Edit Story (Ctrl-E) from the

Edit menu, and choose Display Style Names from the Options menu. The story window displays the names of applied styles in the column to the left of the text (see fig. 5.23).

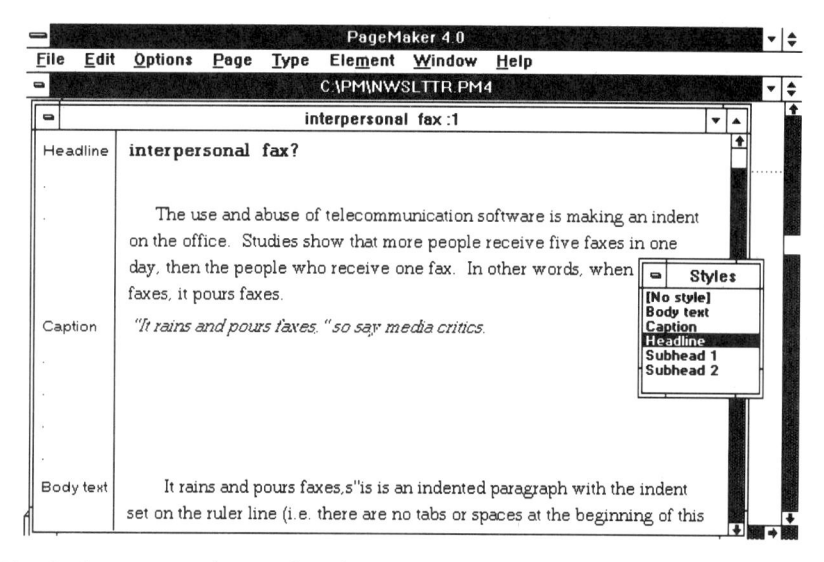

Fig. 5.23. Story window with style names displayed.

Adding New Styles

You can add new styles or edit styles anytime during the layout of the publication. You can add new styles by defining the new style yourself, by basing the new style's attributes on a style in the publication that you are working on, by copying a whole style sheet from another publication, or by importing the style sheet with the imported word processing document.

To define a new style from scratch, go to the Edit Style dialog box by pressing the Ctrl key and clicking No Style in the Styles palette or by choosing the Define Styles command in the Type menu (Ctrl-3) and clicking New in the dialog box (see fig. 5.24). PageMaker displays the Edit Style dialog box (see fig. 5.25).

In the Edit Style dialog box (see fig. 5.26), type the name of the new style. Give the style an easily recognizable name. If you are cloning the new style from an existing style, that style is listed in the Based On field. You can change the Based On style at any time by changing the name in this field or by typing *No style* if you do not want this style to be related to any other. If you edit the style named in the Based On field and change any attributes that are shared by this new style, then the new style also changes.

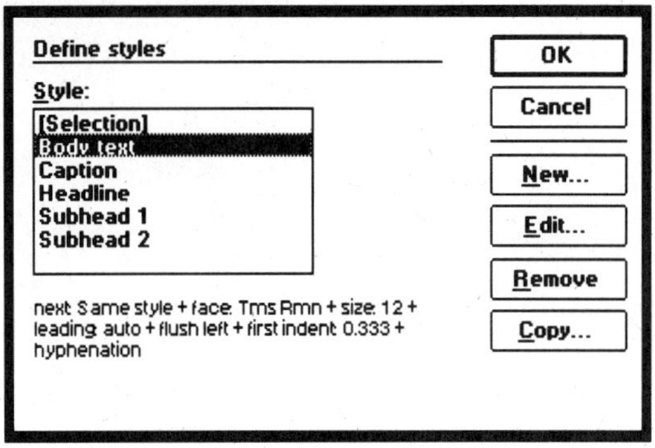

Fig. 5.24. Using the Define Styles dialog box to get to the Edit Style dialog box.

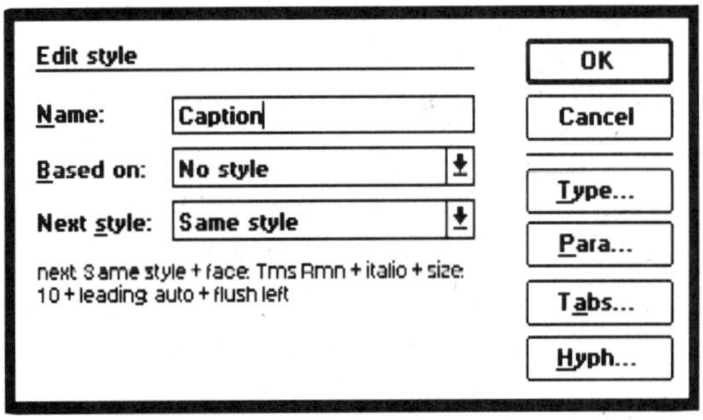

Fig. 5.25. The Edit Style dialog box used to edit styles.

Cloning an Existing Style

If you want to create a new style that is similar to an existing style, click once on the name of the style you want to copy in the Define Styles dialog box, and then click New. The Edit Style dialog box will be set up with the specifications of the cloned style, and you can modify those attributes you want to change them.

Basing a Style on a Formatted Paragraph

To base a new style on the attributes of a formatted paragraph, position the insertion point in the paragraph, choose Define Styles, click Selection in the Define Styles dialog box, then click New. The Edit Style dialog box will be set up with the specifications of the selected paragraph.

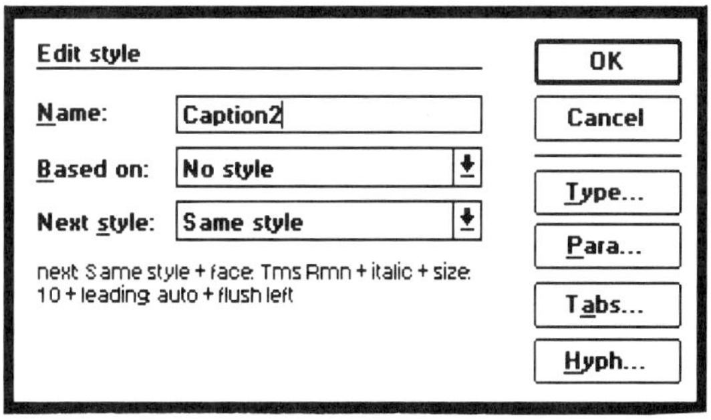

Fig. 5.26. In using the Edit Style dialog box to create a new style based on an old one, the type specifications of the original style are shown.

If you type a style name in the Next Style field, PageMaker starts the next paragraph with the style named as the Next Style after you type a carriage return that ends a paragraph in the current style. The Next Style option is useful for setting the style names for headings that are always one line or one paragraph long and are always followed by another style. For example, Heading Level 1 might be followed by Body Text style. If you set up a style for blank lines that will hold inline figures, the next style may be for the caption. By using this feature you can save time in changing from one style to another.

After you select the name and Based On and Next Style names, click any of the four options to select the new style attributes: Type, Para, Tabs, or Hyph. Using Type modifies the type specifications in the Type Specifications dialog box (see fig. 5.27). Using Para changes specifications in the Paragraph Specifications dialog box (see fig. 5.28). Tabs modifies the indent and tab specifications in the Indents/Tabs dialog box (see fig. 5.29). Hyph affects the options in the Hyphenation dialog box (see fig. 5.30).

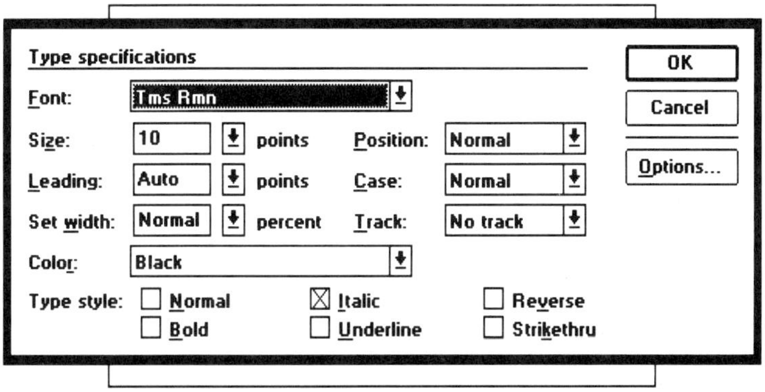

Fig. 5.27. The Type Specifications dialog box.

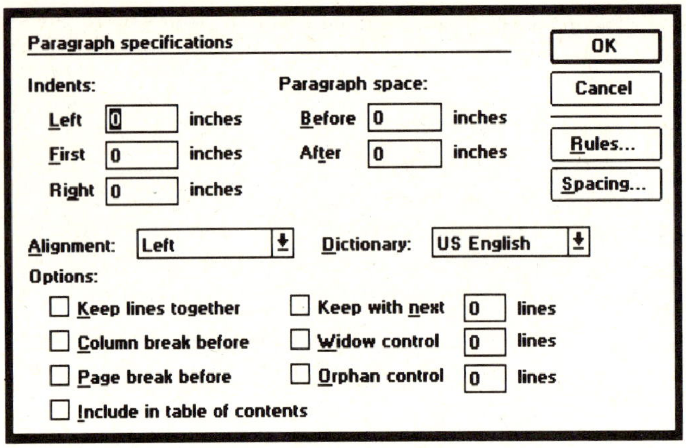

200 Part I: The Production Process with PageMaker

Fig. 5.28. The Paragraph Specifications dialog box.

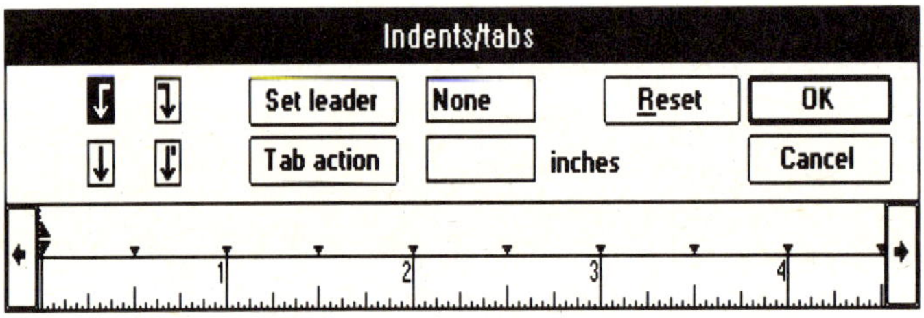

Fig. 5.29. The Indents/Tabs dialog box.

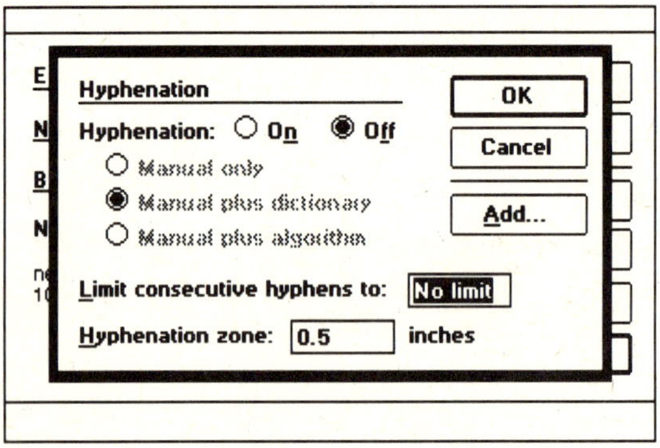

Fig. 5.30. The Hyphenation dialog box.

Copying Styles from Other PageMaker Publications

To copy a style sheet from another PageMaker publication, choose Define Styles from the Type menu to display the Define Styles dialog box, then click Copy. Style names from the copied publication are then added to the list in the Styles palette. If the current publication includes any styles with the same name as styles in copied publications, PageMaker asks whether you want to replace the old styles with the copied ones. If you choose to replace the styles, those styles and all text in the current publication that has been formatted with those styles are changed to match the copied style sheets formatting specifications.

Designing Styles in Your Word Processor

Style sheets created in Microsoft Word and other word processing applications can be imported along with the text into PageMaker if the Microsoft Word import/export filter has been installed. When you import text set with style names, highlight the Retain Format option in the Place dialog box that is displayed when you use the Place command from the File menu. The imported text retains the formatting set in the word processor, and the style names from the word processor become part of the PageMaker style sheet.

If a style sheet has been set up in PageMaker, you can type style names as part of the text in any word processor. PageMaker can read a style name from a word processor if the name is enclosed in angle brackets (< >). The brackets must appear at the beginning of the paragraph for PageMaker to modify the text to the new style (see fig. 5.31). If a paragraph does not have its own style, the paragraph takes on the attributes of the paragraph that precedes it.

When you import text set up with style names, highlight the Retain Format option in the Place dialog box that is displayed when you use the Place command from the File menu. The imported text takes on the attributes of the style in the style sheet of the PageMaker publication.

Removing a Style

To remove a style from the style sheet, choose Define Styles from the Type menu to display the Define Styles dialog box, click on the style name you want to delete, then click Remove. Paragraphs that have been formatted with the deleted style retain their formatting, but they are identified as having No Style in the Styles palette.

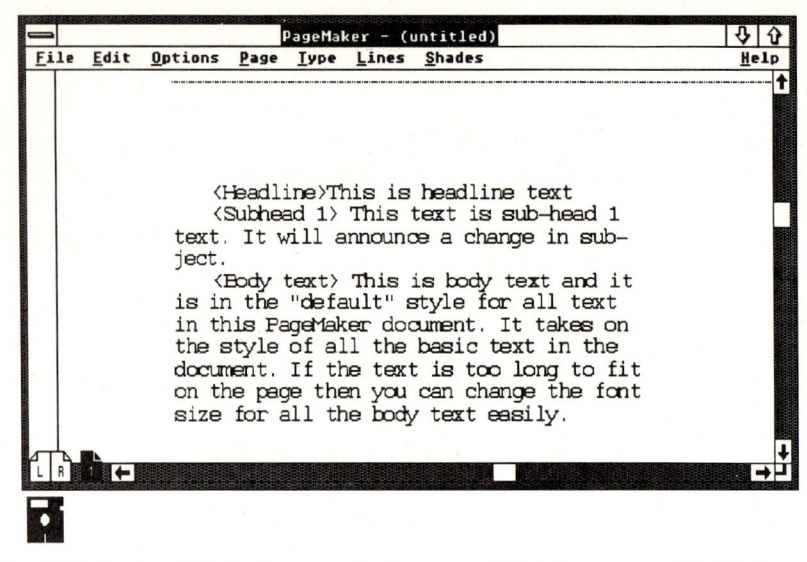

Fig. 5.31. Text as it looks in a word processor with style names added before paragraphs.

Editing Styles

You use the same techniques to edit a style as to create a new style. You can start by choosing the Define Styles command, selecting the style you want to change in the dialog box, and clicking Edit. You also can jump directly to the Edit Styles dialog box by holding the Ctrl key and clicking on the style's name in the Styles palette.

> ### Seeing the Attributes of a Style
> To view the specifications for a particular style, click the Define Styles dialog box in the Type menu. Highlight a style, and then watch as all the style's attributes are listed in the dialog box.

When you edit a style, all text in the publication that has been formatted with that style changes to match the new format. For example, if your style is called *bodytxt2* and you change the font of *bodytxt2* from 10-point Helvetica to 14-point Times Roman, all the text that is labeled *bodytxt2* is changed to 14-point Times Roman when you return to the page layout view.

Formatting Text by Using Styles

To change the style of text, highlight the text tool and select the paragraphs you want to change by clicking somewhere in the paragraph or by using one of the text-selection methods to highlight a series of paragraphs. Choose the Style command from the Type menu to display a submenu of styles and then choose a style from the submenu, or choose a style from the Styles palette.

To display the Styles palette if it is not already shown on the screen, choose Styles Palette (Ctrl-Y) from the Window menu. The Styles palette contains a list of the different styles that have been set up in the publication. When you select text, the style name is highlighted in the Styles palette to show what style name formats the current text (see fig. 5.32). Search the list in the Styles palette for the style you want, highlight that style name, and click once. The text reformats with the new style's attributes (see fig. 5.33).

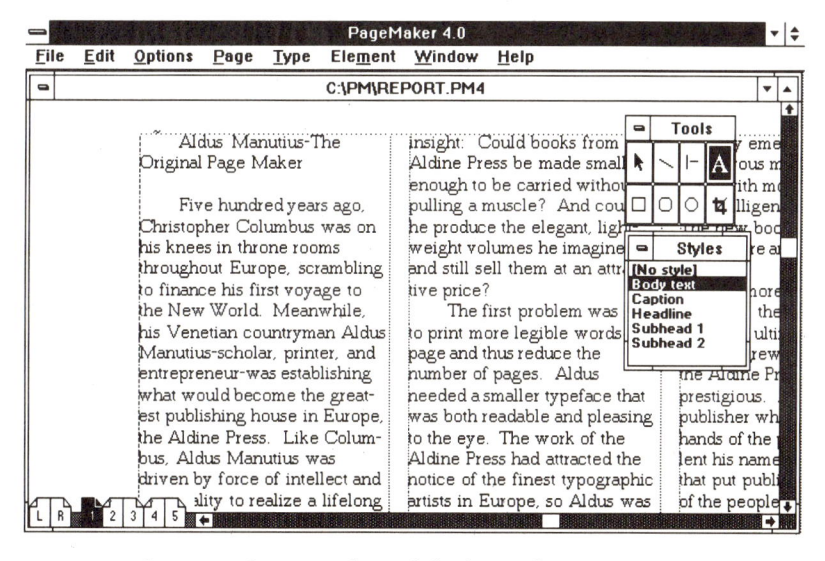

Fig. 5.32. Body text with PageMaker's default attributes.

Copy Fitting

During the page-layout process you will find that copy fitting can be a major problem. What do you do when the text for a four-page newsletter runs to four and a half pages? How do you make a table of numbers fit into a defined area on the page? How can you force two columns to bottom out at the same measure when they consist of different amounts of text?

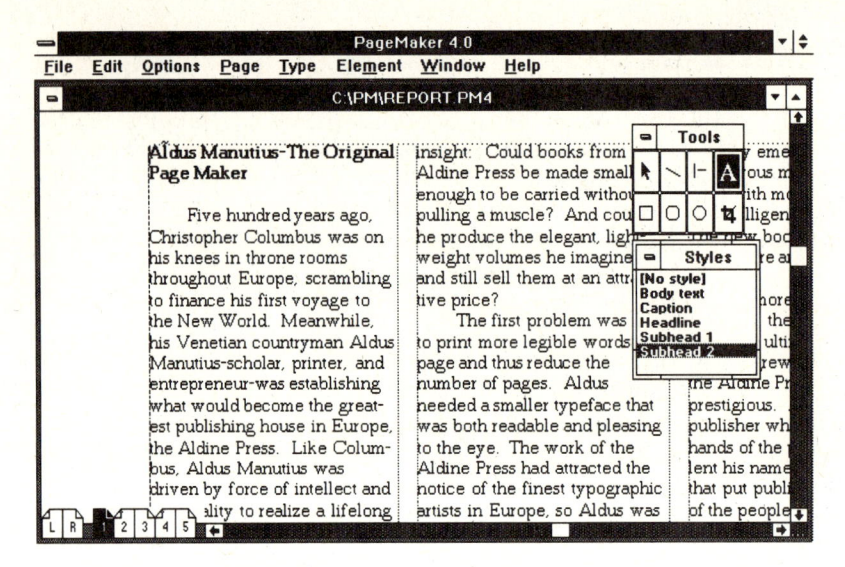

Fig. 5.33. Text modified from Body Text to Subhead2.

PageMaker does not have an automatic vertical-justification feature that fits copy exactly from the top to the bottom margin. To fit copy in a column or on a defined number of pages, you can change the length of the text in a column by using any of the following techniques.

The most direct method of forcing text to fit a designated number of pages or of making two columns the same length is to adjust the length of the text in each column by dragging the bottom windowshade handles up or down. For example, if the text of a four-page price list is two or three lines too long to fit, you might decide to add one line of text to each column by dragging down the windowshades to extend below the bottom page margin. If an article falls a few lines short of filling a two-column page, you can drag up the bottom handle of the longer column to make the two columns end at the same measure on the page.

If you have strict standards about making text meet the bottom margins, or if your extra text is too long to fit by extending the bottom margin on each page, you may need to use one of the following approaches.

Changing the width of the text is one way to change the amount of space that the text occupies. Chapter 3 describes how to change the width of columns *before* they are filled with text; Chapter 4 describes the steps involved in changing the size of text blocks *after* the text has been positioned on a page. Another way to change the size of a text block is to change the point size. These methods work fine for copy fitting if you are designing the document as you go along or designing the text deliberately to fit the space allowed. For very long documents or documents that must match the design specifications, however, changing the width or size of the text is unacceptable.

A better approach is to change the leading (the space between the lines) through the Type Specifications dialog box (see figs. 5.34 and 5.35). If you use small increments, this method is the least disruptive to the basic design. PageMaker enables increments as small as one-tenth of a point. If the text is divided into many columns or text blocks throughout the document, making the copy fit by changing the leading is much faster than changing the width of every text block. Unless you use a style sheet, you cannot globally change the width of an entire publication's text after the text has been placed. You must adjust each text block individually.

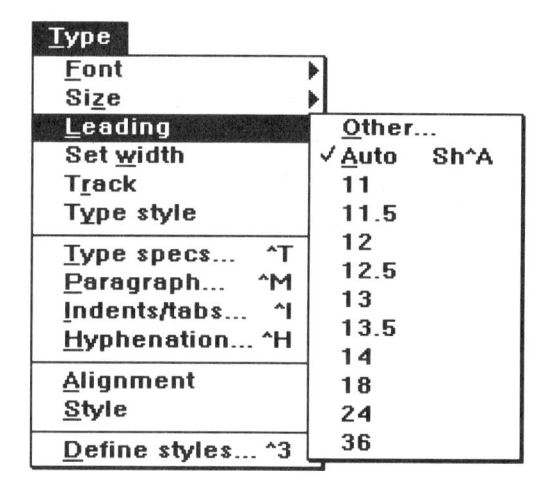

Fig. 5.34. The Leading submenu.

Fig. 5.35. Changing leading by using the Type Specifications dialog box.

> ### Changing All Leading in Copy
>
> You can use the Define Styles command to change the leading or any other style for all body copy. If you did not use a style sheet to format the text, you can change the leading for whole stories by using the Select All command with the text tool inside the text area to select the copy. Next, move through the document and reset the leading on individual headings where necessary.
>
> If you used automatic leading in formatting the body text, you can change the space between lines by choosing the Select All command with the text tool inside the text area to select the copy, and then choosing the Paragraph command. The Spacing button in the Paragraph Specifications dialog box displays the Spacing Attributes dialog box, where you can adjust the formula for automatic leading. Autoleading usually is 120 percent of the point size of the type. You can set this value higher to expand the text or lower to contract the text.
>
> Remember that PageMaker can make adjustments within the nearest one-tenth of a point, so for 12-point type, the smallest increment PageMaker responds to is 1 percent for changing automatic leading, which is fine if you are printing to a high resolution typesetter. A 300-dpi laser printer, however, can handle differences of only one-fourth of a point. The smallest practical increment for changing automatic leading for 12-point type, therefore, is two percentage points if you are printing to a 300-dpi printer.

You also can gain space by scaling tables that were imported as graphics from the Table Editor (see Chapter 4). If you are fitting a table of tabbed text into a space of a specific width, you can change the tabs and, if necessary, the type size. To fit a tabbed table into a space of a set length, you can adjust the leading. You also can adjust the Spacing Attributes settings in the Paragraph Specifications dialog box, which appears when you select the Paragraph command on the Type menu. This setting controls the amount of space between paragraphs. Each line of the table is treated as a paragraph with space Before or After (see fig. 5.36). To fit copy *before* the page layout stage, see Chapter 10.

Table set with no spacing between lines:			Table set with .025-inch spacing between lines:		
2/14	Travel	$398	2/14	Travel	$398
2/14	Food	$30	2/14	Food	$30
2/15	Car Rental	$20	2/15	Car Rental	$20
2/15	Food	$50	2/15	Food	$50
2/16	Travel	$398	2/16	Travel	$398

Fig. 5.36. Adjusting tables by changing the Spacing Attributes settings in the Paragraph Specifications dialog box.

Chapter Summary

Now that you have seen in this chapter and Chapter 4 the range of formatting options that PageMaker provides, you can compare PageMaker's features with the capabilities of your word processing program and decide how to approach any large publication project. Remember that you can do as much formatting in the word processor as you like, as long as PageMaker retains that formatting when you place the text on the page.

Few word processors, however, have the full range of options available through PageMaker for selecting typefaces and sizes and for controlling the amount of space between words, letters, and lines of text. Chapter 3 provides more tips about efficient methods of applying these specifications in the page layout stage. Chapters 9 and 10 offer suggestions on modifying the defaults for these settings, and Chapters 12 through 16 contain examples of the settings used in specific publications. Before you move into the multifaceted design and layout steps, read the Chapter 6 to learn about the sources of graphics for a PageMaker publication.

Working with Graphics

The capability to incorporate graphics and text on a page is one of the characteristics of PageMaker as a page-composition program. PageMaker contains graphics tools that enable you to draw such simple shapes as boxes, ovals, and lines. The new Table Editor feature in PageMaker 4.0 enables you to create tables of rows and columns of text, including rules between rows and columns and shaded cells, and to save them in a graphics format for importing into PageMaker.

PageMaker's Place command also enables you to import graphics created in other programs, such as Windows Draw, In*A*Vision, AutoCAD, 1-2-3, Symphony, Windows Graphics Device Interface (GDI) Metafiles, Windows Metafile (WMF), Encapsulated PostScript (EPS) formats, Windows Paint, PC Paintbrush, and Publisher's Paintbrush. You also can import scanned images saved as PC Paintbrush files or in TIFF format.

In PageMaker, you have three methods of incorporating graphics. You can create new graphics with PageMaker's built-in graphics tools, use the Paste command to bring in graphics from Window's Clipboard, and use the Place command to bring in graphics created in other programs. This chapter introduces you to the alternatives available for adding graphics to a page and demonstrates how to prepare graphics in other programs.

You learn to use PageMaker's tools to create graphics and to import graphics created in other programs. You also learn to use the pointer tool to select, move, and scale graphics and to use the cropping tool to trim the edges from imported graphics. The differences among graphics from various sources are explained, and you learn how imported TIFF images can be manipulated to adjust contrast and brightness.

210 Part I: The Production Process with PageMaker

Chapter 3 introduced the specific applications during page layout for the procedures described in this chapter. Chapter 8 describes the application of color and printing color graphics.

Drawing with the Toolbox Tools

All of PageMaker's built-in graphics tools appear as icons in the toolbox. The toolbox, shown in figure 6.1, is actually a window. You can move the toolbox to any position or hide it by issuing the Toolbox command from the Element menu.

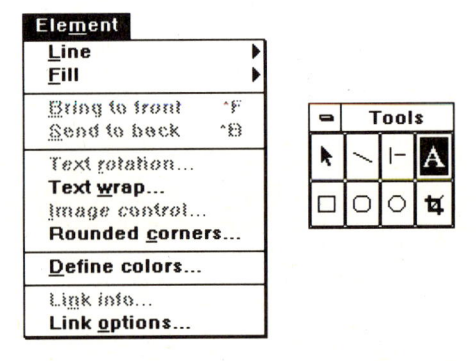

Fig. 6.1. The Element menu and the toolbox.

The toolbox contains eight tools. You have seen how to use the text tool and the pointer tool to select, move, and size blocks of text. In this section, you learn to draw straight lines and create boxes, circles, and ovals with the toolbox's five drawing tools:

- The diagonal-line tool
- The perpendicular-line tool
- The square-corner tool
- The rounded-corner tool
- The oval tool

When you select one of the five drawing tools, the pointer changes to a crossbar. All five drawing tools work the same way. You move the mouse to position the crossbar on the page or pasteboard and hold down the mouse button as you drag the crossbar. The object appears on the screen as you drag. As long as you press the mouse button, you can keep adjusting the size of the object. When you release the mouse button, the graphic is set. To change the size or position of a completed graphic, you must switch to the pointer tool.

Drawing Straight Lines

You use the diagonal-line tool and the perpendicular-line tool to draw straight lines. By using the diagonal-line tool, you can draw lines that cross at any angle; by using the perpendicular-line tool, you can draw only horizontal or vertical lines or lines at a 45-degree angle. When you use the diagonal-line tool, the diagonal lines begin and end exactly at the crossbar points. A perpendicular line begins at the crossbar point and ends at the 45-degree increment nearest the ending crossbar location.

If you need to draw a mixture of perpendicular lines, lines angled at 45 degrees, and lines angled at other than 45 degrees, you can use the diagonal-line tool to draw all three types of lines. To draw with the diagonal-line tool, hold down the Shift key when you want to draw a perpendicular line or a line angled at 45 degrees.

When you draw a diagonal line, PageMaker centers the line on the crossbar, regardless of the line's thickness. When you draw perpendicular lines, the crossbar point marks the *edge* of the line. You can flip a perpendicular line to the opposite side of the crossbar by dragging slightly in the direction you want the line to fall as you are drawing.

Creating Boxes

You use the square- and rounded-corner tools to draw boxes. By using these tools, you can draw rectangles in any proportion. If you hold down the Shift key while you are drawing, you draw squares. The square-corner tool produces boxes with right-angle corners, but you can make them rounded by using the Rounded Corners command on the Element menu after the box is drawn (see fig. 6.2). You also can change rounded corners to square corners or adjust the roundness of the corners with the same command.

You can change the degree of roundness of the corners by using the Rounded Corners command on the Element menu before or after you draw the box. To set the degree of roundness of corners *before* you draw a box, first be certain that nothing on the page is selected (no existing box displays handles). Choose the Rounded Corners command from the Element menu and make a selection in the dialog box. All new boxes that you draw with the rounded-corner tool take on the latest setting for rounded corners.

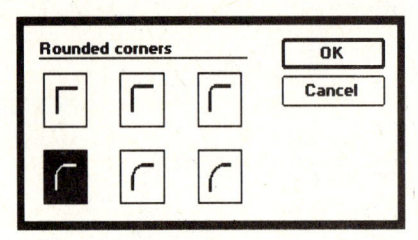

Fig. 6.2. The Rounded Corners dialog box.

To set the degree of roundness of corners *after* you draw a box, first be certain that the box you want to change is selected—you have drawn it or selected it with the pointer tool and it displays eight handles. Choose the Rounded Corners command from the Element menu and make a selection in the dialog box. Only the selected box takes on that setting for rounded corners.

All the boxes you draw in PageMaker have horizontal and vertical edges. You cannot create trapezoids or parallelograms or rotate boxes in PageMaker. You can use the line tools to create a polygon or a box of any angle, composed of separate straight lines, but you cannot fill it with a pattern. You can, however, use other graphics programs to create polygons and import them into PageMaker.

Creating Circles and Ovals

The oval tool enables you to draw circles and ovals. When using this tool, you drag the crossbar diagonally to define the rectangular area into which the circle or oval falls. If you hold down the Shift key while you are dragging the crossbar, you create a circle.

All ovals drawn in PageMaker have horizontal and vertical axes. If you want an oval to have a diagonal axis, you must create the oval in another program and import it into PageMaker. You also cannot draw arcs—segments of circles, as used in pie graphs—in PageMaker, but you can import arcs drawn in other programs.

Editing Toolbox Graphics

You must use the pointer tool to select, move, or scale graphics after you draw or place them on-screen. You cannot select, move, or scale a graphic when other graphics tools are selected. With the other tools, you can draw only new graphics or make menu selections.

Using PageMaker's Tools To Draw Graphics

When you use one of the tools from the toolbox to draw graphics, you can save time in the long run by positioning the crossbar carefully when you start and not releasing the mouse button until you are sure that the graphic is the correct size.

If you make a graphic the wrong size, you can fix it in two ways:

- Press Shift-Del immediately to remove the graphic and then draw the object again.
- Select the pointer tool to change the graphic's size or position, as described in the following section, "Selecting Graphic Objects."

Selecting Graphic Objects

When a line is created with the diagonal-line or perpendicular-line tool and is selected with the pointer tool, the line is framed in two small black squares, called *handles*. When a box is created and is selected with the pointer tool, the box is framed in eight handles. To change a line's length or angle, drag one of these corner handles. To move a line to another position, drag anywhere on the line *except* a corner handle.

To select a single graphic object, first select the pointer tool from the toolbox, then click the pointer tool on any part of the object. The graphic displays the handles: two handles if the object is a line, eight handles if it is a box or an oval. To select one or more objects at a time, hold down the Shift key and click each object. To select all the objects within a rectangular area, hold down the mouse button as you drag the pointer tool diagonally from one corner of the area to the opposite corner. If the graphic object is on a layer below other graphic objects or text blocks, the first time you click with the pointer you select the object on only the top layer. Press Ctrl as you click again to select the object on the next layer down, and continue Ctrl-clicking until the desired graphic is selected.

Moving Objects

After you select a graphic object, you can move or scale it by using the pointer tool. To move one or more selected objects, click the pointer tool on any part of the selection except the handles and drag the object or group to the new location. When you hold down the mouse button to move a graphic object, the pointer becomes a four-directional arrow.

To move a graphic that has a fill pattern, you can click anywhere on the object. To move a graphic object that does not have a fill pattern, place the pointer somewhere on the border. To move a selection along horizontal or vertical lines, hold down the Shift key as you drag.

> *Positioning Graphic Elements Precisely*
>
> To position graphic elements precisely, use the snap-to effect of the nonprinting guides, or work in 200% Size so that you can move objects in fine increments (see Chapter 3).

Scaling Objects

After an object is selected, you place the pointer on a handle and drag to *scale* (stretch or shrink) the graphic. The pointer becomes a two-directional arrow when you hold down the mouse button to scale a graphic.

When you use the pointer tool to change the length or angle of any line, you also can change the angle of the line. If you hold down the Shift key as you drag one of these handles, you force the line to follow a 45-degree path. You can even change a diagonal line to a vertical or horizontal line by holding down the Shift key as you drag a handle. If you do not hold down the Shift key while dragging, you can stretch the line in any direction. You can even change the angle of a line that was originally drawn with the perpendicular-line tool.

You also can change the shape and size of a box by using the pointer tool to select the object and drag one of the handles. The corner handles can be dragged in any direction to change the dimensions of the box, and the handles in the middle of each side of the box can be dragged horizontally or vertically to change one dimension.

After drawing a rectangle, you can change it to a square by selecting the rectangle with the pointer tool and holding down the Shift key as you click or drag any handle. You can change an oval into a circle by selecting the oval with the pointer and holding down the Shift key as you click on any handle.

> ### Watching the Pointer
> When drawing, moving, or scaling a graphic, always be certain that the pointer's appearance reflects your intention before you make a change. A crossbar indicates that you are about to draw a new object. A four-headed arrow indicates that you are about to move the selected objects. A two-headed arrow indicates that you are about to scale an object.

Two-dimensional objects have eight handles, one at each corner and one in the middle of each side. When you drag one of the handles that falls in the middle of a side, you stretch the graphic along one axis only. In other words, you stretch the graphic out of proportion. When you drag one of the corner handles, you stretch the graphic in two directions at once, proportionally.

If you hold down the Shift key while dragging a corner handle, you can create several effects:

- If you used PageMaker's tools to draw the graphic, lines become or remain horizontal or vertical; boxes become or remain squares; ovals become circles; and circles remain circles.

- If you have imported the graphic from another program, you size the graphic proportionally (see fig. 6.3).

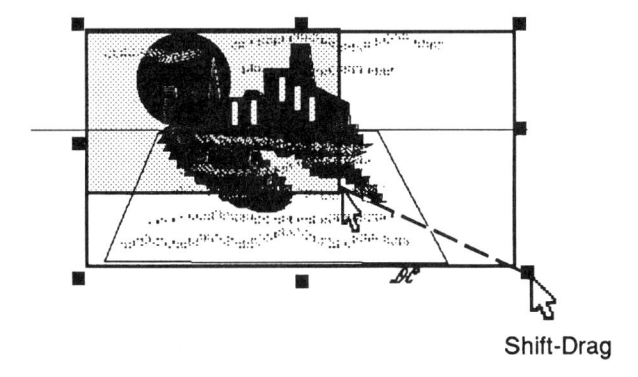

Shift-Drag

Fig. 6.3. *Effects of the Shift key on graphic objects created in another program.*

Changing Lines Widths and Fill Patterns

When you create a new object—line, box, or oval—with one of PageMaker's tools, the object first takes the default line width and fill pattern that you set, or PageMaker's defaults of hairline width and no fill pattern. You can change these settings before or after you draw the object.

You can select line patterns from the Line submenu under the Element menu to change the appearance of any line or the border around any box or oval created with PageMaker's built-in tools (see fig. 6.4). You can fill boxes and ovals with patterns from the Fill submenu (see fig. 6.5). These menus affect only graphics created in PageMaker; they cannot be applied to graphics imported from other programs.

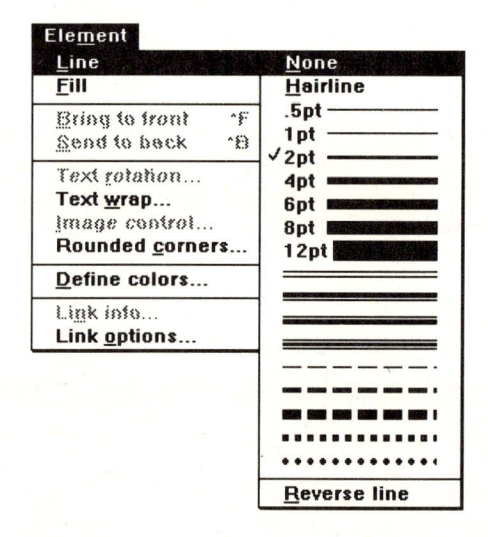

Fig. 6.4. The Line submenu.

You can change the line style and fill pattern by using the Line and Fill commands under the Element menu before or after you draw the box. To set the line style and fill pattern *before* you draw a line, box, or oval, first be certain that nothing on the page is selected. If no existing element displays handles, then choose the Line or Fill command from the Element menu and make a selection from the drop-down menu. All new lines, boxes, and ovals that you draw take the latest settings for line style and fill pattern. The fill pattern setting does not affect lines.

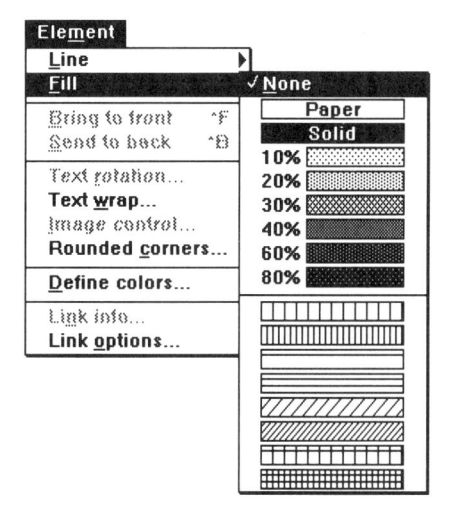

Fig. 6.5. The Fill submenu.

To set the line style and fill pattern *after* you draw a box or oval, first be certain that the element you want to change is selected. After the element displays handles, choose the Line or Fill command from the Element menu and make a selection from the drop-down menu. Only the selected elements take the changed settings.

Importing Graphics Created in Other Programs

For many publications, PageMaker's graphics tools are sufficient—especially when you have no illustrations other than lines, boxes, and ovals. For heavily illustrated material, however, other programs are the primary sources of graphics. You use the Place command from the File menu to import graphics created in other programs. These graphics can be scaled and cropped in PageMaker, but you cannot change the lines or patterns with PageMaker's menus. You must edit the graphics in their originating program.

You use the Place command from the File menu to bring in graphics created in other programs. The entire graphics file is placed in PageMaker as a single graphics object, regardless of how large the graphic is or how many objects are in the original source file. If the graphic includes text, PageMaker retains the font settings specified in the graphics program. Chapter 8 describes how PageMaker handles color graphics.

To meet different needs, PageMaker imports two kinds of graphics from other programs. These two types are object-oriented *vector graphics* and *bit-mapped graphics*. With these basic formats, you can create reports containing AutoCAD designs, newsletters with illustrations created through Windows Paint, magazines containing pictures scanned from photographs, and many other kinds of illustrated materials. With all PageMaker's options for importing graphics, you have the capability of producing high-quality graphics for many types of publications.

Figure 6.6 lists the types of graphics programs that PageMaker supports and displays the icons for each type. You can determine the type of graphic you are importing in two ways. Files created by vector-graphics programs usually have the file extension PIC, PLT, WMF, WMT, or EPS in the name shown in the Place command dialog box, and the placement icon looks like a pencil or a box containing the letters PS (for an Encapsulated "PostScript" file). File names representing bit-mapped graphics usually end with the file extension MSP, PCX, TIF, or IMG, and the placement icon looks like a paintbrush or a box containing a crosshair.

Graphics Program	File Extension	Icon
EPS-format (Encapsulated PostScript)	EPS	PS
Scanned Image	IMG	
	TIF	☒
MacPaint	PNT	
PC Paintbrush	PCX	
Publisher's Paintbrush	PCX	🖌
Windows Paint	MSP	
AutoCad	PLT	
GDI metafiles	WMF	
In•a•Vision	PIC	
Lotus 1-2-3	PIC	✏
PC Paint	PIC	
Symphony	PIC	
Windows Draw!	PIC	
Windows Graph	PIC	
HP Graphic Galery	TIF	
Dr. Halo DPE	TIF	
Hotshot	PCX or EPS	
HPGL plotter files	PLT	
Videoshow Graphics File Format	PIC	
CGM Graphics File Format	CGM	

Fig. 6.6. File name extensions and placement icons for different types of graphics.

Follow these steps to import graphics from other programs into PageMaker:

1. Select the Place command from the File menu.

2. In the Place File dialog box, find the name of the graphics file you want (see fig. 6.7). Use the scroll bars to scroll through the list of names. If you do not see the name of the file you want, click the drive indicator, type the path name, and press Enter. Click the file name and place it. The Retain Format, Convert Quotes, and Read Tags options have no effect on graphics files.

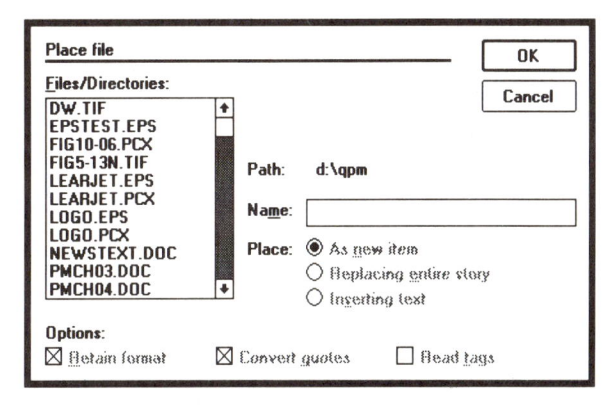

```
Place file                                    OK
Files/Directories:                          Cancel
DW.TIF
EPSTEST.EPS
FIG10-06.PCX
FIG5-13N.TIF
LEARJET.EPS      Path:   d:\qpm
LEARJET.PCX
LOGO.EPS         Name:
LOGO.PCX
NEWSTEXT.DOC     Place: ● As new item
PMCH03.DOC              ○ Replacing entire story
PMCH04.DOC              ○ Inserting text

Options:
☒ Retain format    ☒ Convert quotes    ☐ Read tags
```

Fig. 6.7. *Finding the name of a graphics file.*

3. After you find the name of the file you want to place, select the name by double-clicking it.

   If the graphic to be imported is larger than 64K, PageMaker displays a dialog box with the message

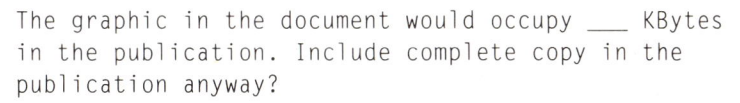

   ```
   The graphic in the document would occupy ___ KBytes
   in the publication. Include complete copy in the
   publication anyway?
   ```

   The actual size of the graphic is shown in the dialog box (see fig. 6.8). If you choose Yes, then the entire original graphic is imported and stored as part of the PageMaker publication. The size of the PageMaker publication is increased by the size of the graphic. If you choose No, PageMaker stores a low-resolution, bit-mapped, screen-display version of the graphic as part of the publication. The original graphic file is *linked* to the publication. When you print the publication, PageMaker looks on the disk for the original graphic file and prints it at high resolution. Chapter 7 describes how to manage linked graphics and text files.

If the imported graphic is smaller than 64K, or after you make a selection in the dialog box for larger graphics, the pointer changes to one of the graphics placement icons shown in figure 6.6.

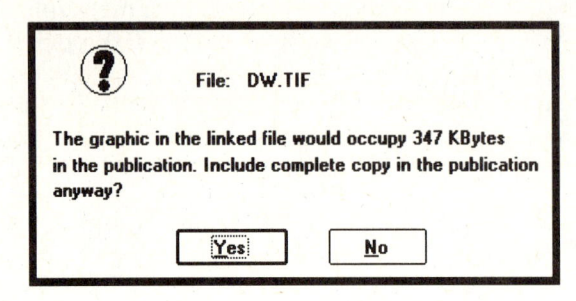

> File: DW.TIF
>
> The graphic in the linked file would occupy 347 KBytes in the publication. Include complete copy in the publication anyway?
>
> Yes   No

Fig. 6.8. *Dialog box offering link option.*

4. Place the icon where you want the top left corner of the graphic to appear and click once. Let the snap-to column guides help you position the graphic placement icon. PageMaker displays the placed graphic framed in eight handles (see fig. 6.9).

If the text tool is selected and the text insertion point is positioned within a text block when you choose the Place command, the graphic becomes an inline graphic.

A graphic imported from another program usually is the same size as in the original program, but you can change the image size or trim edges. You also can adjust the size of a graphic as you place it by using the drag-place feature. To use the drag-place feature, you define the size of the graphic by holding the mouse button and diagonally dragging the graphic placement icon. An outline of a box appears on the page as you hold down the mouse button and drag. When you release the mouse button, the graphic takes the dimensions of the box.

Placing Large Graphics from Other Programs

If the original graphic is much larger than the position reserved on the page, you can size or crop the graphic on the pasteboard before importation. You also can use the drag-place feature to reduce the graphic as you place it.

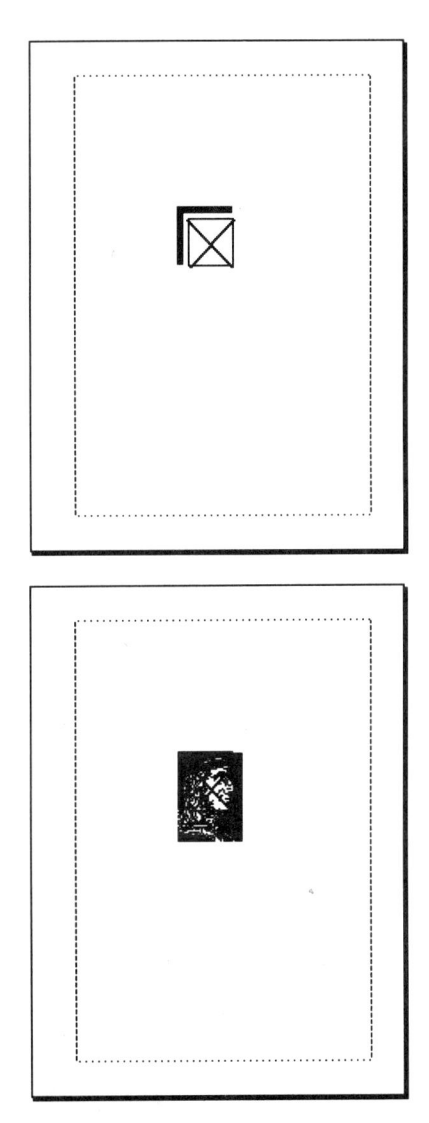

Fig. 6.9. Placing a graphic image on the page.

Object-Oriented Graphics

Object-oriented graphics comprise separate objects—boxes, lines, and ovals—that can be moved independently. PageMaker's built-in graphics are object-oriented graphics, and you can import object-oriented graphics from other programs. Object-oriented graphics are sometimes called *vector graphics* because the lines and patterns that you see are actually stored as mathematical formulas for the vectors composing the image. A *vector*, shown in figure 6.10, is a line defined by a starting point, a directional angle, and a length.

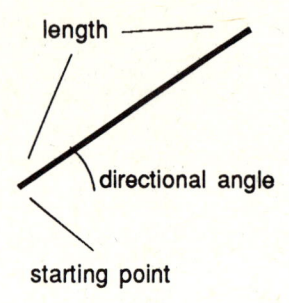

Fig. 6.10. A vector.

Object-oriented graphics are created with drafting programs, draw programs, and spreadsheet graphics. Programs that produce object-oriented graphics that can be placed in PageMaker include Windows Draw (see fig. 6.11), In*a*Vision, AutoCAD, 1-2-3 (see fig. 6.12), Symphony, Windows Graphics Device Interface (GDI) Metafiles, and Encapsulated PostScript (EPS) formats (see fig. 6.13).

Fig. 6.11. Two graphics created in Windows Draw.

Chapter 6: Working with Graphics **223**

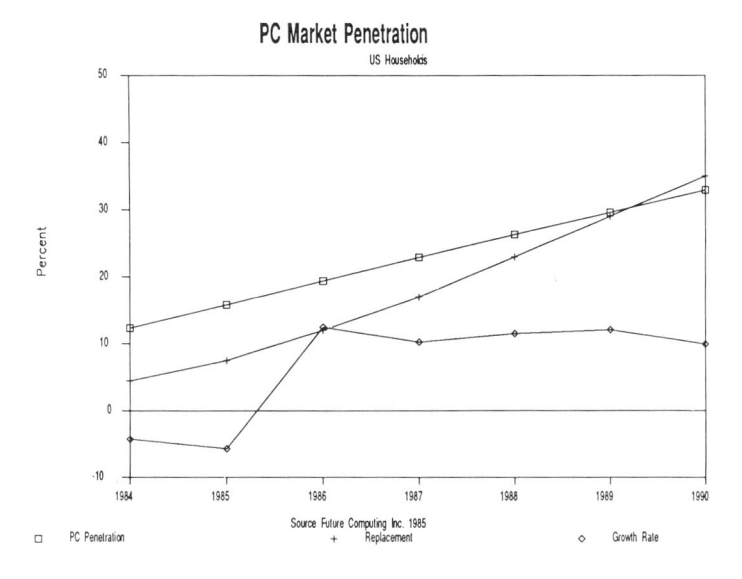

Fig. 6.12. *A graph created in 1-2-3.*

Fig. 6.13. *Graphics drawn with Adobe's Illustrator program to create Encapsulated PostScript (EPS) code.*

Because these vector graphics are defined mathematically, they are clarified during the printing process to create crisp line art and precise fill patterns. Vector graphics, therefore, are considered better-quality images for line art than bit-mapped graphics.

Encapsulated PostScript Format

Encapsulated PostScript format files can be created by using draw programs or by direct coding in the PostScript programming language. If you create the image directly in code, when you place the image in PageMaker, you see only a box reserving the space for the graphic. If you use a program that creates a screen image and the encapsulated code—CorelDRAW!, Micrografx Designer, or Adobe's Illustrator—when you place the EPS file in PageMaker, you can see the graphic and scale or crop it as you would any other graphic. Figure 6.13 shows an example of these graphics.

> ### Using the Primary Sources of EPS Files
> You can use Adobe Illustrator or Aldus FreeHand on a Macintosh to create graphics and save them in Encapsulated PostScript format (IBM Windows version). You can telecommunicate that EPS file as text from the Macintosh to a PC and place the graphics in PageMaker.

Bit-Mapped Graphics

Bit-mapped graphics are composed of a pattern of dots, or *pixels*, rather than being stored as mathematical formulas. This type of graphic comes from paint programs, such as Windows Paint, PC Paintbrush, or Publisher's Paintbrush. Figure 6.14 shows a bit-mapped graphic drawn with Windows Paint.

Because bit-mapped images are composed of dots, rather than whole objects, bit-mapped images cannot be broken easily into separate elements: boxes, circles, and lines. Objects are not *layered* one above the other as they are in PageMaker. When a circle is drawn on top of a square, for example, in the intersection the dots that compose the circle actually replace the dots that composed the square.

Bit-mapped images are not smooth like vector graphics when printed. Bit-mapped graphics, therefore, are generally considered inferior to vector graphics for most line art. Bit-mapped images, however, are superior for scanned images and for fine art images that call for air-brush effects.

Note concerning on-screen versus printed bit-mapped images: Some bit-mapped graphics may seem distorted on-screen, but they print well if the original graphic was not distorted. Graphics generally look best displayed on the same equipment used to create them. For example, a graphic created on equipment using a Hercules Graphics Card may look distorted when placed by PageMaker on equipment with an EGA graphics card or a different monitor.

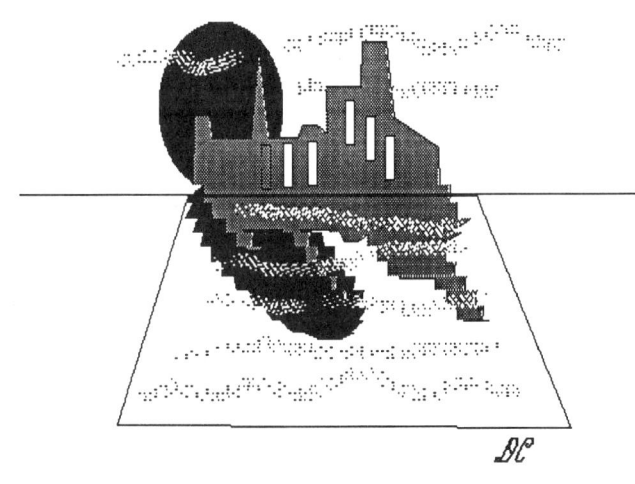

Fig. 6.14. *A bit-mapped image drawn with Windows Paint.*

Using Object-Oriented Graphics

Use object-oriented graphics rather than bit-mapped graphics for line art whenever possible. Bit-mapped graphics have a jagged appearance and take much longer to print.

When bit-mapped graphics are required, do not include text in the file in the paint program. Place the graphic portion in PageMaker and use PageMaker's text tools to add captions and labels.

Scanned Images

Scanned images also are bit-mapped images, but the latest scanning applications enable you to store images in your choice of graphic format: the IMG format created by the scanning program; the paint-type formats supported by PageMaker; PIC format; or Microsoft's tag image file format with the file extension TIF, which is a bit-mapped format that enables higher resolution than most paint programs.

Images can be edited in a paint program or in a program that enables you to edit IMG, PIC, or TIF files before inserting the files into PageMaker. Scanners that create images that can be saved in one of these formats include those made by Canon, Datacopy Corporation, DEST Corporation, Microtek Lab, Inc., and Ricoh Systems, Inc.

You can scan line art, such as a graphic logo, and save it in PIC format. PIC is an object-oriented format, but the scanned image is not stored as layered elements or as separate, editable objects as they would be if you created the logo from scratch by using a drawing application.

You can scan continuous-tone images, such as photographs or artwork created with brushes or charcoals, and save them in PIC format; these images are more commonly saved in a paint or TIFF format. Save continuous-tone images in paint format if you are using them *for position only* to show where a halftone will be stripped in at the print shop. Save them in TIFF format if you plan to print the scanned image as part of the final page layout. Good-quality scanned photographs can look like halftones when printed, even though the images may look coarse on your low-resolution screen (see fig. 6.15).

Fig. 6.15. A scanned image.

> **Scanning Resolution**
>
> If your scanner offers a choice of resolutions, choose the one that matches your printer's resolution. The image may seem rough on low-resolution screens but should look better when printed (see fig. 6.16).

300 dots per inch

72 dots per inch

Fig. 6.16. Scanned images at 72 and 300 dots per inch.

Editing Imported Graphics

You can select, move, and scale imported graphics by using the same techniques as for selecting, moving, and scaling graphics created with PageMaker's tools.

When you move or scale graphics imported from other programs, the speed of the drag can make a difference. If you drag quickly, the graphic image disappears as it changes, and you see only the outline of the area that the graphic fills. When you finish dragging the object and release the mouse button, the graphic reappears on-screen in the new size or location. If you drag slowly, you can see the entire image changing as you work.

When you change the size of some bit-mapped images in PageMaker, you may notice that parts of the image show a moiré pattern: a grid of perpendicular and diagonal lines. You can avoid this effect by using PageMaker's *magic stretch* feature, which jumps to fixed reduction and enlargement settings. The higher the resolution of your printer, the finer the adjustments you can get in magic stretch. Select the graphic with the pointer tool. To retain original proportions, hold down the Shift key as you are stretching the graphic. To activate magic stretch and jump to the best scales for printing, hold down the Shift and Ctrl keys as you are stretching (see fig. 6.17).

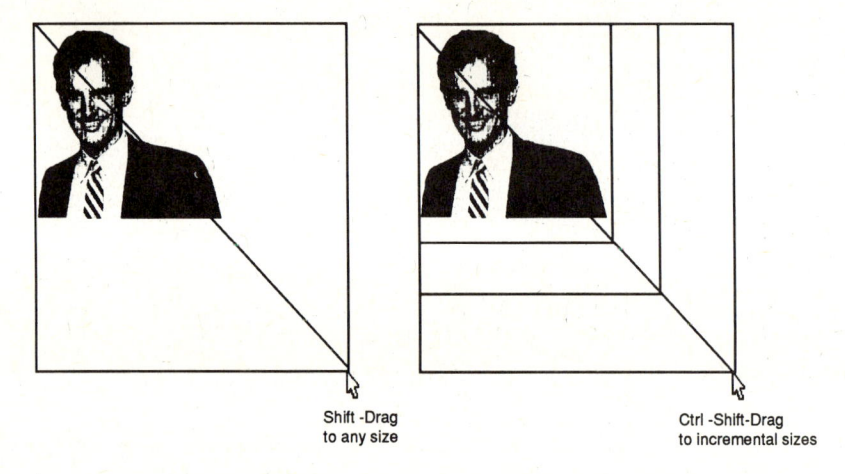

Shift-Drag to any size

Ctrl-Shift-Drag to incremental sizes

Fig. 6.17. Proportionate scaling and magic stretch.

Trimming Imported Graphics

The cropping tool trims edges from a graphic without changing the size of the rest of the graphic. You can crop or trim graphic objects brought in from other programs, but you cannot crop graphics drawn with PageMaker's built-in graphics tools.

To crop a graphic, select the cropping tool in the toolbox and then select the graphic. Click the cropping tool on the graphic to display the handles. Place the cropping tool over any handle and drag. You can trim horizontally or vertically by dragging one of the middle handles; you can trim diagonally by dragging one of the corner handles.

If you hold down the Shift key while dragging one of the corner handles, the cropped image retains the proportions of the original image. If you crop a graphic too much, you can drag the handles to enlarge it again.

The full image is stored with or linked to the PageMaker publication, and you always have the option of returning to the original full-size image by using the cropping tool to expand the graphic by dragging one of the handles. You also can move the image around inside the crop frame by placing the cropping tool anywhere on the graphic, except on a handle, and dragging (see fig. 6.18). In the figure, the image is moved to the left but retains the same proportions.

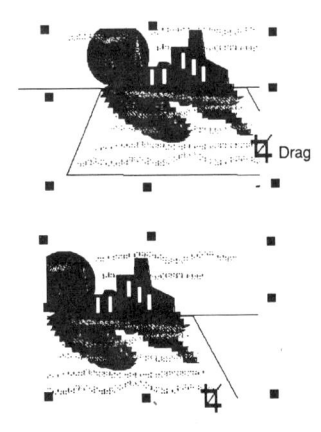

Fig. 6.18. Changing the view of the image without changing the size of the frame.

Controlling Paint and TIFF Graphics Image

You can use the Image Control command to change the appearance—lightness, contrast, screen pattern, screen angle, and lines per inch—of imported graphics that are stored in paint or black-and-white TIFF graphic formats. First select the graphic you want to change, and then choose Image Control from the Element menu to display the Image Control dialog box (see fig. 6.19).

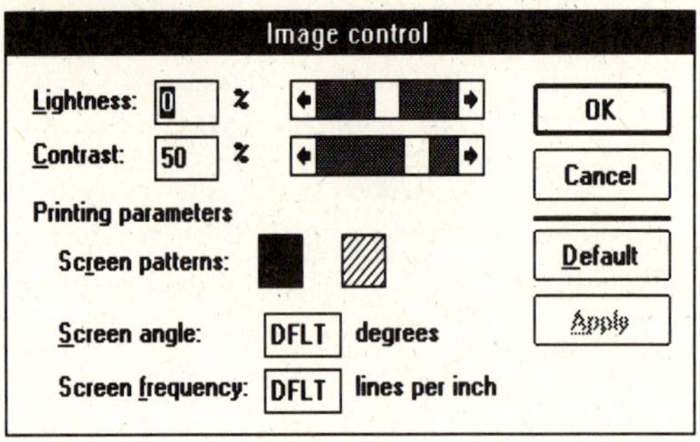

Fig. 6.19. The Image Control dialog box.

The Image Control dialog box is a window that can be moved on the screen by dragging the title bar to enable you to set up the screen display for the best view of the graphic as you change the settings. You can try different settings: click Apply to view the effects without closing the dialog box, click Reset to change the settings to what they were originally, click Cancel to close the dialog box without changing the graphic, or click OK to close the dialog box and change the graphic.

One of three options in the left corner is checked and indicates the type of graphic selected when you open the dialog box:

- Black and White indicates a paint image composed of solid black and white dots with no gray-scale information.

- Screened indicates a gray-scale image. You also can click Screened for a black-and-white image if you want to change the screen from a dot pattern to a line pattern.

- Gray is displayed when a TIFF image is selected and if your monitor supports gray-scale images. Otherwise, Gray is dimmed and TIFF images are identified as Screened.

The next three options affect how the screen is handled when printing the image (see fig. 6.20):

- You can choose a normal Screen Pattern of dots or diagonal lines for special effects.

- PageMaker usually uses the default Screen Angle that is built into the printer—usually 45 degrees—but you can change this angle.

Chapter 6: Working with Graphics **231**

- If Screen Frequency is set to DFLT, default, then PageMaker uses the printer defaults for lines per inch (lpi). The defaults usually are 90 lpi for PostScript imagesetters and lower for laser printers. By entering a frequency here, you override all printer defaults.

Default dot screen   90 lines per inch dot screen   30 lines per inch dot screen

Default line screen (45 degrees)   Default line screen, 90 lines per inch   90-degree angle line screen

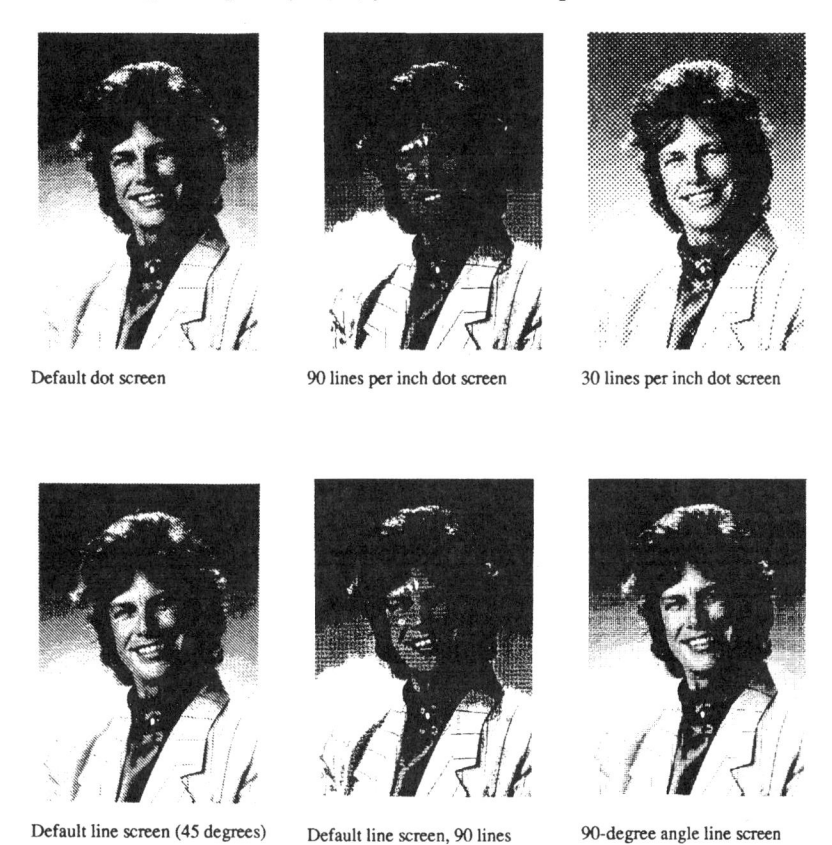

Fig. 6.20. *Examples of different screen settings: default dot screen, default line screen, 45-degree angle, 90-degree angle, 90 lpi, and 30 lpi.*

The next options affect the appearance of individual dots within the image:

- Click on the arrows beside Lightness to make the entire image darker or lighter.

- Click on the arrows beside Contrast to make light areas of the image lighter or darker relative to the surrounding background.

Pasting Graphics from the Clipboard

Besides using PageMaker's graphics tools to create an object or using the Place command to import graphics, you can cut, copy, and paste objects through the Windows Clipboard. The Clipboard is a temporary storage area that contains the objects most recently cut or copied in the Windows environment. The items in the Clipboard are replaced each time the Cut or Copy command is used, and the Clipboard is erased when you close Windows.

To use the Clipboard, you first select one or more objects on-screen. With the Cut and Copy commands under the Edit menu, you put the selected text or graphic into the Clipboard. The next time you use the Paste command, the graphic from the Clipboard is positioned in the center of the screen, unless the text tool is active and the text insertion point is positioned within a text block, in which case the pasted graphic becomes an inline graphic, as described later in this chapter.

A graphic from the Clipboard can be cut or copied from the current PageMaker publication, another PageMaker publication, or a graphics program you are running under Microsoft Windows. (See Chapter 2 for a description of running multiple programs under Windows.) You can bring graphics directly from one PageMaker publication to another only by using the Clipboard.

Losing Links through the Clipboard

Caution: Items copied within PageMaker, from one location in a publication to another or from one publication to another, retain all linking information (see Chapter 3). Items copied from another application into PageMaker through the Clipboard also retain linking information. You should, therefore, use the Place command rather than Copy and Paste to get graphics from other Windows applications into PageMaker.

Making duplicates of a graphic and using these duplicates to create drop shadows is a common use of the Clipboard. First, draw the top layer of the graphic by using one of PageMaker's tools. Use the Fill command under the Element menu to create a fill pattern. With the Copy command, you create a duplicate graphic in the Clipboard, and with the Paste command, you bring the duplicate back onto the same PageMaker page. To select the shadow pattern, you use the Fill command again. Move the shadow to the desired position (see fig. 6.21). Select the Send to Back command on the Element menu. Figure 6.22 shows the finished figure with the drop shadow in place.

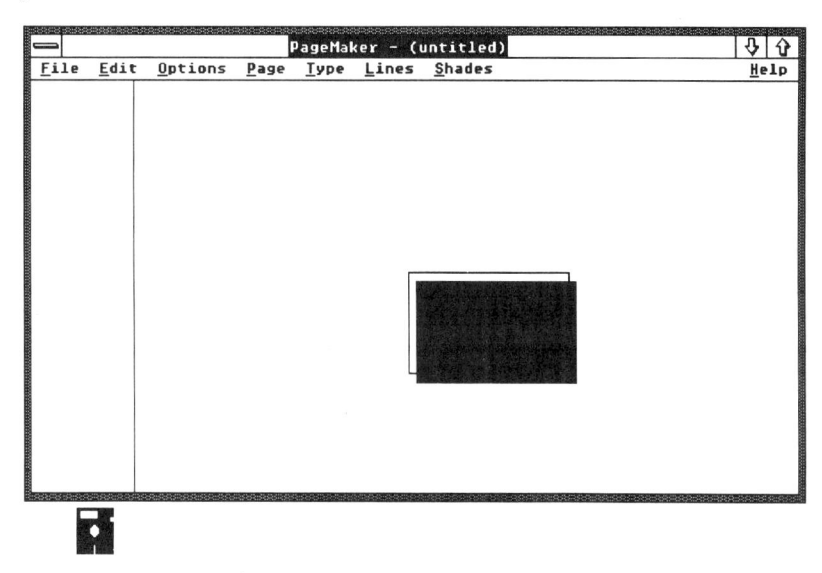

Fig. 6.21. The drop shadow moved to the desired position.

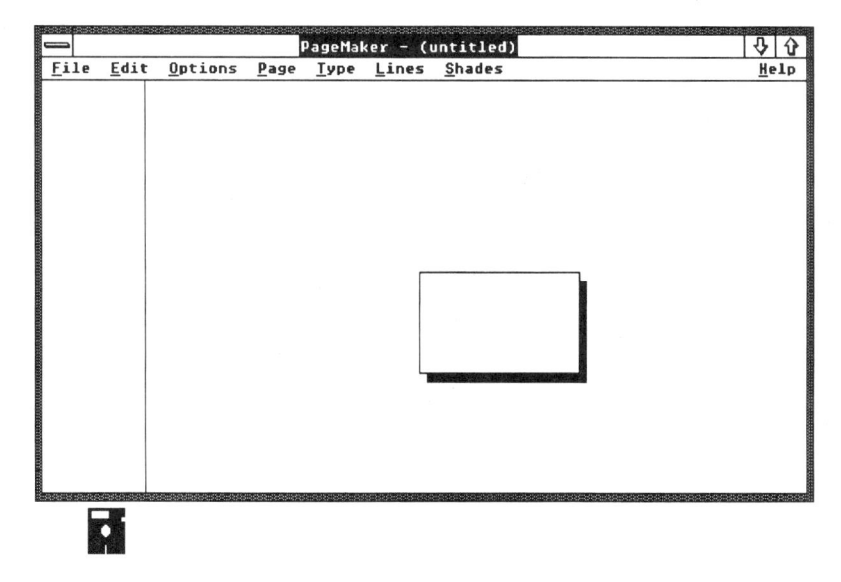

Fig. 6.22. The final graphic with the drop shadow in place.

Layering Objects

PageMaker is a three-dimensional system in the sense that you can place objects next to each other, and you can layer objects, as shown in figure 6.23. The first object placed, drawn, or typed in a series usually becomes the bottom layer; and the last object is the top layer. You should change the order of the layers by using the Send to Back and Bring to Front commands on the Element menu. You also can work through the stack by Shift-clicking to select objects below another object.

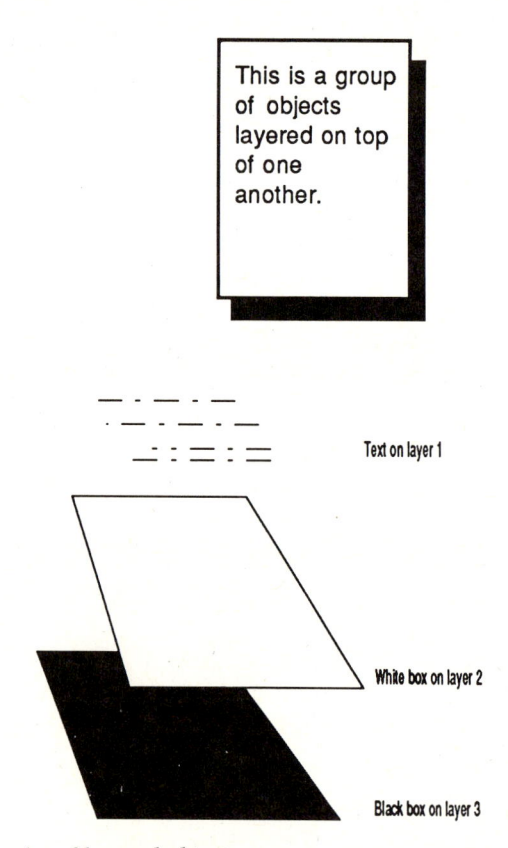

Fig. 6.23. Examples of layered objects.

Placing Objects in the Background

The Send to Back command sends a specific object to the bottom layer in a series. You can use this command, for example, to make shaded boxes the background for a particular area. You also can use the Send to Back command to access objects several layers below the top layer. This procedure is an alternative to holding down the Ctrl key as you click to select objects on different layers (see the section "Selecting Graphic Objects" earlier in this chapter).

Bringing Objects to the Foreground

The Bring to Front command brings a selected object to the top layer in front of any other unselected objects. When you are arranging a series of objects on the screen, you may find this command a useful alternative to the Send to Back command.

The Bring to Front command especially is useful when you are dealing with more than two layers of objects. When only two objects are layered, you can select the top one by clicking it with the pointer. You then use the Send to Back command to uncover the object below.

When many objects are layered, however, the pointer tool cannot reach an object through the other layers. You may be able to select the target object easily with the selection marquee by dragging the pointer tool to the flashing selection marquee. After editing or moving the object, use the Send to Back command if necessary.

When you edit text or move a graphic, it becomes the top layer on that page. You may need to use the Send to Back command to return the text or graphic to the proper order, even though you did not use the Bring to Front command.

Wrapping Text around Graphics

You can wrap text around graphics with PageMaker's Text Wrap command on the Element menu. The Text Wrap dialog box enables you to choose different options for wrapping text. Under Wrap Option, you decide whether the text should overlap the graphic, wrap around the rectangular space occupied by the graphic, or wrap around the irregular—nonrectangular—shape created by the graphic. You can set the Text Flow to wrap to the next column, wrap below the graphic, or wrap on both sides of the graphic, if it is narrower than the column. You also specify the Standoff, the distance between the graphic and the text. Manually wrapping graphics by creating different text blocks is an option, but using PageMaker's automatic text wrapping usually is more efficient (see Chapter 3).

Remember that the best approach is to build each page completely before going on to the next. You will find, however, that many approaches to laying out a page are available. The following figures show different methods of wrapping text around a graphic.

The first text-wrapping method forces the text to jump over the graphic. Follow these steps for this text-wrapping method:

1. To force the text to jump over one graphic, first position and size the graphic on the page (see fig. 6.24). Use the pointer tool to select the graphic.

Fig. 6.24. The graphic positioned and sized on the page.

2. Choose Text Wrap from the Element menu.

3. Select the icon for a rectangular graphic boundary, the middle icon in the top row (see fig. 6.25).

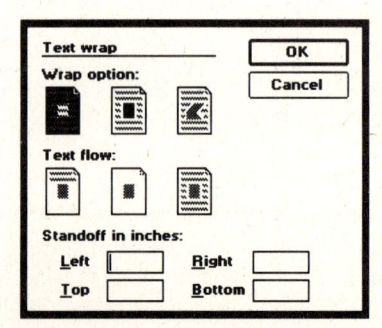

Fig. 6.25. The Text Wrap dialog box with the icon for a rectangular graphic boundary and the Standoff in inches set to zero.

4. Set the Text Flow icon for text jumping over the graphic, the middle icon in the second row.

5. In the Standoff in inches text boxes, type the amount of space that you want between the graphic and the text, the *graphic boundary*.

6. Using the Place command dialog box from the File menu, flow your text on the page. The text continues after the graphic (see fig. 6.26).

Fig. 6.26. The text jumping over the graphic.

The second text-wrapping method wraps text around a graphic. Follow these steps for this method:

1. Place and size the graphic in the column. Use the pointer tool to select the graphic (see fig. 6.27).

2. Choose Text Wrap from the Element menu.

3. Select the icon for a rectangular graphic boundary.

4. In the Standoff in inches text boxes, type the amount of space between the graphic and the text.

5. Set the Text Flow icon to wrap around the text (see fig. 6.28).

6. Place the text (see fig. 6.29).

By setting the Text Wrap option without a graphic selected, you set the default, which applies to all subsequently placed graphics.

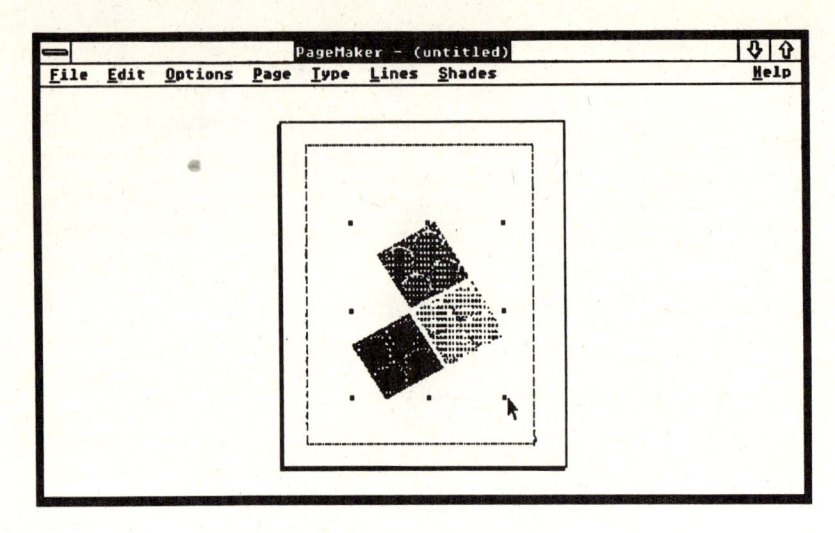

Fig. 6.27. *The graphic positioned and sized on the page.*

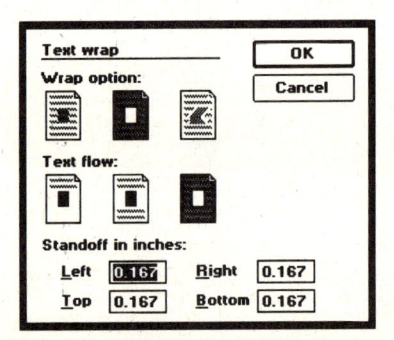

Fig. 6.28. *The Text Wrap dialog box with the icon selected for a rectangular graphic boundary, Standoff in Inches set, and Text Wrap set for wrapping around the graphic.*

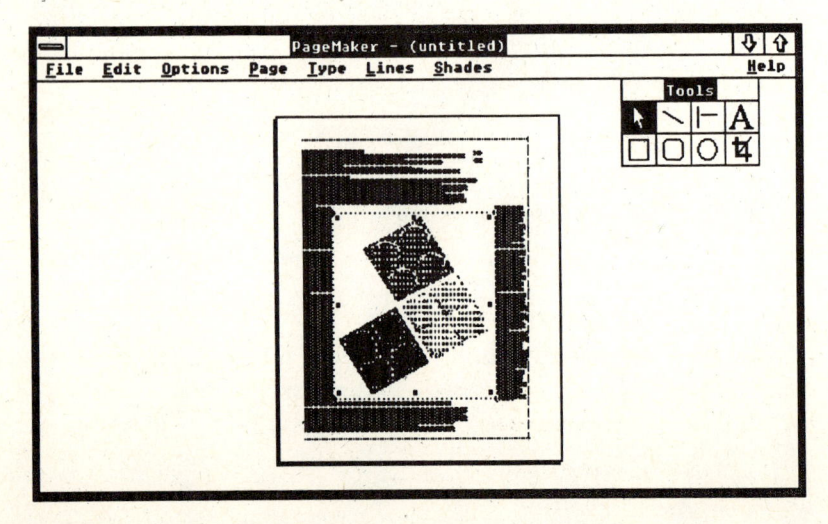

Fig. 6.29. *The text wrapped around the graphic.*

Creating a Custom-Shaped Graphic Boundary

All graphics in PageMaker have rectangular boundaries unless you customize the boundary around the graphic. A custom boundary can take any shape you want and can create interesting design options on the page.

To create a custom boundary, follow these steps:

1. Click on the graphic and highlight the Text Wrap command in the Element menu (see fig. 6.30).

2. Select the third Wrap Option, the rectangular boundary in the Text Wrap dialog box. Click on the last Text Flow option, which forces the text to wrap on all sides of the graphic (see fig. 6.31).

3. Click OK. Diamond-shaped handles appear around the graphic boundary (see fig. 6.32).

4. To change the shape of the boundary, drag the diamond-shaped handles to form a new shape (see fig. 6.33). You can add more diamond-shaped handles by clicking on the graphic boundary where you want the new handle to appear. To erase a handle, drag it on top of another handle.

5. After the custom boundary is in place, use the Text Flow option to choose whether you want the text to flow around part or all of the graphic (see fig. 6.34).

> ***Regulating Text Flow***
>
> **When changing the shape of the graphic boundary, hold down the space bar to stop text from flowing until all the boundaries have been readjusted.**

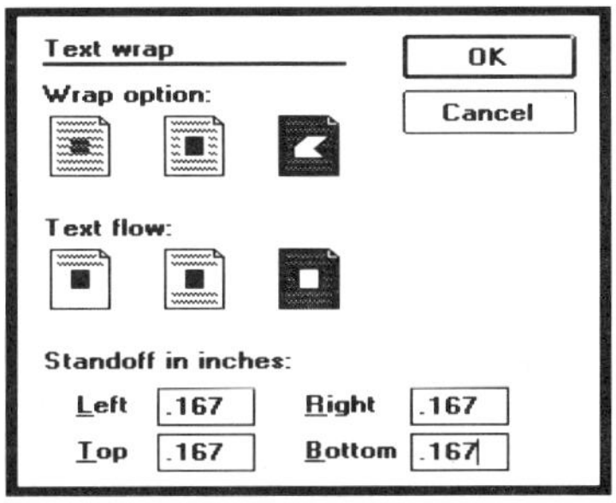

Fig. 6.30. *The Text Wrap options for the custom-shaped graphic.*

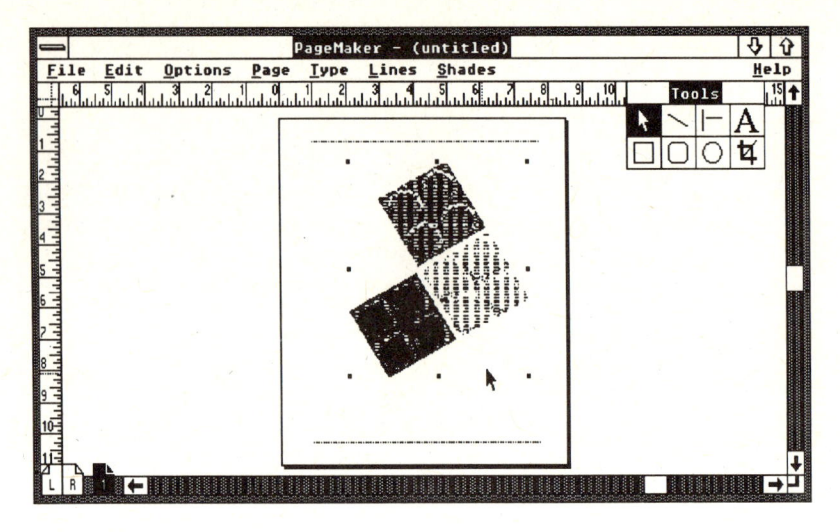

Fig. 6.31. A custom-shaped graphic.

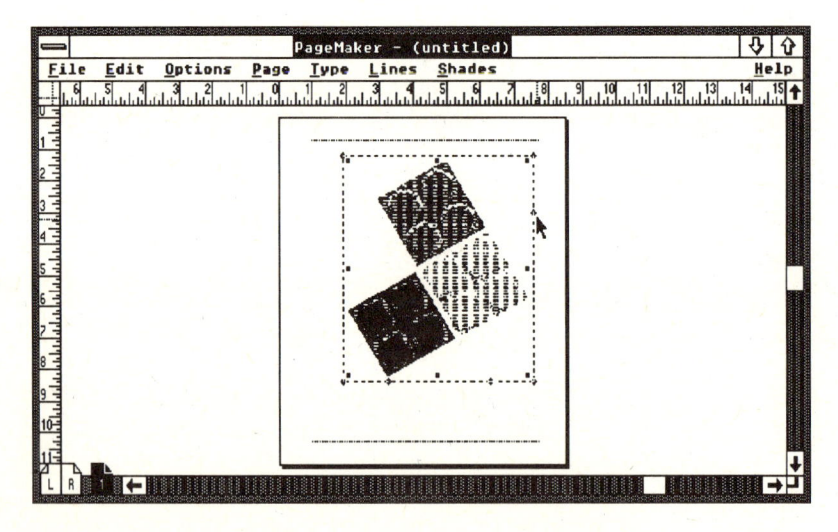

Fig. 6.32. Diamond-shaped handles around selected graphic.

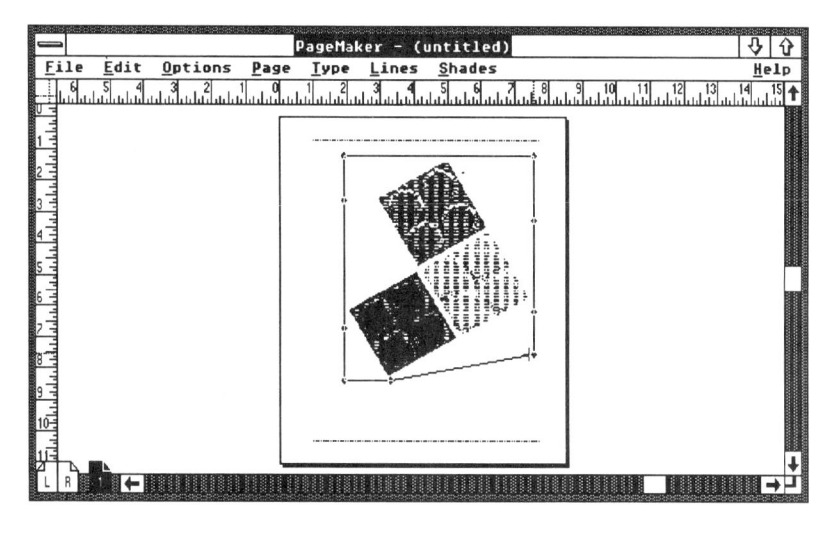

Fig. 6.33. Forming a new graphic shape.

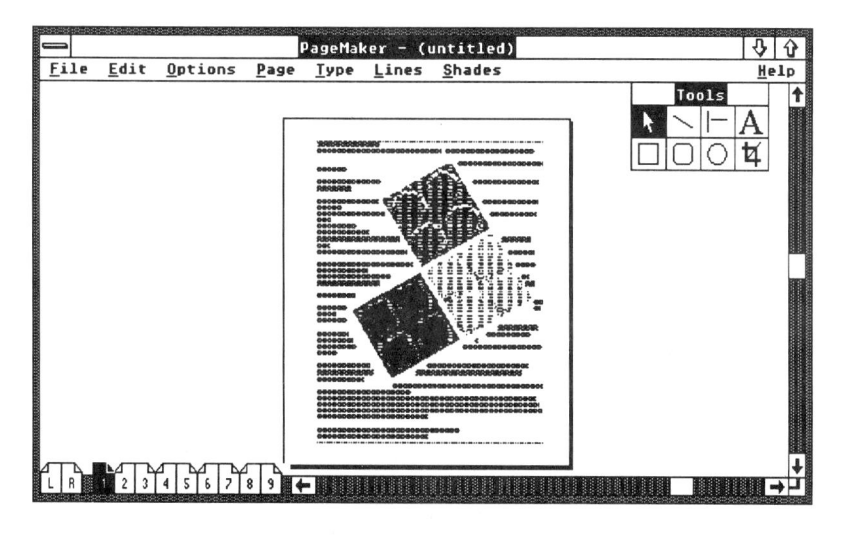

Fig. 6.34. Text wrapped around a custom-shaped graphic.

Using Inline Graphics

4.0 PageMaker 4.0 introduces the capability to position *inline graphics*, graphics that are part of the text and move with the text. This capability is useful for incorporating symbols as part of a sentence, as shown in figure 6.35, and for positioning figures next to captions when you want them to move with the text flow, as shown in figure 6.36.

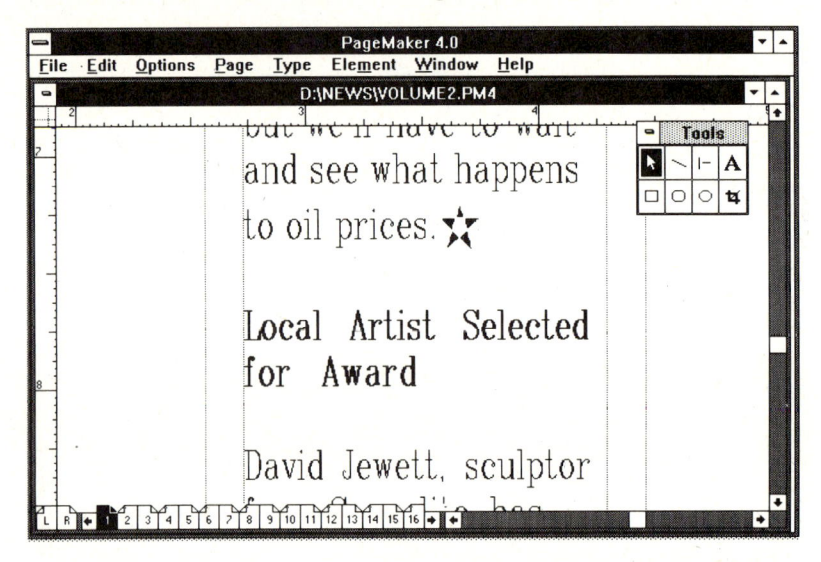

Fig. 6.35. Inline graphics can be symbols incorporated within a sentence.

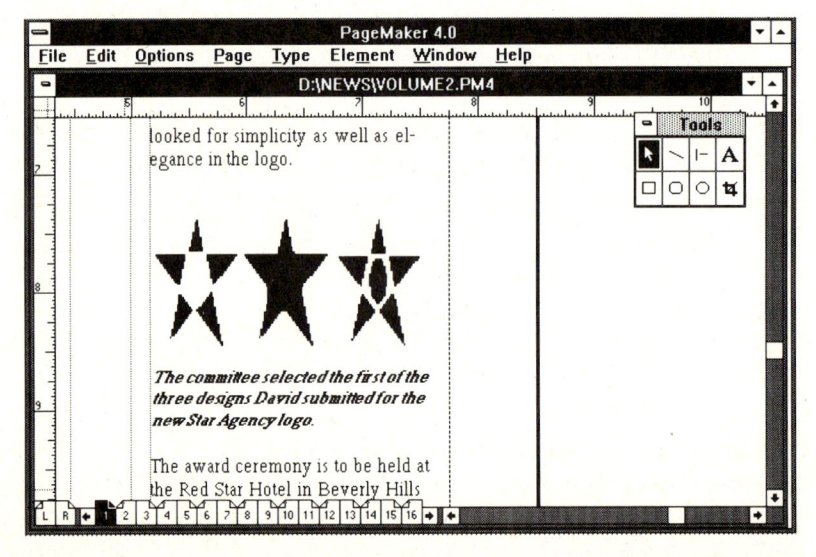

Fig. 6.36. Inline graphics can be figures above a caption and part of the text flow.

Creating an Inline Graphic

You can use three methods to create an inline graphic. The first method can be used in Layout view or in Story view and works with any graphic created using PageMaker's tools or a graphic that has been imported.

Follow these steps to use the first method:

1. Select a graphic that is already part of the PageMaker publication and choose Cut or Copy from the Edit menu.

2. Select the text tool and position the text insertion point in the text where you want the inline graphic to appear.

3. Choose Paste from the Edit menu.

The second method of creating an inline graphic is applicable only in Layout view and only to graphics that are imported into PageMaker.

Follow these steps to use the second method:

1. Select the text tool and position the text insertion point in the text where you want the inline graphic to appear.

2. Choose Place from the File menu.

3. Select the graphic you want to import as an inline graphic from the Place dialog box.

The third method can be used to import an inline graphic in Story view. The following steps comprise the third method:

1. Position the text insertion point in the text where you want the inline graphic to appear.

2. Choose Import from the Story menu.

3. Select the graphic you want to import as an inline graphic from the Import dialog box (see Chapter 4).

Inline graphics display handles when selected, and they can be scaled and cropped like any other graphic in Layout view. You can apply color to inline graphics and manipulate them through the Image Control command if they are paint or TIFF images. Story view is represented by a graphic symbol only and cannot be manipulated as a graphic unless you return to Layout view (see Chapter 4).

Inline graphics can be formatted like any text. You can use commands under the Type menu to set indents, leading, tracking, and kerning, as described in Chapter 5. You can adjust the baseline by dragging the graphic up or down with the pointer tool in Layout view, but you cannot drag an inline graphic from one line of text to another. To move an inline graphic, you must select it, choose the Cut command, then position the text insertion point at the new location, and choose Paste.

Including Symbols in Text

Special symbols commonly are embedded within text. Many software manuals, for example, use symbols to represent special keys outlined in boxes, such as the function keys and the Ctrl and Alt keys. PageMaker 4.0 enables you to insert inline graphics as part of the text flow so that they move when the text moves. This insertion is an alternative to creating the symbols as a font, and each method offers its own unique benefits.

If you want to insert the symbols as a graphic, use a graphics application to create them, or use PageMaker's built-in graphics tools if the symbols are simple lines, rectangles, or ovals. Scale the symbols to the desired sizes in the graphics application before importing them into PageMaker. You can scale graphics in the page layout application. If you scale graphics in the graphics application, however, graphics will be the same size every time you import, and you eliminate the inconvenience of repeatedly scaling the graphic.

To create a symbol or set of symbols as a font, you must use a font-generating application, such as Fontrix (Data Transforms Inc.) or Publisher's Type Foundry (Z-Soft). After the font is created and loaded into the system, you can insert the symbols in the text by typing the keyboard characters you assigned for each symbol and using the Font command from the Type menu to select the symbol font.

The advantage of creating the symbols as a font is that you can input them while typing in the word processor or the page layout program. You also can easily and consistently scale them through the type-scaling commands. In PageMaker 4.0, you can search and replace characters and fonts. If you set the symbol to the letter E, you can quickly type the text using the letter E as the symbol, and then search for the whole word E and replace it with the letter E in the symbol font.

Handling Figure Captions

In most cases, you want text blocks to be linked continuously throughout a publication, article, or story. Figure captions usually are an exception to this rule, unless you position the figures as inline graphics so that they flow with the text. If you do not want PageMaker to move figures and captions when you edit the text preceding the caption, the following three methods of separating captions from text are available:

- You can type each caption individually in PageMaker.

- You can use a word processor and type all the captions in a separate caption file. You then place that file as a stream separate from the rest of the text. This procedure is useful if you do not know exactly where you will put each figure in the final publication.

- You can type the captions into the main text file. When you place the text, use the Cut and Paste commands to separate the captions from the body of the text and make them individual unlinked blocks.

Chapter Summary

Now that you know what alternatives are available for adding graphics to a page, you can make decisions about using PageMaker or another program to create graphics. Chapter 10 offers more specific advice about making design specifications for graphics from diverse sources. Chapter 6 took you through the steps involved in laying out a publication, incorporating the information you learned in Chapters 3 through 5, and provided tips about using PageMaker's tools during the layout process.

Managing Large Documents and Linked Files

Not all documents produced with PageMaker are fliers and brochures. You also can produce large documents with PageMaker. This chapter contains information to help you create such publications. PageMaker 4.0 introduces the following advanced features that simplify the production of long documents and complex documents composed of large imported graphics:

- The link feature has been enhanced so that you can link external text and graphics files and specify whether the external file is dynamically linked. That way, the PageMaker publication reflects changes to the external file.

- The Book command enables you to join a series of separate PageMaker publications as a single document, so that you can print the whole series in one step and opt to have PageMaker number all pages sequentially from one publication to another.

- PageMaker 4.0 also can generate a table of contents and an index.

This chapter concludes with additional suggestions for organizing your disk files for large projects and work groups.

Managing Linked Text and Graphics Documents

4.0 PageMaker 4.0 introduces the option of linking external sources of text and graphics to the publication, so that changes in the external file are incorporated in the PageMaker version of the graphic or text when the publication is opened or updated through the Links command under the File menu.

With the linking feature, you also can control the size of a PageMaker publication. Scanned-image files, often stored at 300-dpi resolution, can be quite large, sometimes larger than 256K. Rather than including the full image in the publication, with PageMaker 4.0 you can show a low-resolution version of these images in the publication, then link the larger, external graphics file for use in printing.

Linking Graphic Files

4.0 When you use the Place command from the File menu to import a graphic into a publication, PageMaker checks the size of the graphic file. If the file is smaller than 64K, then the entire graphic is imported and stored as part of the PageMaker document. If the file is larger than 64K, PageMaker 4.0 displays a dialog box with the following message (see fig. 7.1):

```
The graphic in the document would occupy xxx KBytes in
the publication. Include complete copy in the
publication anyway?
```

(The actual size of the graphic appears where you see xxx above.)

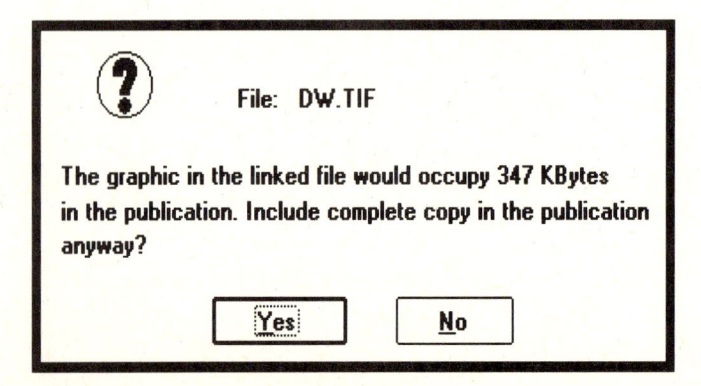

Fig. 7.1. The dialog box offering the Link option.

Chapter 7: Managing Large Documents and Linked Files **249**

If you choose Yes, the entire graphic is imported and stored as part of the PageMaker publication. The size of the PageMaker publication is increased by the size of the graphic. If you choose No, then PageMaker stores a low-resolution, bit-mapped, screen-display version of the graphic as part of the publication. The original graphic file is *linked* to the publication. When you print the publication, PageMaker looks on the disk for the original graphic file and prints it at high resolution. If PageMaker cannot find the linked file when you print the publication, it displays the message shown in figure 7.2.

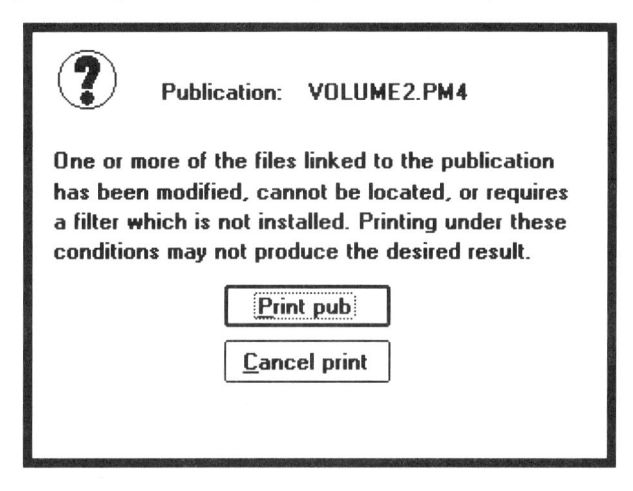

```
Publication:  VOLUME2.PM4

One or more of the files linked to the publication
has been modified, cannot be located, or requires
a filter which is not installed. Printing under these
conditions may not produce the desired result.

        [ Print pub ]
        [ Cancel print ]
```

Fig. 7.2. PageMaker looks for the scan file when printing the PageMaker publication.

If you choose to print, then PageMaker prints the publication using the low-resolution versions of the graphics files that are stored as part of the publication. If you want to be sure that the original, high-resolution versions of the graphics files are used, click Cancel and relink the large files, as described later.

Storing Linked Graphics Files

Store scanned-image files and other large graphic files in the same directory as your publication. If you copy the publication to another disk, copy the graphics files, too. Without the linked graphics files, the images print at low resolution, even on high-resolution printers.

Setting Default Link Options

You can set up the default for link options before importing graphics or text into a publication. If you choose the Link Options command from the Element menu when no publication is open, you can set the defaults for all new publications. If you choose the Link Options command when a publication is open and no graphics or text are selected, you can set the defaults for all new graphics placed in that publication (but this does not change the link options that have been set up for graphics that have already been placed in the publication). In either case, the Link Options dialog box is displayed (see fig. 7.3). (If you choose the Link Options command when a graphic or text is selected, you can set the linking options for that element only, as described later in this chapter.)

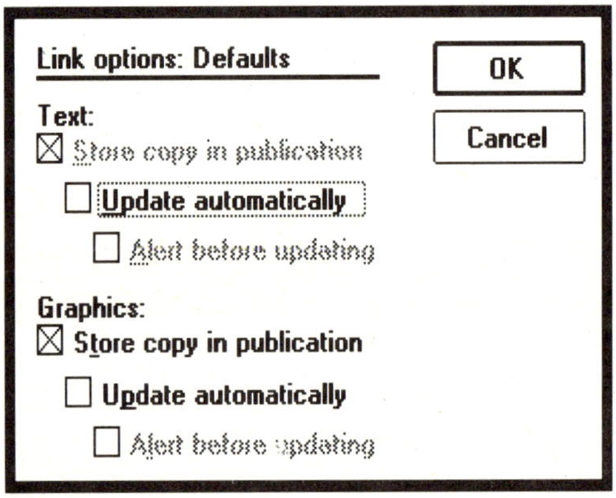

Fig. 7.3. The Link Options dialog box.

The Store Copy in Publication option is grayed out in the Link Options dialog box for text and EPS graphics because all imported text and EPS files are stored in full as part of the publication. You always can print the publication without access to the external files.

If you select Store Copy in Publication for graphics (and no graphics were selected when you opened the Link Options dialog box), then all graphics that are subsequently imported are stored in full as part of the publication, and you can print the publication without accessing the original graphics files. The PageMaker publication file size, however, will be larger if you store graphics as part of the publicaton rather than link imported graphics.

You can opt to update the text or graphics when you open a publication if the original file has been modified since first placing or last updating the imported document. If Update Automatically is not checked on the Link Options dialog box, changes to the original file are not reflected in the

PageMaker publication. If you select Update Automatically, you also may choose Alert Before Updating to have PageMaker display an alert box before updating a changed file. With the alert box, you can choose on a case-by-case basis whether to update each changed graphic or story.

Changes made through the Link Options dialog box when no text or graphics are selected do not affect the link options of text and graphics already imported and linked. Only new imports take on the new defaults.

If you choose the Link Options command when an imported graphic or story is selected, the options you choose apply to that graphic or story only. This process is the same as clicking the Link Options button in the Links dialog box, described later in this chapter.

Checking or Changing Link Settings

Use the Links command under the File menu to view and manage the linkages in a publication. The Links dialog box (see fig. 7.4) lists all imported documents and the page on which they appear in the publication. This dialog box lists all documents—text and graphic files—imported into the PageMaker publication, giving their name, file type, and the page number on which they appear.

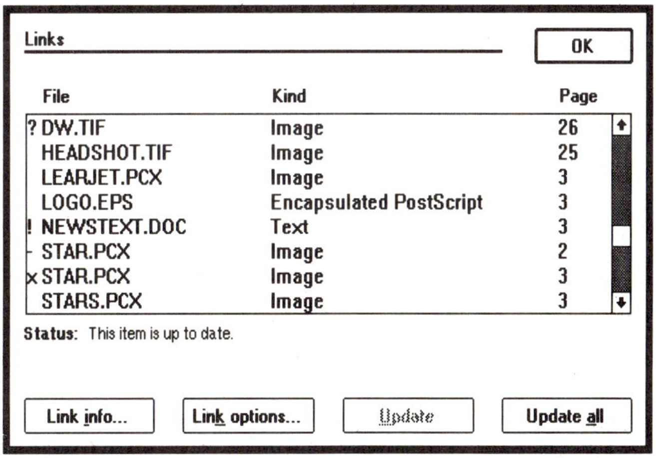

```
Links                                              OK

   File              Kind                    Page
 ? DW.TIF            Image                    26
   HEADSHOT.TIF      Image                    25
   LEARJET.PCX       Image                     3
   LOGO.EPS          Encapsulated PostScript   3
 ! NEWSTEXT.DOC      Text                      3
 - STAR.PCX          Image                     2
 x STAR.PCX          Image                     3
   STARS.PCX         Image                     3

Status:  This item is up to date.

  [ Link info... ]  [ Link options... ]  [ Update ]  [ Update all ]
```

Fig. 7.4. The Links dialog box shows one of each indicator type.

If no symbol appears before the file name, the item is updated—it has not been changed since last updated or imported. Table 7.1 lists the link status indicators and their meanings. The link status indicators are displayed at the left of each appropriate file name.

**Table 7.1
Link Status Indicators**

Status Indicator	Definition
?	A question mark indicates that the file is missing. It has been moved, deleted or updated, and PageMaker cannot find it. If you click the file and then click Link Info at the bottom of the Links dialog box, you can redirect PageMaker to the moved or renamed file, as described later.
+	A plus sign indicates that the external file has been modified since you put it in or updated it in the PageMaker publication. If you select the file and click Update in the Links dialog box, or if you click Update All, then the modified version of the file is brought into or linked to the PageMaker publication.
–	A minus sign or hyphen indicates that the external file has been modified since being placed or updated in the PageMaker publication, but you have instructed PageMaker not to update this element. Select the file and choose Link Options on the Links dialog box to change to automatic updating, or select the element and choose Update to update the selected element.
!	An exclamation point indicates that the internal and external versions of the file have been updated since being placed or updated in the PageMaker publication. If you select the file and click Update on the Links dialog box, the external version of the file replaces the internal version, and changes made to the internal copy are discarded.
x	An x indicates that the publication is not storing a complete copy of the external file; that is, the publication is storing a low-resolution version of a high-resolution external document that must be available when printing.

Chapter 7: Managing Large Documents and Linked Files 253

Status Indicator	*Definition*
*	An asterisk next to a file type (in the Kind column) indicates that the file needs a filter to be printed, and PageMaker cannot locate the filter. Run SETUP.EXE in the PM4 directory (as described in Chapter 2) to copy the appropriate filters from the original set of PageMaker installation disks.

The Page column lists the page numbers on which the imported element appears, or the column may show one of the following indicators:

- Page #?   The linked inline graphic is in a story that has not been placed on a page yet; that is, the story is in the Story Editor (described in Chapter 3). (Inline graphics are described in Chapter 6.)

- LM   The linked item is on the left master page.

- RM   The linked item is on the right master page.

- PB   The linked item is on the pasteboard.

- OV   The linked inline graphic is a part of the text overflow in a text block that has not been fully flowed.

- UP   The linked text element is an open story that has not yet been placed.

Clicking the Link Info button in the Links dialog box displays another dialog box detailing information about the selected file (see fig. 7.5). To display this dialog box, you can select a file and click the Link Info button, or simply double-click on a file name in the Links dialog box. You also can display this dialog box for a selected object by choosing the Link Info command from the Element menu.

The left side of the Link Info dialog box lists the files on the system that can be linked to a PageMaker publication. You can rejoin or change the link to the currently selected element by double-clicking on a different file name, clicking once on a file name and then clicking Link, or by typing a different file name in the Name text box on the right side of the dialog box. (You must type the full path if the file's drive and directory do not appear in the Path space above the Name text box.) The file you select becomes the new link to replace the element selected when you open this dialog box.

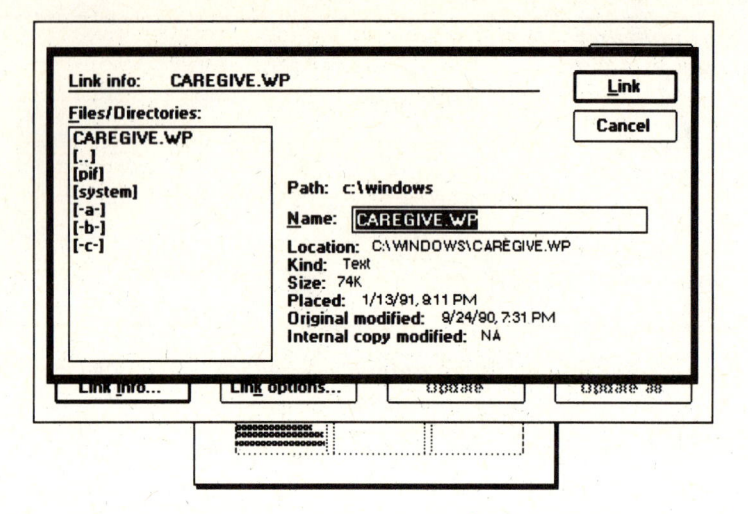

Fig. 7.5. The Link Info dialog box.

Other information in the dialog box includes the following:

Location	Drive, directory, and name of the file
Kind	Type of file
Size	Size of the file, or NA if not known
Placed	Date and time the file was last placed in the publication
Original modified	Date and time the external file was last modified
Internal copy modified	Date and time the element was last modified in the publication

Changing Link Options for Individual Files

When you click Link Options in the Links dialog box, you get a dialog box that enables you to change the link options for the currently selected graphic (see fig. 7.6) or text file (see fig. 7.7) only. You get this same dialog box if you choose the Link Options command from the Element menu when a text block or imported graphic is selected. This dialog box is an abbreviated version of the dialog box that you get when you choose the Link options command from the Element menu to change the defaults when no text or graphic files are selected.

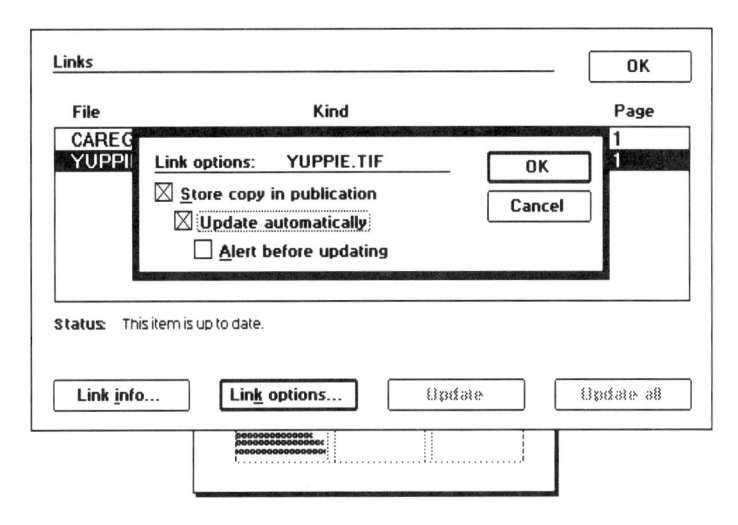

Fig. 7.6. The Link Options dialog box when a graphic is selected.

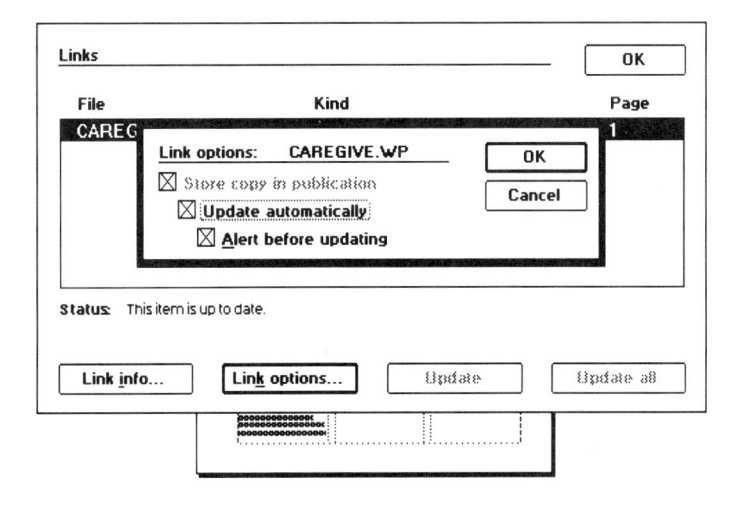

Fig. 7.7. The Link Options dialog box when text is selected.

The entries in these dialog boxes were described in detail earlier in this chapter.

Updating Linked Files

If you click Update in the Links dialog box, you replace the current internal version of a file with the latest external version. This option is dimmed if the two versions are already up-to-date. If the internal and the external versions are modified, PageMaker displays a warning asking you to confirm that you want to discard the changed internal version.

Clicking Update All updates the internal version of all elements that now are not up-to-date *and* for which Update Automatically has been checked in the Link Options dialog box. (Links for which automatic update has been turned off must still be updated individually.)

Updating Text Files with Inline Graphics

Caution: If you link a text file and then add inline graphics to that file in PageMaker, you lose those graphics if you update the text file with a changed external file. If you expect to be updating external text files, don't import inline graphics until you update the internal text file through the Links command for the last time. Inline graphics are described in detail in Chapter 6.

Using the Book Command

PageMaker 4.0 introduces the Book command, which enables you to associate a number of separate PageMaker files as a single, long publication. PageMaker uses this book list to assemble all parts of the publication in printing, in numbering pages, and in generating an index or a table of contents.

To create a book list, open the first publication in the series. This publication should be the table of contents, the front matter, or the cover page of the publication. Choose Book from the File menu. The Book Publication List dialog box lists the books on the right and all directories and PageMaker publications on the left (see fig. 7.8). To add a PageMaker publication to the book list, double-click on the publication name in the left window, or click once on the name and then click Insert.

Newly selected publications are added at the end of the book list. You can rearrange the order of the publications by clicking on individual file names and then clicking Move Up or Move Down. You can remove a publication from the book list by selecting the name and clicking Remove. (This maneuver does not delete the file from the disk; it only removes the file name from the list.)

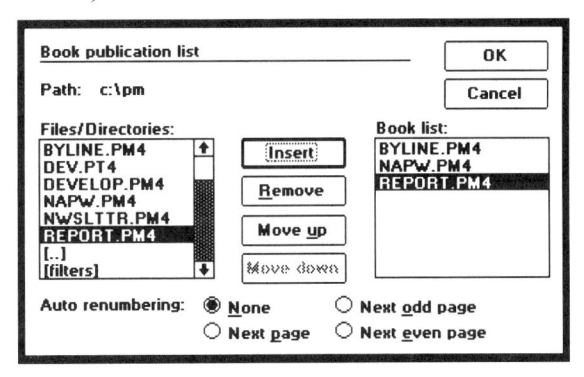

Fig. 7.8. The Book Publication List dialog box.

When you choose Print, Create Index, or Create TOC (described later in this chapter) with a publication open, PageMaker prints the index or generates the table of contents for the entire book—including all publications in the book list—and numbers the pages according to the sequence of the list. When the book list is associated only with the first publication in the book, the entire book is assembled only when the first publication is open and you use one of the book-related commands. You can generate an index or table of contents for individual chapters by opening any part of the book except the first file.

Note that the Book feature changes page numbers if you do not check Restart Page Numbering in the Page Setup dialog box, as described in Chapter 3. Check the Restart Page Numbering option only if you want the page numbering of each section of the publication always to begin with the page number specified in the Start Page # dialog box for that section (displayed when you use the New command from the File menu to begin a new publication, or whenever you choose the Page Setup command from the File menu).

The Book feature, however, does not insert pages to fill gaps between sections; you must insert blank pages at the end of chapters that end on odd-numbered pages; for example, if the next chapter starts on an even-numbered page and you want to print a sheet for each page number. Chapter 3 describes how to insert blank pages.

Creating a Table of Contents

4.0 PageMaker 4.0 introduces a new feature for generating a table of contents. You can identify lines or paragraphs within the text to be included in the table of contents and then generate the list including page numbers. You can generate a table of contents for a single publication or for a series of publications that are associated through the Book command. The table of contents becomes a new story that you can place and edit in your publication.

You can select lines to be included in the table of contents after you finish building a publication, but the process of planning an outline usually precedes the writing (even if the outline itself changes during the writing process). If you know the outline before you start building the PageMaker publication, you can determine how many of the outline heading levels you want to include in the table of contents and set them up for inclusion through the style sheet specifications (as described in Chapter 5).

Identifying Table of Contents Entries

To include a line or paragraph in the table of contents, select the text tool from the toolbox and position the text insertion point in the paragraph. Choose the Paragraph command from the Type menu, and check Include in Table of Contents in the Paragraph Specifications dialog box (see fig. 7.9).

Alternatively, you can make the table of contents attribute a part of a style by using the Define Styles command to enter the Paragraph Specifications dialog box, as described in Chapter 5.

If you want to remove an entry from the table of contents, you can uncheck the Include in Table of Contents box for selected paragraphs or styles. Other entries on this dialog box are described in Chapter 5.

Generating a Table of Contents

If you know how many pages the table of contents requires, insert the appropriate number of blank pages at the beginning of the document before generating the table of contents. You also can put the table of contents in a separate publication that's linked to the rest of the document through the Book command (described earlier in this chapter), and number the table of contents pages with Roman numerals (through the New or Page Setup commands described in Chapter 3). You also may generate the table of contents twice: once to place the table of contents and determine how many pages it requires, a second time to generate correct page numbering. Plan on generating a printed version of the table of contents at least twice: once for proofing, followed by editing before the second and (possibly) final generation.

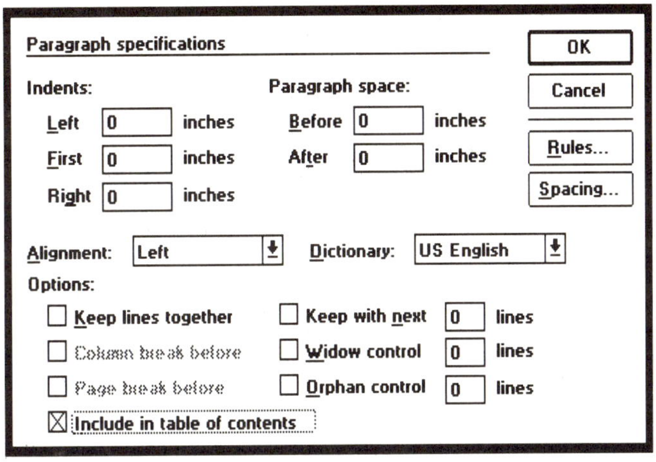

Fig. 7.9. The Paragraph Specifications dialog box with Include in Table of Contents checked.

If you want the table of contents to be a separate PageMaker publication, use the New command from the File menu before you generate the table of contents. Save the new publication as the table of contents, and use the Book command (described earlier in this chapter) to select all the publications that are to be included in the table of contents. Generate the table of contents with this new publication open.

To generate the table of contents, open the publication and choose Create TOC from the Options menu. If the table of contents is to cover a series of publications, the open publication should be the one that associates all related publications through the Book command, as described earlier in this chapter.

When the Create Table of Contents dialog box is first displayed (see fig. 7.10), PageMaker assigns the title "Contents" at the top of the table of contents text, but you can change this title to any title you want (up to 30 characters long) or delete the title entirely. You also can opt to replace the existing table of contents (if you have generated one previously), or generate the new table of contents without replacing the old one. (This capability is helpful if you want to compare the two tables of contents.)

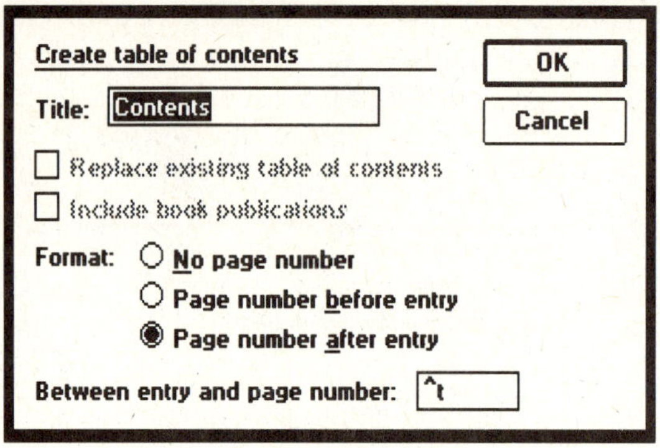

Fig. 7.10. The Create Table of Contents dialog box.

If your publication is part of a book list (as described earlier in this chapter), you can opt to generate the table of contents for the current publication only or for all the publications in the book list.

You can format the table of contents by choosing not to print page numbers, to print page numbers before each entry, or to print page numbers after each entry. You also can set the character to appear between the entry and the page number, usually a tab, typed as a caret and a lower-case letter *t* (^t) in the dialog box.

Click OK to generate the table of contents. PageMaker then searches the publications for table of contents entries, collects them, and formats them. Depending on the publication's size and the number of table of contents entries, this process can take several minutes.

If you replace the existing table of contents, that text is replaced in the current publication. If you don't replace the current table of contents, or if this is the first time you are generating the table, PageMaker generates the table, and the mouse pointer changes to a loaded text icon if you are in Layout view. You can place the table of contents in the publication just as you place imported text, as described in Chapter 3. If you are in Story view when you generate the table of contents, PageMaker opens a new story window for the table of contents. Choose Place from the File menu to return to Layout view and place the table of contents as a new story.

When generating a table of contents, PageMaker creates special styles to use if the paragraphs to be included in the table of contents are formatted using a style sheet. With generated style names, PageMaker precedes the original paragraph style name with `TOC`. The default font for table of contents is Times Roman, with the size and type style (bold, italic, or normal) matching the original paragraph. The tab stops for each heading level are copied from the original paragraphs in the text.

After generating the table of contents, you can revise the table's style by using the Define Styles command as described in Chapter 5. If you change the name of the generated styles (or import TOC styles from another publication), however, PageMaker reverts to generating the standard styles when you regenerate the table of contents.

Editing a Generated Table of Contents

You can edit the text of a generated table of contents the same way you edit any text in PageMaker. The better method, however, is to make any changes to the table of contents by editing the headings in the publication and through the Paragraph or Define Styles commands, then regenerate the table of contents.

The table of contents shows page numbers in the format set up through the Numbers option in the Page Setup dialog box (displayed with the New command or the Page Setup command from the File menu as described in Chapter 3).

Production Notes in a Table of Contents

You can use the table of contents feature to log production notes during work in progress. This method is especially useful when working in a team, so that you can distribute the printed list of missing or unfinished parts and make sure that each person knows what holes he or she must fill.

Production notes that are appropriate for printing in the table of contents of a work-in-progress include general comments about missing or unfinished elements, such as

```
Figure 2.3 to be created
More text to come from author
```

Create a special style (as described in Chapter 5) for production notes and set it up to be included in the table of contents. Type the production notes at points throughout the text where elements are missing or unfinished. When you generate the table of contents, the production notes print out under each section heading, including the page numbers. Delete the production notes when you add the missing elements, before printing the final document.

Creating an Index

PageMaker 4.0 introduces a new index feature that automates indexing to the greatest extent possible. If you have created an index manually—by finding the words in the final manuscript, typing the words and the page numbers, and then sorting them somehow—you can appreciate PageMaker's capability to sort the entries and assign page numbers.

The process of creating the index entries in the first place, however, is no trivial task. Creating a good index requires time as well as forethought. Some rules to good indexing follow:

> **Be consistent.** If you are going to make entries under "soups," for example, don't refer to "broths" separately. Instead, if you want to list the word "broths" in the index, refer the reader to the listings under "soups." Also, be consistent in spelling and capitalization of entries. If you index some entries as "soups" and others as "Soups," they appear as two separate entries in the final index.
>
> **Be concise.** If you want to list 10 different references to "soups," don't repeat the same 10 listings under synonyms such as "broths." Refer the reader to one listing only.
>
> **Be comprehensive.** Make sure that the index refers to all the topics a reader may want to look up.

The following sections describe the *mechanics* of indexing in PageMaker.

Identifying Index Entries

You can create index entries in Layout view or in Story view, but Story view offers the advantage of the Find command on the Edit menu so that you can search for words to index. You also can see index markers in Story view, to see which words have been indexed.

To identify an index entry, select a word or phrase to be indexed, or position the text insertion point next to the topic in the text and choose Index Entry from the Options menu. If a word or phrase is selected, the Add Index Entry dialog box (see fig. 7.11) displays the selected phrase in the level 1 topic field. If the text insertion point is positioned in the text but no text is selected, the level 1 field is empty. If the text insertion point is not positioned, the page reference option is dimmed.

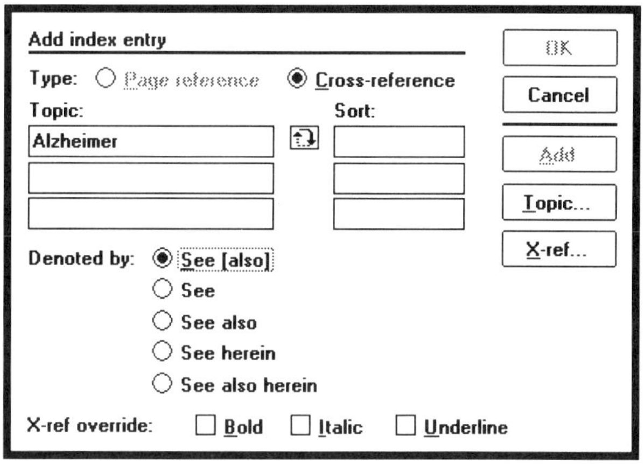

Chapter 7: Managing Large Documents and Linked Files **263**

Fig. 7.11. The Add Index Entry dialog box with Cross-Reference selected.

The two Type options give you a choice between adding a topic with a page number reference or a topic with a cross-reference. The rest of the options, except the Topic and Sort fields, change depending on which option is selected. (These options are described in the following section.)

The Topic option includes three fields to accommodate three heading levels. The topic you type or display in the first heading level field will be indexed in alphabetical sequence with all other level 1 headings in the index. There must be an entry in the first heading level if you want to type a topic in the second heading level field. Level 2 headings will be indexed in alphabetical sequence below the level 1 headings with which they are associated. Similarly, there must be level 1 and level 2 entries if you want to make a level 3 entry, and level 3 headings will be indexed below the level 2 headings with which they are associated. You can edit or type text in any of the three fields, or you can position the cursor in a field and click the Topic button to choose from a list of topics already set up for this publication. (The Topic button is discussed later in this chapter.)

Fast Index Entry

To create an index entry without going through the Add Index Entry dialog box, select the text you want as the level 1 index entry (in Layout view or Story view) and press Ctrl-Shift-; (Control-Shift-semicolon). PageMaker creates an index entry with default indexing options, shown when you open the Add Index Entry dialog box.

You can click on the looped arrow icon at the right of the level 1 topic field to move topics from one level to another.

You can make entries in the Sort fields to specify sorting different from the spelling shown in the topic list. For example, if a topic starts with a number, such as "2 megabytes," it is sorted as a symbol and appears at the beginning of any alphabetical list. You can force the "2 megabytes" entry to sort under "T" by typing *two* in the Sort box next to the heading. You also should use the Sort boxes to set initial-cap entries to sort with lowercase entries as appropriate. (Otherwise, "soups" and "Soups" appear as two entries.)

You also can use the Sort fields to force words with accents to sort in the same order as words without accents. Normally, PageMaker sorts words with accent marks to follow the same word without accents. For example, "elan" sorts in front of and separate from "élan." To force "elan" and "élan" to sort as the same word, you can type *elan* in the sort box next to the "élan" index entry.

Whether you are creating a page reference or a cross-reference, you can click OK to close the dialog box and record the changes to the index, click Cancel to close the dialog box without recording any changes to the index, or click Add to record the current entry without closing the dialog box. You also can select from a list of index topics by clicking the Topic button, as described later in the chapter.

Selecting Page Reference Options

If you select the Page Reference option in the Add Index Entry dialog box, the dialog box displays five options for identifying the range of pages that cover the topic, plus the option of setting these particular page numbers in bold, italic, or underline (to distinguish them from other page numbers listed under the same topic). Figure 7.12 shows the Add Index Entry dialog box with the Page Range options listed.

The Page Range options make it easy for PageMaker to determine the page range and adjust the range when page breaks change:

- Click Current Page if the topic is mentioned on one page only.

- Click To Next Style Change if the topic ends when the paragraph style changes. This option is useful if the next style change indicates a new heading, but you need to be cautious in using this option if the next style is a figure caption, for example, or some other style that does not end the topic. In the latter case, use To Next Use of Style instead.

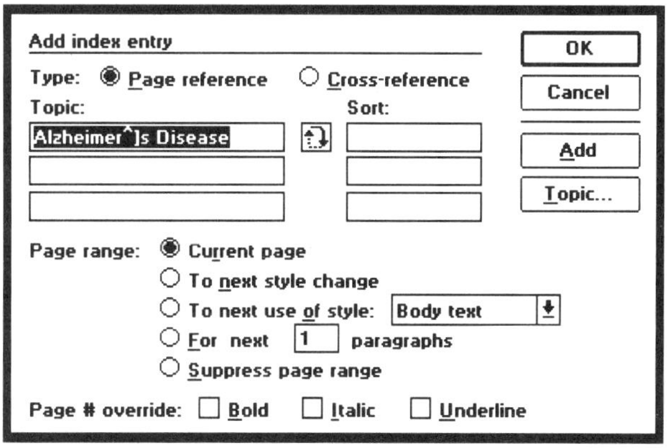

Chapter 7: Managing Large Documents and Linked Files 265

Fig. 7.12. The Page Range options after selecting Page Reference.

- Click To Next Use of Style and then click the arrow to the right of style name to display and select from a drop-down list the style name that marks a change of topic.

- Click For Next __ Paragraphs and enter the number of paragraphs that mention the topic. This option is less reliable than the preceding two options because you must update the number of paragraphs in this dialog box if editing adds or deletes paragraphs in the text.

- Click Suppress Page Range when you want to create a major topic that prints on a line of its own without page references, above a series of level 2 headings that do have page references, or cross-references.

You can select any number of the Page # Override options to distinguish the current page numbers from other page numbers that reference the same topic. If the style for the index is normal, clicking Italic makes these page numbers print in italic. If the style for the index is italic, however, clicking Italic makes these page numbers print normal.

Setting Topics and Page Numbers Differently

If you want the topic to print as normal text and *all* the page numbers to print in italic, click Italic once, when you make the first index entry; this setting becomes the default for all subsequent entries unless you change it again. You should make this decision before starting the indexing process. Otherwise, you must edit each index entry individually if you change your mind.

Selecting Cross-Reference Options

If you select the Cross-Reference option in the Add Index Entry dialog box, the dialog box displays five options to denote the phrasing of the cross-reference and the option of setting this particular cross-reference in bold, italic, or underline (again see fig. 7.11). The five options for denoting phrasing are listed as follows:

See [Also] is the default setting that enables PageMaker to choose the phrasing. PageMaker then uses See if no page number references are under this topic, or See Also to refer readers to the current entries and the entries in the cross-reference.

See Herein refers the reader to the other level 2 or level 3 entries under the current topic.

See Also Herein refers the reader to the page references in the main entry as well as the other level 2 or level 3 entries under this topic.

As with page number references, you can select any number of the X-ref Override options to distinguish the current page numbers from other page numbers that reference the same topic. For example, if the style for the index is normal, clicking Italic makes these reference topics print in italic. If the style for the index is italic, however, clicking Italic makes these topics print normal.

Selecting the Topic button enables you to choose from a list of topics under which this cross-reference will be indexed, and the X-ref button enables you to choose from a list of topics to be referred to in the cross-reference.

Selecting Topics from a List

When you click the Topic button in the Add Index Entry dialog box, you see the Select Topic dialog box (see fig. 7.13). You get a similar dialog box (see fig. 7.14) when you click the X-ref button in the Add Index Entry dialog box when Cross-Reference is selected. Use these dialog boxes to select a topic from a list of existing topics rather than type one. This way, you ensure that the spelling, case, and phrasing is identical to other entries.

You can use the scroll bars to scroll through the list of topics. You also can select the section of the alphabet you want to view by clicking the arrow at the right of the current section and choosing from the drop-down Topic Section list, or clicking Next Section to view the next alphabetical section that contains topic entries.

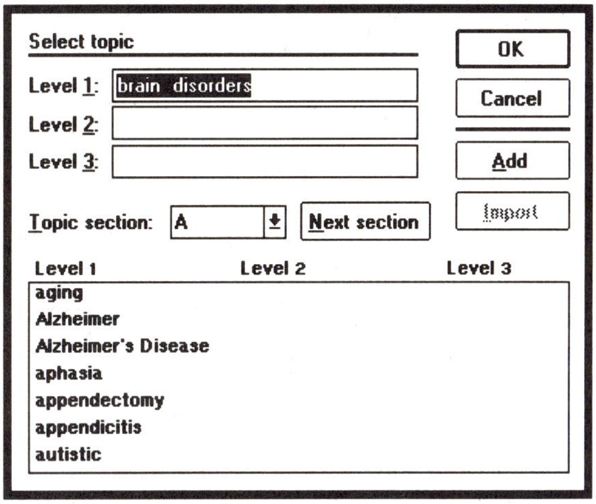

Fig. 7.13. The Select Topic dialog box.

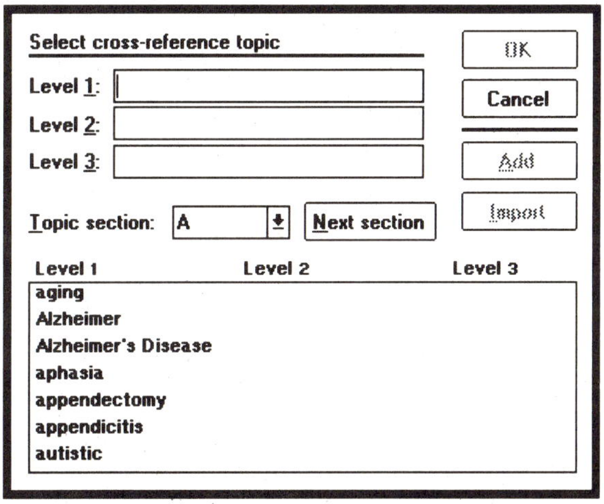

Fig. 7.14. The Select Cross-Reference Topic dialog box.

Topics you choose here are assigned the page number of the current text insertion point if Page Reference is selected in the Add Index Entry dialog box. The topics are cross-referenced if Cross-Reference is selected and you click the Topic button in the Add Index Entry dialog box. The topics become the topics being referred to (that is, "See" or "See also" topics) if Cross-Reference is selected and you click the X-ref button in the Add Index Entry dialog box.

To choose a topic from the Select Topic dialog box, highlight the desired topic and click OK. PageMaker returns you to the Add Index Entry dialog box and inserts the selected topic in the Topic edit boxes. If you choose a topic and click Add, PageMaker adds the topic as an index entry at the current text insertion point (for page references) or as a cross-reference entry, and keeps the Select Topic dialog box open so that you can add more topic references at the same insertion point in the text.

Click Import in the Select Topic dialog box to import the topic list from the indexes of every other publication in the book list associated with the current publication. This feature helps ensure consistency. Only topics you select (and press Add or OK) appear in the index of the current publication.

> ### Adding New Level 2 or 3 Entries
> You can type new level 2 and level 3 entries in the Add Index Entry dialog box, then click the Topic button to display the Select Topic dialog box. Select the level 1 topic and hold the Ctrl key when you click OK. Even if the level 1 topic in the Topic list showed level 2 entries, only the level 1 topic is entered in the Add Index Entry dialog box, retaining the level 2 and level 3 entries you typed.

Editing the Index

If you are new to indexing, then plan to generate the index more than once to refine the entries until the final index is as consistent, concise, and comprehensive as you can make it. You can add, change, delete, and reorganize entries through the Show Index command or by working directly in Story view.

Using the Show Index Command

You always can generate and print the index, as described in the following section, but you can save time in the first round of edits by using the Show Index command from the Options menu, which lists all topics and page references or cross-references (see fig. 7.15). The index includes entries for all publications in the book list. To view the index entries for the current publication only, press the Ctrl key as you choose Show Index from the menu.

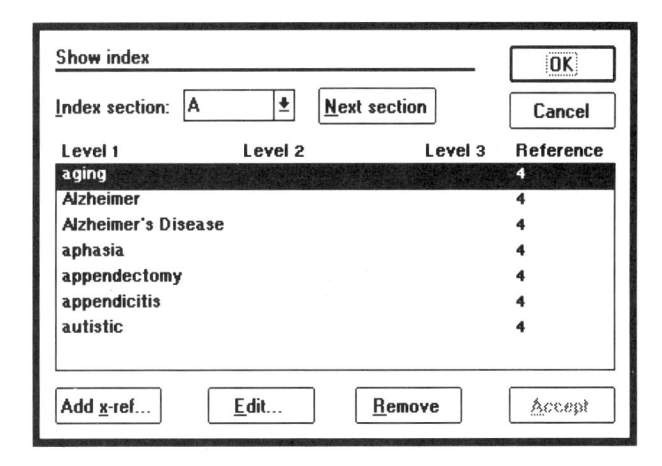

```
Show index                                    OK
Index section: A  ▼  Next section            Cancel
Level 1        Level 2         Level 3      Reference
aging                                        4
Alzheimer                                    4
Alzheimer's Disease                          4
aphasia                                      4
appendectomy                                 4
appendicitis                                 4
autistic                                     4

Add x-ref...   Edit...    Remove       Accept
```

Fig. 7.15. The Show Index dialog box.

The Show Index dialog box shows three levels of index entries and their page numbers. The page number column also may list one of five codes for text not placed on numbered pages:

- PB   Text is on the pasteboard.
- LM   Text is on the left master page.
- RM   Text is on the right master page.
- OV   Text flows beyond the margins in Layout view.
- US   Text is in an unplaced story in Story view.

You can use the scroll bars to scroll through the index. You also can select the section of the alphabet you want to view by choosing from the drop-down Index Section menu, or click on Next Section to view the next alphabetical section that contains index entries.

When you click the Add X-ref button in the Show Index dialog box, PageMaker displays the Add Index Entry dialog box. This dialog box is the same as the Add Index Entry dialog box described earlier, but the Page Reference option is grayed out. You cannot add page reference entries through the Show Index command—only cross-references.

When you select an index entry by highlighting it in the Show Index dialog box and then click the Edit button, PageMaker displays the Edit Index Entry dialog box. This dialog box is the same as the Add Index Entry dialog box described earlier.

When you select an index entry by highlighting it in the Show Index dialog box and then click the Remove button, the page reference entry is removed from the index but the *topic* remains in the index. You can remove unreferenced entries when you generate the index using the Create Index command, described later in this chapter.

You can click Accept to save the changes to the index without closing the dialog box.

Shortcuts in the Show Index Dialog Box

PageMaker offers five keyboard shortcuts for deleting and restoring index entries through the Show Index dialog box.

Two shortcuts reverse your recent actions: Press Alt and click the Add X-ref button to delete all entries added since last choosing Accept or opening the Show Index dialog box. Press Alt and click the Remove button to restore all entries deleted since last choosing Accept or opening the dialog box.

Three shortcuts enable you to remove index entries globally: Press Ctrl-Alt and click Remove to delete all page references. Press Ctrl-Shift and click Remove to delete all cross-references. Press Ctrl-Alt-Shift and click Remove to remove all index entries.

Working in Story View

PageMaker stores an index marker next to each entry, and these markers are displayed in Story view as small white diamonds in black squares (see fig. 7.16). You can cut, copy, paste, or delete index entries as you would any text by selecting the index marker in Story view and using the commands for cutting, copying, pasting, or clearing under the Edit menu (or their keyboard shortcuts), as described in Chapters 3 and 4.

You can change an individual entry by selecting the index marker in Story view and choosing the Index Entry command. You can change entries in the dialog box as described in the preceding section.

You can search for index markers in Story view by using the Find command and searching for a caret and a semicolon (^;).

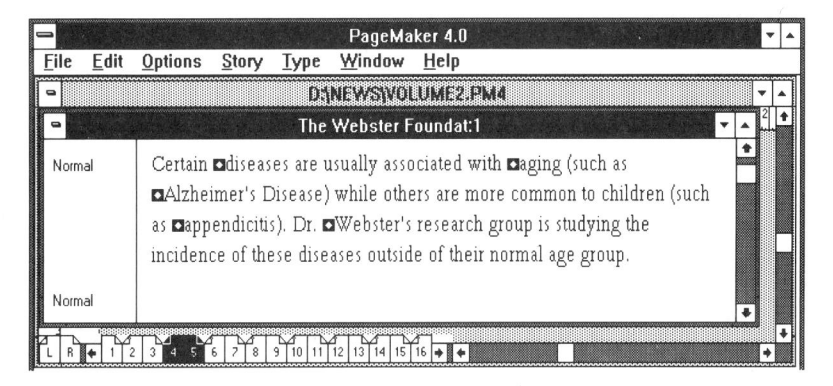

Fig. 7.16. Story view shows index markers as black-and-white diamonds.

Generating an Index

After you create, review, and edit your index entries, use the Create Index command from the Options menu. Using this command generates the index as text that you can place on pages in the PageMaker publication and print. No matter how much you edit the index using the methods described in the preceding sections, plan on generating a printed version of the index at least twice—once for proofing, followed by more editing before the second and (possibly) final generation.

If you want the index to be a separate PageMaker publication, use the New command from the File menu before generating the index. Save the new publication as the index, and use the Book command (described earlier in this chapter) to select all the publications that are to be included in the index. Generate the index with this new publication open.

When the Create Index dialog box is first displayed (see fig. 7.17), PageMaker assigns the title "Index," which appears at the top of the index text, but you can edit this title to any title you want (up to 30 characters) or delete the title. You also can opt to replace the existing index. (If you are generating a second index without replacing the old one, include a version number as part of the title so that you know which one is more recent.)

If your publication is part of a book list (as described earlier in this chapter), you can opt to generate the index for the current publication only or check Include Book Publications to generate the index for all the publications in the book list.

Part I: The Production Process with PageMaker

Fig. 7.17. The Create Index dialog box.

Check Remove Unreferenced Topics to remove topics without page numbers or cross-references. Unreferenced topics can develop when you import topics from another index but do not use them, or when you delete page references through the Story Editor or the Show Index command. Checking this option does not remove the entries in which you elect to Suppress Page Reference.

You can format the index by clicking the Format button in the Create Index dialog box. The Index Format dialog box (see fig. 7.18) is displayed, enabling you to include or exclude section headings and determine the paragraph format of index entries. (The Index Entry command, described earlier, enables you to set the *character* formats for the index entries.)

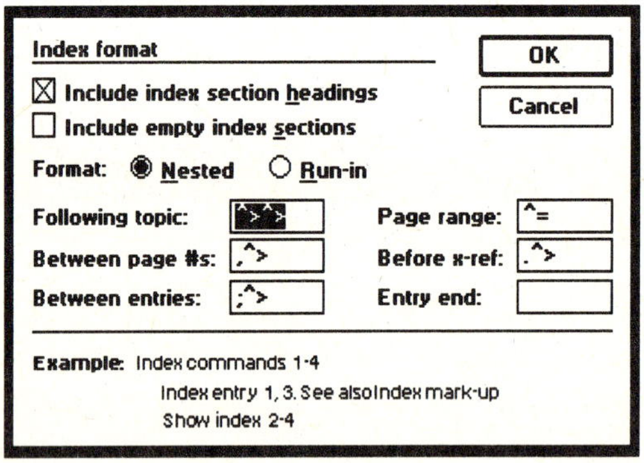

Fig. 7.18. The Index Format dialog box.

Check Include Index Section Headings to include headings that mark the beginning of each alphabetical section of the index (that is, A, B, C, and so on). If this option is not checked, the headings do not appear, but more spacing appears between alphabetical sections. Click Include Empty Index Sections if you want headings for alphabetical sections under which no entries exist. Empty sections include the phrase "No entries."

The Format option enables you to choose between two paragraph formats: Nested (in which each entry is a separate paragraph, with progressive indentation for different levels) or Run-In (in which all levels fall into one paragraph per entry). An example of the current selection is displayed at the bottom of the dialog box.

The last six options in the dialog box enable you to specify characters to appear following a topic, between page numbers, between entries, between a page range, before a cross-reference, and at the end of an entry. Commonly used separators include a semicolon, an en-space (represented by a caret and a greater than symbol [^ >]), or an en-dash (represented by a caret and a hyphen [^ -]).

Click OK in the Index Format dialog box to return to the Create Index dialog box, then click OK to generate the index. PageMaker then searches the publications for index entries, collects them, sorts them, and formats them. The process may take several minutes.

If you opted to replace the existing index, that text is replaced in the current publication. If you opt not to replace the current index, or if this is the first time you are generating the index, then PageMaker generates the index and the mouse pointer changes to a loaded text icon if you are in Layout view. You can place the index in the publication just as you place imported text, as described earlier in this chapter. If you are in Story view when you generate the index, PageMaker opens a new story window for the index. Choose Place from the File menu to return to Layout view, and place the index as a new story.

After you generate the index, PageMaker applies the specified styles to the title, section headings, index entries, and topic references. If these styles do not already exist in the style sheet for the publication, PageMaker creates them when it creates the index. Generated style names include Index Title, Index Section, Index Level 1, Index Level 2, Index Level 3, and Index Run-In.

After you generate the index, you can revise index styles by using the Define Styles command as described in Chapter 5. If you change the name of the generated styles, however, PageMaker reverts to generating the standard styles again if you regenerate the index.

Editing a Generated Index

You can edit the text of a generated index the same way you edit any text in PageMaker. A better idea, however, is to make any changes to the index through the Create Index or Show Index commands, and then regenerate the index.

The index shows page numbers in the format set up through the Numbers option in the Page Setup dialog box (displayed with the New command or the Page Setup command from the File menu).

> ### *Production Notes in Index*
>
> You can use automatic indexing to flag and list missing information within paragraphs in a work-in-progress. For example, you may insert dummy text to hold a place for missing words or phrases, such as
>
> > Giuseppe Verdi was born on date? in city?
> >
> > See page ?? for more information about Giuseppe Verdi.
> >
> > Continued on page ??
>
> You can index the missing element only—such as "date?"—or, better yet, index enough of the phrase so that you know which date is missing. The automatic index lists the phrase you index and the page number.
>
> If you are using the index feature only for production notes, you can set all entries to level 1. Otherwise, precede every "production" entry in the index with a special character (such as a question mark), or create a level 1 entry called "000 Production Notes" and set all production notes as level 2 entries under this heading. (By putting a symbol or 000 at the beginning of the level 1 index entry, you print all these entries at the beginning of the index. Use ZZZ instead if you want all notes to appear at the end of the index.) Delete the index entries when the questions are resolved.

Organizing Your Disk Files

Organizing your disk files before you start building a document in PageMaker is a good idea, especially if the document you are building is very large or uses a great deal of different source files. Part III of this book offers detailed suggestions about organizing large projects and a few basic guidelines that can save you much trouble in the long run.

Decide on Naming Conventions

No matter how you organize your files, developing logical naming conventions is a good idea. Decide on the conventions to use for all new files created during the project. The first goal is to be able to find documents easily and know what they contain. One helpful guideline is to name the different parts of the document so that they appear sequentially when you view them alphabetically. For example, a chapter document may be named CHAP1 or CH1 or 1, but you don't want a set of documents related to one book to use all different naming standards, i.e., CHAP1, CH2, 3, 04, and so forth.

If two or more people are involved in the production process, the disk organization and file-naming conventions should be determined by the production manager and announced to the production crew. File organization and naming conventions may be incorporated into the list of standards and review items as guidelines for moving or renaming files as they move through the production process.

Copy All Project Files onto One Hard Disk

If possible, assemble all source files—the text and picture files as well as the PageMaker templates and publication files—onto one primary hard disk. This disk can be your internal hard disk if your computer is the primary workstation for page layout activities, or it can be the file server if you are on a network and several people are involved in the final document production. This hard disk can be a separate hard disk or a removable hard disk if you need to carry the files from one station to another.

Set Up Project-Specific Directories

Try to set up a single directory on the hard disk for each document or publication, and move all of the text and graphic files into that directory. If many files are involved, then divide the main document directory into subdirectories. Some publishers like to keep text sources in one directory and graphic elements in another. Another way of dividing the files is to put the text and graphics files related to a single chapter together in a directory, so that you end up with one directory per chapter.

The publication-specific directory also can include a directory of the fonts used in the publication. Copies of these fonts can be stored in the Windows or PageMaker directory, but if you keep a set in the publication directory you easily can remember to take copies when you move the publication to another system to be printed.

Back Up All Files Regularly

Keep all files related to one document in a single directory.

These few steps are worth taking before you begin assembling text and graphics on a page. Taking time with these preliminaries can save you hours over the life of a large project. Applying these simple steps to small projects also is easy.

Reviewing Some Workgroup Scenarios

Until now, you have learned some general rules and guidelines for organizing disk files in a large project. The next sections present a scenario of how these ideas may be applied in workgroups.

Networked Workgroup Scenario

A networked workgroup is a group of computers, each with a local hard disk, hooked up to a common file server through which the computers can share files. The following sections describe how you might organize a publication project in a networked environment.

The File Server

The *file server* in a network is a computer with a hard disk. Depending on the size of the hard disk, the file server stores the following types of files:

- The files for the project. These files include linked files, publication files, imported text files, and templates. Some projects may be so large that the file server's entire hard disk is devoted to the project files.

- Other files shared among workstations, such as clip art and other shared files that are not project-specific

- Printer fonts, which must be stored on the file server if printing is spooled through the server. Let local workstations copy only those fonts that are in use on active projects.

Individual Workstations

Individual workstations store the following types of files on their local hard disks:

- The project files now in progress on that workstation. These files are copied from the file server, used at the local workstation, then copied back to the file server. (See the following section, "Backup Procedures.")

- Printer fonts that are in use on active projects

- Applications and utilities that are commonly or now used, including PageMaker

If your workgroup shares one room, or if the project is well-managed and the group has good communication between members, you may not need to take extra precautions so that two people do not start working on copies of the same file at once. If procedures are followed correctly and a project coordinator monitors the status of each file as work progresses, you can prevent someone from working on a file that is not the latest version of that file.

Remember: If the group is widely dispersed in a building, if recommended procedures aren't followed, if the project is too large, and the pace is too fast, or if chaos reigns, accidents can happen.

By far the most efficient method of tracking the master copy of a document is through the attention of a project coordinator. The coordinator should maintain and post a log of each document's status, such as the one shown in figure 7.19. Notice that the log tracks changes to externally linked graphics files as well as changes to PageMaker documents.

Disk File Name	Master File Start date	WIP Station ID	Date	Back to Master Date	WIP Station #ID	Date
CH01	4/1	SV	4/3	4/5	DB	4/8
CH02	4/1	SV	4/6	4/8		
CH03	4/1					
Linked Graphic A	4/1					

Fig. 7.19. Example of a log of disk files.

Backup Procedures

The master files—or the most recently printed files that are still works-in-progress—are stored on the file server. When a file is to be modified, copy it to a local workstation. Under this system, the file server is the backup for whatever files are actively being used at local workstations. When the work is finished, copy the file from the local workstation back to the file server.

If the work in progress on each workstation will require more than a day, then you may want each workstation user to copy current works-in-progress back to the file server at the end of each day to serve as interim backups. Be sure to maintain a copy of the most recently *printed* version of the documents; do not copy the work-in-progress files over the most recently printed "master" file on the file server. Instead, copy the interim versions into a separate directory, or add a suffix such as WIP (work-in-progress) to the file names.

When the entire project is finished, copy all files from the file server only onto floppy disks or removable hard disks for storage. You should keep copies of all disk files at least until the final document has been mass-produced and distributed. You can erase the disk files later if storage space is limited. If you are producing a newsletter or a magazine, for example, you can erase the disk files after each issue is printed.

At the end of each project, you can collect parts of the document that can be reused and store them as part of a template for use in later documents.

Nonnetworked Workgroup Scenario

If your group does not share files through a file server, or if some members of the group are not on the network, you can use the following procedures to manage large projects.

The Master Files

If your workgroup does not share files through a network, the master files for a project can be stored on one of the workstation's hard disks and individuals can go to the master workstation to get copies of files as needed. In this case, the master workstation can be set up exactly as described in the previous section. If the files are too large to fit on floppy disks, you can use one of the following methods to copy files from the master workstation to other workstations:

- Instead of using a workstation's hard disk as the master, put all master files on an extra, external hard disk. Move this external hard disk to each workstation and copy files as needed.

- If each workstation has a removable hard disk drive, the master files can be stored on one or more removable hard disk cartridges that can be moved from station to station.

- If each workstation has a modem, or if your group has at least two modems and two phone lines, you can transfer large files directly from one workstation to another through the phone lines.

Individual Workstations

Individual workstations can be set up as described for networked groups.

Backup Procedures

The master files—or the most recently printed files that are still works-in-progress—are stored on the designated master disks. When a file is to be modified, copy it to a local workstation. Under this system, the master disks are the backup for whatever files are actively being used at local workstations. When the work is finished, copy the file from the local workstation back to the master disk.

Chapter Summary

You can create any publication in PageMaker without using any of the features or suggestions presented in this chapter, but you should find these features indispensable if you produce many or very large documents. The following two chapters describe how to print PageMaker publications. Chapter 8 describes the process of setting up a printer and printing a publication, and Chapter 9 describes how to create and apply colors to a publication and make color separations.

8

Printing

Your ultimate goal in the production process is to print your publication on a high-resolution printer. Sometimes this output becomes the distribution copy or copies. More often, the output becomes the *camera-ready pages* from which the document is reproduced with photocopying or offset-printing equipment. In this chapter, you learn the differences among various printers' capabilities. You learn how to install the printer (during the process of installing Windows or PageMaker), how to select the printer for a publication (if you are using more than one printer), and how to print a publication. You also learn how to add new fonts to your printer and to the list of fonts in the Type Specifications dialog box. Finally, you learn how to create a disk file that includes all of the printer-language instructions needed for printing the publication—including linked graphics—and how to prepare your publications to be printed at another location, such as a service bureau.

Knowing Your Printers

Before designing publications for PageMaker, you should become familiar with the capabilities of your printer. Not all printers can take advantage of all PageMaker features (reverse type and white lines, for example). Some printers produce graphics and text at higher resolution than other printers. Some printers require certain sizes of special paper or film; others can use many different sizes of lightweight stock. The list of available fonts also varies from printer to printer. Generally, you will want to design your publications with your final-copy printer in mind.

Printers Supported by PageMaker and Windows 3.0

The printing devices available for personal computers fall into six categories: character printers, plotters, dot-matrix printers, ink-jet printers, laser printers, and phototypesetters or imagesetters. Of these, only the last two types normally are used for the final printing of a PageMaker publication. One reason is that laser printers and phototypesetters can handle outline fonts and produce typeset-quality publications. Another reason is that laser printers and phototypesetters can print at much higher resolutions than dot-matrix printers and ink-jet printers.

Publications created with PageMaker can be printed on all PostScript printers (such as the Apple LaserWriter II NT and NTX, the IBM Personal PagePrinter, and the QMS ColorScript printer), all PostScript-language imagesetters (such as the Linotronic and the Agfa Compugraphic 9600G), and the Hewlett-Packard (HP) LaserJet series of printers and compatible printers that use HP's Printer Control Language (PCL 4 and PCL 5). You also can print on other printers that are compatible with Windows 3.0, including dot-matrix printers such as the IBM Proprinter and Epson LQ series. PageMaker does not support plotters.

To print on any supported printer, four conditions must be met: (1) The *printer* must be installed (i.e., physically attached to your system), (2) the printer *driver* must be installed through Windows 3.0, (3) the printer driver must be assigned to an active *port* (the location at the back of your computer to which the printer is physically attached), and (4) the printer must be selected as the *target printer*. This chapter discusses how to meet these conditions.

Resolution

One difference among printers is the resolution with which they print. *Resolution* is a measure of the density in which text and graphics are printed and usually is specified in dots per inch (dpi). Laser printers, such as the Apple LaserWriter and Hewlett-Packard LaserJet, print at 300 dpi. This resolution is considered high compared to most dot-matrix printers, which print at 120 dpi, but is considered low compared to typesetting equipment or imagesetters, which can print as many as 3,386 dots per inch.

The higher the resolution, the smoother the appearance of the edges of text and graphics. The lower the resolution, the greater the jaggedness of the edges. Some printers have a range of settings for resolution, as shown in table 8.1. Most printers can print pages of text at the higher resolutions. Pages containing graphics, however, may overload some printers' processing capabilities unless the printers are set to lower resolution for graphics or more memory is added. (Lowering the graphics resolution usually does not impair the resolution of text.)

**Table 8.1
Resolutions of Some Printers Compatible with PageMaker**

Printer	*Resolution Settings*
LaserWriter	300
LaserJet	300, 150, or 75
Linotronic 100	1200, 900, 600, or 300
Linotronic 300	2400, 1200
QMS ColorScript 100	300

Paper Stock, Size, and Print Area

Printers vary in the type of paper (stock) and the size of paper they can handle. The printer manufacturer's specifications tell you what types and sizes of paper can be used in the printer. Most laser printers can take any lightweight paper stock; special paper stocks are available with a slightly glossy coating that helps the toner print solid black areas. Phototypesetters and imagesetters use photosensitive film that is developed using a chemical process, yielding the best results for solid black areas and fine typography. The film comes in rolls (allowing variable page sizes) and can be solid (white) or transparent. Ink-jet printers usually require special papers with a wax coating.

Regardless of paper size, the area on which a printer can print is limited: usually a border at the edges of the paper is used for gripping the paper as it goes through the printer. Print area is further limited by the printer's memory; the border around large paper sizes may therefore be larger than the border around small paper sizes.

If the printer's instruction manual does not list the maximum print area, you can check it yourself by setting up a PageMaker publication that is the same size as the maximum paper size handled by the printer. Use the PageMaker rectangle tool to draw a box that overlaps all four edges of the paper, and assign it a shade of gray or black. When you print the page, the printer's maximum print area will be revealed by blank borders at the edges of the paper.

If you plan to create designs with elements that "bleed" off the edges of the paper, you need to make the page size of the publication smaller than the maximum print area of your printer.

Types of Fonts

Some printers (such as those that use a daisywheel) are limited to printing the characters that are physically on their print elements. Dot-matrix printers and laser printers, on the other hand, can change the appearance of the characters they print by switching to a different font. Printer fonts differ in how their character shapes are defined and how they are accessed by the printer. (Fonts are discussed in greater detail in Chapter 10.)

Character Definition

The shapes of characters in a font usually are defined in one of two ways. Your choice of printers is greatly increased because PageMaker uses both bit-mapped fonts and outline fonts.

Each character in a *bit-mapped font* is composed of a pattern of dots. Bit-mapped fonts generally take up more memory than outline fonts and print more slowly. The printed results, however, are typically crisp and true to the font design, especially in high resolution. Bit-mapped fonts cannot be scaled—you must have every size of every font you intend to use installed on your printer. If you enter a point size that is not available, PageMaker substitutes the next smaller available size for the bit-mapped font. You also cannot rotate, expand, or condense bit-mapped fonts. You need to install both portrait and landscape versions of these fonts if you intend to print publications in both of these page orientations. Bit-mapped fonts commonly are used in PCL 4 printers, such as the Hewlett-Packard LaserJet series. (Some PCL 4 printers, such as the LaserJet IID and the LaserJet IIP, enable you to use portrait fonts as landscape fonts, and vice versa.)

Outline fonts are just that—font outlines that the printer interprets and prints like bit-mapped fonts. Because outline fonts print faster and can be scaled, they are more flexible than bit-mapped fonts. (In PageMaker, you can scale fonts from 4 to 650 points, in one-tenth-point increments.) Outline fonts also can be expanded, condensed, and rotated using PageMaker's commands. These fonts are commonly used with PostScript printers, although many other types of printers—such as the LaserJet III series of printers and other PCL 5 printers—use outline fonts because of their printing speed.

> **Using a Type Manager**
>
> You can install a type-management program—such as Adobe Type Manager—to increase the number and flexibility of fonts on a PCL 4 printer. A type manager can generate scalable fonts even for printers designed to print only bit-mapped fonts, and it can accommodate rotated, expanded, and condensed text.

Access

A major difference among printers is the number of built-in fonts (see table 8.2). Built-in fonts are, in effect, part of the printer's circuitry. A font built into the printer is always available for any publication.

Sometimes printer fonts are available in replaceable cartridges that can be inserted into the printer. For example, the Hewlett-Packard LaserJet Series II has one built-in font (12-point Courier), and you can add more fonts on cartridges. The choice of fonts depends on which cartridge is loaded in the printer and selected in the Target Printer dialog box (displayed when you select the Target Printer command on the File menu). The Apple LaserWriter has four built-in typefaces (Courier, Times, Helvetica, and Symbol), each available in any size and style (normal, boldface, italic, and boldface italic).

Table 8.2
Built-In Fonts of PageMaker-Compatible Printers

Printer	Fonts
LaserWriter	Times, Helvetica, Courier, Symbol (all sizes, all styles)
LaserWriter Plus	Times, Helvetica, Courier, Symbol, Avant Garde, Bookman, New Century Schoolbook, Helvetica Narrow, Palatino, Zapf Chancery, Zapf Dingbats (all sizes, all styles)
LaserJet and LaserJet Plus	Helvetica 14 point

continues

Table 8.2 *(continued)*

Printer	Fonts
Cartridge A	Times 10-point normal
	Times 10-point bold
	Times 10-point italic
	Times 10-point bold italic
	Times 8-point normal
	Courier 12-point normal
	Line printer 8-point light
Cartridge B	Helvetica 14 point
	Times 10-point normal
	Times 10-point bold
	Times 10-point italic
	Times 10-point bold italic
	Times 8-point normal
	Courier 12-point normal
	Line printer 8-point medium
Linotronic	Times, Helvetica (all sizes, all styles)

PageMaker includes the width tables (required for printing) and screen fonts (required for displaying fonts on the screen) for all the fonts listed in table 8.2 and some additional downloadable fonts as well. A width table assigns the space for each alphabetic character, number, and symbol in a given font. A screen font is a bit-mapped version of the outline font used in printing the text. Screen fonts are used to display text on-screen.

Fonts that are neither built into the printer nor included in the printer's cartridges can be transferred (downloaded) to the memory of some printers. You must purchase downloadable fonts from the printer manufacturer or a software developer who makes downloadable fonts. Adobe Systems is one of the primary sources for downloadable PostScript fonts. Bitstream is a popular source of downloadable bit-mapped fonts for the Hewlett-Packard LaserJet Plus, Series II, and 500 Plus printers.

The steps involved in downloading fonts to a printer are discussed in the section "Downloading Soft Fonts."

Installing the Printer

Instructions for installing a printer are given in the manufacturer's printer manual. The first step is to use a cable to connect the printer to your computer. After you connect your printer (or printers), you must install your printer's driver through the Windows installation program or the Control Panel before you can print a publication. PageMaker does not install printer drivers itself, but through PageMaker's Print command you can access the installation capability of the Windows Control Panel.

The Windows installation program displays a list of printers supported by Windows and prompts you to select the printers you are using. (These installation steps are discussed in detail in Chapter 2.) Select all the types of printers that you might use for your publications, whether the printers are hooked up to your computer or to another computer that you will use for final printing.

Even after you have installed Windows, you can define your printer setup through the Windows Control Panel, where you can add printers to the list of those already available and change printer connections. The PageMaker Print command (on the File menu) also enables you to install new printer drivers. You can change the specifications for individual printers by means of the Print command and the Target Printer command (also on the File menu). After you have installed several printers, you can use PageMaker's Target Printer command to set up the target printer for a particular publication and change its specifications before you start printing. (Because PageMaker composes the publication for the target printer, you should specify the target printer before you start the publication. If you need to change the printer while working on the publication, PageMaker reformats the document to the new printer's specifications.) Both the Print command and the Target Printer command are discussed in this chapter (see the section "Using the Print Command" and also "Choosing the Target Printer through PageMaker" in the section "Installing the Printer").

Adding Printers through the Windows Control Panel

You can install a new printer driver or change the printer specifications using the Control Panel that is part of Windows 3.0. To use the Control Panel, start Windows 3.0 and choose Main from the Windows menu if that window is not already displayed. The Control Panel icon is displayed in the Windows main window (see fig. 8.1).

Part I: The Production Process with PageMaker

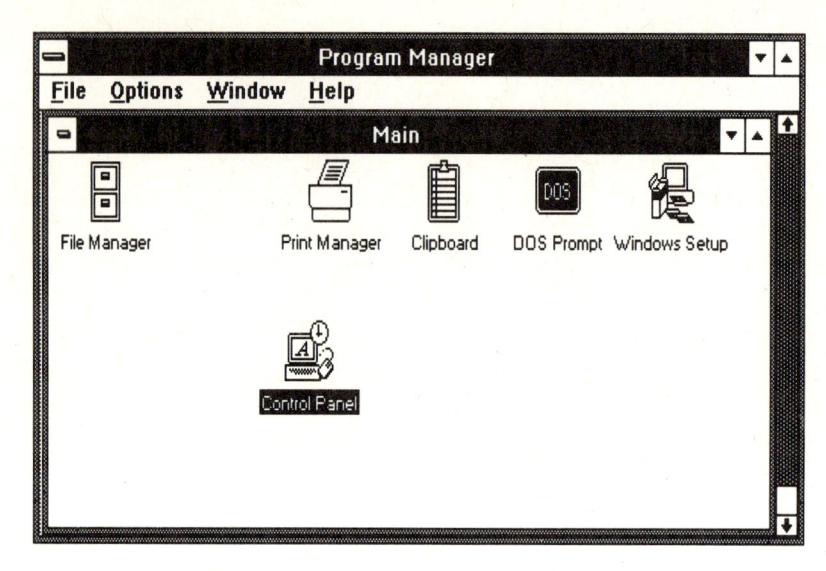

Fig. 8.1. The Control Panel icon in the Windows main menu.

Next, double-click the Control Panel icon. The Control Panel window displays a number of icons (discussed in Chapter 2), including the Printers icon (see fig. 8.2).

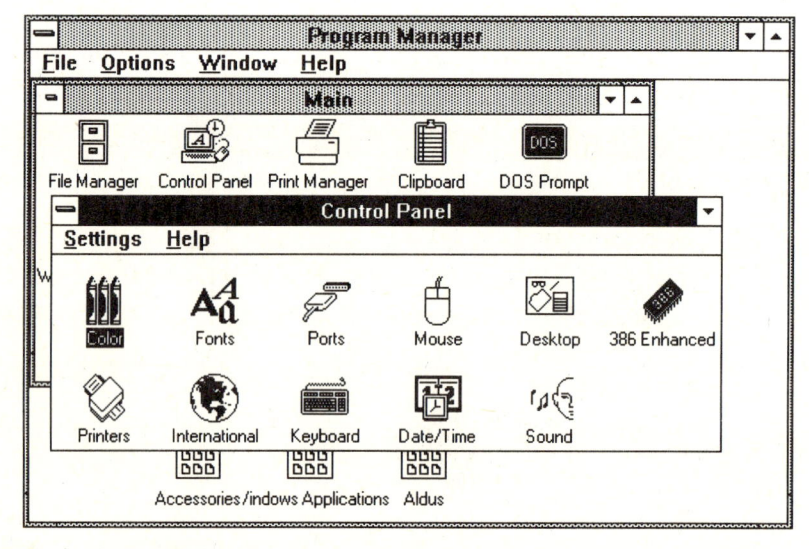

Fig. 8.2. The Control Panel window shows the Printers icon.

Double-click the Printers icon to display the Printers dialog box, which shows the list of currently installed printers and the ports to which they are assigned (see fig. 8.3). By using the Add Printer button, you can add a new printer driver. By selecting the Configure button on the right side of the dialog box, you can change a currently installed printer's physical port assignment.

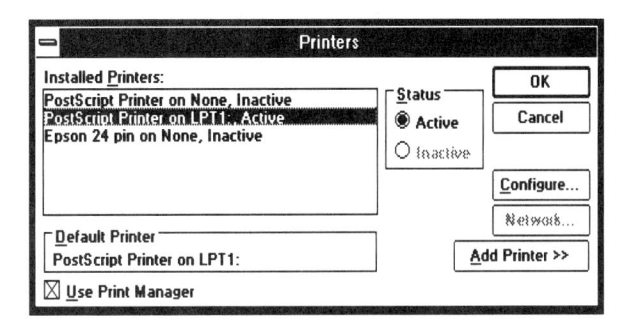

Fig. 8.3. *The Printers dialog box.*

Adding a Printer Driver

For PageMaker's Target Printer command to list a printer, you need to install the printer driver for that printer. A *driver* is software that "translates" information sent from your computer into a form the printer can recognize. Microsoft Windows comes with many printer drivers. The printer manufacturer also might supply a driver that updates or supplements the drivers that come with Windows.

To install a new driver through the Control Panel, click Add Printer in the Printers dialog box (displayed when you double-click the Printers icon). The dialog box expands to include a scrolling window listing the types of printers supported by Windows 3.0 (see fig. 8.4). Use the scroll bars to scroll through the list and find the type of printer you want to install, then double-click on the printer name (or click once on the printer name to select it and then click Install).

Windows prompts you to insert in drive A the disk with the driver or to specify the appropriate path to the printer driver. Insert the disk (supplied with Windows or by the printer manufacturer) and click OK. After you insert the correct driver disk, Windows installs the driver automatically.

You also can add a printer driver by means of the Print command in PageMaker: Choose Print from the File menu, click Setup in the Print dialog box, and then click Add Printer in the next dialog box. The rest of the process is the same as that used in the Windows Control Panel.

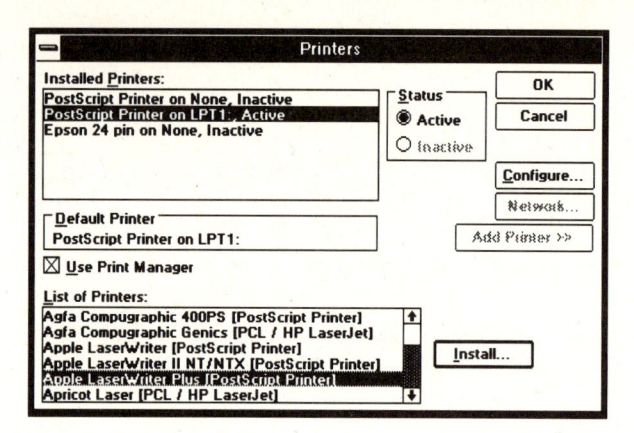

Fig. 8.4. The Printers dialog box expanded when Add Printer is selected.

Updating a Printer Driver

You also use the Control Panel to install a newer version of a driver that you already have installed. Treat the newer version as a completely new driver, and follow the procedure for adding a new driver discussed in this section. Windows knows whether a printer driver for that type of printer is already on the system and prompts you to confirm that you want to replace the old driver.

Changing Printer Connections

You must connect your printer to a port. Typically, LPT1, LPT2, and LPT3 are parallel ports; COM1 and COM2 are serial ports. Normally, you hook up your computer and printer before installing Windows, and you are prompted to specify which ports the printers are connected to during the Windows installation. If your system has only one communications port but you use two different printers, you may need to change the cable connections each time you change printers. You not only change the physical cable connection, you also must use the Control Panel to declare the change.

If you change the cable connections between your computer and printer, you must use the Control Panel to tell Windows and PageMaker where to send the printed pages. Open the Control Panel window and double-click the Printers icon, click on the printer name in the Installed Printers list to select it, and click the Configure button. In the Printers—Configure dialog box, click on the name of the port to which the printer is now connected (see fig. 8.5).

Fig. 8.5. The Printers—Configure dialog box.

Changing Printer Options

Besides selecting the type of printer and assigning a printer port, you can tell Windows the source of the paper (automatic feed, manual feed, or a paper tray), the size of the paper, and the orientation of the paper (tall or wide). You also can specify a percentage for enlarging or reducing the printed page on some printers, or specify a font cartridge for printers that use cartridges. Open the Control Panel window and double-click the Printers icon, click on the printer name in the Installed Printers list to select it, and click the Configure button. In the Printers—Configure dialog box, click Setup to display the dialog box that enables you to set the options for paper source, size, and orientation. This dialog box is printer-specific: The options available vary depending on the printer selected. Figures 8.6 and 8.7, for example, show the dialog boxes for the Apple LaserWriter Plus and Hewlett-Packard LaserJet III, respectively.

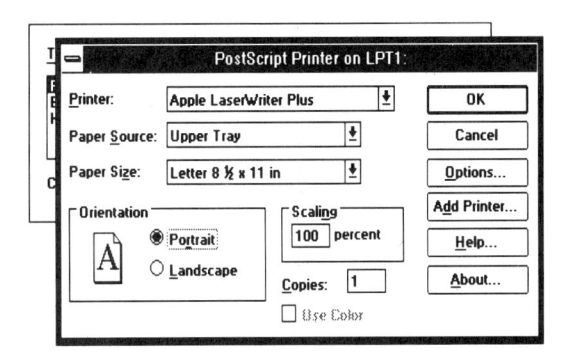

Fig. 8.6. The dialog box for the Apple LaserWriter Plus printer.

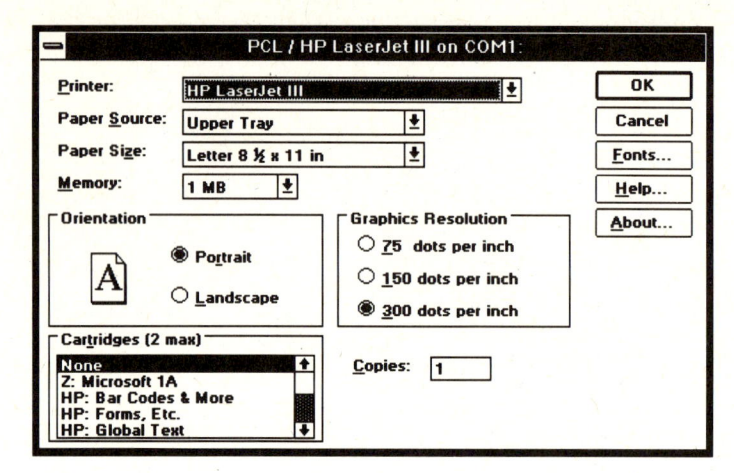

Fig. 8.7. The dialog box for the Hewlett-Packard LaserJet III printer.

Click the arrow to the right of the Printer option to display a drop-down menu that lists all the printers supported by Windows. If you select a printer for which the driver is not installed, you must install the driver for that printer (see the methods of installation discussed in this section).

Click the arrow to the right of the Paper Source option to select a paper tray or to select Manual Feed from the drop-down menu. Click the arrow right of the Paper Size to select a paper size. The Paper Source and Paper Size drop-down lists show the options specific to the type of printer you have selected.

Most printers enable you to choose Portrait or Landscape orientation. (Some dialog boxes list these options as Tall and Wide.) Portrait, or Tall, orientation is the way you usually print on a piece of letter-size paper (11 inches of text on 8 1/2-inch-wide paper); the longer measurement is the vertical measurement. Landscape is the same as Wide orientation; the longer measurement is the horizontal measurement. If your printer supports Landscape orientation, you can choose Portrait or Landscape for any size paper.

PostScript printers enable you to reduce or enlarge the printed image by entering a value in the Scaling Percent box. You also can specify a default number of copies to be printed; this number can be overridden through the Print dialog box in PageMaker (see "Specifying the Number of Copies" in the "Using the Print Command" section of this chapter). Finally, if you are printing on a color printer, you can choose Use Color (that is, print in color) if you want.

> ***Your Printer May Restrict Orientation***
>
> ***Caution:*** Some printers do not print well in Landscape orientation. For some reason, they have to work harder, take longer, and sometimes drop information. In printers such as the LaserJet, some downloadable fonts cannot be used in both Portrait and Landscape orientation on a single page. It is a good idea to create a short sample document in Landscape orientation and try printing it before you embark on a large or complex project that requires Landscape orientation.

Printer resolutions and font-cartridge names are shown in scrolling windows for PCL printers. In the dialog box in figure 8.7, you can choose from 21 cartridges (see Chapter 10 for examples of the different fonts on each cartridge) and from graphics resolutions of 75, 150, or 300 dots per inch (dpi). Letters have more jagged edges at the lower resolutions, but the quality of text is not dramatically lowered, and the pages are printed faster. Lower resolutions are good for printing drafts during the production process. Also, some pages with complex graphics or large bit-mapped images cannot be printed at 300 dpi without overloading the printer's memory.

Changing the Default Printer

If you have only one printer hooked up to a port at a time, that printer becomes the default printer for PageMaker and all Windows applications. If you have printers hooked up to two or more ports, you can change the default printer by choosing from the Default Printer list in the Printers dialog box (displayed when you click the Printers icon on the Windows Control Panel).

When no publication is open, you also can use the Target Printer command on PageMaker's File menu to specify the default printer used by PageMaker, or you can open a publication and use this command to specify the target printer for that particular publication without changing the default printer for all other publications.

Choosing the Target Printer through PageMaker

When you design and produce any publication, one of the first questions you need to ask yourself is this: What printer will be used for the final camera-ready pages?

In many cases, you use the same printer throughout the entire production sequence, from early proofs to final masters. In fact, most installations probably have only one printer (or only one type of printer if more than one printer is available). If the printer on which you will be printing the final version of your publication is different from the printer you will be using for drafts, then you need to specify the final printer as the *target printer* before you start building your publication. You specify the target printer using the Target Printer command. (You select the current draft printer through the Print command, discussed in "Using the Print Command.")

The target printer specified through the Target Printer command should be selected once, when you first start a publication, and never changed. If you change the target printer after you have started a publication, PageMaker substitutes fonts as necessary and the stored publication changes. On the other hand, if you change only the printer used for drafts of a publication (using the Print command on the File menu), the text is recomposed to match the new printer's fonts as closely as possible, but PageMaker adjusts letter and word spacing to correspond with the line breaks as they will appear when the target printer is used. The stored publication remains unchanged.

If you change the target printer for a publication, PageMaker asks you whether you want to recompose the entire publication to match the new printer's capabilities (see fig. 8.8).

Fig. 8.8. PageMaker's response to changing target printers while working on a publication.

> ### *Changing Target Printers*
>
> ***Caution:*** If you switch the target printer of an existing publication, be prepared to adjust for differences in fonts, print area, and the printer's capability to handle rotated, expanded, and condensed text. In addition, graphics may need to be resized to match the new target printer's resolution. All of these adjustments are likely to affect the spacing of your publication, including line breaks and overall text length.
>
> A type manager reduces or eliminates font substitution problems that can occur when you switch target printers. (Type managers are described in Chapter 10.)

If your system has only one printer or one type of printer with only one set of fonts, you can set the target printer once during the program installation process and never change it. If your system has more than one printer but the printers are all of the same type—for example, all Hewlett-Packard LaserJets with the same cartridge—you can use the Print command on the File menu to change from one printer to another at any time without changing the target printer specification.

If you have more than one type of printer or a cartridge printer with more than one font cartridge available, choose the Target Printer command from the File menu to specify the printer and click Setup to choose the cartridge you are using before you build your publication (see fig. 8.9).

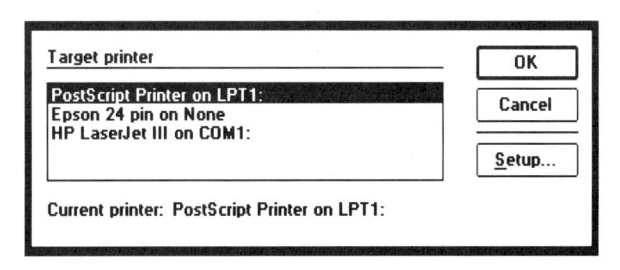

```
Target printer                            OK
┌─────────────────────────────────┐
│ PostScript Printer on LPT1:     │     Cancel
│ Epson 24 pin on None            │
│ HP LaserJet III on COM1:        │
│                                 │     Setup...
└─────────────────────────────────┘
Current printer: PostScript Printer on LPT1:
```

Fig. 8.9. The Target Printer dialog box used to specify the target printer.

The Target Printer dialog box lists the names only of the printer drivers set up during the initial Windows installation steps or added through the Windows Control Panel (see "Adding Printers through the Windows Control Panel: Adding a Printer Driver" in this section). This list can include printers that are not physically hooked up to your system. To choose a target printer, click once on a printer name to select it and then click OK. To check or change the target printer setup, click once on the printer name to select it and then click the Setup button, or simply double-click on a printer name. PageMaker then displays the same dialog box you access with the Printers icon in the Windows Control Panel (by double-clicking the Printers icon, clicking Configure in the Printers dialog box, and clicking Setup in the Printers—Configure dialog box; see "Changing Printer Options"). Figure 8.10 shows the Printer Setup dialog box.

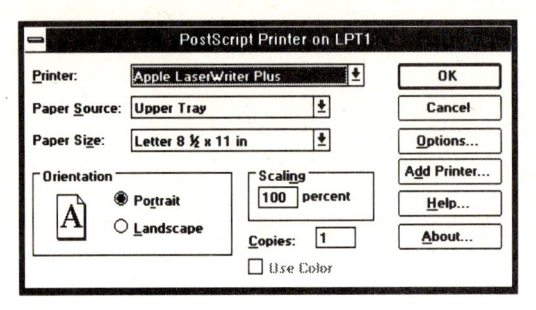

Fig. 8.10. The Printer Setup dialog box for the Apple LaserWriter Plus printer.

When you access this dialog box through the Control Panel, you set the specifications for each printer installed on your system, and these choices become the default specifications when you choose a printer through any application. When you access this dialog box through the Target Printer dialog box in PageMaker, you set the printer specifications for the target printer in the current publication only.

You can set the default values for number of copies, orientation, paper size, paper tray, printer memory, graphics resolution, and font cartridge in this dialog box and change these settings for individual printings in the Print dialog box (displayed when you select the Print command on the File menu).

Printing at Lower Resolutions

Use lower-resolution printing during the early stages of a project for faster printing of draft copies.

If you run into memory-overload problems while you are printing a publication at 300 dpi, try printing it at 150 or 75 dpi or print the graphic separately.

Downloading Soft Fonts

If the printers you have installed use only built-in fonts or font cartridges (see "Knowing Your Printers: Types of Fonts"), you can begin printing publications immediately. Many printers, however, also use fonts that come in the form of software (i.e., files on disks) that can be purchased from various sources. These fonts sometimes are called *soft fonts* because they are not "hard-coded" into chips in the printer or in the printer font cartridge. They also are called *downloadable fonts* because you must either send, or download, them to the printer before printing begins or let PageMaker automatically download them as needed during the printing process. Before you use soft fonts, you must first install them and decide whether to download them permanently or temporarily.

Installing Soft Fonts

In order to have access to a soft font in PageMaker, you must let the Windows environment "know" that the new font is available. To do so, you must have a printer font metrics (PFM) version of the font. PFM files are not themselves downloadable printer fonts, but they contain the character spacing and kerning information PageMaker needs to space characters proportionally on the screen and in print.

If you are planning to print the final version of your publication on another system—or send it to a service bureau for printing—you do not need the printer fonts, but you should have the PFM files for the fonts (PFM file names have the extension PFM). If you are printing the final version on your own system, you need the actual printer fonts for your printer in order for those fonts to appear in your printed output.

Some font manufacturers provide PFM versions on their disks. Follow the manufacturer's instructions for copying the PFM fonts from the manufacturer's disk to your hard disk. Copy the fonts into the WINDOWS directory or into a new font subdirectory you create. Make a note of the identification numbers the installation program assigns during this process.

PageMaker comes with an assortment of PostScript PFM files. When you choose the PostScript Font Metrics option during the PageMaker installation process, additional PFM (printer font metrics) and FON (screen fonts) files are copied to your PageMaker directory, in a subdirectory called METRICS. These files are used in imagesetter-targeted publications when your system is updated with the following typefaces:

Helvetica Narrow (PFM only)

New Century Schoolbook (PFM only)

Palatino (PFM only)

ITC Avant Garde (PFM only)

ITC Bookman (PFM only)

ITC Zapf Chancery (FON and PFM)

ITC Zapf Dingbats (FON and PFM)

If you do not have a particular PFM file, the printer driver that comes with Windows can generate a generic PFM file, but the printed effects are not as good as those from a custom PFM file.

After you have acquired and installed the PFM files for the fonts you will be using, update the WIN.INI file, or use the Soft Font Installer for PCL printers.

Updating WIN.INI

In many cases, the list of installed fonts is expanded in the WIN.INI file whenever you install a new font using a Windows-compatible font installer program, such as the Soft Font Installer for PCL printers. Sometimes you are asked to specify which fonts you want to install when you install a new printer or Windows application that comes with fonts, but in many cases that installation process simply loads all the fonts that come with the product.

If the installation program does not update WIN.INI for you, or if you use DOS copy commands to copy fonts into the system, you need to update WIN.INI yourself. Before you update your WIN.INI file, be sure that you have either followed the printer installation procedure during the Windows 3.0 setup program or configured at least one active PostScript printer through the Windows Control Panel (see "Adding a Printer Driver" in the "Installing the Printer" section of this chapter).

To give Windows and PageMaker access to the additional PFM files needed to print imagesetter-targeted publications, use the following procedure for updating WIN.INI:

1. Change to the WINDOWS directory and make a backup copy of WIN.INI. For example, if you are already in Windows 3.0, open File Manager. Find WIN.INI in your Windows 3.0 directory and select (highlight) the file. Click on the File menu name and choose Copy (or press F8) to display the Copy dialog box. Type *winini.sav* in the

To box, and press Enter (or choose Copy). A copy of WIN.INI is saved as WININI.SAV in the WINDOWS directory.

2. Double-click on the notepad icon in the Program Manager's Accessories Group window to open Notepad.

3. Click on the File menu name and choose Open. In the Directories scroll box, double-click on the METRICS subdirectory (of the PAGEMAKER directory). With the cursor, select the contents of the Filename box and then type:

   FONTME.TXT

   Press Enter or click OK.

4. Scroll to the following list of PFM files and select the entire list:

   softfonts=22

   softfont1=c:\pm\metrics\ag_____.pfm

   softfont2=c:\pm\metrics\agbo____.pfm

   softfont3=c:\pm\metrics\agd_____.pfm

   softfont4=c:\pm\metrics\agdo____.pfm

   softfont5=c:\pm\metrics\bd_____.pfm

   softfont6=c:\pm\metrics\bdi_____.pfm

   softfont7=c:\pm\metrics\bl_____.pfm

   softfont8=c:\pm\metrics\bli_____.pfm

   softfont9=c:\pm\metrics\hvn_____.pfm

   softfont10=c:\pm\metrics\hvnb____.pfm

   softfont11=c:\pm\metrics\hvnbo___.pfm

   softfont12=c:\pm\metrics\hvno____.pfm

   softfont13=c:\pm\metrics\ncb_____.pfm

   softfont14=c:\pm\metrics\ncbi____.pfm

   softfont15=c:\pm\metrics\nci_____.pfm

   softfont16=c:\pm\metrics\ncr_____.pfm

   softfont17=c:\pm\metrics\pb_____.pfm

   softfont18=c:\pm\metrics\pbi_____.pfm

softfont19=c:\pm\metrics\pi_____.pfm

softfont20=c:\pm\metrics\pr_____.pfm

softfont21=c:\pm\metrics\zc_____.pfm

softfont22=c:\pm\metrics\zd_____.pfm

PFM Directories

Caution: Before you update the WIN.INI file, you easily can use Notepad to edit the directory/path names of PFM font file names to reflect different font locations. That is, if you choose to locate PFM files in any other directory—for example, C:\PSFONTS—you need to include this path in the text that you paste into the WIN.INI file, such as

softfont1=c:\psfonts\ag_____.pfm

and so on. Also, note that the PFM file names must be 8 characters long, in either letters alone or combinations of letters and underline characters. The 3-character file name extension is always PFM, which identifies these files as printer font metrics files.

---

5. Choose Copy from the Edit menu.

6. While still in Notepad, open the file WIN.INI located in your WINDOWS directory.

7. Find the first [PostScript,<port>] label for the target printer that is to be used for imagesetting output only (such as a Linotronic).

   These labels appear at the beginning of PostScript printer port sections in WIN.INI. For example, you may find the following:

   [PostScript,COM1]

   or

   [PostScript,FILE]

8. Place the cursor just below the [PostScript,<port>] label, click to create an insertion point, and choose Paste from the Edit menu (or press Shift-Insert).

   If you already have PostScript soft fonts installed, then other soft font entries may already exist in the printer sections of the WIN.INI file. To avoid conflict, you need to edit WIN.INI using Notepad to include the additional lines in continuous, numerical order. For example, suppose that two fonts already exist in the WIN.INI printer sections, introduced by a line that reads:

softfonts=2

You need to paste in the text for the 22 additional soft fonts after the two existing fonts; then edit the "softfonts=" line to read:

softfonts=24

Finally, edit the 24 lines of text that follow to reflect the correct numerical order (i.e., "softfont1" through "softfont24").

> *Note:* You should have no more than one "softfonts=" line to indicate the total number of soft fonts in each PostScript printer port section.

9. Repeat step 8 for any other printers you anticipate using for imagesetter-targeted publications. Do not repeat step 8 for laser printers that might not support Adobe PostScript soft fonts.

10. Choose Save from the File menu, and then choose Exit to close Notepad. Make sure that you save the WIN.INI file in the WINDOWS directory.

11. To install screen fonts, consult "Adding and Deleting Screen Fonts" in the "Working with PageMaker's Font List" section of Chapter 10. If you choose not to install screen fonts, exit and restart Windows to activate the modified WIN.INI settings.

Note that these PFM files are available to other Windows applications (besides PageMaker) that use soft fonts.

Unfortunately, every installed font takes up space in memory and can thus make applications run more slowly. Some applications, such as PageMaker, are slowed even further by the fact that they read the specifications of every font in the list when you use a command that references the list of fonts. The longer the list, the longer the command takes to execute.

You can add and delete fonts through the Windows Control Panel, and you should delete fonts that you never use. If you normally produce many publications using different fonts, you can create a different WIN.INI file for each publication or set of related publications that uses a different font set.

To create different WIN.INI files, first make lists of the fonts that you need for each set of publications. For example, suppose that publication set A (reports) uses only Times and Helvetica, and that publication set B (a newsletter) uses only Palatino. To each list of fonts add Helvetica, which is the font used in most Windows dialog boxes; without Helvetica, the dialog boxes are difficult to read.

Next, start Windows. Make a copy of the WIN.INI file that includes all of the installed fonts and name the copy WIN.ALL. Use the Windows Control Panel to delete all of the fonts except those that are used in publication set A. The WIN.INI file is automatically updated with the new font list. Make a copy of the new WIN.INI file and name it WIN.A.

Repeat this step for each publication set. In this two-set example, you would next use the Windows Control Panel to delete all of the fonts in the WIN.ALL file except those that are used in publication set B (do not delete Helvetica). Again, the WIN.INI file is automatically updated with the new font list. Make a copy of the new WIN.INI file and name it WIN.B.

You now have three different versions of the WIN.INI file—named WIN.ALL, WIN.A, and WIN.B—each with a different set of fonts. Whenever you want to start Windows with one of these font sets, make a copy of the file and name it WIN.INI (replacing the current WIN.INI) and restart Windows.

Using the Soft Font Installer for PCL Printers

PageMaker provides a Soft Font Installer to install soft fonts on your PCL printer. Using the Target Printer command in the File menu, select (highlight) a PCL target printer. Click Setup to see the printer-specific dialog box (or double-click the target printer). Click the Fonts button to display the Printer Font Installer dialog box (see fig. 8.11).

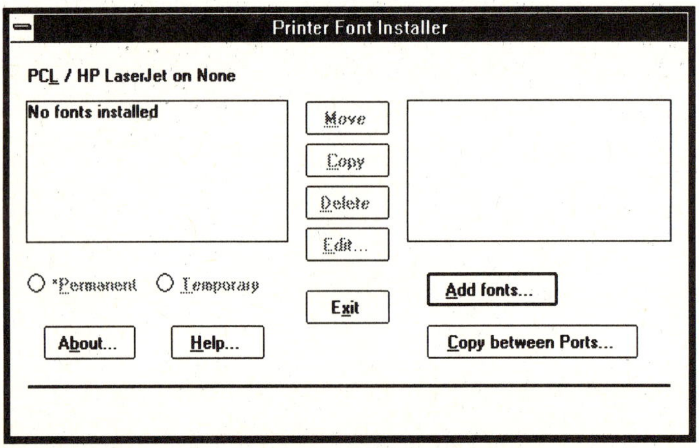

Fig. 8.11. The Printer Font Installer dialog box for PCL printers.

Next, click Add Fonts. The Add Fonts dialog box asks you where the program can find the fonts that you want installed. In the scroll box to the right, the installer lists the names of all the soft fonts in the path you specify. Select the font you want by clicking it. If you want to install more than one font, hold down the Shift key as you click. Hold down the Ctrl and Shift keys and click the mouse if you want to select all the fonts listed.

After you have selected the fonts, you are asked to specify which directory the fonts should be copied to. The installer copies the fonts and the PFM files to your hard disk. You can specify that you want the fonts to be loaded permanently to your hard disk by clicking the Permanent option in the dialog box; click Temporary if you want the fonts to be loaded only when they are used. If you select Permanent, PageMaker updates your WIN.INI file. Click the Copy Between Ports button if you want the fonts to be available through ports other than the one to which the currently selected printer is attached. Remember: Turn on your printer before you start Windows if you use permanently downloaded fonts. To view the new fonts on-screen, you must use a type manager program or add the screen fonts through the Windows Control Panel. See "Adding and Deleting Screen Fonts" in the "Working with PageMaker's Font List" section of Chapter 10.

Downloading Permanently or Temporarily

The first step involved in using a soft font is to follow the manufacturer's instructions, which usually involve running a utility program for downloading the fonts to your printer or your hard disk. This utility program comes with the font. In this step, the downloaded fonts are assigned numbers by which the printer identifies them. You also specify whether the fonts are to be downloaded permanently or temporarily.

To say that a font is permanently downloaded is slightly misleading. The only truly permanent fonts are hard-coded into the printer; these fonts, by definition, are not downloadable. They are resident in the printer's ROM or in a cartridge.

Permanently downloaded fonts are available during an entire work session. At the beginning of a session, you download a font into the printer's memory, where the font remains until the printer is turned off. Because permanently downloaded fonts remain in the printer's memory, it can print publications more quickly. The amount of memory remaining for processing each page, however, is limited by the number of fonts downloaded. You may experience problems printing pages with graphics when several fonts are downloaded.

Temporarily downloaded fonts are sent to the printer's memory while a publication is being printed. When the printer finishes printing the publication, the temporarily downloaded font is flushed out of the printer's memory. Printing tends to be slower with temporarily downloaded fonts because the fonts are downloaded each time the publication is printed. Temporarily downloaded fonts have the advantage of releasing memory space when the font is not being used.

Permanently downloaded fonts are used most often for body text in smaller sizes (10, 12, or 14 points). Temporarily downloaded fonts usually are specialty fonts, such as headlines or decorative fonts, which are used less frequently.

Downloading Fonts Automatically

You can add lines of instructions in your WIN.INI file to download fonts to your printer at the start of your workday. (See the procedure for updating WIN.INI outlined in "Installing Soft Fonts" in this section.) If you use this method, you need to turn on your printer before you start Windows so that the printer accepts the downloaded fonts.

Permanent downloading is advisable if you normally use the same number and style of fonts in your publications, such as company letters or documents that always use a specified type style.

Erasing Permanent Fonts

If you permanently download any fonts at the beginning of the day, and you run into memory problems when you print pages with graphics that do not use those fonts, you can flush the fonts out of the printer's memory by turning off the printer. When you turn the printer back on, print the pages with graphics first, before you permanently download the fonts again.

Most printers can handle no more than 16 soft fonts per page and 32 soft fonts per publication. (Even this maximum depends on the size of the font because larger fonts take up more memory.) These limits are considerably smaller for printers with limited memory available. For example, a 512K printer may be able to hold only 10 text fonts that are 9 or 10 points in size. The advantage of temporarily downloading fonts is that the printer's memory is completely cleared between print jobs. With permanently downloaded fonts, you must turn the printer off, then on again, to clear the memory.

As noted in Chapter 4, a font is a particular combination of typeface and style (and sometimes point size). Some printers require that each combination of typeface, style, and size be downloaded as a separate font; other printers—PostScript printers, for instance—can print any size of a specific typeface and style after the font is downloaded. To use the entire family in the Palatino typeface on a PostScript printer, for example, you need to download only four different styles: normal, boldface, italic, and boldface italic. For design suggestions, along with a discussion of other production considerations such as the choice of fonts for publications, see Chapter 10.

Using Soft Fonts

After you install a soft font in your system and let Windows know where it is, try using the font in a publication. Select the font in the Type Specifications dialog box, which is displayed when you select the Type Specs command on the Type menu. If you have trouble printing the publication, either of two problems may be the reason:

- The page has graphics that cannot be processed when the fonts are permanently downloaded.
- You have used too many fonts on one page or in one publication.

Remember that different typefaces, styles, and sizes take up different amounts of memory and that different types of graphics also make different demands on memory. Before you design a long publication with downloadable fonts, try printing one or two sample pages with representative graphics as well as text that uses all the fonts called for in the design. If you have trouble printing these sample pages, change your design by reducing the number of fonts you use or by simplifying the specifications for illustrations.

Using the Print Command

The Print command—located on the File menu and available only in Layout view—is used throughout the production process to print preliminary versions and final copies of publications. Because this command is so frequently used, it has a keyboard shortcut: Ctrl-P. Invoking the command causes PageMaker to display a dialog box in which you specify the number of copies and range of pages to be printed, as well as other special options (see fig. 8.12). These options include reducing or enlarging pages, printing miniature "thumbnails" of each page, printing crop marks on pages that will be trimmed for final production, printing large-format pages on smaller sheets of paper, and changing the printer selection. Not all printers support all of the options shown in the dialog box. Options that are not supported by the currently selected printer are missing from the dialog box or displayed in gray. If you want to keep all the default options, click OK to print. Each of the options is described under the next headings.

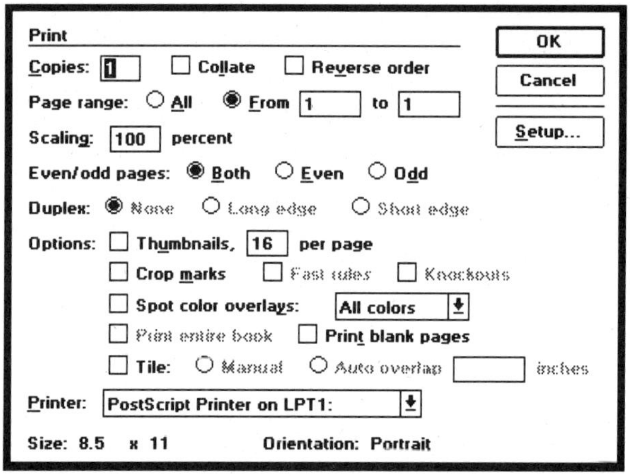

Fig. 8.12. The Print dialog box.

> ***Saving Your Publication before Printing***
> Immediately before issuing the Print command, you should save your publication. Complex pages (those with large bit-mapped images, for example) sometimes can cause a printer to malfunction and force you to reboot your computer. When you reboot, you lose some data. Even if you lose only one page of changes, you can save yourself a significant amount of time and aggravation by saving your publication before you begin to print.

Specifying the Number of Copies

When you specify how many copies you want to print of each page, you can indicate whether they should be printed in reverse order and whether they should be collated. If you are printing only one copy of a publication, PageMaker normally prints from the beginning to the end of the publication.

If your printer outputs pages face down, the pages come out in the correct order. If your printer outputs pages face up, however, the printed stack of pages come out in reverse order. In this case, choose Reverse Order to force the final stack of pages to be output in the correct order.

If you are printing more than one copy and choose the Collate option, PageMaker prints one complete copy of the entire publication before it prints the next copy. This option is useful when you want to review the first copy while the other copies are printing or when you are printing final copies for distribution.

Collating saves you the time you would spend sorting the copies manually, but the process often involves significantly longer printing time. When copies are not collated, the printer processes each page only once and prints multiple copies immediately from the same drum image. During collation, the printer must process each page for each copy—that is, it reprocesses the drum image for each sheet of paper printed. You can speed up printing by setting the printer to make multiple, uncollated copies.

Printing a Range of Pages

PageMaker's default setting is to print all pages of the publication. But suppose that you need to make changes that affect just a few pages or that you want to print the finished parts of a publication still in process. Instead of printing the entire publication, you can print a specific range of pages. Enter the beginning and ending page numbers in the From and To boxes of the Print dialog box. These entries are remembered when you save the publication, so you should always check that you are printing the pages you want—and not a previous page selection.

Reducing and Enlarging Pages

Some printers—such as PostScript printers—can print percentage reductions or enlargements between 25 and 1,000 percent. If you are using this type of printer, you can enter a percentage reduction or enlargement in the Scaling box in the Print dialog box. The top left corner of each page, as shown on-screen, remains the top left corner of the printed page; all enlarging or reducing is done to the right and down.

The results of printing enlargements are predictable: If you scale a page to be larger than the printer paper, you lose part of the right and bottom edges of the page. You can print these missing portions of the page using the Tile option (see "Printing Parts of Pages" in this section).

The results of printing reductions may not be what you expect. Only the graphics and text blocks that actually touch the page on-screen appear on the printout. Graphics and text blocks that overlap the page and pasteboard are printed, but elements that fall totally onto the pasteboard are not printed in a reduction.

> ### Working in Large Scales
>
> Suppose that you are using very small point sizes for text throughout a publication or that you have more columns than fit on an 8 1/2-inch-wide page. In these cases, you can work in larger point sizes on a tabloid-size page on-screen and then print the publication at 50 percent to fit on an 8 1/2-by-11-inch page.
>
> Note that the Scaling specification in the Print dialog box overrides the scaling specification in the printer-specific dialog box that is accessed through the Windows Control Panel or the Setup button in PageMaker's Print dialog box (see "Adding a Printer Driver" in the "Installing the Printer" section of this chapter).

Printing Double-Sided Copies

Usually, you print all pages (both even-numbered and odd-numbered) of a publication in succession, each on a single side of a piece of paper. In a double-sided publication, these single-sided master pages are output back-to-back by photocopying or offset printing.

Printing without a Duplex Printer

If you want to print double-sided pages directly through a laser printer, however, and the printer does not have duplexing capabilities, use the Odd Pages option to print only odd-numbered pages first. Check the Reverse Order option, flip the stack over, feed it into the printer, and print only even-numbered pages on the back of the odd-numbered pages.

The Even/Odd Pages options are not available when you are printing spot color overlays, thumbnails, or tiles.

> ### *Printing Double-Sided Copies*
>
> ***Caution:*** The orientation of the paper tray and the position of output pages vary from printer to printer, and you may need to add an extra (even-numbered) blank page to the end of a publication with an odd number of pages before you print it. You should experiment with a short (three- to five-page) double-sided publication before trying to print a large publication double-sided through a laser printer. Be sure to check the Print Blank Pages option (see "Printing Blank Pages" in this section).
>
> Also, some printers do not allow passing paper through a second time. Refer to the documentation that came with your printer.

Printing with a Duplex Printer

If your printer has duplexing capabilities—such as the Hewlett-Packard LaserJet IID and the LaserJet 2000—you can select the Duplex option to print on both sides of the paper. The specification you select for duplex printing depends on the page orientation and the binding edge.

If your page orientation is Tall and the publication will be bound along the left vertical edge, select Long Edge. If your page orientation is Tall and the publication will be bound along the top edge, select Short Edge. Conversely, for a Wide page orientation, select Long Edge if the publication will be bound along the top and Short Edge if the publication will be bound along the left side.

Note that the Duplex specification in the Print dialog box overrides the duplex specification in the printer-specific dialog box that is accessed through the Windows Control Panel or the Setup button in PageMaker's Print dialog box (see "Adding a Printer Driver" in the "Installing the Printer" section of this chapter).

Printing Thumbnails

The Thumbnails option enables you to print miniature versions of up to 64 publication pages per printed page, with facing pages paired, as shown in figure 8.13. Not all printers support this option. For example, LaserJet printers and clones and dot-matrix printers do not print thumbnails, but

PostScript and DDL printers do. If the currently selected printer does not have thumbnails capability, this option is displayed in gray in the dialog box. Thumbnails can be handy reminders of the contents of a publication, and they can be used as planning tools during the design and production process, as discussed in Chapter 10.

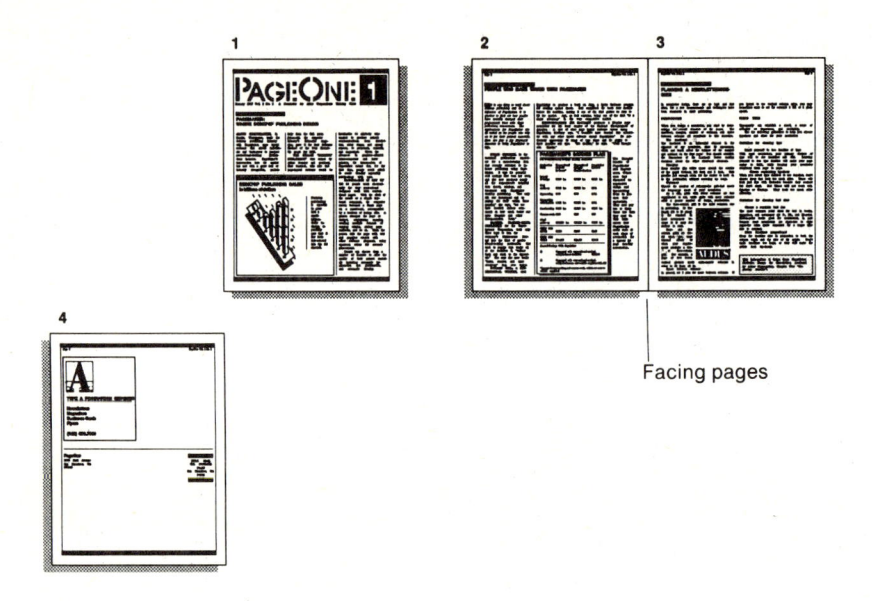

Fig. 8.13. Example of publication printed with the Thumbnails option.

Printing Crop Marks

You can use the Crop Marks feature to generate the marks traditionally used to indicate where the pages are cut when trimmed to their final size (see fig. 8.14). This option is available only when you are printing on a paper size that is at least 1/2 inch longer and wider than the page size specified for the publication. You also can use the Crop Marks feature when you are printing a reduced page size using the Scaling factor discussed in "Reducing and Enlarging Pages" in this section. This option also produces registration marks if you print spot-color overlays (see Chapter 9).

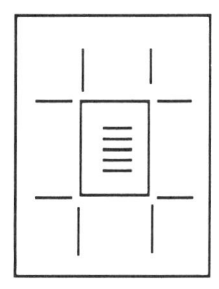

Fig. 8.14. Printing crop marks when page size is smaller than paper size.

Using Fast Rules

Check Fast Rules to speed up the printing of vertical and horizontal rules and boxes drawn with PageMaker's tools. PageMaker sends the dimensions of the rule or box to the printer instead of a bit-mapped image. Leave Fast Rules unchecked when you are printing spot-color overlays with knockouts.

Printing in Color

PageMaker enables you to add spot color to your publications. These images can be printed on a color or a black-and-white printer, or they can be prepared for commercial color printing by printing spot-color overlays (separate page printouts for each color). PageMaker has built-in support for color printers; images are automatically printed in color unless you specify otherwise. If the printer does not have color capability, the images are printed in black-and-white.

If you are printing spot-color overlays, check Knockouts when you want PageMaker to leave blank those areas where other colors overlap. Objects are cut out on each overlay according to the order in which they are drawn or layered on the page. Leave this option unchecked if you want your commercial printer to cut out the overlapping colors for you.

Chapter 9 discusses in detail the use of color and shows you how to prepare your publications for spot-color overlays and for offset printing.

Printing Books

Check Print Entire Book if the current publication includes a book list of related PageMaker publications and you want to print all of the publications. Do not check this option if you want to print the current publication only. This option is displayed in gray if the current publication does not include a book list. The Book command is discussed in Chapter 7.

Note that when you print from a book list, the print specifications of the current publication temporarily override, but do not change, the print specifications stored with each publication in the book list.

Printing Blank Pages

Usually, PageMaker does not print the blank pages in a publication—pages that contain nothing but master page elements. You can check Print Blank Pages to force all pages of the publication to print. Usually, you would leave this option unchecked when printing drafts for editing or proofing, but check this option for the final printing so that every page of the publication is represented by a numbered printed page. This option is not available if you are printing spot-color overlays.

Printing Parts of Pages

With the Tile option, you can print pieces of large pages on smaller paper. A common application of the Tile option is to print tabloid-size, 11-by-17-inch pages on 8 1/2-by-11-inch paper, as shown in figure 8.15. You can assemble the "tiled" sheets into one piece for reproduction, or you can use them as proof sheets only. (You can print the final version of a tabloid page on a Linotronic typesetter's 12-inch wide roll of photosensitive paper without using the Tile option.)

When you "tile" pages, you can select the Auto Overlap option and specify by how much you want the images on each tile to overlap. (You set the minimum amount for tiling overlap, but PageMaker tries to give you as much overlap as possible and may exceed the amount that you specify). You need to account for the fact that most printers cannot print closer to the edge of the paper than approximately 1/3 inch, and some printers cannot print closer than 1/2 inch.

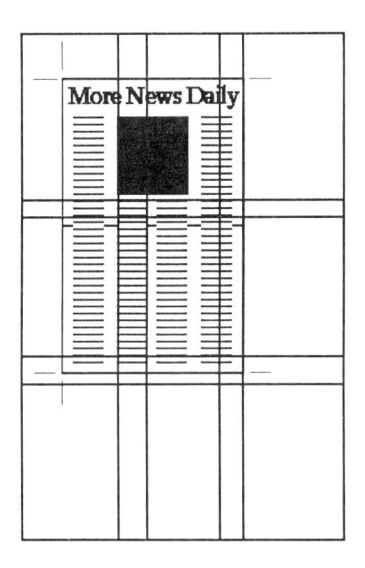

Fig. 8.15. A tabloid-size page printed on 8 1/2-by-11-inch paper with the Tile feature and a full page printed with crop marks on a Linotronic typesetter.

You also can manually force parts of the printed images to overlap when you assemble them into one large page. Select the Manual option and define the limits of each tile piece by moving the zero point on the ruler line. For example, print one tile with the zero point at the top left corner of the page, then move the zero point to mark the top left corner of the next tile and print again.

> **Avoiding Manual Tiling of Facing Pages**
>
> When you use PageMaker's manual tiling feature, make sure that the Facing Pages option is turned off. Because facing pages have a single zero point, you would have to move the zero point twice as many times to tile a facing-page publication.

Selecting the Printer

Two methods of selecting a printer for a publication are available. The target printer is set up by means of the Target Printer command (see "Choosing the Target Printer through PageMaker" in the "Installing the Printer" section of this chapter). The current printer—which may or may not be the same as the target printer—is set up in the Print dialog box (displayed when you select the Print command on the File menu). The target printer is the printer intended for the final printing of your publication, whereas the current printer specified in the Print dialog box can be either the target printer or a draft printer.

The Printer window of the Print dialog box displays the currently selected (highlighted) printer, along with a list of other printers installed on your system (see fig. 8.12). This list shows the printers that are physically hooked up to your system and installed through the Control Panel (see "Installing the Printer")—it is not a comprehensive list of all the installed printer drivers (which can be displayed with the Target Printer command). You can change the current printer selection by clicking another printer name (if other names are displayed).

If you change the type of printer for a publication, the text is recomposed to match the new printer's fonts as closely as possible; in addition, based on information taken from the target printer driver, PageMaker adjusts letter and word spacing to correspond with the line breaks as they will appear when the target printer is used. The printed draft will therefore look similar to but may not exactly match the final publication. The stored publication remains unchanged, and the Layout view continues to show how the publication will look when it is finally output on the target printer.

Changing Printer Specifications

The current selections for paper size and orientation are displayed at the bottom of the Print dialog box. You can change these settings for the current publication, and other printer specifications, by clicking the Setup button in the Print dialog box. PageMaker then displays the same dialog box you access with the Printers icon in the Windows Control Panel (by double-clicking the Printers icon, clicking Configure in the Printers dialog box, and clicking Setup in the Printers—Configure dialog box; see "Changing Printer Options" in this section).

When you access this dialog box through the Control Panel, you set the specifications for each printer installed on your system, and these become the default specifications when you choose a printer through any application. When you access this dialog box through the Print dialog box in PageMaker, however, you set the printer specifications for the current printer and the current publication only. Changes made through the Print command do not affect settings made through the Target Printer command (see "Choosing the Target Printer through PageMaker" in the "Installing the Printer" section of this chapter).

Page versus Paper Orientation

Caution: Usually, publications set up with Portrait *page* orientation in the Page Setup dialog box are output on printers set up with Portrait *paper* orientation in the Print dialog box. Similarly, Landscape pages are printed on Landscape paper. If the orientation of the page differs from the orientation of the paper, PageMaker displays a warning message before printing. Choosing different orientations for pages and paper has the effect of rotating the entire page image 90 degrees on the paper (see fig. 8.16).

Model Airplane Contest

Top 3 Win a Trip to Palm Beach
in the cockpit of a Cessna!
1st place also wins $5,000
2nd place $2,000, 3rd $500

Rules

1. Models must be constructed of paper and balsa wood and glue only.
2. Model must be between 8 and 12 inches long and wide.
3. Entries must be received by midnight, August 30.
4. Send for official entry form and more details.

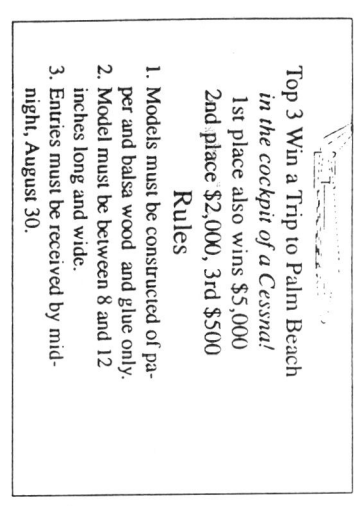

***Fig. 8.16.** Portrait page (left) printed to paper set up with Landscape orientation (right).*

Using the Print Manager

After you complete your entries in the Print dialog box and click OK, PageMaker prepares each page for printing and either prints it directly or sends it to the Print Manager—a print spooler that is part of the Microsoft Windows 3.0 operating environment. The Print Manager enables any program running under Windows to perform all its print processing quickly and to store the results on the computer's hard disk. You thus can resume working with the program while printing is in progress.

While PageMaker is preparing each page for printing, the program displays a dialog box with a changing message about the current status of the printing process (see fig. 8.17). As each page is printed or prepared for the Print Manager, PageMaker highlights the icon for that page in the lower left corner of the Publication window. When PageMaker finishes its part of the printing process, you can resume working on the publication or run any other program under Windows.

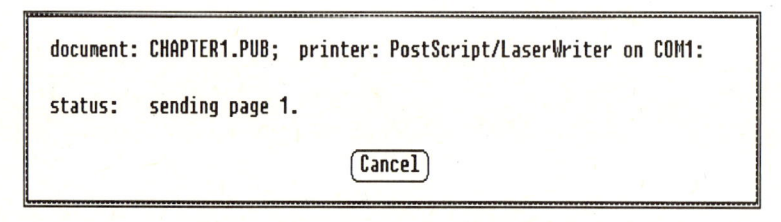

```
document: CHAPTER1.PUB;  printer: PostScript/LaserWriter on COM1:

status:    sending page 1.

                         ( Cancel )
```

Fig. 8.17. Dialog box showing the status of the printing process.

Note that if you close the Windows environment, you terminate the printing process.

If you send more than one file to the printer, the Print Manager lines up the files and feeds them to the printer in the order in which you sent them. You can view the list of files in the print queue, temporarily stop the active printing process, and reorder the priority of jobs in the queue by displaying the Windows main window and double-clicking the print manager icon. The resulting window (see fig. 8.18) shows the list of jobs in the print queue. Click the Pause button to stop printing temporarily; click the Resume button to resume printing. Select a job and click Delete to remove it from the print queue.

The dialog box in figure 8.18 shows that the publication is being printed on an Apple LaserWriter Plus printer attached to the COM1 port. Nothing else is printing or waiting to be printed.

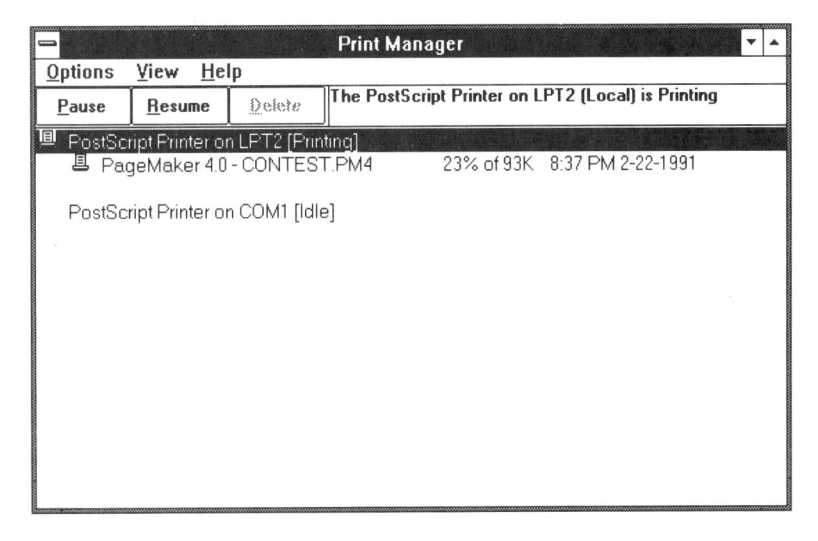

Fig. 8.18. The Print Manager dialog box.

Open the Options menu on the Print Manager menu bar to set a selected job to Low Priority, Medium Priority, or High Priority. Within each category, jobs are printed in the order submitted.

Saving Time Spooling and Printing

You can allocate more RAM to the spooler so that it works faster. Before you begin printing, open the Print Manager window from the Control Panel and select Priorities. Choose High instead of the default Low.

Small print jobs take almost as long to spool as to print. Spooling is most useful for long jobs (10- to 100-page files). You can turn off your spooler in the WIN.INI file so that print jobs go directly to the printer.

If you are working on a network with its own spooler, your publications will print faster if you turn the Print Manager off: Double-click the Control Panel icon in the Windows main window, double-click the Printers icon, and click Use Print Manager to remove the X from the checkbox.

Stopping the Printing Process

You can stop the printing process by clicking Cancel in the dialog box that PageMaker displays while pages are being formatted for the print spooler (see fig. 8.17). The dialog box disappears when PageMaker completes its portion of the printing process. You still can cancel printing by using the Control Panel to open the Print Manager window and then clicking the Delete button. If more than one publication is in the queue for printing, you can use this command to remove selected publications before they start printing.

Printing a Publication to a Disk

Instead of printing a publication on a printer, you can print the publication to a disk file. This single, printable disk file of the publication includes all linked graphics and downloadable fonts. You then can print the file using the COPY command under DOS (i.e., you do not need Windows 3.0 or PageMaker to print the file), or you can use the Print command under Windows 3.0 (i.e., you do not need PageMaker).

When you want to transfer a publication to another system, printing to disk is especially useful in the following circumstances:

- The other system does not have PageMaker installed

- You do not want to worry about having all the linked files or providing instructions to the operators on the other system about how the files are linked

- The PageMaker publication is too large to fit on a floppy disk; you can create several printable files by printing a few pages at a time to disk

- You want to transmit the publication by modem

Editing Printable Disk Files

Caution: You cannot use PageMaker to edit a file that has been printed to disk. This process creates an ASCII file that contains PostScript code. You can use a text editor, however, to modify this ASCII file if you know the PostScript language.

> ***Printing Disk Files with Downloadable Fonts***
>
> ***Caution:*** When you are using downloadable fonts in a publication, those fonts must be listed under the FILE port (that is, [PostScript, FILE]) in the WIN.INI file for them to be included in your print file (see the discussion on updating the WIN.INI file in "Installing Soft Fonts" in the "Downloading Soft Fonts" section of this chapter).
>
> If the fonts in the publication are not permanently downloaded to the printer used for the final version, you must download the soft fonts as temporary fonts when you print the file (see "Downloading Soft Fonts" in this chapter).

Creating a Printable Disk File

To create a printable disk file of a PageMaker publication, choose the Print command from the File menu, click Setup in the Print dialog box, then click Options to display the Options dialog box. In the Print To area, click Encapsulated PostScript File (see fig. 8.19).

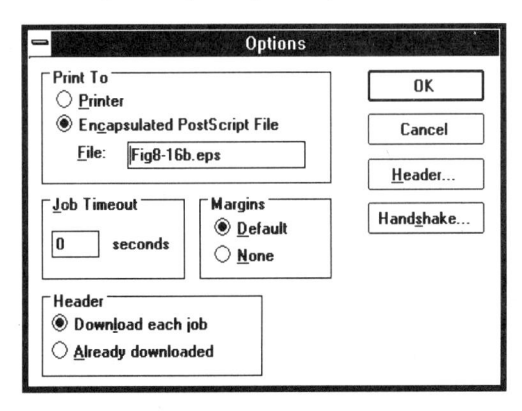

Fig. 8.19. *Encapsulated PostScript selected in the Options dialog box.*

Printing the Disk File from DOS

To print the disk file from DOS, at the DOS prompt type the command *copy* followed by the name of the file to be printed (including the path to the file) and the name of the port to which the printer is attached. For example, you type

    COPY C:\BOOK1\CH01.PRN COM1:

to print the file named CH01.PRN, stored in the BOOK1 directory on drive C, on the printer attached to the COM1 port.

Printing the Disk File from Windows 3.0

The Windows Print command prints a listing of the Encapsulated PostScript code, not the page image. To print the PostScript code disk file from Windows, start Windows 3.0 and choose Main from the Windows menu if that window is not already displayed. Double-click the File Manager icon in the Windows main window, double-click the name of the directory where the disk file is stored, and click the name of the disk file to select it. Choose Print from the File menu, confirm the name of the file to be printed in the dialog box, and click OK to start the printing.

Changing Systems

If you take your PageMaker publication from one system to another, you need to take the following files with you besides the PageMaker file itself:

- All linked graphics files used in the publication
- Printer fonts used in the publication (or a list of fonts, so you can make sure that they are installed in the other system)

Copy linked graphics files into a single directory with the PageMaker publication. Use the Save As command and click the Copy Files Required for Remote Printing option in the dialog box, which also copies special files such as the track-kerning resource file that is needed in printing. (The Copy All Linked Files option includes files that are not required for printing. Use this option for archive or backup purposes only.)

Using Service Bureaus

You might want to use a service bureau to print your final publication on a printer or typesetter that has a higher resolution than your own printer.

Before you prepare your PageMaker files for output by a service bureau, you should verify the format in which they prefer to receive your publication files and the printer fonts they have available. Some service bureaus may request that files be printed to disk in PostScript format (see "Creating a Printable Disk File" in this section), which they can download to the imagesetter.

You should always keep a backup of your files, especially when taking them from one machine or system to another.

Chapter Summary

As you can see, the printing process can be simple if you are using only the fonts built into your printer. If you want to add downloadable fonts for your publications, the process involves several steps outside of PageMaker before you create the publication. The number of different fonts you can use on one page or in one publication is limited by the amount of memory in the printer and the size of the fonts you are downloading.

If you have only one printer in your office, workshop, or studio, and you are using only fonts hard-coded into your printer, the printing process is straightforward: You select the Print command on the File menu. If you have more than one printer to choose from, you can use the Target Printer command to select the final printer for a particular publication. Use the Control Panel to add or remove printer and font names from the lists shown in dialog boxes. Also use the Control Panel to switch printer connections or to change the option settings for a particular printer.

Before you design a large publication that calls for downloadable fonts, experiment a little. Do the same before deciding whether to use permanently or temporarily downloaded fonts. Chapter 10 further discusses different fonts and factors to take into account when you use them.

9

Making Color Separations

One of the biggest obstacles to using color in offset-printed communications in the past was cost. But each color adds only 10% to offset printing costs—it is the *prepress* costs that are the greater expense in most color productions. Traditionally, the term "prepress" has been used to describe the steps that the print shop goes through to prepare a page for printing from the time the mechanical is delivered until the printing plate is actually made from a negative.

If the page is to be printed in one color and is composed solely of text and line art, the traditional prepress steps are simple: Photograph the page and develop the negative. If the page is to be printed in more than one color, then the print shop needs to make color separations of the page and prepare one negative for each color to be printed, selectively concealing (masking) other colors and trimming areas where colors overlap (traps) and edges where colors meet (butts). These traditional methods take a great deal of time, use sophisticated cameras and other equipment, and require a considerable level of skill; they are therefore costly. PageMaker has built-in functions that automatically perform many of these steps, so the prepress process takes less time, uses less expensive equipment, and requires less specialized skills.

PageMaker enables you to assign colors to text and graphics and to preview the colors on a color monitor, to print spot-color overlays in black and white on any laser printer or PostScript typesetter, and to print color pages on a color printer. (PageMaker prints spot-color separations but not process-color separations. The difference between spot color and process color is discussed in "Printing in Color with Offset Printing" in this chapter.)

PageMaker's spot-color feature is useful for several purposes:

- Designing color publications and previewing the colors on a color monitor
- Creating color comps (examples) of different design ideas
- Creating spot-color overlays for offset printing
- Printing color pages and overhead transparencies on a color printer

This chapter explains how to use PageMaker's color features, when to use color printers, how offset printers produce color, and how to prepare mechanicals for color printing.

Assigning Spot Colors in PageMaker

You assign colors to text or graphics in PageMaker by first defining the color and then applying it, as described in the following sections. Colors appear as black, white, and shades of gray on a monochrome monitor and in color on a color monitor. The accuracy with which the printed colors will match the displayed colors depends on the number of colors your hardware supports and on the differences between electronic display technology and printing technology.

When you create colors in PageMaker, you actually set up a color sheet that applies to all the colors in a publication, just as a style sheet applies to all the text. As with style sheets, you can edit and remove colors from a color sheet and copy colors from one publication's color sheet to another.

PageMaker can print *spot-color overlays (spot-color separations)*, which means that it prints an object or objects (text or graphics) on separate sheets for each color. The objects on these sheets are *registered* (lined up) on the final composite page (see fig. 9.1). This capability makes it easy to prepare camera-ready film for most spot-color printing jobs.

PageMaker provides a basic default color palette that includes three colors that you can change or delete (Blue, Green, and Red), plus three colors that are always available: [Paper], [Black], and [Registration]. [Paper] indicates opaque, which is white (or a color of your choice). [Black] is always black, which is the initial default color for all text and graphics, and the color definition for [Black] cannot be changed. [Registration] is the color you assign to elements that you want PageMaker to print on every spot-color overlay, such as registration marks that you add manually (see "Crop Marks and Registration Marks" in the "Printing in Color with Offset Printing" section of this chapter).

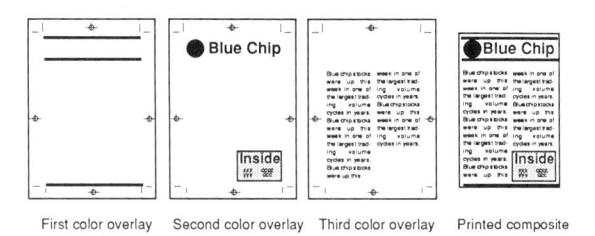

Fig. 9.1. Spot-color overlays printed from PageMaker.

Use the buttons in the Define Colors dialog box (displayed when you select the Define Colors command on the Element menu) to work with color definitions. From this dialog box you can create a new color, edit an existing color definition (change how a color looks), copy a color sheet from one publication to another, or remove a color from the color sheet. When you click on a color name to select it, the color is displayed in the Color box at the top of the dialog box. You can edit the existing colors in the default color palette, including the [Paper] color but excluding [Registration] and [Black]. You can remove or rename any color that does not appear in brackets in the dialog box.

Editing Existing Colors

You can edit colors by choosing Define Colors from the Element menu to display the Define Colors dialog box, which lists the colors already defined (see fig. 9.2).

You edit a color either by double-clicking on the color in the Define Colors dialog box or by clicking once on the color to select it and then clicking the Edit button to display the Edit Color dialog box (see fig. 9.3). You also can display the Edit Color dialog box by holding down the Ctrl key and clicking on a color name in the Colors palette (see "Applying Colors" in this chapter).

In the Edit Color dialog box you can change the name of a color by replacing the name shown in the Name field. You also can change the color model and the color percentages used to define the color. You can adjust the defining characteristics of a specific color by using any one of three color models: RGB (red, green, and blue), HLS (hue, luminance, and saturation), or CMYK (cyan, magenta, yellow, and black). The number of slide bars and slide bar labels changes to reflect the color model you choose.

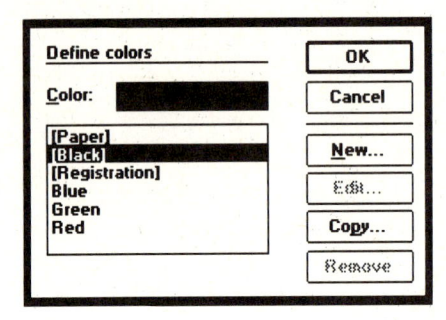

Fig. 9.2. The Define Colors dialog box with the default color names.

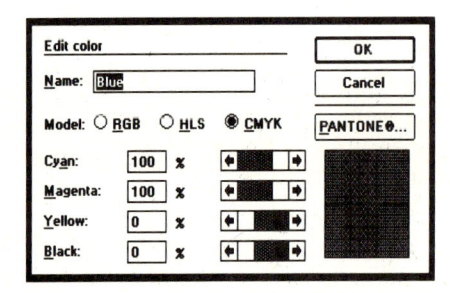

Fig. 9.3. The Edit Color dialog box.

In the RGB, HLS, and CMYK color systems, you mix colors by varying the percentages of their defining values: You either type numbers in the text boxes near each scale name or scroll the slide bars. Percentages range from 0 to 100 percent for all values (except hue, which ranges from 0 to 359 degrees). You can use a color reference guide available from art supply stores to help determine the percentages, or you can mix colors on-screen and preview the results of various percentage settings (if you have a color monitor). The rectangle in the lower right corner of the Edit Color dialog box displays the original color in its lower half and the new mixed color in its upper half. Click OK to accept the new color, or click Cancel if you decide to keep the original color.

You also can define a color using the Pantone Matching System (PMS) by clicking the Pantone button to display the Pantone Color dialog box (see fig. 9.4). The Pantone Matching System is a standard used by designers and commercial printers for specifying colors and mixing spot-color inks. The colors in the Pantone Color dialog box are listed in the same order as in the *Pantone Color Formula Guide 747XR*, a color swatchbook available from most art supply stores.

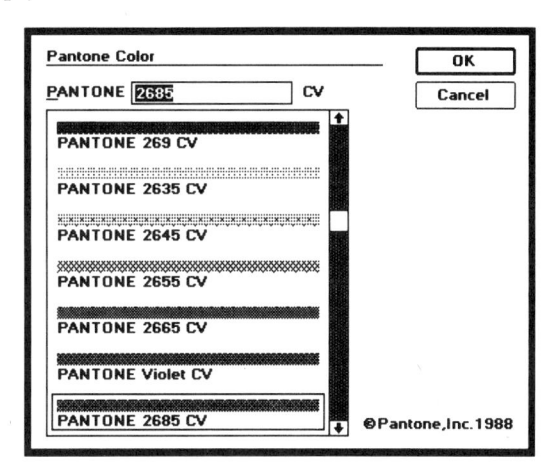

Fig. 9.4. The Pantone Color dialog box.

You select a specific PMS color either by using the scroll bar to locate the color and clicking on the color name or by typing the PMS color number in the box at the top of the dialog box and clicking OK. PageMaker then returns you to the Edit Color dialog box, where you can either click OK to add the PMS color to your color palette or edit the color.

Editing a Pantone Color

Caution*:* If you choose the Crop Marks option when you print spot-color overlays, PageMaker prints the color names you have assigned on each overlay. Because Pantone color names and numbers have very specific meanings to commercial printers, it is a good idea to change the name of any color you edit that is based on a Pantone color.

When you close the Edit Color dialog box, the Define Colors dialog box remains open. Click Close to close the box and record all changes, or click Cancel if you decide not to record any changes or additions.

> ### *Choosing a Color System*
>
> The choice of a color model to work with in the Edit Color dialog box depends entirely on your personal preference—the color model does not affect how the color is displayed on the screen or printed. You can match most colors using any color model.
>
> The RGB color model is the one used to display colors on computer monitors, and it is used in mixing colors for printing in some countries (but not the United States). Traditional graphic artists are accustomed to working with the HLS system when they create new colors. If you are not familiar with the HLS system, you probably should stick with the CMYK or Pantone color models, which generally are used in offset printing in the United States. The Pantone system—with the aid of a Pantone color swatchbook— is the most efficient method of assigning colors when you have a monochrome monitor.

Creating New Colors

To create a new color, choose Define Colors from the Element menu. PageMaker displays the Define Colors dialog box (see fig. 9.2 again).

To create a new color, double-click on the [Black] or [Registration] color name, or select any other color and click New. PageMaker then displays the Edit Color dialog box (see fig. 9.3 again). You also can display the Edit Color dialog box for a new color by holding down the Ctrl key and clicking on the [Black] or [Registration] color name in the Colors palette (see "Applying Colors" in this chapter).

Type the name of the new color in the Name field, where the blinking cursor appears. If the name you type is not on the palette, PageMaker adds the new name to the color sheet but does not delete or change any existing names. If you type a name already on the palette, PageMaker prompts you to use a different name (you must click the Edit button in the Define Colors dialog box if you want to change an existing color definition). If you type a reserved Pantone color name (Process Black, Process Yellow, Process Magenta, or Process Cyan), PageMaker prompts you to use a different name—Pantone colors must be selected through the Pantone Color dialog box (see "Editing Existing Colors" in the "Assigning Spot Colors in PageMaker" section of this chapter).

Removing Colors

You can remove a color from the color sheet by choosing Define Colors from the Element menu, choosing a color, and then clicking Remove in the Define Colors dialog box. Text and graphics to which the removed color has been assigned become black. You cannot remove the three basic colors defined by PageMaker: [Paper], [Black], and [Registration]. Removing a color from the current publication's color sheet does not affect the color sheets of other publications.

Copying Colors

You can copy the color sheet from another publication to the current one by choosing Define Colors from the Element menu and clicking Copy in the dialog box. The Copy Colors dialog box displays a list of the other publications whose color sheet you can copy (see fig. 9.5). Scroll through the list to find the name of the publication you want.

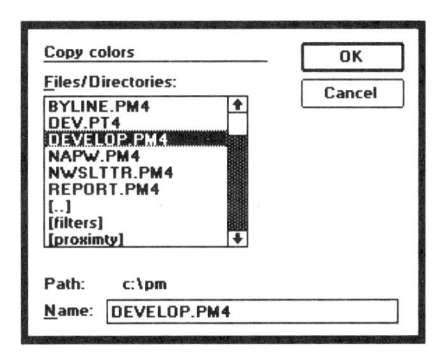

Fig. 9.5. The Copy Colors dialog box.

You can select a disk drive and directory path as you do in similar dialog boxes, such as the Open, Place, Save As, and Export dialog boxes. Double-click the parent directory symbol ([..]) to change to the next higher directory on the current drive; double-click the name of a drive (usually [-A-], [-B-], or [-C-]) to change to that drive, or type a path name in the text box and click OK to display the publications in the specified directory.

Choose the publication whose color sheet you want to copy by double-clicking the publication name or by selecting the publication name and clicking OK. When you click Close in the Define Colors dialog box, all the colors defined in the selected publication are copied into the current publication. If an existing color shares the same name as a color you are copying, PageMaker asks whether you want to replace the existing color with the copied color definition.

Applying Colors

To apply a color, first display the Colors palette by either choosing Color Palette from the Window menu or using the keyboard shortcut, Ctrl-K. The Colors palette displays a scrolling list of all the colors you have defined by means of the Define Colors command. You can resize the palette window in the same way you size any window: Position the cursor along the edge of the palette until the cursor changes to a double-headed arrow, and drag the edge of the palette until it is the size you want. You can make the palette large enough to display the full list of all colors you have created, or you can keep the palette small (to allow more room on-screen for the page layout and pasteboard) and use the scroll bars to move through the list of colors. You close the Colors palette by double-clicking the palette's Control menu icon (in the top left corner), by choosing the Color Palette command from the Window menu whenever it has a check mark next to it, or by using the keyboard shortcut, Ctrl-K.

When the Colors palette is displayed, you assign a color to an object (text or graphic) by selecting that object and then clicking a name in the Colors palette (see fig. 9.6). You can select more than one object at a time and then assign one color to the whole group. If all the selected objects are already assigned the same color, that color is highlighted in the Colors palette. If the selected objects are assigned different colors, no color is highlighted in the Colors palette.

Fig. 9.6. The Colors palette.

You can assign a color to selected text (individual characters or a range of text), graphics created with PageMaker's graphics tools, and graphics imported from other graphics applications.

Applying Color to Text

You apply color to text by first selecting the text with the text tool and then selecting a color from the Colors palette. (You also can assign color to text by means of the Type Specs command, on the Type menu, as discussed in Chapter 5.) Text color can be included in a style sheet definition. You can assign colors to text and anchored graphics while in Story view, but the color is not displayed until you return to Layout view.

Applying Color to PageMaker Graphics

You can apply color to lines, rectangles, and ovals created with PageMaker's drawing tools. In choosing colors for lines, remember that color in thin lines appears lighter than the same color applied to a larger, solid area.

You can assign a color to any two-dimensional object, such as a box or an oval, created with PageMaker's graphics tools. Because fill patterns affect colors besides black, any of the fill patterns displayed in the Fill submenu of the Element menu can be applied. You also can make the object's border stand out. An object with no fill (a fill of None selected from the Fill submenu) shows only a border in the selected color; an object with no border (a border of None selected from the Lines submenu of the Element menu) appears only as a filled interior in the selected color and pattern. By selecting appropriate border and fill patterns, you can get solid borders around lighter-colored interiors. The Fill submenu is shown in figure 9.7.

Because an object can have only one color, however, the border and fill will have the same color. If you want the fill color to be different from the border color, create two identical objects to be overlapped. Using the Line and Fill submenus of the Element menu, assign to one of the objects the color you want for the border and a fill of None; assign to the other object the color you want for the fill and a border of None.

If you're working with only a limited number of colors, such as black and one accent color, you can create additional visual interest, and the feeling of a multicolor piece, by using PageMaker's rectangle tools and the Fill submenu of the Element menu to create screens with spot color. For example, a 30-percent screen of red produces a pink tint. You can combine, therefore, a variety of tints of one color on a page to get more variety when printing with only one or two ink colors. Color tints can be attractive when printed in large blocks or across a whole page. In addition, with a light tint, you can overprint type in black or most other colors. Be careful about overprinting type, however; color tints such as grays may not provide enough character definition.

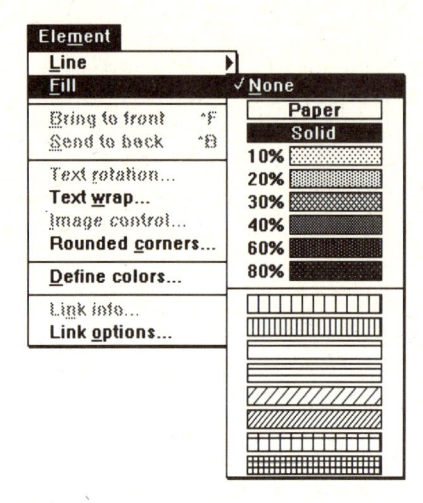

Fig. 9.7. The Fill submenu.

Applying Color to Imported Graphics

Graphics imported from other graphics applications with the Place command can be assigned one color. You cannot, however, assign colors only to parts of such graphics. Multicolor graphics created in other applications and imported into PageMaker may be displayed in color, but PageMaker cannot always match the colors chosen in the original graphics applications, and PageMaker may not be able to separate the image into spot-color overlays. PageMaker usually imports color graphics in black or in a single color set as the default color on the Colors palette (with the Color Palette command on the Element menu). If you want to assign several colors to an imported graphic in PageMaker, you can use the source graphics application to cut the graphic into separate parts, store each part as a separate file, and import each part as a separate object that you can place and color in PageMaker.

PageMaker displays the colors you assign to black-and-white bit-mapped images, but it does not display the colors you assign to Windows Metafiles, EPS files, or color TIFF images. Imported color TIFF images cannot be color separated directly with PageMaker, but you can get process color separations of PageMaker publications by using other separating systems or software (see "Preparing a PageMaker Publication for Process Color Printing" in the "Printing in Color with Offset Printing" section of this chapter).

Proofing Colors On-Screen

On-screen color proofing, or *soft proofing*, is a method currently being used only for preliminary and position proofing. Soft proofing is not reliable as a final proofing technique because using the color on monitors to simulate the color of ink on paper is extremely difficult.

Most monitors are based on a cathode ray tube (CRT) that displays colors by electrically stimulating phosphors on the surface of the tube. The transmitted color is made up of dots of the additive primaries (red, green, and blue) that make up white light. These dots, or *screen pixels*, are fixed in size and position. CRT displays create different colors by varying the intensity of pixels. If red and green pixels are stimulated at the same intensity, for example, the result is yellow. If the intensity of green is reduced, the result is orange.

Printed color, on the other hand, is reflected; it is made up of dots of the subtractive primary colors—yellow, cyan, and magenta—plus black. Different colors are created by varying the size of the dots (the density of the printed ink).

When you proof color pages on your monitor, be sure that all color images are correctly linked to your publication (discussed in Chapter 7), that detailed graphics are set to display at high resolution by means of the Preferences command (on the Edit menu, discussed in Chapter 3), and that your monitor is set to display as many colors as your graphics card allows.

> ***Displaying a Single Image at High Resolution***
> To display a single image at high resolution when the Preferences resolution is set to Normal or Gray Out, press the Ctrl key as the image starts to appear on the screen. This procedure works whenever PageMaker displays or redisplays the page; when you move to a different page, change the view of the page.

Printing in Color with Color Printers

You can print color pages with PageMaker directly on color dot-matrix printers, thermal-transfer printers, ink-jet printers, and film recorders supported by Microsoft Windows and PageMaker. For example, the QMS ColorScript 100 color printer is a 300-dpi PostScript thermal printer that can serve for color proofing or for short-run color productions. Currently, most high-resolution color printers use an ink-jet technology, creating images by spraying minute droplets of ink. Printing a color publication is no different from printing a black-and-white publication. If the printer you select in the Print dialog box (displayed when you select the Print command on the File menu or press Ctrl-P) has color capabilities, PageMaker prints the publication in color. If you print a color publication on a black-and-white printer, PageMaker converts the page image to monochrome black and shades of gray.

If you intend to print a publication on a color printer, you need to know what colors the printer is capable of reproducing and define colors that match the printer's colors. If you are using a high-resolution PostScript color printer, you should be able to print any color you want. If you are printing on a low-resolution dot-matrix printer, however, your choice of colors is more limited.

Inexpensive dot-matrix color printers can cost less than $1,000. The trade-offs for the low cost can include low resolution, slow printing speed, a limited color palette, poor color quality, and banding (streaks across the printed image that result from a moving carriage). Nevertheless, a dot-matrix color printer can be a worthwhile investment for in-house presentations and for printing proofs of color images that might later be output elsewhere on a printer of greater capability. Dot-matrix color printers are available from Epson, Canon, Brother, Toshiba, and others.

The next step up is color ink-jet printers. Their prices range from less than $1,400 (the Hewlett-Packard PaintJet) to more than $8,500 (the Howtek PixelMaster), and they offer higher resolution and better color than dot-matrix printers. The wide price range in this group reflects the variation in color quality and the range of resolutions (up to 180 dpi on the PaintJet, 300 dpi on the Howtek).

At the high end, color printers can cost as little as $6,000 (the Calcomp Color Master) or as much as $80,000 (DuPont Imaging Systems' 4Cast). In this category are thermal printers that use heat to seal color pigments in a wax or plastic coating onto Mylar, laser printers that use color toner cartridges, and printers that use thermal dye technology to produce output approaching the quality of photographs. Prices for most thermal printers fall between $10,000 and $24,000, and include printers made by Kodak, Mitsubishi, QMS, Tektronix, and Versatec. These printers offer the best output, but the high investment must be justified by a high volume of color printing. For this reason, most people take disk files to a service bureau for color output of this quality.

Besides compatibility and the cost of the printer itself, you need to figure the cost of supplies into your decision to buy a color printer. For best results, most ink-jet or thermal color printers require either special coated paper or special transparent film if the printer accommodates overhead transparencies. In addition, you need to stock a good supply of color ribbons, ink cartridges, or toner cartridges. You will be surprised at how quickly the color supply dwindles when you are printing full-page color images with solid color backgrounds.

Many color print jobs, especially large-volume runs, are best handled by an offset print shop (discussed in "Printing in Color with Offset Printing"); however, some color publications can be printed on a color printer. The following sections explain some of the jobs you probably can handle easily without taking your work to an offset print shop.

Comps or Proofs

Color printers are often used to print *comps* (to give a client an idea of how a design looks in color) or *position proofs* (to show the position and general color of elements on a page). You can print full-color images on a single page, or you can print separated spot-color images on separate sheets of acetate. Printing color on acetate is a good way to check the registration of separated colors. Although these proofs often look extremely similar to the screen display of some color monitors, some people object to using position proofs as final proofs because they do not predict color press results accurately enough.

Short-Run Color Publications

Color printers also can be used for short-run color publications. If you need more than a few color copies, the slow printing speed and cost of color cartridges or inks make it more economical to print only one color master and then reproduce that master on a color copier. For very large quantities, you will want to use offset lithography—the traditional printing press. Offset printing has its own set of considerations and specialized vocabulary, discussed in "Printing in Color with Offset Printing" in this chapter.

Presentation Materials

Presentation materials, such as overhead transparencies, are rarely offset printed because they are needed in such low quantities. Three methods of creating color images for presentations are commonly used: printing on a color printer, coloring a black-and-white image by hand, and overlaying adhesive color acetates.

You also can print the images on paper, which often yields a crisper image, and reproduce them with color photocopiers or color photoprocessors, or you can photograph the images to make slides. Color printers offer the option of printing on clear acetate, which is useful for color overlays to check registration and for multicolor overhead transparencies.

If you do not have a color printer, you can use PageMaker to design on-screen color images, print them in black-and-white on acetate, and color the images yourself. You can color a black-and-white image by hand with a brush and color inks or with color pens. You need to be sure that the inks you are using adhere to the transparent film and will not bleed across boundaries on paper. Coloring by hand this way requires skill and patience to ensure even coverage and to avoid streaking.

You also can add color to printed images by using traditional paste-up techniques. Unless you are skilled with pens or brushes, you get the best results by overlaying printed images with adhesive color acetates, available at art supply shops. You can lay a sheet of color over the printed image, trace over the area to be colored using a cutting edge, and pull the color away from those parts of the image not to be colored (see fig. 9.8).

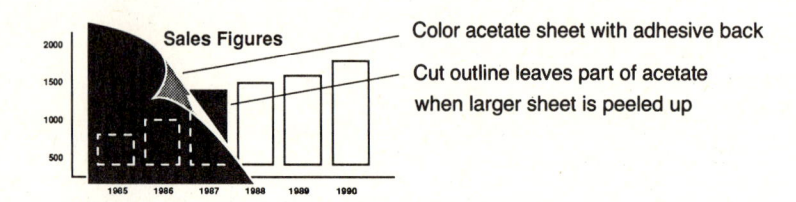

Fig. 9.8. Use a cutting edge to trace over an area to be colored.

Printing in Color with Offset Printing

When you need a color publication printed, especially in large quantities, usually you first print it in black-and-white on a PostScript printer or typesetter and then send it to an offset print shop to be printed in color. Even if a color printer is available, the offset print shop needs black-and-white mechanicals, also called *camera-ready masters*. (Printing in only one color is the same as printing in black-and-white.) For multicolor printing, on the other hand, each page element to be printed in a particular color must be separated from elements to be printed in other colors because each color requires a different printing plate.

Offset printing offers two ways of producing colors on a page: *spot color* and *process color*. Both methods require you to separate colors, but the separations are different, depending on which method you use. For spot color, each color is printed on a separate overlay and made into a separate printing plate; ink is mixed to match precisely each color used on the page, and each ink well on the press is loaded with a different mixed color. For process color, each color is split into its primary components (cyan, magenta, yellow, and black), and each ink well on the press is loaded with one of these colors.

Making good color separations traditionally is a difficult, exacting process. Many highly trained artisans have specialized in color separation all their lives. They work like surgeons to meticulously cut the edges around artwork where two colors meet on a page (traps and butts). If the trim is off by as much as the width of the knife edge, the two colors will overlap or have a gap between them.

PageMaker can print separated spot colors; each color is printed on a separate sheet of paper or transparency with crop marks and registration marks to show how the overlays are to be aligned. PageMaker 4.0, however, does not produce color separations for four-color process printing, but other separating systems or software can produce process color separations of PageMaker publications (see "Preparing a PageMaker Publication for Process Color Printing" in this section).

Understanding Spot-Color Offset Printing

To understand spot color, think of a pen plotter. The plotter can print in as many as four different colors of ink, but you cannot superimpose an area of one color on another—the resulting color would be muddy.

Offset-printing presses produce spot color in much the same way. The printer mixes several colors of ink to match each color indicated by the design. The ink colors are usually mixed according to formulas given in swatchbooks for Pantone Matching System (PMS) colors. Each press ink well is then filled with one custom-mixed color.

Because the spot colors never overlap on the final page, you can print a single camera-ready version of the page and on a tissue overlay mark instructions that tell the printer which parts are to be printed in each color. The printer then creates several negatives of the page and selectively blocks out sections of each negative to make several plates, each plate containing the parts of the page image to be printed in a particular color. Because PageMaker can print spot color separations automatically, this process can save the time it would take to block out different color elements on the negatives.

If the press has only one ink well, the printer runs the job once with one color, allows the pages to dry, cleans the ink well and rollers, fills the ink well with the next color, loads the next plate, and runs the dry pages for the next color. Many print shops have presses that can print two or more colors in one run, but in any case each color requires a separate plate, or color separation.

Deciding between Spot Color and Process Color

The procedure for printing spot color is labor-intensive and time-consuming; drying time alone can add days to a multiple-color print run done on a one-color press. Waiting time is shortened when you use a press that can print two or more colors in one run (industrial-strength dryers can help set one color before the sheet reaches the next set of rollers), but you still pay extra for each color the printer has to mix and load on the press. This method is often used to print a publication with just one, two, or three colors.

Publications that call for more than a few colors are usually printed using a four-color press always loaded with cyan, magenta, yellow, and black ink. With this technique, called *process color*, you can produce an infinite number of colors by printing a fine pattern of dots with the three subtractive primary colors plus black. If you stand back and look at the page normally, your eye is tricked into seeing the solid colors that result from mixing the primaries, but if you magnify a color image from any newspaper or magazine, you can see the patterns of non-overlapping dots in the three colors (plus black). If you are producing a publication that uses more than a few spot colors, you may choose to use the four-color process in the final printing; however, PageMaker cannot produce the process color separations for you.

Because four-color presses are designed to print all the colors in one run, the printer never needs to change the colors in the press. For this reason, you may choose to print spot color as process color—that is, to let the print shop separate each color into the three primary colors plus black (PageMaker cannot do this for you).

If you want to use the four-color process for final reproduction, you still can use PageMaker's color feature to produce color proofs (on a PostScript color printer) or to view colors on-screen, but you need to let the print shop make the final color separations for you, using traditional screening or photographic techniques.

Printing Spot-Color Overlays

To print spot-color overlays, choose Print from the File menu, and check Spot Color Overlays in the Print dialog box (see fig. 9.9). All page elements assigned a particular color are printed together on a sheet, and each color is printed on a different sheet. If you do not want to print all colors, click the arrow right of the color selection box (next to the Spot Color Overlays option) to choose specific colors from a drop-down list.

If the page size is smaller than the paper size and you choose the Crop Marks option in the Print dialog box, PageMaker prints the name of each color in the area beyond the page margins. Otherwise, you need to label each overlay with the color you intend the offset printer to use (see "Marking Mechanicals for Solid Spot Color" in this section).

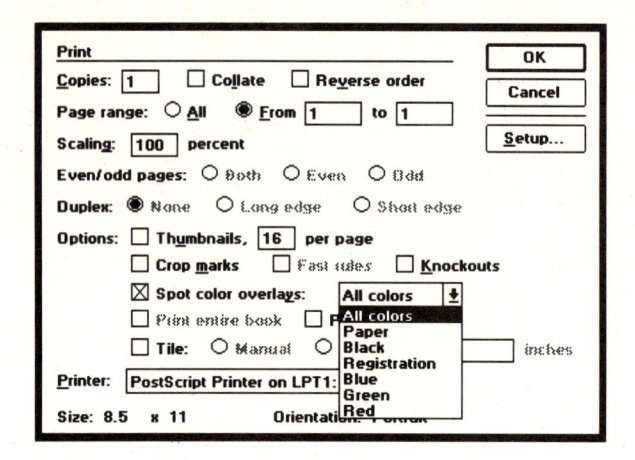

Fig. 9.9. The Print dialog box with Spot Color Overlays selected.

Crop Marks and Registration Marks

If the page size specified in the Page Setup dialog box (displayed when you select the Page Setup command on the File menu) is smaller than the paper size, you should select the Crop Marks option in the Print dialog box. When this option is selected, PageMaker prints crop marks and registration marks on each sheet (see fig. 9.10). *Crop marks* indicate where to trim a page to create the final page size. *Registration marks* help the printer check and align the plates used in printing different colors.

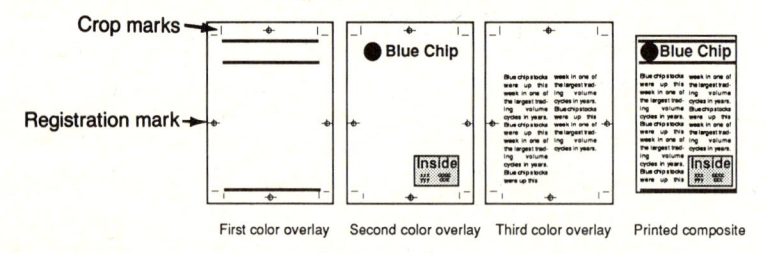

Fig. 9.10. Printed page showing crop marks and registration marks.

If the page size is the same as the paper size, the crop mark feature is not available; however, you should add registration marks manually to help the printer align the overlays. To add the registration marks manually, on the master page draw one registration mark like the one shown in figure 9.11. Use PageMaker's oval tool and straight-line tool with hairline line width. Select the entire graphic and choose [Registration] from the Colors palette (the Color Palette command on the Window menu or its keyboard shortcut,

Ctrl-K) or from the Define Colors dialog box (displayed when you select the Define Colors command on the Element menu). Copy and paste the registration marks around the four sides of the master page in the margins. The registration marks, and any elements assigned the [Registration] color name in the Colors palette, are included on all overlays printed with the Spot Color Overlays option.

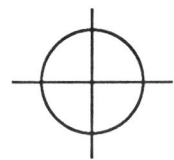

Fig. 9.11. Registration mark composed of a circle and two straight lines.

When you deliver the overlays to the print shop, be sure to instruct the printers to delete the registration marks on the final plates.

Knockouts (Traps and Butts)

If you're using more than one color, but elements of different color don't touch each other, printing is fairly simple. However, if elements touch—for example, if you have purple type in the middle of an otherwise solid red circle (a *trap*)—their colors must meet precisely in the separated overlays. If the colors are even a hairline out of register, you see the mistake in the printed piece, either as a dark line where the colors overlap or as a gap between the colors (see fig. 9.12). You usually want the two colors to overlap at the adjoining edge—the *butt*—only by a point or so (about the width of an X-ACTO blade).

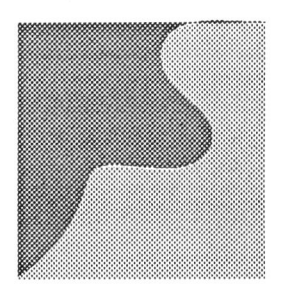

Perfect registration, colors meet but do not overlap

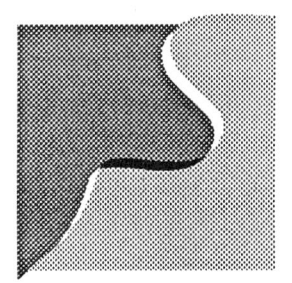

Registration off slightly, gaps show as white lines, overlapping colors yield muddy line

Fig. 9.12. Adjacent spot colors must meet exactly, without gap or overlap between them.

PageMaker enables you to print two overlapping spot colors using the Knockouts option in the Print dialog box (displayed when you select the Print command on the File menu or press Ctrl-P). With this option selected, each element is printed in its color with the space required by the overlapping element cut out (see fig. 9.13). These knockouts, however, butt each other exactly (without any overlap), so this technique may not yield the most accurate results—you may end up with poor registration between the two colors. Your printer may prefer that you deliver separate overlays without knockouts (see fig. 9.14).

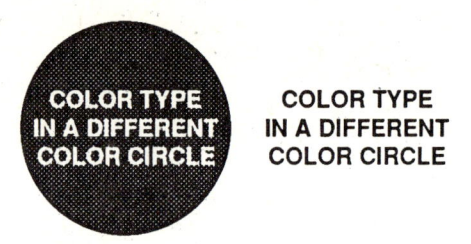

COLOR TYPE IN A DIFFERENT COLOR CIRCLE   **COLOR TYPE IN A DIFFERENT COLOR CIRCLE**

First color overlay   Second color overlay

Fig. 9.13. Overlapping colors printed with the Knockouts option.

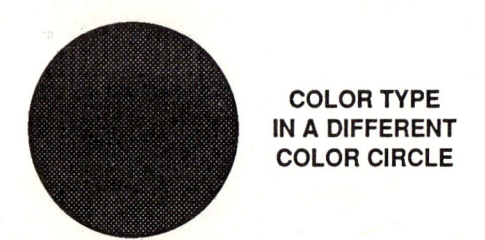

COLOR TYPE IN A DIFFERENT COLOR CIRCLE

First color overlay   Second color overlay

Fig. 9.14. Overlapping colors printed without the Knockouts option.

If you don't want to be responsible for registration, you can prepare your mechanical as a *keyline*: an unseparated single-page printout. Using the circle example, you place the circle (as an outline) and the type on one mechanical, and on an overlay write instructions for color specifications, such as "Circle prints PMS 282. Type prints PMS 141 and traps in circle."

Marking Mechanicals for Solid Spot Color

If you decide not to use PageMaker to print spot-color overlays (see "Printing Spot-Color Overlays" in this section) but to let the printer separate spot color, you have to print the page without the Spot Color Overlays option and mark your black-and-white mechanical with instructions about which page elements are to be in which colors. You can write these instructions directly on the mechanical (keyline mechanical) using a nonreproducible blue ink pen or pencil, or you can write them on a tissue overlay. The printer photographs the mechanical once for each color and masks out any unwanted images from each set of films.

When you output a page to which spot colors have been assigned, you get one page for each color in the publication (see fig. 9.10). A page output as a mechanical produces black-and-white sheets, but one sheet contains elements that are to be printed in black ink, and each of the other sheets contains those elements assigned a specified color. Registration marks on each output page indicate how the colors should overlay. If you print the output on Mylar (or another type of clear polyester film overlay), you can mount the spot-color sheets over each other and check the registration yourself.

Specifying Colors for Offset Printing

In addition to indicating which page elements should be in color—or physically separating them yourself—you also must specify on your mechanical what colors you want. You can specify color in a number of ways. For example, you can give the printer a sample of the color you want—a piece of paper, a company logo, and so on—and ask the printer to duplicate the color as closely as possible.

A more precise way of specifying color is to use a color-matching system, such as the Pantone Matching System (PMS). PMS ink swatchbooks, Toyo, and other brands are available at any graphic arts supply store. Printers usually can get most of these types of inks, or they can mix the inks they have to match your swatch.

Ink swatchbooks generally include a wide range of inks, printed on coated and uncoated paper. This difference is crucial because the appearance of the ink varies a great deal depending on the type of paper. In general, inks appear more brilliant on coated papers, softer and duller on uncoated papers.

Swatchbooks usually present inks grouped according to *hue* (place in the color spectrum, as in red versus blue), *saturation* (amount of color, as in red versus pink) and *luminance* (amount of brightness, as in dull red versus fire-engine red). You often see two colors side by side with the same hue but different saturations. Near each color sample there is usually information about how the color is created—what primary colors in what proportion make up this color (see fig. 9.15). By taking some time to understand and use a swatchbook, you actually can learn a great deal about color. For example, you may be surprised to find that the difference between two apparently dissimilar colors can be as little as 10 percent cyan and 5 percent black.

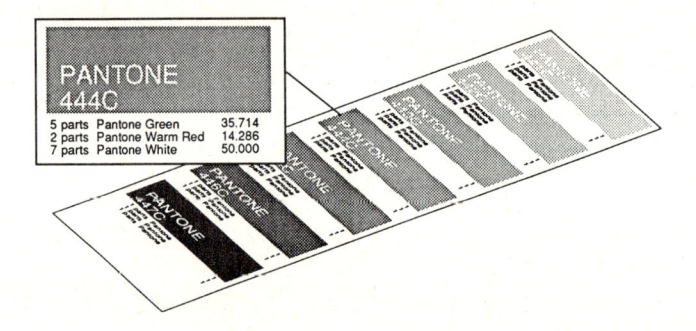

Fig. 9.15. Close-up of PMS swatch with ink density information.

Specifying Colors for Type or Thin Elements

Caution: You should be careful when specifying colors for type or for thin graphic elements such as rules. Swatches usually are printed in one-inch strips or squares; however, colors look different when printed as a thin headline or rule. When printed in a thin line, bright colors look duller; dark colors, such as a deep blue, may look black; and light colors, such as pastels, may nearly disappear. To visualize exactly how your printed color will look, use a piece of white paper to cover up all but a small piece of the swatch. Try to have paper on hand exactly like your printing stock; even white paper comes in a range of hues.

Preparing a PageMaker Publication for Process Color Printing

Although PageMaker 4.0 does not produce color separations for four-color process printing, you can get process color separations of PageMaker publications by using separating systems or software such as Publisher's Prism from Insight Systems, which produces four-color process separations from *any* printable PostScript page description. (Chapter 8 discusses the creation of printable PostScript files from a PageMaker publication.)

Four-color process printing is the only method used to print continuous-tone color images (such as color photographs). If your publication includes continuous-tone color images, you will want to create color separations using PageMaker's Open Prepress Interface (OPI), which links PageMaker to sophisticated color prepress systems. You then can use a low-resolution color scanner on your own PC to create a full-page layout to show the prepress house or the print shop how to position and crop the image. You then can take your disk files to a prepress service, which will transfer your full-page layout into its system for the final color processing and output the color separations for the layout—exactly as you planned it. These services actually scan your original color photograph with a highly sensitive scanner and replace your low-resolution image. Nevertheless, you have saved some of the prepress costs by going as far as you can on your own.

Equally valuable, these prepress services can serve as a liaison to printers and color trade shops. Although prepress services may themselves have the equipment to do appropriate desktop-color page makeup for many jobs, most also work closely with traditional suppliers. They are knowledgeable about the most effective ways of combining the capabilities of desktop systems and other equipment, and they can help you work within your budget to achieve the best results.

The OPI link is a feature new in PageMaker 4.0 for the PC. (The Macintosh version of PageMaker offered the OPI link for more than a year before it was available on the PC.) For more information about the use of PageMaker with OPI, as well as the availability of OPI-compatible prepress systems in your area, check with your local prepress house.

Chapter Summary

The future of printing is color. Color printing is expensive, however—even if you can avoid the cost of making color overlays, the masters used in making plates to print each color.

Under the impact of electronic technology, the publishing process is changing across the entire spectrum of production. To understand and adapt to the changes in methods, roles, and relationships, you must understand the entire process. If you have never worked with color, you should find out more about how offset printers produce color. If you already are familiar with color printing, you should see how the separations produced by PageMaker—spot-color overlays, color comps, and final printed publications—compare with traditional color productions.

This chapter concludes Part I of *Using PageMaker 4 for Windows*. You now understand the basics of using PageMaker throughout the production process. Part II (Chapters 10 and 11) introduces you to professional typography and design concepts in order to help you design effective publications. Part III (Chapters 12 through 16) brings together all these ideas by presenting finished publications and explaining how they were designed and created using PageMaker. If you are unfamiliar with design concepts, read Part II before you explore Part III.

Part II

Designing and Producing Different Types of Publications

Includes

Typography
PageMaker as a Design Tool

Part II focuses on how you can apply to your PageMaker publications the typography and design concepts used by professional typesetters and text designers. In Part II you learn what kinds of fonts, sizes, and styles of type are available for your printer, how fonts are installed, and how fonts are created. You also learn how to select fonts for a publication, how to create special effects such as drop caps, and how to use leading and kerning to adjust the spacing of text. In addition, you learn how to design a PageMaker publication, how to use master pages and template systems, and how to prepare pages for an offset printer.

10

Typography

Designers and typographers have a unique set of terms for identifying the text in a publication: fonts, drop caps, leading, kerning, and many others. In this chapter, you learn how to view a PageMaker publication in these terms. You learn what fonts are, how fonts used by various printers differ, and how to add new fonts to the PageMaker menus. You see the importance of knowing what typefaces, sizes, and styles are available to your printer before you start the design process. You learn how to set up your design specifications—including special effects such as drop caps—using PageMaker's menus. And you learn to estimate the amount of text that fits on each page and to make fine adjustments in spacing to fit copy into a defined space.

Regardless of whether you, as a designer or typographer, are writing the design specifications for a publication or are using PageMaker to set up the master template, you need to know how PageMaker works before you plan your publication. In this chapter, you not only learn something about how professional typesetters and designers determine what fonts to use in a publication; you also learn how to specify them for a production team that uses PageMaker.

Understanding Fonts

The word *font* is related to the French verb *fondre*, which means "to melt or cast." The term once referred literally to the trays of cast metal letters that printers used to compose a publication. Each tray, or font, included all letters of the alphabet that were of a specific size and appearance (see fig.

10.1). For example, one tray held only 10-point Times italic letters, another tray held only 10-point Times bold, and so on. A font, then, was a particular combination of size, typeface, and style.

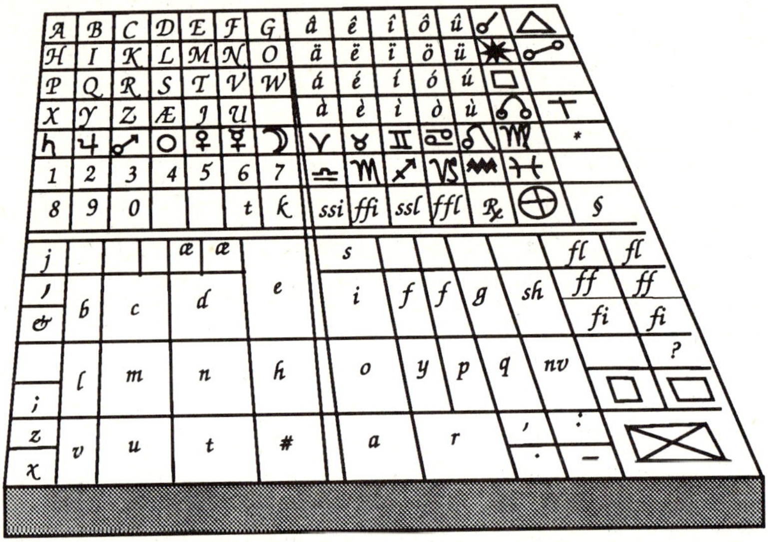

***Fig. 10.1.** A font, or tray of cast metal letters, from 1747.*

More recently, however, the word font has come to mean only the name of a typeface, such as Times or Helvetica. The word has this meaning in PageMaker's Type Specifications dialog box (displayed when you select the Type Specs command on the Type menu). This definition makes sense for the new computer fonts based on formulas, such as PostScript fonts. In these fonts, each letter of the alphabet is cast, or designed, only once to define the shape of the letter. This information is stored as a complex curve-fitting equation. A printer that uses a programming language such as PostScript or DDL to create text can produce any size of a typeface for which the printer "knows" the shape of each letter.

If you are told that a printer is limited to a certain number of fonts per page or per publication, you must know which meaning of the word *font* applies. Some printers are limited to four fonts in the more traditional sense: for example, 10-point Times Roman, 10-point Times italic, 10-point Times boldface, and 10-point Times boldface italic. For other printers, a limit of four fonts means four typefaces: Times, Helvetica, Courier, and Palatino.

When you create the design specifications for the type in a PageMaker publication, you need to be specific about which printer you are using as well as which fonts (typefaces, sizes, and styles). This chapter's section on "Working with PageMaker's Font List" provides tips for selecting fonts.

Typeface

In the traditional sense, a *typeface* is a set of characters with the same basic shape for each letter. The Times typeface, for example, includes all sizes and styles of type that are variations of the same basic designs for each letter of the alphabet. Typefaces are broadly grouped into two kinds: serif and sans serif, examples of which are shown in figure 10.2. A *serif* is a fine cross-stroke that projects across the end of the main stroke of a letter (the tiny marks across the top and bottom of the lowercase i, for example). *Sans serif* means "without serif."

> Times is a serif typeface.
> **Helvetica is a sans serif typeface.**

Fig. 10.2. Serif and sans serif typefaces.

Typefaces also are often classified as body-copy typefaces or display typefaces. *Body-copy typefaces* are commonly used for most text and are legible in small sizes (measured in units called points). *Display typefaces* are used in display ads and logos, headings in publications, and headlines in newsletters. Display typefaces can be ornate and usually are set larger than 12 points (see fig. 10.3).

> Body type can be as small as 9 points.
> Body type can be as large as 12 points.
> *Display typefaces*
> *are usually designed for larger sizes.*

Fig. 10.3. Body-copy type and display type.

When used on computers and laser printers, typefaces often are divided into two other categories: bit-mapped fonts and outline (curve-fitting) fonts (see fig. 10.4). *Bit-mapped fonts*, which are printed as patterns of dots, may appear jagged at the edges when printed (in the same way that screen fonts appear jagged on-screen). Some bit-mapped fonts are designed to be printed at higher resolutions, and these fonts can look as good as outline fonts when produced on most laser printers. Because bit-mapped fonts are hard to scale to different sizes, the font designer must develop a different set of designs for each size. Stored as a pattern of dots, these fonts usually take up a great deal of space in the printer's memory while a page is being printed.

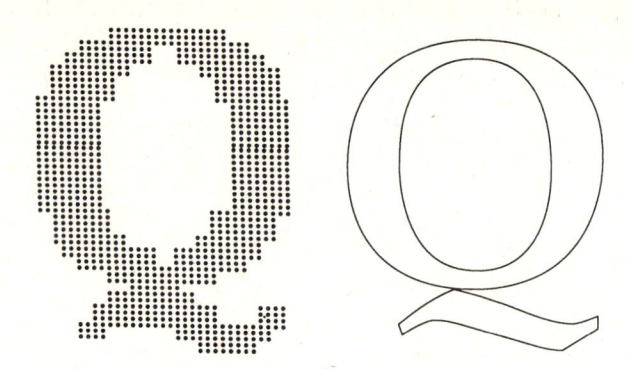

Fig. 10.4. Bit-mapped and outline (curve-fitting) fonts.

Outline fonts (also called *curve-fitting fonts*) are defined by curve-fitting mathematical formulas. These typefaces can be scaled to any size or made boldface or italic by the changing of a few variables in the formulas that define the shapes of the letters. PostScript, for example, is a curve-fitting language; choosing PostScript fonts when printing with a PostScript printer or typesetter ensures a smooth finished product. Because fonts stored as formulas take up less space in the printer's memory than do bit-mapped fonts, you can download more of these outline fonts at one time.

The list of typefaces, or fonts, in PageMaker's Type Specifications dialog box (displayed when you select the Type Specs command on the Type menu) varies depending on which printer drivers you have installed, which printer you have selected as the target printer, and which fonts you have added (or deleted). PageMaker supports a wide range of typefaces, sizes, and styles that not all printers can handle. By clicking the Fonts icon in the Windows 3.0 Control Panel window, you can add a new screen font to the menus (see "Adding and Deleting Screen Fonts" of the "Working with PageMaker's Font List" section of this chapter.) You cannot, however, print the publication in that font unless you also install it on the printer (see Chapter 8).

Knowing Your Printer

If you do not know whether a particular typeface is installed on your printer, select that typeface in the Type Specifications dialog box. If no sizes are listed for that typeface, it is not installed on the target printer.

In your publications, you can use fonts that your printer does not support. For example, you can specify a PostScript printer as your target printer but take the finished publication to a service bureau for printing on a Linotronic typesetter. Although you can use your own dot-matrix printer for drafts, note that the printer converts the fonts to supported fonts or prints them as bit-mapped fonts. This substitution may be acceptable for printing draft copies, but the appearance of the publication may change significantly when you switch from one printer to another. If you plan to use your own printer throughout the entire production cycle, be sure that your design specifications call for fonts that are supported by your printer.

Size

Typesetters measure the size of type in points. The word *point* is related to the French verb *poindre*, "to prick." A point was the smallest possible mark that a printer could make on a page—about 1/72 inch. An inch, therefore, contains approximately 72 points.

Originating during the same time period in which the words *font* and *serif* were introduced, the term *leading* (rhymes with "heading") once referred to thin strips of metal (lead) that were inserted between lines of type to add vertical space in a column or tray of set type. For example, a type specification of 10/12 Times Roman ("10 on 12 Times Roman") calls for 10-point Times Roman letters with 2 points of leading between lines.

This system of measure is the same as the picas and points listed in the Preferences dialog box (displayed when you select the Preferences command on the Edit menu) and used on the ruler lines (see Chapter 6). The larger 12-point unit, the *pica*, is used to measure distances on the page but is not usually used in defining type size. A 1.5-inch distance on the page is measured as 9 picas, for example, but a 1.5-inch-high character is measured as 108 points.

Originally, the size of type was measured as the full height of the cast letter or type block. This measurement included some space above and below the letter so that two lines of type would not touch each other. Because the width and exact position of the type on the block is determined by the original designer of each typeface, the apparent sizes of the letters may vary greatly among different typefaces. Figure 10.5 shows 36-point letters from an assortment of typefaces. Note the differences.

Ay Ay Ay Ay Ay Ay Ay

Fig. 10.5. *Letters with the same nominal size that look larger or smaller in different typefaces.*

The Type Specifications dialog box, accessed by choosing Type Specs from the Type menu, displays the sizes available for the currently selected typeface (see fig. 10.6). With PageMaker, you can specify any size between 4 and 650 points, in one-tenth-point increments. Usually, however, you want to use the sizes supported by your printer, which might not include the full range supported by PageMaker. PostScript printers can handle any size, including sizes larger than 650 points. You also can import graphics that use larger fonts.

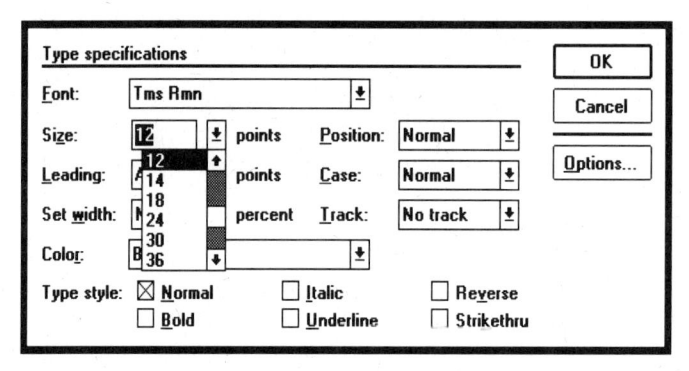

Fig. 10.6. The Type Specifications dialog box.

Generally, body copy is set between 9 and 12 points. Headlines are usually larger. Business cards and classified ads can be smaller, using 7- or 8-point type. Text smaller than 6 points is difficult to read in most typefaces and is rarely used.

Style

The third basic element of the traditional font is *style*. Styles listed on the Type Style submenu of the Type menu and in the Type Specifications dialog box include Normal, Bold, Italic, Underline, Strikethru, and Reverse. You also can set the case to Normal, All Caps, or Small Caps. Figure 10.7 provides some examples. Any of these variables can be part of the design specifications.

As is true of size, not all styles shown on PageMaker menus are supported by all printers. You want to use the styles that your printer supports. You need to become thoroughly familiar with the capabilities and limitations of your printer by testing your design ideas in short (one- or two-page) publications before building long documents. Create a test publication with every combination of the typefaces, styles, and sizes that you plan to use in your publication. Avoid being shocked by last-minute discoveries of what your printer cannot do.

Black type:
Normal
Bold
Italic
Bold Italic
SMALL CAPS

Reverse type:
Normal
Bold
Italic
Bold Italic
SMALL CAPS

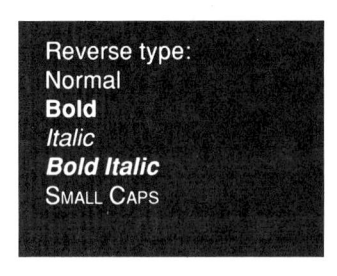

Fig. 10.7. Examples of type styles available on a PostScript printer.

Some downloadable typefaces are available in *families*, each style of which you must install separately. For instance, you install the boldface style of a typeface separately from the italic set. The style appears in the list of typefaces, as shown in figure 10.8. A listing of I Helvetica Oblique (*I* indicates italic) means that the font I Helvetica Oblique has been designed and customized as italic rather than derived from normal Helvetica by automatic formulas. You get better-looking type, therefore, by choosing I Helvetica Oblique than by choosing Helvetica and making it italic through the Type menu. If you choose a customized style such as I Helvetica Oblique and then select the Italic style setting on the Type menu, you produce a double-italic effect, which may be difficult to read.

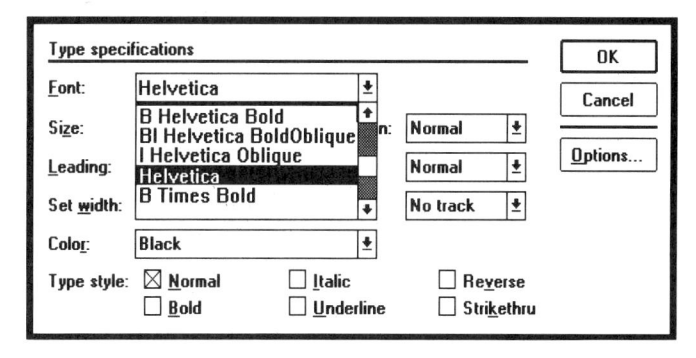

Fig. 10.8. Style as part of the typeface name on the menu.

Working with PageMaker's Font List

Chapter 5 explains how to use PageMaker's Type Specs command (on the Type menu) to change type specifications. This chapter examines the Type Specifications dialog box in terms of the typefaces and fonts listed there. You learn how to change the default font and add typefaces and fonts to or delete them from the list in the dialog box.

Changing the Default Font

The default font is usually 12-point Times Roman or the closest equivalent available for the target printer. If 12-point type is not available, PageMaker uses the next smaller available size. The default font determines the appearance of new text typed directly into PageMaker and of unformatted text (with the file extension TXT) placed in PageMaker from another program.

If during a work session you want to change the default font for the current publication, select the pointer tool in the toolbox before you make a new selection with the Type Specs command. To change the default font for this session and all future PageMaker sessions, choose the Type Specs command when all publications are closed. This change is saved in the file PM4.CNF.

Installing Fonts

Installing a new font is usually a two-step process:

1. Install the new font so it will display on PageMaker's Font submenu and in the Type Specifications dialog box (i.e., as a screen font) by using the Control Panel.

2. Install the new font on the printer.

The following sections tell you how to install fonts on your computer and printer.

Adding and Deleting Screen Fonts

When you add a typeface or font to the list in PageMaker's Type Specifications dialog box, you are adding a *screen font* to the system—a font file with the extension FON. PageMaker then knows, from the font's width table and kerning table, exactly how to display it on-screen.

You can add new screen fonts by using the Fonts utility that comes with Windows 3.0, represented by an icon in the Control Panel window. (Remember that the Control Panel is a Microsoft Windows utility that you can start by double-clicking the Control Panel icon in the Windows 3.0 main window. See Chapter 8 for more information about using the Control Panel.)

To use the Control Panel, start Windows 3.0 and choose Main from the Windows menu if the Main window is not already displayed. Double-click the Control Panel icon displayed in the Main window. The Control Panel window displays a number of icons (discussed in Chapter 2), including the Fonts icon (see fig. 10.9).

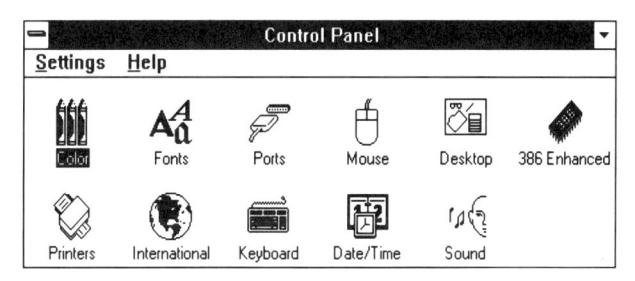

Fig. 10.9. The Control Panel window shows the Fonts icon.

Double-click the Fonts icon to display the Fonts dialog box, which shows the list of currently installed fonts (see fig. 10.10). The Remove and Add buttons on the right of the dialog box enable you to remove a selected font from the list (delete it from the WIN.INI file) or add a new font or size.

To delete a font from the list, first click on the font name to highlight it, then click the Remove button. If you click the Add button, PageMaker displays a dialog box through which you locate the fonts to be installed (see fig. 10.11).

A type manager can expand the availability of fonts on both your screen and your printer. If you are not using a type manager (discussed in "Using a Type Manager" in this section), you may want to install every size of each font you plan to use. Otherwise, fonts may appear distorted on the screen.

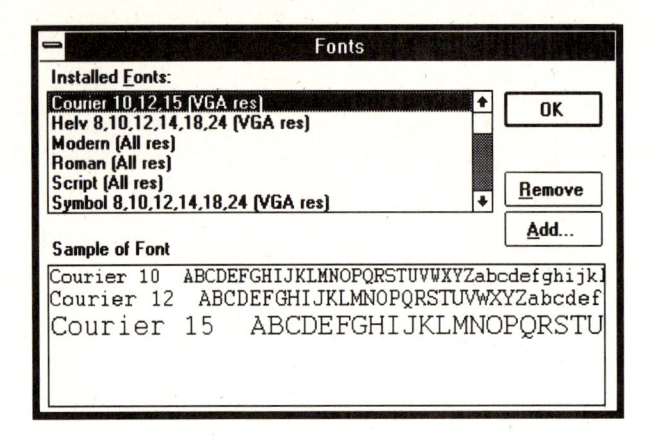

Fig. 10.10. The Fonts dialog box.

Fig. 10.11. The Add Font Files dialog box.

Note, however, that screen fonts can take up a lot of space on your hard disk, and fonts currently being used require a lot of memory. You can create and print a publication without using a type manager and without having matching screen versions of every printer font you use. When you don't have a screen version of a printer font, Windows supplies the screen font that most closely matches it. Even when font substitution occurs, line endings and page breaks on-screen are accurate.

When you add screen fonts to the PageMaker menu, you must be sure to add those same fonts to your printer.

Adding Printer Fonts

For a printer to print any font correctly, the printer also must know about the font. Unlike the screen, however, which uses a relatively low-resolution bit-mapped font, the printer uses a high-resolution bit-mapped font or an outline font (determined by a curve-fitting formula). Available fonts vary from printer to printer. Essentially, three types of *printer fonts* are available, each with its own method of installation: built-in fonts (built directly into the printer), cartridge fonts (stored on a font cartridge), and downloadable fonts (transferred from the computer's memory, or downloaded, into the printer's memory).

Built-In Printer Fonts

Built-in printer fonts are installed by the manufacturer. They are always available for any publication. Ideally, every font would be built into the printer. Unfortunately, fonts take up space, so most printers have few or no built-in fonts.

Many PostScript printers come with the same set of fonts as were originally built into Apple's LaserWriter Plus and are now built in to the LaserWriter NTX: Times, Helvetica, Courier, Symbol (primarily Greek letters and mathematical symbols), Avant Garde, Bookman, New Century Schoolbook, Helvetica Narrow, Palatino, Zapf Chancery, and Zapf Dingbats (all symbols). Figure 10.12 shows the LaserWriter Plus typefaces. Each of these fonts, except Zapf Chancery, can be printed in any size or style listed on the menu.

> Times
> Helvetica
> Helvetica Narrow
> Courier
> Symbol: Συμβολ
> Avant Garde
> Bookman
> New Century Schoolbook
> Palatino
> *Zapf Chancery*
> Zapf Dingbats: ✹✧☆✦

Fig. 10.12. *LaserWriter Plus's 11 built-in typefaces.*

The Linotronic Model 100 and 300 typesetters come with Times and Helvetica built in. All other typefaces are downloaded as the pages are being printed. The number of typefaces that you can download at one time is limited by the amount of memory in the typesetter (see the discussion of downloadable fonts in this section), unless you are using fonts permanently downloaded to a hard disk attached to the typesetter.

Cartridge Fonts

Cartridge fonts are similar to built-in fonts but are built into removable cartridges rather than hard-wired into the printer. The number of fonts available for a specific publication depends on the cartridge installed at the time of printing. Chapter 8 explains how to tell Windows and PageMaker which cartridge is installed.

The Hewlett-Packard LaserJet is one example of a cartridge printer. Dozens of different font cartridges for the LaserJet are available; many cartridges include groups of fonts suitable for a particular purpose, such as publishing newsletters. If you do not have a cartridge, the default font is 12-point Courier (which is a built-in font). The LaserJet's memory is too limited to accommodate any downloaded fonts. The Hewlett-Packard LaserJet Series II also is a cartridge printer, but its expanded memory enables you to download fonts to the printer. The LaserJet Series III can accept cartridges, but it also comes with two built-in scalable fonts (Times and Helvetica) and a megabyte of RAM for downloading more fonts.

Downloadable Fonts

Downloadable fonts differ from both built-in and cartridge fonts in that they are not coded directly into hardware. Instead, they take up memory space (in random-access memory, or RAM) when downloaded to the printer. (Chapter 8 explains how to install downloadable fonts.) PageMaker supports most of the downloadable fonts sold by various manufacturers, such as those from Adobe Systems, Inc., (which offers a wide range of downloadable fonts for PostScript printers) and Bitstream (which also makes downloadable fonts for Hewlett-Packard printers and others).

You can download additional fonts to a printer that has built-in RAM, but the printer's memory and the typefaces selected determine the number of downloadable fonts the printer can handle at once. You can try to get around the printer's limitations by restricting the number of fonts in individual text blocks in the PageMaker publication. In other words, you can have as many downloadable fonts on a page or in one publication as you like, so long as each text block has no more downloadable fonts than the printer can handle. (See "Choosing the Fonts" in the "Planning Your Design Specifications" section of this chapter.)

Using a Type Manager

A type manager is a program that uses outline-font technology to generate characters of virtually any size for both your screen and printer. A type manager represents your final, printed publication on-screen more accurately than is possible without using a type manager. Several page-design options (such as manual kerning, rotating text, expanding text, and condensing text) become much easier when you can see the fonts accurately on-screen. Screen fonts generated by a type manager require less hard disk space than do other screen fonts.

To take full advantage of a type manager's capabilities, you need to change the settings in the Screen Font Options dialog box (select the Preferences command from the Edit menu and click Other in the Preferences dialog box). Change the settings of Stretch Text Above and Vector Text Above to 600 or higher to make sure that you can see the outline fonts in the large sizes a type manager provides.

A type manager also increases the number of fonts available on your printer. The effect on your publication depends on the type manager you are using, the fonts you have installed, and the printer you are using. Refer to your type manager's instruction manual for information on how the type manager can expand the font capabilities of your printer.

Note that although a type manager usually will increase the font capabilities of your printer, it also can slow down the printing process. If you are using a type manager that is designed to work with your printer (for example, if both your printer and type manager use bit-mapped fonts), you will have the increased flexibility of outline fonts with little difference in printing time. If, however, you are using a type manager designed to work with a different printer standard (for example, if you have a PCL-language printer, like the Hewlett-Packard printers, and your type manager uses PostScript fonts), then each character generated by the type manager will be treated as a graphic. In this case, printing will take longer using the type manager's fonts than it would if you were using the printer's original fonts.

> ### Using a Type Manager Economically
> If your type manager uses a different font standard than your printer usually works with, use the regular printer's fonts for body text and the type manager's fonts only for large text such as headings.

Planning Your Design Specifications

Planning the design specifications of your publication involves many steps. You must determine how many fonts are available with your printer, which typefaces and how much leading to use, whether headlines and titles should be kerned, and how to handle captions. You also should plan for special text elements such as symbols and mathematical formulas.

Choosing the Fonts

The first step in the design process is to list all the built-in fonts in the printer you plan to use for the publication's final production. In addition, you must know which cartridge fonts and downloadable fonts you can access. With this information, you can list in your design specifications all the different fonts available for use.

> **Shortening Printing Time**
> Downloaded fonts can take a long time to print. If time is a concern, stick to the built-in fonts.

The second step is to list the number of fonts that you plan to use in a particular publication. One reason for limiting the number of fonts involves design considerations. The best designs use only a few fonts on each page. Another reason for limiting the number of fonts is a practical one: Some printers cannot handle more than a few fonts per page or per cartridge. A third factor in determining the number of fonts is the number of different text elements in the publication. Such elements can include:

- Chapter openings, section openings, or feature article headlines
- Different levels of headings or headlines
- Body copy
- Figure captions
- Labels within figures
- Footnotes
- Special sections, such as sidebars, summaries, and tables

Now match the items on the two lists—the list of the fonts available (or that you want to use) and the list of the different elements within the publication (see fig. 10.13).

Available fonts:	Document elements:
8-point Times Roman	Figure labels
10-point Times Roman	Body copy
10-point Times Bold	Subhead
10-point Times Italic	Figure captions
14-point Helvetica Bold	Headlines

Fig. 10.13. *Beginning the type-specification process.*

Printing a Type Sample Sheet

If you are not familiar with the different typefaces in the Type Specifications dialog box, or if you do not know which ones your printer supports, make and print a dummy copy using each option on the menu. Figure 10.14 shows some type samples.

If you are accustomed to having all your publications printed on a daisy-wheel printer or a similar printer that produces letter-quality output, you may find a comparatively wide range of fonts rather confusing. If so, you can approach the type specifications for a publication in two ways.

The fastest way to acquire a sense of design and develop good design specifications is to study and imitate published works similar in structure to your publication. Match your design specifications as closely as possible to those of the published document. Select fonts similar to those used for headings, body copy, and captions in the published document. You do not have to match the typefaces exactly, but try to substitute typefaces in the same category (serif or sans serif, Roman, italic, boldface, and so on). Examples of publications with different type specifications are shown in Part III of this book.

```
┌─────────────────────────────────┐
│ We offer...                     │
│ Times                           │
│                                 │
│ 8 9 10 11 12 14 18 24           │
│                                 │
│ **Bold**                        │
│ *Italic*                        │
│ ***Bold Italic***               │
│                                 │
│ Helvetica                       │
│                                 │
│ 8 9 10 11 12 14 18 24           │
│                                 │
│ **Bold**                        │
│ *Italic*                        │
│ ***Bold Italic***               │
│                                 │
│ ▬▬ Reverse type (all fonts) ▬▬  │
└─────────────────────────────────┘
```

Fig. 10.14. *A type sample sheet.*

A second approach to creating type specifications is to study the underlying principles that designers and typographers follow. Some guidelines are listed here:

- Do not use more than two typefaces in a publication. Usually, one typeface is serif; the other, sans serif. Use variations in size and style to distinguish among different text elements.

- Use variations in size rather than boldface type to distinguish the different heading levels. One common exception to this rule is the lowest heading level, which may be boldface in the same size and typeface as the body copy.

- Use italic rather than underscored text in body copy. (Underscored text is a convention developed for use in publications printed on letter-quality printers that cannot print italic.)

- Use all caps as a deliberate design strategy rather than as a way to show emphasis or to differentiate heading levels. Use variations in size instead of all-caps text to differentiate headings. One common exception to this rule occurs when the list of available fonts is too limited to accommodate all heading levels. In this case, you can use all caps to distinguish between two heading levels in the same font.

Few publications can follow all these guidelines without making some exceptions. Some of the most common exceptions have been mentioned. One mark of a good designer is knowing when and how to break the rules.

Mixing Typefaces

As stressed in the design guidelines, you should stick to one or two different typefaces—usually a serif and a sans serif typeface—and use variations in size and style to differentiate elements.

You will find that using only one typeface whenever possible makes the production process more efficient. One convenience of using only one typeface (with different sizes and styles) is that you can globally change to any other typeface without affecting the different sizes and styles set up in the text. For example, you can select a whole story or article and change its typeface from Times to Helvetica. In PageMaker 4.0, you can search for and change text attributes through the Story Editor (discussed in Chapter 4), so you can globally change Times to Helvetica in a block of text that mixes typefaces.

Starting with one typeface can be handy if you want to generate quickly several variations on a basic design without using a style sheet or if you use one printer or cartridge for all drafts and switch to a different printer, cartridge, or downloadable font for the final printing. Another pragmatic reason for using one typeface is that you can save formatting time in PageMaker or your word processing program.

The number of typefaces you choose can be affected by a printer that uses permanently downloaded fonts. Because these downloaded fonts are not stored in the printer's permanent memory (ROM) or in the printer cartridge, they take up space in the printer's temporary memory (RAM). You usually cannot download more than a few fonts at a time. On some printers, you also may not be able to print high-resolution graphics when the downloaded typeface is required.

> ### Breaking Pages into Multiple Text Blocks
> You can get around the limit on the number of a printer's downloadable fonts by breaking text into separate blocks, as shown in figure 10.15. You can print pages that use many different fonts if you use temporarily downloaded fonts (see Chapter 7) and if each individual text block on the page uses no more than the maximum number of downloadable fonts for the printer.

At the other extreme, you may have good reasons for using many more than two typefaces. For example, you may have to use all the fonts on an eight-font cartridge to achieve the required differentiation of text elements. Publications such as magazines and newsletters, which use different formats in different sections, may employ more than four typefaces throughout the publication, even though each page, feature, or advertisement uses only one or two typefaces. Figure 10.16 shows an example of a publication that uses all four typefaces on a Hewlett-Packard cartridge.

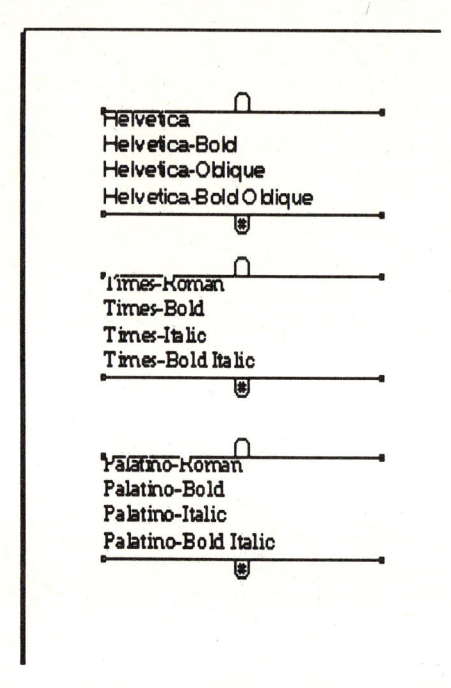

```
Helvetica
Helvetica-Bold
Helvetica-Oblique
Helvetica-Bold Oblique

Times-Roman
Times-Bold
Times-Italic
Times-Bold Italic

Palatino-Roman
Palatino-Bold
Palatino-Italic
Palatino-Bold Italic
```

Fig. 10.15. Printing a page with more than three or four downloadable fonts.

Choosing Automatic or Forced Leading

If you have training in traditional typesetting, you probably are accustomed to specifying the exact leading (the space between lines) as well as the type size. PageMaker, however, has an automatic leading feature. If you do not specify otherwise, the program determines the leading based on the point size of the type. The leading is roughly 120 percent of the point size (rounded to the nearest half-point). See figure 10.17 for examples.

The use of automatic leading is a production convenience rather than a design principle. If you change the point size of all or part of the text, the leading changes to match the new size. You can, however, override the automatic leading. You can manipulate the leading to achieve a custom look or to make copy fit a column or a certain number of pages (see "Fitting Copy within a Defined Space" in this chapter).

PageOne 1

PAGEMAKER: WHERE DESKTOP PUBLISHING BEGINS

ALDUS CORPORATION, in Seattle, Washington, leads the desktop publishing industry with PageMaker, page layout software that allows individuals and businesses to produce professional-looking publications in-house. PageMaker's introduction into the market has met with a great deal of industry recognition, particularly from the press. *Infoworld*, the computer industry's influential magazine, gave it the Best Software Product of the Year Runner-Up award for 1985.

THE PHRASE, "DESKTOP PUBLISHING," was coined by Aldus founder and president, Paul Brainerd, who saw that page-layout software would be invaluable to anybody who wanted to produce printed communications, from newsletters, order forms, and annual reports, to proposals, manuals, and magazines. Given the advances in graphics-oriented microcomputers and laser printers, the introduction of PageMaker meant that, for the first time, people could afford to create visually appealing publications with ease.

PAGEMAKER LETS PEOPLE WORK electronically the way professional designers work with conventional pages. With the click of the mouse, or a simple keyboard command, the computer screen becomes a blank page on a pasteboard, accompanied by a toolbox of design aids. A person arranges the page as desired, establishing margins, creating columns of varying widths, adding page numbers, and so on. Then the person fills the page with text and graphics created with other software programs, using on-screen rulers and dotted lines for accurate placement.

INDIVIDUALS AND CORPORATIONS alike have turned to PageMaker as the most reliable way to publish high-quality, low-cost materials, from brochures to 300-page books and technical manuals.

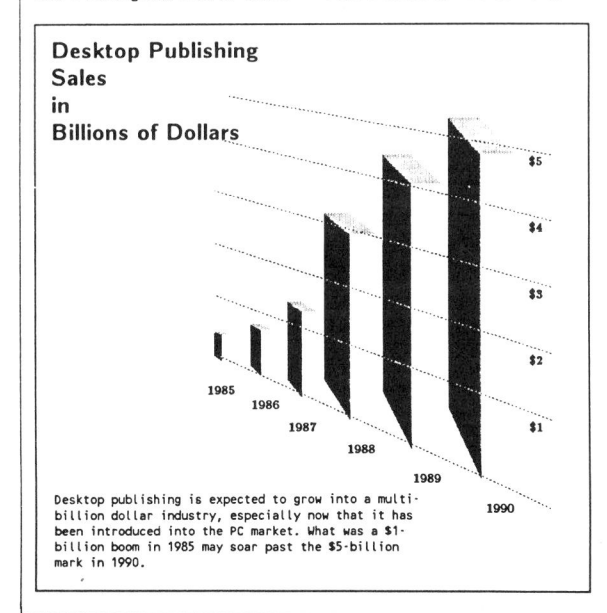

Desktop Publishing Sales in Billions of Dollars

Desktop publishing is expected to grow into a multi-billion dollar industry, especially now that it has been introduced into the PC market. What was a $1-billion boom in 1985 may soar past the $5-billion mark in 1990.

Fig. 10.16. An example of a publication that uses all four typefaces (eight fonts) on a Hewlett-Packard LaserJet cartridge.

Automatic leading for 10-point Times is 12 points, or 10/12.

Automatic leading for 12-point Times is 14.4 points, or 12/14.5.

Automatic leading for 14-point Times is 16.8 points, or 14/17.

Fig. 10.17. *Examples of automatic base-to-base leading.*

Creating Large Initial Caps

The leading for any line is determined by the largest characters in that line. If you want to create large initial caps, you must adjust the leading for the large letter or place the letter as a separate text block. The first example in figure 10.18 shows a 24-point initial cap with automatic leading in a line of text that is otherwise 8-point type. In the second example, the leading on the 24-point letter has been changed to zero. (You can use a leading measure smaller than the type size when the text has no letters with descenders or is all uppercase.)

Creating Drop Caps

To create drop caps such as the S in the bottom part of figure 10.18, you cut the letter out or type it on the pasteboard. You then can make the large letter a separate text block and use tabs to indent the first few lines of text, or you can make the first few lines a separate text block (for justified text). (See Chapter 5 for more information on indenting and justifying text.)

PageMaker 4.0 offers a second way of creating drop caps: Set them as subscripts and adjust their size and position. Figure 10.19 shows an example of a drop cap.

The following steps show how the drop cap shown in figure 10.19 was created:

1. Type the paragraph. In this example, the text is set in 18-point Times.

2. Select the first letter (S) and use the Type Specs command on the Type menu to set the letter larger than the rest (in this case, 72 points). Position the letter as a subscript: Click the Options

button in the Type Specifications dialog box and set the Subscript size to 100% of point size and the Subscript position to 50% of point size.

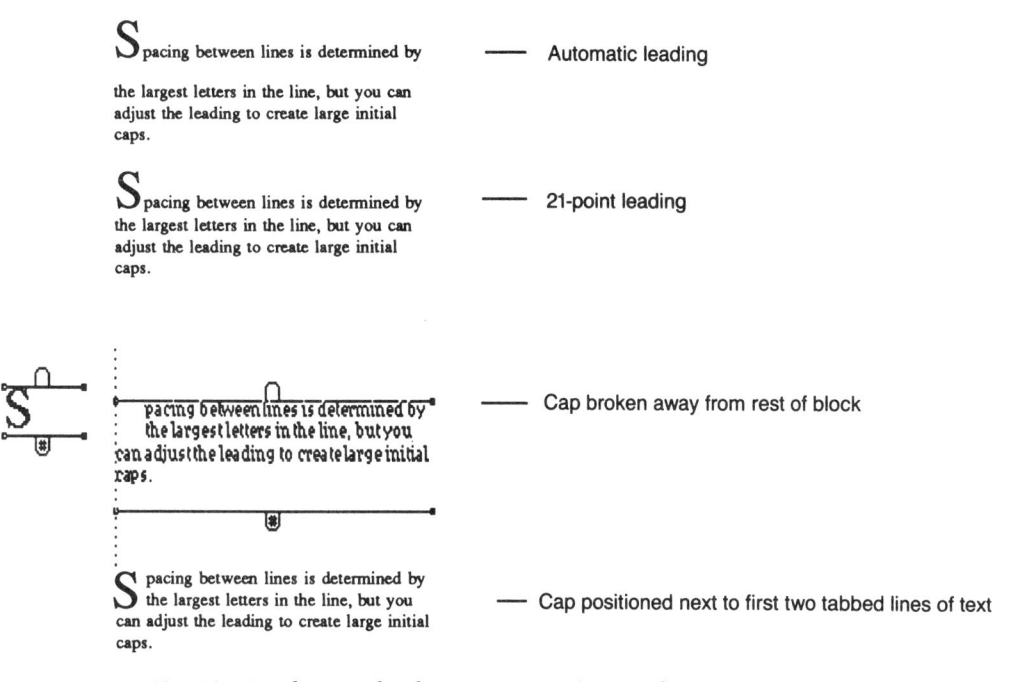

S̲pacing between lines is determined by the largest letters in the line, but you can adjust the leading to create large initial caps. ——— Automatic leading

S̲pacing between lines is determined by the largest letters in the line, but you can adjust the leading to create large initial caps. ——— 21-point leading

——— Cap broken away from rest of block

S pacing between lines is determined by the largest letters in the line, but you can adjust the leading to create large initial caps. ——— Cap positioned next to first two tabbed lines of text

Fig. 10.18. Adjusting leading to create 24-point drop caps.

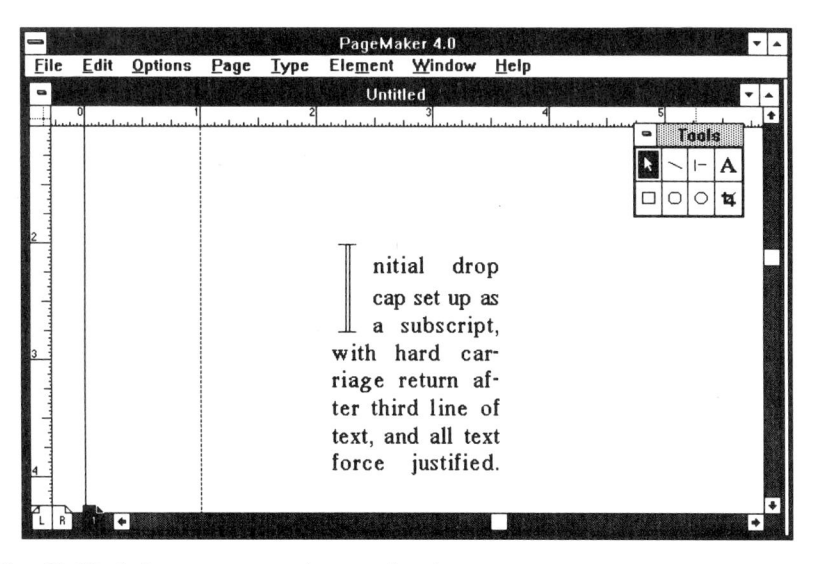

Fig. 10.19. A drop cap created as a subscript.

3. Select the entire paragraph and use the Leading command or the Type Specs command (on the Type menu) to set fixed leading (in this case, 20 points).

4. Position the cursor by clicking it on the first line, and use the Indents/Tabs command on the Type menu to display the Indents/Tabs ruler. Hold down the Shift key and drag the bottom half of the Left Indent marker to a position that forces the second and third lines of the paragraph into position right of the drop cap (in this case, 0.344 inches). The first line remains flush; in effect, it is indented −0.344 inches. (Paragraph indentation is described in Chapter 5.)

5. Press Enter after the third line to force a new paragraph, and use the Indents/Tabs command to reset the left indent to the zero point on the Indents/Tabs ruler.

6. Select both paragraphs and use the Alignment command on the Type menu to set them to Force Justify.

You can apply your own variations of this technique to create other drop caps.

Kerning Headlines and Titles

Headlines and titles—such as figure titles, newsletter banners, and advertising copy—should stand out from the body copy of the publication. Because design principles require that you use size rather than boldface to differentiate and emphasize these elements, your headlines and titles probably will be large and need to be kerned. *Kerning* is the fine adjustment made to the spacing between certain pairs of letters to give the overall text an even appearance.

Using Automatic Kerning

As noted in Chapter 5, PageMaker applies the basic kerning formulas to any text larger than 12 points in size, as indicated in the Spacing Attributes dialog box, which is displayed when you select the Paragraph Specifications command on the Type menu (see fig. 10.20). If you want to kern smaller headings and titles, you can change the minimum point size indicated in that dialog box. For example, suppose that you are producing a brochure in which the body copy is 9 points and the headings are 12 points. If the design specifications for the publication require kerned headings, you can use the Spacing option in the Paragraph Specifications dialog box to change the minimum nonkerning point size to 10.

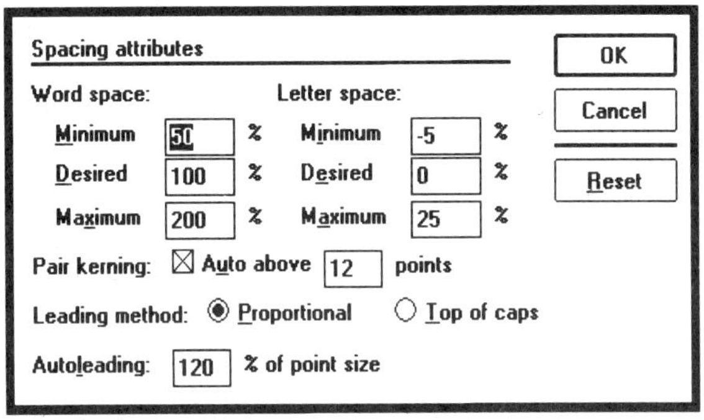

Fig. 10.20. The Spacing Attributes dialog box.

Using Manual Kerning

By using PageMaker's manual kerning option, you can adjust the space between any two letters. You use this procedure on a case-by-case basis—not as a global type specification.

Print the publication and examine the headlines for pairs of letters with unwanted space between them. As explained in Chapter 5, the space is caused by the widths and the angles of the two adjacent letters. For example, the opposite edges of the capital A and the capital V have similar slopes. Without kerning, when the letters A and V are adjacent in a word, as in KNAVE, the space between the A and the V appears to be much wider than the spaces between any of the other letters.

To change the space between two letters manually, select the text tool from the toolbox. Place the text-insertion point between the two letters you want to kern. To decrease space between letters, hold down the Ctrl key as you press the Backspace key. To increase space between letters, hold down Ctrl and Shift keys and press the Backspace key. With each press of the Backspace key, you change the space between the letters by 1/24th the usual space assigned to that font (see fig. 10.21).

AV —— Automatic kerning

AV —— Ctrl-Backspace to decrease space

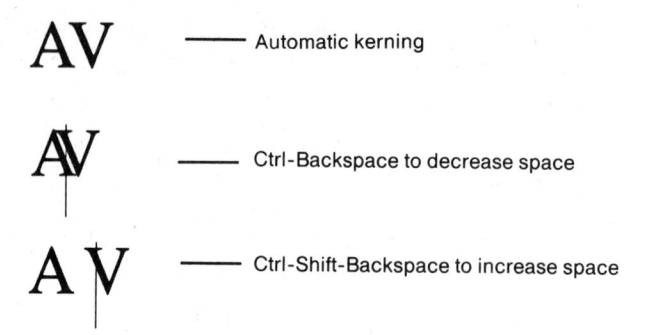

A V —— Ctrl-Shift-Backspace to increase space

Fig. 10.21. *Kerning text manually.*

Handling Captions

In any publication, you want to be sure to treat like items consistently, including captions, figure titles, and labels within figures. Consistency can be difficult to achieve when you are bringing figures into PageMaker from other programs. Will the graphing program be able to match the fonts used in figures from other drawing packages? Will the figure be scaled larger or smaller after it is in PageMaker? As the designer, you need to specify how captions, figure titles, and figure labels are to be handled in each program serving as a source of illustrations for the publication.

To ensure consistency, you may decide to enter all figure titles and captions directly in PageMaker. But you still have to specify the font you want to use for labels within the figures. Furthermore, you may need to account for changes in type size that result when you shrink or enlarge a figure in PageMaker. As explained in Chapter 6, when you change the size of a graphic imported from another program, you also change the size of the type used in that graphic. If you know that you will be shrinking a figure by 50 percent, for example, the illustrator may need to make the type in the drawing program twice as large as the type in the final publication.

Inserting Symbols in Text

It is not uncommon to see special symbols embedded within text. For instance, many software manuals use symbols to represent special keys outlined in boxes, such as the function keys and the Ctrl and Alt keys. Some magazine publishers use a symbol to indicate the end of an article.

PageMaker 4.0 enables you to insert "inline graphics" as part of the text flow; they move when the text moves. Using graphic symbols is an alternative to creating the symbols as a separate font, and each method offers its own unique benefits.

If you want to insert a symbol as a graphic, use a graphics application to create it or use PageMaker's built-in graphics tools if the symbol is made up simply of lines, rectangles, or ovals. Scale the symbol to the desired size in the graphics application before importing it or anchoring it in PageMaker. (Even though you can scale a graphic in PageMaker, you can be sure that the graphic is the same size every time you import it—and thus eliminate the inconvenience of repeatedly scaling the graphic—if you scale it in the graphics application instead of PageMaker.)

The advantage of creating a symbol as a graphic is that you probably already have a graphics application if you have been doing much desktop publishing. As an alternative, you can use a scanner to input the symbol if it already exists on paper.

To create a symbol or set of symbols as a font, you must use a font-generating application such as Fontrix (from Data Transforms Inc., of Denver, Colorado) or Publisher's Type Foundry (from Z-Soft of Marietta, Georgia). After the font is created and loaded into the system, you can insert the symbols in the text by using the Font command under the Type menu to select the symbol font and then typing the keyboard characters you assigned for each symbol.

The advantage of creating symbols as a font is that you can input them while typing in the word processor or in PageMaker. You also can easily and consistently scale them by means of the type-scaling commands. In PageMaker 4.0, you can search for and replace characters and fonts (see Chapter 5). For example, if you assign a symbol to the letter E on the keyboard, you can type the text using the letter E in place of the symbol; you then can search for the whole word E and replace it with letter E in the symbol font.

Creating Fractions in PageMaker

PageMaker has no built-in functions for creating mathematical formulas, but this section describes two techniques you can use in PageMaker 4.0 to create mathematical formulas without resorting to a font-generating application.

Creating a Fraction within a Sentence

If you want to create a simple fraction within a sentence, you can compose it of superscripted and subscripted characters that are kerned manually to print one above the other.

For example, to create a fraction composed of one single-digit number over another single-digit number, you first type the two numbers (such as a 1 and a 2, as shown in the first row of fig. 10.22). Select the first number (the numerator) and use the Type Specs command from the Type menu to set it as an underscored superscript; then select the second number (the denominator) and use the Type Specs command to set it as a subscript (column 2 of figure 10.22).

Finally, position the cursor between the two numbers and manually kern the two characters by holding the Ctrl key as you press the Backspace key to tighten the space between them until they are aligned with each other (column 3 of figure 10.22).

To make the fraction meet the baseline of the rest of the text, select both numbers, choose the Type Specs command from the Type menu, and click the Options button to get the Type Options dialog box. Set the Super/Subscript size to 45 percent of point size, the Superscript position to 40 percent of point size, and the Subscript position to 0 percent of point size. The results are shown in column 4 of figure 10.22.

$$12 \quad \frac{1}{2} \quad \frac{1}{2} \quad \frac{1}{2}$$

$$212 \quad \frac{1}{2\ 2} \quad \frac{1}{22} \quad \frac{1}{22}$$

$$2112 \quad \frac{11}{2\ 2} \quad \frac{11}{22} \quad \frac{11}{22}$$

Fig. 10.22. Steps in creating fractions within a sentence: Row 1 shows a single-digit number over a single-digit number, Row 2 shows a single-digit number over a double-digit number, Row 3 shows a double-digit number over a double-digit number.

To create a fraction composed of a single-digit numerator over a double-digit denominator, type the numerator between the other two digits, set as an underscored superscript. Set the two digits of the denominator as subscripts, and kern the spaces between each pair of numbers manually to create the effect shown in row 2 of figure 10.22.

To create a fraction composed of a double-digit numerator over a double-digit denominator, type the two digits of the numerator (set as an underscored superscript) between the other two digits. Set the two digits of the denominator as subscripts, and kern the spaces between the end pairs of numbers manually to create the effect shown in row 3 of figure 10.22.

Creating Stand-Alone Mathematical Formulas

You can use the new "paragraph rules" feature of PageMaker 4.0 (described in Chapter 5) to create mathematical formulas on lines of their own (i.e., not embedded in a paragraph of normal text). Figure 10.23 shows a complex formula.

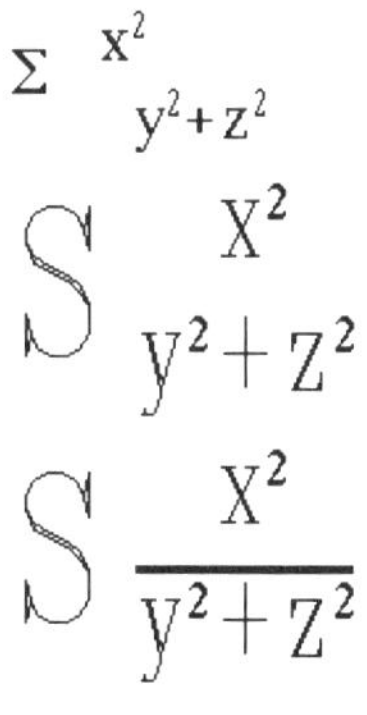

$$\Sigma \quad \frac{x^2}{y^2+z^2}$$

$$S \quad \frac{x^2}{y^2+z^2}$$

$$S \quad \frac{x^2}{y^2+z^2}$$

Fig. 10.23. Evolution of a complex formula.

For example, to create the formula shown in figure 10.23, you follow these steps:

1. Type the characters *Sx2* on one line, then press Enter and type *y2+z2* on the second line. In our example, these characters are set in 24-point Times.

2. Select the first letter (S) and use the Type Specs command on the Type menu to set the letter larger than the rest (in this case, 72 points). Position it as a subscript: Click the Options button in the Type Specifications dialog box and set the Subscript size to 100% of point size and the Subscript position to 50% of point size. In our example we set the "S" in symbol font to get the large sigma shown in figure 10.23.

3. Use the Type Specs command to set each 2 as a normal superscript.

4. Position the cursor on the second line, and use the Paragraph command on the Type menu to display the Paragraph Specifications dialog box. Specify a Left Indent wide enough to force the second line into position right of the large subscripted first letter in the formula (in this case, 0.656 inches), then click the Rules button to display the Paragraph Rules dialog box. Set up a 4-point rule (in our example) above the paragraph, set to the width of the text. Paragraph indentation and paragraph rules are described in Chapter 5.

5. To center the top line over the bottom line in the formula, insert a tab or spaces between the first letter in the formula (the sigma) and the rest of the characters on the first line.

All of these steps are shown in figure 10.23.

You can apply your own variations of this technique to create other formulas. Note that the sigma in the formula will appear as an S in some views on-screen, but it will print as a sigma.

Fitting Copy

Copy fitting is the process of making text fit into a predefined area: a column, a page, or a specific number of pages. *Copy casting* is the process of predicting how much space a given amount of copy will require or how much copy will fit a given space. In this section, you learn how a designer estimates how copy will fit *before* it is placed in PageMaker, and you will learn several methods of fitting copy after the copy has been written and edited.

Copy Casting

Traditionally, professional designers have approached the problems of copy casting from two angles. First, based on the design specifications, you can estimate how many words (or characters) can fill the space allotted. Magazine editors use this method when they ask authors to write articles of a specified word length. Second, you can take the text from the author and either estimate how much space the text will fill or make up design specifications that will force the text to fit a specified area.

Before placing a whole text file in PageMaker, you should estimate the amount of text that will fit and compare this figure with the text provided by the authors. If the amount of text provided differs significantly from the amount required, you can force the copy to fit by adjusting the margins in PageMaker before you place the text. Alternatively, you can use the word processing program to edit the copy until it is the desired length.

Casting from a Typecasting Reference Book

One traditional method used in copy casting is to refer to the typecasting reference book. This book, available at most bookstores, shows examples of text in various sizes and with different leadings. From these examples you can choose the look you want for your body copy. Also provided is the average number of characters per pica for each font. Your word processing program may be able to give you a character count for your text, or you yourself can count the number of characters per page or per line of printed copy. You also may use a type gauge to measure the type against a specific column width and length to estimate the number of lines of final copy. You use another measuring guide or gauge to determine the number of lines per inch at various leadings. The sequence of calculations goes something like this:

1. Select a font to be used for the text.

2. In the typecasting reference book, look up the average number of characters per pica.

3. Determine the number of characters in the word processing file by using the word processing software or a word-counting utility.

4. Divide the total number of characters by the average number of characters per pica to estimate the total number of picas required by the text.

5. Divide the total number of picas by the column width in picas to estimate the total number of lines of final copy.

6. Look up the number of lines per column inch for the leading you will be using.

7. Divide the total number of lines by the number of lines per column inch to estimate the number of column inches of final copy.

8. Divide the number of column inches of final copy by the number of column inches per page to estimate the total number of pages.

Because this method of casting copy or estimating length is tedious and has a wide margin of error, many typesetters instead use a second method.

Casting Sample Pages

In this second method of casting copy, you lay out one or two sample pages in PageMaker, using the font that will be used for normal body copy, and estimate the number of characters that fit on a page. This character count is often converted to an estimated number of words to be assigned to the author. The steps for this method are as follows:

1. Type one paragraph exactly 100 characters (or words) long.
2. Set the type in the specified font.
3. Duplicate the paragraph as many times as necessary to fill the column or page.
4. Count the number of paragraphs required to fill the column or page and multiply that number by 100 to get an estimated character (or word) count per column or page.
5. Multiply the estimated count per column or page by the number of columns or pages to determine the maximum character (or word) count.
6. Use the word processing program or utility to count the number of characters in the publication.
7. Divide that number by the number of characters per final column or page to estimate the number of columns or pages that will be filled.

Using a Formula

A third method of fitting copy is to take a 100-character paragraph of text and set it in the exact width used throughout the publication. Set copies of the same paragraph in different sizes or with different leadings, and measure the depth of each variation. You can estimate roughly the total number of column inches for the publication by using the following formula:

$$\text{Total number of column inches for the publication} = \text{Column inches required per 100 characters} \times \frac{\text{(Total number of characters in text files)}}{100}$$

None of these copy-casting techniques absolutely guarantees that copy will fit the space allowed. You therefore still need to do final copy fitting directly in PageMaker by adjusting one or more of the following variables: column width, leading, hyphenation zone, and word and letter spacing (for justified text).

Adjusting the Column Width

If you are accustomed to traditional typesetting techniques, you probably have specified text in terms of the width of each column. PageMaker, however, defines a page in terms of the number of columns and the space between columns. Because you cannot enter the column widths directly, you should establish your design specifications in terms of the number of columns and the space between them rather than the width of the text column.

> **Determining the Best Text Width**
>
> Here is one rule of thumb for determining the best width of text:
>
> The best line width (column width) is equivalent to 60 characters of the specified typeface, size, and style.
>
> Columns that are too narrow (much shorter than 60 characters in line length) have awkward line breaks and hyphenation. Lines that are too long are hard for the reader to follow.

You should determine the final column width before you create a new publication and stick with that column width throughout the production. You cannot automatically change all column widths throughout a PageMaker publication after the text has been placed on the pages. To change existing text, you have to adjust the width of each text block manually, or you have to export the text and then import it onto new pages that have the changed column specifications.

Adjusting the Leading

After the design specifications are established, the most common and preferred method of fitting copy is to change the leading rather than change the specifications for typeface, size, or style.

Whether you use PageMaker's automatic leading feature or specify the exact leading yourself, you always can make fine adjustments in the leading to fit copy into a defined space. Figure 10.24 provides examples. You can specify leading in half-point increments in the Type Specifications dialog box (displayed when you select the Type Specs command on the Type menu). To make copy fit, you can change the leading for the entire publication, for selected text elements, for style tags, or for selected pages. Leading is described in detail in Chapter 5.

This paragraph is exactly 100 characters long. This paragraph is exactly 100 characters long.	This paragraph is exactly 100 characters long. This paragraph is exactly 100 characters long.	This paragraph is exactly 100 characters long. This paragraph is exactly 100 characters long.	This paragraph is exactly 100 characters long. This paragraph is exactly 100 characters long.
12/12 Times	12/14 Times	12/auto	12/15 Times

Fig. 10.24. *12-point Times with different leading specifications.*

When you adjust leading, be consistent. Change the leading on all the body copy rather than on individual paragraphs. If you cannot change or do not want to change the leading for an entire article or publication, change the leading for whole pages and keep it the same across columns on a single page.

Using Hyphenation and Justification

PageMaker hyphenates text automatically unless you use the Hyphenation command on the Type menu to turn hyphenation off for selected publications or individual paragraphs (see Chapter 5). Hyphenated text takes up less space than unhyphenated text.

You also can change the amount of space the text requires by changing the alignment: Justified text tends to take up less space than unjustified text. The reason is that the justification process can reduce the space between words and between characters within words; unjustified text has standard spacing between words and letters.

Besides using the hyphenation and justification settings to fit copy to a page, you can achieve unusual effects by changing the hyphenation zone on unjustified text. Make this adjustment with the Spacing command and dialog box. You can use a large hyphenation zone to exaggerate the ragged right margin or to minimize hyphenation without turning it off entirely. (See Chapter 5 for more information on the hyphenation zone.)

Justified text usually calls for hyphenation, especially when the columns are narrow. Unhyphenated justified text tends to have more *rivers*—wide areas of blank space running down through several lines of type, caused by forced spacing between words.

Controlling Word and Letter Spacing

Unless you have some special effects in mind, you should keep PageMaker's defaults for word and letter spacing and tracking. Most publishers are likely to accept PageMaker's defaults for these settings. Changing word and letter spacing should be the last resort in copy fitting. You may want, however, to change these settings as a deliberate design strategy for special publications, such as advertisements and brochures.

You can help fit justified text into a specific space by adjusting the spacing between words and letters. With the Spacing option in the Paragraph Specifications dialog box (displayed when you select the Paragraph command on the Type menu) you can specify the acceptable size ranges for the spaces inserted between words and letters during the justification process. These ranges are given as percentages of "normal" space for the font.

If you think that you can improve your publication's appearance by reducing the spacing between words, you should first consider the tradeoffs. With a wide allowance for spacing between words and letters, justified text may be flooded with wide rivers of blank space, but fewer words are hyphenated. Justified text with a narrow spacing allowance is likely to be highly hyphenated.

Changing the Track setting in the Type Specifications dialog box (displayed when you select the Type Specs command on the Type menu) also adjusts the amount of space required by text. This technique can be used to expand or condense all of the text (in a newsletter, for example), but it is most useful in condensing selected lines (such as headings) just enough to pull up short widow lines. Note that if you plan to kern the space between characters manually—in a headline, for example—you should always set the tracking value first, then kern the letters.

Chapter Summary

This chapter provided information about fonts and copy fitting to help you design your publications for PageMaker. You have weighed some of the considerations involved in choosing fonts for a publication and in working with built-in, cartridge, and downloadable fonts. You also have learned how to fit copy into a defined space and how to estimate the amount of space required before you place the text on the page in PageMaker.

The next chapter offers more tips on the overall design of a publication, including the development of an underlying grid structure and the creation of template files, which enable you to complete large projects more efficiently.

11

PageMaker as a Design Tool

PageMaker, a tremendous design tool in many ways, is outstanding in at least four respects:

- You can use PageMaker to sketch out rough ideas for designs to be reviewed with the rest of your team or your client. (The term client can include managing editors, publication department managers, or end-user groups—anyone with whom the designer must share decisions.)

- You can use the structure PageMaker provides for organizing specifications for the production team.

- You can create template systems and style sheets to ensure that all parts of a publication follow the same specifications.

- You can select from 17 different line styles (in black or white), 16 different shade patterns, and a full spectrum of colors to add designer touches to any publication. You can see how these options are used in some of the examples in Part III.

This chapter discusses what you must consider in any publication design and offers tips about how you can use PageMaker as a design tool. The design considerations are given in the sequence you follow in PageMaker when you build a publication from scratch. You first see how you use PageMaker to develop a series of different design ideas for a project. Next, you learn what goes into a template system so that you can create a series of publications with the same design. Finally, you learn how the designer can work ahead of the production team, sketching the layout of each page of the publication before the text and graphics from other programs are placed on the pages. Desktop publishers often play all these roles. If you are the designer, production team, author, and editor, you can learn how to follow the steps of all these professionals.

In practice, some of these steps may be done first on paper rather than at the computer; in fact, the designers on some teams may never touch the mouse. Whether you—as the designer—are simply writing out the design specifications or actually setting up the master template, you should know how PageMaker works before making your specifications. For example (as mentioned in Chapter 10), you cannot enter column widths directly. PageMaker defines a page in terms of the margins, the number of columns, and the space between columns. Your specifications, therefore, should be in terms of the number of columns and the space between them, rather than the width of the column itself. (You can move column guides to get an exact width, but you miss the advantages of PageMaker's automatic column guides.)

Traditionally, a designer becomes involved in a production only after the writing is complete or well under way. If the project team is small, however, and the authors are willing, some design specifications can be incorporated into the text during the writing stage. For instance, if you plan the design ahead of time, you can let the authors know whether they should type two carriage returns between paragraphs and indent the first line of each paragraph. Other design details, such as the page size and margins, can be decided later—after the writing but before the text is placed in PageMaker. In other words, you can wait to develop some design specifications until after you learn what text and graphics are required for the publication.

This chapter shows you how to prepare your design specifications in terms of PageMaker's commands and capabilities.

Creating Design Alternatives

You can use PageMaker to create a series of quick *comps* of different designs for a publication before you decide on the final design. A designer's comp is a comprehensive layout of a design idea, usually done by hand with pencils, rulers, and colored pens. The advantages of sketching out your ideas with PageMaker rather than using pencil and ruler are threefold:

- Copying and moving elements on a page is easy if you are working on a single design.

- Making copies of the first design and modifying it to create alternative designs is an efficient design practice.

- Showing clients crisp text and graphic elements printed on a high-resolution printer makes an effective presentation.

Identifying the Essential Elements

One step in the design process is to identify the essential elements of the publication to be created. For example, suppose that you are creating a newsletter. Although the production manager views the elements in terms of articles that must be written by various authors, the designer uses another perspective to view the newsletter. The designer may list the newsletter's design elements as the following:

- Page size and margins
- Underlying grid structure
- A style sheet for the text elements
- Running heads and running feet
- Two different page formats (right and left)
- Three heading levels
- Four types of graphics
- Spot color

In addition, this particular publication may include one or more of the following special considerations or constraints that affect the design:

- Feature articles requiring special placement
- Sidebars or pull quotes distinct from the rest of the text on a page
- Custom graphics requiring special placement

For this proposed publication, you use PageMaker as a design tool and let the program's built-in text and graphics features create representations of your basic design elements. For example, use shaded boxes to show where graphics will be placed and crop marks to show the page size. To enhance the design, you use ruled lines; figure 11.1 shows how PageMaker illustrates design ideas for the chapters of a book. You also may use "greek text" to show the position and size of text on a page. The phrase *greek text* refers to any text used to represent the font, but not the content, to be used on a page. Typesetters use standard block paragraphs that are called greek, but the text looks more like Latin ("Lorem ipsum dolor sit..."). This use of the term *greek* differs from that used to describe the appearance or display of text in the Fit in Window view, where text in small point sizes appears as gray bars on the screen.

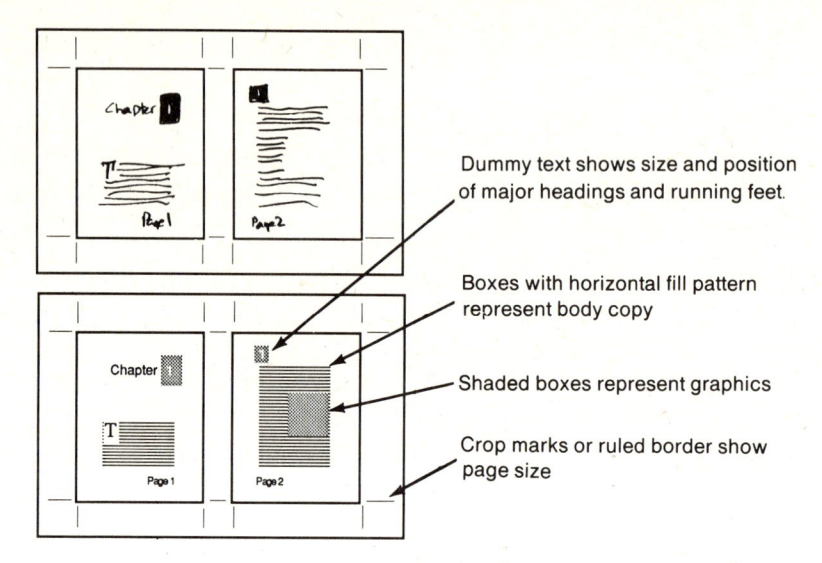

Fig. 11.1. Rough page comps done by hand and made with PageMaker.

After you create the basic elements of your publication, you can modify the design or rearrange the elements on the page to develop variations. Rather than create a different PageMaker publication to represent each design idea, you use one design publication to create and show many pages of design variations (see fig. 11.2).

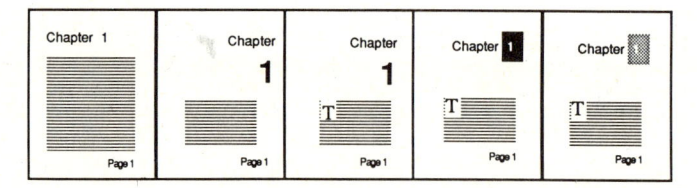

Fig. 11.2. Example of a design publication with variations.

PageMaker enables you to do the following:

- Create representations of all the basic design elements once and store them on the pasteboard
- Use the Copy and Paste commands to place individual design elements on each page layout
- Change type specifications (specs) or style tags of selected text as needed to represent each new design
- Add a new page for each new design idea

- Use greek text as a marker to develop design ideas and then replace the greek text with imported text while maintaining the form of the original design

> ### *Making Duplicates of the Basic Design Elements*
>
> Store all the basic design elements on one side of the pasteboard (see fig. 11.3). In starting a new design idea, use the Copy and Paste commands to move all the basic elements from one side of the pasteboard to the other, and move the duplicated elements onto the new page to create a new design. After completing one design, insert a new page and repeat the copy and paste operation to begin building a second design (see fig. 11.4).

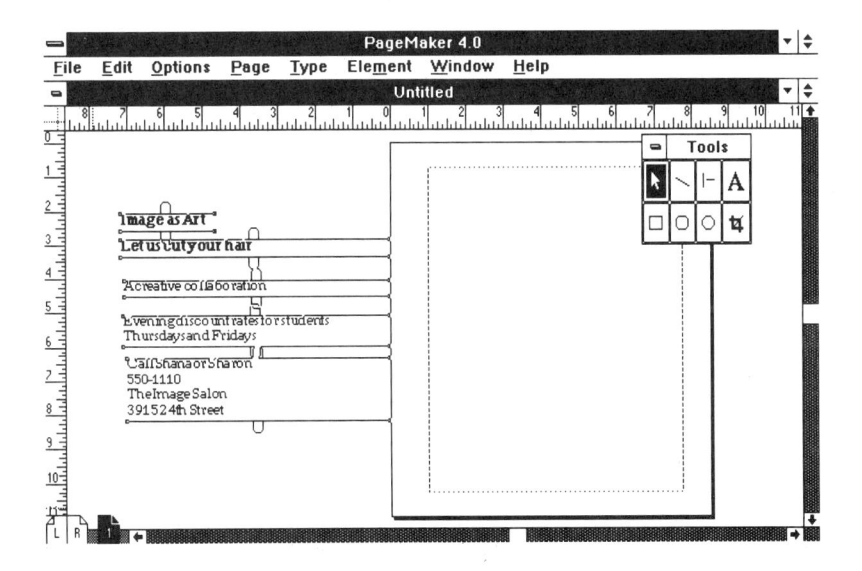

Fig. 11.3. Basic elements shown on the pasteboard.

Looking at Unique Design Features

The master-page elements for the initial design publication should include only specifications that are known and unchangeable. If all the elements of the design are open to change, you may leave the master pages blank in a design publication. (Master pages are described in Chapter 3.)

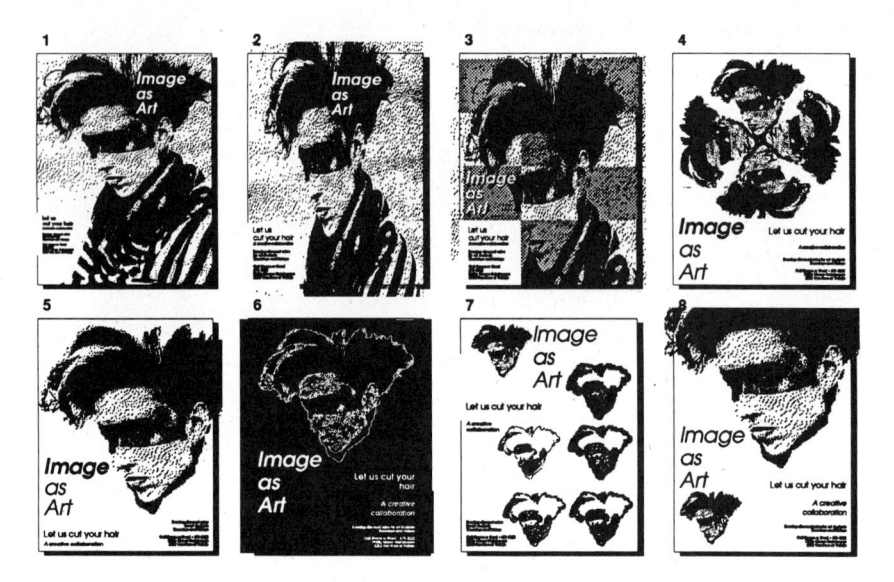

Fig. 11.4. *A series of design ideas for a one-page flier.*

Many elements to be positioned on the master pages of finished publications are considered variable elements during the design phase. You enter these variable elements directly on the numbered pages of the publication.

Although you place the actual text and graphics in final publications, you can create representations of the basic elements in your design publication. You need not know the exact text or contents of the publication to rough out a design idea. You can use dummy text for headlines or headings, sample text for body copy, and black or gray boxes for figures. When using the Place command to place text in a PageMaker publication, you can select whether the new text will be "replacing entire story" or placed as a "new item." You also can replace graphics by the same method. In this way, you can place sample text and, when your design is complete, quickly replace it with the correct copy for your publication. (The Place command is described in Chapters 3, 4, and 6.)

If the trim size of the publication will be smaller than 8 1/2 by 11 inches, you can use a solid border in the design publication to represent the edges of the pages. This border enables you to see how the final pages will look when trimmed. In the final publication, however, you should use crop marks rather than solid lines to indicate the edges of the paper (see fig. 11.5). Otherwise, the solid lines may show in the final publication—especially if the pages will be folded into signatures before being trimmed. (A *signature* is a single sheet of paper on which an even number of pages is printed—usually 16 or 32. The pages are arranged so that the signature can be folded and trimmed to create a booklet or a small section of a larger publication.)

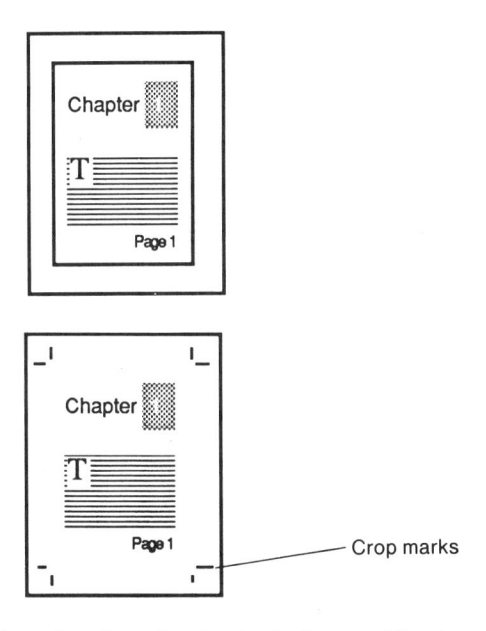

Fig. 11.5. Solid lines showing trim size in design specification, replaced by crop marks in printed copy.

After you choose one design idea, you translate this idea into the specifications for PageMaker and the other programs used to construct the parts of the publication. Ideally, you then sit down at the computer with PageMaker and build the basic template system for the final publication.

Building a Template

Whenever you start a new publication, you must go through a certain series of steps and commands to set up the pages before you begin placing text and graphics from other programs. In traditional terms, you define the design specifications for the publication. In PageMaker, you make selections in the Page Setup dialog box and add grid lines and other elements on the master pages.

A template is a PageMaker publication that embodies the basic design specifications (see fig. 11.6). The basic grid system for each page appears on the template. The template also includes common elements that will appear within the publication in specific locations or at repeated intervals. For example, a newsletter template might include a style sheet, a basic grid structure on the master pages, parts of page one (such as the newsletter banner), and parts of other pages (such as the masthead), or an area for a mailing label. A template is set up with all the defaults tailored to match the design specifications for the publication.

Fig. 11.6. Thumbnails of a template for a four-page newsletter.

The next sections describe the process and benefits of creating templates—publications that already are set up with a standard design that can be shared by many publications. To create a template, first create a publication with standard, shared elements. When you use the Save command the first time, or whenever you use the Save As command, you have the option of saving the document as a Publication or as a Template. To use a template, choose Open from the File menu, select the template for your publication, and click OK. A template opens as a new, untitled publication that you can continue building without affecting the original template.

After you create a template, you can clone it to create a series of publication files that follow the same design specifications. For example, a long document may have one template that is cloned to create a series of sections or chapters that follow the same design specifications. A short document produced on a regular basis, such as a newsletter, may have one template from which every issue is cloned. Some documents may be composed of sections that follow different design specifications, requiring a series of templates—one for each different section layout.

The benefit of using templates is that the activities described in the following sections are executed only once during the production cycle instead of once for every new file in the full document. As you follow the design steps for publications, you soon see how much time you can save by using a series of templates for large publications.

> ### Using PageMaker's Templates
>
> PageMaker comes with a collection of templates that have been created by professional designers for Aldus. Instead of making your own templates from scratch, you can use these templates for proposals, newsletters, reports, and slides. If you opted to install the templates during the installation process, the templates are stored in the template subdirectory of PageMaker:
>
> C:\PM4\TEMPLATE
>
> To modify a template, open the template as an untitled publication, adapt it to your publication, and then save the copy as a new template for current and future use.

Defining the Standards

Before you lay out your page grid, you should define the basic defaults and standards you will use throughout the publication. These defaults and standards include the page size and orientation, the margins, the target printer, and the unit of measure. After a publication has been opened, these specifications are stored with the publication.

In the following sections, these standards are discussed in the sequence in which they appear as you build a template. You must specify page size, orientation, and margins in the Page Setup dialog box before you can set the target printer and unit of measure for a publication. Remember that most of the commands mentioned in this chapter already have been described in detail in Chapters 3 through 9, and we mention them here simply as they apply to creating templates.

Defining the Page Setup

You define the paper size and orientation through the Page Setup dialog box when you open a new publication (see fig. 11.7). By setting these standards in a template, you ensure that all other templates cloned from that template will have the same page size and orientation.

```
Page setup
Page:  Letter                                    OK
Page dimensions:  8.5  x  11  inches             Cancel
Orientation:  ● Tall  ○ Wide                     Numbers...
Start page #:  1    Number of pages:  1
Options:  ☒ Double-sided   ☒ Facing pages
          ☐ Restart page numbering
Margin in inches:
    Inside  1         Outside  0.75
    Top     0.75      Bottom   0.75
Target printer:    PostScript Printer on LPT1:
```

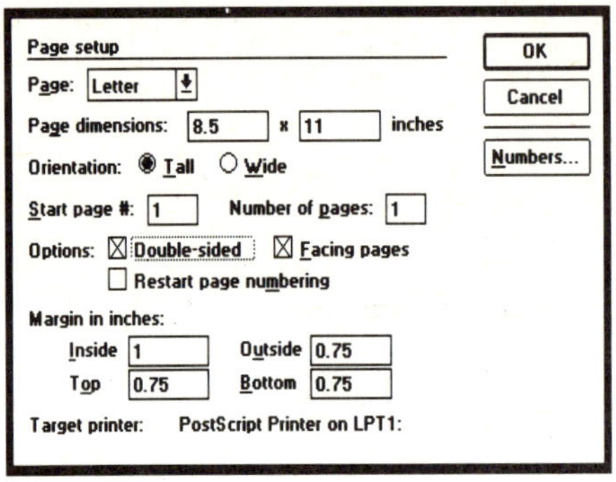

Fig. 11.7. Choosing page size and orientation for a new publication.

Most publications have the same page size for all sections, but the orientation of the pages, which can be Tall or Wide, may vary from section to section. For instance, you may have a set of appendixes with financial reports that must be printed wide to accommodate many columns of numbers. In this case, you set up two templates: one for all tall pages and one for all wide pages.

Although the page size is usually the same as the final publication after it is mass produced, bound, and trimmed, you can deliberately specify larger page sizes for special layouts. For example, you may specify that you are printing on 8 1/2-by-11-inch paper and use that setting as the board size for designing a 6-by-9-inch booklet, as shown in figure 11.8. You can use nonprinting guides, margins, and columns to define the 6-by-9-inch layout area and use the area beyond that to print project-control information, registration marks, and instructions to the printer. The printed pages also can show crop marks that you draw on the master pages because the automatic crop marks feature does not accurately show the page size in this case.

The margins defined in the Page Setup dialog box apply throughout a publication. Each section of the publication that requires different margins should have a separate template (see fig. 11.9).

Alternating Tall and Wide Pages

If your pages contain only text, you can rotate all the text blocks on a page to give the page a wide orientation. If your pages include graphics, you can set up tall and wide pages using two different files. In this case, you might want to rotate the text of the running headers and footers in the wide publication so that they match the position of the headers and footers in the tall publication. (Chapter 5 describes how to rotate text.) You also need to insert blank pages as necessary where the pages alternate between tall and wide, to maintain correct page numbering.

You can insert wide page layouts in tall publications by using this trick: create the wide pages in a separate document, then save each page in EPS format (as described in Chapter 8). Open the EPS page in a drawing application that supports EPS formats and enables rotation, and rotate the page image 90 degrees. Finally, place the rotated page image in the tall publication.

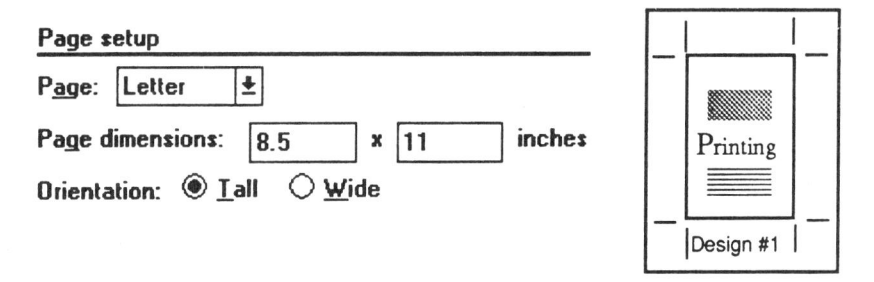

Fig. 11.8. 6-by-9-inch booklet pages defined as 8 1/2 by 11 in dialog box and printed on 8 1/2-by-11-inch paper with crop marks and project-control information on the master pages.

If the margins remain the same throughout but the column guides differ between pages or sections, you can work from one master template and use PageMaker's Column Guides command from the Options menu to change column settings. Part III shows you examples of publications with changing column settings.

The margins are not necessarily the same as the limits of the text and graphics that appear on a page. PageMaker enables you to position text and graphics beyond the margins. The side margins determine the width of the column guides. The bottom margin determines where text stops flowing when placed in a column. Elements that can fall outside your margins might include ruled lines around pages, vertical and horizontal rules that are part of the design, and running heads and feet (see fig. 11.10). You must make sure, however, that your printer can print these areas (as explained in Chapter 8).

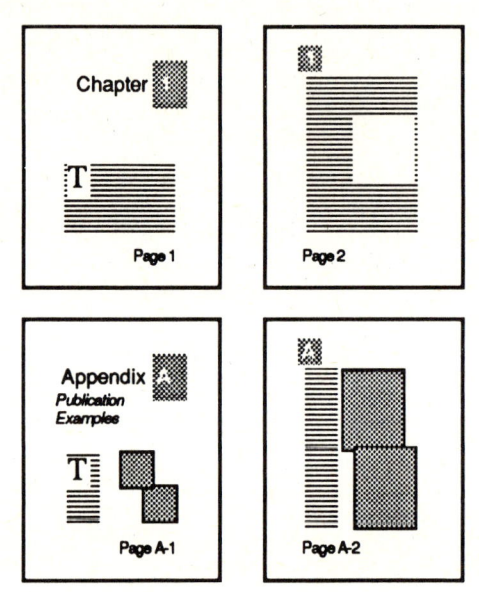

Fig. 11.9. Separate templates for sections of the publication requiring different margins.

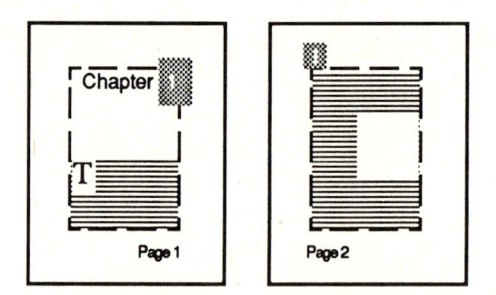

Fig. 11.10. Margins do not limit all text and graphics.

If you are accustomed to defining page layouts by width of text rather than width of margins, you must convert your specifications to the terms used by PageMaker. For example, if you want the text to be 6 inches wide on an 8 1/2-inch-wide page, the total amount of space available for both the inside and the outside margins is 2 1/2 inches. In other words, if you know what the margins are and what the page size is, as specified in the Page Setup dialog box, you can calculate the width of the text with the following formula:

text width = (page width) − (inside margin measure + outside margin measure)

If you know the page size and the text width, you can calculate the margin allowance with this formula:

total space available for inside and outside margins = page width − text width

You can use variations of these formulas to determine the top and bottom margins or to calculate the measured depth allowed for text on each page.

You can use an expanded version of the following formula to calculate the widths PageMaker will set up for columns when you use the Column Guides command:

$$\text{column width} = \frac{(\text{page width} - (\text{inside} + \text{outside margin measures}) - (\text{space between columns} \times (\text{number of columns} - 1)))}{\text{number of columns}}$$

Identifying the Target Printer

As you begin to build your template, you first should decide the printer you will use. If you have more than one printer or cartridge available on your system, you make this selection once by defining the target printer in the template with the Setup Printer command on the File menu. From this point, all publication files cloned from this template will have the same target printer specifications. The target printer selection dictates certain font selections for the rest of the design (see Chapter 9).

Selecting a Unit of Measure

If you give all your design specifications in the same unit of measure, you can set your preferences in the template so that the same unit of measure applies to all files made from the template. Use the Preferences command under the Edit menu. If you give your specifications in two or more different measures (inches for margins but points for type, for instance), select the unit of measure in which you prefer to view the ruler line. You also can set different units of measure for the vertical and horizontal rule. The Preferences dialog box is shown in figure 11.11.

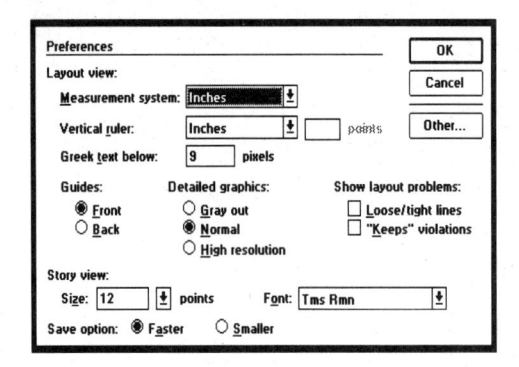

Fig. 11.11. Setting the unit of measure in the template.

Displaying Rulers

During the design phase, you must turn on the rulers (using the Rulers command from the Options menu) to lay out your grid precisely. If you leave the rulers on in the template, they are displayed automatically in all publications made from the template. During the production phase, the automatic ruler lines are convenient for scaling or cropping graphics.

Whenever possible, state your design specifications as a measure from the zero point on the ruler line. Usually, this reference point is the top left corner of the page or the tops of the inside edges of double-sided publications created with the Facing Pages option (see fig. 11.12). If your design specifications require a different zero point, you should make the position of the zero point on the page a part of the design specifications.

Setting Defaults on the Type Menu

Although some text formatting might occur in your word processing program, you can set the defaults for the body copy by having the body text take on the default settings as you import the text. From then on, all publications cloned from the template retain the default settings you have set. Any new text typed in PageMaker and any placed text files (with a TXT extension) automatically take on the template's default settings.

To change the defaults for an entire publication, make selections on the Type menu after selecting the pointer tool rather than the text tool. These settings are discussed more comprehensively in Chapter 10, "Typography."

Fig. 11.12. Design specifications in reference to zero point.

Setting Defaults on Style Sheets

After you create a style sheet, all text takes on the characteristics you set for the body text, including the attributes for the Tabs, Type, Paragraph, and Indents dialog boxes. The style sheet enables you to work with many different elements at once, not just the type specification. (See Chapter 5 for more information on style sheets).

Creating a Grid System

The best publication designs are based on underlying grids that position elements throughout publications. Using PageMaker, you can define the grid and other printing elements, such as ruled lines and folios, on master pages. Nonprinting grid lines in PageMaker include page margins, column guides (up to 20 columns per page), and up to 40 nonprinting ruler guides per page or pair of facing pages. Simple grid structures that involve one, two, or three columns are relatively easy to work with; but complex grids usually offer more design possibilities (see fig. 11.13). For example, the variety in a one-column grid structure can be achieved only by varying the type specifications and paragraph indentations. A two-column grid structure offers the added possibility of graphics and text expanding to full-page width on selected pages. A three-column grid offers at least three page variations.

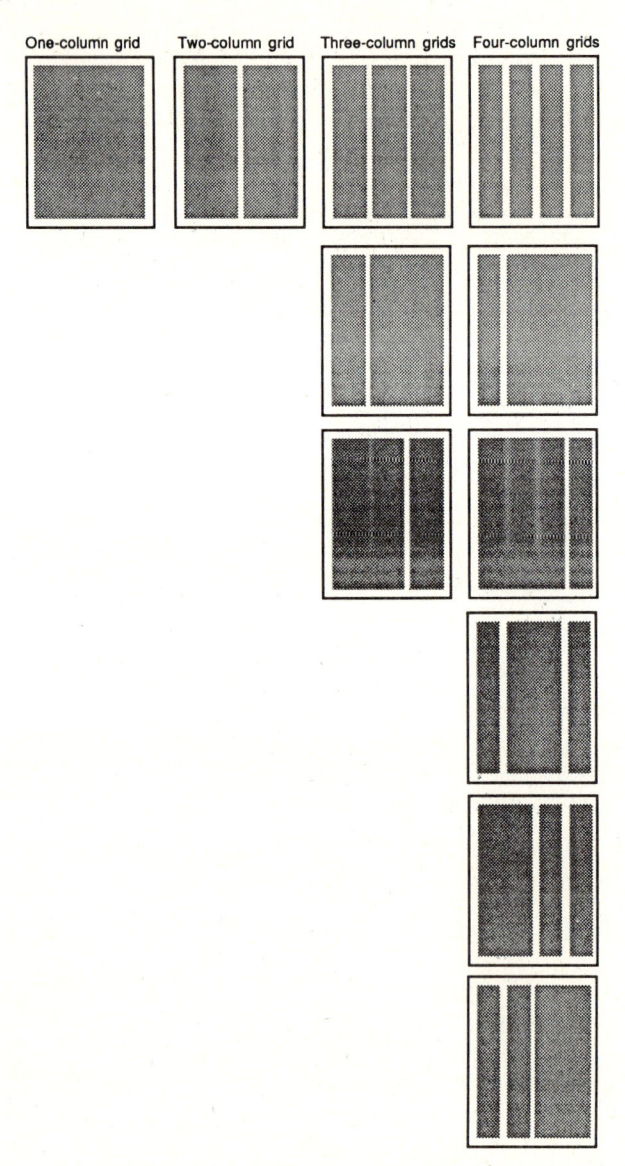

Fig. 11.13. Grid structures showing design possibilities.

For even spacing, you can set up a grid structure with PageMaker's Column Guides command. You do not have to leave the column guides fixed to follow the grid. For example, to set up the grids shown in figure 11.14, you first set up three column guides to divide the page in thirds. You then move ruler guides to divide the page into thirds. Next, set up two columns and drag the center column guides to the first or second marker, as in the first column of figure 11.14. The second and third columns of figure 11.14 show the same technique applied to a four-column grid.

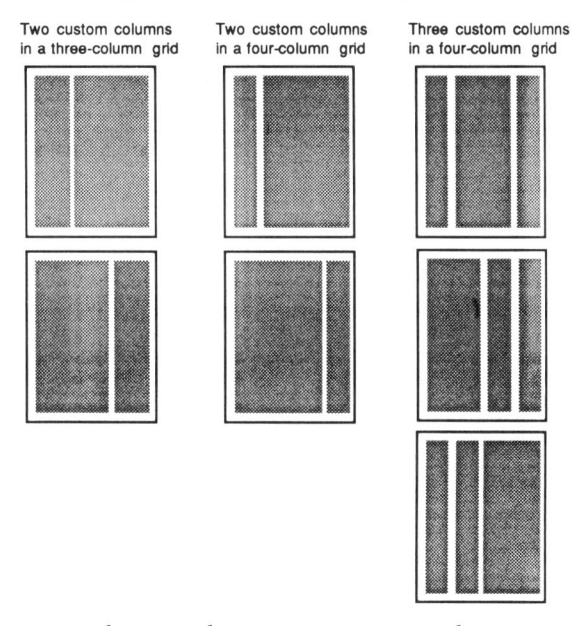

Fig. 11.14. Moving column guides to create custom grid settings.

The spacing between the columns usually is set to a default width of 0.167 inch, or one pica. You can make this space wider if you plan to insert hairline rules between columns, but in general, keeping the space between columns less than 2 picas is good design practice.

> ### Using Columns as Grid Markers
> You can set the space between columns to zero and use the Column Guides command to help divide the page into equal parts. Pull ruler guides into position over the column edges to hold the divisions, and then reset the space between columns to create the guides you want to use to define the text.

Publications with the same grid on every page are much easier to produce than publications that switch between variations in the grid. A common variation, the mirror-image page layout, is particularly hard to handle (see fig. 11.15). Individual page layout is not difficult, but chaos can ensue if you have to insert or delete a page after the publication is laid out. When you work with mirror-image designs, your best option is to insert or delete an even number of pages to keep all the subsequent page layouts intact.

Fig. 11.15. Mirror-image page design.

If you must create mirror-image grid designs, specify all measures starting from the inside edges of the paper. Remember that in double-sided, facing-page publications, PageMaker sets the zero point on the ruler lines at the inside margin. On the left master page, the zero point is set at the upper right corner; on the right master page, the zero point is set at the upper left corner.

Identifying Common Text and Graphic Elements

Most of your text probably will be brought in from other programs. Some elements, however, are repeated throughout the publication. In a template, these repeated elements can appear on the master pages, on the pasteboard, and on some numbered pages.

Elements that appear in the same position on every page belong on the master pages. Every page holds running heads and running feet, as well as the graphic elements of the basic page design. The master-page running head and foot of a template, however, are only place holders (see fig. 11.16). Although you position these elements with the correct type specifications and alignment, the text of each publication created from the template probably will change. When you clone the template, one of your first steps is to change the text of the running head and running foot.

Chapter 11: PageMaker as a Design Tool **401**

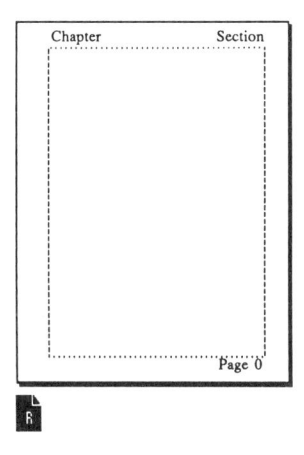

Fig. 11.16. The running heads and feet on the template.

In addition to the elements that belong on the master pages, other elements may be repeated irregularly throughout the publication. You create these items once and then store them on the pasteboard. Whenever you need the repeated elements, you can duplicate them with the Copy and Paste commands from the File menu (see fig. 11.17).

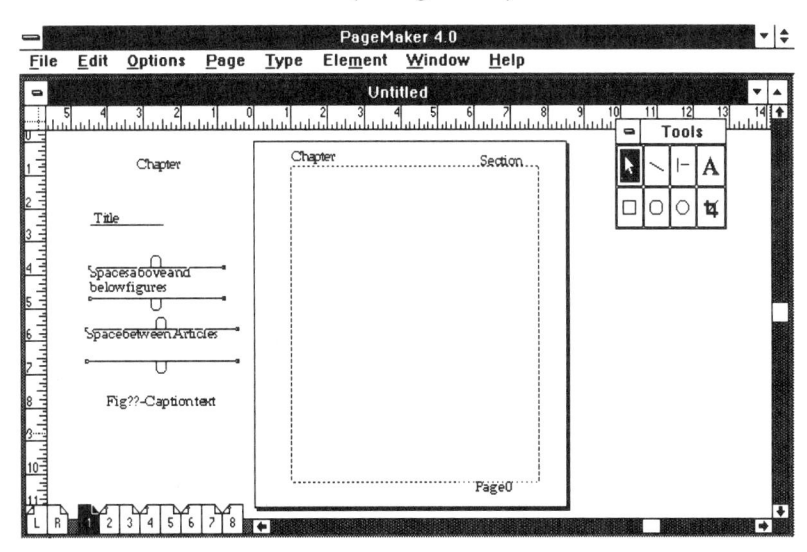

Fig. 11.17. Commonly used elements on master pages and pasteboard.

For example, you can use the pasteboard to store a graphic symbol that appears at the end of every article in a newsletter or magazine. When you reach the end of an article, you simply copy the symbol from the pasteboard.

Just as you create text place holders for the running head and running foot, you create standard dummy text blocks for headlines or captions within the publication and store them on the pasteboard. If your publication includes display ads in predetermined sizes, you can store the correct size boxes on the pasteboard. You then use the Copy and Paste commands from the File menu to duplicate and position the blocks as you lay out the pages.

Adding Standard Elements to Numbered Pages

Besides the elements positioned on the master pages or stored on the pasteboard, your publication may contain elements that appear predictably on certain numbered pages. For example, the template for a newsletter should include the banner from the first page (see fig. 11.18). If all issues of the newsletter are always the same length, you may be able to predict the positions of the subscription information and other permanent features. You also can add place holders for the headline text for feature articles that start on the first page.

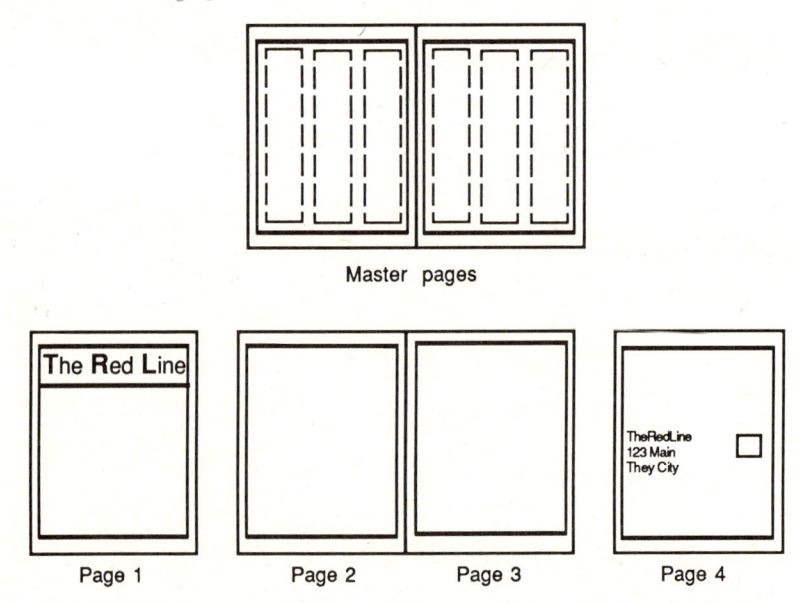

Fig. 11.18. Newsletter templates with standing elements on fixed numbered pages.

> **Storing Dummy Headlines on the Pasteboard**
> On the pasteboard, store templates for headlines. Use templates that include dummy text and are one-, two-, or three-columns wide.

Determining the Number of Templates Required

You already have seen that a separate template file is required for each unique page size, orientation, and margin setting. In addition, you can use templates to handle any other essential differences among sections of your publication. For example, if the basic format of running heads and feet changes between major sections of a publication, you need more than one template (see fig. 11.19). On the other hand, if the only difference between sections is the number of columns, one template may suffice.

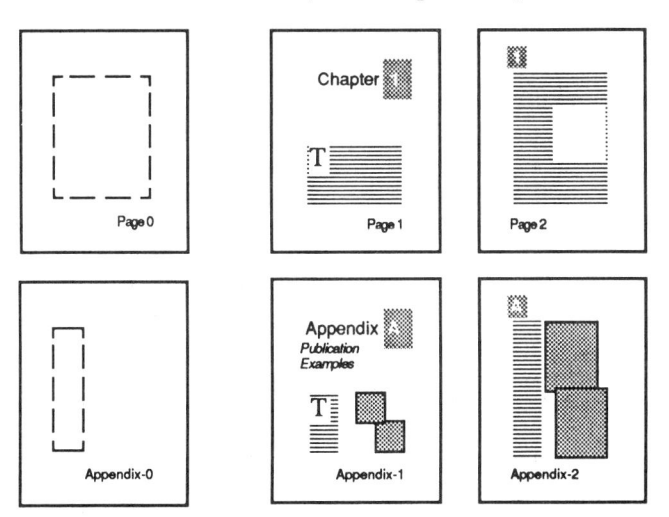

Fig. 11.19. A multiple-template system.

Create separate templates if any of the following conditions occur:

- Page size varies
- Page orientation changes
- Master-page elements change (except the text of running heads and feet)
- Basic grid changes

Adding Instructions for Working with the Template

If the person designing the template is not the same person who uses it in production, the designer should list the steps necessary for working with the template. The steps can be simple—serving primarily as reminders of each step. For example, a designer may list the following instructions:

1. Open the template and immediately save it under a new name.
2. Change the running heads and feet on the master pages.
3. Change the volume and date information on the first page, below the newsletter banner.
4. Place the table of contents on the first page before placing the feature article.
5. Delete these instructions.
6. Continue placing text and graphics as specified for the current issue. To catch the attention of the production staff, you can type instructions directly on the template's pasteboard, the right master page, or the first page (see fig. 11.20). The production person can move the instructions or delete them after reading.

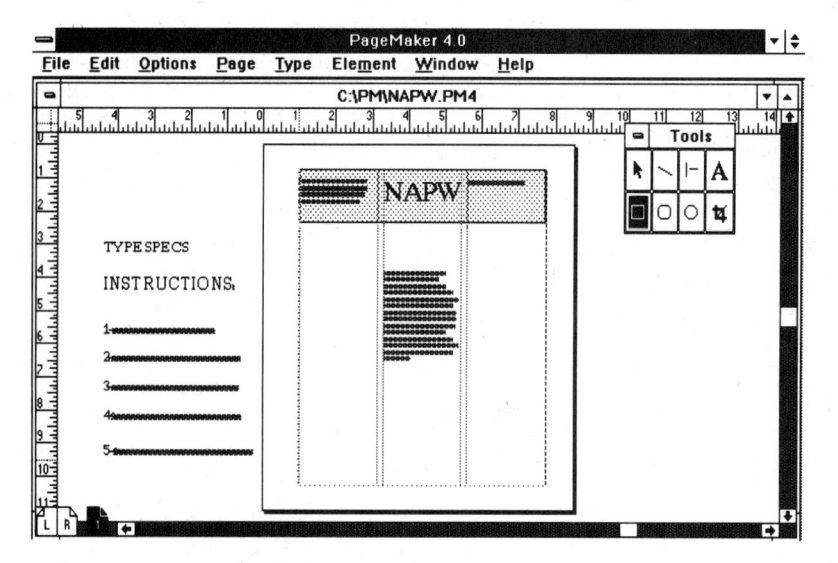

Fig. 11.20. Type specifications and instructions for using the template.

Creating Specifications for Other Programs

Chapter 10, "Typography," presents most of the necessary considerations for selecting fonts for different text elements. You can put some specifications—such as those for the position and format of running heads and feet—directly into your PageMaker template. You can implement other specifications—such as type specifications or style sheet tag names—with your word processing program. Line widths and fill patterns can be set up as default values in the PageMaker template. These items also can be stored as defined elements on the pasteboard or applied in the graphics programs you use to create the content of the publication.

A designer should have a good idea of the number and sources of graphic elements that go into the publication. Knowing the capabilities and limitations of the available programs, the designer must specify how each illustration should be treated. What are the size limitations or preferences for the figures, for example? If you are following a grid system, each figure's width must match the increments allowed by the grid. For instance, a two-column grid allows only two figure widths (one column wide or full-page width); a three-column grid allows three different figure widths; a four-column grid allows four widths; and so on.

The designer must answer other questions. What fonts, styles, and sizes will be used in illustrations and their captions? Will the figures be enlarged or reduced during page composition? Will photographs and other special illustrations be pasted up by hand or scanned into the computer? You can write out these specifications, or you can use the programs that create illustrations to create figure templates just as you use PageMaker to create publication templates.

Your design specifications for body copy, captions, and figure titles should include directions for paragraph alignment (left, right, justified, or centered) and spacing between paragraphs. The designer must consider convenience and speed of production. Some formats can be handled by menu selections in PageMaker and most word processors. Other formats require special treatment and may slow down the production process.

Designing Page Layouts before Entering Content

Publications with complex grid systems require the designer's attention throughout the production cycle. That attention is especially important for magazines and newsletters that incorporate various sizes of display ads throughout the publication. The designer can work ahead of the production team to specify where ads are to be placed and how articles should jump from one page to another.

Traditionally, a designer would draw pencil roughs of each page, or thumbnail sketches. This term originally meant that the sketches could be literally as small as a person's thumbnail because the sketches were intended to be quick to produce. PageMaker's Thumbnails option on the Print dialog box creates miniature versions of the pages of the publication. (This option is available only on PostScript and DDL printers, not on dot-matrix or LaserJet II printers.) For example, you can make rough page layouts with shaded boxes and article titles for every page of a magazine or newsletter and print the thumbnails as a guide for building the publication (see fig. 11.21). This same rough file can be used as the starting point in placing the finished text and graphics files on each page. Another set of thumbnails may be printed to check the final layouts (see fig. 11.22).

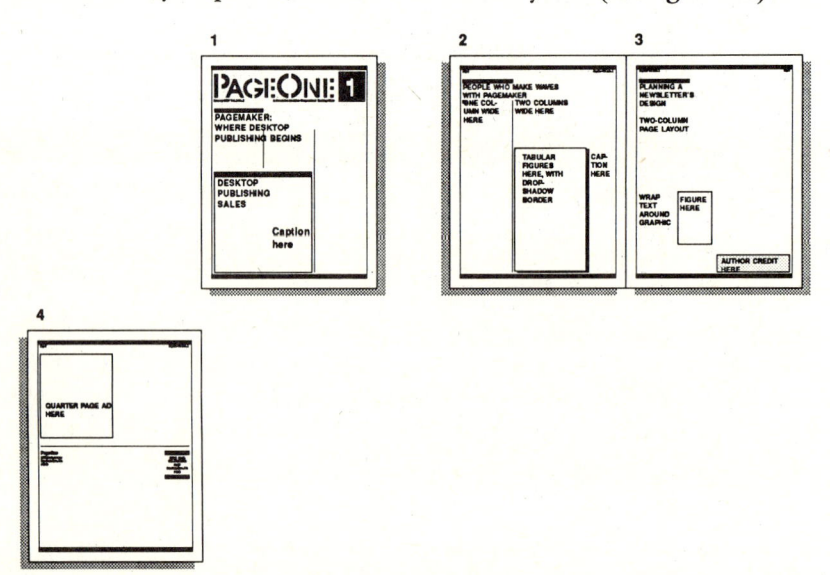

Fig. 11.21. Thumbnail printouts of rough page layouts.

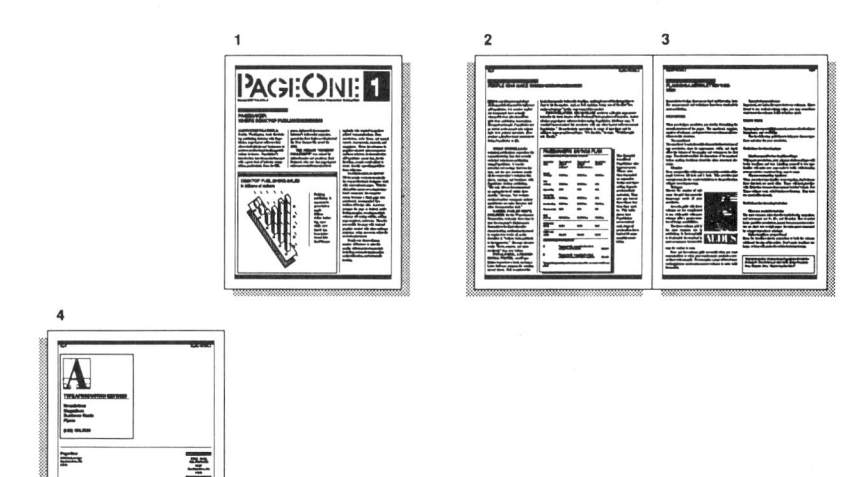

Fig. 11.22. Thumbnail printouts of finished page layouts.

> ### *Building a Page Layout like a Painting*
>
> A publication does not have to be built from front to back, page by page. You can construct a publication in layers, just as painters work on canvas. The painter first pencils the rough outline on the canvas and then gradually adds layers of paint.
>
> In PageMaker, the basic grid system is the painter's penciled sketch. You can use shaded boxes to reserve certain areas for planned graphics and particular articles. The text and graphics that you bring in from other programs to replace these place holders are like the painter's gradually added layers of paint.

During both the design and production phases, you can work on views of facing pages for double-sided publications. Working on both pages can be an advantage when you want to consider the overall impact of the open publication or you want to create graphic images that bleed across from one page to the other.

Be careful when you design page layouts that bleed off the edges of the paper or across facing pages. The top of figure 11.23 shows how part of an image that bleeds across two pages can be lost in the edges of the paper, depending on the type of printer you use. To solve this problem, specify a page size that is smaller than the paper size (see the bottom of figure 11.23). You can determine the margin limits by printing a page covered by a solid black or shaded box.

Center of image is lost at the edges of the pages in a bleed across 8.5x11 pages

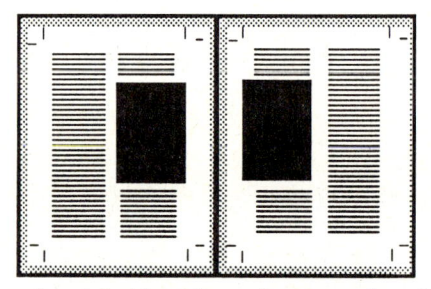

Full image is printed to edges of crop marks when the page size is smaller than 8.5x11

Fig. 11.23. Handling bleeds.

The designer may be called in again after the PageMaker publication goes to production. (Refer to Chapters 3 through 9 for the production process following the design step.) The final design activities are described in the following paragraphs.

Going beyond PageMaker

For some publications, the final pages for distribution are printed on a laser printer. In most cases, however, you make multiple copies with a photocopier or an offset printer.

After the final pages of the publication are printed on a high-resolution printer, some final preparation may still be required before the pages are ready for reproduction. This preparation can include manual paste-up of figures that could not be produced on the computer, photograph mark-up for halftone processing, and color overlays to specify multiple-color printing.

Some artwork may be impossible to render using the computer—for example, photographs or original artwork that feature fine charcoal or airbrush techniques. In this case, you leave space for the special artwork on the PageMaker page and paste in the artwork by hand on the final version before you make multiple copies of the publication.

If you plan to paste up many elements, you may want to lay all the pages down on *boards*—heavy white paper that keeps the pages flat and prevents pasted-down elements from peeling or curling.

If you are using photographs, you can scan them into the computer and then place them on the PageMaker page (see Chapter 6), or the print shop can use a camera to create *halftones*. A halftone is composed of dots, like a scanned image; but most scanned images are saved at low resolutions (between 72 and 300 dpi), whereas halftones have many more dots per inch.

To save time, you can use solid black boxes to reserve space for photographs on the PageMaker pages (as shown in fig. 11.23). Otherwise, you can use a scanned image of the photograph to indicate the exact size and cropping required. You should check with your print shop before you set up pages for halftones to see whether they prefer to receive your pages with black boxes or with the for-position-only scanned images in place.

> ### *Scanned Images versus Photographs*
>
> If the final publication will be printed on a porous paper like newsprint, a 300-dpi scanned image can look as good as a photographic halftone.
>
> If the final publication will be produced on glossy paper, 300-dpi scanned images may be too coarse for the final product. Still, you can scan, place, scale, and crop your PageMaker image to show the camera operator how to handle the original photograph (see fig. 11.24).

If you plan to have color in your publication, PageMaker can help you prepare the publication for commercial color printing. PageMaker's Spot Color Overlays feature in the Print dialog box prepares the publication by printing separate sheets for each color used in order to simplify the process of making printing plates for each color. For example, if your headlines and footers are magenta, your text is black, and your graphic is light blue, PageMaker prints three copies of that one page. The headlines and footers print on one page, the text on another, and the graphic spotted for color on a third. You can print a master page and label your color choices for the commercial printer, as shown in figure 11.25.

Fig. 11.24. Using a scanned image to bold the place of a halftone in the final production.

When commercial printers make plates for the publication, they look on each printed page for registration marks, or symbols that line up the images. If your publication size is smaller than the page size, registration marks automatically print on every page when you select Spot Color Overlays in the Print dialog box. If your publication leaves no room on the page, place the registration marks on the master page by using the Graphics menu. Using the Color Palette command in the Options menu, assign the color [Registration] to the graphic (see fig. 11.26). The registration marks will appear on each page—even on the pages that have spot color overlays.

Chapter 11: PageMaker as a Design Tool **411**

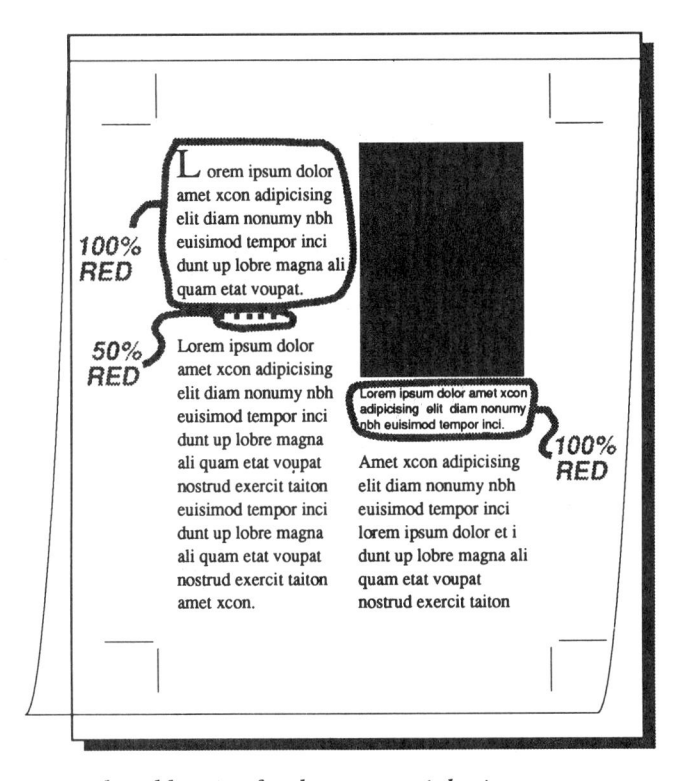

Fig. 11.25. Sample publication for the commercial printer.

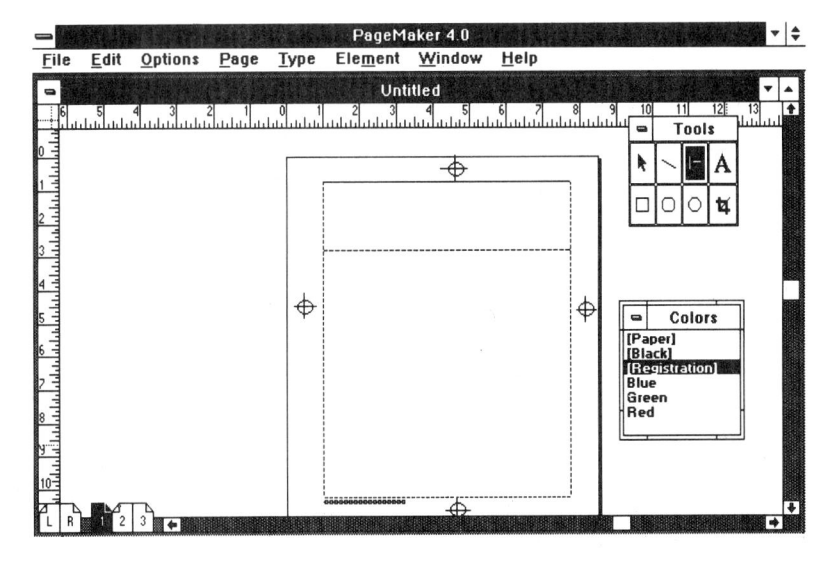

Fig. 11.26. Setting up master pages with registration marks.

Chapter Summary

In Chapters 2 through 11, you have learned all the steps needed to produce a PageMaker publication. In particular, Chapter 11 offered tips for designing a publication using PageMaker's tools. The next part of this book provides examples of more than 30 publications that were produced using PageMaker. You can find notes about how the principles given in Chapters 2 through 11 were applied in each publication.

Part III

Examples of Publications Created Using PageMaker

Includes

Creating Business Reports, Books, and Manuals

Creating Newsletters and Similar Publications

Creating Overhead Transparencies, Slides, and Handouts

Creating Brochures, Price Lists, and Directories

Creating Fliers and Display Ads

The chapters in Part III present examples of publications that were created using PageMaker. These documents illustrate specific applications of the procedures and principles covered throughout the book and demonstrate the wide range of designs possible with PageMaker. You will be able to develop your own designs with the help of the sample pages, sample templates, and Page Setup dialog boxes provided with many of the examples. Whether you need to create a business report or a brochure, the examples in Part III will help get you started.

12

Creating Business Reports, Books, and Manuals

In this chapter, you learn some specific design and production ideas that apply to reports, manuals, and books. Whether you are producing a 300-page textbook, a 30-page business proposal, or a 10-page list of illustrated steps for a procedures manual, these publications share many characteristics (see fig. 12.1). For example, these publications are usually longer than documents like the newsletters, handouts, fliers, and other types presented in the following chapters. The full publication often is composed of several PageMaker files, so these types of documents are good candidates for template systems and the Book and link features of PageMaker 4.0. Even if your document has fewer than 999 pages (the maximum allowed in PageMaker 4.0), dividing the material into several files still makes good sense in many cases. In this chapter, you will find tips on when and why to divide a document into several files.

Another common characteristic is size. Most business reports and many manuals are published in 8 1/2-by-11-inch format. Books frequently have smaller dimensions, and this chapter shows you how to prepare a document for smaller finished-page sizes.

The publications in this category have similar formats. These documents usually have a one-column format, although some have a second column for headings, captions, and figures. Traditionally, most business reports are single-sided documents, whereas manuals and books are usually double-sided documents. In this chapter, you learn how and when to use PageMaker's single-sided, double-sided, and facing-pages options.

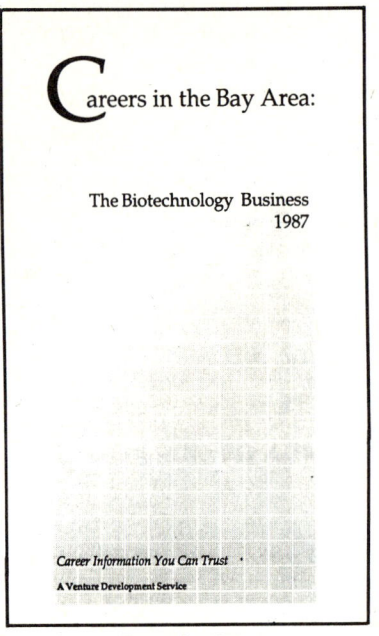

416   Part III: Examples of Publications Created Using PageMaker

Example 12.1

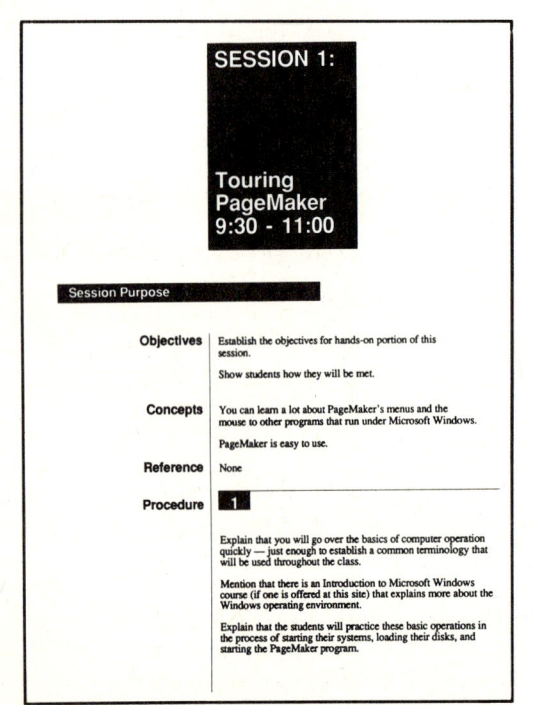

Example 12.2

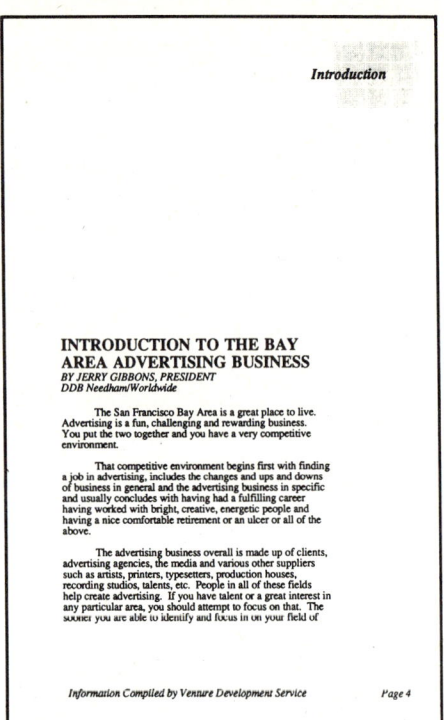

Example 12.3

Fig. 12.1. Examples of the publications in this chapter.

This chapter focuses on the specific design and production ideas that apply to the types of documents just described. You can apply the same design principles and production tips to any publication in this general category: long publications composed of several sections or chapters. You see how the general design principles and production tips have been applied to the examples.

Design Principles

The design principles developed by book designers can be applied to business reports and manuals. For example, because reports and manuals are longer publications, the use of white space and running heads makes the documents more attractive and easier to use. The design principles presented in these examples range from tips for creating the design, to page layout, to choice of typefaces. By applying these principles, you can produce publications with a professional appearance; they are uncluttered and unified in design.

Many of these principles apply to all types of publications, not just those in this chapter. Their applications to reports, books, and manuals are described generally in this section, and then the same principles are repeated and applied specifically to the appropriate examples.

Don't be afraid of white space.

White space is any area of a page that does not have text or graphics. The principle of allowing white space in the basic design applies to any document but is worth special mention in this chapter because this principle has not been applied to many publications of the types presented. Traditionally, business reports have been produced with the same margin settings as those used for letters, memos, minutes, and agendas rather than designed specifically to allow white space on the pages. Books usually have minimal white space, leaving only enough room at the edges for the reader's thumbs to hold the book open without covering the text.

Perhaps in the interest of cutting printing costs, contemporary books tend to have smaller margins (less white space) than the classic proportions shown in figure 12.2. More white space in the design usually means more pages. Depending on the content of the book and how it will be used, however, you can increase the apparent white space without increasing the total number of pages by using a smaller size type, a different typeface, or tighter leading. Figure 12.3 shows the relative amount of space required if you lay out the same text in different grids and fonts.

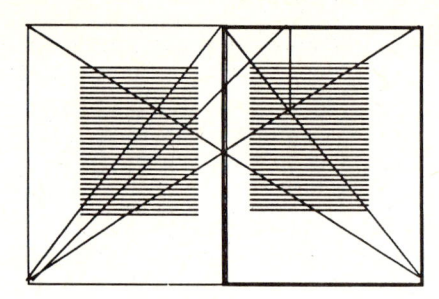

Fig. 12.2. Determining the classic proportions for book design.

Use a grid system.

The traditions of book design and production are older than any of the other principles discussed in this book. Gutenberg's Bible, for instance, shows traces of the grid system he used to lay out his pages. A few decades later a book named *De Divina Proportione*, written by Fra Luca Pacioli and illustrated by Leonardo da Vinci, applied the rules of classic proportion to book design. Contemporary designers still study this master work and apply the same principles in new book designs. Later, Renaissance designers used basic geometry and rules of proportion to design books (as well as buildings, rooms, and paintings). One classic method of defining the margins of a book is shown in figure 12.2. As you can see, the facing pages are crossed with a pattern of straight lines to determine the margins.

Many methods of deriving grids are based on classic proportions. You also can develop the grids for your publications by imitating similar documents that you admire. Whichever method you choose, the underlying grid for your publication merits some forethought. Chapter 11 and the examples in this chapter show how PageMaker's master-page feature enables you to lay out a grid system for a publication.

Use only one or two different typefaces in a document.

As explained in Chapter 10, "Typography," and Chapter 11, "PageMaker as a Design Tool," the type-specification process involves listing each different element of the document that requires type specifications. For reports, books, and manuals, the list may include the following:

   Body copy

   Running heads

   Running feet

Chapter or section titles

One or more subhead levels

Figure captions

Figure labels

Table headings

Table data

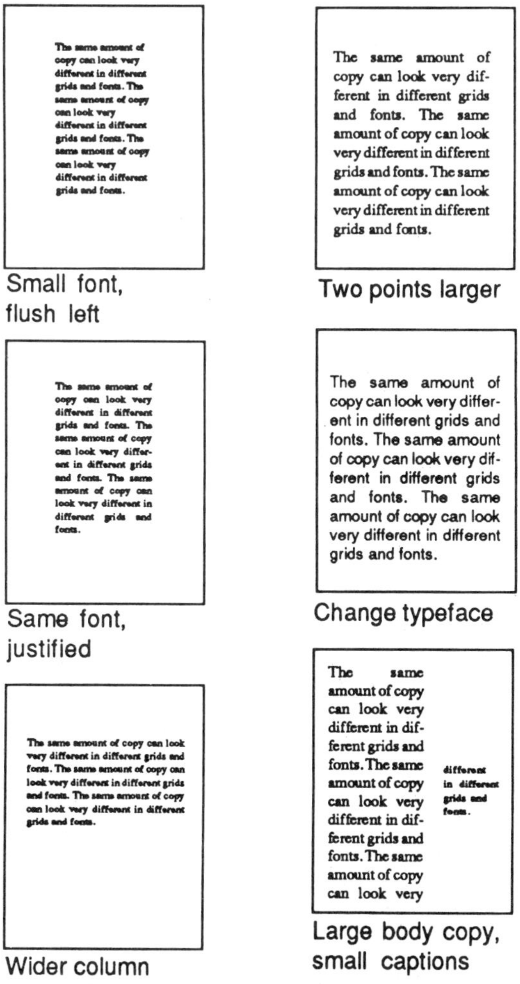

Small font, flush left

Two points larger

Same font, justified

Change typeface

Wider column

Large body copy, small captions

Fig. 12.3. The same amount of copy in different grids and fonts.

Each element may be subdivided into several other elements that require more type specifications. In the running feet, for example, you may want the page number in boldface type and the section name in italic. A common tendency is to use a different font for each element, a good idea within limits. The majority of book designers, however, follow the guiding principle of simplicity in design. If you study other published works, you see that most books use only one or two different typefaces, with variations in size and style used sparingly.

Apart from the design principle of simplicity, one reason for having few type changes in a PageMaker publication is that some laser printers are limited to 8 fonts per page or per publication. Some of the examples in following chapters show how as many as 14 different elements can be distinguished by 8 or fewer fonts.

On the other hand, most current published works use a greater variety of fonts than the traditional business report, which may feature one size of plain Courier and Courier boldface. When you switch your business reports from a letter-quality printer to a laser printer, the wide selection of fonts may seem confusing at first. The best approach in designing your first reports is to imitate the type specifications used in professionally designed documents that are similar to yours, such as the examples shown in this chapter. After you become familiar with the underlying design principles, you easily can design your own long documents.

Table 12.1 lists some of the typefaces commonly used in these types of documents. You can see that the more decorative typefaces such as Zapf Chancery are not recommended for the publications in this chapter and that the list of typefaces commonly used in books and manuals is much more limited than the list for business reports.

Use all capitals (uppercase text) as a deliberate design strategy rather than as a method for emphasizing text or indicating a heading.

If you use a letter-quality printer, you probably use uppercase type to add emphasis or to distinguish headings. Uppercase letters still can be part of your deliberate design strategy when other size or style variations are not possible. Do not use uppercase letters, however, just because the author used uppercase letters in the rough copy. Long headings can be difficult to read when the text is all uppercase. Consider changing all-uppercase headings to upper- and lowercase letters and setting them in boldface or italic.

Only one example in this chapter uses uppercase text as a deliberate design strategy. In Example 12.4 (a manual that uses one template to switch between two grids), the most common head is "FYI" (to indicate "For Your

Information"). All the other heads are short phrases ("OVERVIEW," "TRY IT," "NOTES," and "SUMMARY"); they are set in all capitals to carry the same weight visually as the FYI heads.

Table 12.1
Typefaces Commonly Used in Reports, Books, and Manuals

(Y = used, N = not used)

Typeface	Reports	Books	Manuals
ITC American Typewriter	Y	N	N
ITC Avant Garde	Y	N	Y
ITC Benguiat	Y	N	N
ITC Bookman	Y	N	Y
Courier	N	N	N
ITC Friz Quadrata	Y	N	Y
ITC Galliard	Y	Y	Y
ITC Garamond	Y	Y	Y
Glypha	N	N	Y
Goudy Old Style	Y	Y	Y
Helvetica	Y	Y	Y
ITC Korinna	Y	N	Y
ITC Lubalin Graph	Y	Y	Y
ITC Machine	N	N	N
ITC New Baskerville	Y	Y	N
New Century Schoolbook	Y	Y	Y
Optima	Y	Y	Y
Palatino	Y	Y	Y
ITC Souvenir	Y	Y	Y
Times	Y	Y	Y
Trump Mediaeval	Y	Y	Y
ITC Zapf Chancery	N	N	N

Use running heads and running feet to help readers find topics.

This principle is applicable to any long document—including magazines—but the rule is a mandate in reference books and manuals. Besides the page number, you should include the section or chapter name in the running heads or running feet. Place the names near the outer edges of the pages for easy reference. This principle is applied in all but one of the examples in this chapter.

Treat all figures consistently in the fonts, line weights, and fill patterns you use.

In the past, business-report figures came from a single source: one spreadsheet program on a letter-quality printer, or a team of one illustrator and one typesetter. Consistency becomes a more important issue when you start using PageMaker to assemble graphics from many different sources, such as a spreadsheet program, a drawing program, and PageMaker's built-in graphics tools. Some figures may be used full-sized in the final document, but others may need reducing or enlarging in PageMaker. To keep line weights consistent throughout the publication, you may want to use heavier lines in the drawing program if the figure will be scaled smaller in PageMaker, or use lighter-weight lines if the figure will be scaled larger. If possible, choose fill patterns that are common to all the graphics programs you will use. Be sure that your final figures have consistent type specifications. You can standardize captions by making them a part of the word processing text files instead of the graphics files. You can set up a style tag for the captions in your word processor if you use a style sheet. For labels within your figures, you may need to establish standards for the fonts to be used in your drawing program. For example, if your report includes many graphs and your spreadsheet program has fewer available fonts than PageMaker, you may want to match the fonts in all your images to the spreadsheet graphics. This principle is included here even though its application is not demonstrated by the examples selected for this chapter. For specific applications, see the examples in Chapter 14.

Be sure that the space between text and graphics is the same for all figures, and the space between adjacent text blocks is uniform.

You should know and declare your ideal standards for positioning graphics and text and for positioning adjacent text blocks. Your specification may be as simple as "roughly center the graphic between the adjacent text blocks," but even this simple guideline is worth stating explicitly. Don't assume that graphics will fall naturally into place. For graphics, use the Text Wrap command to create standoff between text and graphics. (See Chapter 6 for information on wrapping text around graphics.) To position graphics between text blocks that are not wrapped around the graphic—such as two separate stories—or to position two text blocks relative to each other, you can use the technique described in the following tip.

Text on each page should bottom out to margin.

Book designers traditionally have followed the principle that the text on every page should end at exactly the same point. This goal is easy to accomplish for books that are primarily body copy without graphics or subheadings, such as the traditional Victorian novel. The principle becomes increasingly difficult to apply the more your document incorporates complicating factors, such as

- Subheadings within each chapter or section
- Figures
- Footnotes
- Tables that cannot be broken across pages
- Limitations for widows and orphans

Creating Spacing Guides on the Pasteboard

As an alternative to using text wrap and type specifications to control the spacing between figures and text, or between text blocks (such as between articles in a newsletter), you can help the production process by setting up text blocks as spacing guides and storing them on the pasteboard of the template.

Use PageMaker's text tool and Type Specs command to create a text block with handles that are separated by the distance called for in the specifications. For example, type the words *Space between articles* and set the text in a point size that makes the text block's handles a measure of the distance you want. You need to type and format a separate text block for each spacing specification (see fig. 12.4).

When you need to check the spacing between two objects on the page, use the Copy and Paste commands to copy the spacing guide from the pasteboard to the page. You then can use the spacing guide to position the objects, as shown in figure 12.5. When the two objects are aligned correctly, delete the duplicate guide on the page.

This type of spacing guide is applied in Examples 12.4 and 12.5.

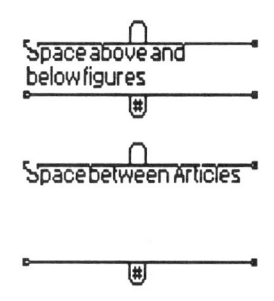

Fig. 12.4. Use a spacing guide to position graphics and text.

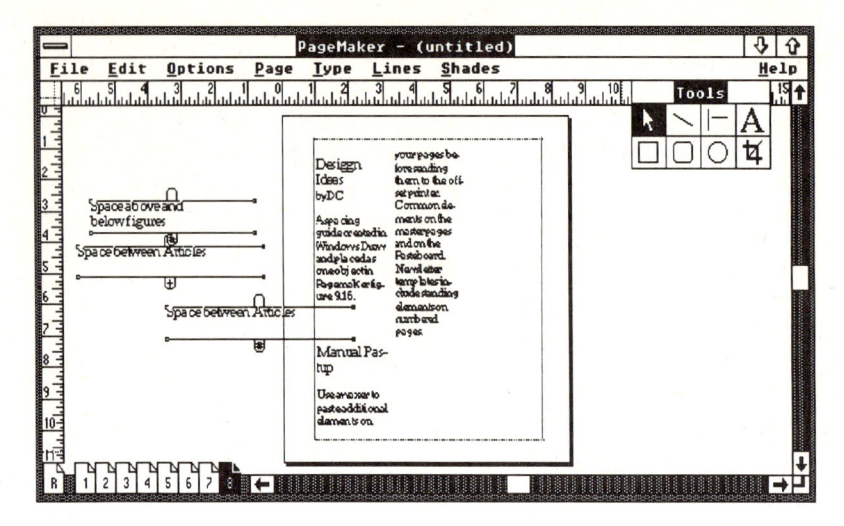

Fig. 12.5. Copying the spacing guide to the page to align separate text blocks.

You can alter the leading (line spacing) around subheadings and the space around figures to make small adjustments in the length of the text on a page. In many documents, however, you will find that bottoming out all pages to the same point is impossible. Alignment can be especially tricky if you follow the common conventions regarding widows and orphans. These terms are used to describe the situation in which one line of a paragraph is separated from the rest of the paragraph by a page break or a column break (see "Copy Fitting" in Chapter 10).

In some documents, you may plan ragged bottom margins as a deliberate design strategy. In general, however, let PageMaker's bottom margin define the maximum length of the text. As shown in the following examples, PageMaker's bottom margin is not always the same as the limits of text on the page layout: In these examples, the running heads and feet always fall outside the page margins that are defined in the Page Setup dialog box.

Let the same graphic elements carry the theme throughout the document.

As explained in Chapter 11, PageMaker's master pages can include graphic elements that appear on every page, such as shaded boxes and ruled lines. You also can use graphics to set off headings in the text and to highlight important points. You can see how common graphic elements (black boxes, ruled lines) are applied in Examples 12.2 and 12.4. In many published books, the cover design has no relation to the inside page layouts; but a common graphic theme is often used on the cover as well as inside pages of business reports, catalogs, directories, annual reports, and other documents. This technique is applied in Example 12.1.

Production Tips

The production tips in this chapter can be applied to any long document composed of several sections or chapters. The tips help you produce your publications more quickly and efficiently than you might be able to do without following these suggestions. The tips range from creating separate templates for different sections to preparing text in a word processor before you start PageMaker.

Many of these tips apply to other types of publications, such as the magazines and newsletters described in Chapter 13 and the brochures described in Chapter 15. The application to reports, books, and manuals is described generally in this section; then, with the examples, the same tips are repeated along with explanations of their specific application to that example.

Make each section or chapter a separate PageMaker publication.

Several good reasons exist for breaking a long document into smaller parts and saving each as a separate file, even if your document has fewer than 999 pages (PageMaker's limit for one file):

- Small files are faster to save and to print.

- You must make separate files of any sections requiring a different page orientation because you cannot mix tall and wide pages in one publication file. For example, an appendix with tables of figures may require a wide format, but the rest of the document appears in tall format.

- You may want to start with a different master-page grid for different sections of the book (see the following tip).

- When the document is divided into several PageMaker publication files, you can set different running heads or feet for each section, making an easy reference for readers.

- If your document is long or includes many graphics, you may need to break the document into sections to keep file sizes small enough to fit a backup on one floppy disk.

- If different sections of the document will be completed at different times but not necessarily in sequence, you can begin each new section when it is ready. This way, you can have different sections of the publication in different stages of the production process.

- You can divide the PageMaker production tasks among several people on the production team.

- If a file is damaged, you lose only part of the work you have done. The production practice of dividing a document into parts is especially pertinent to the long publications in this chapter and is more rarely applied in the shorter publications described in Chapters 13 through 16.
- PageMaker 4.0 enables you to link related PageMaker publications through the Book command.

Build a master template for all sections.

If the final document will be composed of several files, build a master-template file from which all the other files are cloned. Chapter 11, "PageMaker as a Design Tool," offers suggestions for building template systems. You can see how those ideas are applied in each template used in the examples in this chapter.

If you expect to update sections of the document periodically without reprinting the entire book, include section numbers in the page-numbering system and let each section start with page 1.

This useful production trick may conflict with design ideas and the offset printer's preferences; but using section numbers as part of the page numbering system (1-1, 1-2, 1-3, ... 2-1, 2-2, and so on) is the best way to handle frequently changed *living* documents, such as procedures manuals. PageMaker's page-numbering feature cannot handle letter suffixes added to inserted pages (23a, 23b, 23c, for example); but within one section you can number all pages sequentially by using a compound page number that includes a fixed section number and a changing suffix (23.1, 23.2, 23.3).

This tip should be applied only to manuals that are updated frequently. The best practice is to number consecutively all pages in a document. You can specify the starting page number for each section in the Page Setup dialog box. None of the examples in this chapter uses compound page numbers.

For longer documents, set up a style sheet and format the text by typing the tags in the word processing program.

Consistency in formatting is an important key to good design. Style sheets are especially helpful in ensuring consistency from one document to another, because you can use the same style sheet for different publications. For example, after a style sheet has been set up for a newsletter, you can use the same style sheet for all subsequent issues simply by loading that style sheet into each new issue's file; you need not re-create the style sheet for each document. This technique ensures consistency between chapters of a book or any series of documents that share the same design.

Prepare all character and paragraph formatting in Story view rather than Layout view.

Ideally, to simplify PageMaker production, you perform all editing and formatting in the Story Editor introduced with PageMaker 4.0. This method is faster than working in Layout view, and fast formatting is especially appropriate for long documents that consist primarily of text. Besides the type specifications, formatting can include using hanging indents to create flush-left heads over indented copy—a format that is often misinterpreted or poorly designed as a two-column format (see fig. 12.6). A hanging indent is a format in which the first line of the paragraph is set flush left and all subsequent lines are indented.

To create the format shown in the top of figure 12.6, set up a hanging indent with a tab set at the indentation point; then enter a tab at the beginning of each paragraph to indent it. Subsequent lines of the paragraph are indented automatically as the text wraps.

> ### Testing Your Specifications in PageMaker
> Before going too far into the production of a long document, test your specifications and plans by placing text formatted in the word processor into PageMaker so that you can see what formatting elements are preserved. This procedure saves you from spending extra time formatting in the word processor, only to discover most of the formatting is lost in PageMaker. (When you tag text for your style sheet in your word processor, you can choose Retain Format under the Place command to force the text to retain much of its formatting.) If the authors use more than one word processor, test each program's text before completing your strategy for formatting text.

Examples

The examples in this chapter have been selected to demonstrate a variety of formats and to illustrate various applications of the design principles and production tips that are described in the preceding sections. As noted in those sections, not all the principles and tips that apply to books can be demonstrated in these few examples, but the design principles that are not specifically applied in these examples are illustrated in some of the examples in the chapters that follow. The five examples presented in this chapter are:

Example 12.1. A One-Column Format with Graphic Section Openings

Example 12.2. A One-Column Format with Flush-Left Heads

Example 12.3. A Two-Column Tabular Format with Small Type

Example 12.4. One Template Used To Switch between Two Grids

Example 12.5. Section Cover Pages

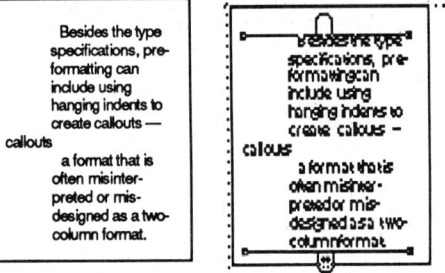

Format callouts using hanging indents when you DO want the callouts to flow with the rest of the text.

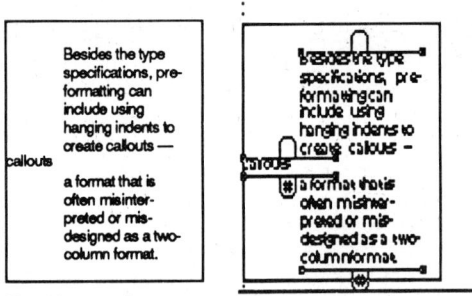

Break text into unlinked blocks when you do NOT want the callouts (or figure captions) to flow with the rest of the text.

***Fig. 12.6.** Preformatting that includes hanging indents.*

Example 12.1. A One-Column Format with Graphic Section Openings

The report used in this example is designed to accommodate relatively simple text formatting in a one-column grid that maximizes white space by using wide margins. The text also is more readable because of the narrow column that results from the wide margin settings. This same design can be applied to any business report; the generous running heads (16-point Times with a graphic background) make this design especially applicable to relatively short reports that are composed of many short sections.

This design probably is not good for a reference manual or training guide, however, without considerable expansion of the type specifications table to accommodate a wider variety of subheads and other visual aids. Books and long reports probably would not use running heads as large as the ones in this report, but a similar design could be used on chapter or section opening pages, with a narrower top margin on subsequent pages.

Description

This limited-distribution report is reproduced in 8 1/2-by-11- inch format with a tall orientation. The grid and graphic elements on the inside pages of this report are designed to carry out a theme that originates with the report cover's design (see fig. 12.7). The final document—one in a series of documents that will be published over time—contains fewer than 999 pages and is stored as one publication file. The text is made up of one source file for each section, a mailing list of names and addresses, and a text file of captions for full-page figures. The figures, not shown here, are reprints of articles from other sources and are pasted in manually.

Always Obtain Written Permission To Reprint

Caution: When you include information or excerpts from other published works, as in Example 12.1, be sure to obtain written permission from the original publisher. Also, cite in your document the origin of the material.

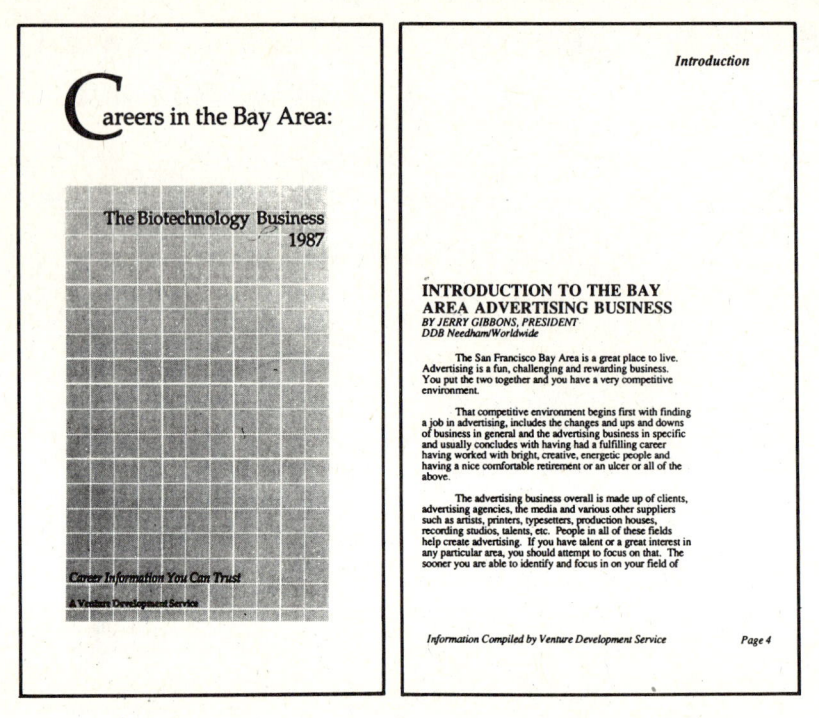

Fig. 12.7. Final printout with a cover-page design that sets the page theme throughout the document.

Design Principles

All the design principles described at the beginning of this chapter are present in this report. The two principles that are especially well illustrated by this example are repeated and described here.

Don't be afraid of white space. In this report, the left and right margins are more than 2 inches, and the top margin is 3.5 inches. The running heads and running feet extend beyond these margins to give each page the feel of a full-page grid with a great deal of white space. The relatively short length of each line of text makes the copy easy to read.

Let the same graphic elements carry the theme throughout the document. A gray rectangle crossed with white (reverse) lines is used on the cover and a smaller gray box with white lines is repeated in the top right corner of every page as a background for the running heads.

Production Tips

In final form, this document is double-sided. Because the margins, heads, and feet are identical on every page of the report, it requires only one master page; the publication is set up in PageMaker as a one-sided document.

Although the final number of pages was not known in advance, the plan was not to exceed 32 pages. An initial setup of 32 pages was specified in the Page Setup dialog box on the template to save repeated use of the Insert Pages command.

The wide margins define the limits of the text placed from word processing files. Figure 12.8 shows how these specifications are set up in the Page Setup dialog box.

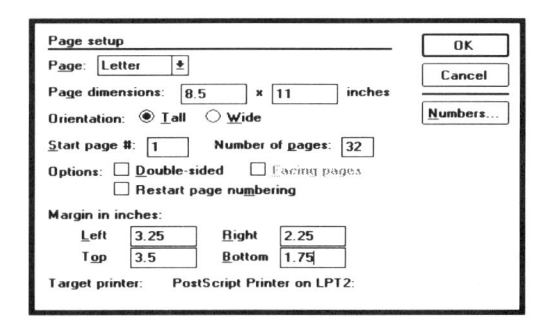

Fig. 12.8. Page Setup dialog box for one-column format with graphics.

The Template

The master page of the template includes the graphic that appears in the upper right corner of every page (see fig. 12.9). The normal default for type specifications—flush left, 12-point Times—holds for this publication. A style sheet also is set up for the document. The body copy tag uses the same default type setting. The first line of a body copy paragraph is indented 0.25 inch as set up in the Paragraph command. By using the style tag, you do not have to press the Tab key for each paragraph. Because the author originally had inserted a blank line between paragraphs, the designer decided to let this convention stand, rather than use the Paragraph command to set the space between paragraphs. Figure 12.10 shows that only four different style tags are used throughout this publication: titles, headings, bylines, and body copy.

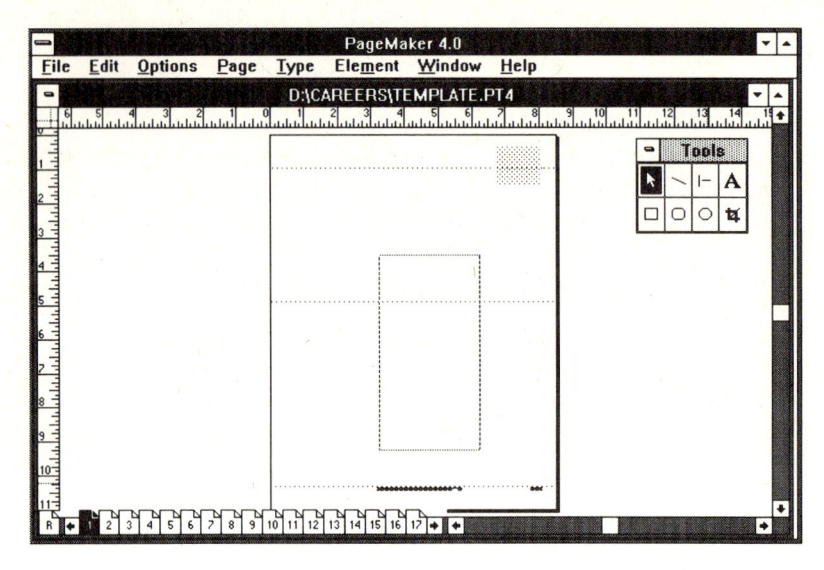

Fig. 12.9. The template with the graphic used in the upper right corner of every page.

Style name	Type specifications
Chapter Titles	16-point Times Bold Italic, Flush right (all other elements will be flush left)
Level 1 Headings	18-point Times Bold
Bylines	12-point Times Italic
Body copy	12-point Times, first-line indent of .25 inches, extra carriage return between paragraphs
	Auto leading used throughout

Fig. 12.10. Type specifications table for one-column format with graphics.

Production Steps

The following steps can be used to produce this publication after the master template is set up as shown in figures 12.8 and 12.9.

1. Type and format text files in the word processing program. Type the appropriate tag for each paragraph while you are in the word processing program. Double space between paragraphs. Store the files in the subdirectory for this report (see Chapter 4).

2. Open the PageMaker template document for this series of reports and modify the master pages and cover page to reflect the new report name. Save the modified template under the new report name (for more information, see Chapter 3).

3. Working in Fit in Window view, place text with the Autoflow command in the Options menu (see "Typing and Bringing Text into PageMaker" in Chapter 4).

4. Return to the beginning of the document and, working in 50% Size, correct the format where necessary and open spaces for figures. Cut the flush-right chapter titles from the text block and paste them over the graphic in the upper right corner of each page. Keep a duplicate of the section title on the pasteboard to use on subsequent pages of the same section. During this step, place the captions on the pasteboard and use the Cut and Paste commands as needed to copy the captions to the pages (see fig. 12.11). See Chapters 3 and 6 for full details about this procedure.

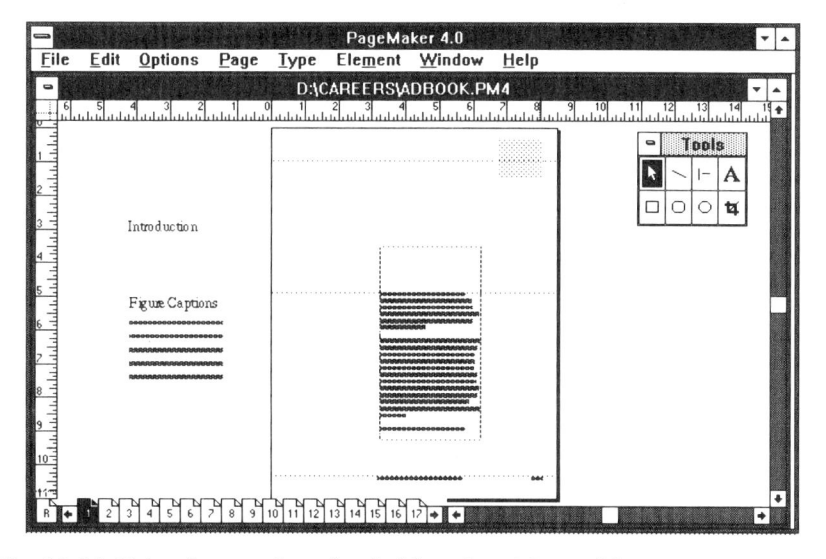

Fig. 12.11. Using the pasteboard to hold section titles and figure captions.

Preparation for Reproduction

All graphics are pasted by hand into page areas reserved for the graphics. All figures are enlarged or reduced photographically to fit the space before pasting. These limited-run reports are reproduced on photocopying equipment at a light setting so that the cut edges of the pasted figures do not show.

The starting point for any new report consists of the two master template files designed for this series: one PageMaker template (TEMPLATE.PT4) and one template for the word processor used to type the text (TEMPLATE.DOC).

(The times estimated for each step in the production cycle and the actual times spent on each step can be entered into a text file named CONTROL.DOC for invoicing or project management.) If you have more than one workstation in your production environment, store the template on a floppy disk designated as the authorized source for any new reports. In this way, enhancements made to the template from any station can be saved on the floppy (as well as the hard disk) for use by the entire production staff.

Each time a new report is produced, the word processing template is used to type and format the text files that compose the report. The master PageMaker template then is opened and saved under the new report name and the text is flowed into that file. Figure 12.12 shows the disk-file organization for this report.

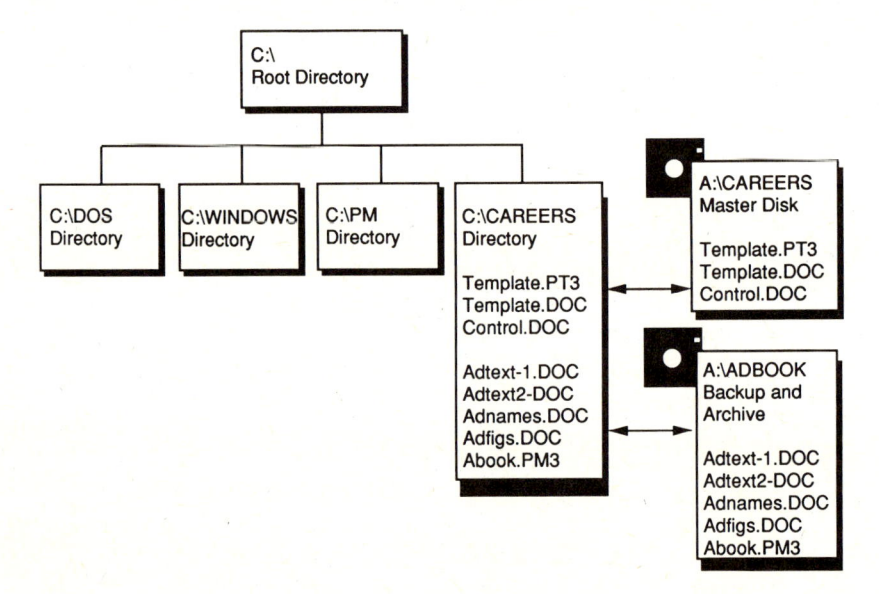

Fig. 12.12. Disk-file organization for one-column format with graphics.

Each report's text files and PageMaker file fit on one floppy disk when the document is complete. This floppy serves as a backup throughout the production cycle, and the same floppy disk becomes the final archived version of the report. If the report is very large or includes many graphics, you can use the Link command to manage the imported graphics as external files, rather than storing them as part of the PageMaker publication. If you divide the report into several PageMaker publications and you want to number all pages sequentially or generate an index or table of contents, use the Book command to link the publications.

Example 12.2. A One-Column Format with Flush-Left Heads

Designed for easy reference, this manual consists of sections with many subheads. As in Example 12.1, the text is more readable because of the narrow column. In this case, the narrow right column of text is achieved by using a hanging indent. This same design can be applied to manuals, textbooks, and business reports that use many subheads in the text. This design, however, probably would not be good for a publication with few subheads.

The production process could be simplified significantly by changing the design slightly to eliminate the use of reverse type. In this particular case, the black boxes with reverse type are printed in a second color of ink, giving the finished pages a lighter feeling than is produced by the black images shown here. (For more information on printing in color, see Chapter 8.)

Description

This procedures manual identifies subsections with reverse-type heads that appear flush to the left margin. The numbers of the steps in each procedure are printed in boxed reverse type. One text file is created for each procedure. Each new procedure starts on a new right-hand page in this double-sided document. Figure 12.13 shows the final printouts of two pages.

Design Principles

All the design principles described at the beginning of this chapter are present in this report. Four principles that are especially well illustrated by this example are repeated and described here.

Use only one or two different typefaces in a document. This manual uses Helvetica and Times, the two typefaces that are built into the Apple LaserWriter. The full type specifications table is shown in figure 12.14. Only five different fonts are used from these two typefaces. As a result, the final publication looks clean and simple, without distractions from the content.

Don't be afraid of white space. The white space is achieved by reserving the left third of the page for section headings. Extra space also is allowed below headings and between rules and type for each step.

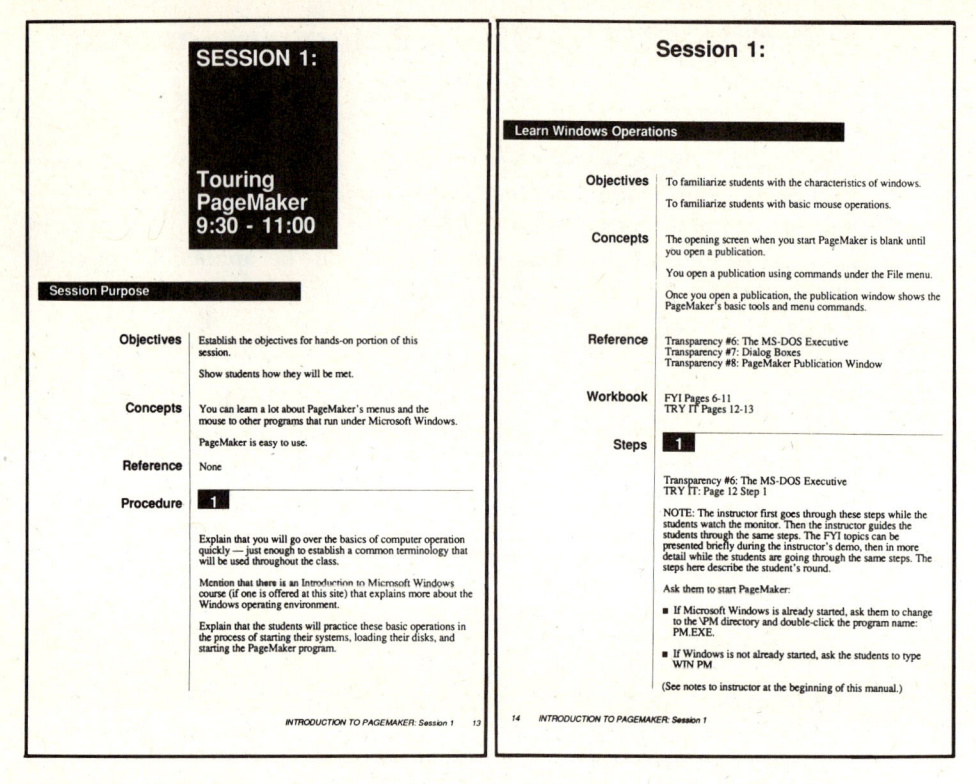

Fig. 12.13. Final printout of pages in one-column format with flush-left heads.

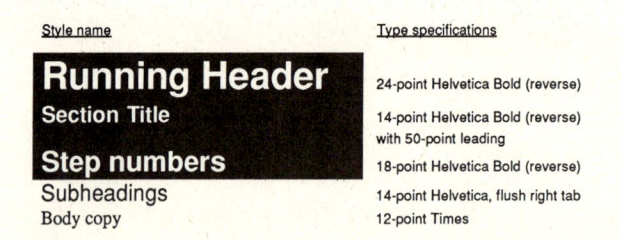

Fig. 12.14. Type specifications table for one-column format with flush-left heads.

Use running heads and feet to help readers find topics. The running heads give the session number; the running feet show the page number at the outside margin along with the document title and session number. The use of the session number in both running heads and running feet means that each session is a separate PageMaker publication, so the running heads and feet can be entered on the master pages.

Let the same graphic elements carry the theme throughout the document. The graphic theme used is white type on black boxes. These black boxes are printed in a second color when the document is mass produced, giving the final book an attractive and unified appearance. Working with white type can be a production headache, however, because you can lose type on the page when it is not on a black box. (See the tip "Working with Reverse Type," following the production steps for this example.)

Production Tips

In this case, the text was first formatted in the word processing program, and all body copy is formatted with a hanging indent. All the text in this manual uses the same ruler line: the left margin of the section titles is the same as the left margin in PageMaker (see fig. 12.15). From the margin, the first tab is the flush-right tab set at 2.25 inches from the left margin and used by section subheads. The second tab positions the first line of all body copy at 2.5 inches from the left margin—the position of the hanging indent. A third tab is set up for tabs after bullets in short lists.

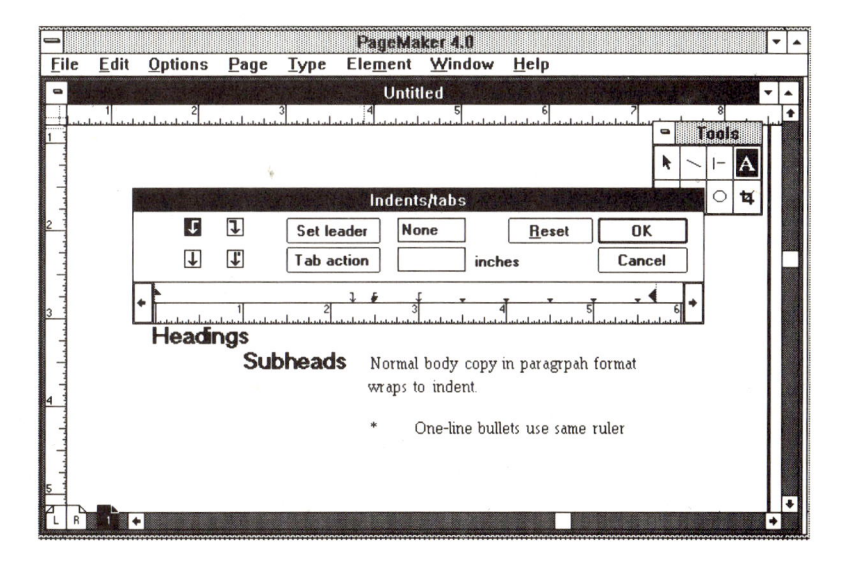

Fig. 12.15. The ruler line used for all text in one-column format with flush-left heads.

The reverse type is set up as normal (black) type in the word processing program because the word processor does not support reverse type. The specification is changed to reverse type after the document is placed in PageMaker.

The Template

Figure 12.16 shows the template's margin settings in the Page Setup dialog box. The master pages of the template for this manual are set up with one column. The master pages show horizontal and vertical ruler guides for positioning the running head and foot and vertical rule. The printed elements on the master page include a vertical rule and the running heads and feet (see fig. 12.17). The running head appears in reverse type on a black backdrop. The pasteboard holds black boxes and the ruled lines used throughout the document.

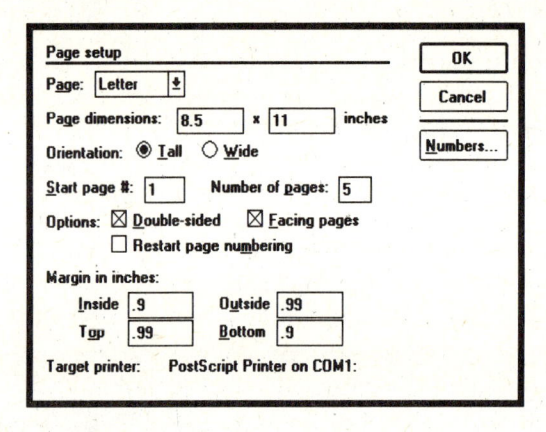

Fig. 12.16. Page Setup dialog box for one-column format with flush-left heads.

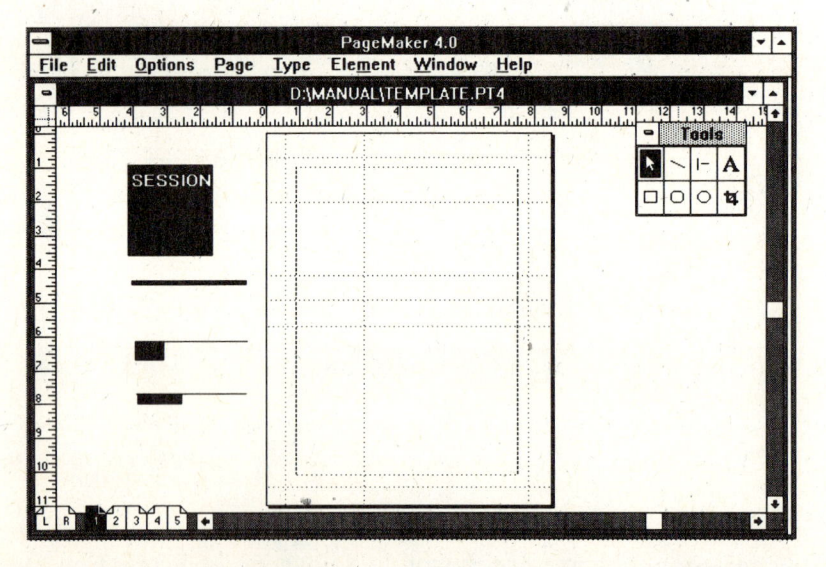

Fig. 12.17. The template, including repeated graphic elements on the pasteboard and on the master pages.

Production Steps

The following steps produce this publication:

1. Type and format the text files in the word processing program, and store them in this manual's subdirectory on the hard disk. Format the text with a hanging indent and the three tab settings shown in figure 12.15.

2. Build one PageMaker template document for this manual, as shown in figures 12.16 and 12.17. Store the template in the manual's subdirectory, and clone the template to continue the manual for each new section when one section fills more than 999 pages, or when one section reaches the maximum number of bytes that will fit on your back-up disks.

3. Working in Fit in Window view and using the Autoflow command in the Options menu, place text on consecutive pages.

4. Go back to the beginning of the document, and working with the text tool in Actual Size view, make the necessary formatting corrections.

5. Return to the beginning of the document and work in Actual Size view with the pointer tool selected. At the beginning of this sweep, copy the predesigned black box and ruled line (for step numbers) from the pasteboard of the template (as shown in fig. 12.18) into the Windows Clipboard. Avoid using the Copy and Cut commands for other objects (so as not to replace the Clipboard contents). At each new step number, perform the following:

    Paste the black box and ruled lines from the Clipboard.

    Position the black box over the step number.

    Use the Send to Back command.

    If you opted not to use automatic widow control, supported by PageMaker 4.0 through the Paragraph command, adjust for widows and orphans on each page (by dragging the bottom windowshade handle of the text) before placing the black boxes on subsequent pages.

6. Go back to the beginning of the document and scroll through with the text tool selected, and do the following:

    Select each step number.

    Choose Reverse from the Type menu.

    Check the alignment of the black box.

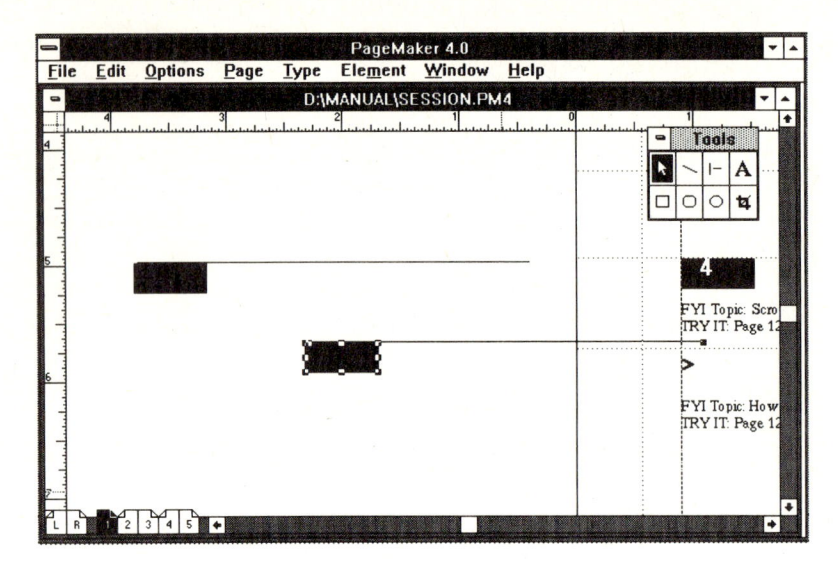

Fig. 12.18. Black boxes ready to be pasted into the Clipboard and then pasted in place on the pages.

To move the black box, you need to select the pointer tool. You select the box *under* the text block by clicking the box. If the box does not highlight, select the Bring to Front option on the Edit menu. Repeated switching from the pointer to the text tool can be time-consuming, and this factor is one of the inconveniences of working with layered designs. If you select the incorrect text to reverse, highlight the text again, and select Reverse; the text reverts to black type.

This example created reverse type on a black background by backing the reverse type with a graphic element, but you can create reverse type backed by paragraph rules if the text is 20 points or smaller.

Working with Reverse Type Larger than 20 Points

When working with reverse type larger than 20 points, you must use a graphic element as backdrop to the type rather than a paragraph rule. As a production aid, put a nonreverse character at the end of the text (see fig. 12.19). If the reverse text falls on a white ([Paper]) background, you still can see where the reverse text is in relation to other text and graphics.

Reverse<

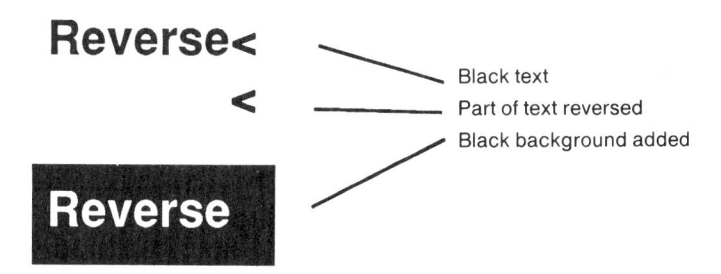

- Black text
- Part of text reversed
- Black background added

Reverse

Fig. 12.19. A nonreverse character placed at the end of reverse text.

> ***Working with Reverse Type Smaller than 20 Points***
>
> When working with reverse type smaller than 20 points, you can use the paragraph rules feature of PageMaker 4.0 rather than use a graphic element as backdrop to the type. Select the text to be made reverse on a black background, then choose the Paragraph command from the Type menu and click the Rules option in the Paragraph Specifications dialog box. In the Paragraph Rules dialog box, set 12-point rules (the largest available, or smaller if the text is smaller) above and below the line of text. Click the Options button in the Paragraph Rules dialog box to get the Paragraph Rule Options dialog box, and specify the distance of the top rule above the baseline, and a distance for the bottom rule to be below the baseline. These distances depend on the size of the type, the thickness of the rules, and the amount of black you want above and below the type.

◆4.0◆

All text and PageMaker files for this document are stored in one subdirectory on the hard disk (see fig. 12.20). If the publication is very large or uses many graphics, you use the Link command from the File menu to manage the graphics as external files, rather than storing the graphics as part of the PageMaker publication. If you divide the document into several PageMaker publications and you want to number all pages sequentially or generate an index or table of contents, use the Book command from the File menu to link the publications.

When making backups and archiving the final files, you copy all the text files on one floppy disk and all PageMaker files on another floppy disk because the text and publication files together are too large to fit on a single floppy disk.

```
                    ┌─────────────────┐
                    │ C:\             │
                    │ Root Directory  │
                    └─────────────────┘
```

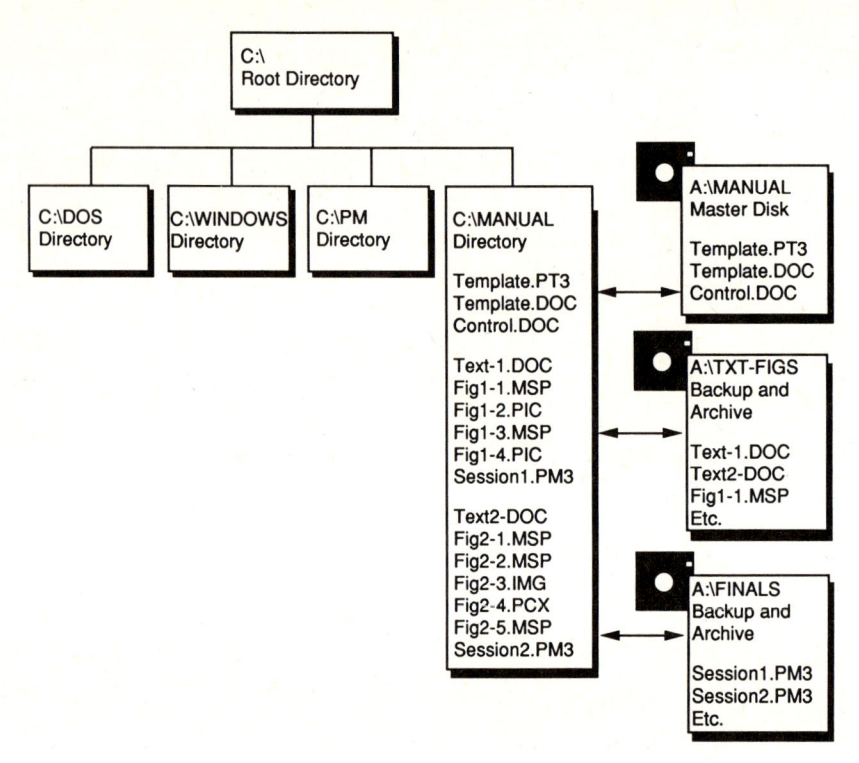

```
┌──────────┐ ┌──────────┐ ┌──────────┐ ┌─────────────────┐      ┌─────────────────┐
│ C:\DOS   │ │C:\WINDOWS│ │ C:\PM    │ │ C:\MANUAL       │      │ A:\MANUAL       │
│ Directory│ │ Directory│ │ Directory│ │ Directory       │      │ Master Disk     │
└──────────┘ └──────────┘ └──────────┘ │                 │      │                 │
                                        │ Template.PT3    │ <──> │ Template.PT3    │
                                        │ Template.DOC    │      │ Template.DOC    │
                                        │ Control.DOC     │      │ Control.DOC     │
                                        │                 │      └─────────────────┘
                                        │ Text-1.DOC      │
                                        │ Fig1-1.MSP      │      ┌─────────────────┐
                                        │ Fig1-2.PIC      │      │ A:\TXT-FIGS     │
                                        │ Fig1-3.MSP      │      │ Backup and      │
                                        │ Fig1-4.PIC      │ <──> │ Archive         │
                                        │ Session1.PM3    │      │                 │
                                        │                 │      │ Text-1.DOC      │
                                        │ Text2-DOC       │      │ Text2-DOC       │
                                        │ Fig2-1.MSP      │      │ Fig1-1.MSP      │
                                        │ Fig2-2.MSP      │      │ Etc.            │
                                        │ Fig2-3.IMG      │      └─────────────────┘
                                        │ Fig2-4.PCX      │
                                        │ Fig2-5.MSP      │      ┌─────────────────┐
                                        │ Session2.PM3    │      │ A:\FINALS       │
                                        └─────────────────┘ <──> │ Backup and      │
                                                                  │ Archive         │
                                                                  │                 │
                                                                  │ Session1.PM3    │
                                                                  │ Session2.PM3    │
                                                                  │ Etc.            │
                                                                  └─────────────────┘
```

Fig. 12.20. Disk-file organization for one-column format with flush-left heads.

Example 12.3. A Two-Column Tabular Format with Small Type

The questionnaire in this example is designed to fit the greatest number of questions on a page by using narrow margins and a relatively small point size for the body copy (9-point Helvetica). This same design can be applied to many list formats (see Chapter 15, "Creating Brochures, Price Lists, and Directories"). This design would not be good for a book or reference manual without considerable revision of the type specifications to make the text larger. Books and reports would probably not use a different head at the top of each column, as this questionnaire does. This example is presented here primarily for its demonstration of working with tabs and small point sizes.

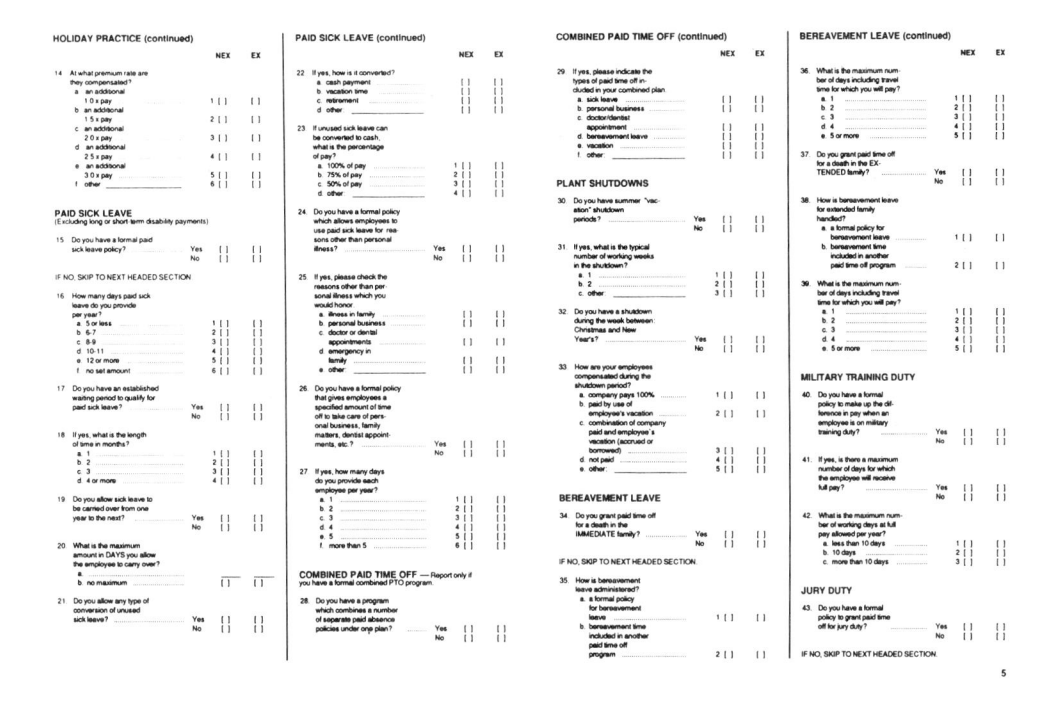

Fig. 12.21. Printout of pages of questionnaire in two-column tabular format.

Description

This questionnaire is set up to be exactly 32 pages long, set in 2 columns of 9-point type. All tabs are set in the word processing program, where all the text is prepared. Figure 12.21 shows the final printouts of two pages.

Design Principles

Many of the design principles that were described at the beginning of this chapter are applied in this report. For example, although the goal is to put a great deal of material on each page, the use of two columns and varying tabs creates white space. The heads are consistent and set in all capital letters to give emphasis and unify the document. One principle does merit special note.

Text on each page should bottom out to the margin. In this case, the overriding rule is to keep the full set of answer choices together with each question, rather than break a series of answers across columns or pages. If the two columns are unequal on a page, leading is added above subhead titles, or the longer column is shortened by moving the last question into the next column.

Production Tips

Work in large type through the initial text-editing rounds so that the production staff and proofreaders can read the text easily (see fig. 12.22). Convert to a smaller typeface for the last editing rounds. By using style sheets to tag the text, you have the advantage of changing the typeface in one easy step. Set tags and tabs in the word processing program before starting the page-layout process.

For first edit rounds:

Work with larger text	12-point Helvetica.
Before placing in PageMaker, change all text to match the body copy specs:	9-point Helvetica with 10-point leading.

Then sweep through to set:

Main headings	12-point Helvetica Bold (centered)
Subheads	10-point Helvetica on 18-point leading

Fig. 12.22. Type specifications table for two-column tabular format.

Change the default type specification to 9-point Helvetica by editing the tag. This font is used in the questionnaire (except for the column headings and other exceptions noted). After all the text is placed, adjust the leading to make sure that the text fits the prescribed number of pages.

The Template

The template file includes dummy text to be used for the column headings for each page and horizontal guides to mark the positions of the column heads. The first page of the template suppresses the master-page elements and begins with a lower guide for placing text. Figures 12.23 and 12.24 show the Page Setup dialog box and master pages for the template.

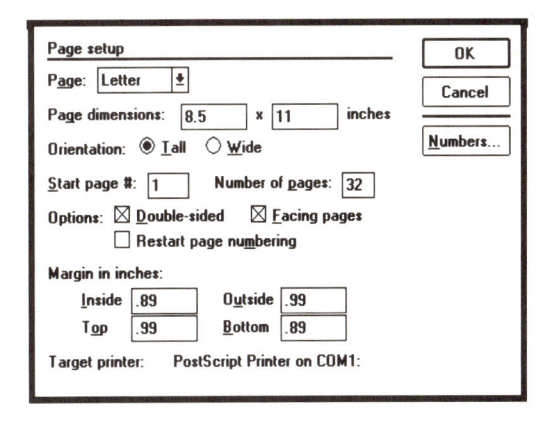

Fig. 12.23. Page Setup dialog box for two-column tabular format.

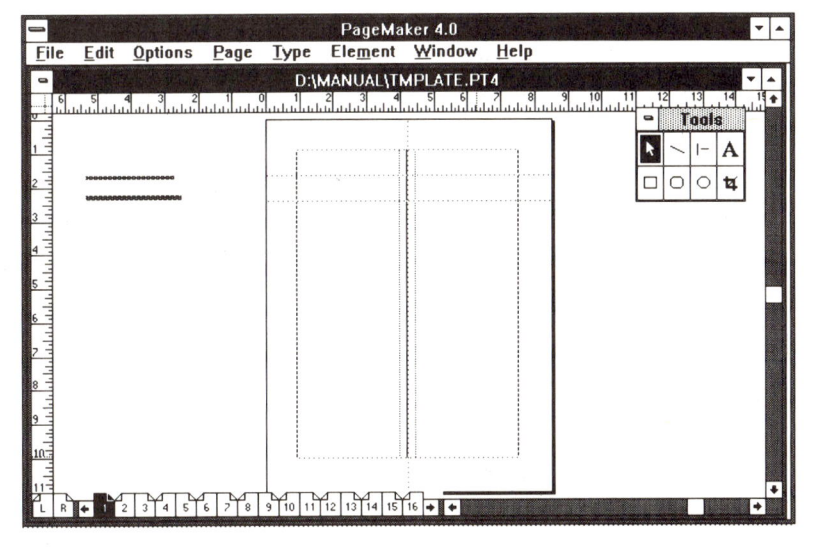

Fig. 12.24. The template for two-column tabular format.

Production Steps

To create this design, follow these steps:

1. Prepare text in a word processing file. Work in 12-point type through the initial editing rounds. Set tabs far enough apart to show columns correctly in the draft printouts from the word processing program.

2. Start a new PageMaker publication and set the margins and column guides on the master pages as shown in figures 12.23 and 12.24. Check the definitions you set for the style sheet. Modify the tags if necessary to automatically change the imported text to 9-point type and to change the tabs on the ruler lines.

3. Working in Fit in Window view and using the Autoflow command, place all text on all pages.

4. If the final text does not fit in the 32 pages allowed, edit the body copy tag to change the leading to shrink or stretch the text. Be sure to leave enough room at the end of the document to accommodate the adjustments to be made in step 6.

5. If the text still does not fit the number of pages allowed, scroll through the file in Actual Size and selectively change the spacing around each heading or between questions.

6. Go back to the beginning of the document and scroll down each column in Actual Size view. You then must force subheads and orphaned or widowed lines into the preceding or next column.

   Use the Copy and Paste commands for headings at the tops of consecutive columns. Tag the text as headline 1 to set the typeface and space around the head. Copy and Paste the word *continued* from the pasteboard to follow headings that repeat (see fig. 12.25).

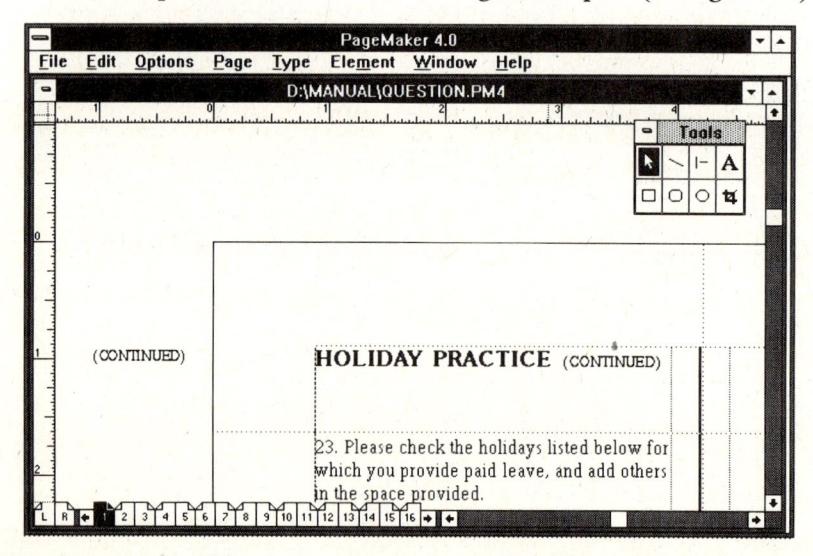

Fig. 12.25. Text for the word "continued" is copied from the pasteboard of the template when needed.

Because this document is composed of one text file (QUESTION.DOC) and one PageMaker file (QUESTION.PM4), both files can be stored in the main directory and backed up on one floppy disk with one command:

COPY QUESTION.* a:

Example 12.4. One Template Used To Switch between Two Grids

The training manual in this example has a format that alternates between two different page designs: one with a narrow left column and a wide right column, the other with three columns. These two layouts are used throughout the publication. This design is rather tricky to work with, and it can be a production headache if you don't set up procedures like those described here.

The same production tips offered here can be modified as appropriate and applied to any publication that uses two or more page layouts within each file. In this case, the two-column pages usually have few graphics compared to the amount of text. The three-column pages are heavily illustrated with graphics. If these pages were laid out as two-column pages with the graphics in the first column and the text in a wide second column, the final book would be at least 30 percent longer.

Description

The design for this manual calls for page formats that alternate between two and three columns. Because different page formats are not confined to alternating pages or separate sections, the trick is to devise master pages that can serve both formats. Figure 12.26 shows examples of printed pages from this document.

Design Principles

Many of the design principles described at the beginning of this chapter are applied in this training manual. The use and spacing of graphic elements is especially important in this publication, as well as the inclusion of ample white space. Note how the following principles particularly enhance the final publication.

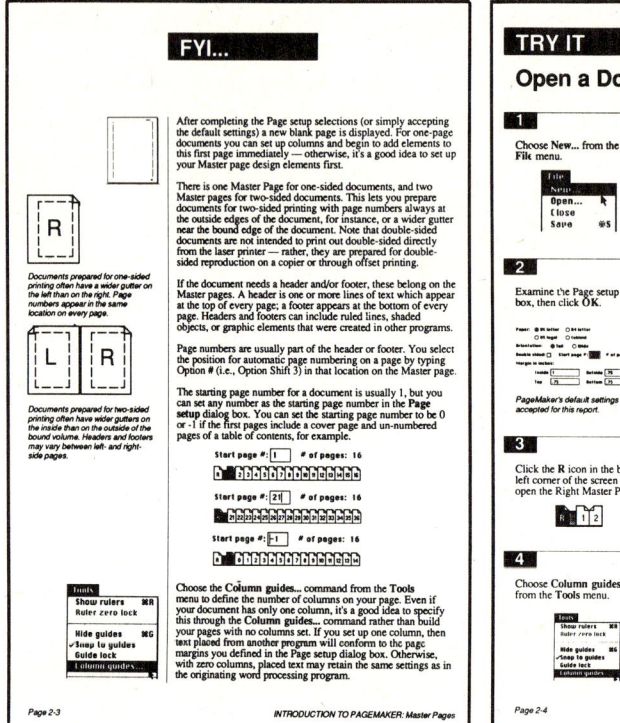

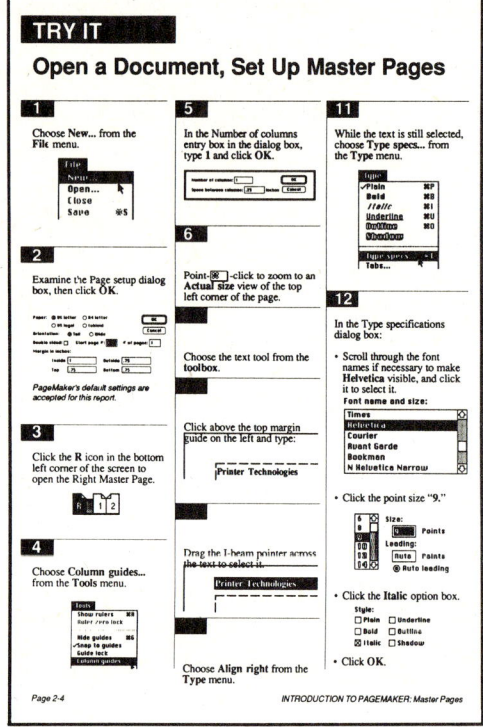

Fig. 12.26. Printout of manual using two grids.

Let the same graphic elements carry the theme throughout the document. The common graphic themes are reverse type on black boxes, hairline rules between columns, and horizontal rules between steps. These elements make finding information easy and allow emphasis of the steps.

Don't be afraid of white space. White space occurs primarily on the two-column page layouts where wide spaces are allowed between paragraphs in order to accommodate figures in the narrow column. On three-column pages, the columns are allowed to be ragged at the bottom margin so that a step is not broken across columns. This publication deliberately violates the principle that text on each page should bottom out to the margin.

Use running heads and feet to help readers find topics. The running feet on left-hand pages show the session number; the feet on right-hand pages show specific subtopics. This manual is the only example in this chapter that uses uppercase text as a deliberate design strategy. Because the most common head is "FYI" (For Your Information) and all the other heads are short phrases ("OVERVIEW," "TRY IT," "NOTES," and "SUMMARY"), all heads are set in uppercase so that they carry the same visual weight.

Be sure that the space between text and graphics is the same for all figures. Spacing guides are used to position all graphics and captions and to separate one step from the next. Careful spacing gives the page a clean, balanced appearance.

Production Tips

All text is formatted in the word processing file as flush left with no indents. One tab is set at 0.3 inches for bulleted lists and commands. Figure 12.27 shows the six fonts from two typeface families that are used throughout the document.

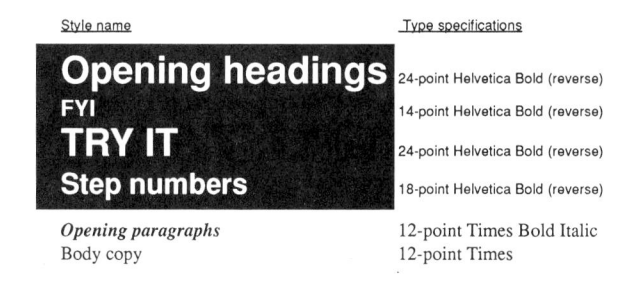

Style name	Type specifications
Opening headings	24-point Helvetica Bold (reverse)
FYI	14-point Helvetica Bold (reverse)
TRY IT	24-point Helvetica Bold (reverse)
Step numbers	18-point Helvetica Bold (reverse)
Opening paragraphs	12-point Times Bold Italic
Body copy	12-point Times

Fig. 12.27. *Type specifications table for manual using two grids.*

The Template

The Page Setup margins define the limits of the text for both formats (see fig. 12.28). Vertical rules on the master pages fall outside these limits (see fig. 12.29). Two-column guides on the master pages are customized. The default line style is changed to hairline rule.

Fig. 12.28. *Page Setup dialog box for manual using two grids.*

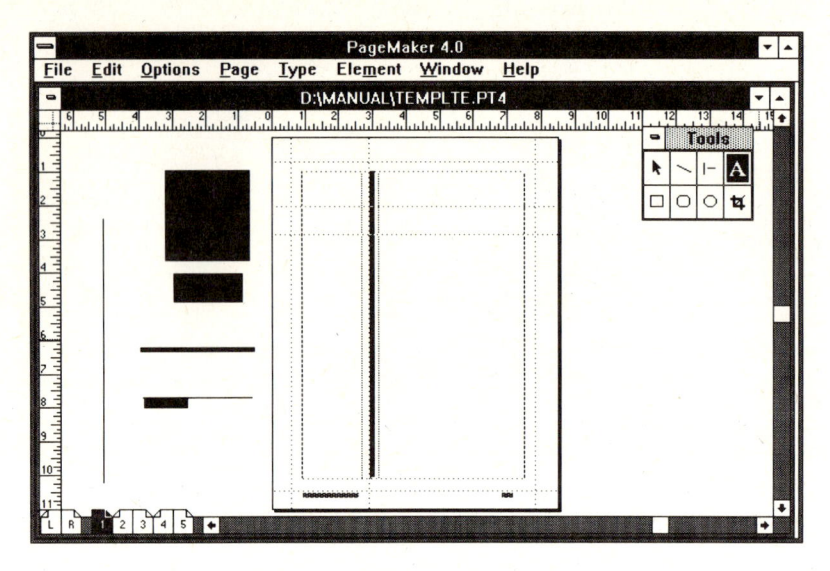

Fig. 12.29. The template for manual using two grids.

> **Using Thumbnail Printouts for Production Notes**
>
> When the template for the publication is complex, print thumbnails of the template and mark them up with instructions to the production team (see fig. 12.30).

Production Steps

To create the publication, take the following steps:

1. Prepare all text files flush left, with one tab for bulleted lists.

2. Set up the template with a customized two-column format on the master pages (see fig. 12.31 for this procedure).

3. As you go through the document, note the following:

    When you need a page in format 1—two columns—keep the master-page elements.

    When you need a page in three-column format, use the Column Guides command from the Options menu to set up three columns, and use the Copy and Paste commands to move the vertical rule from the pasteboard into the space between columns 2 and 3.

Chapter 12: Creating Business Reports, Books, and Manuals **451**

The trick to this alteration is that the column width set up automatically by the Column Guides command is exactly the same as the first column width of the customized format.

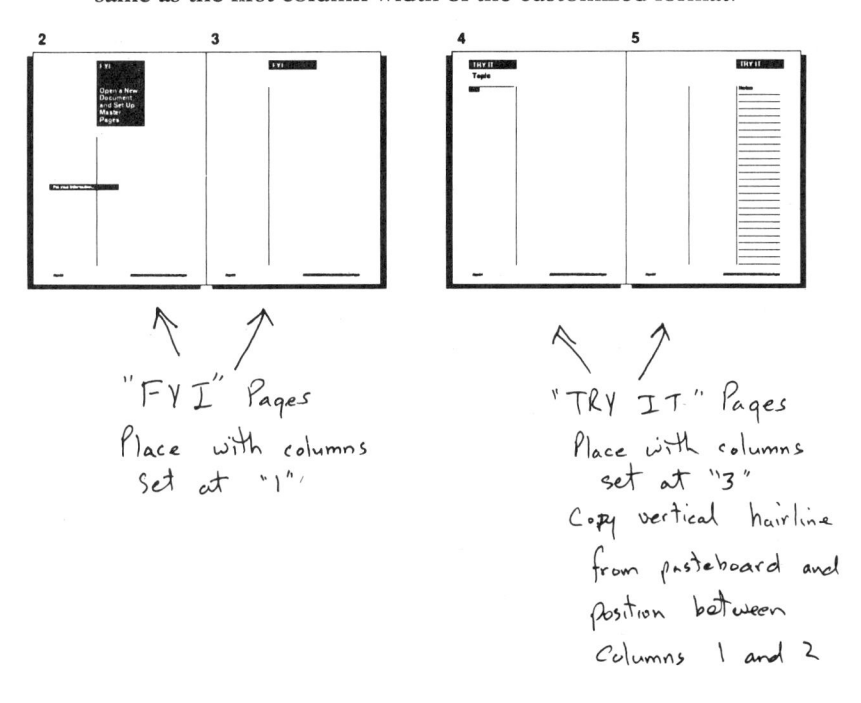

Fig. 12.30. Thumbnails of the template for manual using two grids.

"FYI" Pages
Place with columns set at "1".

"TRY IT" Pages
Place with columns set at "3".
Copy vertical hairline from pasteboard and position between Columns 1 and 2.

All text files and PageMaker documents for this manual are stored in the same subdirectory (see fig. 12.32). If the publication is very large or uses many graphics, you can use the Link command to manage the graphics as external files, rather than storing them as part of the PageMaker publication. If you divide the report into several PageMaker publications and you want to number all pages sequentially or generate an index or table of contents, use the Book command to link them.

Part III: Examples of Publications Created Using PageMaker

Use the Column guides command to set up three columns.

Move the middle column guides to match the vertical ruler guides you just created.

Use the Rulers command to display rulers, and move vertical guides to overlap the guides between columns one and two.

Draw a vertical hairline between columns one and two.

Use the Column Guides command to select two columns.

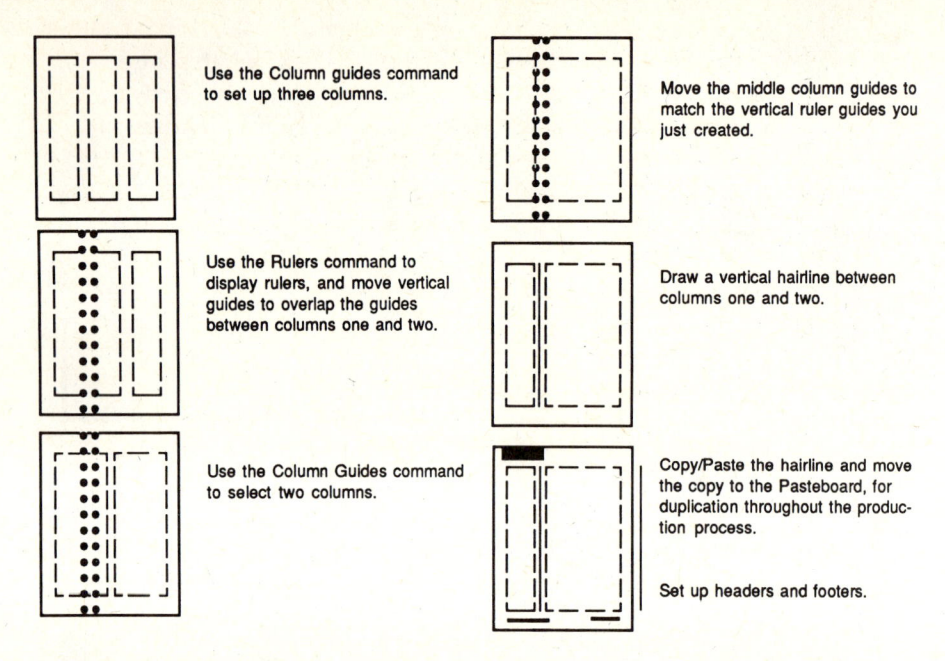

Copy/Paste the hairline and move the copy to the Pasteboard, for duplication throughout the production process.

Set up headers and footers.

Fig. 12.31. *Setting up the template with a customized two-column format on the master pages.*

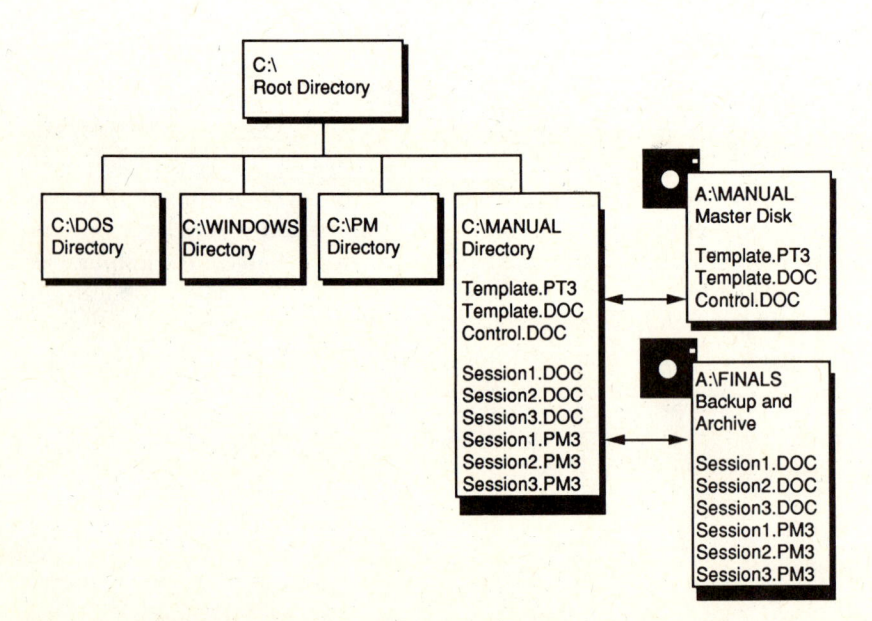

```
                    C:\
              Root Directory
      ┌──────────┬──────────┬──────────┐
   C:\DOS    C:\WINDOWS   C:\PM    C:\MANUAL         A:\MANUAL
 Directory   Directory  Directory  Directory         Master Disk

                                   Template.PT3      Template.PT3
                                   Template.DOC      Template.DOC
                                   Control.DOC       Control.DOC

                                   Session1.DOC      A:\FINALS
                                   Session2.DOC      Backup and
                                   Session3.DOC      Archive
                                   Session1.PM3
                                   Session2.PM3      Session1.DOC
                                   Session3.PM3      Session2.DOC
                                                     Session3.DOC
                                                     Session1.PM3
                                                     Session2.PM3
                                                     Session3.PM3
```

Fig. 12.32. *Disk-file organization for manual using two grids.*

Example 12.5. Section Cover Pages

The section, or chapter, cover pages in this example are created as a single-sided publication with a repeated graphic on the master page. Each numbered page of the publication contains only the new section or chapter name. The cover pages are printed without page numbers and inserted between the sections of the final document. This example is provided to show a simple technique for producing a series of cover pages that use the same basic design. You can apply this technique to any publication that uses graphic cover pages for each section.

Description

Each cover page shows the product logo on a gray background. Examples of pages from this publication are shown in figure 12.33. Because these pages contain no text, the design principles are not applicable.

Fig. 12.33. Final printout of section cover pages.

Production Tips

These cover pages are prepared for printing on 8 1/2-by-11-inch paper, but they are to be part of a document trimmed to 6 by 9 inches. The pages therefore can accommodate the bleed from the larger paper and show crop marks as well. If the final pages were to be 8 1/2-by 11 inches, the page size selected in this dialog box would be even larger in order to accommodate the bleed. (As explained in Chapter 11, bleed is the term used in offset printing to describe pages on which the inked area runs to the trimmed edges of the final document.)

This document is set up as single-sided because all the pages are right-hand pages, even though the larger document into which they are inserted is double-sided. The margin settings reflect the limits of the text, not the bleed or the trim. The Page Setup dialog box settings used for the template are shown in figure 12.34.

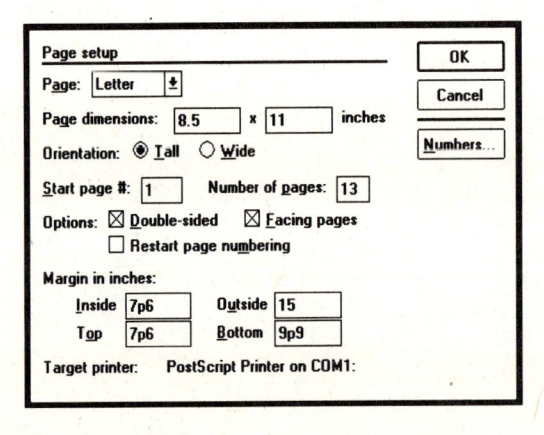

```
Page setup                                          OK
P_age: | Letter  ± |                              Cancel
Page dimensions: | 8.5 | x | 11 |   inches
Orientation: ◉ Tall   ○ Wide                      Numbers...
Start page #: | 1 |   Number of pages: | 13 |
Options:  ☒ Double-sided   ☒ Facing pages
          ☐ Restart page numbering
Margin in inches:
    Inside  | 7p6 |    Outside | 15  |
    Top     | 7p6 |    Bottom  | 9p9 |
Target printer:     PostScript Printer on COM1:
```

Fig. 12.34. The Page Setup dialog box for section cover pages.

The Template

The master page of the template includes the logo and the gray background, with guides to show the position of the section name (see fig. 12.35). Crop marks on the master page show the printer where to trim the printed covers. The pasteboard includes a skeletal text block that can be moved with the Copy and Paste commands and modified for each section.

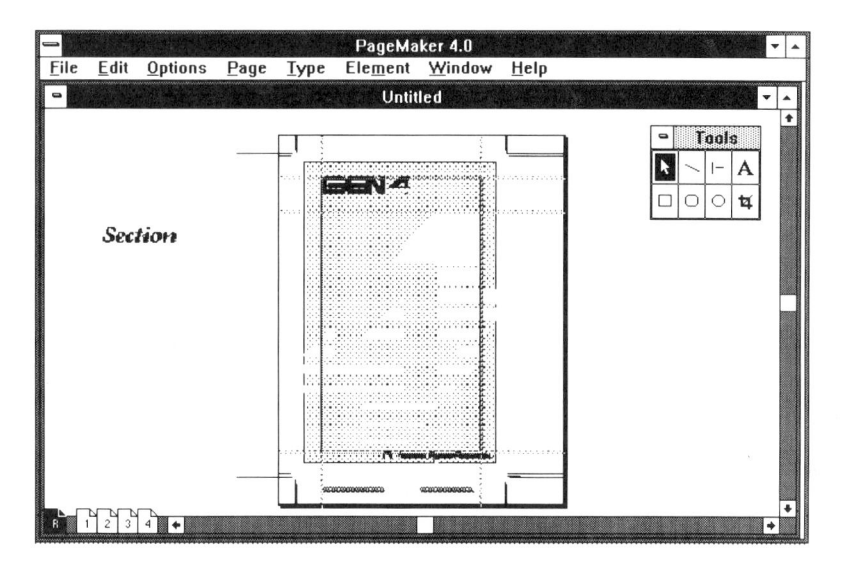

Fig. 12.35. The template for section cover pages.

Production Steps

The design steps are simple, as follows:

1. Set up the background design on the master page of the template and type dummy text on the pasteboard according to the type specifications to be used for all section titles.

2. Go through each cover page, and use the Copy and Paste commands to move the text from the pasteboard to the cover page background. Change the text to reflect the new section names.

Preparation for Reproduction

All the pages call for a bleed at the edges (see fig. 12.36). Usually, this design means that the color must be printed beyond the trim area. The pages with bleeds therefore should be delivered to the offset printer as a set separate from the rest of the document. Include a note stating that the pages call for a bleed. Pages like these often are handled separately because larger paper and more cuts are required than for other pages. Page numbers outside the bleed area indicate where each page will be inserted into the finished document.

Fig. 12.36. Cover page designed for a bleed at the edges.

Chapter Summary

This chapter has presented general descriptions and specific applications of the design principles and production tips that apply to long documents, such as books, manuals, and reports. After studying the examples in this chapter, you should be better equipped to design your own long documents, set up the templates, and implement efficient production procedures. If you are new to PageMaker and long document production, remember to take a small portion of the text through the entire production cycle before you finalize the full cycle of production steps in your project plan.

Finally, try to avoid setting tight production deadlines—or even trying to predict the completion date—for your first large production project with PageMaker.

13

Creating Newsletters and Similar Publications

Magazines, newsletters, and newspapers have become so much a part of our daily lives that many readers take these publications for granted. Readers expect the design and layout to be inviting and the information precise. Publishers of these documents create special touches that complicate the production process. These activities include kerning headlines, wrapping text around graphics, and varying page layouts. At the same time, producers of magazines, newsletters, and newspapers face more pressure to meet the deadline than any other publishers. The demand for efficiency in production techniques, therefore, is especially important.

The following are four characteristics that distinguish these types of publications:

- The publications use at least two columns, usually more, in the underlying grid. The number of columns can change from page to page.

- The flow of text for a single article or story can jump from one page to a point several pages later.

- The documents are usually produced as a series. A document of the same basic format and length is produced at regular intervals.

Part III: Examples of Publications Created Using PageMaker

- The documents often call for special layouts that may involve kerning headlines, wrapping text around graphics, or pasting display ads from one PageMaker document into another.

Figure 13.1 demonstrates all these characteristics.

Fig. 13.1. Examples of the documents in this chapter.

These features and other characteristics involve their own special design and production problems and practices. These special concerns are explained and illustrated in this chapter. After you understand the underlying principles, you can apply the suggestions in this chapter to other types of documents.

Using PageMaker helps you with newsletters and similar publications. You can use PageMaker to plan your designs and therefore save yourself time. After you have a good design for a newsletter, for example, you can use the master pages for every issue; you don't need to create formats again. PageMaker also eases such typesetting chores as kerning, wrapping text, and using different typefaces.

Design Principles

The design principles that apply to newsletters are derived from the long traditions of newspaper and magazine publishing. Because newsletters are relatively short, their design is particularly important. You need to convey information in a limited space and in an uncluttered, attractive format. The principles stressed in this chapter address these needs and range from the number of typefaces and the use of ruled lines to considerations of margins and provision of ample white space.

Some of these principles apply to all types of publications, not just those mentioned in this chapter. This section provides a general description of the application of these principles to newsletters, magazines, and newspapers. With each example, the applicable principles are repeated and accompanied by a description of their specific application to that example.

Use only one or two different typefaces in a document.

Magazines and newsletters often use many more typefaces than the business reports, books, and manuals shown in the preceding chapter, particularly when the magazine or newsletter includes display ads. The basic principle of simplicity, however, remains the best guide. Table 13.1 shows some of the typefaces commonly used in magazines and newsletters. In these publications, display ads often contain a wide variety of typefaces, but headlines and body copy use only one or two.

Table 13.1
Typefaces Used in Magazines and Newsletters

(Y = used; N = not used)

Typefaces	*Newsletters*	*Magazines*
ITC American Typewriter	Y	N
ITC Avant Garde	Y	N
ITC Benguiat	Y	Y
ITC Bookman	Y	Y
Courier	N	N
ITC Friz Quadrata	Y	Y
ITC Galliard	Y	Y
ITC Garamond	Y	Y
Glypha	Y	Y
Helvetica	Y	Y
ITC Korinna	Y	N
ITC Lubalin Graph	Y	Y

continues

Table 13.1 *(continued)*

Typefaces	Newsletters	Magazines
ITC Machine	N	N
ITC New Baskerville	Y	Y
New Century Schoolbook	Y	Y
Optima	Y	Y
Palatino	Y	Y
ITC Souvenir	Y	Y
Times	Y	Y
Trump Mediaeval	Y	Y
ITC Zapf Chancery	N	N

Use variations in the grid to help distinguish different sections of the magazine.

You probably have seen how some newsletters and magazines distinguish sections by giving them different grid structures. Figure 13.2 shows an example. The main feature begins on a facing-page spread. A graphic, the story title, and one column of text fill the left-hand page. The feature continues on the right-hand page with three columns of text. Another variation might be to have letters to the editor occupying three columns and the articles, two columns. Example 13.2 uses this technique.

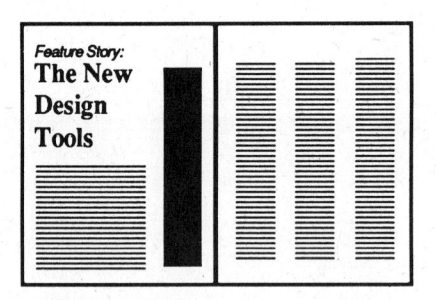

Fig. 13.2. Varying the grid structure to distinguish sections.

Use ruled lines to set off the grid of the pages.

In addition to using nonprinting guides to design your pages, you can use PageMaker's ruled lines to enhance the appearance of the pages. For example, designers often drop hairline rules between columns of text. This technique is demonstrated in examples in this chapter. You also can set ruled lines that are part of the paragraph specifications for text in PageMaker 4.0 (see Chapter 5).

All columns on all pages should bottom out at the same point.

This rule is more strictly applied in magazines than in most newsletters or any other type of document described in this book. The problems associated with alignment are compounded when you add subheadings in an article, have strict rules about the spacing around graphics and between paragraphs, and do not allow widows and orphans. You may need to adjust the space around headings and figures to force columns to meet the bottom margin.

On the other hand, a ragged bottom margin, as illustrated in figure 13.3, allows more flexibility in copy fitting. The ragged margin is better than an even margin that stops above the bottom of the grid. This strategy is used deliberately in Example 13.1 (see the second page in figure 13.7). Other examples in this chapter also illustrate bottom alignment and provide production tips for copy fitting.

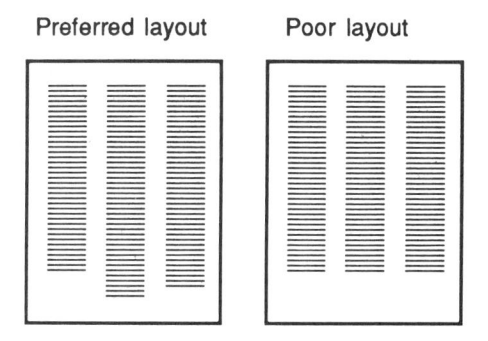

Fig. 13.3. Deliberately making a bottom margin ragged.

Don't be afraid of white space.

Applications of this principle vary greatly. Some magazines—*The New Yorker*, for instance—fill every column completely with small type. This kind of design can be attractive as well as functional; it produces the greatest number of words in the fewest number of pages. Good designers can make designs like this work, but if you are just beginning to learn the ins and outs of page layout, you should follow the rule of allowing some white space on the pages. In the examples in this chapter, you will see that white space occurs primarily around article titles and subheads. This practice is common to newsletters and newspapers.

Provide estimates of the number of characters per column for contributors and editors.

Providing character-count estimates is something that most professional editors do as a matter of course when they make an assignment. These estimates help eliminate the many problems that arise when you begin to lay out the pages. You need to estimate the amount of space allocated for the text of each article, and type specifications for the article determine the number of words that will fit in the space. Chapter 10 describes methods of counting characters and copy casting before placing the text in PageMaker.

Production Tips

This chapter discusses documents that are laid out in several columns and use figures of varying widths. The production tips are applicable at all stages of creating these kinds of publications—from building the publication to taking it to a printer. You learn, for example, when to use a drawing program to create banners and when and where to place a table of contents. You learn how to handle documents with many illustrations and how to scale figures and pictures to column widths. The tips also tell you how to adjust spacing in multiple-column publications and how to ready your publication for printing. Many tips in this chapter apply to other types of publications, such as the booklets described in Chapter 15. This section describes how the tips apply generally to newsletters, magazines, and newspapers. In the examples, the pertinent tips are repeated with explanations of their specific applications.

If your printer cannot handle large type sizes, use a scanned image or a paint figure for the banner.

If you use a font cartridge that does not have large display type, you can create a banner by scanning large type. You also can create the banner by using large type in a paint file. The scanned image provides the best quality on the printout if the image is saved as a high-resolution image. In either case, you probably need to clean up the image pixel-by-pixel to get smooth edges. The results always are of lower quality than if you use type in PageMaker up to 650 points. (For examples of scanned and paint-type graphics, see Chapter 6; for examples of bit-mapped characters, see Chapter 10.)

If your publication includes a list of contents that can vary in length, place or type the list before filling the rest of the page.

Rather than placing long articles on the pages first, type or place elements that cannot be jumped to later pages. The list of contents is just one example of this kind of element. You do not need to know the exact page numbers when you first type the table of contents, but you do need to know the number of articles that will appear in the issue and the lengths of the titles.

The calendar of events on page 1 in figure 13.7, for example, must be placed before the rest of the page is laid out. Similarly, the list of contents at the top right corner of page 1 in figure 13.12 must be placed before the rest of the page can be completed.

Use a spacing guide to position text and graphics and to adjust the spaces between articles.

Precise spacing is especially important in newsletters and magazines. Set text offset specifications in the Text Wrap dialog box for controlling the distance of text wrapped around graphics. Use the Paragraph Specifications dialog box to specify space between sections within stories. See Chapter 12 for a description of using dummy text blocks as spacing guides that adjust the space between adjacent stories and between graphics and adjacent text blocks. You will see such spacing guides on the pasteboard of the template for Example 13.2 in this chapter (see fig. 13.18).

Scale pictures and figures to precise column widths.

A picture can span more than one column, but all pictures should conform to the grid lines. A picture can be one column, two columns, or three columns wide in a three-column grid design, for example, but should not be 1.5 columns wide unless your grid is designed to accommodate this variation. For example, figure 13.20 shows the layout of a page of figures that range from one-half column wide to two columns wide.

Pages with several figures look best if the figures are aligned with other pictures or headlines.

Figure 13.4 provides examples of various layouts that follow or violate this guideline. The pages on the left in the example make one edge of each figure align horizontally or vertically with the edge of another figure on the page. The pages on the right do not follow this rule. As a result, the pages on the right lack balance and look haphazard.

Use black boxes to reserve space for photographs that need halftones dropped in by the printer.

When offset printers prepare plates for pages that require halftones, the preparers usually black out the space on the camera-ready mechanicals so that the camera creates a clear *window* in the negative. You can save the printer this extra step by using PageMaker's black boxes to reserve space for halftones. The camera-ready master pages are printed directly from Page-Maker in black images on white paper. The photographic negative is prepared by the offset printer; the print image is transparent on a black background. The plate made from the negative has a raised surface that picks up ink from the roller and lays the ink on the paper. The plate is a mirror image of the final page.

Fig. 13.4. Aligning figures with other figures or headlines.

> ### Talking to Your Printer before Preparing Final Camera-Ready Pages
>
> If you have not used the offset-printing process before, ask what form of camera-ready pages your printing service prefers. Also ask how the printing charges may change if you do more or less of the preparation yourself. Use white boxes to reserve space for line art that will be pasted in before copy is sent to the printer.

The printer wants to lay halftones on transparent windows in the negative (created by black boxes on the camera-ready page), but the paste-up artist usually wants to paste figures down on a white background. Figure 13.5 shows how you can type the name or number of the figure in the space reserved for each figure. To draw the white box to size, you use PageMaker's square-corner tool. To type the figure number in the box, you use PageMaker's drag-place feature: Select the text tool and drag the I-beam inside the figure area to define the text's width before you start typing.

Use a template for all issues.

The template systems for newsletters and magazines may be elaborate compared to those for most other types of documents. In some of the examples that follow, you see how comprehensive a template can be. Figure

13.18 shows a template for a tabloid with 13 different place holders for type specifications, several spacing guides, and three different page layouts. Chapter 11 provides a full discussion of template systems.

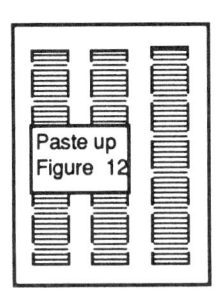

Fig. 13.5. Identifying the figure to be pasted in.

Use a style sheet for all issues.

The style sheet *tags* enable you to specify the format specifications for a particular paragraph of text. Style sheets give your publication a consistent appearance by ensuring that minor headlines, captions, and other text in the publication are consistent throughout the document. You can set font specifications and paragraph formats for a document by defining attributes once for each style name, or tag, in the style sheet.

Do all character formatting in advance, using a word processor, or in Story view in PageMaker.

This suggestion carries extra weight for magazines and newsletters. When you are working under the pressure of a regular deadline, you need to use the best tools available for each function. As explained in Chapter 4, word processors and the Story Editor in PageMaker 4.0 are more efficient than working in Layout view in PageMaker for editing and formatting text. Word processors and the Story Editor are faster because they do not need to perform all the additional screen-imaging functions required for the Layout view display.

Use pull-out quotes to extend copy that falls very short of filling the space allowed.

Pull-out quotes are short sentences excerpted from the text, printed in larger type, and set off from the rest of the page by boxes or lines. Magazines and newsletters frequently use pull-out quotes to fill space and to emphasize points from the article. A pull-out quote usually is set four to six points larger than the body copy (see fig. 13.6).

Fig. 13.6. Using pull-out quotes to fill space or emphasize specific text.

You can use a style tag for pull-out quotes, or you can create them manually. To help estimate the number of lines you need, you use formulas based on your type specifications. The following are examples of formulas based on 16-point type with 18-point leading and a 0.25-inch margin for a ruled line above the pull-out quote:

Number of Lines in Quote	Number of Inches Added
1	.5
2	.75
3	1.00
4	1.25
5	1.5

Use leading changes to make fine adjustments in copy fitting.

If the final text does not fit into the space allowed, change the leading of the body copy for selected columns, pages, or articles. As mentioned in Chapter 10, leading changes should be made consistently in adjacent columns and on facing pages. The quickest way to make text fit into a specific space is to select a whole article and change the leading globally to shrink or stretch the text. By using style sheets, you can change the leading by editing the tags for the body text and other tags in the publication. You may need to scroll through the columns in Actual Size mode to check for widows and orphans. The alternative is to scroll manually through pages and adjust the leading for segments of text. This technique, however, is slower and involves displaying more dialog boxes.

Avoid spanning articles across separate PageMaker publications if you divide a single issue into small pieces.

The 999-page limit enforced by PageMaker is unlikely to present a problem for magazines and newsletters, but you may want to divide a single issue into several PageMaker publications, especially if they contain many graphics. Remember that you do not want to build a single publication file too large to be backed up on one floppy disk.

Confine each text file or story to a single PageMaker file, if possible. Otherwise, the text blocks will not be linked between documents; if the blocks are not linked, problems can arise when the text is edited.

Examples

This chapter contains two examples of newsletters. The first example is a two-page newsletter, every issue of which contains the same basic elements. The second example is a tabloid newsletter prepared for two-color printing.

> Example 13.1. A Two-Page Newsletter with Repeated Basic Elements
>
> Example 13.2. A Tabloid Newsletter Prepared for Two-Color Printing

Example 13.1. A Two-Page Newsletter with Repeated Basic Elements

The two-page newsletter in this example is designed for ease of production by a group of volunteers who have many other, perhaps more pressing, responsibilities. The trick is that the newsletter always contains the same set of features, each of which is always the same size and occupies the same position on the pages. A collection of extra copy and artwork—house ads, helpful tips, and interesting quotations—is available for use in a month when a feature is short or missing.

The techniques used here can be applied to any publication that is produced regularly by a group whose primary function is not publishing. Such publications include newsletters produced by volunteer staff, house organs produced by administrative staff, and event calendars with descriptions of the offerings produced by educational institutions and seminar agencies.

Description

This two-page newsletter uses a three-column format that routinely presents the calendar of events for a seminar agency. The contents always follow the same basic formula:

- A calendar of events of varying length, always on page 1
- A feature article about the main event (300-400 words), always on page 1
- An article about secondary events (300-400 words), always on page 1
- An article about a person or agency, usually one of the event leaders or sponsors, of 200-250 words, which can start on page 1
- An article of 300-400 words, which offers information on a topic of general interest to the readers, usually written by one of the seminar leaders and found on page 2
- No more than three miscellaneous fillers, such as house ads, special announcements, short tips, and notable quotations

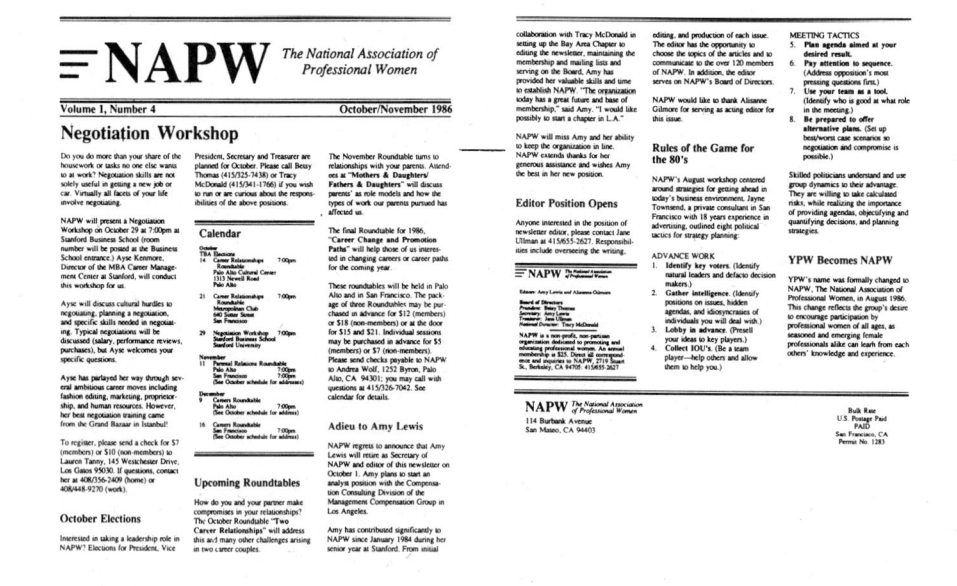

Fig. 13.7. Printout of two-page newsletter.

Using the same basic design elements enables each contributor to know exactly how many words to write. And if one contributor fails to meet the deadline for copy, the editor can fill the space with one of the canned house ads, tips, or quotations. A spacing guide is included in the template as a standard for the minimum space allowed between articles, but this space can be increased as needed to make the articles fill the pages. These loose standards make this publication easy to lay out.

Design Principles

The design principles listed at the beginning of this chapter generally have been applied in this newsletter. Four of those principles have been applied in a way that intentionally simplifies the production process. Because the producers of the newsletter are not professional publishers, following these principles is especially important.

Use only one or two different typefaces in a document. Only one typeface, Times, is used, in five fonts, as shown in the type specifications table in figure 13.8. This relatively short list of elements helps simplify the production of the newsletter.

Style name	Type specifications
Logo	127-point Times
Banner Tag	18-point Times Italic
Volume/Issue ID	14-point Times Bold
Main Article Title	24-point Times Bold
All Other Titles	14-point Times Bold, 24-point leading
Body Copy	10-point Times, auto leading
Calendar text	8-point Times
Masthead	7-point Times

Fig. 13.8. Type specifications table for two-page newsletter.

Use ruled lines to set off the grid of the pages. Horizontal rules are used to set off standing elements, such as the Calendar and the masthead information. All rules except one use the *double-line option*, also called an *Oxford rule*, from the Lines menu. Figure 13.10 shows that on page 1 of the newsletter, two-column-wide ruled lines are stored for future placement around the calendar text.

Provide estimates of the number of characters per column for contributors and editors. The length of each feature is standard. The total newsletter is 7,500 characters, about 1,500 words. Before beginning an assignment, a writer knows how long it should be. The editor's primary concern is that the assignment not exceed the expected word count. If an article is too short, the extra space can be filled with a house ad, tip, or short quotation.

All columns on all pages should bottom out at the same point. This general rule is not rigidly applied in this case. If a contributor writes too much or too little, columns are left uneven; the text is not edited to change the length, and the leading is not changed.

Production Tips

The production tips offered here can be applied to any publication for which a primary goal is simplicity in the production process. The tips include ways to deal with material that comes in varied formats and suggestions for setting up the template. You also are led through all the steps of the production process for this kind of publication.

Sources of Data

You usually can expect a wide range of sources for the text in any publication that consists of articles by a number of different authors, unless you are producing an in-house newsletter for which all the contributors use the same computer system. Because the newsletter is only two pages long, the editor can type short articles directly into PageMaker if they are not supplied on disk. All text formatting is done in PageMaker.

The Template

Figure 13.9 shows the Page Setup dialog box for the newsletter. The template is set up with two pages, and the relatively wide margins provide white space that helps balance the wide spacing between articles.

The template, shown in figure 13.10, uses a simple three-column format. The first page contains a standing banner and two ruled lines that will be positioned around the calendar. Page 2 contains the masthead information and mailing label area. A list of production steps is stored on the pasteboard for easy reference.

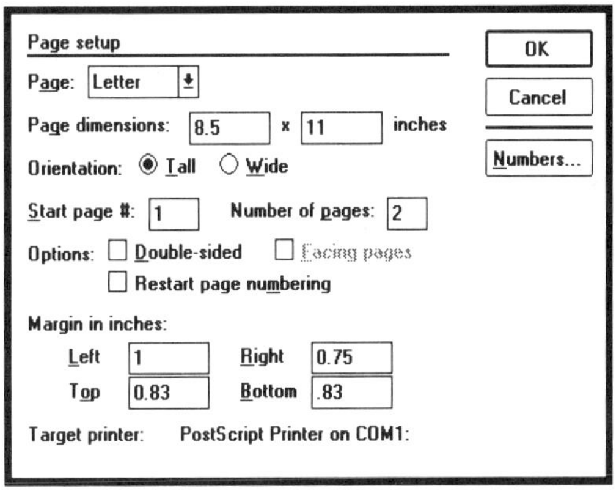

Fig. 13.9. Page Setup dialog box for two-page newsletter.

Production Steps

To aid the creators of this quarterly newsletter, the following steps appear on the pasteboard of the template. These steps apply to this specific newsletter, but you can apply them easily to any publication of this type.

1. Collect all text files, either on disk or paper. The target character count is 7,500 for the entire newsletter, about 1,500 words, including the Calendar but excluding the standing items on the template.

2. Open the template for this newsletter. Save the template, with a new name that includes the issue number, such as VOL1-04.PT3. All files for the newsletter begin with the same letters or numbers, such as 04-ART1.TXT, and 04-ART2.TXT.

3. On page 1, change the issue identification below the banner. (See the section "Design Principles" for suggestions for creating banners.)

4. While working in Actual Size or 70% Size, type or place each article in the space allowed and format text as you go (see fig. 13.8 for fonts and tags).

5. If the final text is too long to fit within the two pages allowed, change the leading in the body text to shrink the text. You may need to scroll down each column to check for widows and orphans and to make fine adjustments to the space between articles.

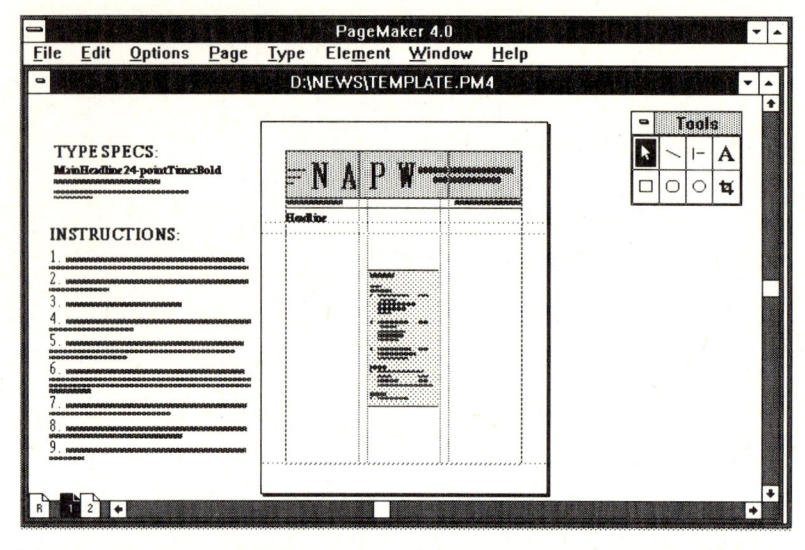

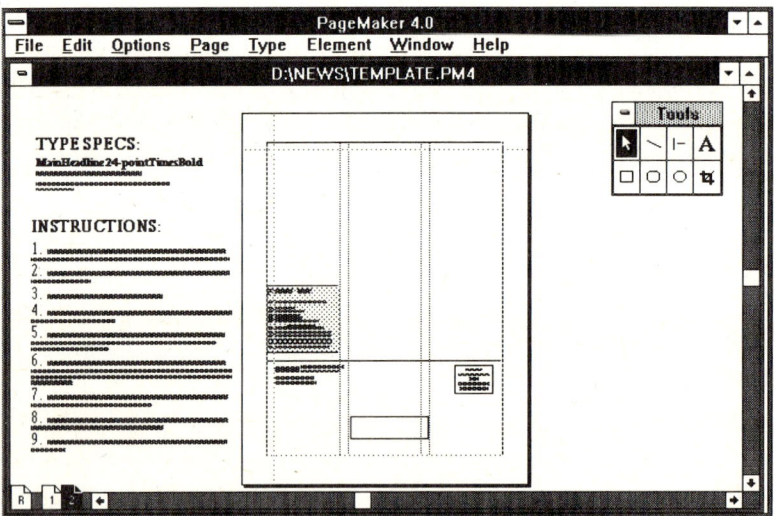

Fig. 13.10. Template for two-page newsletter.

6. If the text is too short to fill the number of pages allowed, add a house ad or a famous quotation from the files. Fill empty space with items from the text files named HOUSEADS.DOC or QUOTES.DOC or from one of the graphics files named HOUSEAD1.PIC or HOUSEAD2.PIC. Names of your files may differ; you may choose to rename the quotations by the dates they are used, such as Q-DEC91.DOC.

You also can increase the spacing between articles.

7. Before printing the final master copy, print the newsletter on a laser printer for proofing. Be sure that the event coordinator or other director sees a copy before it is sent to the print shop.

8. Print the newsletter on a laser printer, and send the camera-ready pages to the printing company. Specify type, color, and weight of the paper and the number of copies.

9. Copy the PageMaker file for this issue to the archive disk named NEWS or any name you choose, and delete all text files from the hard disk.

> ### Adding Space around Article Titles
> When changing the spacing between sections throughout a document, copy a blank line of the desired spacing into the Clipboard; sweep through the document; and at each break, do the following:
>
> 1. Triple-click to select the blank line.
>
> 2. Press Ins to replace the selected line with the blank line stored in the Clipboard.

For all issues of this newsletter, all work is done in one directory (see fig. 13.11). Only the PageMaker version of each issue, along with the template, is saved on the archive disk. If the imported graphics are very large, you can use the Link command to manage the graphics as external files, rather than storing them as part of the PageMaker publication.

Example 13.2. A Tabloid Newsletter Prepared for Two-Color Printing

The newsletter used in this example is more similar in design and format to a newspaper than to most newsletters. The tabloid-size 11-by-17-inch pages are printed in tiled pieces on 8 1/2-by-11-inch paper for the editing reviews, and the final camera-ready pages are printed full size on a Linotronic 300 typesetter.

The design and production tips provided here can be applied to any newsletter or newspaper publication, particularly publications consisting of many different articles, figures, and photographs. The tips that specifically address two-color printing can be applied to any two-color publication; these tips also can be adapted for three- and four-color jobs.

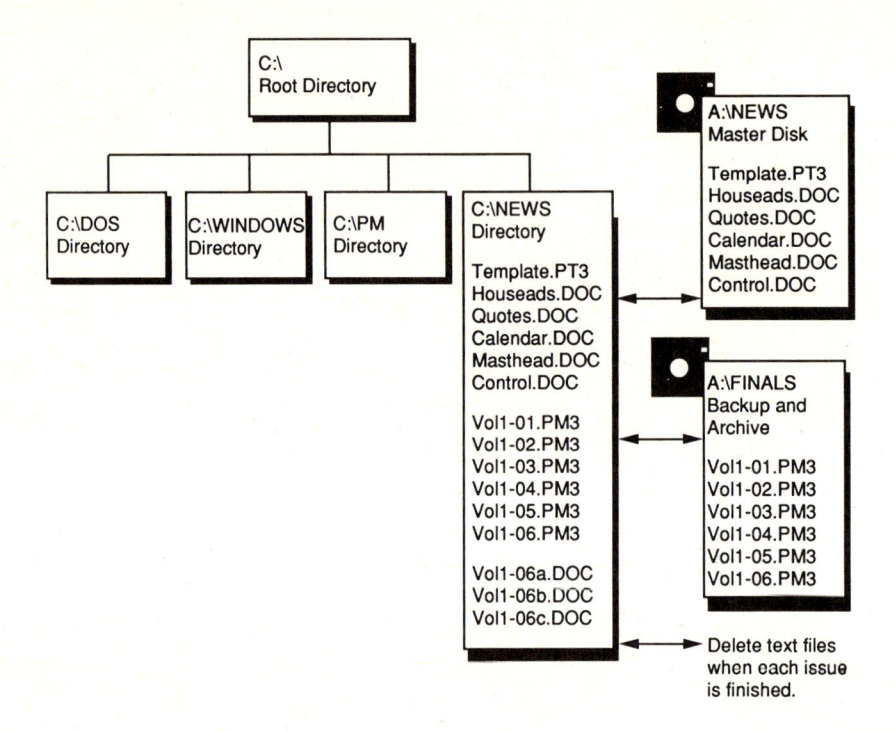

Part III: Examples of Publications Created Using PageMaker

```
C:\
Root Directory
├── C:\DOS Directory
├── C:\WINDOWS Directory
├── C:\PM Directory
└── C:\NEWS Directory
      Template.PT3
      Houseads.DOC
      Quotes.DOC
      Calendar.DOC
      Masthead.DOC
      Control.DOC

      Vol1-01.PM3
      Vol1-02.PM3
      Vol1-03.PM3
      Vol1-04.PM3
      Vol1-05.PM3
      Vol1-06.PM3

      Vol1-06a.DOC
      Vol1-06b.DOC
      Vol1-06c.DOC

A:\NEWS Master Disk
  Template.PT3
  Houseads.DOC
  Quotes.DOC
  Calendar.DOC
  Masthead.DOC
  Control.DOC

A:\FINALS Backup and Archive
  Vol1-01.PM3
  Vol1-02.PM3
  Vol1-03.PM3
  Vol1-04.PM3
  Vol1-05.PM3
  Vol1-06.PM3

→ Delete text files when each issue is finished.
```

Fig. 13.11. Disk-file organization for two-page newsletter.

Description

The tabloid-size newsletter shown in figure 13.12 is assembled from text contributed in various forms by many different authors. The production process involves a considerable amount of coordination among contributors, editors, and the production staff. Because the people involved are scattered over a wide geographic area, files are telecommunicated through a modem. The files usually can be telecommunicated as ASCII text or directly from the word processing programs used by the project.

The final telecommunication occurs when the production group sends the finished PageMaker files to the editorial group for the final review. The editors make changes directly to the files and send them back to the production group. The files then are printed to a Linotronic typesetter using the Spot Color Overlays command in the Print menu to create color separations. The separations will be used for the two-color black-and-red commercial printing.

Fig. 13.12. Printout of tabloid newsletter.

Design Principles

All the design principles described at the beginning of this chapter are applied in this report. Some principles, however, are particularly well illustrated. The tabloid makes effective use of ruled lines, white space, and variations in the grid. Estimates of character counts are essential for this kind of production.

Use variations in the grid to distinguish different sections of the newsletter. The three pages shown in figure 13.12 provide good examples of grid variations: the basic grid is four columns; the Corporate Directory heading is two columns wide; and a page of graphs and tables includes tables and graphs that vary from one-half column to two columns wide. These grid variations help differentiate sections and maintain the reader's interest, as well as accommodate a variety of formats.

Use ruled lines to help set off the grid of the pages. This design uses hairline rules between columns and horizontal rules above article titles (see figs. 13.12 and 13.13). These rules set off different types of material and highlight the variations in the grid.

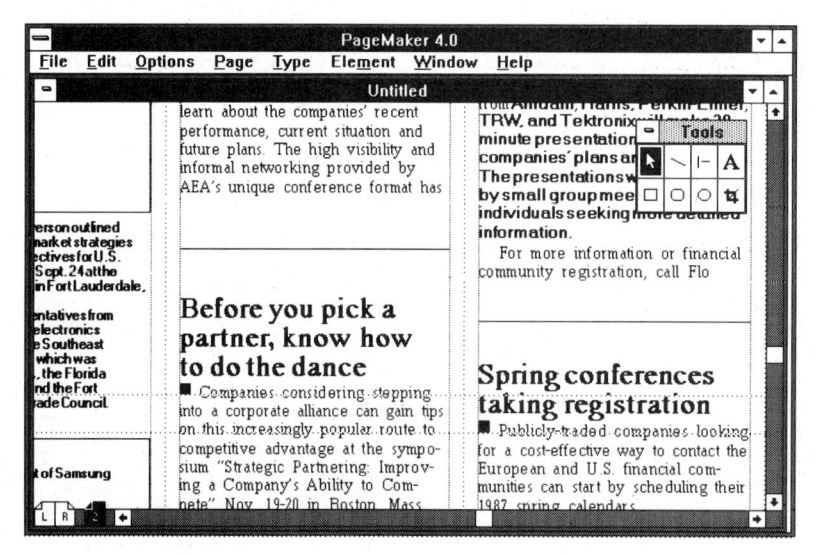

Fig. 13.13. White space and hairline rules above the headlines.

Provide estimates of the number of characters per column for contributors and editors. The character counts for each article are assigned to the writers initially, but the final count may change when figures are added. The editors expect to do a great deal of editing after they receive the text from various sources.

All columns on all pages should bottom out to same point. This rule is strictly followed in this newsletter, as in most newspapers, which are the models from which this design is derived. As you can see in figure 13.12, the pages are carefully aligned at the bottom margin of the grid. This alignment produces a neat, clean tabloid newspaper.

Don't be afraid of white space. White space is achieved primarily by leaving a great deal of space above headlines (see fig. 13.13). Otherwise, the page layouts are very dense. Again, this design strategy deliberately imitates most newspaper designs.

Production Tips

To produce a tabloid of this size and complexity every month, the production team and editors must use every trick they can to make production as smooth and efficient as possible. The following anecdote illustrates this process.

A tabloid produced by conventional methods had required 200 person-hours for the full production. Expecting to save a great deal of time, the production team switched to desktop publishing. The team members took a one-day class in PageMaker and engaged a designer experienced in PageMaker to build the first template, which took four days.

The first issue took more than 400 hours to produce. Much of that time was spent learning how to use PageMaker efficiently and adapting the specifications to PageMaker's options. By the time the team had produced the sixth issue, however, the total production time was reduced to less than 40 hours—less than a quarter of the time previously required.

The tips and tricks provided here are not complete *cookbook recipes* for producing this newsletter. Many details have been excluded because they were specific to this team's word processing programs, graphics programs, and editorial standards. The suggestions, however, do provide a good overview of what this type of production entails, and the ideas can be adapted to any large or complex publication project.

Sources of Data

The authors' manuscripts come in all forms. When authors and editors are using the same network, files are immediately accessible to the editors. Authors in the same building with editors and the production crew deliver the files on disks. Other authors telecommunicate their text through modems. Occasionally, an author submits a manuscript on paper only. The editors work on the files in any word processor available and type the stories that were received on paper. The editors then give the files to the production group with marked-up thumbnails of the template, which indicate where each story should be placed (see fig. 13.14).

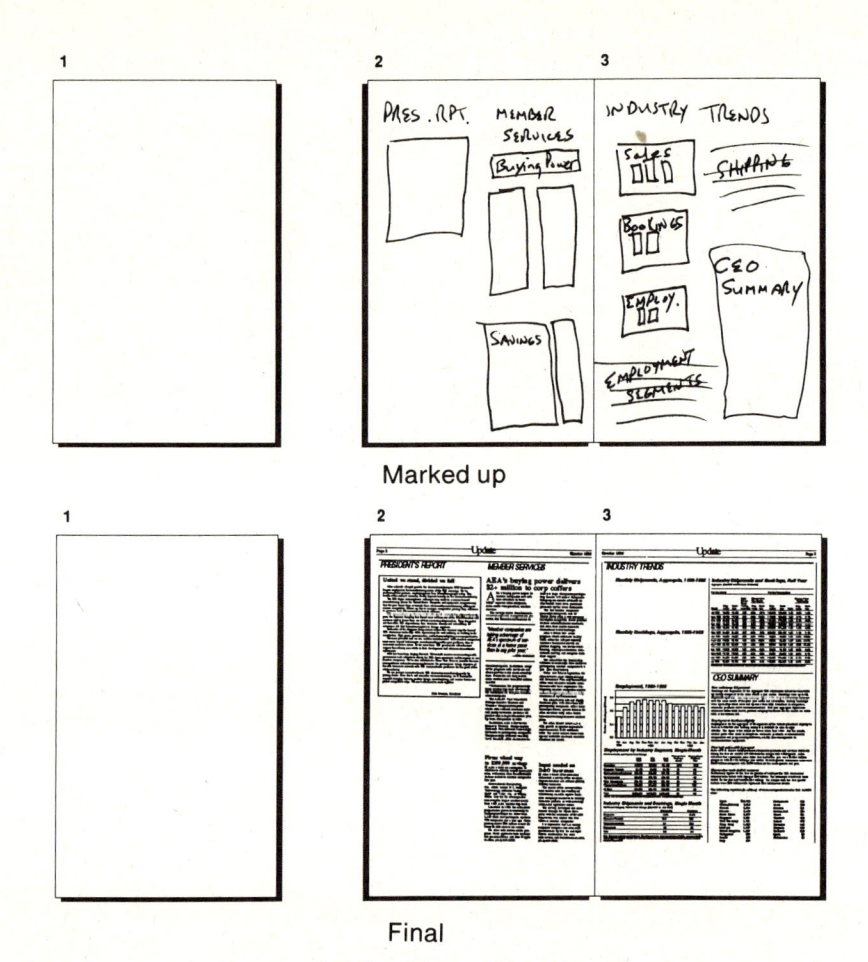

478 Part III: Examples of Publications Created Using PageMaker

Fig. 13.14. Marked-up thumbnails of the template showing where text is to be placed.

If the disk files and telecommunicated files for the text have not been formatted, the production staff converts the files to the word processing program and then does the formatting. If the files have been formatted in one of the word processing programs that PageMaker supports, production places the files in PageMaker. Most word processors cannot handle the wide variety of fonts used in this newsletter (see fig. 13.15); therefore, much formatting is done in PageMaker. The large initial drop cap used in the opening paragraphs of certain articles must be positioned in PageMaker rather than in the word processing program.

Logo/banner	Created in Windows Draw and stretched to 160-point Times
Volume/Isuue ID	14-point Times

Headlines:

3-col. Headlines	36-point Times Bold, 25-point leading
2-col. Headlines	27-point Times Bold, 24-point leading
1-col. Headlines	18-point Times Bold, auto leading
SUBJECT HEADINGS	24-point Helvetica, all caps
Body Copy Body Copy Body Copy Body Copy	11-point Times, 12-point leading, 3-line initial drop cap, paragrpahs indented 1 pica
Words highlighted within text	10-point Helvetica Bold, 12-point leading
Large Captions within text	18-point Helvetica Italic, centered, 2-point rule above and below
"INSIDE"	18-point Helvetica Bold Italic, 33-point leading, all caps
Inside text	14-point Helvetica Bold italic, 14-point leading, extra line between paragraphs
Photo Captions	8-point Helvetica Bold, 9-point leading
Subheads within articles	12-point Times Bold

Fig. 13.15. Type specifications table for tabloid newsletter.

Tagging Text in the Word Processing Program

To save production time, provide the writers with a list of tags so that they can tag text in their word processing program when possible. PageMaker recognizes tag names that are put at the beginning of the paragraph and are surrounded by < > brackets: <Title> before the article title, <Body copy> before the body text, and <Subtitle> before the subheading. Each paragraph that does not have a tag name at its beginning takes on the attributes of the preceding paragraph.

> ### Requesting ASCII Text Files
>
> For the best and most efficient results, the authors should use the same word processing program that the production team uses. If this is impossible, ask the authors to save their files as text-only (ASCII) files, and let the production team format the text with a word processor that PageMaker supports.

The Template

The Page Setup dialog box in figure 13.16 indicates that this newsletter has a tabloid format. Not all laser printers can handle the narrow inside and outside margins (0.33 inches); some printers force a minimum margin of 0.5 inches. The template initially is set up with three pages; the first page, the second page, and a special page of graphs. Additional pages are added when needed. As is evident in the production steps that follow, this 12-page newsletter can be developed as several PageMaker publications so that the production team can distribute the work more equally.

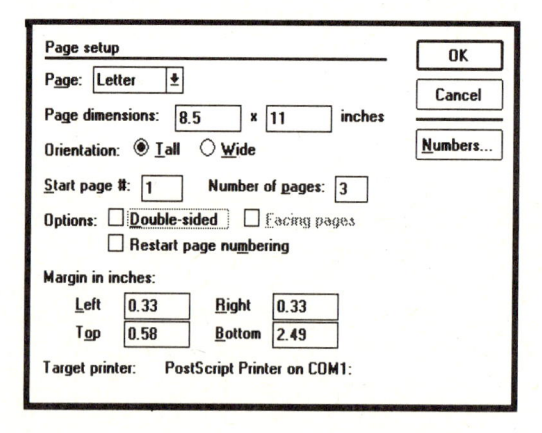

Fig. 13.16. Page Setup dialog box for tabloid newsletter.

> ### Dividing a 12-Page Tabloid into Several PageMaker Files
>
> The template is set up as a three-page document. Each page or series of consecutive pages is started from this template, but a single issue is stored as three or more different PageMaker files (see fig. 13.17). With this arrangement, a group of people can share the production and editing tasks. Use the Book command to link the files.

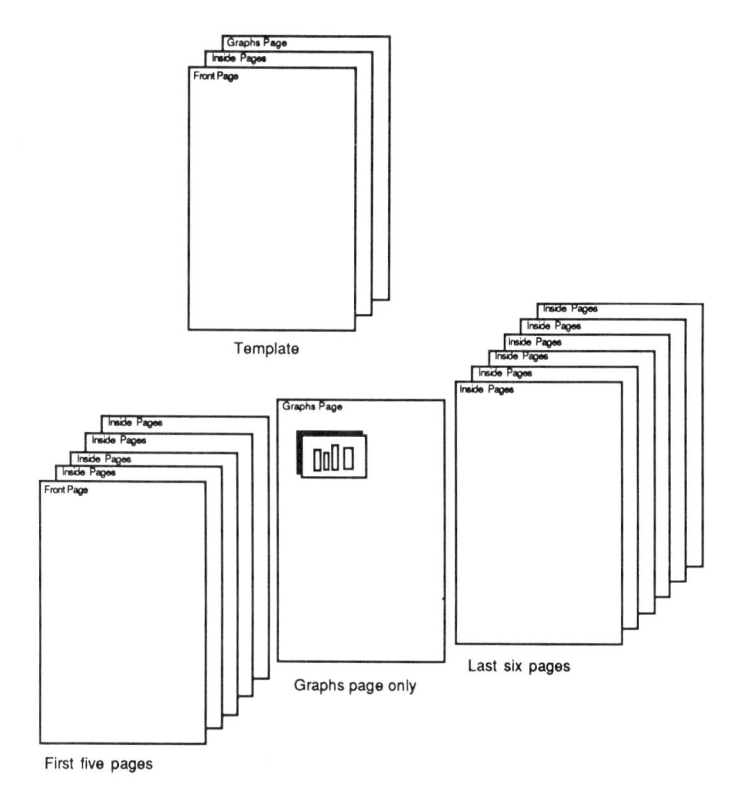

Fig. 13.17. Developing the tabloid newsletter in several files.

The template for this complex document is an essential production aid for each issue (see fig. 13.18). The master pages are set as 4-column formats with running heads. Standard elements, including ruled lines, 13 different text place holders, and several spacing guides, are stored on the pasteboard. Page 1 of the template includes the banner, a box where the contents are listed, and a ruler guide for starting articles on this page. Page 2 includes the masthead information, and page 3 contains drop-shadow boxes where graphs and tables will be placed.

Building the template requires more than 40 hours. The design is based on specifications that match previous issues created by using traditional typesetting and paste-up methods. Forty hours includes time to build one page, to print it by using PageMaker's Tile feature, and to write specifications for the production staff and the authors and editors, who previously did not participate in typesetting and formatting.

The editors use thumbnails to mark the locations of articles. To create thumbnails, the editors open the template document and use the Insert Pages command to create a 12-page empty document. They then print the empty document with the Print command Thumbnails option (see fig. 13.19).

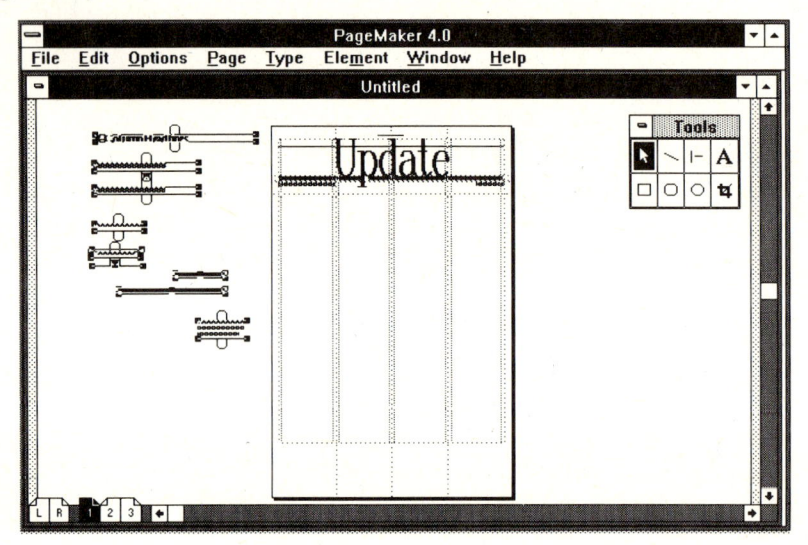

Fig. 13.18. Template for tabloid newsletter.

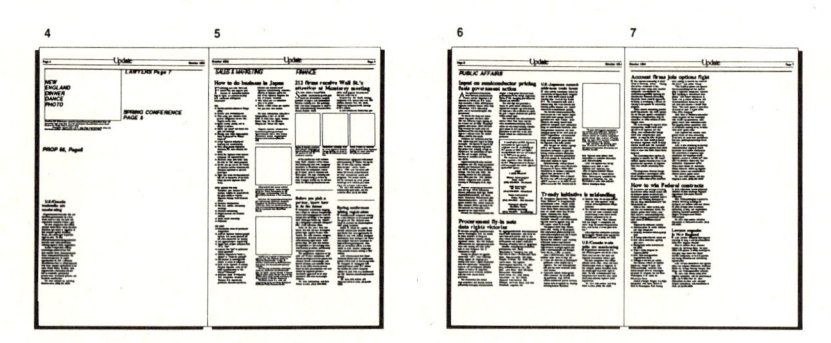

Fig. 13.19. Thumbnails for tabloid newsletter.

> **Printing Reductions of Each Page Instead of Using Thumbnails**
>
> Because the newsletter itself is assembled as several different files and because the tabloid pages are so complex, thumbnails are not practical for viewing finished pages. Using a percentage reduction to print quick miniatures of each finished page produces more helpful results. By using PostScript, for example, you can print the pages at a 45-percent reduction, from the Print command Scaling option, to fit on one sheet of 8 1/2-by-11-inch paper. These reductions can be used for control and review purposes but not for detailed proofreading or final production.

Production Steps

If the production group uses more than one PageMaker file to build the publication, each file or partial publication must include sequential pages; the stories must be self-contained within that file. Anytime during the production cycle, the pages or groups of pages may be at different stages in the following sequence of steps:

1. The staff collects the text files from contributors.

2. The editorial staff edits each article before passing it to the production group. The editors mark the dummy thumbnails for positioning articles and graphics.

3. The production staff formats the text if necessary.

4. The production staff positions each article and places black boxes where photographs will be printed or white boxes where pictures or line art will be.

5. A senior editor reviews the first printouts of the composed pages. These pages are printed in pieces on 8 1/2-by-11-inch paper, by using the Print command Tile option. If the copy is too short, the editor adds copy or pull-out quotes to fill space. The editor also makes notes to the production staff if any headlines need to be kerned manually.

6. After each page is laid out and edited so that all columns are aligned, a member of the production group scrolls through each column, measures all spaces around headings and figures against the spacing guide, and adds ruled lines around article titles and pull-out quotes. The standard ruled lines are stored on the pasteboard and placed on the pages with the Copy and Paste commands. Headlines are kerned manually.

7. The final pages are printed full size on a Linotronic 300 typesetter.

Pages with graphs require special handling:

1. Graphs are created by using a spreadsheet graphing program to create the bars or lines.

2. The graphs are then opened in Freelance Plus, where additional formatting is performed.

3. The graphs are placed in PageMaker, where drop-shadow borders mark the positions, as shown in figure 13.20.

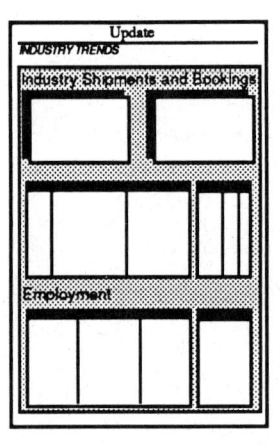

Fig. 13.20. Using drop-shadow boxes to mark the positions of graphs that appear in every issue.

Preparation for Reproduction

The final full-size typeset pages are marked for the printer. Color separations are printed using the Spot Color Overlay option in the Print menu for pages that have color. Tissue overlays show where halftones must be stripped in (see fig. 13.21). The photographs supplied to the printer may need to be marked for sizing and cropping.

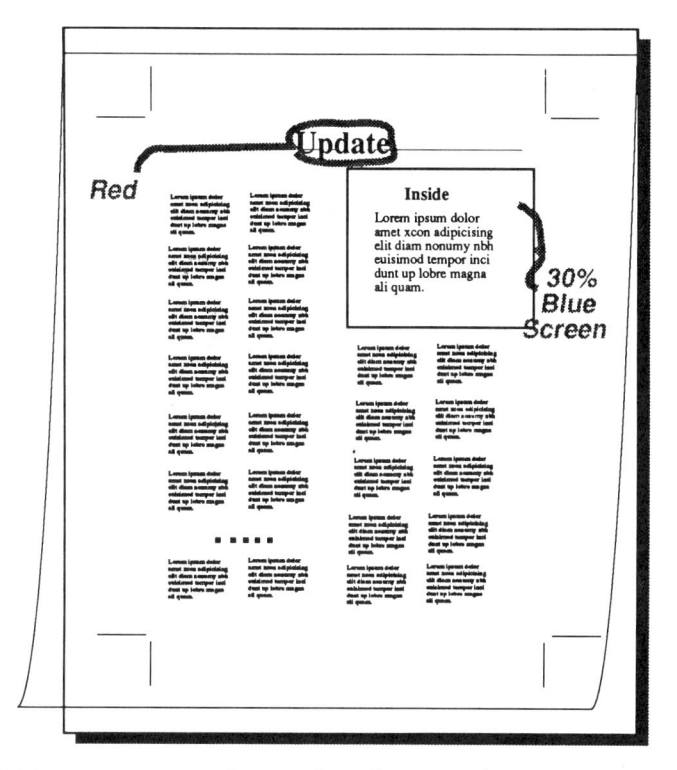

Fig. 13.21. Using tissue overlays to show the printer how to separate the image for color printing.

Besides the template, the second factor in making each issue's production run smoothly is a careful organization of disk files (see fig. 13.22). The team must be able to use the file names to distinguish one article from another within an issue. The team also must be able to distinguish between the latest version of an article and earlier versions that may have been left on disks or archived.

If the imported graphics are very large or numerous, you can use the Link command to manage the graphics as external files, rather than storing them as part of the PageMaker publication.

In naming files, the team follows certain conventions:

- All names begin with the issue number and are located in a subdirectory for that issue. Volume number is not necessary because it can be deduced from the date of the file.

- Signed articles are identified with the author's initials; three letters work best.

- Text and graphics files are distinguished by suffix only. See Chapter 6 for a list of graphics file suffixes and their meanings. The PageMaker file names include issue number and page numbers.

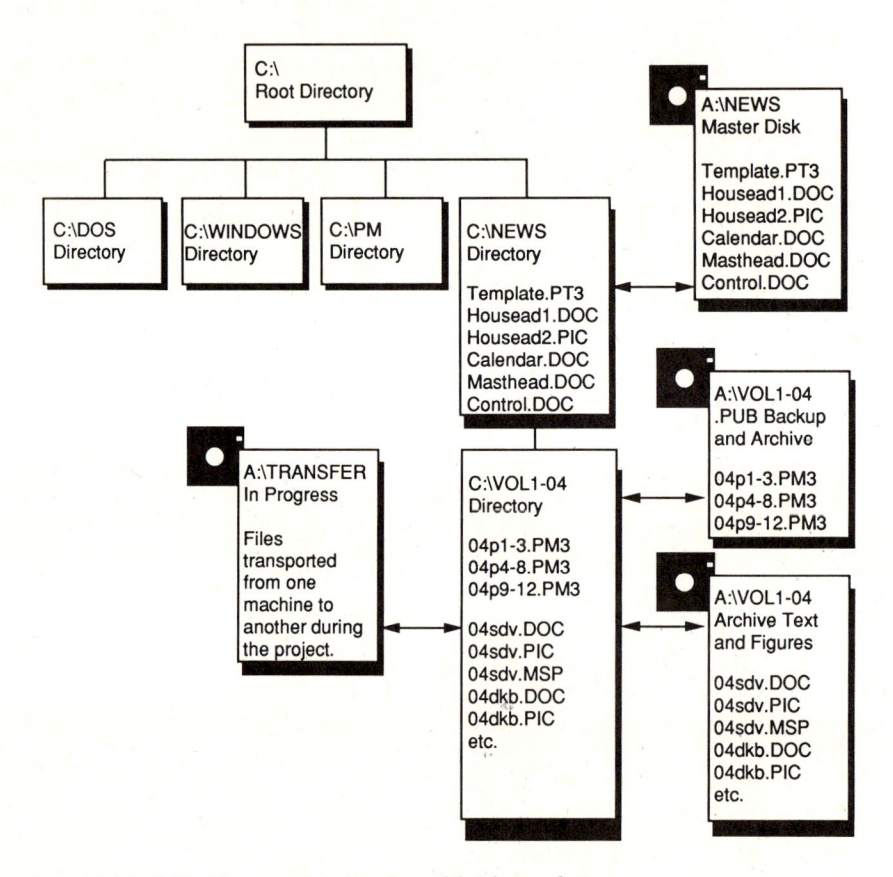

```
C:\
Root Directory
├── C:\DOS Directory
├── C:\WINDOWS Directory
├── C:\PM Directory
└── C:\NEWS Directory
    Template.PT3
    Housead1.DOC
    Housead2.PIC
    Calendar.DOC
    Masthead.DOC
    Control.DOC
    │
    └── C:\VOL1-04 Directory
        04p1-3.PM3
        04p4-8.PM3
        04p9-12.PM3
        04sdv.DOC
        04sdv.PIC
        04sdv.MSP
        04dkb.DOC
        04dkb.PIC
        etc.
```

A:\NEWS Master Disk
Template.PT3
Housead1.DOC
Housead2.PIC
Calendar.DOC
Masthead.DOC
Control.DOC

A:\TRANSFER In Progress
Files transported from one machine to another during the project.

A:\VOL1-04 .PUB Backup and Archive
04p1-3.PM3
04p4-8.PM3
04p9-12.PM3

A:\VOL1-04 Archive Text and Figures
04sdv.DOC
04sdv.PIC
04sdv.MSP
04dkb.DOC
04dkb.PIC
etc.

Fig. 13.22. Disk-file organization for tabloid newsletter.

The members of the production team keep current versions of their files on their hard disks in separate subdirectories set up for each issue. The staff members remove files from their hard disks when they send files to another computer for further changes. Each team member has a floppy disk reserved for each issue and backs up each file before sending it. The members also keep current the date and time stored in their systems so that questions about the most recent version of a file can be resolved by looking at the date of the file.

After the issue is printed, all current files are copied from all hard disks to one or more floppy disks and stored with other archived data away from the office.

Chapter Summary

The two examples presented in this chapter illustrate two extremes of production. The short newsletter has a relatively simple format and relaxed standards; the newsletter is easy to produce by a team whose primary function is *not* publishing. The tabloid-size newsletter, on the other hand, involves complex grid variations and strict production standards, which are applied by a team of professionals. The design and production tips provided at the beginning of the chapter and illustrated by the examples give you a good overview of the factors involved in producing a newsletter, magazine, or newspaper. You can apply these ideas to your own newsletter production and other publications.

14

Creating Overhead Transparencies, Slides, and Handouts

Desktop publishing usually is associated with books, reports, newsletters, and magazines, but PageMaker is also an excellent tool for creating presentation materials. You can develop tables and graphs in other programs, place them in PageMaker, and then add captions and topic summaries with PageMaker's text tool. To produce overhead transparencies, you can use a color printer, a laser printer, or a typesetter to print the images on clear acetate. If you want 35mm slides for a presentation, you can print the images on paper and then photograph the printed sheets.

Examples 14.1 and 14.3 in this chapter are designed specifically as overhead transparencies or slides (see fig. 14.1). Although examples 14.2 and 14.4 are designed as printed handouts, all examples share the following characteristics:

- Presentation materials consist of a series of similar parts.

- The items are primarily graphics, and words usually appear in a large type font.

- Each item requires in PageMaker some extra touches that are not possible in the graphics programs that create the graphs and diagrams.

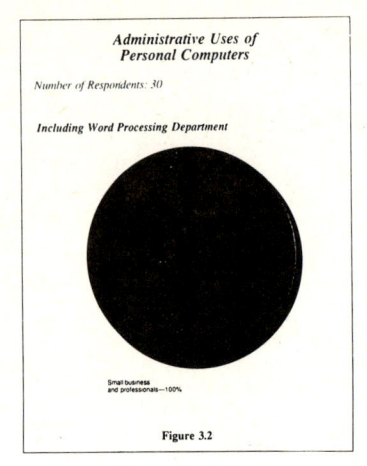

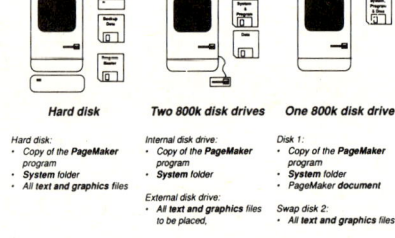

490 Part III: Examples of Publications Created Using PageMaker

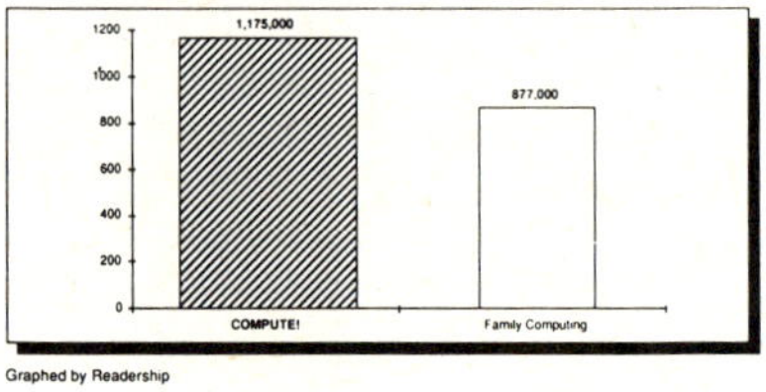

Fig. 14.1. Examples from the documents in this chapter.

Chapter 14: Creating Overhead Transparencies, Slides, and Handouts **491**

> ### Using Thumbnails To Help Prepare Your Presentation
> Use the Thumbnails option in the Print command dialog box to print a capsule summary of the topics for reference during the presentation (see fig. 14.2). Make notes on the thumbnails about the points you want to emphasize.

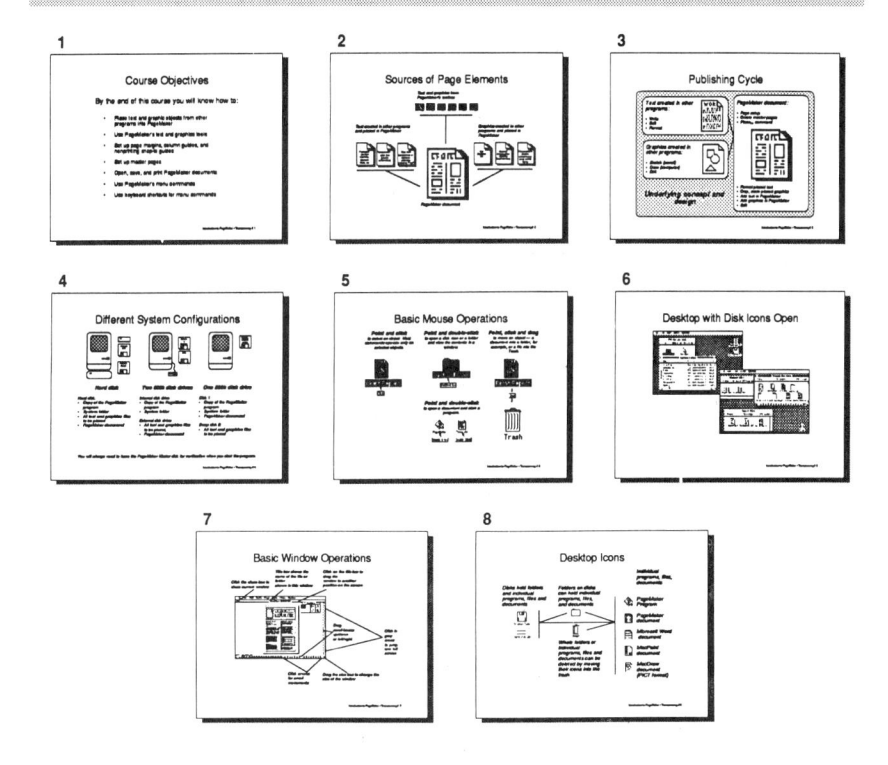

Fig. 14.2. Thumbnails used to help prepare presentation notes.

Design Principles

The design principles for presentation materials are derived from a mixture of basic design traditions, advertising guidelines, good training practices, and the technology of projecting images for an audience. The principles emphasized in this chapter concern the selection and sizes of typefaces, the amount and content of text, and the sizes of images.

Several guidelines are dictated by the dimensions of the final product; for instance, slides are usually 35mm by 24mm. Other guidelines are borrowed from the advertising industry because the best presentation materials are similar to billboards and display ads. These principles are described generally in this section, but applied to specific examples later in this chapter.

Select only one or two typefaces. Keep headings of the same level the same size. Keep similar text on all images in the same typeface.

This guideline is difficult to follow when graphic images come from different programs with different fonts. The number of fonts available in your spreadsheet-graphing program is probably smaller than the number of fonts available in your drawing program. PageMaker probably has more fonts than either your spreadsheet or your drawing program. Before you make the final specifications for a set of presentation materials, you should know all the font options of the programs you are using, as well as which fonts your printer can handle. Consult Chapter 10 for additional suggestions for controlling type specifications when images are drawn from several sources. Table 14.1 shows the typefaces commonly used in presentation materials.

Table 14.1
Typefaces Used in Tables, Graphs, and Overhead Transparencies

(Y = used; N = not used)

Typefaces	*Tables*	*Graphs*	*Overheads/Slides*
ITC American Typewriter	Y	Y	Y
ITC Avant Garde	Y	Y	Y
ITC Benguiat	N	N	N
ITC Bookman	N	Y	Y
Courier	Y	N	N
ITC Friz Quadrata	N	N	Y
ITC Galliard	Y	Y	Y
ITC Garamond	Y	Y	Y
Glypha	Y	Y	N
Goudy Old Style	N	N	Y
Helvetica	Y	Y	Y
ITC Korinna	Y	Y	N
ITC Lubalin Graph	Y	Y	Y
ITC Machine	Y	Y	Y
ITC New Baskerville	N	N	N
New Century Schoolbook	Y	Y	Y
Optima	Y	Y	Y
Palatino	Y	Y	Y
ITC Souvenir	N	N	Y

Typefaces	Tables	Graphs	Overheads/Slides
Times	Y	Y	Y
Trump Mediaeval	Y	Y	Y
ITC Zapf Chancery	N	N	Y

Try to limit the text on each overhead transparency or slide to no more than 25 words.

The number 25 is somewhat arbitrary. Although you set different limits for different purposes, brevity usually increases effectiveness. Billboard designers do not exceed 7 words if possible—and billboards have a strong impact. You also may have difficulty reading and understanding slides and overhead transparencies with too many words in small type.

You may set your limit at 50 words per page or more, especially if the text is on a handout rather than projected on a screen. The important point is to recognize that presentation and overhead materials require special attention to word count and point size.

Give graphs descriptive titles.

Your graph and table titles should include enough information to be meaningful. The graph title "1987 Income," for example, conveys little information. Use more descriptive titles, like those used in newspapers and magazines. For example, the title "1987 Income Shows Increased Widget Sales Relative to Other Categories" shows viewers the purpose of the graph.

For images that will be projected as slides or overhead transparencies, use large point sizes for the text.

For overhead transparencies, one rule of thumb is that the image on the paper (not the projected image) should be easy to read from approximately 10 feet (see fig. 14.3). For most audiences, this rule means that important words should be set no smaller than 36 or 24 points.

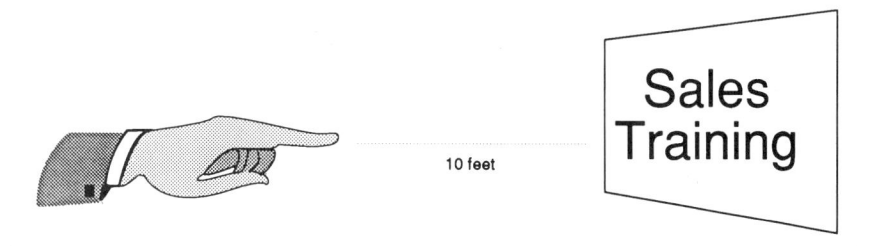

Fig. 14.3. Printout for overhead transparencies—readable at 10 feet.

For slides, an image on 8 1/2-by-11-inch paper should be easy to read from 7 feet (see fig. 14.4). This rule means that the text is 18 or 24 points in size, slightly smaller than the text for overhead transparencies.

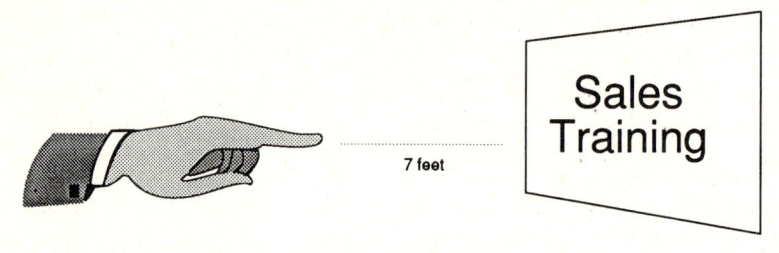

Fig. 14.4. Printout for slides—readable at 7 feet.

For overhead transparencies, fit all images into a 7-by-9-inch area.

This rule applies particularly to framed overhead transparencies, because a transparency frame usually has a 7 1/2-by-9 1/2-inch window (see fig. 14.5). You can specify a page size of 7 by 9 inches in the Page Setup dialog box, or you can set the margins of an 8 1/2-by-11-inch page to confine the text and graphics to a 7-by-9-inch area.

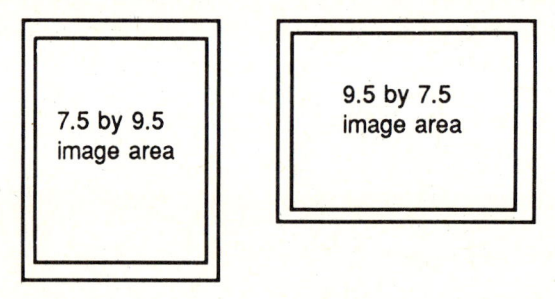

Fig. 14.5. Overhead transparency proportions.

The 7-by-9-inch ratio is a good guide to follow even when the images are not framed. Viewing conditions may restrict some people in the audience from seeing the edges of the overhead, but the center of the image should be visible to everyone in the room. If you want to use the same visual material for slides and transparencies, the image area measurement limitations used for overheads are also appropriate for use with 24mm-by-35mm slides. Another advantage of these presentation sizes is that your graphic images benefit from being surrounded by white space.

For materials to be made into slides, set all images within an area of approximately 3:2 proportions.

Frames for 35mm slides usually have a 35mm-by-24mm clear window. You should design your graphics—especially slide images with a ruled border—within this 3:2 proportion. If you are not using 35mm film for your slides, calculate the proper proportions based on the final size of your slide window. Use the following formula:

$$\frac{\text{slide width}}{\text{slide height}} = \frac{\text{PageMaker image width}}{\text{PageMaker image height}}$$

For example, if you decide to use a width of seven inches for your images, you can calculate the proportional height using this formula:

$$\text{PageMaker image height} = \text{PageMaker image width} \times \frac{\text{slide height}}{\text{slide width}}$$

If possible, design all the images in a series to use the same page orientation.

This consistency makes the production steps easier than mixing tall and wide pages in a series. If the material being presented is not consistent in orientation, you must develop the presentation materials in two or more different PageMaker publications.

Production Tips

The production tips in this chapter are specifically applicable to presentation materials to be projected on a screen. The tips explain ways to produce high-quality material easily. With these tips, you frequently can eliminate one or more production steps, thereby increasing efficiency.

The reasons for applying the following tips are described in general terms in this section. Some of the same tips are repeated with the examples, accompanied by explanations of their specific applications to that example.

Use automatic page numbering to number the set in sequence.

You can use PageMaker's automatic page-numbering feature to number the images used in a presentation. In this way, you easily can find the images in the PageMaker document when you want to update selected materials. If you do not want the numbers to show when you are projecting the images, use a small point size for the page number (12 points or less) and place the page numbers at the bottom of the image area (see fig. 14.6). This trick is used in all the examples in this chapter.

Part III: Examples of Publications Created Using PageMaker

```
┌─────────────────────┐
│                     │┐
│   Sales  Training   ││┐
│      Seminar        │││┐
│                     ││││┐
│       ┌─────────────┤││││
│       │ Overhead #1 ├┘│││
│       ├─────────────┤ │││
│       │ Overhead #2 ├─┘││
│       ├─────────────┤  ││
│       │ Overhead #3 ├──┘│
│       ├─────────────┤   │
│       │ Overhead #4 ├───┘
│       ├─────────────┤
│       │ Overhead #5 │
└───────┴─────────────┘
```

Fig. 14.6. Automatic page numbering for a set of presentation materials.

If the page sequence changes for particular presentations, or if presentations are shortened by omitting images, you still can use the automatic page-numbering feature to number the master set and print alternate numbers on each page in the same small font.

If you use a laser printer for the final output, use a gray screen rather than solid black areas for the best projection image.

If your laser printer's toner cartridge is at peak performance, you can get solid black areas to print evenly on special laser paper. Even with a good cartridge, however, black areas may print unevenly on acetate sheets for transparencies. This unevenness is exaggerated when the image is projected. You can reduce the effects of uneven toner by using gray fill patterns instead of solid black (see fig. 14.7).

To create overlays, copy the complete image on several pages; then delete portions of the image from each page.

To create a set of overhead transparencies with overlays, first create the whole image on one page in the PageMaker publication. Copy the complete image to subsequent pages—one for each overlay. Go back to the first page and delete the parts of the image that appear on the subsequent overlays. On each following page, delete all parts of the image except what appears on that single overlay. An example of a set of overlays is shown in figure 14.8.

You can achieve a similar effect when you prepare slides. Build the full image first, then copy the complete image to subsequent pages. Keep the full version on the last page in the series, and delete selected elements from each page preceding the full image (see fig. 14.9).

Pages in a series for overlays of overhead transparencies do not repeat the same elements, but each page in a series of slides maintains elements from the previous pages and adds new elements.

Chapter 14: Creating Overhead Transparencies, Slides, and Handouts **497**

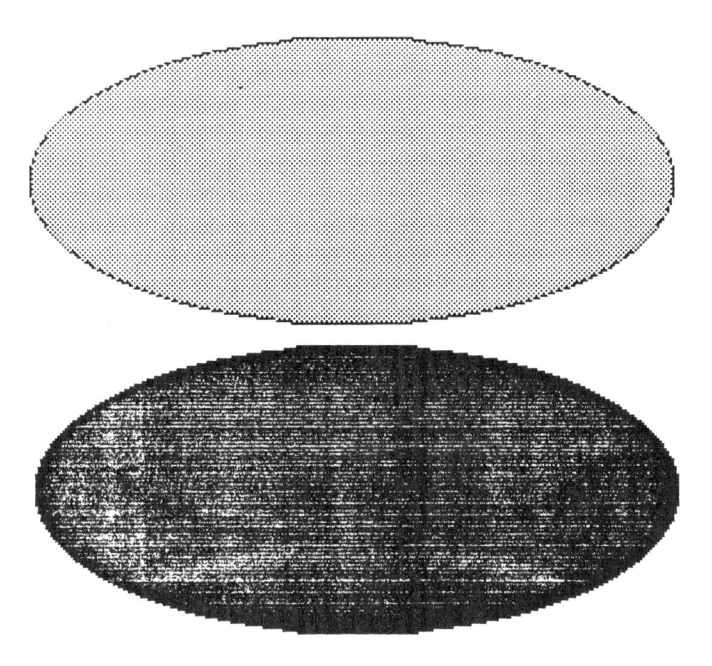

Fig. 14.7. Gray areas print and project better than solid black areas that wash out when printed on some laser printers.

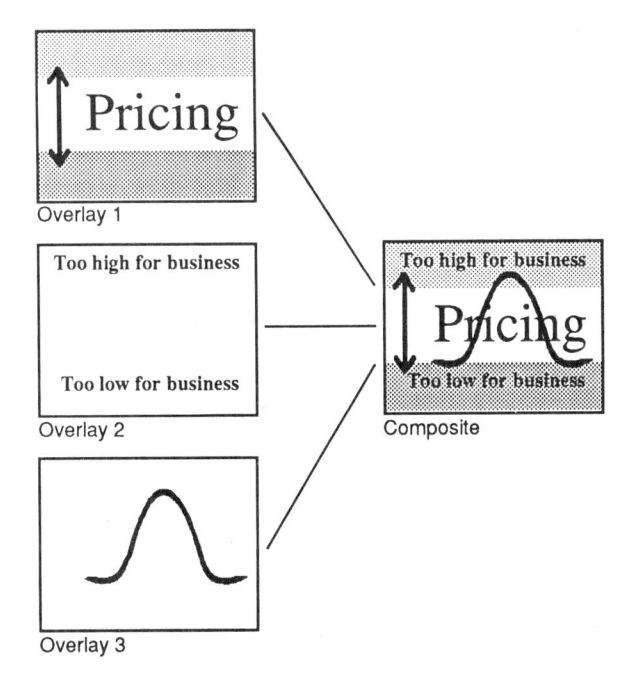

Fig. 14.8. In a series of overhead overlays, each page includes elements that are unique to the page.

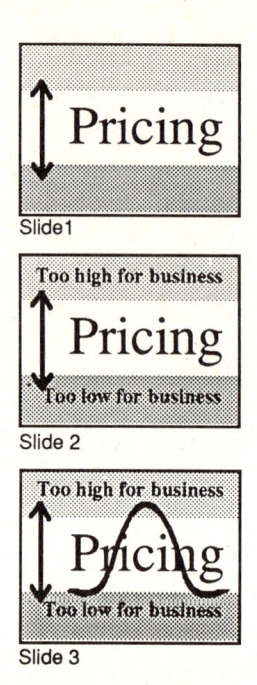

Fig. 14.9. *In a series of slides, each page includes all of the elements from the previous page plus new elements.*

Examples

The following examples demonstrate a variety of formats and illustrate various applications of the design principles and production tips discussed in the preceding sections. The four examples are the following:

    Example 14.1. A Series of Transparencies of Graphs in the Same Format

    Example 14.2. A Handout Showing Tabular Figures and Graphs

    Example 14.3. A Series of Transparencies with Varied Formats

    Example 14.4. A Handout Showing a Table with Shaded Columns

Example 14.1. A Series of Transparencies of Graphs in the Same Format

The series of pie graphs in this example is designed to report the results of a survey or questionnaire. Each pie graph represents a different question and the responses of a specific set of respondents. The production tips for this example apply to many similar situations, such as a series of sales reports on the same list of products (in which each pie represents a different geographical region or purchasing group), a series of stock reports (in which each graph represents a different stock), or a series of profit-and-loss projections for a new company or a new product (in which each graph represents a different set of assumptions about advertising expenses, pricing, and market penetration).

Description

This overhead presentation is composed of a series of pie graphs generated with a spreadsheet graphing program (see fig. 14.10). The percentage labels and part of the legend were retained from the graphing program, but the graph title and legend tags were cropped off when the image was placed in PageMaker. The legend text, graph titles, and captions then were added with PageMaker's text tools. Note that the titles are consistent in the use of font and point size, the organization of each graph is similar, and the numbering of the graphs is done in a consistent and meaningful way.

Design Principles

All the design principles described at the beginning of this chapter are applied in this report. Choices of typeface and the size of the type are especially important in these transparencies. Appropriate design principles discussed earlier in this chapter are repeated here in italic, and then applied to this example.

Select only one or two typefaces. Keep headings of the same level the same size. Keep similar text on all images in the same typeface. In this example, the choice of fonts in the spreadsheet graphing program is the limiting factor. The percentage labels around each pie graph are preserved from the graphing program because typing and locating the labels in PageMaker

500 Part III: Examples of Publications Created Using PageMaker

would be too time-consuming. The legend text and graph titles are typed in PageMaker in larger type sizes than those available with the graphing program.

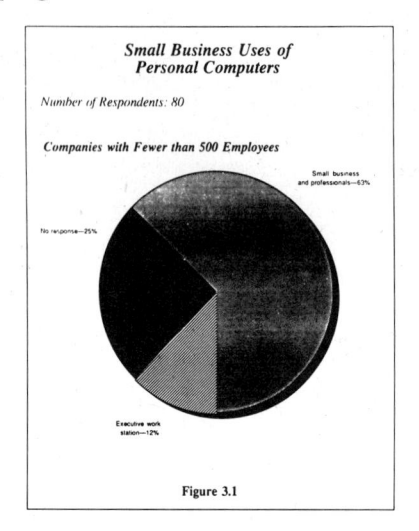

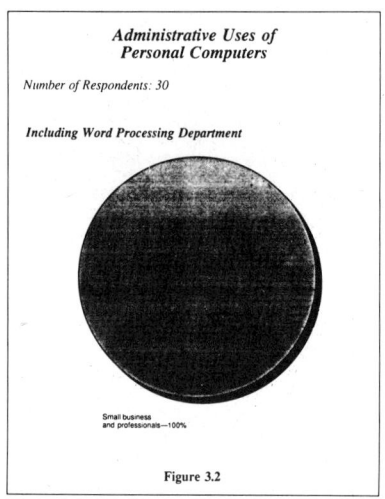

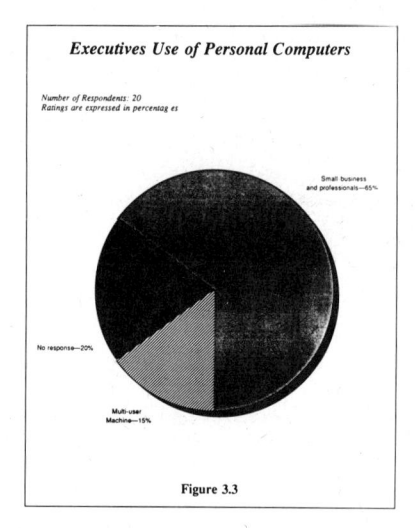

Fig. 14.10. Printout of a series of graphs in the same format.

For images that will be projected as slides or overhead transparencies, use large point sizes for the text. As already mentioned, the graphing program's titles are not large enough for effective presentation material. PageMaker's tools are used to add text in the larger type sizes required for presentations.

Production Tips

Producing transparencies is easy in PageMaker because the process is the same as that for producing any publication. Usually, you use only one template. For the best results, you need to be especially careful about printer settings, as explained in the following production tip.

If you use a laser printer for the final output, use a gray screen rather than solid black areas for the best projection image. The drop shadow around each pie is filled with a 40 percent screen. This arrangement eliminates the risk of uneven toner that could occur if the drop shadow were solid black (see figs. 14.10 and 14.13).

The Template

The Page Setup dialog box is used to set the margins that show the limits of the image area on each page (see fig. 14.11). The margin settings force an image area of 6 by 8 inches—well within the 7-by-9-inch limits recommended for transparencies.

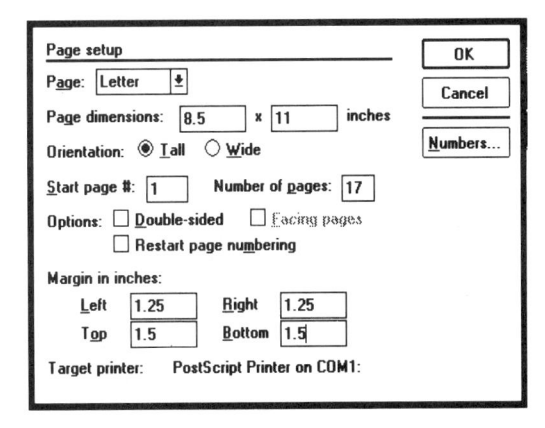

Fig. 14.11. Page Setup dialog box for a series of graphs in the same format.

The master page for this series includes the text of the legend, positioned to match the legend from the graphing program (see fig. 14.12). The graph title on each page is copied from a text block stored on the pasteboard of the template. The drop-shadow circles are created in PageMaker, stored on the pasteboard, and copied to each page.

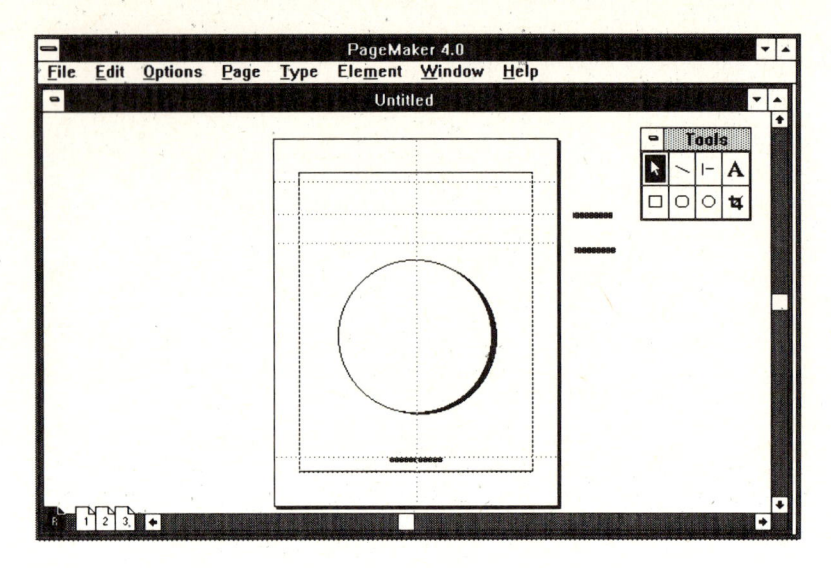

502 Part III: Examples of Publications Created Using PageMaker

Fig. 14.12. Template for a series of graphs in the same format.

Production Steps

Creating the series of graphs in this example is not difficult. If you take particular care with the first page, developing the others is simple. Take the following steps to produce this series of graphs:

1. Determine the content of the presentation.

2. Create a sample graph with the graphing program and use the Place command from the File menu to place the sample in PageMaker to check the size and position of the image. Based on this test, refine the specifications in the graph program (if your graph program enables you to adjust final graph size or font sizes).

3. Begin to build the template for the series by typing the legend text and page numbers on the master page. Draw a border around the image area and set guidelines for positioning the graphs. Type text in the size to be used for each graph title, and place the text on the pasteboard.

4. Create the drop shadow using PageMaker's circle tool and place the drop shadow on the page.

5. Place the sample graph (from step 2) on the page, and check the position of the legend text and the size of the drop shadows (see fig. 14.13). Make sure that the longest graph title fits on the page.

Chapter 14: Creating Overhead Transparencies, Slides, and Handouts **503**

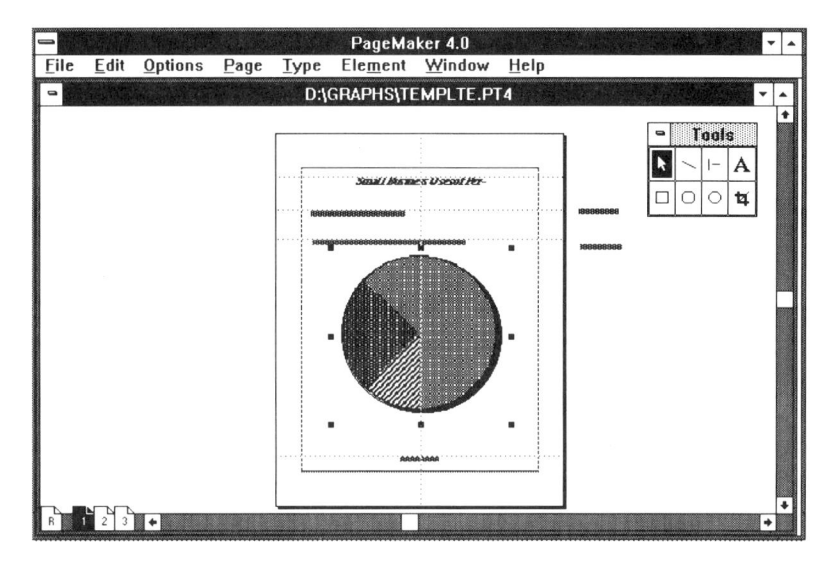

Fig. 14.13. Checking one sample graph against the template.

6. Create all the graphs with a graphing program that can transfer to PageMaker.

7. Place each graph in PageMaker, using the Place command from the File menu. Copy the title text block from the pasteboard, and type the current graph title before cropping out the graph title and legend text from the graphing program.

8. Save the file each time you complete a page.

All the graphs in this example are saved under file names that are shown in the alphabetical listing in the Place command dialog box. This order means using 01, 02, 10, and so on, instead of 1, 2, 10, and so on (see fig. 14.14). Otherwise, for example, the file GRAPH11 would precede GRAPH2 in the list of figures in the Place File dialog box. If the presentation is very large, you can use the Link command to manage the graphs as external files, rather than storing them as part of the PageMaker publication.

Example 14.2. A Handout Showing Tabular Figures and Graphs

Instead of a single presentation before a group, you sometimes may want to give each person information to keep. This practice is particularly good for presenting detailed or technical information, which probably cannot be absorbed in a single viewing.

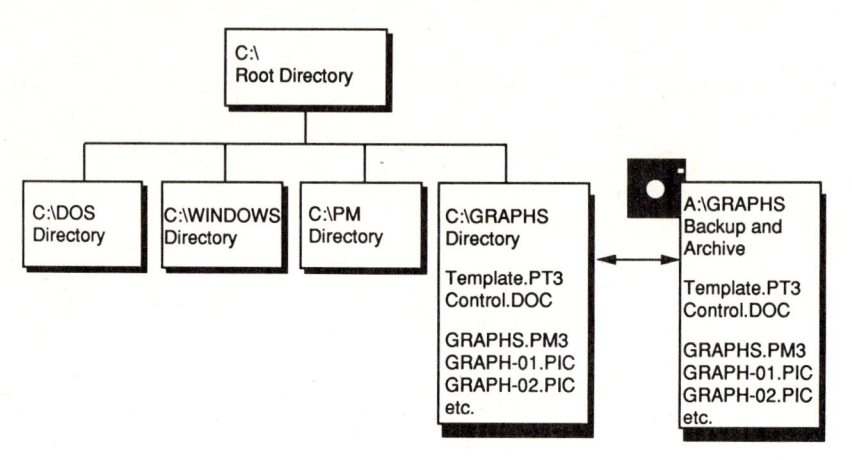

Fig. 14.14. Disk-file organization for a series of graphs.

Description

The images in this example are designed as handouts rather than overhead transparencies or slides. The goal is to show a table of statistics on the same page as a graph of those values (see fig. 14.15)—a combination that is not easy to achieve with a spreadsheet program alone. In fact, most spreadsheets do not support this feature.

Design Principles

All but one of the design principles given at the beginning of this chapter have been applied to this set of handouts. The exception is that you do not need to limit the text to 25 words if you count the entries in the tables of numbers. These figures are set in a small point size in order to leave white space on the pages. The small sizes are acceptable because these materials are handouts rather than overheads.

Production Tips

The production tips used for these handouts are different from those used in producing transparencies, as given at the beginning of this chapter. In the description of the template, however, and in the steps for production, you will find valuable instructions and shortcuts.

TOTAL ADULTS
Magazine Readership
SPRING 1986 MRI

	Totals	**COMPUTE!**	Family Computing
UNWGT	20330	**218**	186
(000)	170599	**1898**	1517
VERT%	100.00	**100.00**	100.00
HORZ%	100.00	**1.11**	.89
INDEX	100	**100**	100

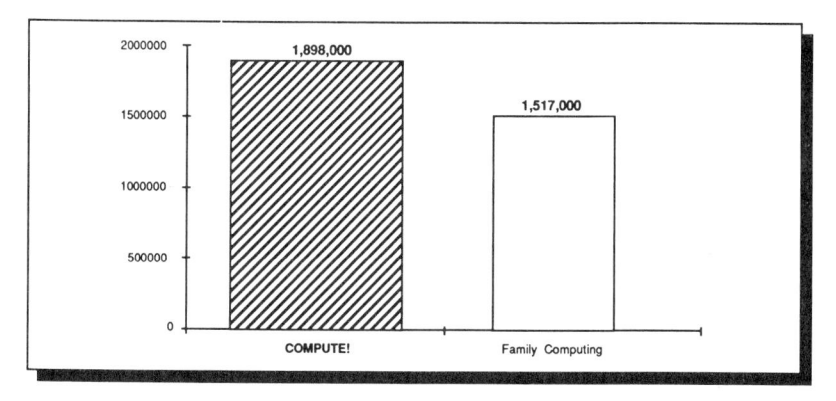

Fig. 14.15. Printout of page containing a table and graphs.

The Template

The template for the image in this example includes a ruled grid on the master page (for the tabbed text) and a drop-shadow border for the graphs. The numbers themselves are set up as tabbed dummy text stored on the pasteboard along with dummy text for the graph titles (see fig. 14.16). Ruler guides on the master page mark the positions of the title and table.

Production Steps

Some of the production steps for a series of transparencies also apply to these handouts. Combining tabular material with graphs, however, requires additional steps.

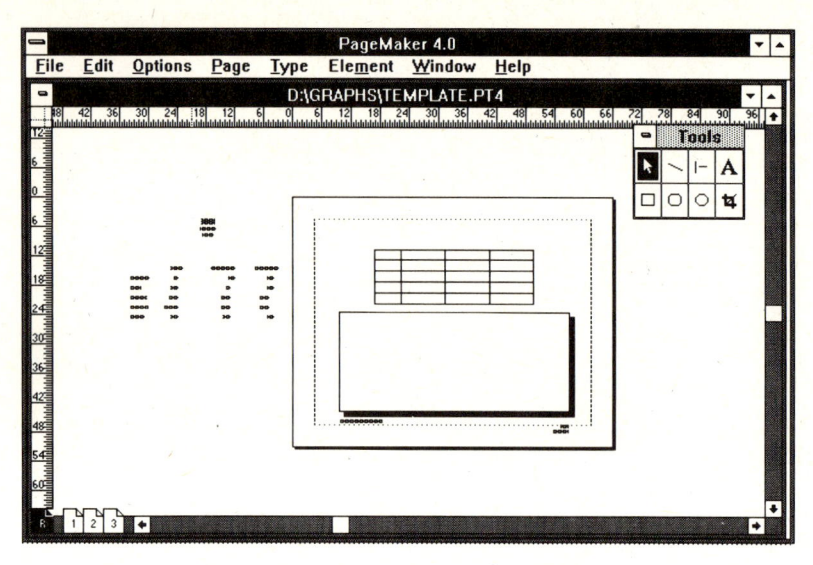

Fig. 14.16. The template for combined table and graphs.

1. Determine the content of the presentation.

2. Begin building the template for the series. Create the drop-shadowed grid using PageMaker's square-corner and perpendicular-line tools. Place the grid on the master page.

3. Type the tabbed numbers as a text block using dummy numbers, and set the tabs to match the grid. Place the tabbed dummy numbers on the pasteboard. (You could instead use the Table Editor to create the data, but typing the data directly into PageMaker is just as fast when the tables are small and simple and numerous.)

4. Create one sample graph with the drawing or charting program, and place the sample in PageMaker to check the size and position of the image. Based on this test, refine the specifications for the drawing program.

5. Make sure that the longest graph title fits in the area allowed before you specify the type size for the titles.

6. Create all the graphs with the drawing program.

   Because the graphs in this example are bar graphs and can be created easily in a drawing program that offers a wide range of formatting options, a spreadsheet graph program is not used. A template file is created with the drawing program and copied for each bar graph (see fig. 14.17). The template includes all the basic elements. Only the length of each bar needs to be adjusted.

877,000

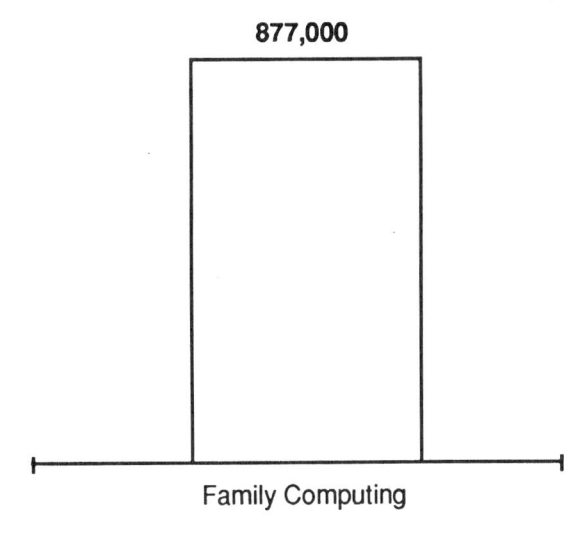

Family Computing

Fig. 14.17. Graph template from the drawing program.

7. Place each graph in PageMaker. Crop the graph titles entered in the drawing file, and re-create them using the dummy title text from the PageMaker template pasteboard.

8. Copy the tabbed dummy-number text block onto each page, and then edit the numbers (see fig. 14.18).

	Totals	COMPUTE!	Competitor
UNW GT	75	4	0
(000)	455	45	0
VERT%	0.27	2.37	0.00
HORZ%	100.00	9.89	0.00
INDEX	100	889	0

Fig. 14.18. Tabbed numbers and grid created with PageMaker tools.

9. Save the file each time you complete a page.

As in Example 14.1, the list of graph file names in the Place Command dialog box is in sequential order (see fig. 14.19). This order means using 01, 02, 10, and so on, rather than 1, 2, 10, and so on. (Otherwise, the file GRAPH11 would precede GRAPH2 in the list of figures in the Place file dialog box.) If the presentation is very large, you can use the Link command to manage the graphs as external files, rather than storing them as part of the PageMaker publication.

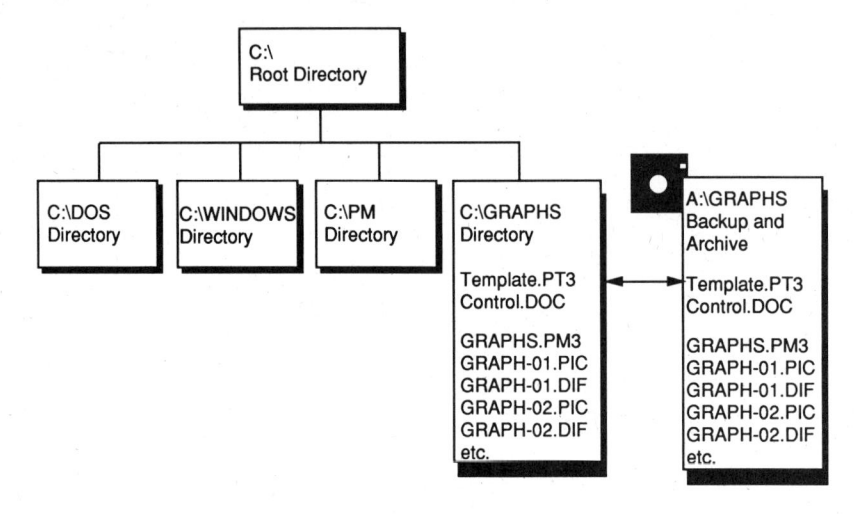

Fig. 14.19. Disk-file organization for a series of tables and graphs.

Example 14.3. A Series of Transparencies with Varied Formats

Frequently, you may want to combine different formats in a single presentation. For example, you may need an opening page with a scanned image or a list of points to be presented. You then may want to include graphs, tables of different sizes, and more explanatory material. This example shows you how to combine formats into a unified presentation.

Description

This set of overheads presents topics and concepts with a variety of formats (see fig. 14.20). The graphics include both figures from a drawing program and bit-mapped screen dumps. The grid has been changed from page to page to accommodate page-wide captions as well as titles and narrow figure labels.

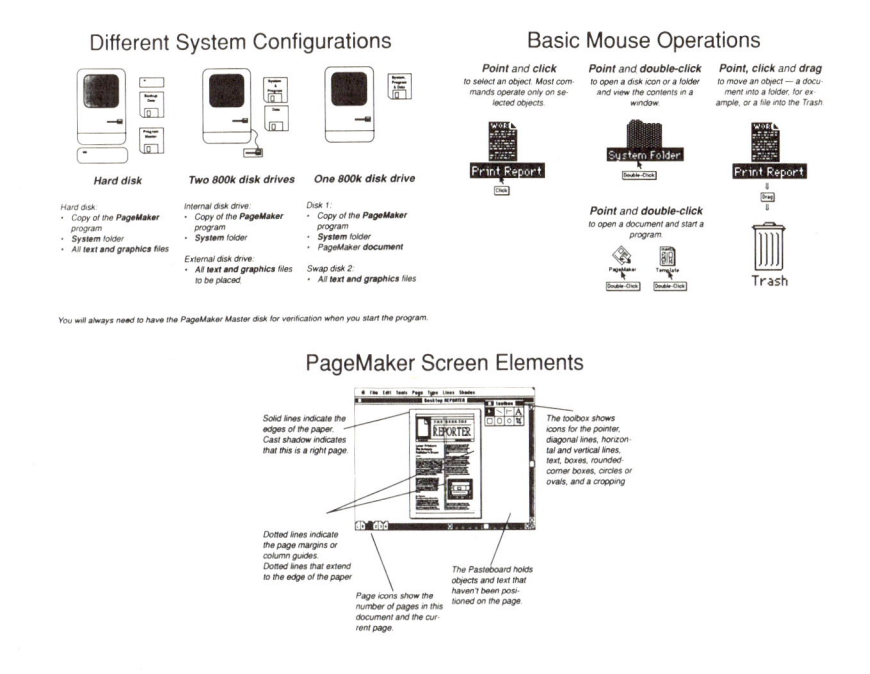

Fig. 14.20. Examples of varying formats in a single presentation.

Design Principles

Most of the design principles listed at the beginning of this chapter are demonstrated in this set of transparencies, but two exceptions merit some discussion. As mentioned previously, guidelines are just that: guidelines. At times, you will have valid reasons for exceptions. The two principles to be excepted are repeated here in italic, and then applied to this example.

Try to limit the text on each transparency to no more than 25 words. For this example, the number of words was extended to 50 to accommodate some of the detailed bulleted lists and figure captions. This exception to the rule is acceptable in this case because of the classroom setting in which these transparencies are used. Each transparency remains projected on the screen for several minutes as the instructor describes the concepts in detail.

For images that will be projected as slides or overhead transparencies, use large point sizes for the text. The smallest point size used on these transparencies is 16 (see fig. 14.21). In all the figures, Helvetica is used in four different sizes: 40, 26, 20, and 16 points. The relatively small 16-point captions are still easy to read because Helvetica is a sans serif typeface with individual characters that are actually larger than the same characters in 16-point Times.

Style name	Type specifications
Figure Title	40-point Helvetica, centered
	(all other elements will be flush left)
Subhead	26-point Helvetica, flush left
Bulletted lists	20-point Helvetica, flush left
Captions	16-point Helvetica Italic
	Auto leading used throughout

Fig. 14.21. Type specifications table for a series of transparencies with varied formats.

Production Tips

An important trick in this example is using automatic page numbering to number the set (as in every example in this chapter). The other primary production tip is to use the Column Guides command from the Options menu to change from one column to four columns as needed for each transparency (see the production steps).

The Template

The template for this example, shown in figure 14.22, consists of a master page with the basic grid laid out in ruler guides. Dummy text for each type of element is stored on the pasteboard. A spacing guide is provided for positioning text and graphics on a page. The running foot on the master page includes the page numbers.

Production Steps

The steps for producing this series of transparencies are similar to those for developing other transparencies. Before you begin production, create the text blocks you need and store them in the pasteboard. Proceed with the following steps:

Chapter 14: Creating Overhead Transparencies, Slides, and Handouts

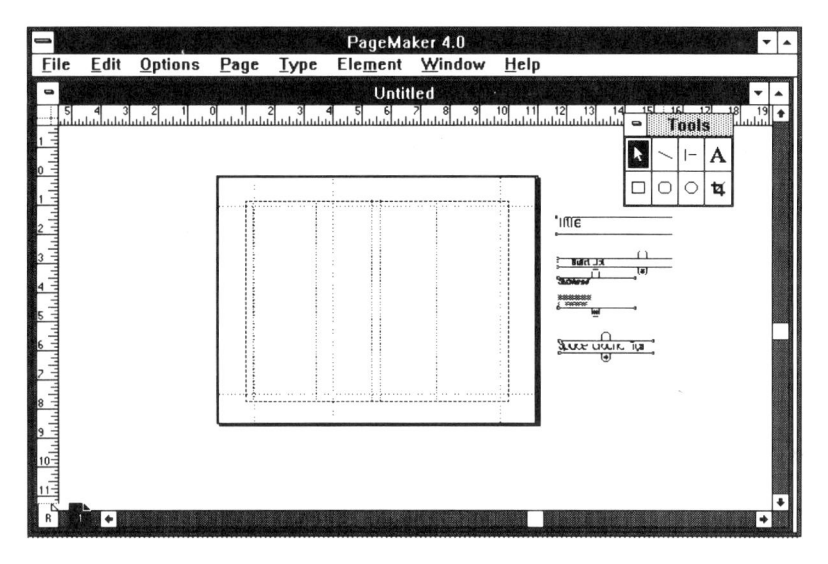

Fig. 14.22. The template for a series of transparencies with varied formats.

1. Develop the complete list of figures and decide which ones require placement of files from the drawing program or bit-mapped screen dumps.

2. Determine the maximum size for each figure; draw the figures to size in the drawing program.

3. Make the screen dumps using a screen-dump utility.

4. Open the PageMaker template and begin building each page. Clone the main heading text from the pasteboard first.

5. Place figures from other programs on each page before typing the captions. Use the Standoff option in the Text Wrap command to set the graphic boundary around the figures; clone the quarter-page-width text blocks from the pasteboard and type the appropriate text.

6. Make a rough layout of figures with captions to decide how many vertical grid lines are involved, and then use the Column Guides command to lay out the vertical grid. The column guides help position the figure labels, not define the width of the labels.

7. Determine the final layout of figures with captions and save the file each time you complete a page.

All screen dumps and figures from the drawing program are saved under file names that appear in the proper sequence in the alphabetical listing in the Place File dialog box. This order means using 01, 02, 10, and so on, rather than 1, 2, 10, and so on (see fig. 14.23). If the presentation is very large, you can use the Link command to manage the figures as external files, rather than storing them as part of the PageMaker publication.

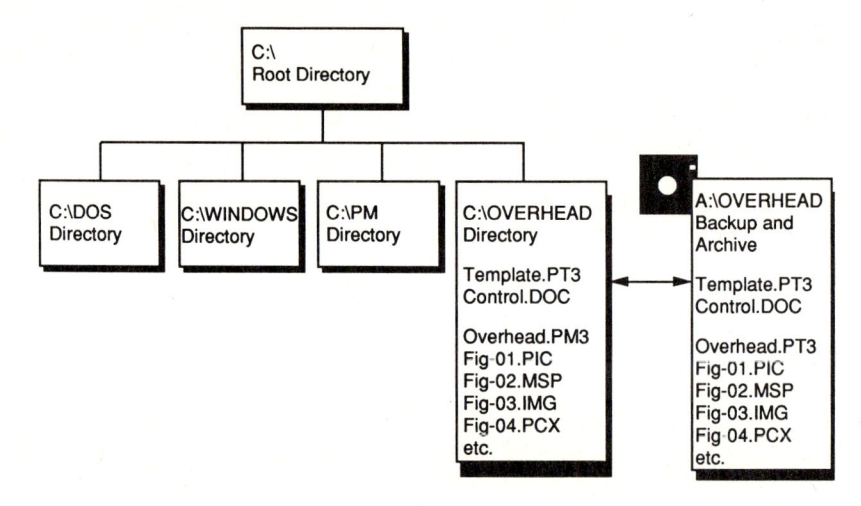

Fig. 14.23. Disk-file organization for a series of transparencies with varied formats.

Example 14.4. A Handout Showing a Table with Shaded Columns

This example shows how a shaded box created with PageMaker's square-corner tool can be used to highlight information that otherwise might be "lost in a sea of numbers" in a table. As in the first two examples in this chapter, the repeated use of the same format (with different figures on each page) enables you to position the gray box once on the master page, along with the ruled lines that set off the figures.

Description

This presentation series repeats a table of figures with the same column and row headings (see fig. 14.24), but each page shows the figures for a different time period. Every page uses a gray background to highlight the figures for the presenter's product against those of the competitors. You must use a very light gray background (no more than 10 percent) for readability.

HOME/PERSONAL COMPUTERS
SPRING 1986 MRI

		TOTALS	READ BYTE	**READ COMPUTE**	READ FAMILY COMPUTING	READ PERSONAL COMPUTING
TOTALS						
	UNWGT	20330	231	**218**	186	342
	(000)	170599	1466	**1898**	1517	2655
	VERT%	100.00	100.00	**100.00**	100.00	100.00
	HORZ%	100.00	0.86	**1.11**	0.89	1.5
	INDEX	100	100	**100**	100	100
HOUSEHOLD OWNS						
	UNWGT	2480	114	**134**	103	158
	(000)	19958	782	**1175**	877	1321
	VERT%	11.70	53.34	**61.91**	57.81	49.76
	HORZ%	100.00	3.92	**5.89**	4.39	6.62
	INDEX	100	456	**529**	494	425
APPLE COMPUTER						
	UNWGT	339	22	**17**	14	24
	(000)	2471	162	**209**	141	181
	VERT%	1.45	11.05	**11.01**	9.29	6.82
	HORZ%	100.00	6.56	**8.46**	5.71	7.32
	INDEX	100	763	**760**	642	471
COMMODORE						
	UNWGT	738	25	**63**	41	51
	(000)	6208	222	**537**	376	575
	VERT%	3.64	15.14	**28.29**	24.79	21.66
	HORZ%	100.00	3.58	**8.65**	6.06	9.26
	INDEX	100	416	**778**	681	595
IBM						
	UNWGT	205	19	**6**	8	21
	(000)	1557	95	**34**	50	122
	VERT%	0.91	6.48	**1.79**	3.30	4.60
	HORZ%	100.00	6.10	**2.18**	3.21	7.84
	INDEX	100	710	**196**	361	503

		TOTALS	READ BYTE	**READ COMPUTE**	READ FAMILY COMPUTING	READ PERSONAL COMPUTING
GRAPHIC TABLET						
	UNWGT	123	6	**6**	5	8
	(000)	928	30	**30**	18	39
	VERT%	0.54	2.05	**1.58**	1.19	1.47
	HORZ%	100.00	3.23	**3.23**	1.94	4.20
	INDEX	100	376	**291**	218	270
PLOTTER						
	UNWGT	58	3	**3**	1	3
	(000)	411	21	**15**	2	15
	VERT%	0.24	1.43	**0.79**	0.13	0.56
	HORZ%	100.00	5.11	**3.65**	0.49	3.65
	INDEX	100	595	**328**	56	235

For more information on how COMPUTE! best serves your advertising needs in reaching the home market of personal computers owners, please call:

1. *New England & Mid-Atlantic*
   Bernard J. Theobald, Jr 212 315-1665
   Tom Link 212 315-1665
2. *Southeast & Foreign including Canada*
   Harry Blair 919 275-9809
3. *Midwest, Southwest, West & British Columbia*
   Jerry Thompson Chicago 312 726-6047
   Lucille Dennis Texas 713 731-2605 • Colorado 303 595-9299 • California 415 348-8222

COMPUTE! Publications Inc
825 Seventh Ave, New York, NY 10019

*Source: Spring 1986 MRI

Fig. 14.24. Printout of tables.

Production Tips

One production tip in particular is emphasized in this example. Type titles and column headings with PageMaker's tools, but use a word processor to prepare the rows of data. This tip is especially important here because the table has so many rows and columns of data. Remember that tabs can be repositioned in PageMaker if needed. The time required to produce this set of handouts, however, could double if you use PageMaker alone to prepare all the text.

The Template

The template in this example includes the table title, column headings, and slug at the bottom of the page (see fig. 14.25). A ruled line separates the headings from the rest of the text. Ruler guides show the positions of the rows of data and the time-period subhead. Dummy text for the time-period entry is stored on the pasteboard.

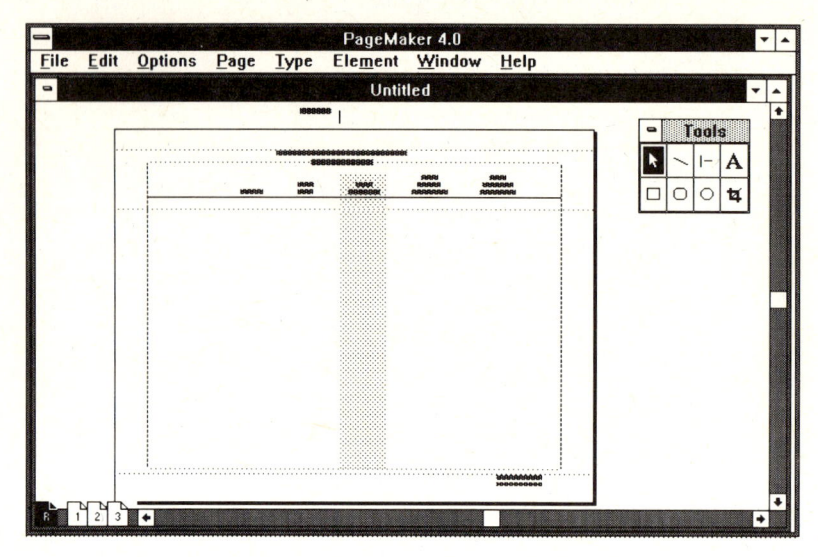

Fig. 14.25. The template for a table with shaded columns.

This design uses Palatino and Helvetica in a limited variety of sizes and styles, as listed in figure 14.26.

Style name	Type specifications
MAIN HEAD	14-point Palatino Bold, 14-point leading, all caps, centered on page
SUBHEAD	12-point Helvetica, all caps, centered on page
COLUMN HEADS	11-point Palatino, all caps, centered in column
PRODUCT NAMES	11-point Palatino, 18-point leading, all caps, flush left
Numbers	11-point Helvetica, 12-point leading, flush right in column
Slug (at bottom of page)	9-point Helvetica, flush left

Fig. 14.26. Type specifications table for a table with shaded columns.

Production Steps

Because of the columns and the shading, constructing this handout involves more steps than the preceding examples. For good results, work carefully through the following procedure.

1. Collect the data and determine the number of columns and rows of data required for each table. Create one sample table in a spreadsheet or the Table Editor before building the PageMaker template.

2. Open a PageMaker publication and place the sample table on the master page for use in setting up the guides.

3. If the table is imported as text, you can set the text with the desired type specifications, and use PageMaker's Indents/Tabs command to set the tabs that distribute the columns evenly across the page. Tabs can be aligned to the right of the text or on the decimal points. Change the leading to make the rows fit the page length. If necessary, change the type specifications to make the data fit the width of the page. Make a note of the tab settings used in PageMaker, and set the same tabs in the word processor.

4. Draw a gray box (10 percent) to cover the column to be highlighted on every page, and use the Send to Back command from the Element menu to place the gray box behind the text.

5. Type the column headings at the top of the text block on the master page; delete the text of the sample table from the master page.

6. Add the text of the table title at the top of the master page.

7. Type the dummy text for the time period on the pasteboard. Use horizontal ruler lines to mark the positioning of the time-period text and the top of the tabular text on the page.

8. Draw a two-point rule below the column heads. Type the slug at the bottom of the master page.

9. In the spreadsheet, type the data for all pages of the presentation. Save the data as a single file, and then save the file as text-only.

10. Open the template, and begin placing the tabular data on the first page. Set tabs as noted in step 3. Be sure that the tabs are the same throughout the document.

11. Continue placing data on all the pages, saving the publication at regular intervals.

This publication has only five files: the original spreadsheet data, the text-only spreadsheet data, the formatted word processing file, the PageMaker template, and the finished publication (see fig. 14.27). If this set of materials is used only for this presentation and will not be re-created with different data, the template file can be the final publication, leaving only one PageMaker file in the system.

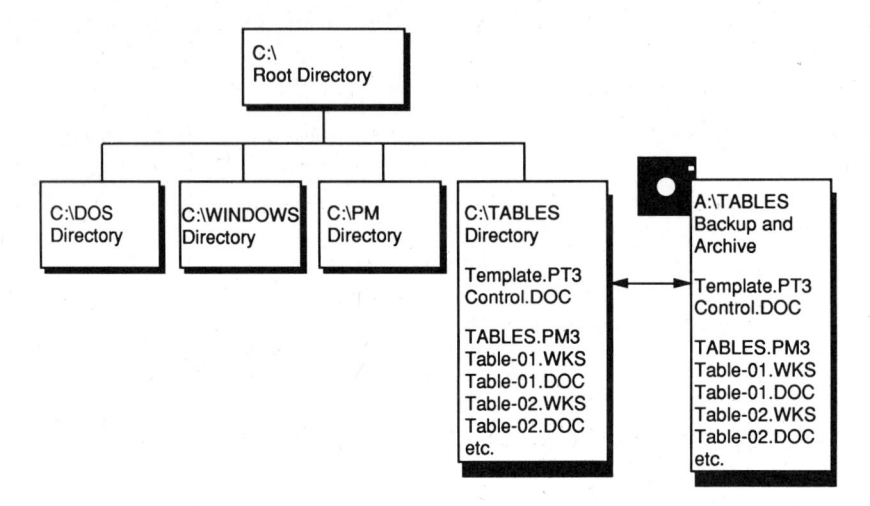

Fig. 14.27. Disk-file organization for a handout showing a table with shaded columns.

When archiving the files, you can discard the text-only file. If, however, you expect to change the figures extensively for next year's presentation, save the spreadsheet data. Replacing old entries in each column with new entries should be easy as long as the row and column headings remain the same. If you expect minor changes, you can update the PageMaker file directly. If you expect to change many entries in scattered rows and columns, save the formatted text file for those changes.

Chapter Summary

Transparencies, slides, and handouts are used frequently in almost all business settings. With PageMaker, you can create effective presentation materials in less time and at less expense than with other methods. As demonstrated in the examples in this chapter, you have few limitations as to the formats and combinations you can use. You also can save the files so that you can use the same templates to create new transparencies.

15

Creating Brochures, Price Lists, and Directories

This chapter shows you how to use PageMaker to create brochures, price lists, and directories (see fig. 15.1). These documents are grouped together because they are promotional materials, but they appear in a wide variety of forms.

Brochures frequently are designed to fit on 8 1/2-by-11-inch paper folded into three panels, or as four (or more) 8 1/2-by-11-inch pages printed on 11-by-17-inch paper and folded in half. These formats are economical because they don't require special cutting and they fit neatly into standard business envelopes. Price lists often are produced in one of these formats unless the lists are very long and in booklet form. In either case, price lists usually are mailed in standard business envelopes. Directories and membership lists can be longer than brochures and price lists, and some lists are bound as books rather than stapled as booklets. Regardless of the final trim size, PageMaker easily handles all these formats.

In a PageMaker file, brochures usually are only one or two pages long, although the finished document may be folded into four or more panels, as in Example 15.1. Example 15.2 is four pages long; it is printed on 11-by-17-inch paper and folded in half. Some of the tips in this chapter also can be used to produce longer brochures, such as the booklets in the third and fourth examples. (See Chapter 12 for more tips on producing longer documents.)

518 Part III: Examples of Publications Created Using PageMaker

Example 15.1

Example 15.2

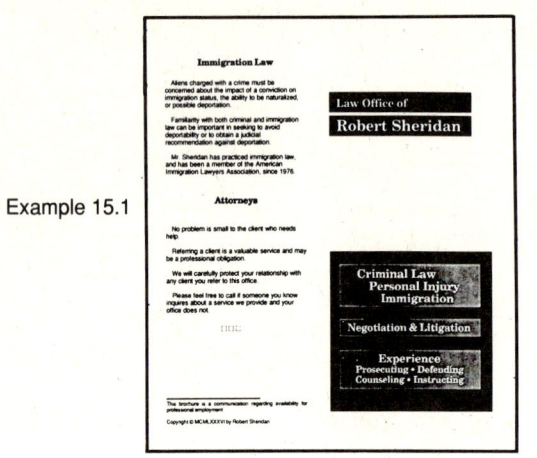

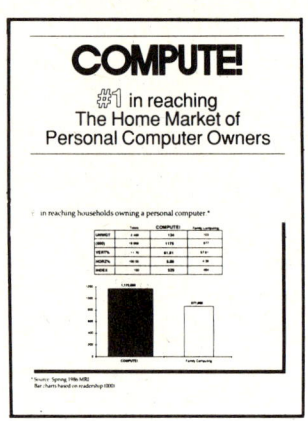

Example 15.2

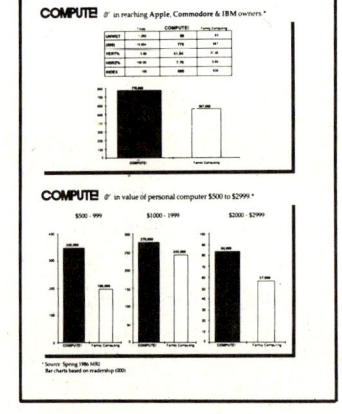

Example 15.3

Example 15.4

Example 15.5

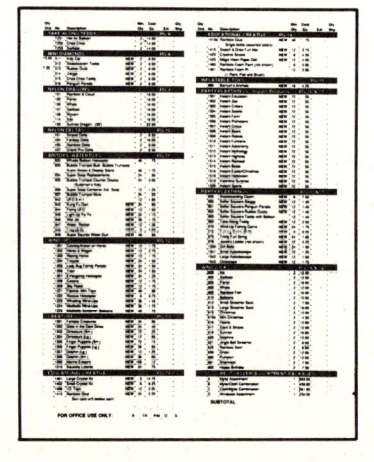

Fig. 15.1. Examples of documents in this chapter.

Price lists can be any number of pages long. The tabbed-list format shown in Example 15.5 (a tabloid price list) can be used for restaurant menus, wine lists, parts lists, inventories, telephone lists, and many other documents. Long lists, like member lists, can be derived from spreadsheet data or database files. Example 15.3 (a membership directory) shows how a database file can be converted to a list.

The longer publications in this category are often a nonstandard size because the final pages may be trimmed and folded. If the directory or price list is more than eight pages long, the booklet can be stapled or bound.

Design Principles

Many documents in these categories follow the basic design principles recommended throughout this book (particularly in Chapters 10 through 14), but you will find exceptions to the guidelines when applied to brochures in general (and to the publications in Chapter 16). Two design principles merit a full discussion in this chapter: the use of white space and the limit on the number of different typefaces used.

Don't be afraid of white space.

White space is especially important if the publication presents your product or service to your clients and the general public. For example, a price list also may serve as a detailed catalog of your products, with illustrations to attract the readers' interest or to explain the value of a special offer. Increased white space can improve the overall effectiveness of the publication as a sales tool.

Decreased effectiveness can occur if you put too many words in a brochure or list of members or services. The final document appears uninviting, and readers may ignore anything written in small type.

When you work with a small format, opening up white space may translate into writing less copy or using fewer illustrations. If you are creating a brochure for a small business, you probably want to give the readers as much information as possible but, at the same time, save printing and postage costs by holding down the number of pages. If you are writing your own copy, follow the example of professional copy writers, who can get a point across in the number of words specified by the designer. By choosing your words carefully, you can get a few important points across and influence the reader to call for your service or come to your store.

Adding pages to your publication design sometimes can be done without significantly increasing the printing or production costs. If you start out with a specific number of pages as a goal and find that this page limit creates a crowded design, you should check into the cost of adding pages.

This guideline is often relaxed in functional reference listings such as telephone directories for an association, a company, or a department and for long inventory lists or price lists used for reference rather than for marketing. If you have a great deal of information in a repetitive format, as in a price list for a large store or warehouse, the reader can find a specific product more easily if the information is compact.

Use only one or two different typefaces in a document.

Table 15.1 shows some of the typefaces used for the types of publications presented in this chapter. Notice that brochures can use almost any typeface, but lists usually are limited to typefaces readable in small sizes.

Table 15.1
Typefaces Used for Brochures, Price Lists, and Directories

(Y = used; N = not used) *Typefaces*	*Brochures*	*Price Lists*	*Directories*
ITC American Typewriter	Y	N	N
ITC Avant Garde	Y	Y	Y
ITC Benguiat	Y	N	Y
ITC Bookman	Y	N	N
Courier	N	N	N
ITC Friz Quadrata	Y	N	Y
ITC Galliard	Y	N	Y
ITC Garamond	Y	N	N
Glypha	N	Y	Y
Goudy Old Style	Y	N	N
Helvetica	Y	Y	Y
ITC Korinna	Y	N	N
ITC Lubalin Graph	Y	N	N
ITC Machine	Y	N	N
ITC New Baskerville	Y	Y	N
New Century Schoolbook	N	Y	Y
Optima	Y	N	N
Palatino	Y	Y	Y
ITC Souvenir	Y	N	N
Times	Y	Y	Y
Trump Mediaeval	Y	Y	Y
ITC Zapf Chancery	Y	N	N

The choice of typeface sets the tone of the piece. Brochures often use decorative or unusual typefaces for the headings and sometimes for the body copy. The typeface you choose can convey a sense of seriousness, elegance, or frivolity. If you are not sure how different typefaces affect the reader, you should stay with the traditional faces rather than experiment with more decorative ones. Traditional typefaces (and their modern adaptations) include American Typewriter, Avant Garde, Bookman, Galliard, Garamond, Goudy, Helvetica, Korinna, Lubalin Graph, New Baskerville, New Century Schoolbook, Optima, Palatino, Times, and Trump Mediaeval. Decorative typefaces include Benguiat, Friz Quadrata, Machine, Souvenir, and Zapf Chancery.

In addition to the preceding principles, use the following guidelines (discussed in Chapters 12 and 14) for promotional materials:

- Use all capital letters as a deliberate design strategy rather than as a method for emphasizing text or showing a heading.
- Treat all figures consistently: fonts, line weights, and fill patterns.
- Be sure that the space between text and graphics is the same for all figures.
- Use the same graphic elements to carry the theme throughout the document.
- Use ruled lines to help set off the grid of the pages.
- All columns on all pages should bottom out to the same point.

These principles, and the two discussed in detail in the preceding paragraphs, are repeated in the examples along with comments about their applications to the specific examples.

Production Tips

The first production tip has been mentioned repeatedly throughout this book, but the second tip is unique to the list formats in this chapter. The application of these tips to promotional materials is described generally in this section. In the "Examples" section, specific tips are repeated with explanations of their applications to the specific examples.

Use templates if you are producing more than one brochure.

If you are designing a series of brochures describing different products offered by the same company, you can develop one template and clone it for each brochure. If you are a designer with many clients, however, you may want each brochure you produce to be unique, and therefore you should not use a template system.

Regardless of how the details of the designs change from one brochure to another, you still can create a template for any series of brochures with the same paper size and number of folds. Figures 15.2 and 15.3 show two types of templates for folded brochures. The text typed on each page of the template shows the sequence of the panels when the brochure is folded.

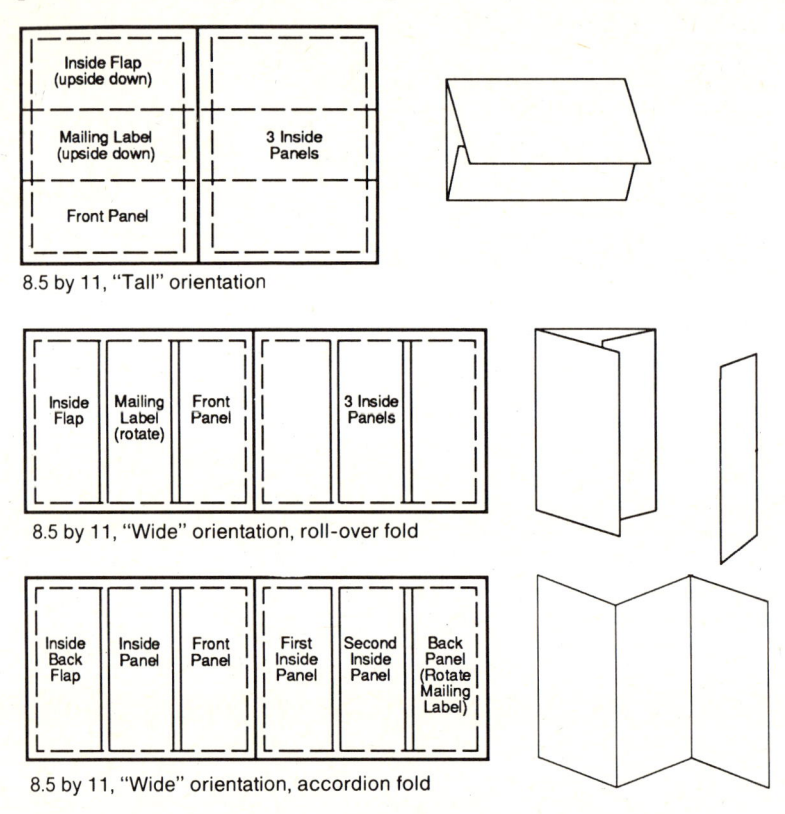

8.5 by 11, "Tall" orientation

8.5 by 11, "Wide" orientation, roll-over fold

8.5 by 11, "Wide" orientation, accordion fold

Fig. 15.2. Templates for three-panel brochures.

If your laser printer forces a wide margin around large paper sizes, you can solve this problem by using the trick described in the discussion of Example 15.1. In the template for the four-panel, legal-size brochure, 8 1/2-by-11-inch paper was used to get around the margins imposed by the laser printer. See the production tips for the four-panel brochure for an explanation of why this procedure was required.

8.5 by 14, "Tall" orientation, two half-folds

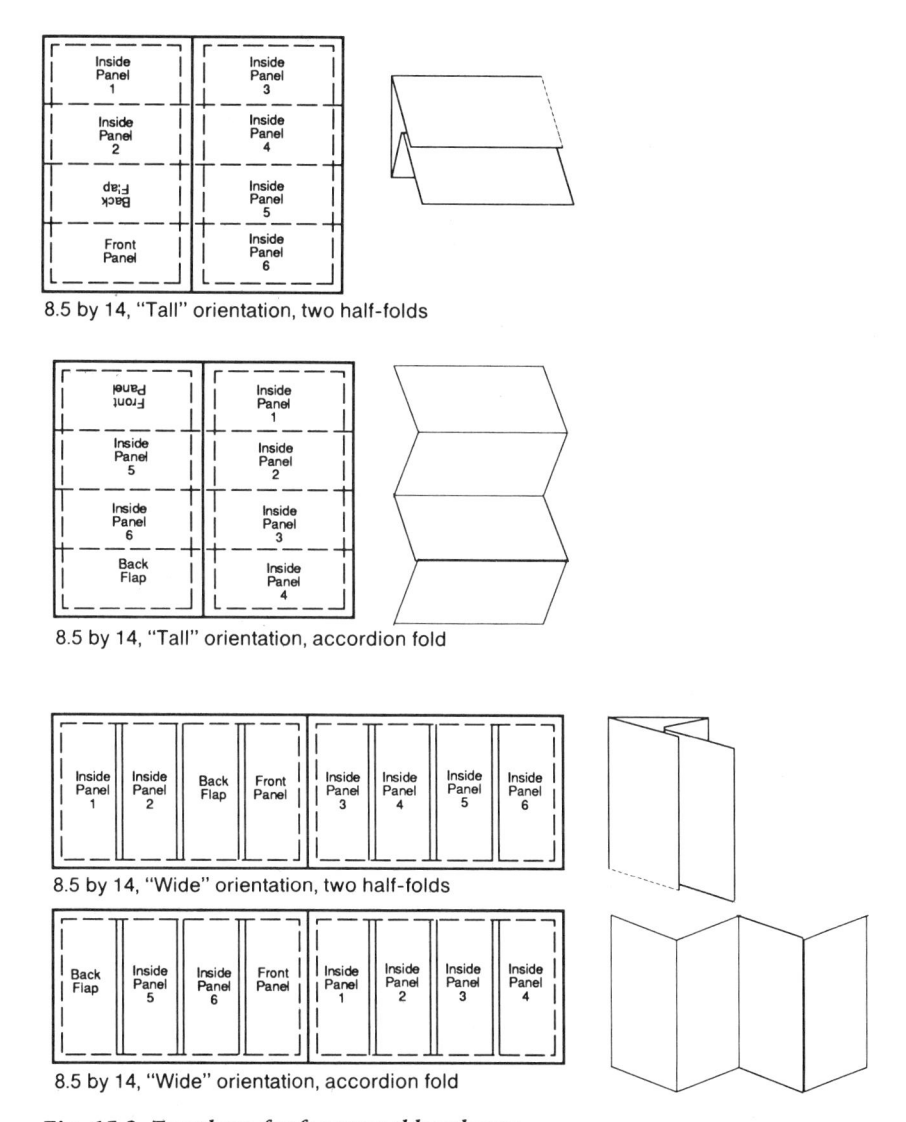

8.5 by 14, "Tall" orientation, accordion fold

8.5 by 14, "Wide" orientation, two half-folds

8.5 by 14, "Wide" orientation, accordion fold

Fig. 15.3. Templates for four-panel brochures.

Compensate for ragged-right text by setting unequal right and left margins.

The need for a balanced appearance is evident in all the examples. Because of the ragged-right text, the right margin may appear to be different from the left. You can compensate for this visual difference by using a wider left margin setting or a narrower right margin.

For brochures containing mostly graphics with little text, add text to the page after you have positioned your graphics.

In many brochures, graphics are the major design strategy. When the graphics are the most important factor of the page layout, you can save time by changing the text to fit the graphics instead of trying to change the graphics to fit the text.

Take a small amount of data from a spreadsheet or database through a test run of the complete production cycle before you complete the specifications for a long list.

If you are converting data from a spreadsheet or a database, you should run a small sample of the data through the production steps before you complete your design specifications. In this way, you can develop a list of specific required steps and learn how many design specifications can or must be handled in the database or spreadsheet. Examples 15.3 and 15.4 use database lists, and the discussion outlines the steps required to convert the data into text for PageMaker.

Brochures, price lists, catalogs, and service directories can be illustrated with photographs or computer art. For handling artwork in these examples, follow the principles presented in Chapters 12 and 13:

Use black boxes to reserve space for halftone photographs dropped in by the printer.

Use white boxes to reserve space for line art to be pasted in before being sent to the printer.

Examples

The examples in this chapter demonstrate the wide range of formats PageMaker can produce. You also learn how to use databases to produce different kinds of promotional and informative publications. The following examples are presented in this chapter:

Example 15.1.   A Four-Panel Brochure Printed on Two Sides

Example 15.2.   A Four-Page Brochure Consisting of Many Repeated Elements

Example 15.3.   A Two-Column Membership Directory Derived from a Database

Example 15.4.   A Single-Column List of Products with Descriptions, Prices, and Suppliers

Example 15.5.   A Tabloid Price List with Horizontal and Vertical Rules

Example 15.1. A Four-Panel Brochure Printed on Two Sides

The brochure in this example is designed to be printed on two sides of 8 1/2-by-14-inch (legal-size) paper and folded into four panels. This same design can be adapted for any folded document. (Refer to figures 15.2 and 15.3 and the accompanying discussion to see how templates can be used for folded brochures.)

Description

This brochure may surprise you. Even though the final brochure is printed on 8 1/2-by-14-inch paper (a size PageMaker supports), the page size is 8 1/2 by 11 inches. The final printouts are pasted on the 8.5-by-14-inch layout. The screens behind some of the text in the final printed piece are created by a photographic halftoning process (see fig. 15.4). Although PageMaker creates screens, they are used in this example for draft reviews only, not for the final camera-ready printouts. The production tips for this four-panel brochure describe why PageMaker's screens were not used.

Design Principles

Two design principles merit special mention in this case. The use of white space gives a pleasing uncluttered appearance, and unity is achieved by repeating the graphics.

Don't be afraid of white space. Keep text to a minimum. This brochure violates this guideline. The writer on this project was given no word count at the beginning, and the designer had no idea how long the delivered text would be. As a result, in early drafts of this brochure, the text filled every page from margin to margin. After seeing the first draft, the designer worked closely with the writer to reduce the number of words to fit the space and leave more white space on each page, but the pages are still somewhat crowded.

Let the same graphic elements carry the theme throughout the document. In this case, shaded backgrounds are used throughout the brochure. This simple graphic element unifies the panels. These screens are created with PageMaker's square-corner tool for the draft review cycles, but they are removed for the final printout and added as halftones by the offset printer.

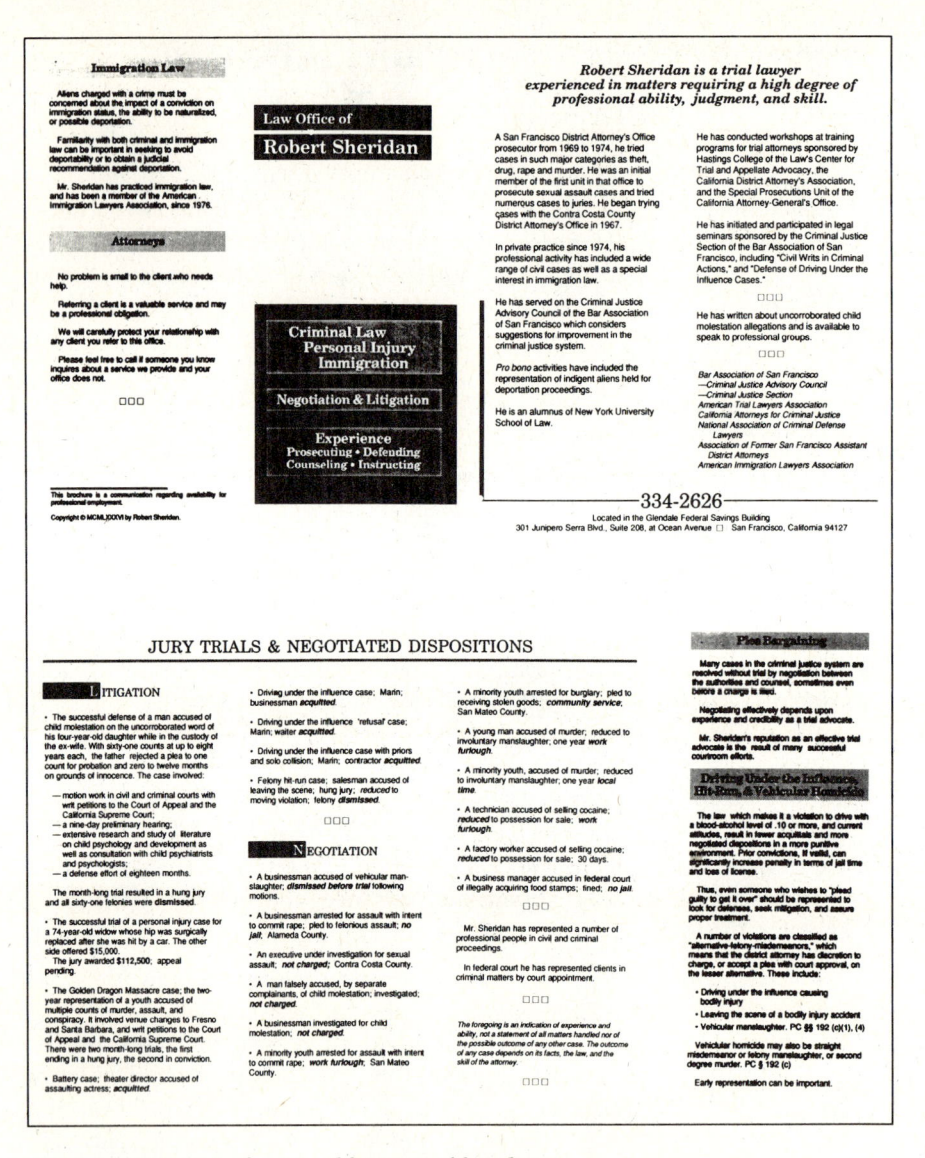

Fig. 15.4. Printout of pages of four-panel brochure.

Production Tips

The trick to producing this brochure is to create it as four 8 1/2-by-7-inch pages. The pages are pasted in place manually before the document is reproduced. You may wonder about the advantage of using an 8 1/2-by-7-inch page because PageMaker has an option for producing 8 1/2-by-14-inch pages—the final size for this brochure. The answer is not obvious until you consider the way the different printers work.

This brochure is designed to be printed on an Apple LaserWriter printer, which does not print all the way to the edges of the paper. One edge of the paper is used by the grippers inside the printer. (Offset printers also require 0.25 inch at the edge of the paper for the grippers on the press.) The other three edges of the paper are defined by the PostScript code inside the printer.

Apple's engineers designed the printer this way to conserve memory. The larger the image area, the more memory is used. The engineers, therefore, made the maximum image area for the printer slightly larger than 8 inches by 10.5 inches—taking about one pica away from the top and bottom of a page, and about 1.5 picas away from the sides. In printer's terms, this allowance yields a maximum of 300 pixels per inch, or 90,000 pixels per square inch. When this 90,000-pixel limit is applied to 8 1/2-by-14-inch pages, the margins around the edge become even wider (see fig. 15.5).

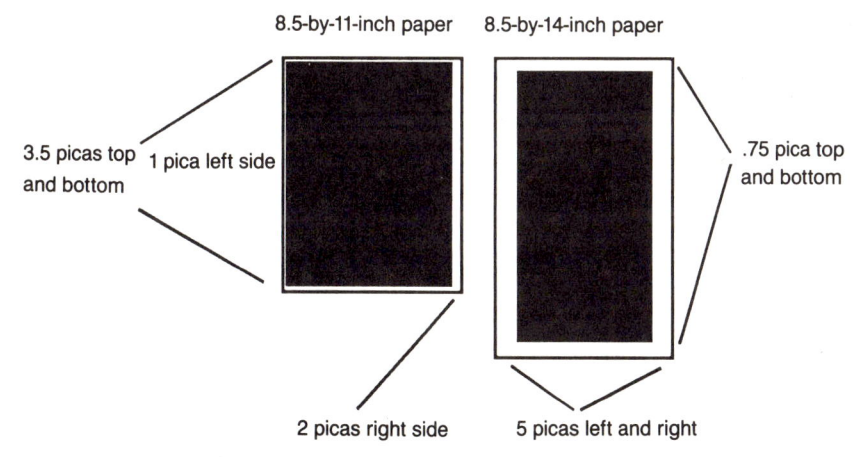

Fig. 15.5. Printing full-page black boxes to determine printer-imposed limits on a page.

You can test the limits for any printer by opening a PageMaker document, drawing a black or shaded box to cover the entire page, and printing the page. On a LaserWriter printer, the 8 1/2-by-11-inch pages have margins of 1 pica at top and bottom and 1.5 picas on the sides. The 8 1/2-by-14-inch pages have top margins of 3.5 picas and side margins of 5 picas. On a Hewlett-Packard LaserJet printer, these margins are even wider. On a Linotronic typesetter the printer might use, however, you can print an image larger than 11 by 17 inches without a forced margin around the image.

These limitations are not a problem for most documents, but when you are designing a small brochure you want the freedom to come within 0.25 inch of all sides—the same limit imposed by the offset printer unless you pay the extra charges for printing bleeds (elements that cross a cut edge in the final document). (The problem is eliminated with the Linotronic typesetter, which has no limits and uses 12-inch-wide film.)

Figure 15.6 shows the Page Setup dialog box for this brochure. Notice that the template uses a page size of 8 1/2 by 7 inches (half legal size) with Tall paper orientation. If the printer could have handled the full-size page layout, as a Linotronic typesetter can, the template would have been set up with a page size of 8 1/2 by 14 inches and Wide orientation. To center each panel in the completed folded brochure, the space between columns is entered (in the Column Guides dialog box) as twice the size of the outside margins.

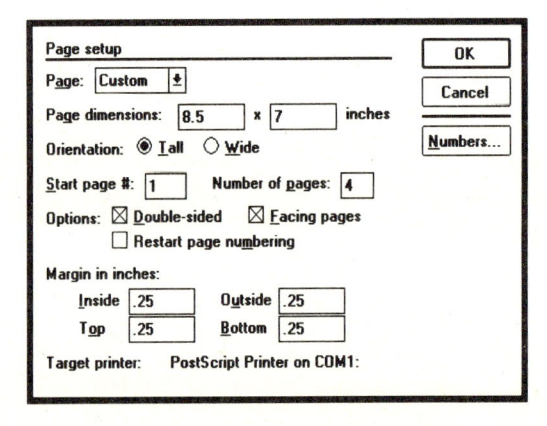

Fig. 15.6. Page Setup dialog box for four-panel brochure.

Bleeding across Paste-Up Lines

When designing pages that will be pasted together for final reproduction, do not cross seamed edges with gray fill patterns: use solid white or black only. Otherwise, when you paste the pages together, you can see the seam where two edges of a gray pattern meet. Figure 15.7 shows thumbnails indicating how the parts of Example 15.1 are printed.

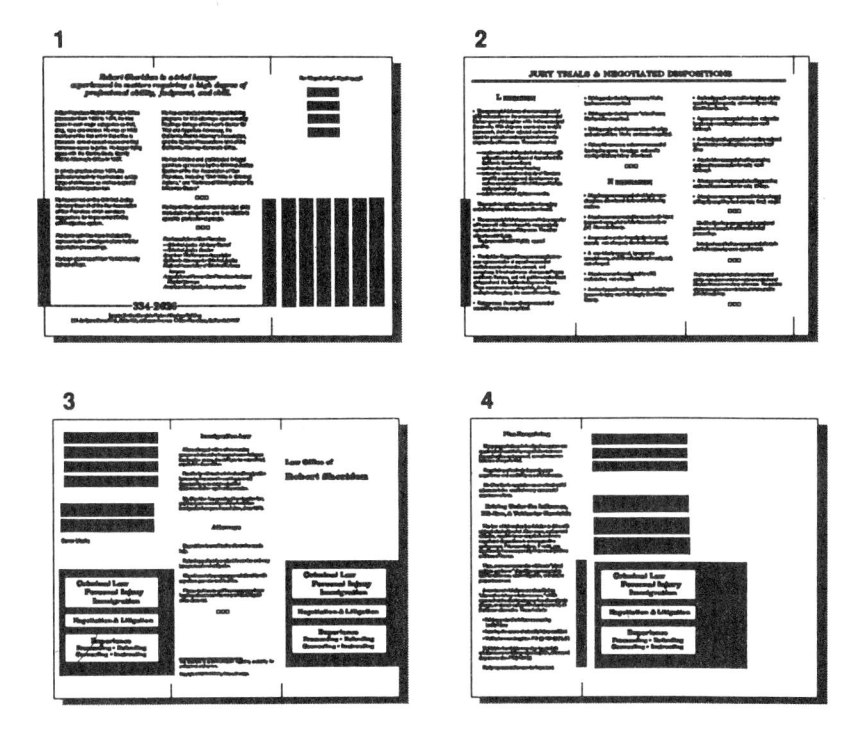

Fig. 15.7. Thumbnail printouts showing how pages are divided.

Production Steps

The production steps for this brochure follow much the same pattern as those for other publications. You need to pay close attention, however, to the order of the pages so that the text flows in the correct sequence after the layout is pasted up (see step 3).

1. Open the template for this brochure and save the template under the brochure's name.

2. Type and format all text in the Story Editor, using a style sheet. See Chapter 5 for information on formatting text using style sheets.

3. Close the story window by clicking the Control menu icon in the upper left corner. Working in Fit in Window view, place all text on all panels of the template. Notice that the text file starts in the right-hand column of page 1— the front cover panel when the brochure is folded. The text flows through segmented columns to page 4 of the template. The last column on page 4 flows to the first column on page 1.

4. Starting with the first panel, go through the document in Actual Size view and make adjustments, adding black or screened boxes behind text.

5. For the screens in the design, use PageMaker's square-corner tool and shading for the draft versions. Delete these shaded boxes for the final printout.

6. Print the final document on 8 1/2-by-11-inch paper, and paste the pages in the correct locations to create the 8 1/2-by-14-inch master for reproduction.

Using Screens for the Four-Panel Brochure

Chapter 14 recommends that for slides and transparencies you use gray screens instead of solid black areas if the final output is produced on a laser printer. If you use offset printing to produce a large quantity of brochures, however, gray screens may not produce the effect you want.

If you create gray screens using PageMaker and have your brochure offset printed, the text or the screen may not print clearly. When the camera is set to pick up a fine screen—a 10-percent fill pattern, for example—the photographic process may darken each character of the text and at the same time blur the edges of characters. If the camera is set to sharpen the text, the 10-percent screen may disappear in the photographed image. In other words, if the image includes very light gray tones or a wide range of gray tones, you will have trouble finding a camera setting that picks up the 10-percent screens and also produces the correct darkness for text and for screens darker than 10 percent.

If your final output will be offset printed, use tissue overlays and let the offset printer's camera operator make the screens rather than use PageMaker's shading, as done with the brochure in figure 15.8. Also, with this method, you can produce screens of a higher resolution (more dots per inch) than the 300-dpi resolution of the laser printer.

Preparation for Reproduction

Instead of using PageMaker's fill patterns to create the gray tones on the page, you can let the offset printer use a camera to create the percentage screens as halftones. After the initial proofing and editing rounds of the

Chapter 15: Creating Brochures, Price Lists, and Directories **531**

brochure with mixed percentages of fill patterns, change all the boxes in the PageMaker version to solid black (behind reverse type) or white (behind black type) and use tissue overlays to tell the camera operator what percentage screen to use (see fig. 15.8). This adjustment adds only a small charge to the printer's bill.

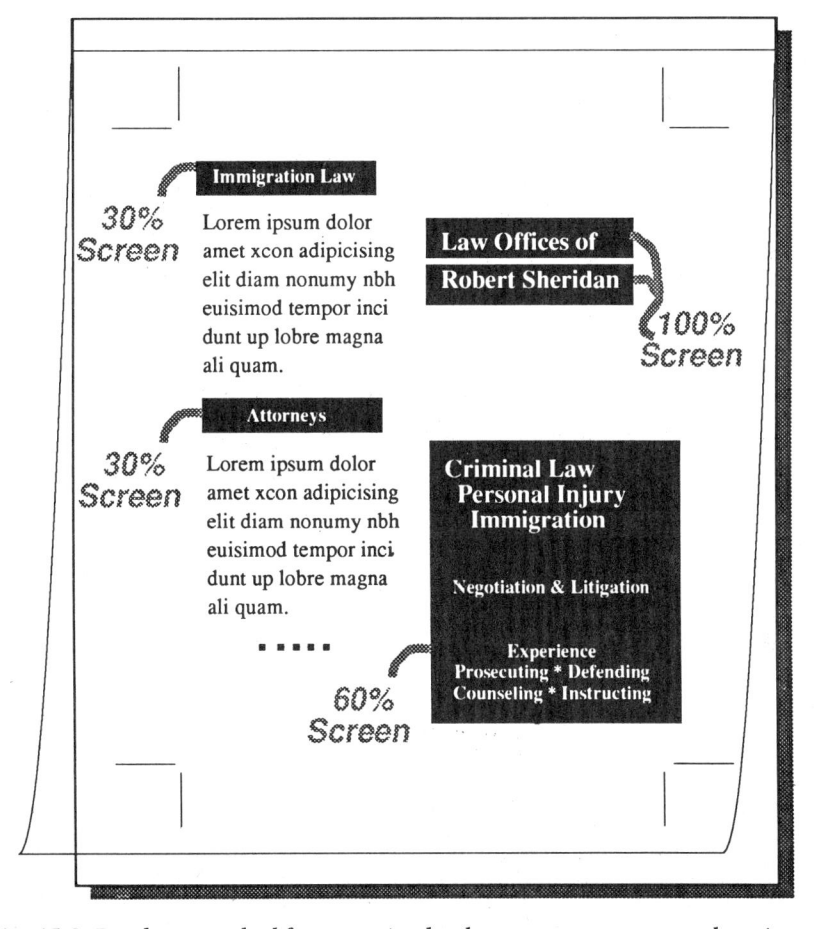

Fig. 15.8. Brochure marked for screening by the camera operator at the print shop.

Example 15.2. A Four-Page Brochure Consisting of Many Repeated Elements

This 8 1/2-by-11-inch brochure is printed on 11-by-17-inch paper and folded in half. Because of the many duplicate elements in the brochure, this example illustrates the use of dummy text and graphics stored on the pasteboard of the template. The design and production tips can be applied to any publication that uses the same elements on every page (with changes to the text or content but not to the format).

Description

This four-page brochure is composed of text and graphics created using PageMaker's tools, plus graphs from Lotus 1-2-3 (see fig. 15.9). All text was typed directly into PageMaker. The logo, COMPUTE!, was kerned manually. The final 8 1/2-by-11-inch pages are offset printed on 11-by-17-inch sheets, which are folded in half.

Design Principles

Many of the design principles described at the beginning of this chapter and in Chapters 10 through 14 are applied in this publication. The four principles best illustrated by this example are repeated and described in this section.

Use all capital letters as a deliberate design strategy rather than as a method for emphasizing text or showing a heading. In this case, the word "COMPUTE!" is in uppercase and the letters are kerned to meet the designer's specifications. This customization of the text creates a unique logo. The logo is kerned once, duplicated, and scaled to various sizes. Whenever this logo is used, the same relative kerning adjustments are applied. The kerning adjustments are preserved when text is sized in PageMaker. (For more information about kerning in PageMaker, see Chapters 5 and 10.)

Treat all figures consistently: fonts, line weights, fill patterns. The same two fill patterns are used in every bar graph in this example. All graphs are scaled to the same size, and all line weights and labels are the same size. This consistency helps highlight the significant differences—the data variations—in the figures.

Let the same graphic elements carry the theme throughout the document. Each graph is framed in a drop-shadow border. This border helps the reader group related information on the page.

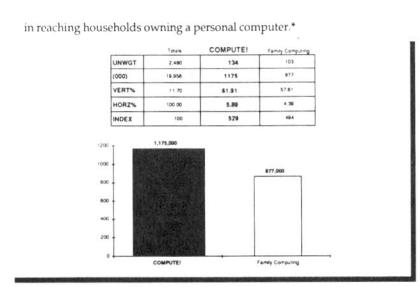

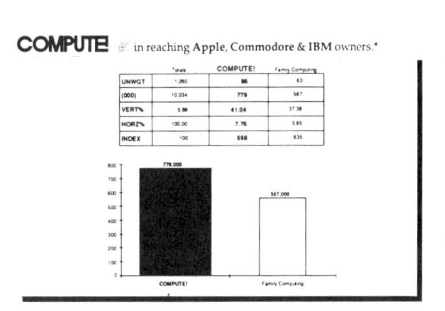

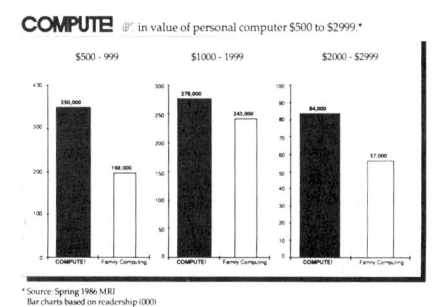

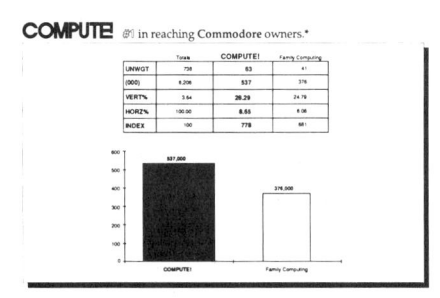

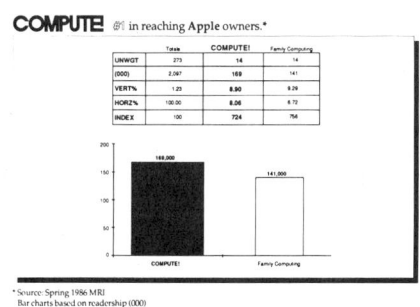

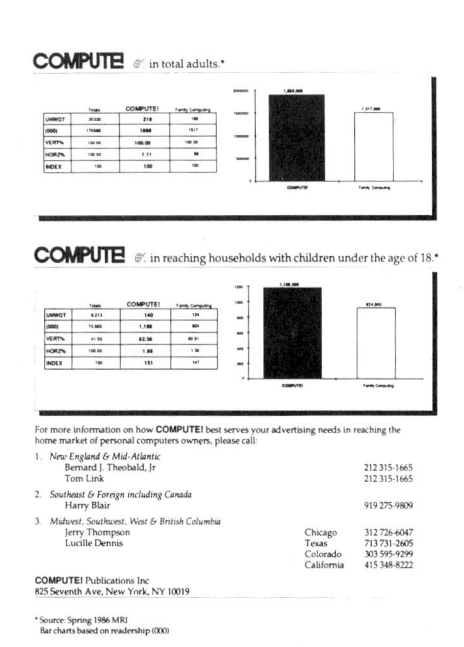

Chapter 15: Creating Brochures, Price Lists, and Directories **533**

Fig. 15.9. Printouts of pages of four-page brochure with repeated elements.

Select only one or two typefaces and use the same sizes for headings and other text on all images. If you are producing a long brochure, consider using style sheets to make the document consistent in appearance. The brochure uses only two typefaces, and a total of seven different fonts (see fig. 15.10). Except for the axis labels on the bar graphs, which are generated by 1-2-3, all text is typed directly into PageMaker and "cloned" from the pasteboard elements.

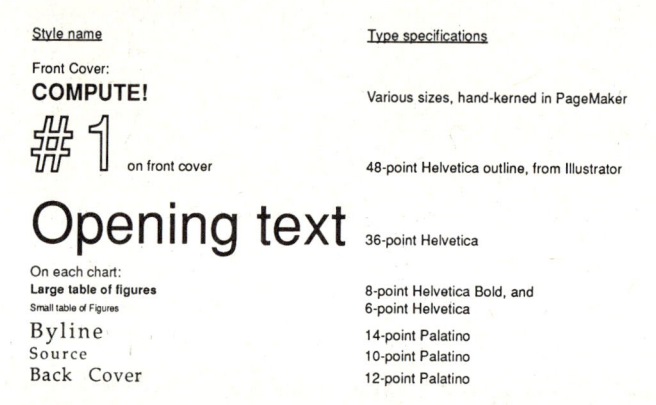

Style name	Type specifications
Front Cover: **COMPUTE!**	Various sizes, hand-kerned in PageMaker
#1 on front cover	48-point Helvetica outline, from Illustrator
Opening text	36-point Helvetica
On each chart: **Large table of figures** / Small table of Figures	8-point Helvetica Bold, and 6-point Helvetica
Byline	14-point Palatino
Source	10-point Palatino
Back Cover	12-point Palatino

Fig. 15.10. Type specifications table for four-page brochure with repeated elements.

Production Tips

The graphs are created in 1-2-3. All options for the size of the graphs, size of the axis labels, and fill patterns are specified in advance, and the same specifications are used for every graph. When placed in PageMaker, the graphs are cropped down to the axis labels; the titles and legends are removed. The drop-shadow border and all other text are added in PageMaker.

The Template

The template is set up as a double-sided document, but the Facing Pages option is not used (see fig. 15.11). This technique leaves a wider pasteboard area for storing the standard drop-shadow box and table of data that appear

Chapter 15: Creating Brochures, Price Lists, and Directories

on every graph (see fig. 15.12). The pasteboard holds dummy text for all text elements repeated on every page, including the tabular information framed in ruled lines created with PageMaker's perpendicular-line tool. A spacing guide is provided for positioning the bar graphs within the drop-shadow borders.

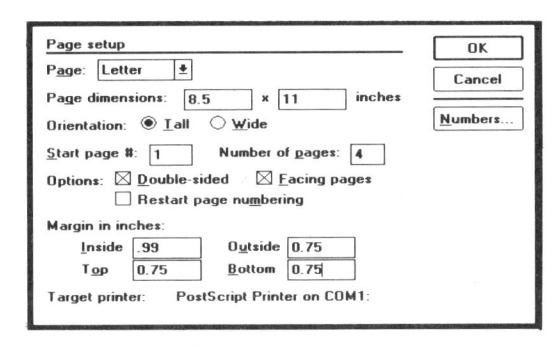

Fig. 15.11. Page Setup dialog box for brochure with repeated elements.

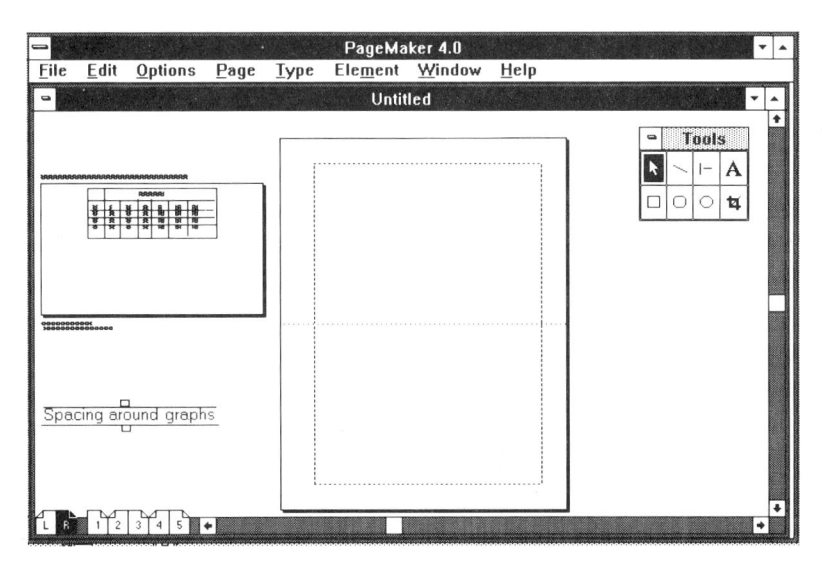

Fig. 15.12. The template with spacing guides and drop-shadow boxes on the pasteboard.

Production Steps

This type of publication uses the pasteboard to great advantage. To produce this brochure, work through the following steps:

1. Open a new publication to build the template and set up the margins as shown in figure 15.11.

2. Type the logo on the pasteboard in 127-point Helvetica and manually kern the letters to tighten the entire word. Make two copies of the logo. Change one copy to 14-point and one to 8-point Helvetica using the Type Specs command from the Type menu. Store all three sizes on the pasteboard.

3. Type the dummy text for the byline and source for the graphs and place these two text blocks on the pasteboard.

4. Using Pagemaker's text tools, tab settings, and the dummy data, create the table for the first graph. Draw a box around the text and add horizontal and vertical rules. Place the entire table (text and graph) on the pasteboard (see fig. 15.13).

	Totals	COMPUTE	Competitor
UNW GT	75	4	0
<000>	455	45	0
VERT%	0.27	2.37	0.00
HORZ%	100.00	9.89	0.00
INDEX	100	889	0

Fig. 15.13. A tabbed block of text framed by PageMaker's ruled lines.

5. Save the template.

6. Go over each page in Fit in Window view. Copy and paste the drop-shadow box, its contents, and the title dummy text from the pasteboard to the page and place each graph.

7. Go back to the first page and, working in Actual Size view, edit the text as needed to adapt it to each graph.

8. Save the publication.

Preparation for Reproduction

If you can, print the final version of this brochure on a Linotronic typesetter to produce solid black drop-shadows. If you use a laser printer for the final output, use a coated paper stock for the best image or spray the final pages with a matte finish to darken the solid black areas before you send the document to the offset printer. You can purchase matte-finish spray in any local art supplies store. (Hair spray also produces the matte effect.)

During production, all the 1-2-3 PIC files are stored on the hard disk in the same subdirectory as the PageMaker document (see fig. 15.14). Later, you can copy all these files to the same backup disk. If you use the Link command to link the graphs to external files, you easily can update the graphs periodically and rebuild the brochure quarterly or annually using new data.

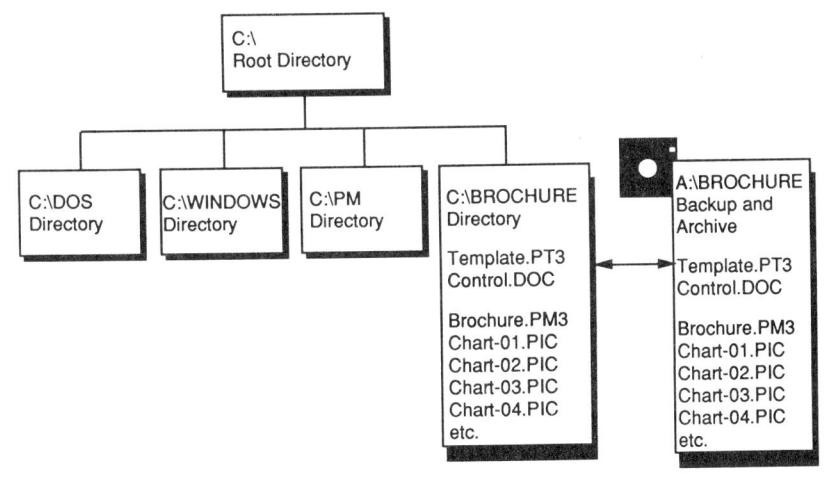

Fig. 15.14. Disk-file organization for brochure with graphs.

Example 15.3. A Two-Column Membership Directory Derived from a Database

This directory is designed as a two-column layout on narrow pages. The list of names and addresses is converted from a database format into text. The design and production methods used in this example can be applied to any directory, regardless of the page size or number of columns. The conversion steps used for the database information can be adapted for any publication that uses a database or spreadsheet file as a primary source of text.

Description

This 80-page booklet lists the names, addresses, and telephone numbers of more than 1,500 members of a professional association (see fig. 15.15). The information is converted from a database to a word processing file and formatted before being placed in PageMaker.

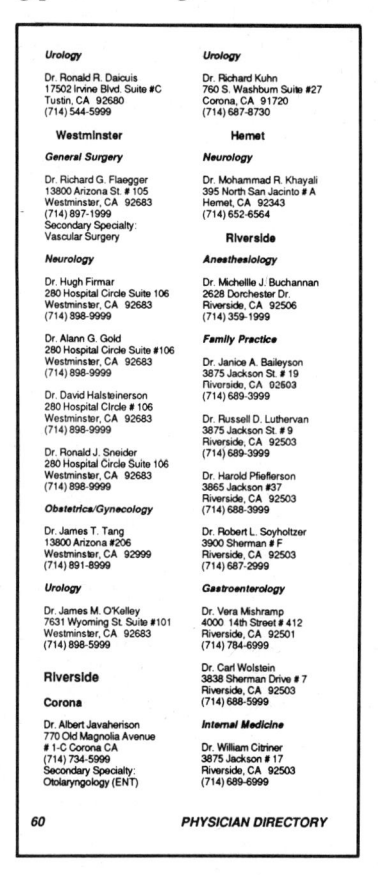

Fig. 15.15. Printout of one page of membership directory.

Design Principles

The design principles discussed throughout this book are generally followed in this example. Two principles in particular merit comment here.

Don't be afraid of white space. In this document, the white-space guideline is relaxed because the final product is a functional reference list like a telephone directory. Most of the white space is achieved by leaving a wide bottom margin between the lists and the running foot. A blank line (two carriage returns) is left between entries.

Use only one or two different typefaces in a document. The typeface used throughout this list is Helvetica (see fig. 15.16). This typeface is clean-looking and easy to read in small point sizes.

Style name	Type specifications
Main Title	14-point Helvetica
Level 1 Head	12-point Helvetica Bold, flush left
Level 2 Head	10-point Helvetica Bold, centered
Level 3 Head	8-point Helvetica Bold Italic, flush left
Listings	8-point Helvetica

Fig. 15.16. *Type specifications table for two-column membership list.*

Production Tips

The primary trick for production involves making a detailed list of the steps needed before going through the full production process.

(The rather convoluted process demonstrated by this example can be considered a worst case scenario in terms of data conversion. Some database programs offer the option of saving data formatted as a mailing list so that the word processing step is not required, and some programs even have the capability of switching the order of the data and adding new fields without going through a spreadsheet.)

Take a small amount of data from a spreadsheet or database through a test run of the complete production cycle before you complete the specifications for a long list. The text-preparation steps in this project require many global search-and-replace operations in the word processing file. Because of the large volume of data in this project, each global search takes nearly 20 minutes. One wrong global replacement adds at least 40 minutes to the total production time (20 minutes to reverse the changes, 20 minutes to perform the correct replacements). You should run a short selection of the data through the production cycle. From this run, prepare a detailed list of steps to reduce the risks of major mistakes in text preparation and increased production time.

Initially, the data is stored in a database format. Converting the data to a spreadsheet format provides a convenient way to switch the order of the information and to add three columns for the title, secondary specialty tag, and a comma between city and state (see fig. 15.17). After the data is sorted by the column labeled Specialty 1, print the data from the spreadsheet program as a reference during production. Delete the Specialty 1 column, save the data as text-only, and format it with a word processing program.

Last Name	First Name	Initial	Building/Suite	Street	City	State	Zip	Phone	Specialty 1	Specialty 2		
Miller	Stuart	L.	Suite 708	12 W. 6th	New York	NY	10010	345-123	Cardiollogy	Vascular		

Title	First Name	Initial	Last Name	Building/Suite	Street	City	State	Zip	Phone	Tag	Specialty 2	
Dr.	Stuart	L.	Miller	Suite 708	12 6th	New York	NY	10010	345-12	Secondary Specialty:	Vascular	

Fig. 15.17. Changing the order of the fields and adding columns in a spreadsheet program.

The Template

The template is set up on a 4-by-9-inch page with the inside margin slightly larger than the outside margin (see fig. 15.18). Because the lists have a ragged right margin, the column margins have been shifted by dragging them manually to the right of the page margins on each page. This technique gives a balanced appearance (see fig. 15.19). Otherwise, the text would appear to be left of center.

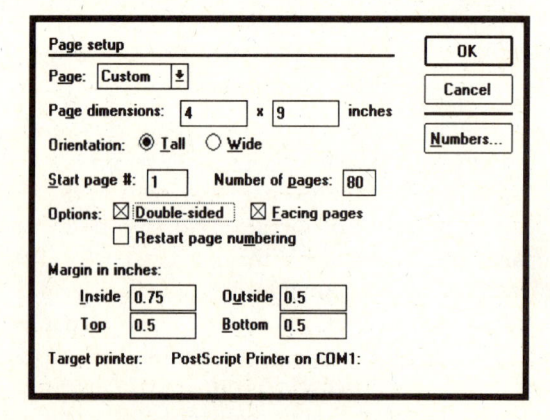

Fig. 15.18. Page Setup dialog box for the membership list.

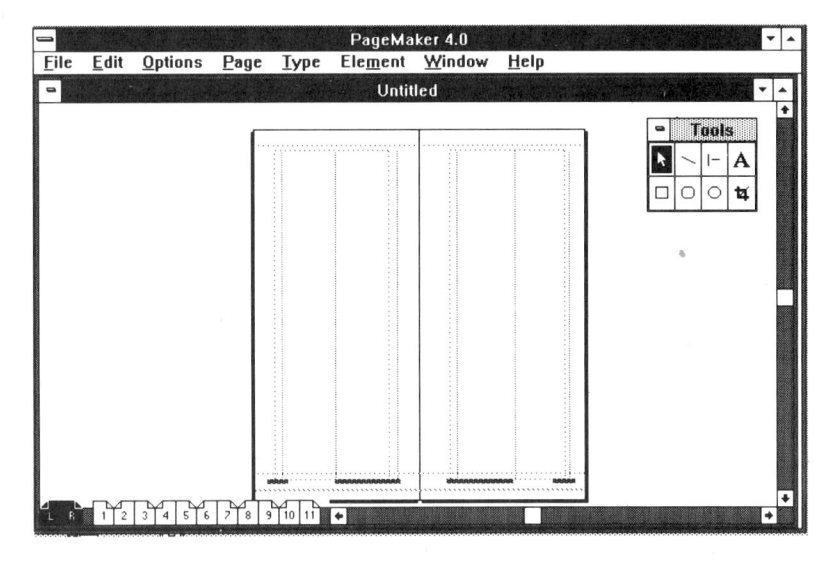

Fig. 15.19. The template for the membership list, with column margins manually shifted to the right.

Production Steps

Producing this two-column list from database material requires more steps and more attention to detail than the other examples given in this chapter. The following steps guide you through the entire process:

1. Select a small portion of your data and take it through the entire process, carefully noting the steps required for full database conversion.

2. Use the small sample of data to estimate the number of pages required for different designs and type specifications. The final design specifications are tempered by considerations of white space, readability, function, and printing costs. The final design in this example accommodates about 16 names per page set in 8-point Helvetica (see fig. 15.20).

3. Convert the data to a spreadsheet format (again see fig. 15.17). Save the data as text-only information. If this conversion results in commas between the items of information, use a word processor and globally change the commas to tab characters. The spreadsheet program interprets each tab as a new column.

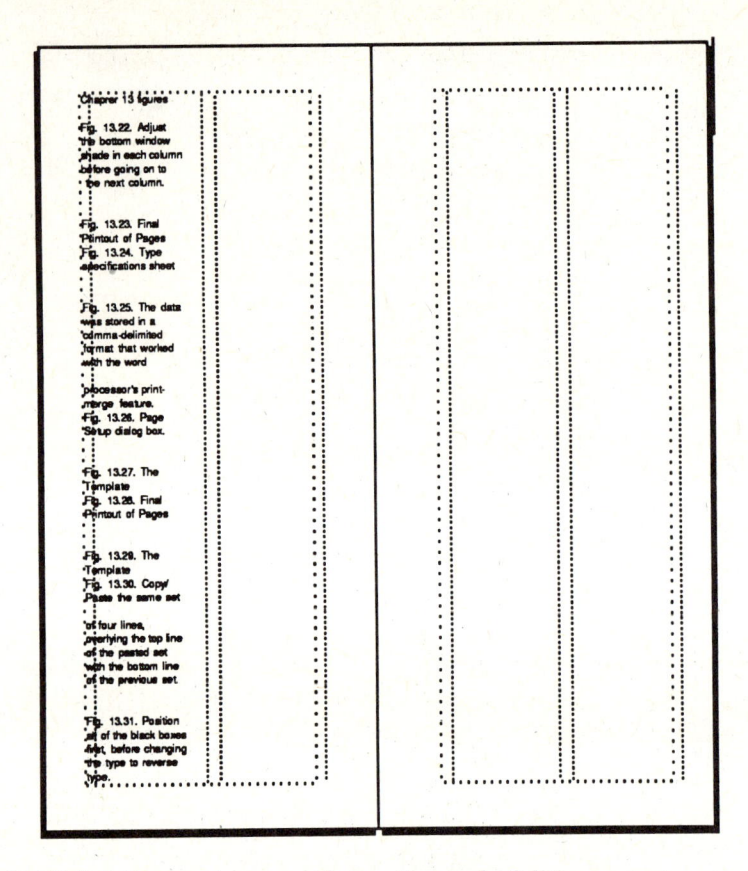

Fig. 15.20. Printing one page sample to estimate the full page count.

4. Open the spreadsheet file and move each first name and initial to precede the last name. Insert three new items: the title, Dr., before each name; the comma between city and state; and the phrase "Secondary Specialty" where applicable.

5. Sort the data by Specialty 1 and print the list from the spreadsheet for use as a reference. Save the spreadsheet.

6. Delete the Specialty 1 column. Before each data column, add a blank column (before Building/Suite, City, Phone, and Tag). Each blank column begins a new line in the final version. Under a new file name, save the data from the spreadsheet as text-only information.

7. Open the template and go through the document in Fit in Window view, placing the text in columns on each page.

8. Perform global changes and detailed edits in the Story Editor. In this case, four separate global searches are required:

    - To add a blank line after each entry, change all single carriage returns to two carriage returns.

    - To convert the blank columns inserted in step 6 to carriage returns in the word-processed files, change each "(tab)(tab)" to "(carriage return)".

    - Change the column of commas between city and state (added in the spreadsheet) from "(tab-comma-tab)" to "(comma-space)".

    - Change all remaining tabs to spaces.

9. Scroll through the document in Actual Size view. Enter the subheads as needed. In most cases, exactly 16 names fit on each page; but if any entry is broken across columns or across pages, adjust the bottom windowshade to force the whole name and address into the next column or page.

    Note that if you choose to edit the text using a word processor—before placing the text in PageMaker—you can tag the subheads in the word processing program so that they look like this:

    <SUBHEAD>Neurology

10. Print all the pages and proofread them against the spreadsheet printout (from step 5) and for formatting.

Example 15.4. A Single-Column List of Products with Descriptions, Prices, and Suppliers

The product list in this example is designed as a catalog for a fund-raising auction. This same format can be adapted for any directory including sentences or paragraphs of descriptive information in addition to names and addresses, or for a product catalog including product descriptions, prices, and product numbers. The list of products easily could have been a list of people (with descriptions of achievements or skills), a list of companies (with descriptions of services or product lines), a list of restaurants (with reviews of what they offer), and so on.

Description

This 48-page booklet lists more than 100 products to be auctioned in a fund-raising event (see fig. 15.21). The listing for each product includes the product name, list price, a brief description, and the name and address of the supplier. Text is wrapped around the large-type item numbers. The page size is designed to accommodate paid advertisements exactly the size of a standard business card (2 by 3 1/2 inches).

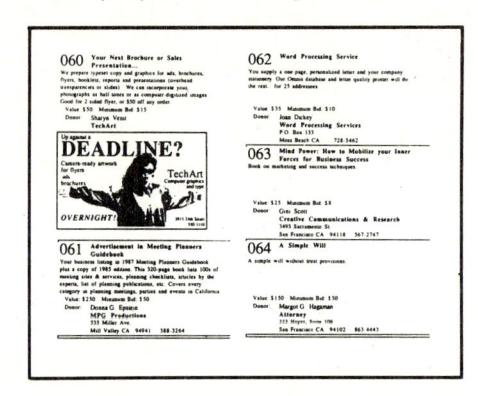

Fig. 15.21. Printout of one page of a list of products.

Design Principles

Besides the general rules related to consistency in design, two principles deserve special mention here.

Don't be afraid of white space. The white space on these pages is produced by indenting the name and address of the donor for each product. Product descriptions are allowed a maximum of five lines each.

Use only one or two typefaces in a document. The Times typeface is used for text throughout this booklet, and Helvetica is used for product numbers (see fig. 15.22). This simplicity helps balance the variety of typefaces in the business cards and display ads supplied by advertisers and pasted up manually on the final printouts.

Style name	Type specifications
000	Product numbers, 24-point Helvetica
Product Title	10-point Times Bold
Product Description	10-point Times
Company Name	10-point Times Bold

Fig. 15.22. Type specifications table for single-column product list.

Production Tips

The original data is stored in a comma-delimited file, which is the source file. A word processing program is used to merge print the data for the product lists into a merge-print file (see fig. 15.23). The trick in this case is that the merge-print file is sent to a disk instead of to the printer. (Note that not all word processing programs can print to a disk.)

Comma-delimited format

001,Your Next Brochure,"We prepare typeset copy and graphics for ads, brochures, fliers, booklets, reports, and presentations (overhead transparencies or slides). We can incorporate your photographs as half-tones, or as computer-digitized images. Good for 2-sided flier, or $50 off any order.",50,15,Grace Moore,TechArt,3915 24th Street,San Francisco,CA,94114,(415) 550-1110

001

Your Next Brochure
We prepare typeset copy and graphics for ads, brochures, fliers, booklets, reports, and presentations (overhead transparencies or slides). We can incorporate your photographs as half-tones, or as computer-digitized images. Good for 2-sided flier, or $50 off any order.
Value: $50   Minimum bid: $15
Donor: Grace Moore
                   TechArt
                   3915 24th Street
                   San Francisco, CA 94114
                   (415) 550-1110

Merge-print file

Fig. 15.23. Data stored in comma-delimited format and the merge-print formatted file.

Because the data already has been edited and corrected, little processing is required. The same data is used to send form letters to the donors to confirm their participation, to send them formal invitations and complimentary tickets to the event, and to send thank-you notes after the event. This data also is used to merge print all the materials used on the night of the auction, such as item tags (produced on mailing labels) and item lists for the auctioneer and the staff members collecting the payments.

The Template

The PageMaker template is set up to print three items per page in a small (4 1/2-by-6 1/2-inch) booklet format (see figs. 15.24 and 15.25). The 0.5-inch margins result in a column width of exactly 3.5 inches, the width of a standard business card and the size of the ads used throughout the booklet. A ruled line is stored on the pasteboard of the template and placed between the product entries. A 2-by-3.5-inch border also is stored on the pasteboard and used to mark the positions for ads to be pasted in manually.

Production Steps

Unlike other examples, this publication requires steps to merge the data before you place it in PageMaker. You may need to adapt these steps to meet the requirements of your own word processor.

1. Enter the data in the merge format used by your word processor.

2. Merge print the formatted data to a disk file, including carriage returns and character-formatting specifications (again see fig. 15.23).

3. Create the boxes used to mark the positions of the ads. Store these boxes and the necessary rules on the pasteboard.

4. Place the formatted text in the PageMaker template. Break the product number and description into separate text blocks and use the techniques described in Chapter 6 to wrap the text around each product number (again see fig. 15.21).

5. Copy and paste the boxes from the pasteboard to the appropriate pages to reserve space for the advertisers' cards to be pasted in manually.

6. Print all the pages and proofread the results before pasting business cards on the final version.

Chapter 15: Creating Brochures, Price Lists, and Directories

Fig. 15.24. Page Setup dialog box for the product list.

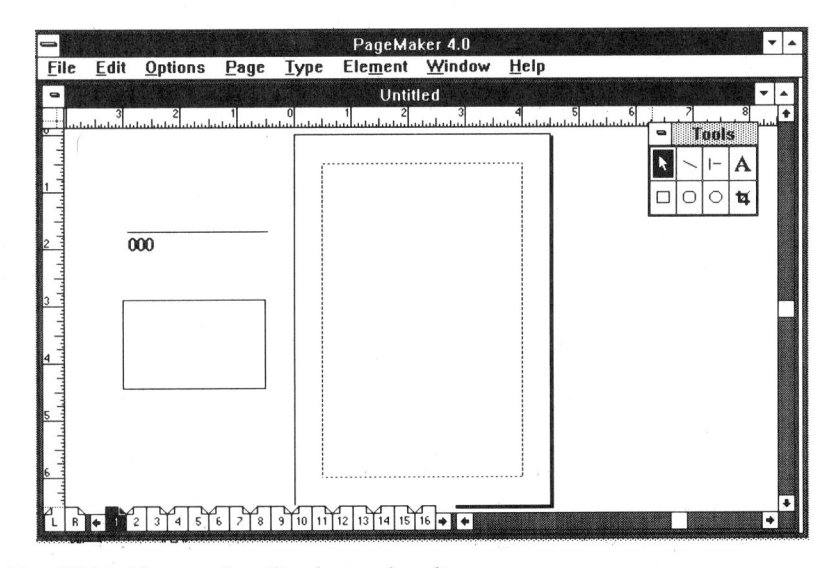

Fig. 15.25. The template for the product list.

Preparation for Reproduction

Advertisers' business cards are pasted by hand into the boxes reserved for them. Business cards supplied by advertisers should be white cards with black text and graphics. Cards in colored inks or on colored paper may require photostating to get a good black-and-white image.

Example 15.5. A Tabloid Price List with Horizontal and Vertical Rules

The order form in this example is organized into seven columns: quantity ordered, product number, description, minimum quantity, unit price, total price, and quantity shipped. The same design principles and production tips can be adapted to any tabbed list format, including restaurant menus, wine lists, telephone lists, inventory lists, or other price lists. The only absolute requirement is that all the data for each entry fit on one line.

Description

The price list in this example is formatted easily using PageMaker 4.0's paragraph rules (see fig. 15.26).

Fig. 15.26. Printout of pages of the tabloid price list.

Production Steps

Follow these steps to create the listing:

1. Set up the simple template shown in figure 15.27 and place the text in PageMaker.

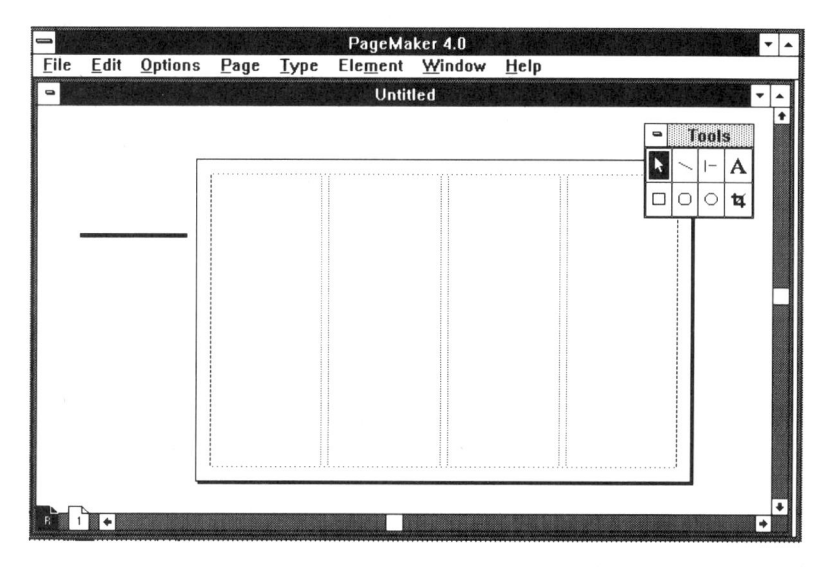

Fig. 15.27. The template for the tabloid price list.

2. Format the text in the Story Editor, setting left, right, center, and decimal tabs as needed. Set up horizontal rules between lines as appropriate by using the Rules option through the Paragraph command. The reverse type is set in PageMaker in a later step.

3. Scroll down each column in Actual Size view to make adjustments as necessary before you reverse the heading type and add the black boxes and hairline rules required by this design.

4. Draw a hairline border around one column and copy and paste the border to the other columns. You can adjust the length of the box to create two different borders in the first column of the price list.

5. Draw one vertical hairline down one column and copy and paste

the same line in the correct position across the column. Copy and paste this set of lines to all other columns.

6. After you have positioned all the vertical hairlines, go back to the beginning and scroll down each column in 200% Size view, deciding where to put the black boxes behind reverse-text headings.

7. Draw one black box the appropriate size and copy the box to the pasteboard. Paste the box over each heading and use the Send to Back command to position the box behind the text. Don't change the text to reverse type until you have positioned all the black boxes.

8. Scroll through the publication once more with the text tool selected. Change each heading, now invisible as black type on black boxes, to reverse type. You also can use PageMaker's style sheets to change text to reverse type by tagging the text to be reverse type. Triple-click to select the whole line and select Reverse Type from the Type menu.

9. Save and print the publication.

Chapter Summary

In this chapter, you have seen examples of publications that use unusual formats: folded brochures, small booklets, and tabloid-size price lists. You also have seen how information stored in a database, spreadsheet, or mail-merge format can be converted to text and placed in PageMaker. The design principles and production tips illustrated in this chapter can be applied to a wide variety of brochures and lists and adapted to meet your specific needs. By studying these examples, you can make your own designs more effective and your production steps more efficient.

16

Creating Fliers and Display Ads

Throughout this book, the focus has been on multiple-page publications that repeat the same basic master-page elements on every page and apply the same type specifications throughout. In this chapter, you learn how you can use PageMaker to produce one-page fliers and display ads like the ones shown in figure 16.1. One example demonstrates how a simple resume can be turned into a marketing tool. You also see how to use PageMaker to generate a series of different designs for one flier. Finally, you learn how to create a series of ads for different franchisers who offer the same product. The fliers and display ads discussed in this chapter share two important characteristics:

- The documents are usually only one or two pages long in a PageMaker file.
- Fliers and ads are often a nonstandard size—the final pages may be trimmed and folded.

Design Principles

The design principles in the previous chapters apply generally to the publications in this chapter, but you are likely to find more exceptions to the rules in this category—fliers and ads—than in any other. Some of the common exceptions are described in this section to give you an idea of how and why fliers and ads can break the rules.

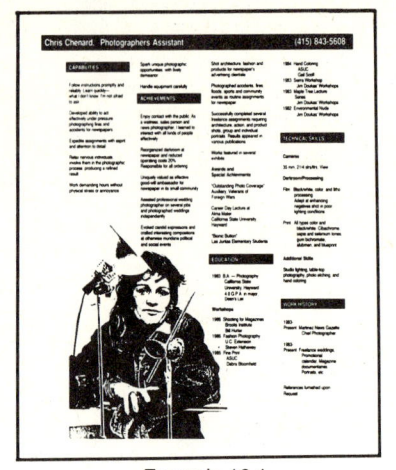

Example 16.1

Example 16.2

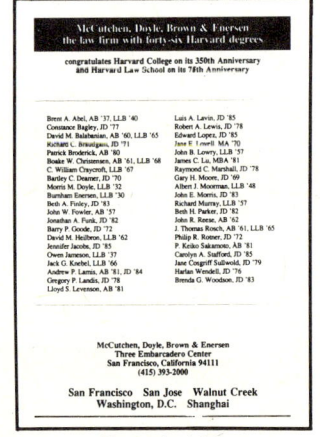

Example 16.3

Example 16.4

Fig. 16.1. Examples of fliers and display ads.

Keep text to a minimum.

Following this guideline can be difficult when you work with small formats. When designing a small ad or flier, most people tend to include as much information as possible about the product or service. Too many words in an ad, however, can make the final image uninviting. Readers simply may not read text printed in a small point size. By choosing your words carefully, you can get a few important points across and still convince the reader to call or come to the event or store.

Try to follow the rule of thumb that has evolved from the billboard industry: express the message in seven words or fewer. Examples 16.2 and 16.4 apply this principle. Examples 16.1 and 16.3, on the other hand, are exceptions to this rule. In these cases, a small point size is used to fit the large number of words in a small space and still leave white space on the page or in the ad.

The choice of font sets the tone of the piece.

Ads and fliers often use decorative or unusual typefaces for the headings and sometimes for the body copy as well. Different typefaces can convey a sense of seriousness, elegance, or frivolity. If you are not sure how typefaces affect the reader, you should probably stay with traditional typefaces rather than experiment with more decorative ones.

For instance, in developing Example 16.2 in this chapter, the designer experimented with several typefaces and finally chose Avant Garde to set the tone in a flier for a hair salon. In contrast, Example 16.3 is a display ad for a law firm that requires the more serious traditional tone of a serif font such as Times.

Use only one or two different typefaces in a document.

You can use almost any font in a flier or ad, but the same rule applies here as with all other publications: use only one or two typefaces. The use of too many fonts in a small space causes the ad or flier to look busy and detracts from the message. For instance, Example 16.1 uses only Helvetica Narrow. The designer calls attention to headings by using reverse type instead of another typeface.

Don't be afraid of white space.

If you skim through any magazine, you are likely to find several full-page ads that leave most of the page blank. These are extreme examples of this principle, but they usually make their point well.

You sometimes may deliberately violate this rule. As already mentioned, Examples 16.1 and 16.3 use small point sizes for the type in order to gain white space. Some of the variations in Example 16.2 have absolutely no white space because the scanned image fills the whole page, but the impact of the flier is still strong (see fig. 16.7). The scanned image itself invites the reader's attention, and few words are required to get the message across.

Use all capital letters as a deliberate design strategy rather than as a method for emphasizing text or showing a heading.

You should avoid using all uppercase letters in long blocks of text. Remember that all uppercase text can be difficult to read, especially in sentences.

On the other hand, you can use all capitals rather than a larger point size to make a few words stand out on the page. You also can use uppercase for a heading rather than change the typeface. Figure 16.2 uses uppercase text and reverse type to emphasize the headings for each section. Uppercase text has the greatest impact if the words or phrases are short. You often can improve the appearance of uppercase text by manually kerning the spaces between certain pairs of letters. (Refer to Chapters 5 and 10 for information about kerning.)

Production Tips

Many production tips that improve productivity when you are creating long documents are irrelevant for one-page documents like those illustrated in this chapter. Other production tips are unique to one-page ads and fliers. Here are some production tips to keep in mind for documents like the resume and ads in this chapter.

Compensate for ragged-right text by setting unequal right and left margins.

The need for a balanced appearance is evident in these examples. Because of the ragged-right text, the right margin may appear to be different from the left. You can compensate for this visual discrepancy by using different margin settings to balance the page.

Store background boxes on the pasteboard to use behind text. Copy boxes to the page as you need them.

Several examples in previous chapters and the resume in this chapter use background boxes. Using the rectangle tool (described in Chapter 6), you can create the box just once, store it on the pasteboard, and paste it on the page in as many different locations as you need.

For ads containing mostly graphics with little text, create your text on the pasteboard and copy text to the page after you have positioned your graphic.

In many ads, the graphic fills most of the available space. As a result, the position of the graphic is the most important factor of the page layout. Text is frequently short and to the point. You can save a great deal of time by positioning the graphic before you place the text. Changing the text to fit the graphic is much easier than trying to change the graphic to fit the text.

If your ad includes a border, remember to set the overall ad size—including the border—in the Page Setup dialog box.

If you use a border in your ad, you need to set the page size so that it accommodates the border and the margin surrounding the border.

If your ad includes a border, set margins inside the border narrower than the margins between the edge of the page and the border.

The border should be an integral part of the entire design. If the margins inside the border are larger than those outside, the final product will not be as attractive or unified as it should be.

Examples

Many of you will find this chapter's examples the most useful in the book because one-page fliers and ads are used frequently. With PageMaker you easily can produce short fliers and ads and modify the designs with only a few additional steps. The examples in this chapter range from a resume to a series of one-page ads. Some use scanned images, and others rely entirely on type. Following are brief descriptions of the examples:

  Example 16.1. A Photographer's Resume with a Scanned Photograph

  Example 16.2. A One-Sided Flier with Several Design Variations

  Example 16.3. A Series of Display Ad Designs with Varied Borders

  Example 16.4. A Series of Ads in the Same Format for the Same Service

Example 16.1. A Photographer's Resume with a Scanned Photograph

This resume is included under the category of fliers and ads because the creative use of a scanned image and reverse text transforms this list of credentials into a promotional piece. The piece conforms to the 8 1/2-by-11-inch full page that most employers or interviewers are accustomed to receiving from individuals, but the four-column format and the large scanned image in the lower left corner give the resume the impact of a flier or brochure describing a service. This example provides one clear lesson: PageMaker can transform any traditional format—resume, memo, agenda, balance sheet—into a marketing tool that can help sell whatever is being presented.

Description

This resume comes from a photographer, and has been dressed up with a scanned photograph (see fig. 16.2). The final version was printed on a Linotronic typesetter and then sent to an offset printer for reproduction.

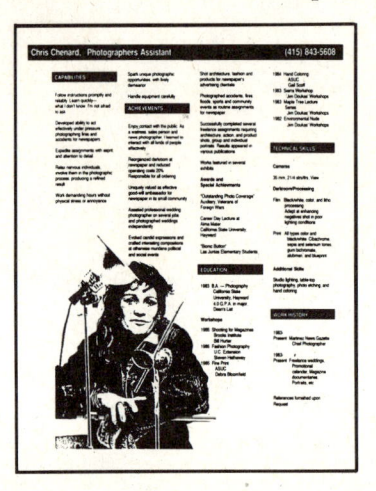

Fig. 16.2. Printout of resume.

Design Principles

In this example, one design principle—keep text to a minimum—is stretched in order to list all the photographer's awards and qualifications. The danger of overcrowding the page is reduced by using a small point size of a narrow typeface: Helvetica Narrow. To compensate for the small size of the section headings, the designer uses all uppercase letters and reverse type. The final effect is a well-balanced composition in a clean, readable typeface with adequate white space.

Don't be afraid of white space. Even though the resume contains a great deal of text, the resume uses white space to distinguish the sections and make reading easy. Notice the white space between columns and the four points of leading between each head and following text.

Use only one or two different typefaces in a document. This resume uses Helvetica Narrow throughout (see fig. 16.3). Helvetica Narrow is a compact, clean, readable typeface that helps support the photographer's image as a fine artist and sophisticated technician. Using this typeface also enables the designer to use more text without creating a crowded effect.

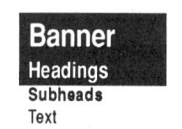

Banner	16-point Helvetica Narrow Bold, reverse type
Headings	11-point Helvetica Narrow Bold, reverse type
Subheads	9-point Helvetica Narrow Bold
Text	9-point Helvetica Narrow, 10-point leading, extra line between paragraphs

Fig. 16.3. Type specifications table for photographer's resume.

Production Tips and the Template

The inside margin is wider than the outside margin, as specified in the Page Setup dialog box shown in figure 16.4; but both margins appear equal on the page (refer to fig. 16.2). The unequal margin settings compensate for the effect of ragged right text. The pasteboard of the template includes a black box that is copied and pasted behind the reverse text of each heading (see fig. 16.5).

Fig. 16.4. Page Setup dialog box for the resume.

Production Steps

As mentioned previously, creating a one-page document is less complicated than creating longer publications. The steps for producing this resume are given in detail. As you follow the procedure, consult the figures for settings and positions.

1. Format the text with a word processing program. Use tabs, not spaces, to indent lines as needed.

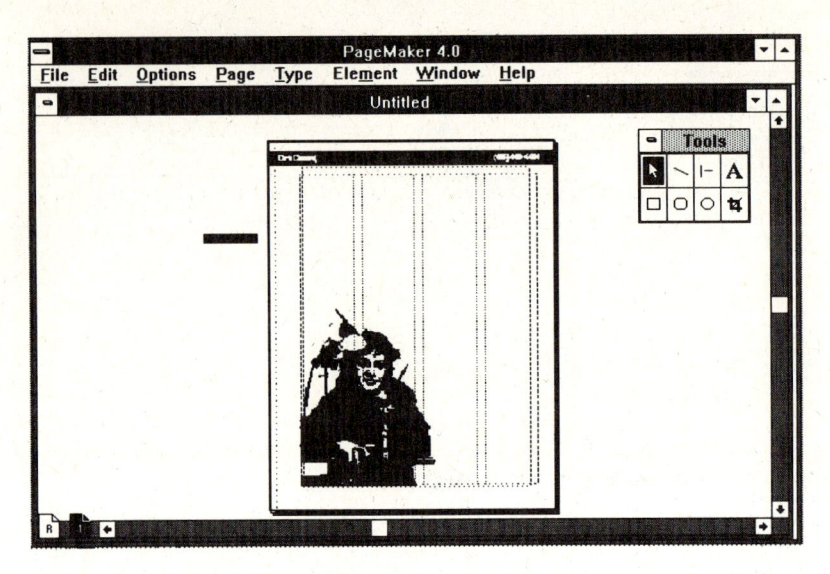

Fig. 16.5. Template for the resume.

2. Scan the image, and use PC Paintbrush, Windows Paint, or the scanning software program to clean up the image. In this case, all the pixels in the background—anything not part of the photographer's head and body or the light stand—are erased to convert the rectangular photo image into an irregular shape that becomes more visually integrated with the text.

3. Open a new PageMaker publication, following the page setup and column settings shown in figures 16.4 and 16.5.

4. Working in the Fit in Window view, place the scanned image in position. Crop and scale the image if necessary.

5. From the Options menu, select the Text Wrap command. Highlight the icon that wraps text rectangularly. (Text is prevented from wrapping on the outside of the graphic if the graphic is next to the outside margin.) Select the Text Flow icon to flow text all the way around the graphic. Create a custom graphic boundary around the graphic, as explained in Chapter 6.

6. In the Fit in Window view, place the text, using the Autoflow command in the Options menu. If you select Autoflow, text jumps to the top of the next column when a graphic is encountered. If Autoflow is off, text stops at the graphic.

7. Change to the Actual Size view, and move down each column, changing the headings to reverse type and adding black boxes as backgrounds for the headings. To reverse the type and add the black boxes, do the following:

   First, draw a black box around the first heading in a column. Use the Send to Back command from the Element menu to place the box behind the text, and use the Copy command from the Exit menu to copy the box to the pasteboard.

   Move to each heading and paste the black box from the pasteboard. Position the box over the heading and use the Send to Back command.

   Go back to the beginning and use the text tool to make the headings reverse type.

8. Print drafts on the laser printer.

9. Print the final copy on the Linotronic typesetter to get crop marks and solid black areas that reach the edge of the paper (see fig. 16.6).

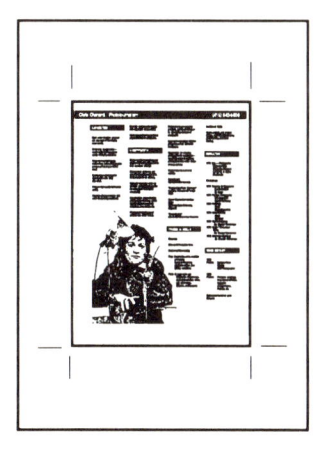

Fig. 16.6. Printed resume with crop marks.

Preparation for Reproduction

You must inform the offset printer that you want part of the image to bleed off the paper. Keep in mind that the bleed adds to the printing charges because of the oversize paper and trimming required. Otherwise, no particular preparation is necessary, because the crop marks are printed by the Linotronic.

> **Printing Black Areas**
>
> Even if your laser-printer cartridge is printing black areas poorly so that they appear unevenly gray, the image often blackens when converted to offset printing plates. True grays are retained when you use gray fill patterns composed of black dots. See the warning in Example 14.1 about using a wide range of gray tones.
>
> If you are not using a typesetter to produce solid black images, use coated paper stock in the laser printer. You also can darken the image printed on the laser printer by spraying the page with a matte finish (available in any art supply shop). This trick works best with uncoated paper.

Example 16.2. A One-Sided Flier with Several Design Variations

The approach used in designing this flier can be applied to any one-page document. The trick is to place all the basic elements on the pasteboard and then copy and paste them onto each page of the design publication, making a different arrangement of elements and testing different type specifications and paragraph formats on each page. The result is a series of design ideas that you can review with your team or client.

Description

This flier began as a series of nine designs that used the same text but different graphics as backgrounds. In the end, three different designs were selected for reproduction on three different colors of paper (see fig. 16.7). The fliers were mailed to the same individuals on a mailing list at three-month intervals, and a different flier was used each month. In this way, the prospective customers were reminded three times of this service, and the variations of the same design helped renew the readers' interest for each mailing.

Production Tips and the Template

The few words required for this piece were typed on the pasteboard of the template. Several different scanned images were candidates for use in the final design. The designer placed each of these images on a separate page and then copied and pasted the text from the pasteboard and modified the text to create different design ideas.

Fig. 16.7. *Printouts of a flier with several designs.*

You may need to keep track of the series of variations but not want to use page numbers on the ads themselves. You can print thumbnails of the entire design file, as the designer did for this example. The thumbnails show the design on each page of the template with the corresponding page number (see fig. 16.8). The numbers give quick access to any variation both before and after the final design is chosen. In this way, the full-size printouts of the pages are not cluttered with page numbers that are not part of the design.

Fig. 16.8. Thumbnails showing the design on each page.

Production Steps

The production steps for this example are simple. The greatest attention is given to placing the different versions of the image and fitting the text with the image.

1. Create a PageMaker publication with the text of the flier on the pasteboard.

2. Go through the document in the Fit in Window view, adding pages as needed. Place a different scanned image on each page, or position the same image in a different location on each page. Some of the scans in this case were deliberately distorted (stretched out of proportion).

During this step, copy and paste the text from the pasteboard into position on each page, but don't change the type specifications.

3. Go through the document in the Actual Size view. You can work from front to back or vice versa. Change the type specifications and break the type into different blocks on each page to create unique designs.

4. Print thumbnails of all the designs and choose the one you want.

5. Delete all unwanted variations from the file.

6. Print the variations as you need them.

Example 16.3. A Series of Display Ad Designs with Varied Borders

Like the preceding example, this example demonstrates how to use Page-Maker to produce design variations. The new twist in this case is that the final printout is pasted into a larger publication as a display ad. You can apply the recommendations about using special paper for the final printout to any ad or publication that will be pasted manually on larger pages or boards.

Description

This series of display ad designs is similar to Example 16.2 in at least two ways: All the text is predetermined (a list of associates in a law firm), and the size of the ad is predefined (a full-page ad in a booklet). The designer, however, can make variations in the border style and in the type specifications and text layout (see fig. 16.9). For example, the address information is set in different type specifications, and the size of the box is varied.

Production Tips and the Template

Use the Page Size setting in the Page Setup dialog box to define the size of the ad (including the border), and set narrow margins inside the border area (see fig. 16.10). Store the text and a box the size of the ad border on the pasteboard in the template (see fig. 16.11). Both the page setup and the template are straightforward. You can follow the settings shown in the figures without using complicated procedures.

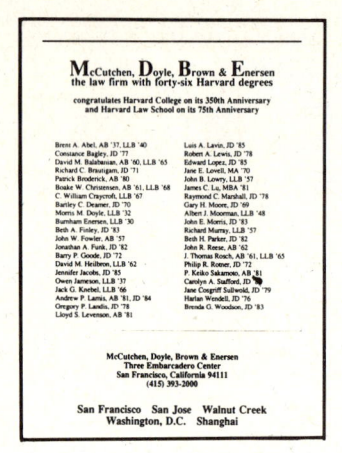

564 Part III: Examples of Publications Created Using PageMaker

Fig. 16.9. Printouts of the series of display ads.

Fig. 16.10. Page Setup dialog box for the series of ads.

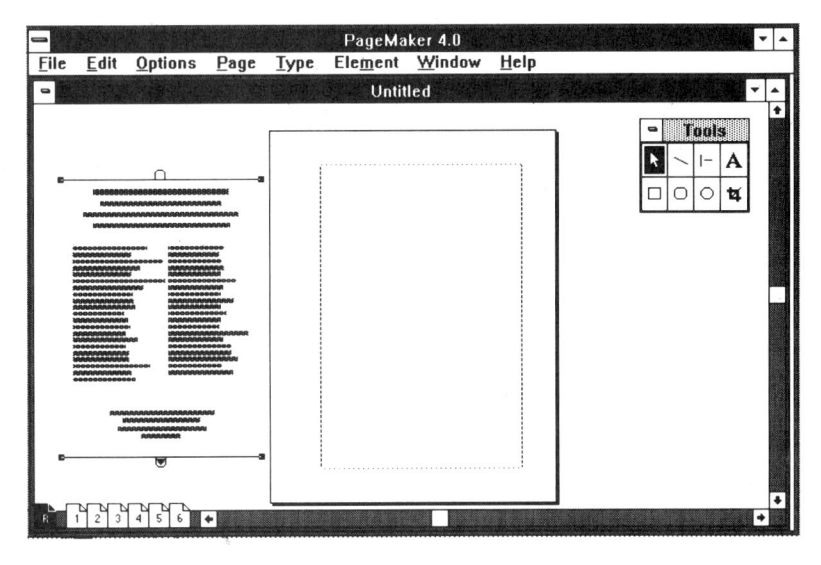

Fig. 16.11. Template for the series of ads.

Production Steps

This example leans heavily on the use of the pasteboard. By creating borders and rules and storing them on the pasteboard, you easily can create variations in the final document.

1. Open a new publication with the Page Setup specifications shown in figure 16.10, and type or place the text of the ad on the pasteboard. Use PageMaker's square-corner tool to draw a border (or borders) the size of the ad, and store the box on the pasteboard.

2. On each page of the template, copy and paste the text block from the pasteboard to the page, and change the type specifications as desired.

3. On some pages, copy and paste the box border from the pasteboard onto the page, or draw horizontal rules to enhance the design.

4. Print all pages, and choose the final design.

Preparation for Reproduction

Ads to be sent to other publications for insertion should be printed on the Linotronic typesetter or photostated. If you are sending laser-printer output, use laser paper or coated stock to get the best black image and to provide the best surface for pasteup. If you are using regular bond paper, you may want to include a note that the camera-ready copy you are delivering is on regular bond paper. Otherwise, production staff who are unfamiliar with laser printing may think that you are delivering a photocopy instead of an original. (This common misunderstanding should occur less frequently in the future, as more production departments start using laser printers.)

Example 16.4. A Series of Ads in the Same Format for the Same Service

This example demonstrates a new angle in developing a series of ads. Whereas Examples 16.2 and 16.3 develop a series of different designs, this example produces a series of ads that use the same design. Only the store location and phone number are different on each ad. The economy lies in using a central design department to develop ads for dealers in widely separated locations. You can apply the same approach to similar situations in which the same service is offered by different franchisers in different regions, or perhaps when you need to produce a series of announcements for the same seminar or special event that will be held in different cities or on different dates.

Description

Example 16.3 shows a series of ad designs from which only one is chosen. In this case, a series of nearly identical ads is created for different stores that offer the same service (see fig. 16.12).

Production Tips and the Template

The trick is to lay out the basic ad design on the master page (see fig. 16.13). On each page in the document, only the store address and phone number are changed. As you can see, the template holds the graphic elements and dummy text. Other text is stored on the pasteboard and used as needed.

Chapter 16: Creating Fliers and Display Ads **567**

Fig. 16.12. Printouts of pages for series of ads.

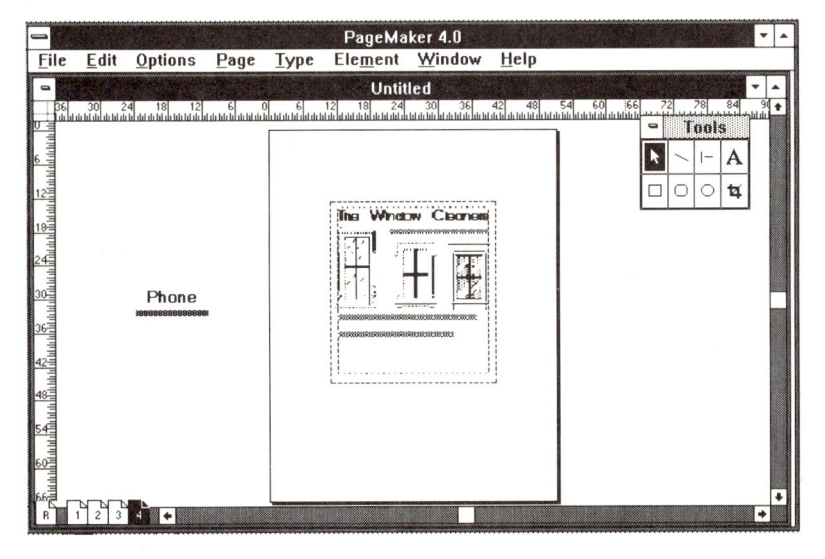

Fig. 16.13. Template for series of ads.

Production Steps

Because this ad has only one design, only one master page is needed. The variation is achieved with the text.

1. Lay out the ad design on the master page. For the address and phone lines, store dummy text (set in the correct type specifications) on the pasteboard.

2. On each page of the document, copy and paste the address and phone lines from the pasteboard to the page, and change the information as appropriate.

Chapter Summary

The examples in Part III of *Using PageMaker 4 for Windows* illustrate PageMaker's wide range of uses and helpful features for producing professional documents. No matter what equipment you may be using—dot-matrix printer, laser printer, or typesetter—PageMaker guarantees high-quality output. Whether your publishing projects are large or small, PageMaker has the capabilities to produce high-quality published documents that just a few years ago could be generated only by professional designers and typesetters.

With PageMaker, professional quality is available to individuals, businesses, and nonprofit, educational, and government organizations. Whether you produce books and manuals or single-page fliers and ads, Part III can help you with each stage—designing, creating, and printing the professional documents you need for your job. The examples in this section of the book will get you started toward making PageMaker a true publishing tool.

Glossary

Actual Size.   A command on the Page menu. Shows in the publication window a page approximately the size in which that page will be printed, depending on the screen's characteristics.

Alignment.   The positioning of lines of text on a page or in a column: aligned left (flush left, ragged right); centered; aligned right (flush right, ragged left); or justified (flush on both left and right).

Ascender.   The part of a lowercase letter that rises above its main body. Technically, only three letters of the alphabet have ascenders: *b*, *d*, and *h*. Uppercase letters and the lowercase letters *f*, *k*, *l*, and *t* also reach the height of the ascenders. See also *Descender*.

ASCII.   The form in which text is stored when saved as Text Only, a Save command option available for most databases, spreadsheets, and word processors. ASCII files include all the characters of the text itself (including tabs and carriage returns) but not the non-ASCII codes used to indicate character and paragraph formats. See also *Text-only file*.

Autoflow.   Text placement in which the text continuously flows from column to column and page to page, with PageMaker creating additional pages as needed until all the text is placed.

Bad break.   Term referring to page breaks and column breaks that result in widows or orphans, or to line breaks that hyphenate words incorrectly or separate two words that should stay together (for example, *Mr. Smith*). See also *Nonbreaking space* and *Orphans/widows*.

Baseline.   In a line of text, the lowest point of letters excluding descenders (for example, the lowest point of letters such as *a* and *x*, but not the lower edges of descenders on *p* and *q*).

Bit map.   A graphics image or text formed by a pattern of dots. PC Paint, Windows Paint, and PC Paintbrush documents produce bit-mapped graphics as well as scanned or digitized images. Low-resolution images are sometimes called *paint-type* files, and they usually have a lower number of dots per inch (dpi) than high-resolution images.

Bleed.   Term used to describe a printed image that extends to the trimmed edge of the sheet or page.

Block.   See *Text block*.

Blue lines.   A preliminary test printing of a page to check the offset printer's plates. This test printing is done using a photochemical process (instead of printers' inks) that produces a blue image on white paper. See also *Prepress proofs* and *Press proofs*.

Blue pencil/blue line.   Traditionally, a guideline drawn with a blue pencil or printed in light blue ink on the boards and used for manually pasting up a page layout. The blue ink is sometimes called *nonrepro* blue because the color is not picked up by the camera when a page is photographed to make plates for offset printing. With PageMaker, you can create nonprinting margins, column guides, and ruler guides on the screen to help you position text and graphics; these lines do not appear when the page is printed.

Board.   A sheet of heavyweight paper or card stock onto which typeset text and graphics are pasted manually. See also *Blue pencil/blue line*.

Body copy.   The main part of the text of a publication, as distinguished from headings and captions. See also *Body type*.

Body type.   The type (font) used for the body copy. Generally, fonts that are used for body copy, as distinguished from display type. See also *Body copy*.

Boilerplate.   See *Template*.

Bounding box.   Space defined by dragging the mouse diagonally. Used to place or type text.

Brochure.   A folded pamphlet or small booklet.

Callouts.   In PageMaker, text that points out and identifies parts of an illustration. Also, headings that appear in a narrow margin next to the body copy. See also *Pull-out quote*.

Camera-ready art.   The complete pages of a publication assembled with text and graphics and ready for reproduction. Literally refers to pages ready to be photographed as the first step in the process of making plates for offset printing. See also *Mechanicals* and *Offset printing*.

Caps and small caps. Text in which the letters that are usually lowercase are set as uppercase letters smaller than normal capitals. An option in the Type Specifications dialog box.

Caption. Descriptive text identifying a photograph or illustration. See also *Callouts*.

Carriage return. A line break you insert by pressing the Enter key at the end of a line or paragraph. Sometimes called a hard carriage return to distinguish it from the soft carriage returns, which result from wordwrap at the right margin of a page or right edge of a column.

Check box. In a dialog box, the area you click to turn an option on or off.

Cicero. A unit of measure equivalent to 4.55 millimeters, commonly used in Europe for measuring font size. Use the Preferences command from the Edit menu to select Ciceros as the unit of measure for the ruler lines and dialog box displays. You also can enter a value in Ciceros in any dialog box by inserting a *c* between the number of Ciceros and the number of points; for example, 3c2 indicates 3 Ciceros and 2 points. See also *Measurement system*.

Click. To press and release a mouse button quickly.

Clipboard. A feature of Microsoft Windows; temporarily stores text or graphics cut or copied by the commands on the Edit menu. The Paste command brings the contents of the Clipboard to the page. The Clipboard command displays the contents of the Clipboard.

Close. To choose the Close command from the File menu and stop work on the current publication, or to choose the Close command from the Control menu and leave PageMaker.

Collated. Printed in numerical order with the first page on top of the stack that comes out of the printer. An option in the Print dialog box. Multiple copies are grouped into whole sets of the publication.

Color separations. In offset printing, separate plates used to lay different colors of ink on a page printed in multiple colors. Using PageMaker, you can create masters for color separations by preparing different pages, with each page containing the elements to be printed in one of the colors. If the colors do not overlap, you also can use a tissue overlay to specify colors to the offset printer. See also *Overlay*.

Column guides. Dotted vertical nonprinting lines that mark left and right edges of columns created with PageMaker's Column Guides command.

Column rules. Vertical lines drawn between columns with PageMaker's perpendicular-line tool.

Command button. A large rectangular area in a dialog box; contains a command such as OK or Cancel. You can activate command buttons surrounded by a thick black line by pressing the Enter key.

Comp. Traditionally, a designer's comprehensive sketch of a page design, showing the client what the final page will look like when printed. Usually a full-size likeness of the page, a comp is a few steps closer to the final than a pencil rough and can be composed using ink pens, pencils, color markers, color acetate, pressure-sensitive letters, and other tools available at art supply shops. Created with PageMaker, a comp resembles the finished product, with typeset text, ruled lines, and shaded boxes created in PageMaker. The comp can be used as a starting point in building the final document.

Continued line. See *Jump line*.

Continuous-tone image. An illustration or photograph, black-and-white or color, composed of many shades between the lightest and the darkest tones and not broken up into dots. Continuous-tone images usually need to be converted into dots, either by scanning or by halftone, to be printed in ink or on a laser printer. See also *Halftone*.

Control menu. The Microsoft Windows menu listing commands for working with windows, getting PageMaker help, using the Clipboard, and leaving PageMaker.

Control menu box. Small square displayed in the upper left corner of the publication window. You click this box to select the Control menu.

Control Panel. A Microsoft Windows application program used to add or delete fonts and printers, change printer connections and settings, and adjust mouse and screen settings.

Copy fitting. Determining the amount of copy (text set in a specific font) that will fit in a given area on a page or in a publication. Making copy fit on a page in PageMaker by adjusting the line spacing, word spacing, and letter spacing.

Corner style. See *Rounded-corner tool*.

Crop. To use PageMaker's cropping tool to trim the edges from a graphic to make the image fit into a given space or to remove unnecessary parts of the image.

Crop marks. Lines printed on a page to indicate where the page will be trimmed when the final document is printed and bound. PageMaker prints these marks if the page size is smaller than the paper size and if the Crop Marks option is selected in the Print command dialog box.

Cropping tool. Tool used to trim a graphic.

Crossbar. The shape of the pointer when one of PageMaker's tools for drawing lines and shapes has been selected.

Custom. In PageMaker, a word to describe unequal columns, which you can create in PageMaker by dragging column guides to the desired position.

Cutout. When an image (or text and an image) contains overlapping colors, the first page is printed in one color with the overlapping object cut out of it; the second page is printed with the overlapping object in the second color.

Default. The initial setting of a value or option. Default settings usually can be changed by the operator.

Descender. The part of a lowercase letter that hangs below the baseline. Five letters of the alphabet have descenders: *g, j, p, q,* and *y.* See also *Ascender* and *Baseline.*

Deselect. In PageMaker, to select another command or option or to click a blank area of the pasteboard to cancel the current selection.

Desktop. The menu bar and blank area PageMaker displays when no publication is open.

Desktop publishing. Use of personal computers and software applications like PageMaker to produce copy that is ready for reproduction.

Diagonal-line tool. Tool used to draw a straight line in any direction.

Dialog box. A window or full-screen display that appears in response to a command that calls for setting options.

Digitize. To convert an image to a system of dots that can be stored in the computer. See also *Scanned-image files.*

Dingbats. Traditionally, ornamental characters (bullets, stars, flowers) used for decoration or as special characters within text. The laser font Zapf Dingbats includes many traditional symbols and some new ones.

Directory. A named area reserved on the hard disk where a group of related files can be stored together. Each directory can have subdirectories.

Discretionary hyphen. A hyphen inserted when Ctrl-[hyphen] is pressed. Identifies where PageMaker can divide a word to fit text in the specified line length when Hyphenation is on (as specified in the Paragraph dialog box). The hyphen appears on-screen and on the printed page only if the hyphen falls at the end of a line. See also *Hyphenation.*

Display type. Type used for headlines, titles, headings, advertisements, fliers, and so on. Display type is usually a large point size (several sizes larger than body copy) and can be a decorative font.

Dots per inch (dpi). See *Resolution*.

Dot-matrix printer. A printer that creates text and graphics by pressing a matrix of pins through the ribbon onto the paper. These impact printers usually offer lower resolution (dots per inch) than laser printers and are used only for draft printouts from PageMaker.

Double-click. To quickly press and release the main mouse button twice in succession.

Double-headed arrow. The shape of the pointer tool when a handle, ruler guide, or column guide is being dragged.

Double-sided publication. An option in the Page Setup dialog box for creating a publication to be reproduced on both sides of the sheets of paper. The front side of a page has an odd-numbered page, and the back side has an even-numbered page. See also *Facing pages*.

Drag. To hold down the main mouse button, move the mouse until the object is where you want it, and then release the button.

Drag-place. To drag the mouse diagonally to define the width of a graphic or text as you're placing it and so override the column guides.

Draw-type files. See *Object-oriented files*.

Drop-down menu. A list of commands that appears when you select a menu. In PageMaker, the menu titles appear on the menu bar along the top of the screen, and the menu commands drop down in a list below the selected menu title.

Dummy publication. Traditionally, a pencil mock-up of the pages of a publication, folded or stapled into a booklet, which the offset printer uses to verify the correct sequence of pages and positions of photographs. PageMaker's thumbnails can serve the function of a dummy publication. See also *Template* and *Thumbnail*.

Ellipse. A regular-shaped oval created with PageMaker's oval tool, as distinguished from irregular ovals, which are egg-shaped.

Ellipsis. Series of three dots in text (...), used to indicate that some of the text has been deleted (usually from a quotation). A closed ellipsis (without spaces) appears after every PageMaker command that opens a dialog box (Open...).

Glossary

Em. Unit of measure equaling the point size of the type; for example, a 12-point em is 12 points wide. The width of an em dash or an em space. See also *En*.

En. One half the width of an em. The width of an en dash or an en space. See also *Em*.

Encapsulated PostScript (EPS). A graphic created with PostScript code. Can also be special text effects.

Enter key. Key you press to break a line when the text tool is active or to confirm the selected options in a dialog box. Usually has the same effect as the Return key. See also *Carriage return*.

Export. To send PageMaker text to a word processing file.

Export filter. A process that tells PageMaker how to convert its files so that they can be understood by the word processing program that imports them.

Facing pages. The two pages that face each other when a book, brochure, etc., is open. Also an option used in double-sided publications. Facing pages have an even-numbered page on the left and an odd-numbered page on the right. See also *Double-sided publication*.

Flow text. To click the mouse button to discharge a loaded text icon and place text on a page.

Flush. Aligned with, even with, coming to the same edge as. See also *Alignment*.

Flush right (or right-justified). Text in which lines end at the same point on the right margin. Opposite of ragged right or left-justified. See also *Alignment*.

Folio. Page number on a printed page, often accompanied by the name of the document and date of publication. See also *Running head* and *Running foot*.

Font. One complete set of characters (including all the letters of the alphabet, punctuation, and symbols) in the same typeface, style, and size. For example, 12-point Times Roman is a different font from 12-point Times italic, 14-point Times Roman, or 12-point Helvetica. Screen fonts (bit-mapped fonts used to display text accurately on the screen) can differ slightly from printer fonts (outline fonts used to describe fonts to the laser printer) because of the difference in resolution between screens and printers.

Footer. See *Running foot*. See also *Folio*.

Format. Page size, margins, and grid used in a publication. Also the character format (font) and paragraph format (alignment, spacing, and indentation).

Formatting. Using the type and paragraph attributes to modify the page.

Four-headed arrow. Shape of the pointer when used to drag a selected text block or graphic.

Generic font. A screen representation of alphanumeric characters, which may not look like the printed characters. See also *Font*.

Grabber hand. A PageMaker icon; appears when you press the Alt key and drag the mouse to move around in the window.

Graphic. A line, box, or circle that you draw with PageMaker. An illustration brought into a PageMaker publication from another application.

Graphic boundary. The dotted line around a graphic that limits how close text can get to the graphic.

Greek text (greeked text). Traditionally, a block of text used to represent the positioning and point size of text in a designer's comp. Standard greeked text used by typesetters looks more like Latin: "Lorem ipsum dolor sit amet...". See also *Greeking*.

Greeking. The conversion of text to symbolic bars or boxes that show the position of the text on the screen but not the real characters. Text usually is greeked in the Fit in Window view in PageMaker; small point sizes may be greeked in closer views on some screens. See also *Greek text*.

Grid. The underlying design plan for a page. In PageMaker, the grid consists of nonprinting horizontal and vertical lines (margins, column guides, and ruler guides) that intersect to form a grid.

Guide. A nonprinting line (margin guide, ruler guide, or column guide) created to help align objects on a page. In PageMaker, nonprinting guides look like dotted lines, dashed lines, or blue lines, depending on the screen's resolution and color settings.

Gutter. The inside margins between the facing pages of a document; sometimes describes the space between columns. In some word processors, the gutter measure is entered as the difference between the measures of the inside margin and the outside margin. See also *Margin*.

Hairline. The thinnest rule you can create, usually 0.25 point. (Some laser printers do not support hairline rules.) See also *Rules*.

Halftone. The conversion of continuous-tone artwork (usually a photograph) into a pattern of dots or lines that looks like gray tones when printed by an offset printing press. See also *Continuous-tone image*.

Handles. The eight small black rectangles enclosing a selected shape; the two small rectangles at the ends of a selected line; the small black rectangles at the four corners of a selected text block. You can drag the handles to change the size of the selected object.

Hanging indent. A paragraph with the first line extending to the left of the other lines. You can use a hanging-indent format to create headings set to the left of the body copy. See also *Indentation*.

Hard carriage return. See *Carriage return*.

Hard disk. Disk storage that is built into the computer or into a piece of hardware connected to the computer. Distinguished from removable floppy disk storage.

Header. See *Running head*. See also *Running foot* and *Folio*.

Headline. The title of an article in a newsletter, newspaper, or magazine.

Hierarchical filing system. A disk storage system in which files can be stored in separate directories, which, in turn, can contain subdirectories. See also *Directory*.

Highlight. To distinguish visually. Usually reverses the normal appearance of selected text, graphic, or option (for example, black text on a white background appears as white text on black background).

Hyphenation. Hyphenation can be achieved in several ways: (1) Page-Maker automatically hyphenates text (based on a built-in dictionary) as you place or type text on the page; (2) PageMaker recognizes hyphens inserted by the word processing program; (3) you can activate prompted hyphenation through the Paragraph command and insert hyphens in words that PageMaker displays in a dialog box as the text is being placed on the page; and (4) you can insert *discretionary hyphens* (displayed only when they fall at the end of a line) by pressing Ctrl-[hyphen] within a word. See also *Discretionary hyphen*.

I-beam. The shape of the pointer when the text tool is selected.

Icon. Graphic on-screen representation of a tool, file, or command.

Image area. Area inside the margins of the page; contains most of the text and graphics.

Import. To bring text or graphics into PageMaker from other programs.

Import filter. A process that tells PageMaker how to convert files from other programs for use by PageMaker.

Increment. Distance between tick marks on a ruler. See also *Measurement system*.

Indentation. Positioning the first line of a paragraph (or second and following lines) to the right of the left column guide (to create a left indent), or positioning the right margin of the paragraph to the left of the right column guide (to create a right indent), relative to the other text on the page. In PageMaker, you set indentation through the Paragraph command dialog box or the Indents/Tabs command. See also *Hanging indent*.

Insertion point. A blinking vertical bar where text will be typed or pasted.

Inside margin. Margin along the edge of the page that will be bound. In single-sided publications, always the left margin. In double-sided publications, the inside margin is the left margin of a right-hand page or the right margin of a left-hand page. See also *Gutter* and *Margin*.

Italic. Letters that slope toward the right, as distinguished from upright, or Roman, characters.

Invert. See *Reverse*.

Jump line. Text at the end of an article indicating on what page the article is continued. Also, the text at the top of a continued article, indicating from where the article is continued. Also called a *continued line*.

Justified text. Text that is flush at both the left and right edges. See also *Alignment*.

Kern. To adjust the spaces between letters, usually to move letters closer together. See also *Kerning*.

Kerning. The amount of space between letters, especially certain combinations of letters that must be brought closer together to create visually consistent spacing around all letters. For example, the uppercase letters AW may appear to have a wider gap between them than the letters MN unless a special kerning formula is set up for the AW combination. In PageMaker, letters larger than the point size specified in the Paragraph command dialog box are kerned against a table of kerning pairs. You also can adjust the space between letters manually with the text tool by pressing Ctrl-Backspace to decrease space or Ctrl-Shift-Backspace to increase space. See also *Kern*.

Landscape printing. The rotation of a page to print text and graphics horizontally across the longer measure of the page or paper (usually 11 inches). In PageMaker, the Wide option in the Print command and in the Printer Setup dialog boxes. See also *Orientation* and *Portrait printing*.

Laser printing. Term used to describe printing with a toner-based laser printer. These printers use laser technology—*l*ight *a*mplification by *s*timulated *e*mission of *r*adiation—to project an intense light beam with a narrow bandwidth (1/300 inch in 300-dots-per-inch printers). This light creates on the printer drum a charge that picks up the toner and transfers it to the paper. Some typesetters (such as the Linotronic 100 and 300) also use laser technology with their photochemical processing but usually are referred to as phototypesetters rather than as laser printers. See also *Phototypesetting*.

Layout. The process of arranging text and graphics on a page. A sketch or plan for the page. Also the final appearance of the page. In platemaking, a sheet indicating the settings for the step-and-repeat machine.

Layout grid. See *Grid*.

Leaders. Dotted or dashed lines that can be defined for tab settings. PageMaker offers three types of tab leaders, plus a custom leader option, through the Tabs/Indents command.

Leading. Historically, the insertion of thin strips of metal (made of a metal alloy that included some lead) between lines of cast type to add space between the lines and to make columns align. In modern typography, the vertical space between the baselines of two lines of text. In PageMaker, leading is measured from ascender to ascender between two lines of text and is entered in points in the Type Specifications dialog box. To give an example of the terminology, 12-point Times with 1 point of leading is 1-point leaded type; 12-point Times with 13-point leading is 12 on 13 Times. Type specifications are sometimes written as "12/13 Times."

Letter spacing. Space between letters in a word. The practice of adding space between letters. In PageMaker, unjustified text has fixed letter spacing; justified text has variable letter spacing, which is adjusted within the limits entered in the Spacing Attributes dialog box. See also *Kerning* and *Word spacing*.

Ligatures. Character combinations that are often combined into special characters in a font. For example, some downloadable fonts come with the combinations *fi* and *fl* as special characters.

Line break. The end of a line of text, created by automatic word wrap and hyphenation. See also *Carriage return*.

Line length. Horizontal measure of a column or a line of text.

Line spacing. See *Leading*.

Line style. Appearance of the border of a shape or a line drawn in PageMaker; selected through the Lines submenu.

List box. Area in a dialog box that displays options.

Loaded text icon. The shape of the text icon while placing text—autoflow, manual flow, or semiautomatic flow.

Lock. In PageMaker, using the Lock Guides command to anchor column guides and ruler guides on the current page or to anchor the zero point of the rulers. Locked guides cannot be inadvertently moved during the process of laying out text and graphics.

Logo. A company trademark. Also, the banner on the front cover of a magazine or newsletter. See also *Masthead*.

Main mouse button. See *Mouse buttons*.

Manual text flow. Manually placing text on the page so that the text flows to and stops at the bottom of the column or the first object that blocks the text.

Margin. Traditionally, the distance from the edge of the page to the edge of the layout area of the page. In PageMaker, page size and margins are defined in the Page Setup dialog box. The margins in PageMaker should be used to define the limits of text. Running heads, running feet, and column rules should be outside the margins. See also *Gutter* and *Inside margin*.

Margin guides. Dotted nonprinting lines displayed near the borders of the screen page to mark the margins of a page as specified in the Page Setup dialog box. See also *Margin*.

Master items. Items on a master page; may include text (running heads), graphics (rules), and nonprinting guides (column guides). See also *Master page*.

Master page. Page containing text, graphics, and guides you want repeated on every page in a publication. Opened by clicking the L or R page icon in the publication window. A single-sided publication has only one master page. A double-sided publication has two master pages: left-hand (even-numbered) and right-hand (odd-numbered). See also *Master items*, *Double-sided publication*, and *Single sided*.

Masthead. Section of newsletter or magazine giving its title and details of staff, ownership, advertising, subscription, and so on. Sometimes the banner or wide title on the front cover of a magazine or the front of a newsletter or newspaper. See also *Logo*.

Measurement system. Units chosen with the Preferences command on the Edit menu: inches, decimal inches, millimeters, picas and points, or ciceros and points. The chosen units appear on the rulers and in all dialog boxes that display measurements. You can enter a value in any unit of measure in a dialog box, regardless of the current Preferences selection, by typing the abbreviation for the unit in your entry. For example, 3.5i

Glossary

indicates 3.5 inches, 3p2 specifies 3 picas and 2 points, 3.5m indicates 3.5 millimeters, and 3c2 specifies 3 ciceros and 2 points. See also *Cicero* and *Pica*.

Mechanicals. Traditionally, the final pages or boards with pasted-up galleys of type and line art, sometimes with acetate or tissue overlays for color separations and notes to the offset printer. See also *Camera-ready art* and *Offset printing*.

Memory. Area in the computer where information is stored temporarily while you're working; also called RAM, or random-access memory. PageMaker automatically saves a publication from the memory onto a disk whenever you turn a page or click a page icon; these saves are called *minisaves*. You also can copy the contents of the memory onto disk by using the Save or Save As command.

Menu bar. Area across the top of the publication window where menu titles are displayed.

Minisave. PageMaker's automatic save of a publication whenever you turn a page or click a page icon. Minisaves create temporary documents on disk and do not overwrite the publication file. Use the Save command to overwrite the last saved version of the publication. See also *Memory*.

Moiré pattern. An undesirable grid pattern that may occur when two transparent dot-screen fill patterns are overlaid or when a bit-mapped graphic with gray fill patterns is reduced or enlarged. PageMaker's magic stretch feature (you hold down the Ctrl key as you drag) can help eliminate this effect.

Mouse buttons. The main mouse button, or primary mouse button, is used to carry out most PageMaker actions. Use the Control Panel to specify the main button as the left or right button of a two- or three-button mouse. Some PageMaker commands also use the secondary mouse button on a two- or three-button mouse. See also *Control Panel*.

Negative. A reverse image of a page, produced photographically on a clear sheet of film as an intermediate step in preparing offset printing plates from camera-ready mechanicals.

Nonbreaking space. A special character inserted between two words so that they are not separated by a line break. See also *Bad break* and *Orphans/widows*.

Nonprinting master items. The ruler guides and column guides on a master page. See also *Margin guides* and *Master page*.

Object-oriented files. Draw-type files consisting of a sequence of drawing commands (stored as mathematical formulas). These commands describe graphics (such as mechanical drawings, schematics, charts, and ad graphics) that you would produce manually with a pencil, straightedge, and compass. Usually contrasted with paint-type files or bit maps. See also *Bit map*.

Offset printing. Type of printing done using a printing press to reproduce many copies of the original (in PageMaker, printed on a laser printer). The press lays ink on a page according to the raised image on a plate created by photographing the camera-ready masters. See also *Camera-ready art*, *Laser printing*, and *Mechanicals*.

Option button. In a dialog box, the round area you click to select an option.

Orientation. Page position options: Tall or Wide. In Tall orientation, text runs horizontally across the narrower measure of the page, and columns run down the longer measure of the page. In Wide orientation, text runs horizontally across the wider measure of the page. See also *Landscape printing* and *Portrait printing*.

Orphans/widows. The first line of a paragraph is called an orphan when separated from the rest of the paragraph by a page break. The last line of a paragraph is called a widow when forced to a new page by a page break and separated from the rest of the paragraph. Most publishers generally consider widows and orphans to be bad page breaks (or column breaks). The term widow also is used to describe bad line breaks that result in the last line of a paragraph having only one word, especially when it falls at the end of a column or page. See also *Bad break* and *Nonbreaking space*.

Outline font. A printer font in which each letter of the alphabet is stored as a mathematical formula, as distinguished from bit-mapped fonts that are stored as patterns of dots. See also *Bit map* and *Font*.

Outside margin. The unbound edge of a publication. In single-sided publications, the outside margin is the right margin. In double-sided publications, the outside margin is the right margin of a right-hand page and the left margin of a left-hand page. See also *Margin*.

Overhead transparency. An image printed on clear acetate and projected onto a screen for viewing by an audience.

Overlay. A transparent acetate or tissue covering a printed page; contains color specifications and other instructions to the offset printer. Also, an overhead transparency that is intended to be projected on top of another transparency. See also *Color separations*.

Glossary

Oversize publication. Publication in which page size is larger than paper size. See also *Page size*, *Paper size*, and *Tile*.

Page icon. An icon displayed in the bottom left corner of the publication window. Icons represent the master pages and every regular page. See also *Icon*.

Page number marker. A series of characters (Ctrl-Shift-3) entered on a master page (displayed as 0) or on a regular page (displayed as the current page number). Instructs PageMaker to number pages automatically.

Page size. The dimensions of the pages of your publication as set in the Page Setup dialog box. Page size can differ from paper size. See also *Margin* and *Paper size*.

Paintbrush icon. Shape of the pointer when a bit-mapped (or paint-type) file is being placed.

Paint-type file. See *Bit map*.

Pair kerning. The PageMaker option that automatically changes the amount of space between two letters to create visually consistent spacing between all letters.

Paper size. The size of the printer paper. Standard paper sizes are letter (8.5 by 11 inches), legal (8.5 by 14), European A4 (8.27 by 11.69), and European B5 (6.93 by 9.84).

Pasteboard. The on-screen work area surrounding the pages on which you are working. You move text and graphics to the pasteboard, where they remain when you turn to another page or close the publication.

Paste-up. See *Mechanicals*.

Pencil icon. Shape of the pointer when an object-oriented (draw-type) file is being placed.

Perpendicular-line tool. Tool used to draw a straight line at any 45-degree increment.

Phototypesetting. Producing a page image on photosensitive paper, as when documents are printed on a Linotronic 100 or 300. This process is sometimes referred to as cold type to distinguish it from the older method of casting characters, lines, or whole pages in lead (hot type or hot metal). See also *Laser printing*.

Pica. A unit of measure equal to approximately 1/6 inch, or 12 points. Use the Preferences command from the Edit menu to select picas and points as the unit of measure for the ruler lines and dialog box displays. You also can enter a value in picas and points in any dialog box by typing a *p* between the number of picas and the number of points: for example, 3p2 specifies 3 picas and 2 points. See also *Measurement system*.

Pixel. The smallest unit on a computer display. Monitors can have different screen resolutions (pixels per inch) and different sizes (total number of pixels).

Place. Command used to bring into PageMaker a text or graphics file created in a word processor or graphics program.

Point. To place the mouse pointer on top of an object on the screen.

Point size. The smallest unit of measure in typographic measurement and the standard unit of measure for type. Measured roughly from the top of the ascenders to the bottom of the descenders. A pica has 12 points; an inch approximately 72 points; a point equals 1/12 pica, or 1/72 inch. See also *Cicero*, *Pica*, and *Measurement system*.

Pointer. The on-screen icon that moves when you move the mouse.

Pointer tool. The PageMaker tool used for selecting and manipulating text and graphics. When the pointer tool is selected, the pointer looks like an arrow.

Portrait printing. The normal printing orientation for a page: horizontally across the shorter measurement of the page or paper (usually, 8.5 inches). In PageMaker, the Tall option in the Print command and Printer Setup command dialog boxes. See also *Orientation* and *Landscape printing*.

PostScript. A page-description language developed by Adobe Systems, Inc., and used by the LaserWriter, the IBM Personal PagePrinter, and other high-resolution printers and typesetters.

Preferences. The PageMaker command on the Edit menu used to select the unit of measure displayed on ruler lines and in dialog boxes. See also *Measurement system*, *Cicero*, and *Pica*.

Prepress proofs. Sometimes called blue lines, these proofs are made using photographic techniques. See also *Press proofs* and *Blue lines*.

Press proofs. A test run of a color printing job through the printing press to check registration and color. See also *Prepress proofs* and *Blue lines*.

Print area. The area on a piece of paper where the printer reproduces text and graphics; always smaller than the paper size. See also *Margin*.

Print queue. Files in the spooler waiting to be sent to the printer. Files are sent in the order they are received. See also *Spooler*.

Printer font. A bit-mapped or outline font installed in the printer or downloaded to the printer when a publication is printed. Usually distinguished from the screen font, which displays the text on the computer screen. See also *Bit map*, *Font*, and *Outline font*.

Proofread. To read a preliminary printout of a page and check for spelling errors, alignment on the page, and other features that are not related to the technical accuracy of the content.

Proofs. See *Prepress proofs*, *Press proofs*, and *Blue lines*.

Publication. A collection of pages created with PageMaker by integrating text and graphics files created with other applications and with PageMaker.

Publication window. Window appearing when you start PageMaker. Displays a view of one or two pages, the pasteboard, page icons, pointer, scroll bars, title bar, menu bar, and toolbox window.

Pull-out quote. Quotation extracted from the text of an article and printed in larger type, often set off by ruled lines.

Ragged right. Text in which lines end at different points near the right margin. Opposite of flush right or justified text. See also *Alignment*.

RAM. See *Memory*.

Registration mark. A mark that is added to a document for color printing to line up copies of the same page to aid the printer for spot-color overlays.

Release. To let go of a mouse button.

Resolution. Number of dots per inch used to create an alphanumeric character or a graphics image. High-resolution images have more dots per inch and look smoother than low-resolution images. The resolution of images displayed on the screen is usually lower than that of the final laser printout. Laser printers print 300 dots per inch or more; typesetters print 1,200 dots per inch or more.

Reverse. Text or a graphic on the printed page that appears opposite of normal. Usually, text and graphics are black on a white background; when reversed, they are white on black.

Right-justified. See *Flush right* and *Alignment*.

Roman. Upright text styles, as distinguished from italic. Sometimes used to refer to Normal style, as opposed to Bold or Italic, on PageMaker's Type menu.

Roughs. Traditionally, the preliminary page layouts done by the designer using pencil sketches to represent miniature page design ideas. You can use PageMaker's Thumbnail option in the Print command dialog box to produce the equivalent of roughs. See also *Thumbnail*.

Rounded-corner tool. PageMaker tool used to draw squares and rectangles with rounded corners. You can adjust the degree of roundness with the Rounded Corners command on the Element menu.

Ruler guides. Nonprinting extensions of the tick marks on the rulers, which form horizontal and vertical dotted, dashed, or blue lines on the page. Used to align text and graphics on the page. Select the Rulers command to display the rulers, and then drag the pointer tool from a ruler onto the page to create a guide.

Rulers. Electronic rulers, one of which is displayed across the top of the publication window, and one down the left side. Also, the text ruler displayed by the Indents/Tabs command on the Type menu. Rulers show measures in inches, picas, or millimeters. Use the Rulers command to display or hide the rulers. Use the Preferences command on the Edit menu to select the unit of measure displayed on the ruler lines and dialog box displays. Increments (tick marks) on the rulers depend on the size and resolution of your screen, as well as on the view (Actual Size, Fit in Window, 200%, and so forth). See also *Measurement system*.

Rules. Black lines added to a page—for example, between columns—to improve the design or increase readability of a publication. Created with PageMaker's perpendicular-line or diagonal-line tool. The Lines submenu sets the thickness and style of the rules.

Run-around. See *Text wrap*.

Running foot. One or more lines of text appearing at the bottom of every page. In PageMaker, the running foot is entered on the master pages. Also referred to as the footer. See also *Folio*.

Running head. One or more lines of text appearing at the top of every page of a document. In PageMaker, the running head is entered on the master pages. Also referred to as the header. See also *Folio*.

Sans serif. Typefaces without serifs, such as Helvetica and Avant Garde. See also *Serif*.

Scanned-image files. Bit-mapped files created with hardware that digitizes images (converts a two- or three-dimensional image to a collection of dots stored in the computer's memory or on disk). PageMaker reads the scanned-image files directly from disk.

Scanned-image icon. Shape of the pointer when a scanned-image file is being placed.

Screen. Gray tone usually identified as a percentage. A 100-percent screen is solid black; a 10-percent screen is light gray. Also, any of the other line patterns on the Shades submenu.

Screen font. See *Font*.

Script fonts. Type designed to look like handwriting or calligraphy, such as Zapf Chancery. See also *Font*.

Scroll bar. Gray bars on the right side and bottom of the publication window. Scroll arrows at both ends of each bar enable you to scroll the document horizontally or vertically. Each scroll bar has a scroll box that you drag to change the view within publication window. List boxes also can have scroll bars for viewing long lists of files or options.

Secondary mouse button. On a multiple-button mouse, the left or right button that is not the main button. See also *Mouse buttons*.

Select. To click or drag the mouse to designate the location of the next action.

Selection area. Area of a text block or graphic defined by the handles displayed when you select that text block or graphic. See also *Handles*.

Selection box. A box drawn by dragging the pointer tool to enclose and select more than one graphic or text block at a time. See also *Drag*.

Semiautomatic text flow. Text placement in which the text flows to the bottom of the column and then stops until the text-placement icon is placed at a new spot.

Serif. A line crossing the main stroke of a letter. Typefaces that have serifs include Times, Courier, New Century Schoolbook, Bookman, and Palatino. See also *Sans serif*.

Shade pattern. Pattern selected on the Shades submenu to fill an object drawn with PageMaker. See also *Screen*.

Shape. An object drawn with PageMaker: a square, a rectangle, a circle, or an oval.

Signature. In printing and binding, the name given to a printed sheet of (usually) 16 pages after folding.

Single sided. An option in PageMaker's Page Setup dialog box that is used to set up a publication so that pages are reproduced on only one side of each sheet of paper. See also *Double-sided publication*.

Size. To make a graphic smaller or larger by dragging the handles. See also *Handles*.

Small caps.   See *Caps and small caps*.

Snap-to.   The effect of various types of nonprinting guidelines, such as margin guides, ruler guides, and column guides. These guides exert a "magnetic pull" on the pointer, text, or a graphic that comes close to the guides. Useful for aligning text and graphics accurately.

Snap-to guides.   PageMaker command that, when turned on, causes margin guides, column guides, and ruler guides to exert a "magnetic pull" on the pointer or any text or graphic near the guides.

Soft carriage return.   See *Carriage return*.

Spacing guides.   A PageMaker object used to help measure and standardize the spaces between text and graphics, between headings and body copy, or between any elements on a page. In PageMaker, spacing guides can be stored on the pasteboard.

Spooler.   A Microsoft Windows application for sending files to the printer. PageMaker's Print command sends the publication to the spooler, not directly to the printer. The spooler holds files in the print queue and prints them in the order in which they were received. You can continue working on other files while a file is being printed. See also *Print queue*.

Spot color.   A process that adds solid areas of colored ink to a publication.

Spot-color overlay.   A page prepared so that each color on the page is printed separately and then combined by a commercial printer to form the completed page.

Square-corner tool.   PageMaker tool used to create squares and rectangles with square corners.

Stacking order.   Order in which overlapping text and graphics are arranged on the page and on-screen.

Standoff.   Distance between the graphic boundary and the graphic.

Story.   All the text from one word processing file: all the text typed or compiled at an insertion point outside existing text blocks. Can be one text block or several text blocks threaded together. See also *Text block*.

Style.   One of the variations within a typeface, such as Roman, bold, or italic. See also *Font* and *Typeface*.

Style sheet.   A list of all the tag formats that can be applied to text in a document.

Tag.   Formatting applied to a particular paragraph.

Glossary 589

Target printer. The printer on which you intend to print the final version of your publication. If no target printer is selected, PageMaker uses the default printer chosen when Windows was installed.

Template. A PageMaker publication containing only the layout grid, master pages, estimated number of pages, and boilerplate text and graphics for a periodical or book. Serves as the starting point for creating many similar documents, such as chapters of a book or issues of a newsletter. You add variable items—text and graphics that are not common to all chapters or issues—to the template document and save it under another name so that the original template document remains unchanged.

Text block. A variable amount of text identified by handles (small squares at the four corners of the text block) or by windowshades (two horizontal lines, each with a loop, at the top and bottom of the text block).

Text box. In a dialog box, the area in which you type text.

Text icon. Shape of the pointer when loaded with text.

Text-only file. Text created with another application and saved without type specifications or other formatting. PageMaker reads text-only files directly from disk. See also *ASCII*.

Text tool. Tool used to select text for editing. When this tool is selected, the pointer looks like an I-beam.

Text wrap. Automatic line breaks at the right edge of a column or at the right margin of a page. Also, the capability to wrap text around a graphic on a page layout. In PageMaker, you can wrap text around a graphic by changing the width of a text block (dragging the text handles) or by using the drag-place feature. See also *Carriage return*.

Threaded text. Blocks of text that are connected across the columns on a page and across pages from the beginning to the end of an article. PageMaker threads all words in a file you place or text you type inside an existing text block. When you edit threaded or chained text, PageMaker moves lines across columns or pages to adjust to the new text length. Text typed outside existing text blocks becomes part of a new text block, and all words in that new text block are threaded together.

Thumbnail. A miniature version of a page that is created with the Thumbnails option in the Print dialog box. Used to preview publications. PageMaker prints up to 64 thumbnails on a page. Available on printers with a page-description language, such as PostScript or DDL. See also *Roughs*.

Tick marks. Marks on the rulers showing increments of measure. See also *Measurement system*.

Tile. Used in oversize publications. A part of a page printed on a single sheet of paper. For a complete page, the tiles are assembled and pasted together. See also *Oversize publication*.

Time-out error. Printer stops because it has not received information for a while. Occurs when you are printing complex pages and printer takes a long time to print a large bit-mapped image. Saving before printing helps reduce chances of data loss.

Toggle switch. An on/off switch, command, or option. Used to describe cases in which the same command is invoked to turn a feature on and off. On PageMaker menus, these commands display a check mark when they are on.

Tones. The shades of a photograph or illustration that is printed as a series of dots. Tones are percentages of black, with lower percentages producing lighter tones.

Toolbox window. Window overlapping the publication window and containing icons for the tools you use to work with text and graphics.

Transparency. See *Overhead transparency* and *Overlay*.

Triple-click. To quickly press and release the main mouse button three times in succession.

Typeface. A single type family of one design of type in all sizes and styles. For example, Times and Helvetica are two different typefaces. Each typeface has many fonts (sizes and styles). Sometimes the terms typeface and font are used interchangeably. See also *Font* and *Style*.

Unit of measure. The units marked on PageMaker's rulers, such as inches, picas and points, or millimeters.

Uppercase. See *Caps and small caps*.

Vector graphics. See *Object-oriented files*.

Vertical justification. Dragging the bottom windowshade to adjust the length of a text block, or adjusting the spaces between lines of text (leading) in fine increments to make columns and pages end at the same point.

View. The size of the pasteboard and page as displayed in the publication window. View is determined by selections on the Page menu. The smallest view (Fit in Window) shows either a complete page or two pages (for a double-sided publication with facing pages). The largest view (200%) shows text and graphics in twice the size at which they will be printed.

White space. Empty space on a page, not used for text or graphics.

Widow. See *Orphans/widows*.

Window. On-screen area where you are running a Windows application. Each window has a title bar, menu bar, and scroll bars.

Windowshade. Horizontal lines, each with a loop, that span the top and bottom of a text block. See also *Handles*.

Word spacing. The space between words in a line or a paragraph. In PageMaker, unjustified text has fixed word spacing; justified text has variable word spacing, which is adjusted within the limits entered in the Spacing Attributes dialog box. See also *Kerning* and *Letter spacing*.

Word wrap. The automatic adjustment of the number of words on a line of text according to the margin settings. The carriage returns that result from automatic word wrap are called soft carriage returns to distinguish them from hard carriage returns, which are entered when you press the Enter key to force a new line. See also *Text wrap* and *Carriage return*.

Wrap. See *Text wrap* and *Word wrap*.

WYSIWYG. "What You See Is What You Get" (or "wizzy-wig"). Term describes systems like PageMaker, which display full pages on the screen with text and graphics. Some systems are more WYSIWYG than others in the accuracy of the display.

X-height. A distinguishing characteristic of a font. The height of lower-case letters without ascenders or descenders, such as *x*, *a*, and *c*. Also called the body of the type.

Zero point. The intersection of the two PageMaker rulers at 0 (zero). The default zero point is at the intersection of the left and top margins but can be moved.

Index

1-2-3 spreadsheet software, 209
25% Size view, 107-108
50% Size view, 107-108
75% Size view, 107-108
200% Size view, 107-108
400% Size view, 107-108

A

active pair kerning, 185-186
Actual Size view, 107-108
Add Index Entry dialog box, 262-264
　cross-references, 266
　page references, 264-265
　topics list, 266-268
adding
　tabs, 190
　text in Story Editor, 152
　words to dictionaries, 194-195
aligning
　paragraphs, 178-179
　text to grid, 183-184
Alignment command, 178-179
AppleShare network software, 71

applying colors, 330
　to text, 331
Arabic numerals, 79-80
ASCII text, 133
Auto leading, 171
AutoCAD drafting software, 209
Autoflow option, 127-130
automatic
　hyphenation, 191-192
　kerning, 370-371
　leading, 366-368
　page numbering, 103-104
　text flow, 128-130

B

bit-mapped
　fonts, 284, 351-352
　graphics, 218, 224-225
blocks, 68
　dividing text, 141-143
　merging, 143
　moving, 137-138
　rotating, 144
　sizing, 138-140

body copy typefaces, 351
boldface, 174
Book command, 256-257
Book Publication List dialog box, 256-257
books, 256-257
    designing, 415-456
    printing, 312
    typefaces used in, 420-421
borders around cells in tables, 162-163
Borders command, 162-163
bottom margin, 422-424
boxes, 211-212
breaks between paragraphs, 180-181
Bring to Front command, 235
brochures, 517-550
built-in fonts, 285-286, 359
    LaserJet Plus printers, 285-286
    LaserJet printers, 285-286
    LaserWriter Plus printers, 285
    LaserWriter printers, 285
    Linotronic printers, 286
butts, 341-342

C

canceling printing, 318
captions, 372
    layout, 422
cartridge fonts, 285-286, 360
case, 171-172
cell borders, 162-163
Cell menu, 162-163
centering paragraphs, 178-179
Change Attribute dialog box, 154-155
Change command, 153-156
Change To dialog box, 153
checking spelling, 156-157
circles, 212
    applying color, 331-332
Clipboard, 115
    copying and pasting text, 147-149
    pasting graphics from, 232-233
CMYK color model, 326-328

color, 173-174
Color Palette command, 330-331
color printing, 311, 324-325
    applying colors, 330-331
    butts, 341-342
    CMYK model, 326-328
    comps, 335
    copying colors, 329-330
    crop marks, 340-341
    deleting colors, 329
    editing colors, 325-327
    HLS model, 326-328, 343-344
    imported graphics, 332-333
    knockouts, 341-342
    mechanicals, 343
    new colors, 328
    offset-printing, 337-339
    Pantone Matching System, 326-327, 343-344
    presentation graphics, 336
    printers, 334-335
    process color, 345
    proofs, 335
    registration marks, 340-341
    removing colors, 329
    RGB model, 326-328
    soft proofing, 333
    spot-color overlays, 339-340
    traps, 341-342
color separation
    see color printing
column width, 379
commands
    Alignment, 178-179
    Autoflow, 127-130
    Book, 256-257
    Borders, 162-163
    Bring to Front, 235
    Change, 153-156
    Color Palette, 330-331
    Copy Master Guides, 106-107
    Create Index, 271-273
    Create TOC, 258-261

Index 595

Cut, 115, 143
Define Colors (Edit menu), 325-327
Define Colors (Element menu), 328-330
Define Flow, 164
Define Styles, 197-201
Display Master Items, 105-106
Fill, 216-217
Font, 174
Hyphenation, 191-195
Image Control, 229-231
Import, 152
Indents/Tabs, 187-191
Index Entry, 262-264
Insert Pages, 109-113
Leading, 174, 370
Line, 216-217
Link Options, 250-251
Links, 251-254
Maximize, 51-52
Move, 52
New, 44-46, 72-73
Open, 46-47, 69-70
Paragraph, 171, 258-259
Paste, 115-116, 143
Place, 126, 217-221, 248-249
Print, 305-306
Remove Pages, 109-113
Revert, 117
Rounded Corners, 211-212
Rulers, 396-397
Save, 78
Save As, 78
Select All, 147-148
Send To Back, 234-235
Set Width, 174
Show Index, 268-270
Size (Control menu), 51-52
Size (Type menu), 174
Spelling, 156-157
Style, 196-197
Style Palette, 196-197
Target Printer, 294-296
Text Rotation, 144
Text Wrap, 235-241
Track, 174
Type Specs, 170, 354, 368-369
Type Style, 174
Undo, 116
comps, 335
connecting printers, 290-291
Control menu (Windows), 51
   Maximize command, 51-52
   Move command, 52
   Size command, 51-52
Control Panel (Windows), 357-358
   installing printers, 287-293
   printer drivers, 289-290
converting publications
   from earlier versions of PageMaker, 70
   from PageMaker Macintosh, 71
copy casting, 376-377
   formulas, 378
   sample pages, 378
Copy Colors dialog box, 329-330
copy fitting, 203-205, 376
   column width, 379
   leading, 379-380
Copy II PC Deluxe Option Board file disk drive software, 71
Copy Master Guides command, 106-107
copying
   colors, 329-330
   indents, 191
   master guides, 106-107
   styles, 201
   tabs, 191
   text to Clipboard, 147-149
Create Index command, 271-273
Create Index dialog box, 271-273
Create Table of Contents dialog box, 258-261
Create TOC command, 258-261
crop marks, 310-311, 340-341
cropping tool, 228-229
cross-references (indexes), 266
current printers, 314

cursor movement, 145
curve-fitting fonts
  see outline fonts
custom graphics boundaries,
  239-241
Custom page size, 73-76
Cut command, 115, 143

D

data, importing into tables, 163-164
default font, 356
default formatting settings, 168-169
Define Colors (Edit menu) command,
  325-327
Define Colors (Element menu) command,
  328-330
Define Colors dialog box, 325-330
Define Flow command, 164
Define Flow dialog box, 164
Define Styles command, 197-201
Define Styles dialog box, 201-202
defining styles, 197-200
deleting
  colors, 329
  styles, 201
  tabs, 190
designing publications
  books, 415-456
  brochures, 517-550
  directories, 517-550
  display ads, 551-568
  fliers, 555-568
  fonts, 362-364
  identifying essential elements,
    385-388
  magazines, 457-487
  manuals, 415-456
  master pages, 387-389
  multiple typefaces, 365-367
  newsletters, 457-487
  newspapers, 457-487
  presentation graphics, 489-516
  price lists, 517-550
  reports, 415-456
diagonal-line tool, 211
dialog boxes, 49
  Add Index Entry, 262-268
  Book Publication List, 256-257
  Change, 153
  Change Attributes, 154-155
  Copy Colors, 329-330
  Create Index, 271-273
  Create Table of Contents, 258-261
  Define Colors, 325-330
  Define Flow, 164
  Define Styles, 201-202
  Edit Color, 325-327
  Edit Styles, 197-200
  Export to File, 164-165
  Find, 155-156
  Hyphenation, 191-195
  Index Format, 272-273
  Insert, 161
  Link Info, 253-254
  Link Options, 250-251, 254-255
  Links, 251-256
  Open Publication, 46-47, 69-70
  Page Numbering, 79-80
  Page Setup, 44-46, 72-76, 80-85,
    392-395
  Pantone Color, 326-327
  Paragraph Rule Options, 182-184
  Paragraph Rules, 181-183
  Paragraph Specifications, 171, 175-183
  Place, 132-135
  Place File, 124-126
  Print, 305-314
  Printer Font Installer, 302-303
  Rounded Corners, 211-212
  Select Cross-Reference Topic, 266-268
  Select Topic, 266-268
  Spacing Attributes, 186-187, 370-371
  Spelling, 156-157
  Table Setup, 158-159

Index

Target Printer, 294-296
Text Rotation, 144
Text Wrap, 235-241
Type Options, 171-172
Type Specifications, 169-174, 354
dictionaries, 157
    adding words, 194-195
    dictionary editor, 157
    specifying for paragraphs, 179
directories, 517-550
    directory structure, 40-42
discretionary hyphenation, 193-194
display ads, 551-568
Display Master Items command, 105-106
display size of pages, 54-55
display typefaces, 351
displaying rulers, 396-397
DisplayWrite3 word processing software, 132
dividing text blocks, 141-143
Document Content Architecture, 132
documents
    see publications
DOS, starting PageMaker from, 42
dots per inch (dpi), 12-13
double-sided copies, 308-309
double-sided pages, 80-83
downloadable fonts, 286, 360
    installing, 297-303
        permanently downloaded fonts, 303-305
        temporarily downloaded fonts, 304-305
dpi (dots per inch), 12-13
drag-place option, 130
drawing
    boxes, 211-212, 331-332
    circles, 212, 331-332
    lines, 211, 331-332
    ovals, 212, 331-332
drivers (printers), 289-290
drop caps, 368-370
drop shadows, 232-233

E

Edit Color dialog box, 325-327
Edit menu
    Change command, 153-156
    Cut command, 115, 143
    Define Colors command, 325-327
    Define Flow command, 164
    Paste command, 115-116, 143
    Select All command, 147-148
    Spelling command, 156-157
    Undo command, 116
Edit Styles dialog box, 197-200
editing
    colors, 325-327
    imported graphics, 227-228
    indexes, 268-270
    styles, 202
    tables, 166
    tables of contents, 261
    text in tables, 159-160
Element menu
    Bring to Front command, 235
    Define Colors command, 328-330
    Fill command, 216-217, 331-332
    Image Control command, 229-231
    Line command, 216-217
    Link Options command, 250-251
    Rounded Corners command, 211-212
    Send to Back command, 234-235
    Text Rotation command, 144
    Text Wrap command, 235-241
Encapsulated PostScript (EPS) files, 209, 224
enlarging
    pages, 307-308
    windows, 51-52
entering text, 122-123
Ethernet network software, 71
Export to File dialog box, 164-165
exporting tables, 164-165

F

facing pages, 83-84
figure captions, 244-245, 372
    layout, 422
File menu
    Book command, 256-257
    Links command, 251-254
    New command, 44-46, 72-73
    Open command, 46-47, 69-70
    Place command, 124-126, 217-221, 248-249
    Print command, 305-306
    Revert command, 117
    Save As command, 78
    Save command, 78
    Target Printer command, 294-296
file server (networks), 276-277
files
    Encapsulated PostScript (EPS), 209, 224
    linking graphics files, 248-254
        checking links, 251-255
        updating links, 256
    naming, 275
    organizing, 275-276
    PFM, 297-298
    PM4.CNF, 356
    printing publications to, 318-320
    sizes, 78
    WIN.INI, 298-302
    Windows Graphics Device Interface (GDI) Metafiles file format, 209
    Windows Metafile (WMF) file format, 209
Fill command, 216-217, 331-332
filters, installing, 39-40
Find dialog box, 155-156
first line indents, 176-177, 189-190
Fit in Window view, 107-108

fitting copy, 203-205, 376
    copy casting, 376-377
        column width, 379
        formulas, 378
        leading, 379-380
        sample pages, 378
fliers, 551-568
Font command, 174
Fontrix font generating software, 244, 373
fonts, 170-171, 184-185, 349-350
    bit-mapped, 284, 351-352
    built-in, 285-286
    cartridge, 285-286
    default font, 356
    designing publications, 362-364
    downloadable, 286, 303-305
    layout, 418-421
    leading, 353
    outline, 284-285, 352
    points, 353
    printer
        built-in fonts, 359
        cartridge fonts, 360
        downloadable fonts, 360
        support, 352-353
    scalable, 173
    screen fonts, 357-358
    style, 354-355
    tracking, 173
    type managers, 285, 361
Fonts utility (Windows), 357-358
footers, 400-401, 421
force justifying paragraphs, 178-179
forced leading, 366-368
formatting
    page numbers, 79-80
    paragraphs
        active pair, 185-186
        aligning, 178-179
        aligning text to grid, 183-184
        breaks, 180-181

font, 184-186
indents, 176-177
kerning, 184-185
paragraph spacing, 177-178
rules, 181-183
Story Editor, 427-428
text
case, 171-172
color, 173-174
default settings, 168-169
font, 170-171
leading, 171
position, 171-172
size, 170-171
tracking, 173
type specifications, 169-170
type specifications keyboard shortcut, 175
type styles, 174
width, 173
formulas (mathematics), 375-376
fractions, 374-375

G

generating
indexes, 271-273
tables of contents, 258-261
grabber hand, 54
graphics, 24
applying color, 331-332
bit-mapped, 218, 224-225
boxes, 211-212
circles, 212
colors, 332-333
drop shadows, 232-233
figure captions, 244-245
handles, 213
image control, 229-231
importing, 217-221, 248-249
editing imported graphics, 227-228
trimming imported graphics, 228-229
inline, 242-244
symbols, 372-373
layering objects, 234-235
layout, 422
lines, 216-217
linking graphics files, 248-255
updating links, 256
master pages, 104-105
moving objects, 214
object-oriented, 221-224
ovals, 212
pasting from Clipboard, 232-233
placing, 248-249
scaling objects, 214-215
scanned images, 225-226
selecting objects, 213
straight lines, 211
symbols in text, 244
vector, 218, 221-224
wrapping text around, 235-238
custom boundaries, 239-241
graphics cards, 35
grid
aligning text to, 183-184
in templates, 397-400
layout, 418, 460

H

handles, 127-128, 136-137, 213
hardware requirements for PageMaker, 34-35
graphics cards, 35
memory, 35
printers, 35
scanners, 35-36
headers, 400-401, 421
uppercase letters, 420-421
help, 60-62
hiding master page items, 105-106
HLS color model, 326-328, 343-344

hyphenation, 191-194
Hyphenation command, 191-195
Hyphenation dialog box, 191-195

I

Image Control command, 229-231
Import command, 152
importing
   data into tables, 163-164
   graphics, 217-221, 248-249
      colors, 332-333
      editing imported, 227-228
      trimming imported, 228-229
   styles, 201-202
   tables, 165
   text, 124-126
      formatted text, 132-134
      unformatted text, 133-135
In*A*Vision graphics software, 209
indents, 176-177
   copying, 191
   ruler line, 189-190
Indents/Tabs command, 187-191
Index Entry command, 262-264
Index Format dialog box, 272-273
indexes
   cross-references, 266
   editing, 268-270
   generating, 271-273
   markers in Story view, 270-271
   marking entries, 262-264
   page references, 264-265
   topics list, 266-268
initial caps, 368-369
inline graphics, 242
   creating, 243-244
   symbols, 372-373
Insert dialog box, 161
Insert Pages command, 109-113

inserting
   pages, 109-113
   symbols in text, 372-373
   text, 145
installing
   downloadable fonts, 297-303
   PageMaker, 36-38
      filters, 39-40
      naming directory, 38-39
   printers, 287-293
      connecting, 290-291
      printer drivers, 289-290
   screen fonts, 357-358
italic, 174

J-K

justifying paragraphs, 178-179
kerning, 184-185
   active pair, 185-186
   automatic, 370-371
   manual, 371-372
keyboard shortcuts, 146-147
   cursor movement, 145
   toolbox, 50
   type specifications, 175
knockouts, 341-342

L

LapLink Plus communications software, 71
LaserJet printers
   built-in fonts, 285-286
   resolution, 283
LaserWriter printers
   built-in fonts, 285
   resolution, 283
layering graphic objects, 234-235
layout
   bottom margin, 422-424
   captions, 422

fonts, 418-421
graphic elements, 424
graphics, 422
grid, 460
grid system, 418
headings, 420-421
presentation graphics, 491-492
running feet, 421
running heads, 421
typefaces, 418-421, 459-460
uppercase letters, 420-421
white space, 417-419, 461
Layout view, 68
    entering text, 122-123
leaders (tabs), 190
leading, 171, 186-187, 353
    automatic, 366-368
    copy fitting, 379-380
    forced, 366-368
    initial caps, 368-369
    proportional, 186-187
    top of caps, 186-187
Leading command, 174, 370
left aligning paragraphs, 178-179
left indents, 176-177, 189-190
left-hand pages, 79
Legal page size, 73-76
Letter page size, 73-76
Line command, 216-217
lines, 216-217
    color, 331-332
Link Info dialog box, 253-254
Link Options command, 250-251
Link Options dialog box, 250-255
link status indicators, 252-253
linking graphics files, 248-249
    checking links, 251-254
    checking links of individual files, 254-255
    options, 250-251
    status indicators, 252-253
    updating links, 256

Links command, 251-254
Links dialog box, 251-256
Linotronic printers
    built-in fonts, 286
    resolution, 283
Lotus Manuscript word processing
    software, 132

M

Macintosh, converting PageMaker
    publications from, 71
MacLink Plus communications software, 71
magazines, 457-487
    typefaces, 459-460
magic stretch feature, 228
manual
    hyphenation, 191-192
    kerning, 371-372
    text flow, 127-130
manuals
    designing, 415-456
    typefaces used in, 420-421
margins, 84-85, 392-395
marking
    index entries, 262-264
    table of contents entries, 258-259
master pages, 23, 68, 387-389
    copying master guides, 106-107
    graphics, 104-105
    hiding items, 105-106
MatchMaker file disk drive software, 71
mathematical formulas, 375-376
Maximize command, 51-52
mechanicals, 343
memory, 35
menus
    see name of menu (i.e., Edit menu, Type menu, etc.)
merging text blocks, 143

Microsoft Word word processing software, 132
minisaves, 117
mouse pointer, 55-56
Move command, 52
moving
    graphic objects, 214
    objects, 115
    tabs, 190
    text blocks, 137-138
    windows, 52
    zero point, 101-102
MultiMate word processing software, 132

N

naming files, 275
networks, 276
    backing up files, 278
    file server, 276-277
    workstations, 277-278
New command, 44-46, 72-73
newsletters, 457-487
    typefaces, 459-460
newspapers, 457-487
number of pages in publications, 76-78
numbering pages, 68, 78-79, 426
    automatic page numbering, 103-104
    formats, 79-80
    presentation graphics, 495-496
    restarting page numbers, 83

O

object-oriented graphics, 221-224
offset printing in color, 337-339
Open command, 46-47, 69-70
Open Prepress Interface (OPI), 345
Open Publication dialog box, 46-47, 69-70
opening
    publications, 44-47, 69-70
    story windows, 150-152

Options menu
    Autoflow command, 127-130
    Create Index command, 271-273
    Create TOC command, 258-261
    Index Entry command, 262-264
    Rulers command, 396-397
    Show Index command, 268-270
organizing files, 275-276
orientation, 76-77, 392-393
outline fonts, 284-285, 352
oval tool, 212
ovals, 212
    color, 331-332
overriding units of measure, 86

P

Page menu, 54-55
    Copy Master Guides command, 106-107
    Display Master Items command, 105-106
    Insert Pages command, 109-113
    Remove Pages command, 109-113
Page Numbering dialog box, 79-80
page numbers, 78-79
    automatic page numbering, 103-104
    formats, 79-80
    presentation graphics, 495-496
    restarting, 83
page references (indexes), 264-265
Page Setup dialog box, 44-46, 72-73, 392-395
    double-sided pages, 80-83
    facing pages, 83-84
    margins, 84-85
    number of pages in publications, 76-78
    page number formats, 79-80
    page orientation, 76-77
    page sizes, 73-76
    restarting page numbers, 83
    starting page number, 78-79
    target printer, 87

Index 603

PageMaker
  installing, 36-40
  starting from DOS, 42
  starting from Windows, 42-43
  vs. word processors, 19-24
pages
  display size, 54-55
  double-sided, 80-83
  facing, 83-84
  inserting, 109-113
  left-hand, 79
  master, 23, 68
  numbered, 68
  numbering, 426
  orientation, 76-77, 392-393
  page numbers, 78-79
    automatic page numbering, 103-104
    formats, 79-80
    presentation graphics, 495-496
    restarting, 83
  page size, 73-76
  printing blank pages, 312
  printing parts of pages, 312-314
  removing, 109-113
  right-hand, 79
  single-sided, 80-83
  starting page number, 78-79
  tiling, 312-314
  turning, 113-114
  view, 54-55
  viewing, 107-108
Pantone Color dialog box, 326-327
Pantone Matching System, 326-327, 343-344
paper size, 73-76, 283, 392-393
paper stock, 283
Paragraph command, 171, 258-259
Paragraph Rule Options dialog box, 182-184
Paragraph Rules dialog box, 181-183
Paragraph Specifications dialog box, 175-176
  aligning paragraphs, 178-179

dictionaries, 179
font tables, 184-186
indents, 176-177
kerning, 184-186
leading, 171
paragraph breaks, 180-181
paragraph spacing, 177-178
rules, 181-183
tables of contents, 181
paragraphs
  formatting, 176-187
    Story Editor, 427-428
Paste command, 115-116, 143
pasteboard, 68
  placing text on, 130-131
pasting
  graphics from Clipboard, 232-233
  objects, 116
  text from Clipboard, 147-149
PC Paintbrush graphics software, 209
PCL printers, 282
  installing downloadable fonts, 302-303
permanently downloaded fonts, 303-305
perpendicular-line tool, 211
PFM files, 297-298
  including in WIN.INI, 298-302
Place command, 124-126, 217-221, 248-249
Place File dialog box, 124-126
  placing formatted text, 132-134
  placing unformatted text, 133-135
placing
  graphics, 248-249
  text
    automatic text flow, 128-130
    drag-place feature, 130
    importing text, 124-126
    manual text flow, 127-130
    pasteboard, 130-131
    semiautomatic text flow, 128
PM4.CNF file, 356
pointer tool, selecting text with, 57-60
points, 353

position, 171-172
PostScript printers, 282
presentation graphics, 336, 491-492
    designing, 489-516
    page numbering, 495-496
    typefaces, 492-493
price lists, 517-550
print area, 283-284
Print command, 305-306
Print dialog box, 305-306
    blank pages, 312
    books, 312
    color printing, 311
    crop marks, 310-311
    current printer, 314
    double-sided copies, 308-309
    enlarging pages, 307-308
    number of copies, 306-307
    page ranges, 307
    parts of pages, 312-314
    reducing pages, 307-308
    thumbnails, 309-310
    tiling pages, 312-314
Print Manager (Windows), 316-317
Printer Font Installer dialog box, 302-303
printer font metrics files, 297-298
    including in WIN.INI, 298-302
printers, 35
    bit-mapped fonts, 284
    built-in fonts, 285-286, 359
    cartridge fonts, 285-286, 360
    color, 334-335
    connecting, 290-291
    current printer, 314
    downloadable fonts, 286, 360
    font support, 352-353
    installing, 287-293
        connecting printers, 290-291
        printer drivers, 289-290
    installing downloadable fonts, 297-303
    LaserJet printers
        built-in fonts, 285-286
        resolution, 283

    LaserWriter printers
        built-in fonts, 285
        resolution, 283
    Linotronic 100/300 printers
        built-in fonts, 286
        resolution, 283
    outline fonts, 284-285
    paper size, 283
    paper stock, 283
    PCL, 282
    PostScript, 282
    print area, 283-284
    QMS ColorScript 100
        resolution, 283
    resolution, 12, 282-283
    target printer, 87, 294-296
    Windows-supported, 282
printing publications, 305-306
    blank pages, 312
    books, 312
    canceling printing, 318
    color, 311, 324-325
    crop marks, 310-311, 340-341
    double-sided copies, 308-309
    enlarging pages, 307-308
    number of copies, 306-307
    page ranges, 307
    parts of pages, 312-314
    Print Manager, 316-317
    reducing pages, 307-308
    registration marks, 340-341
    selecting printer, 314
    spot-color overlays, 339-340
    thumbnails, 309-310
    tiling pages, 312-314
    to disk, 318-320
process color, 337-339, 345
proofing colors on screen, 333
proofs, 335
proportional leading, 186-187
Publication window, 47-48

Index

publications, 68
   converting from earlier versions of PageMaker, 70
   converting from PageMaker Macintosh, 71
   creating new, 72-73
   designing
      books, 415-456
      brochures, 517-550
      directories, 517-550
      display ads, 551-568
      fliers, 551-568
      fonts, 362-364
      identifying essential elements, 385-388
      magazines, 457-487
      manuals, 415-456
      master pages, 387-389
      multiple typefaces, 365-367
      newsletters, 457-487
      newspapers, 457-487
      presentation graphics, 489-516
      price lists, 517-550
      reports, 415-456
   double-sided pages, 80-83
   facing pages, 83-84
   margins, 84-85
   new, 44-46
   number of pages, 76-78
   opening, 44-47, 69-70
   page number formats, 79-80
   printing, 305-306
      blank pages, 312
      books, 312
      canceling printing, 318
      color, 311
      crop marks, 310-311
      double-sided copies, 308-309
      enlarging pages, 307-308
      number of copies, 306-307
      page ranges, 307
      parts of pages, 312-314

Print Manager, 316-317
   reducing pages, 307-308
   selecting printer, 314
   thumbnails, 309-310
   tiling pages, 312-314
   to disk, 318
   reverting to last saved version, 117
   single-sided pages, 80-83
   starting page number, 78-79
Publisher's Paintbrush graphics software, 209
Publisher's Type Foundry font-generating software, 244, 373
publishing cycle, 25-30

Q-R

QMS ColorScript 100 printer, 283-285
rectangles, 211-212
   color, 331-332
reducing pages, 307-308
registration marks, 340-341
Remove Pages command, 109-113
removing
   colors, 329
   pages, 109-113
   styles, 201
reports
   designing, 415-456
   typefaces used in, 420-421
resizing windows, 51-52
resolution (printers), 12-13, 282-283
restarting page numbers, 83
Revert command, 117
reverting to last saved publication, 117
RGB color model, 326-328
right aligning paragraphs, 178-179
right indents, 176,-190
right-hand pages, 79
Roman numerals, 79-80
rotating blocks, 144
Rounded Corners command, 211-212
Rounded Corners dialog box, 211-212

rounded-corner tool, 211-212
ruler line, 187-188
    adding tabs, 190
    copying indents, 191
    copying tabs, 191
    deleting tabs, 190
    indents, 189-190
    moving tabs, 190
    tab increments, 190
rulers, 396-397
Rulers command, 396-397
rules, adding to paragraphs, 181-183
running feet, 400-401, 421
running heads, 400-401, 421

S

SAMNA Word word processing software, 132
sans serif type, 351
Save command, 78
Save As command, 78
saving publications, 62-64
    reverting to last saved version, 117
scalable fonts, width, 173
scaling graphics, 214-215
    magic stretch feature, 228
scanned images, 225-226
scanners, 35-36
screen fonts
    installing, 357-358
    type managers, 285, 361
scroll bars, 53
searching and replacing text, 153-156
Select All command, 147-148
Select Cross-Reference Topic dialog box, 266-268
Select Topic dialog box, 266-268
selecting
    graphic objects, 213
    text, 146-147
        keyboard shortcuts, 146-147
        pointer tool, 57-60
        text tool, 57-60

semiautomatic text flow, 128
Send to Back command, 234-235
serif type, 351
service bureaus, 320-321
Set Width command, 174
Show Index command, 268-270
signature, 388
single-sided pages, 80-83
Size (Control menu) command, 51, 52
Size (Type menu) command, 174
size of files, 78
sizing
    tables, 160-161
    text blocks, 138-140
small caps, 171-172
soft fonts
    see downloadable fonts
soft proofing, 333
Spacing Attributes dialog box, 186-187, 370-371
spacing paragraphs, 177-178
spelling checker, 156-157
    dictionaries, 157
Spelling command, 156-157
Spelling dialog box, 156-157
spot color, 337-339
    see also color printing
square-corner tool, 211-212
starting
    PageMaker from DOS, 42
    PageMaker from Windows, 42-43
starting page number, 78-79
stock, 283
Story Editor, 149
    adding text, 152
    formatting paragraphs, 427-428
    index markers, 270-271
    opening story windows, 150-152
    searching and replacing text, 153-156
    spelling checker, 156-157
Story menu
    Import command, 152
straight lines, 211

Index 607

style, 354-355
Style command, 196-197
Style Palette command, 196-197
style sheets
   see styles
styles, 195-196
   copying, 201
   creating, 197-200
   defining, 197-200
   deleting, 201
   editing, 202
   importing, 201-202
   removing, 201
   viewing, 196-197
subscripts, 171-172
   fractions, 374-375
superscripts, 171-172
   fractions, 374-375
symbols, inserting in text, 244, 372-373
Symphony spreadsheet software, 209

T

Table Editor, 158
   creating tables, 158-159
   exporting, 164-165
   importing data, 163-164
Table Setup dialog box, 158-159
tables
   cell borders, 162-163
   creating, 158-159
   editing, 166
   editing text, 159-160
   importing, 165
   importing data into, 163-164
   sizing, 160-161
tables of contents, 181, 258
   editing, 261
   generating, 258-261
   marking entries, 258-259
Tabloid page size, 73-76
tabs, 187-188
   adding, 190
   copying, 191
   deleting, 190
   leader, 190
   moving, 190
Tall orientation, 76-77
target printer, 87, 294-296
Target Printer command, 294-296
Target Printer dialog box, 294-296
templates, 389-391
   footers, 400-401
   grids, 397-400
   margins, 392-395
   page orientation, 392-393
   paper size, 392-393
   rulers, 396-397
   running heads, 400-401
   units of measure, 395-396
temporarily downloaded fonts, 304-305
text
   adding in Story Editor, 152
   aligning to grid, 183-184
   applying colors to, 331
   ASCII, 133
   automatic text flow, 128-130
   blocks, 68
   bottom margin, 422-424
   dividing blocks, 141-143
   drag-place option, 130
   editing in tables, 159-160
   entering, 122-123
   formatting, 168-174
   importing, 124-126
      formatted, 132-134
      unformatted, 133-135
   including symbols, 244
   inserting, 145
   inserting symbols into, 372-373
   manual text flow, 127-130
   merging blocks, 143
   moving blocks, 137-138
   placing, 124-126
   placing on pasteboard, 130-131
   position, 171-172
   rotating blocks, 144

searching and replacing, 153-156
selecting, 146-147
semiautomatic text flow, 128
sizing blocks, 138-140
typing, 122-123
wrapping around graphics, 235-238
 custom boundaries, 239-241
Text Rotation command, 144
Text Rotation dialog box, 144
text tool, 144
 selecting text, 57-60
Text Wrap command, 235-241
Text Wrap dialog box, 235-241
thumbnails, 309-310
tiling pages, 312-314
toolbox, 50-51
 cropping tool, 228-229
 diagonal-line tool, 211
 keyboard shortcuts, 50
 oval tool, 212
 perpendicular-line tool, 211
 rounded-corner tool, 211-212
 square-corner tool, 211-212
 text tool, 144
top of caps leading, 186-187
topics list (indexes), 266-268
TOPS network software, 71
Track command, 174
tracking, 173
traps, 341-342
trimming imported graphics, 228-229
turning pages, 113-114
type managers, 285, 361
Type menu
 Alignment command, 178-179
 Define Styles command, 197-201
 Font command, 174
 Hyphenation command, 191-195
 Indents/Tabs command, 187-191
 Leading command, 174, 370
 Paragraph command, 171, 258-259
 Set Width command, 174
 Size command, 174
 Style command, 196-197
 Track command, 174
 Type Specs command, 170, 354-355, 369
Type Options dialog box, 171-172
type size, 170-171
Type Specifications dialog box, 169-170, 174, 354
 case, 171-172
 color, 173-174
 font, 170-171
 leading, 171
 position, 171-172
 tracking, 173
 type size, 170-171
 width of scalable fonts, 173
Type Specs command, 170, 354, 368-369
Type Style command, 174
type styles, 174
typefaces, 13-14, 351
 bit-mapped fonts, 351-352
 body copy, 351
 books, 420-421
 designing publications, 365-367
 display, 351
 layout, 418-421, 459-460
 magazines, 459-460
 manuals, 420-421
 newsletters, 459-460
 outline fonts, 352
 presentation graphics, 492-493
 reports, 420-421
 sans serif, 351
 serif, 351
typing text, 122-123

U

underscore, 174
Undo command, 116
undoing actions, 116
unformatted text, importing, 133-135

Index 609

units of measure, 395-396
   overriding, 86
updating links, 256
uppercase letters (layout strategy), 420-421

V

vector graphics, 218, 221-224
viewing
   pages, 107-108
   styles, 196-197
views
   25% Size, 107-108
   50% Size, 107-108
   75% Size, 107-108
   200% Size, 107-108
   400% Size, 107-108
   Actual Size, 107-108
   Fit in Window, 107-108
   Layout, 68, 122-123
   Story, 68
views of page, 54-55
Volkswriter 3 word processing software, 132

W

white space, 417-419
   layout, 461
Wide orientation, 76-77
width
   columns, 379
   scalable fonts, 173
WIN.INI file, 298-302
Window menu
   Color Palette command, 330-331
   Style Palette command, 196-197
Windows 3.0
   Control Panel, 357-358
   Fonts utility, 357-358
   installing printers, 287-289
   Print Manager, 316-317
   printers supported, 282
   Starting PageMaker, 42-43
windows
   enlarging, 51-52
   moving, 52
   opening story windows, 150-152
   Publication, 47-48
   resizing, 51-52
   scroll bars, 53
   toolbox
      see toolbox
Windows Draw graphics software, 209
Windows Graphics Device Interface (GDI) Metafiles, 209
Windows Metafile (WMF) files, 209
Windows Paint graphics software, 209
Windows Write word processing software, 132
windowshades, 127-128, 136-137
WordPerfect word processing software, 132
WordStar 2000 word processing software, 132
WordStar word processing software, 132
workstations (networks), 277-278
wrapping text around graphics, 235-238
   custom boundaries, 239-241
WYSIWYG, 14

X-Y-Z

XyWrite word processing software, 132
zero point, moving, 101-102

Computer Books From Que Mean PC Performance!

Spreadsheets

Database Techniques	$29.95
Graphics Techniques	$24.95
Macro Library, 3rd Edition	$39.95
Release 2.2 Business Applications	$39.95
Release 2.2 PC Tutor	$39.95
Release 2.2 QueCards	$19.95
Release 2.2 Quick Reference	$ 8.95
Release 2.2 QuickStart, 2nd Edition	$19.95
Release 2.2 Workbook and Disk	$29.95
Release 3 Business Applications	$39.95
Release 3 Workbook and Disk	$29.95
Release 3.1 Quick Reference	$ 8.95
Release 3.1 QuickStart, 2nd Edition	$19.95
Tips, Tricks, and Traps, 3rd Edition	$24.95
Business Applications: IBM Version	$39.95
Quick Reference	$ 8.95
QuickStart	$19.95
Tips, Tricks, and Traps	$22.95
1-2-3/G	$29.95
1-2-3, Special Edition	$27.95
1-2-3 Release 2.2, Special Edition	$27.95
1-2-3 Release 3.1, 2nd Edition	$29.95
Excel: IBM Version	$29.95
Lotus Spreadsheet for DeskMate	$22.95
Quattro Pro	$24.95
SuperCalc5, 2nd Edition	$29.95

Databases

dBASE III Plus Handbook, 2nd Edition	$24.95
dBASE III Plus Tips, Tricks, and Traps	$24.95
dBASE III Plus Workbook and Disk	$29.95
dBASE IV Applications Library, 2nd Edition	$39.95
dBASE IV Programming Techniques	$24.95
dBASE IV Quick Reference	$ 8.95
dBASE IV QuickStart	$19.95
dBASE IV Tips, Tricks, and Traps, 2nd Edition	$24.95
dBASE IV Workbook and Disk	$29.95
Clipper	$24.95
DataEase	$24.95
dBASE IV	$27.95
Paradox 3	$24.95
R:BASE	$29.95
Reflex, 2nd Edition	$24.95
SQL	$29.95

Business Applications

Lotus Quick Reference	$ 8.95
Introduction to Business Software	$14.95
Introduction to Personal Computers	$19.95
Norton Add-in Toolkit Guide	$29.95
Norton Utilities Quick Reference	$ 8.95
Norton Tools Quick Reference, 2nd Edition	$ 8.95
Quick Reference	$ 8.95
Computer User's Dictionary	$ 9.95
Wizard Book	$ 9.95
Quicken Quick Reference	$ 8.95
Software Tips, Tricks, and Traps	
2nd Edition	$24.95
Computers in Business	$22.95
DacEasy, 2nd Edition	$24.95
Enable/OA	$29.95
Harvard Project Manager	$24.95
Managing Your Money, 2nd Edition	$19.95
Microsoft Works: IBM Version	$22.95
Norton Utilities	$24.95

Using PC Tools Deluxe	$24.95
Using Peachtree	$27.95
Using PFS: First Choice	$22.95
Using PROCOMM PLUS	$19.95
Using Q&A, 2nd Edition	$23.95
Using Quicken: IBM Version, 2nd Edition	$19.95
Using Smart	$22.95
Using SmartWare II	$29.95
Using Symphony, Special Edition	$29.95
Using Time Line	$24.95
Using TimeSlips	$24.95

CAD

AutoCAD Quick Reference	$ 8.95
AutoCAD Sourcebook 1991	$27.95
Using AutoCAD, 3rd Edition	$29.95
Using Generic CADD	$24.95

Word Processing

Microsoft Word 5 Quick Reference	$ 8.95
Using DisplayWrite 4, 2nd Edition	$24.95
Using LetterPerfect	$22.95
Using Microsoft Word 5.5: IBM Version, 2nd Edition	$24.95
Using MultiMate	$24.95
Using Professional Write	$22.95
Using Word for Windows	$24.95
Using WordPerfect 5	$27.95
Using WordPerfect 5.1, Special Edition	$27.95
Using WordStar, 3rd Edition	$27.95
WordPerfect PC Tutor	$39.95
WordPerfect Power Pack	$39.95
WordPerfect Quick Reference	$ 8.95
WordPerfect QuickStart	$19.95
WordPerfect 5 Workbook and Disk	$29.95
WordPerfect 5.1 Quick Reference	$ 8.95
WordPerfect 5.1 QuickStart	$19.95
WordPerfect 5.1 Tips, Tricks, and Traps	$24.95
WordPerfect 5.1 Workbook and Disk	$29.95

Hardware/Systems

DOS Tips, Tricks, and Traps	$24.95
DOS Workbook and Disk, 2nd Edition	$29.95
Fastback Quick Reference	$ 8.95
Hard Disk Quick Reference	$ 8.95
MS-DOS PC Tutor	$39.95
MS-DOS Power Pack	$39.95
MS-DOS Quick Reference	$ 8.95
MS-DOS QuickStart, 2nd Edition	$19.95
MS-DOS User's Guide, Special Edition	$29.95
Networking Personal Computers, 3rd Edition	$24.95
The Printer Bible	$29.95
Que's PC Buyer's Guide	$12.95
Understanding UNIX: A Conceptual Guide, 2nd Edition	$21.95
Upgrading and Repairing PCs	$29.95
Using DOS	$22.95
Using Microsoft Windows 3, 2nd Edition	$24.95
Using Novell NetWare	$29.95
Using OS/2	$29.95
Using PC DOS, 3rd Edition	$24.95
Using Prodigy	$19.95

Using UNIX	$29.95
Using Your Hard Disk	$29.95
Windows 3 Quick Reference	$ 8.95

Desktop Publishing/Graphics

CorelDRAW Quick Reference	$ 8.95
Harvard Graphics Quick Reference	$ 8.95
Using Animator	$24.95
Using DrawPerfect	$24.95
Using Harvard Graphics, 2nd Edition	$24.95
Using Freelance Plus	$24.95
Using PageMaker: IBM Version, 2nd Edition	$24.95
Using PFS: First Publisher, 2nd Edition	$24.95
Using Ventura Publisher, 2nd Edition	$24.95

Macintosh/Apple II

AppleWorks QuickStart	$19.95
The Big Mac Book, 2nd Edition	$29.95
Excel QuickStart	$19.95
The Little Mac Book	$ 9.95
Que's Macintosh Multimedia Handbook	$24.95
Using AppleWorks, 3rd Edition	$24.95
Using Excel: Macintosh Version	$24.95
Using FileMaker	$24.95
Using MacDraw	$24.95
Using MacroMind Director	$29.95
Using MacWrite	$24.95
Using Microsoft Word 4: Macintosh Version	$24.95
Using Microsoft Works: Macintosh Version, 2nd Edition	$24.95
Using PageMaker: Macinsoth Version, 2nd Edition	$24.95

Programming/Technical

Assembly Language Quick Reference	$ 8.95
C Programmer' sToolkit	$39.95
C Quick Reference	$ 8.95
DOS and BIOS Functions Quick Reference	$ 8.95
DOS Programmer's Reference, 2nd Edition	$29.95
Network Programming in C	$49.95
Oracle Programmer's Guide	$29.95
QuickBASIC Advanced Techniques	$24.95
Quick C Programmer's Guide	$29.95
Turbo Pascal Advanced Techniques	$24.95
Turbo Pascal Quick Reference	$ 8.95
UNIX Programmer's Quick Reference	$ 8.95
UNIX Programmer's Reference	$29.95
UNIX Shell Commands Quick Reference	$ 8.95
Using Assembly Language, 2nd Edition	$29.95
Using BASIC	$24.95
Using C	$29.95
Using QuickBASIC 4	$24.95
Using Turbo Pascal	$29.95

For More Information, Call Toll Free!
1-800-428-5331

All prices and titles subject to change without notice.
Non-U.S. prices may be higher. Printed in the U.S.A.

Let Que Help You With All Your Graphic Needs!

Using Harvard Graphics, 2nd Edition

Steve Sagman & Jane Graver Sandlar

Through Version 2.3

Order #1196   **$24.95 USA**

0-88022-608-0, 700 pp., 7 3/8 x 9 1/4

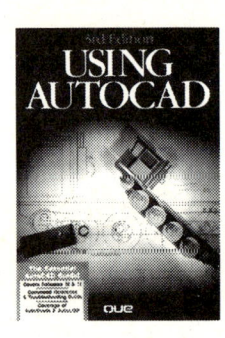

Using AutoCAD, 3rd Edition

Que Development Group

Through Release 11

Order #1218   **$29.95 USA**

0-88022-623-4, 800 pp., 7 3/8 x 9 1/4

More Graphics Titles From Que

CorelDRAW Quick Reference
Que Development Group
Through Version 1.2
Order #1186   **$8.95 USA**
0-88022-597-1, 160 pp., 4 3/4 x 8

Harvard Graphics Quick Reference
Que Development Group
Version 2.3
Order #1084   **$8.95 USA**
0-88022-538-6, 160 pp., 4 3/4 x 8

Using Animator
Craig Sharp
Version 1
Order #1090   **$24.95**
0-88022-544-0, 450 pp., 7 3/8 x 9 1/4

Using DrawPerfect
Stuart Bloom
Version 1
Order #1107   **$24.95 USA**
0-88022-561-0, 400 pp., 7 3/8 x 9 1/4

Using Freelance Plus
Jim Meade
Version 3.01
Order #1050   **$24.95 USA**
0-88022 528 9, 330 pp., 7 3/8 x 9 1/4

Using Generic CADD
Roger Blaylock with Derik White
Through Level 3
Order #983   **$24.95 USA**
0-88022-453-3, 450 pp., 7 3/8 x 9 1/4

Using PFS: First Publisher, 2nd Edition
Katherine Murray
Through Verion 3.0
Order #1183   **$24.95 USA**
0-88022-591-2, 450 pp., 7 3/8 x 9 1/4

Using PageMaker: IBM Version, 2nd Edition
S. Venit & Diane Burns
Through Version 3
Order #953   **$24.95 USA**
0-88022-415-0, 511 pp., 7 3/8 x 9 1/4

Using Publish It!
Katherine Murray
Through Version 1.2
Order #1272   **$24.95 USA**
0-88022-660-9, 350 pp., 7 3/8 x 9 1/4

Using Ventura Publisher, 2nd Edition
Diane Burns, S. Venit, & Linda Mercer
Through Version 2
Order #940   **$24.95 USA**
0-88022-406-1, 621 pp., 7 3/8 x 9 1/4

**To order, call:
1-800-428-5331
or
(317) 573-2510**

Word Processing Is Easy When You're Using Que!

Using LetterPerfect
Robert Beck

A comprehensive guide to this all-new condensed version of WordPerfect! Includes reference for error messages and formatting codes.

Version 1

Order #1277 $22.95 USA
0-88022-667-6, 500 pp., 7 3/8 x 9 1/4

Using Word for Windows
Ron Person & Karen Rose

Complete coverage of program basics and advanced desktop publishing hints. Includes Quick Start lessons and a tear-out Menu Map.

Version 1.0

Order #886 $24.95 USA
0-88022-399-5, 500 pp., 7 3/8 x 9 1/4

Using Professional Write
Katherine Murray

Quick Start tutorials introduce word processing basics and help readers progress to advanced skills. Packed with easy-to-follow examples!

Through Version 2.1

Order #1027 $22.95 USA
0-88022-490-8, 343 pp., 7 3/8 x 9 1/4

More Word Processing Titles From Que

Microsoft Word 5 Quick Reference
Que Development Group

Version 5.5

Order #976 $8.95 USA
0-88022-444-4, 160 pp., 4 3/4 x 8

Using Microsoft Word 5.5: IBM Version, 2nd Edition
Bryan Pfaffenberger

Through Version 5.5

Order #1252 $24.95 USA
0-88022-642-0, 500 pp., 7 3/8 x 9 1/4

Using DisplayWrite 4, 2nd Edition
David Busch

DisplayWrite 4 V2 & DisplayWrite 5 for OS/2

Order #975 $24.95 USA
0-88022-445-2, 438 pp., 7 3/8 x 9 1/4

Using MultiMate
Jim Meade

Version 4

Order #1093 $24.95 USA
0-88022-548-3, 450 pp., 7 3/8 x 9 1/4

Using WordStar, 3rd Edition
Steve Ditlea

Through Release 6.0

Order #1194 $27.95 USA
0-88022-606-4, 500 pp., 7 3/8 x 9 1/4

To Order, Call:
(800) 428-5331
OR (317) 573-2510

Complete Coverage From A To Z!

Que's Computer User's Dictionary

Que Development Group

This compact, practical reference contains hundreds of definitions, explanations, examples, and illustrations on topics from programming to desktop publishing. You can master the "language" of computers and learn how to make your personal computers more efficient and more powerful. Filled with tips and cautions, *Que's Computer User's Dictionary* is the perfect resource for anyone who uses a computer.

IBM, Macintosh, Apple, & Programming

Order #1086 $10.95 USA

0-88022-540-8, 500 pp., 4 3/4 x 8

The Ultimate Glossary Of Computer Terms—Over 200,000 In Print!

"Dictionary indeed. This whammer is a mini-encyclopedia...an absolute joy to use...a must for your computer library...."

Southwest Computer & Business Equipment Review

**To Order, Call:
(800) 428-5331 OR (317) 573-2510**